The Loyalists in
Revolutionary America
1760–1781

A VOLUME IN THE SERIES

The Founding of the American Republic

Planned and initiated by CLINTON ROSSITER

BOOKS PUBLISHED TO DATE

Slavery in the Structure of
American Politics, 1765–1820

DONALD L. ROBINSON

The American Quest, 1790–1860

CLINTON ROSSITER

The Loyalists in Revolutionary America, 1760-1781

ROBERT McCLUER CALHOON

Harcourt Brace Jovanovich, Inc.

New York

Library of Congress Cataloging in Publication Data

Calhoon, Robert McCluer.
The loyalists in Revolutionary America, 1760–1781.

(The Founding of the American Republic)
Bibliography: p.
1. American loyalists. 2. United States—History
—Revolution—Causes. 3. United States—Politics and
government—Colonial period. I. Title.
E277.C24   973.3'14   73–8835
ISBN 0-15-154745-9

First edition
B C D E

FOR DORIS

Preface

THERE have been two sorts of serious historical writing about the loyalists of the American Revolution.* A modest number of books and articles describes the loyalists themselves and deals sparingly with the larger context of Revolutionary society and politics, while an immense body of scholarship concerned with the causes and nature of the Revolution and the character of eighteenth-century American life deals incidentally with aspects of loyalist activity. By synthesizing portions of the rich historical literature on the loyalists and on the Revolution, and by utilizing a wide variety of loyalist testimony, this book seeks to make the loyalists intelligible and comprehensible to readers of early American history. This volume is a study of the loyalists in the original thirteen colonies and states, from the very early stages of the pre-Revolutionary controversy until the cessation of hostilities. Though it is broadly sketched in the Epilogue, it has not been possible to examine the longer-term effect of the Revolution on the loyalists—the exile experiences of perhaps 80,000 loyalists and their dependents who departed or the adaptation of as many as 400,000 who remained in the United States—or the role of the loyalists in the post-Revolutionary settlement: the implementation of the peace treaty and the uses made of confiscated loyalist property.

The first half of the book deals with the critics of colonial resistance during the pre-Revolutionary controversy, almost all of whom became active or passive loyalist neutrals after 1776. Part I examines the colonial leaders who believed that immutable

---

* The great bulk of this scholarship is cited in the text and notes of this book, and the major works on the loyalists are appraised in the Bibliographical Essay, pp. 559–565.

legal, constitutional, and historical rules governed the Empire and necessarily circumscribed colonial liberty, and it surveys the sources and disposition of political power within the British Empire. Part II explores the efforts of other colonists to circumvent strict rules of colonial subordination and to arrange instead practical, improvised accommodation between Britain and the colonies, and it delineates the intangible political tendencies and habits that comprised the "political culture" of pre-Revolutionary America. Part III considers a third and virulent variety of pre-Revolutionary loyalism, the appeal to doctrine by men who regarded all colonial remonstrance and resistance as morally wrong and esthetically abhorrent. With their reactionary philosophy of order and obedience and their profound alienation from the ideology of the Revolution, these men especially merited the title "Tory," and they are here studied against the background of formal thought in the late colonial period to which they made an acerbic, penetrating contribution. Although these three varieties of pre-Revolutionary loyalism developed more or less simultaneously, there was a chronological progression in the themes treated in the first three parts of this book; the enunciation of the principles of imperial administration was largely a response to events in the 1760's and very early 1770's, the search for accommodation became most energetic between 1767 and 1769 and again in 1774 and early 1775, and the appeal to doctrine grew most shrill and intense in late 1774, 1775, and early 1776.

These categories of thought and behavior were among the first casualties of war; with the commencement of hostilities, the pre-Revolutionary enunciation of principle, search for accommodation, and appeal to doctrine receded, became less distinct, and were replaced by more elemental grounds for resisting the Revolution and desiring British victory. Part IV relates the way in which tightly knit New England communities reacted self-protectively during the early stages of hostilities, from 1774 to 1777, to immobilize, disarm, and intimidate "persons inimical" to the cause of liberty. It further locates several significant flaws in New England's social fabric where loyalist defection flourished. Part V examines the middle states of New York, Pennsylvania, New Jersey, and Delaware—a heterogeneous and pluralistic social order, and scene of many of the military operations of the war (from 1776 to 1778—where the most widespread civil conflict between patriots and loyalists occurred. Finally, Part VI locates the widely scattered pockets of loyalist activity throughout the South; during the early stages of the war these areas, which had never been brought fully under the sway of the dominant Whig planter elites, impeded patriot efforts in the South to consolidate control over a large geographical area. Against this background, the latter chapters of Part VI narrate the British invasion of the South from 1779 to 1781, a military operation that depended for its success on loyalist support and that failed largely because the loyalists were too weak, scattered, and unco-ordinated to play the ambitious role assigned them by British military planners.

In following the numerous and varied strands of the story, this book seeks to understand the *motivation*—the compelling reasons, influences, predispositions, and dictates of self-interest, temperament, conscience, intellect, fear, and plain confusion—that impelled the loyalists to act as they did. And, because personal motivation is difficult to establish and verify, the investigation of loyalist motivation is supplemented by an examination of the loyalists' *perception* of their roles in society, their dilemmas as the victims of political upheaval, and their consequent private anguish. The process of giving structure to thoughts and sensations, perception encompasses man's self-image, emotional and intellectual dexterity and stamina, the imperatives that govern him in moments of conscious choice, as well as the predispositions that operate in periods of routine. The co-ordinated study of motivation and perception is less superficial than the cataloguing of attitudes and more manageable than the search for the deeper roots of behavior. It is at this intermediate level that surviving loyalist sources convey the clearest meaning. In quotations, the spelling, capitalization, and punctuation have been modernized except in one obvious instance where original spelling has been retained.

As for terminology, I have not devised precise definitions for the many gradations of thought and behavior that may be classified as anti-Revolutionary, nor have I defined the elusive terms "loyalist" and "Tory." The word "loyalist" did not come into use until late in the war, when exiles in England adopted it as a badge of honor; "Tory" was an ugly epithet hurled at pre-Revolutionary supporters of British authority, which became a more general designation for the King's friends early in the War for Independence. In dealing with the pre-Revolutionary controversy, at least from 1760 to 1774, no label suggesting ultimate allegiance is appropriate because the issue of allegiance had not yet crystallized. Parts I through III of this book, therefore, are concerned with all of the *critics and opponents of the pre-Revolutionary movement.* From 1775 to 1781, there were specific ways in which men clearly identified themselves as adherents of the Crown—bearing arms, seeking protection, going into exile, swearing oaths, or doing business with the British—but there were innumerable shades and degrees of pro-British conduct. Many people tried to avoid any involvement in the struggle and supported one side or the other only when circumstances forced them to do so. This book is concerned with all of those persons who may be described as *opponents* or *victims* of the Revolution. In parts IV through VI, I have used the terms "loyalist" and "Tory" in much the same way as other historians, to identify persons who committed overt acts of opposition to the Revolution. Although Whigs and Tories were not formally constituted groups, these terms have been capitalized in keeping with widely employed usage in modern historical writing.

Acknowledgments

MORE than anyone else, Jack P. Greene enabled me to undertake and complete this study. Over a decade ago, at the Graduate School of Western Reserve University, he introduced me to the study of early American history and directed my initial research on the loyalists. He has continued to be a constant source of encouragement and insight.

The University of North Carolina at Greensboro has supported my work in many ways, and I wish particularly to acknowledge the assistance of the Research Council, the entire staff of the Library, and Richard Bardolph, head of the History Department. Kent Newmyer and Robert W. Lougee arranged for me to teach at the University of Connecticut in 1966–67, where some of the work on the book was done in a lovely setting.

The United States Educational Commission in Great Britain, the Research Foundation of the University of Connecticut, the National Society of Colonial Dames of America, the Research Department of Colonial Williamsburg, and the National Endowment for the Humanities have given generous financial support. A fellowship under the Co-operative Program in the Humanities of Duke University and the University of North Carolina at Chapel Hill provided time to write a portion of the manuscript in 1969–70. Past and present editors of the *Journal of American History, Pennsylvania History,* the *South Atlantic Quarterly,* the *Virginia Magazine of History and Biography,* and the *William and Mary Quarterly* criticized and improved portions of the study and allowed materials first published in their journals to be used here.

The staffs of all the libraries and archives where I worked were unfailingly helpful, and in particular I wish to thank

Acknowledgments

Harriet Lacy, of the New Hampshire Historical Society; Winifred Collins, Malcolm Freiberg, and John Cushing, of the Massachusetts Historical Society; Mr. and Mrs. Leo Flaherty, of the Massachusetts Archives; Magdelena Houlroyd, of the Glassboro State College Library; Albert Klyberg, of the Rhode Island Historical Society; and F. B. Stitt, of the William Salt Library.

Several former students have contributed significantly to my understanding of early American history: Rex T. Lohmann, Paul Ringenbach, Richard Warfle, and William R. Lee, graduate students at Connecticut in 1966–67; and Marsha J. Buckalew, Betty Wolfe, Elaine DeMars, Jimmy McKee, and Samuel Chapin Post, Jr., members of a memorable class on the American Revolution in Greensboro in 1970. Mary Beth Norton, Richard Maxwell Brown, James C. Zeidman, Don Higginbotham, David Maas, and Wallace Brown shared with me the results of their own research. Paul H. Smith, Albert E. Van Dusen, Anne Y. Zimmer, John K. Nelson, David P. Aldstadt, Ronald D. Cassell, and Ernest Swiger read and criticized portions of the manuscript. Stephen MacKinnon, Sharon Ericson, and Kenneth Scott served as research assistants. More recently, Kathleen Swiger performed an array of academic and research tasks with singular efficiency.

My mother proofread several drafts of the manuscript, and Sara Tillery typed it. The late Clinton Rossiter brought his great resourcefulness and infectious enthusiasm to the initial planning of the book and was unfailingly considerate and helpful. William B. Goodman, of Harcourt Brace Jovanovich, extended me the gratifying freedom to write the book in my own way, and when I asked for his assistance he gave valuable counsel. I am much indebted to the historians cited in the notes and Bibliographical Essay, upon whose work I have depended. For their indispensable encouragement and assistance, I am deeply grateful to my friends Converse D. Clowse, Richard O. Curry, Donald C. Lord, and Robert M. Weir. My wife, Doris, has lived with the writing of the book with patience, sympathy, and good cheer.

Greensboro, North Carolina
December 12, 1972

Contents

Contents

Contents

Contents

I

The Enunciation
of Principle

1

James Wright and the Nature
of the Empire

ON October 25, 1765, an excited but good-natured crowd of merchants, waterfront laborers, and artisans milled along the sandy main street of Savannah, Georgia. It was Friday afternoon, and they watched the militia muster to celebrate the fifth anniversary of George III's accession to the throne. By dusk the crowd, now growing in size, was attracted toward the waterfront by a group of men carrying an effigy of a stamp distributor, an imaginary agent of the recently enacted British law requiring tax stamps on all colonial legal documents, newspapers, and commercial transactions. Buoyed along by the day's celebration, the crowd's exuberance mounted until, sometime in the evening, the effigy was "hanged and burnt amidst the acclamations of a great concourse of people of all ranks and denominations." Four days later the traditional celebration of Guy Fawkes Day was also turned into a more threatening demonstration when six sailors from the Savannah docks carted through the town a crude scaffold on which sat a man with his head in a noose, imitating a stamp distributor, and bleating, "No stamps, no Riot Act, gentlemen," in mock pleas for mercy. Shouting obscenities, the sailors carried the scaffold to Machenry's Tavern, where they tied a noose under his arms as well as around his neck and hoisted him into the air in a pantomime hanging, while a large, respectably dressed crowd laughed and cheered. The Stamp Act crisis had come to Georgia.[1]

Although theatrical and full of high spirits, these scenes were part of the most serious crisis ever to occur within the political

[1] Notes are on pages 511–558.

order of the British Empire. In Boston, Massachusetts on August 14, a similar crowd had broken into the home of Stamp Distributor Andrew Oliver and, finding him fled, had demolished his fine furniture; on August 26 the same men wrecked and looted the home of Oliver's kinsman Lieutenant Governor Thomas Hutchinson. Mobs in Rhode Island, New Hampshire, New Jersey, Connecticut, Pennsylvania, and Virginia all demanded that stamp distributors resign their posts or be driven from their provinces. Throughout the colonies royal governors watched this violent response to the Stamp Act, measured their own limited power to compel obedience to the hated law, and declined to act. In Georgia, on the contrary, the contagion did not paralyze imperial government. The colony did come close to defiance of British authority but stopped short of actual disobedience. Tax stamps were actually sold and used in Georgia, as the law required. The reason was Governor James Wright's handling of the crisis from November 1765, when the law went into effect, until the following February, when attempts to nullify the law in Georgia died.[2]

James Wright, Royal Governor of Georgia from 1760 to 1775, was a native American, born in South Carolina, where his father held the Crown post of chief justice and where Wright himself served for twenty years as attorney general. Educated in England and having served as South Carolina's agent in London, he was equally at home with the landowning aristocracy of the Southern colonies and within the bureaucratic administration of the Empire. The two attachments created painful conflicts of interest for many colonists, but to an unusual degree Wright reconciled in his own mind the interests of the Crown and those of the colonies.[3]

Wright's effectiveness as governor of Georgia during the early 1760's rested on his knowledge of the eighteenth-century development of the Southern mainland colonies. He had grown up in South Carolina during that province's phenomenal expansion of the production and exportation of rice and indigo, and he understood the multiple economic causes of such development: English investment capital, enormous importations of slave labor, and the emergence of a metropolis at Charles Town and of subsidiary port towns like Georgetown. Wright also understood the mentality of the planter-merchant elite, who resembled both Virginia's gentry-aristocracy to the north and West Indian planters to the southeast. Like the West Indian planters, the South Carolinians lived in towns, left their estates in the hands of overseers, served as merchants and shipowners, and depended on ever-increasing supplies of slaves to work in the humid, disease-infested lowland plantations. Like the Virginians, the South Carolinian elite were intensely political and made the lower house of their Assembly a powerful and vigilant instrument for weaning power away from royal governors and the royal Council.

Wright's experience in South Carolina equipped him well for the governorship of Georgia. During the 1760's Georgia underwent a transformation in its economy, role in the Empire, social maturity, and identity as an American province, and the strongest single influence for change was the example of its rich, powerful neighbor, South Carolina. After a dismal period as a floundering proprietary colony created in the 1730's as a humanitarian refuge for England's deserving poor and as a defensive buffer between Spanish Florida and South Carolina, Georgia became a royal colony in 1752. The introduction of slavery and the migration of South Carolinian planters into the Georgia low country made the new royal colony a miniature South Carolina, producing rice and indigo on the coastal plantations. With ready investment capital and first crack at choice land, the South Carolinians in Georgia made profits of 25 to 30 per cent on their initial investment. The opportunity to buy more slaves and land tempted the planters to go ever more deeply into debt, and as their holdings and opulence grew, so did their indebtedness to English creditors. The existence of Charles Town—the colonial Charleston—as a major regional port actually fostered the growth of a subsidiary port at Savannah, where Charles Town firms opened branch offices. Georgia's proximity to the lucrative West Indian trade, moreover, enabled Savannah to become independent of Charles Town and made it an important center of trade with England, the West Indies, and North American ports. A native merchant community developed in Savannah during the 1760's by catering to the planters' appetite for expensive English furniture, clothing, and other finished goods. The prosperity of the 1760's and the sudden maturing of the economy attracted from the Carolina back country a steady migration of common folk who took advantage of cheap upcountry land, easy credit, and growing local commerce.

In this development, two royal governors of Georgia—Wright and his predecessor, Henry Ellis—played a vital role. They were patient and skillful negotiators with the Creek Indians at a time when peaceful white-Indian relations were essential to economic development; and the British government supported this work with a generous supply of gifts for use in the ceremonies of Indian diplomacy. Wright was also a military commander during a period when Georgia continued to have strategic importance. He alone among the royal governors of 1765 and 1766 had regular British troops directly under his command—distinct from provincial militia, which the assemblies controlled, and from other British troops in America, who were under the command of General Thomas Gage in New York. Most important, Wright commanded the respect of Georgia's Commons House of Assembly. His fair and firm Indian diplomacy opened new areas of land for speculation and development. He worked closely with the Assembly to improve navigation into the Savannah and Sunbury harbors, encouraged the enactment of inspection laws to eliminate inferior or spoiled export produce, and engineered a discriminatory tax on skins, which made it unprofitable for South Carolinian merchants to buy Georgia pelts and thereby channeled this lucrative trade through Savannah. He lobbied strenuously to influence the Board of Trade in London to permit a 1761 emission of badly needed paper money in Georgia. He won the support of the Assembly in 1762 for his successful effort to secure the ouster of an incompetent Chief Justice. His stand in a border dispute with South Carolina in 1764—ultimately settled in Georgia's favor by the Board of Trade—further enhanced his popularity.[4]

Strong executive leadership was essential to Georgia's growth and maturity, and during the early 1760's Wright's energy, foresight, and luck provided that leadership. His intimate knowledge of British administration and of colonial needs and conditions made him an unusually able Crown official. He was driven, however, not only by heady success and self-confidence but also by the dim apprehension that his position was precarious. The very rapidity of Georgia's growth under royal auspices created subtle, insidious pressures within the colony's society. The elite, the successful planters and merchants, had tasted enough wealth and power to become dissatisfied with their status as slightly junior partners to Wright and the imperial administration he represented. As inhabitants of a young, newly emergent colony without a long tradition of provincialism, Georgians were quick to think of themselves as Americans. Georgia had compressed into one decade the development that had taken other royal colonies more than a half century to achieve. Beneath the outward scene of bustle and order was a morass of uncertainty and complexity. If royal authority should falter as the central organizing force of the colony's development, a fierce power struggle would surely ensue. Wright's lack of pomp or complacency, his brisk and terse dispatch of duties, and his aloofness indicate his understanding of these perils. The Stamp Act crisis brought them into full view.

Wright did not even receive a copy of the Stamp Act until November 22, 1765—three weeks after it had gone into operation. The stamps themselves did not arrive until December 5, nor did Georgia's newly appointed Stamp Distributor, George Angus, arrive until January 5, 1766. Despite this haphazard timing by British officials, Wright spent the month of November preparing to outmaneuver a hastily formed organization of opposition to the Stamp Act known as the "Liberty Boys," composed of anonymous planters who prudently kept their identity secret but hoped to seize the stamps and intimidate the Distributor into resigning his post. Moving quickly, Wright and the royal Council decided to bring the stamps ashore as soon as they arrived and place them under guard. The Governor had a strong advantage in the 120 British troops scattered at five outposts in the province, and he brought fifty-six men and eight officers to Savannah. As soon as the transcript of the act arrived, he posted copies of it and administered to customs officials the necessary oaths, which bound them not to clear ships for departure from Savannah unless customs documents bore tax stamps. It was a bold move. Savannah's merchants considered the Stamp Act a direct threat to their livelihood, for the tax had to be paid in British sterling notes rather than colonial currency and, with the money supply already tight, it therefore threatened to stifle commercial transactions requiring sterling. Moreover, Wright quickly found that virtually everyone in Georgia considered the tax an unconstitutional intrusion of Parliamentary power upon colonial liberty. In the face of this anger and apprehension, Wright managed to wheedle from the most outspoken critics of the tax a promise that they would not physically seize the stamped paper. The paper came ashore on December 6, 1765. Two days earlier, on December 4, Wright had closed the Savannah harbor and prevented the sailing of more than sixty ships, many of them languishing with perishable cargoes and idle crews. The pressure on the merchants worked, and they asked Wright to appoint a temporary stamp distributor so that commerce could resume. The Liberty Boys, who had been biding their time until opposition to the Stamp Act mounted, were caught off guard and hastily gathered a crowd of some 200 to demonstrate against enforcement of the act. Wright responded by posting troops in front of the guardhouse where the stamps were stored, and the crowd drifted angrily but indecisively toward the Governor's home. Carrying his own musket, Wright caught up with the crowd and demanded to know what they were doing. A voice asked whether Wright was going to appoint a temporary distributor, but the Governor ignored the questioner and lectured the crowd on the bad manners of threatening a royal governor. He reminded them that they might call themselves "Sons of Liberty," but that he was truly upholding their liberty by maintaining law and preserving the freedom they enjoyed as British subjects. The crowd grudgingly dispersed but declared it would reassemble if news came of the appointment of a stamp distributor. Wright then collected fifty-four rangers and moved the stamps to more secure lodging in the large storehouse used for Indian presents.[5]

The next day Stamp Distributor Angus arrived in Georgia, and Wright had him brought secretly to his home in Savannah. With both stamps and Distributor secure from harm, the Liberty Boys had little leverage in their effort to prevent enforcement of the Stamp Act. By this point, the merchants were frantic to have the port reopened, and a temporary truce between merchants and Liberty Boys allowed the sale of stamps for customs documents only. On January 7, 1766, the port was unsealed, but it was only a temporary victory for Wright. Near the end of January the South Carolinian Sons of Liberty sent agents into the Georgia back country to stir up new resistance, and a large if undetermined number of insurgents converged on Savannah. While the size and power of the approaching force remained in doubt, Wright boldly disarmed Savannah and sent most of the fifty soldiers at his disposal to move the stamps to a fort on Cockspur Island, where a British man-of-war would collect them. Moving swiftly, the troops returned to Savannah before the back-country force reached the capital. The troops brought with them twenty British sailors, and by February 4 Wright had nearly one hundred armed men under his command. When the back country Liberty Boys entered the town, they assembled on the common and there learned of Wright's removal of the stamps and the arrival of reinforcements. The leaders of the insurgent force began to quarrel, and the band then dispersed.

Wright's ability to outmaneuver the Liberty Boys during the Stamp Act crisis turned upon several critical factors. First, he was the only royal governor with troops under his command. The fifty rangers at his disposal during the crisis were only a token force, but they were a formidable psychological weapon with which to dissuade the Liberty Boys from attempting actual violence. Even more important was Wright's ability to isolate the Liberty Boys from the majority of leading Georgians, who detested the Stamp Act but also feared the effect of violence and disruption on the colony's stability and order. To counteract "inflammatory papers, letters, and messages" sent to Georgia by "the Liberty Boys . . . in Charles Town,"[6] Wright spent countless hours between November 1765 and March 1766 drafting messages to the Assembly and talking informally to men representing every shade of opinion. These negotiations secured a series of agreements between Wright and the leaders of the Assembly that substantially reduced the chances for violent confrontation. In September 1765 Wright did nothing to prevent members of the Assembly from replying sympathetically to an invitation to attend the Stamp Act Congress. The Assembly was in recess when the invitation came, and the Speaker illegally usurped the Governor's prerogative by calling assemblymen into informal session. While the group declined to send a delegation to the congress, it did draft a reply endorsing the principle of united colonial resistance to the Stamp Act. Wright's refusal to disband the September meeting or to denounce its actions "amounted to complicity,"[7] in light of the Governor's usual insistence on his prerogatives. When the Assembly formally opened in October, it endorsed the actions of the September rump meeting as well as the resolutions of the Stamp Act Congress and summarily dismissed as the colony's London agent William Knox, an English bureaucrat who had outspokenly endorsed Parliament's power to enact the Stamp Act. Wright's silence on all of these actions clearly signaled his sympathy with this position.

Governor Wright's restraint in dealing with the Assembly during the autumn of 1765 enabled him to seize the initiative from activist leaders who would risk open defiance of the law to prevent enforcement of the Stamp Act. There was, he implied, an intelligent way to oppose the act. "It is not only our duty but our interest" to behave with "decency and submission" during the crisis and thereby dramatize the need for British "justice" to correct any mistakes made by Parliament. Those who ran headlong into loud defiance could "neither be friends to their King, their country, or to society," for they jeopardized "peace, harmony, and good order."[8] As conservative and rigid as these arguments sound today, they were powerful and relevant considerations in the Georgian society of the 1760's. Georgians knew their young province was held together by fragile social bonds that might disintegrate if rancor, suspicion, or violence alienated groups within the society from each other. Looking back on the crisis during the summer of 1766, after news of repeal of the Stamp Act had quieted the province, a number of Georgians agreed that the Stamp Act had intruded dangerously into the normal political life of the province, giving rise to bitterness, rage, and vituperation which the colony could ill afford. Wright understood and capitalized shrewdly on the fear of disruption.[9]

Wright's victory in the Stamp Act crisis came at a high personal and political price. It left him not so much embittered as emotionally drained and rigidified in the exercise of his office. During his first five years as governor he had carefully garnered a large store of trust and good will from the planter and merchant elite in the province. By insisting on enforcement of the act and persuading the majority of these men to eschew violence, Wright expended his treasury of obligations and confidence and guaranteed that the same men would never indenture themselves to him again. Moreover, the crisis shook Wright's confidence in the intelligence and capacity of British colonial policy. The tardy arrival of the stamps and the Distributor had needlessly jeopardized his control of the situation. The apparently easy success of the Sons of Liberty in neighboring South Carolina in blocking enforcement of the act convinced Wright that acting Governor William Bull was a spineless and two-faced Crown official. Most of all, the Stamp Act shattered Wright's equanimity and composure. He kept his own opinion of the act a carefully hidden secret, but his connivance with the Assembly's protests in September and October 1765 indicated his sympathy with their position. Through his close friend James Habersham, a wealthy merchant and President of the royal Council, Wright gave stronger evidence that he detested the Stamp Act. Both men had recently become widowers and spent many long evenings together during the winter of 1765–66. Habersham's public and private statements, which depicted the Stamp Act as recklessly ill-considered and dangerous, almost certainly reflected Wright's convictions. Habersham, a warm and generous man, believed that his oath as royal councillor to uphold British authority bound him to support a detestable law. "The Crown have as good a right to faithful servants," he explained tersely and with a tinge of bitterness, "as you and I to those we pay wages to." He even suffered the indignity of being warned for his own safety to stay away from his home during the crisis. Feeling "torn to pieces by our present internal distractions," he wrote, with genuine horror, how "dreadful it is to find one's person and property at the disposal of the giddy multitude . . . my heart bleeds."[10] Wright felt the same disgust and apprehension. The presumption of the Liberty Boys in trying to wrest from him his responsibility to enforce the law was, he wrote, "a matter too cutting . . . for a good subject and servant to bear"—about as close as Wright ever came to expressing emotion.[11]

The pattern of his conduct from 1766 onward revealed what a major change the Stamp Act crisis had wrought in his personality, image of himself, and political style. Now he did not hesitate to criticize, in letters to his superiors in London, British policies he considered short-sighted. He pointedly reminded Lord Hillsborough—the conscientious, overbearing Colonial Secretary from 1768 to 1771—that he knew better than any minister in London about the growing crisis of authority in the colonies. Nor did he bother, after 1766, to bridle his impatience when dealing with obstreperous assemblymen. His increased bluntness and self-confidence bordered on arrogance. He looked back on the Stamp Act crisis as the moment when he had been right and almost everyone else in responsible positions in colonial and imperial institutions had been wrong.[12]

Wright was not just licking his wounds. If the Stamp Act crisis had made him a more inflexible man, it had also forced him to re-evaluate the nature of colonial politics. The panicky way Parliament had repealed the Stamp Act, he feared, had only vindicated the colonists who had illegally thwarted its enforcement. Habits of recalcitrance in America, he concluded by 1766, would not "subside" easily. The restoration of harmony between Britain and the colonies would require "time and prudent conduct" by the Crown's servants, for the colonists had imbibed a heady ideology, "strange, mistaken ideas that no power can tax or restrain them but themselves or representatives of their own choosing"; and this conviction was "still fixed" in men's minds and boded only trouble for the future.[13]

Wright's statement was an accurate prediction of the future of colonial-imperial relations and all the more remarkable at a time when repeal of the Stamp Act produced a general feeling of euphoria about future harmony within the Empire. Wright embarked upon the task of restoring tranquillity to Georgia without any illusions, for at the same time that he was becoming a more stubborn, inflexible executive, his perceptiveness increased. From 1766 to 1774 he continued to outmaneuver Georgia's Liberty Boys, although the struggle became increasingly intense. The Commons House tried in 1767 to gain sole power to select and pay the colony's agent in London, and it refused to build barracks for British troops, as required by an act of Parliament. Wright and the royal Council stood firm on both issues, and the Commons retreated. Wright could not prevent a storm of colonial protest over the Townshend duties in 1768

from disrupting Georgia politics, and the Commons passed resolutions endorsing Virginia's and Massachusetts's opposition to the
new taxes before Wright could dissolve the House. In 1771 the
Commons chose its ground more carefully by electing as speaker
a leading Liberty Boy, Noble Wimberley Jones. Wright retaliated by using his power to veto Jones's election, and the Assembly in turn branded this action "a high breach of the privileges
of the House." For the next two years the Commons refused to do
business until its power to select its own speaker was recognized
and while Wright refused to allow any depletion of his prerogative power to approve the House's nominee for the office.[14]

In the short run, time worked in Wright's favor. He spent
nineteen months in England during the impasse over the
speakership, leaving his office in the loyal and capable hands of
acting Governor Habersham. When he returned in February
1773 as Sir James Wright, Baronet, he brought with him permission from the Crown for Georgia to purchase two million acres of
land from the Indians—an immensely popular achievement in
the colony. A rash of Creek Indian attacks on white settlers in
early 1774 and the need for better defenses against the Indians
made the Assembly unusually "dutiful and loyal" while other
colonies were exploding in protest against the Coercive Acts.
Georgia did not even send delegates to the First Continental
Congress at Philadelphia in September. As late as the closing
months of 1774 Wright had resisted every attempt to diminish
the power of the Crown in Georgia. By the middle of the next
summer all this had changed. A provincial Congress replaced the
old colonial Assembly and moved swiftly to align Georgia with
the other rebelling colonies. The provincial Congress first took
control of the militia and then of the courts of law. "The powers
of government," Wright accurately explained, "are wrested out
of my hands."[15]

It was a fitting epitaph for British rule in Georgia. Wright
understood that power was more than negative coercion; it was
also the capacity of government to command respect. He knew
that he had handled power as dexterously as any man in the
Empire, for Wright was that rare kind of individual who rated
his own abilities very highly and took himself utterly seriously
but was at the same time neither vain nor self-deluded. Wright's

observations on the dynamics of the pre-Revolutionary controversy are among the best informed and most discriminating available. He understood that the emotional force of colonial arguments against Parliamentary power was far more powerful than the loyalties and habits upon which Britain relied to hold colonial allegiance. "My Lord," he beseeched Hillsborough to understand in 1769, "the Americans are deeply convinced that they are not represented in the British Parliament and . . . are so enthusiastically possessed with an opinion that they cannot be constitutionally taxed . . . by laws to which they have not consented . . . that *they will never be brought to change their sentiments or acquiesce quietly.*"[16] This change was unalterable, Wright continued, because the colonists had become "intoxicated with ideas of their own importance and power." There was only one remedy. Parliament had to seize the initiative in the controversy and voluntarily renounce its power to tax the colonies, drawing a clear and unmistakable line between colonial rights and British authority. "It seems absolutely necessary to bring these matters to a point and *settle them,*" he told Hillsborough.[17] In no other way could imperial authority regain "its due weight and power."[18]

Bereft of "due weight and power," Wright felt acutely aware, as the pre-Revolutionary crisis deepened, that the only tools at his disposal were maneuver and persuasion. When Hillsborough reprimanded Wright for allowing the Commons to pass resolutions against the Townshend duties, the Governor retorted with a blunt analysis of his position: "I knew well, my Lord, that if I appeared openly to oppose this measure or even reason . . . and endeavour to convince them of the impropriety of it, . . . that considering the temper of the times, I should probably have done more harm than good. I therefore [took] every opportunity . . . of talking the matter over in a private way with individuals."[19] Wright also knew when the time for such prudent retreat had ended and when duty required him to defend colonial obedience in moral terms. "You may be advocates for liberty," he bluntly told the Commons House on January 18, 1775; "so am I, but in a constitutional and legal way. . . . Take heed how you give sanction to trample upon law and government and be assured . . . that where there is no law there can be no liberty. It is the due course of law and support of government which only can insure the enjoyment of your lives, your liberties, and your estates. . . . Don't catch at the shadow and lose the substance."[20]

Wright's claim in 1775 that he was a defender of American liberty was not a hypocritical guise or a desperate taunt. It expressed in clear language the rules that had always governed his conduct as a Crown official. The Empire had given Georgia an institutional framework, military security, and commercial opportunity. Those assets made provincial growth and individual success possible, but Wright knew that there was nothing automatic or guaranteed in this political and social arrangement. It required subjects who would restrain their naturally turbulent natures, and capable, intelligent British officials in both London and provincial capitals like Savannah. Thus considered, imperial authority was a delicate fabric.

2

The Sources and Disposition of Power in the British Empire

THE British Empire at the middle of the eighteenth century was a collection of possessions extending from the banks of Newfoundland and Nova Scotia along the thirteen seaboard colonies from New Hampshire to Georgia. It also included the Bermudas and Bahamas in the Atlantic; the Caribbean sugar islands of Jamaica, Barbados, and the Windward and Leeward islands; coastal Honduras; Gibraltar and Minorca in the Mediterranean; and Guinea, on the west coast of Africa. Finally, there was the territory occupied by chartered trading companies operating around Hudson Bay, in west Africa, and in India. The acquisition, settlement, and exploitation of the Empire were an integral part of England's emergence as a major power from the 1580's, when the first abortive attempts to establish permanent colonies occurred, through 1763, when victory over France in the Seven Years' War added French Canada and Spanish Florida to Britain's overseas possessions.[1] The Empire had meant many things to England. At first, permanent colonies established England's claim to a share of the wealth of the New World. Then overseas possessions impelled England to supplant first Spain, then the Dutch, and finally France as Europe's major colonial and commercial power. The Empire became an outlet for daring investors, restless and ambitious settlers, and religious dissenters. Armed with land grants and governing authority, corporate groups of such men formed the vanguard of colonial expansion during the seventeenth century. Between 1689 and 1713, England created a colonial bureaucracy capable of administering its growing overseas holdings effectively, and thus the Empire became associated with an officialdom. At the same time, the prosperity and rapid maturity of colonial societies created, in the New World, replicas of the mother country that imitated English culture but resisted imperial centralization and political control.[2]

Running through these shifting economic, social, military, bureaucratic, and cultural aspects of empire was one common assumption: colonies existed to enhance the power and wealth of the mother country. This mercantilist belief was expressed and embodied in a series of statutes enacted by Parliament between 1650 and 1764, most notably the Navigation Act of 1660, which established the commercial system after the restoration of Charles II, and the Act of 1696, which revamped its administration under a Board of Trade. These laws required that all trade within the Empire travel in English or colonial ships manned by English or colonial crews. At the heart of this regulatory system was a practice called "enumeration": a statutory list of colonial agricultural staples that could be exported only to the mother country. Customs duties on imports and exports within the Empire added to the income of the Crown and in the colonies defrayed the cost of enforcing the acts of trade. To stimulate the commerce of the Empire a complex system of bounties, subsidies, and exclusive access to the British market promoted the production of staples like naval stores, which received a production bounty; tobacco, which was given a monopoly of the home market; and rice, which after 1730 could be exported directly to the Iberian peninsula. In turn, the colonies were prohibited from manufacturing finished iron, fur hats, or woolen textiles, which might compete with British products.

Under the acts of trade, colonial commerce flourished and Britain became the wealthiest trading nation on earth. This economic dynamism held the Empire together in part because the acts of trade were a patchwork of expedients that only roughly adhered to mercantilist theory. The capricious and arbitrary provisions of the system proved to be unenforceable. There was, for example, a strong bias among British officials toward the sugar-producing British West Indies; there, climate, fertility, and massive slave labor enabled planters and British merchants and investors to reap fabulous profits while at the same time providing Britain with a desirable staple product and making a direct contribution to the British Treasury. As a reward, Parliament passed the Molasses Act of 1733, placing a prohibitive duty on the cheaper and better-grade French molasses imported by New England merchants. The result was widespread smuggling of French molasses. Other arbitrary mercantilist practices aggravated the problem. In theory, Britain was the financial hub of the Empire and export of gold coin to the colonies was forbidden. The colonies could not mint their own coin, and British officials only grudgingly permitted occasional emissions of colonial paper currency. The need for a larger and more responsive money supply heightened the value of illicit trade between the mainland and the French, Spanish, and Dutch West Indies. This commerce not only brought gold into the colonies; the higher profits from illegal free trade in the Caribbean also provided investment capital for mainland merchants seeking to expand their legitimate trade within the Empire. In addition, it was not until the 1760's that the British Customs Service had the manpower or expertise to check cargoes of enumerated goods closely; as a result, some of this trade went to non-English ports, and only a fraction of export duties on legitimate and illicit trade was ever collected. This laxity of enforcement—caused by inefficiency, bribery, and confusion in bustling, crowded ports—actually stimulated the commerce of the Empire. Truly stringent checking of customs papers and searches of cargoes would have seriously hampered the speed and volume of trade. Colonial merchants apparently violated the acts of trade when there was an overriding economic reason to do so. Illicit commerce with the non-English West Indies placed the colonies in an international market and greatly increased the total level of commercial activity within the Empire.[3]

The acts of trade provided much of the legal framework of the Empire, and colonial economic development modified that structure; the Empire was an amalgam of changing laws and practices. How viable and durable was the British Empire as an economic and political unit? Was the unevenness of imperial authority in the seventeenth and eighteenth centuries a healthy stimulant to British and colonial political ingenuity or an impairment of the cohesion of the Empire? These questions have provoked an

enormous amount of historical scholarship, and though historians have reached no agreement on the answers, they have
identified two sets of forces working simultaneously within the
Empire—one binding it more closely together and the other
weakening the efficacy of those ties.[4]

The most important political bonds connecting the thirteen
North American colonies to the mother country were the royal
governments, which replaced decrepit charter and proprietary
administrations. In Virginia, a royal government was set up in
1624; in New York, after its proprietor, the Duke of York,
became King in 1685; in New Hampshire, after its separation
from Massachusetts in 1679; in Massachusetts in 1691; in Maryland from 1689 to 1715; in New Jersey in 1701; in North Carolina in 1729; in South Carolina in 1719; and in Georgia in 1752.*
Royal government brought continuity, a uniform constitution,
and badly needed executive leadership to these colonies. Such
governments were ostensibly based upon the English constitution, with its essential elements of King, Lords, and Commons.
The governor was appointed by and represented the King, and
the Crown supervised his performance with a detailed "Commission" outlining his powers and lengthy "Royal Instructions"
specifying how he should deal with particular problems. His
most important duties were summoning, dissolving, and proroguing (that is, recessing) the Assembly, approving or vetoing
its legislation, and referring the legislation he signed to the Privy
Council in London for further review. The lower, or popularly
elected, house of the Assembly served the functions of the House
of Commons in the English model; the royally appointed Council was roughly the equivalent of the House of Lords. It shared
legislative power with the lower house, though in practice it
could not initiate or modify taxation or appropriation bills. The
Council also served as a local version of the Privy Council, officially advising the governor and being a party to some executive
decisions. The most notable departure from this constitutional
scheme was the Massachusetts Charter of 1691, which allowed the
lower house to elect—subject only to the governor's veto—the
members of the Council. Although the Massachusetts House

* These are the dates of the changeover from proprietary to royal rule in
London, not of the arrival of the new royal governors in America.

tended to choose, and the governor to approve, councillors relatively sympathetic to the policies of the Crown, the Massachusetts Council was an independent body which after 1765 increasingly sided with the lower house against the governor.[5]

At its best, royal government gave order and form to the still fragile and unstable colonial society and brought security and predictability to the task of taming the wilderness and maintaining European standards of civility in a crude, unpolished social setting; it induced colonial leaders to put aside internecine factional strife and co-operate with the governor in the task of promoting the colony's prosperity. William Gooch, Governor of Virginia from 1727 to 1749, persuaded the House of Burgesses to institute a far-reaching program to improve the market value of tobacco through a system of inspection and the destruction of low-quality leaves. He won local support for these reforms by making the inspection fair, honest, and impartial. He overcame opposition from the customs service, which feared that export limitations on tobacco would reduce customs, the value of duties on tobacco, and thereby lower its income.[6] In Massachusetts, Governor William Shirley (1741-1757) succeeded where his predecessors had failed in securing the co-operation of all the major factions in the colony; he engineered this political harmony by persuading the assembly to support expensive military operations against the French in King George's War, 1741-1748, and he bestowed the contracts, commissions, and civil offices that the war created on a wide circle of able provincial leaders.[7]

Benning Wentworth, Governor of New Hampshire from 1741 to 1767, brought such benevolent, stabilizing techniques to the level of an art form. As early as 1637 the first Wentworth settled in the region that later became New Hampshire, and by the middle of the eighteenth century the family was the richest and ablest in the province. Benning Wentworth became governor and acquired extensive authority by constructing a network of influences and alliances within New Hampshire itself, in neighboring Massachusetts, and in London. Wentworth's numerous relatives dominated New Hampshire's chief export trade, lumber. Through John Thomlinson, his close associate in London, Benning Wentworth secured the governorship and also the influential post of surveyor of His Majesty's Forests in North America, an office that regulated lumbering and insured that the British Navy would have a regular supply of masts, spars, and other shipbuilding necessities. Thomlinson also secured for Wentworth and other New Hampshire merchants lucrative contracts to supply lumber for the navy. Acting as governor, Wentworth could create new townships and grant the choice land in these locations to his political supporters. Intermarriage with a few prominent merchant families in Portsmouth made the Wentworths leaders of an aristocracy that acquired its wealth in lumbering, office-holding, land speculation, and commerce. Wentworth's judicious use of patronage and land grants and his lax enforcement of restrictions on lumbering placed the great majority of landowners and merchants of New Hampshire in his debt. The Assembly therefore worked closely with the Governor and relied upon Wentworth's contacts in London to promote the province's interests. A concentration of power, influence, and effectiveness in the Wentworth family gave New Hampshire a stable and prosperous political and social order.[8]

Gooch, Shirley, Wentworth, and Wright brought royal government in America to its most effective level of performance; each man possessed leadership talents that fostered the economic expansion of his province and enlarged the power and wealth of his colony's social elite. But the political institutions that benefited most from prosperity and the growth of aristocracy were the lower houses of assembly. Created during the earliest years of each colony's existence, the assemblies gave power and responsibility to the leading men of the province. By the middle of the eighteenth century each of the assemblies had acquired exclusive power to initiate provincial tax bills and audit its colony's financial records, often the authority to supervise expenditures, and on occasion the power to print paper money. The lower houses acquired extensive control over militia, local government, public works, and Indian affairs. Control of the purse and the responsibility for paying salaries to many Crown officials, however, did not give the assemblies enough leverage to dictate to their governors. But the assemblies could bring specific operations of government to a halt by delaying the payment of a salary, refusing to build a needed fort, or failing to raise and arm militia in time of war. Lengthy debates about the conduct of particular Crown officials or protracted disputes between the lower house and the council could prevent the passage of needed routine legislation and embarrass the governor more than they inconvenienced the public. By steadily enlarging their control over finance and policy and scrutinizing every action of Crown officials, the assemblies transformed American politics during the half century from 1713 to 1763.[9]

The assemblies succeeded partly because they proved to be far more adaptable political institutions than the agencies of the Crown. During the seventeenth century, property qualifications for voting restricted the electorate to less than a quarter of the adult white male population; however, the growing availability of land after 1713 enlarged the electorate so that by the 1760's probably 95 per cent of adult white males could vote in Massachusetts, perhaps 75 per cent in New York, and at least 50 per cent in Virginia. Candidates for the assemblies were almost always men of property and of standing in the colony. Men of humbler station lacked the time, training, and incentive to hold office, and by tradition the bulk of the population deferred to members of the elite. Political contests, then, pitted rival segments of the aristocracy against each other. To win an election a candidate needed both the backing of powerful political sponsors and the approval of the voters. Oratorical eloquence, a reputation for honesty or shrewdness or piety or business acumen, and a respected family name were among the qualities that voters favored. Within the assembly a further screening of talent occurred. Through an elaborate committee system, a core of experienced and hardworking legislators monopolized the power of the assembly. These were the men who did the hard, tedious work of responding line by line to governors' messages; in the process they learned how to distinguish their own ideas about public policy from those propounded by Crown officials and royal governors. The exchange of messages between governors and assemblies forced assemblymen constantly to refurbish and refine the idea that the colonies had a contractual relationship with the mother country—a contract that guaranteed the preservation of representative government and individual liberty.[10] Unintentionally the Crown encouraged the assemblies to think of themselves as bulwarks of liberty, miniature parliaments designed to check and counteract any excessive use of prerogative power by the Crown. Royal instructions to governors cautioned that lower houses were not to exercise "any power or privilege . . . which is not allowed . . . the House of Commons . . . in Great Britain."[11] This comparison was a heady stimulant to colonial politics, for the image that eighteenth-century Americans had of the House of Commons came from the seventeenth century, when the Commons had resisted and whittled down the prerogative power of the Stuart monarchy. At the very least, this tendency to imitate the House of Commons brought regularity and a sense of seriousness to colonial politics.

Despite the apparent maturity and vitality of political institutions in America, the constitution of the Empire was fundamentally unstable. Difficult to diagnose and impossible to correct at the time, this instability had three major underlying causes. In the first place, the executive branches of the royal governments— governors, councils, and other appointed officials—possessed far more formal power than they did informal political influence and leverage.[12] The governor of a colony could summon, prorogue, or dissolve its assembly at will, while in Britain a new Parliamentary election had to be called every seven years and Parliament effectively controlled the duration of its sessions. Governors frequently thwarted hostile resolutions by proroguing assemblies without warning and extending the recesses for long periods of time. The governor had an absolute veto over all colonial laws, and the Privy Council often disallowed laws that the governor allowed to stand; British kings in the eighteenth century had tacitly relinquished authority to disapprove acts passed by Parliament, but royal governors used the veto regularly. Finally, the Crown claimed the power to dismiss royally appointed colonial judges at will, although British judges could be removed only for proven misconduct. In contrast with these formal powers, which exceeded those of the Crown in Great Britain, royal officials in America lacked the informal power that enabled the British government at home to get things done. The governors—except in New Hampshire and, to a lesser extent, in Massachusetts—had little patronage to dispense. Royal councils were intended to provide the governor with a group of wealthy and prestigious advisers who shared with him the responsibility for maintaining British authority; but for a variety of reasons the councils steadily declined in prestige and power and were often more of an embarrassment than a support for the governor. Consequently, many governors felt a galling sense of impotence. "Officers and . . . commissioners are named by the General Assembly," Governor James Glen, of South Carolina, reported in 1748, "and are answerable and accountable to [the Assembly] only. . . . A governor has no power either to reprove or remove them, and indeed it were to little purpose to tell them he is displeased with them, when he cannot displace them. Thus little by little the people have got the whole administration into their hands. . . . No . . . governor [can be] clothed with authority when he is stripped naked of power and . . . can neither reward the virtuous . . . nor displace and punish those that offend."[13] On the one hand, the governors' extensive formal powers aroused deep apprehension and kept the assemblies in a state of defensiveness, while, on the other, the governors' lack of informal influence weakened their capacity to deal firmly and fairly with the assemblies.

The anxiety with which governors and colonial politicians eyed each other's powers prompted both groups to stabilize colonial politics by establishing a network of relationships with highly placed political patrons in England. Ironically, this effort created a second unsettling feature in the colonial structure. Most Crown officials and many colonial politicians depended on allies within the ruling circles in London to intervene with Parliament or agencies of the Crown in a host of mundane matters—appointments, minor changes in the acts of trade, legal decisions of colonial courts that had been appealed to the Privy Council. Thus Benning Wentworth had John Thomlinson; William Gooch had close ties with key political advisers of Robert Walpole; James De Lancey, the most powerful politician in New York during the 1740's and 1750's, owed his position to a network of highly placed allies in London, including the Archbishop of Canterbury. This system of personal transatlantic ties worked well during the first half of the eighteenth century because responsibility for colonial policy was fragmented during those years. Under Robert Walpole, Parliament avoided divisive questions of policy, and the only important Parliamentary legislation affecting the colonies during that period was the passage of the Molasses Act of 1733 at the behest of West Indian planters. As long as an extensive alliance of Whig factions dominated Parliament, the work of governing the colonies was reduced mainly to competition over patronage: the distribution of royal offices in America to deserving supporters of the various factional leaders in British politics. In this situation, highly placed agents of governors and provincial leaders as well as official agents of particular colonies could influence patronage decisions and obstruct efforts by agencies of the imperial bureaucracy to impose truly coercive controls on the colonies.[14]

Intended to stabilize colonial politics by creating intimate lines of communication across the Atlantic, these alliances between colonial and British political figures made the colonies dependent on English political stability and predictability. Beginning in the 1750's, English politics again became highly unpredictable. The Duke of Newcastle, the great patronage broker of the 1730's and 1740's, began to lose his once-magisterial control. The Seven Years' War delayed the disintegration of the Walpolean alliance of Whig leaders in Parliament; as an emergency wartime arrangement, the ministry was jointly led by Newcastle, who kept the House of Commons in line, and William Pitt, who mobilized the war effort and planned the brilliant campaigns that defeated the French in Canada, on the continent, and in the West Indies. But Pitt fell from power as soon as British victory was assured. War, moreover, created vast new wealth for British merchants, and the scramble to share this booty weakened the old London merchant houses and joint stock companies and strengthened newly emerged merchant firms in Bristol, Liverpool, and Glasgow. At the same time, the mercantile interest groups that lobbied Parliament and the ministry became smaller, more specialized, and more numerous than the interest groups of the early eighteenth century.

At this moment of flux in politics and economic life, George II died and his young grandson ascended to the throne as George III. Politically inexperienced but determined not to be manipulated by powerful factions, the new King quickly humiliated Newcastle by offering jobs and influence to opportunists among the Duke's Parliamentary backers and then purging from the government payroll those who remained loyal to Newcastle. In so doing, George III and his adviser, the Earl of Bute, broke the power of the alliance of Whig factions that had governed Britain since 1713. Despite this initial success, it would take the young King ten years to find a ministry that could command a dependable majority in the House of Commons. Into this power vacuum moved not only shortsighted and mediocre ministers like George Grenville, Charles Townshend, and the Earl of Hillsborough, but also the bureaucratic agencies of the Crown that throughout the past half century had sought to make colonial policy and to govern the colonies firmly but that had never had enough power or leadership to make good this ambition. Thwarted in its efforts from 1696 to 1760 to govern the Empire more rigorously, and then successful in securing support for tough colonial policies, the imperial bureaucracy constituted a third source of turbulence within the colonial political order.

The oldest English agency concerned with colonial government was the Privy Council. As late as the reigns of Queen Elizabeth and her successor, James I, the Privy Council was a small and effective body of less than twenty members that advised the monarch and implemented royal policy. Under Charles I (1625–1641) and his son Charles II (1660–1685) the Council lost authority to cliques of favored advisers; the general decline of the King's power following the Revolution of 1688 further reduced the Council's weight; finally, as its size expanded from 52 members in 1714 to 75 in 1760 and 106 in 1782, the Privy Council became an unwieldy ceremonial body that ratified decisions made elsewhere in the executive. Throughout this transformation the Privy Council retained one group of its old powers: settling disputes in the colonies between Crown officials and elected assemblies, reviewing all legislation passed by colonial assemblies, and acting as a final appellate court in judicial cases appealed from colonial courts to London for final adjudication. Usually acting on recommendations from the Board of Trade, the Privy Council disallowed many of the laws passed by colonial assemblies and approved by royal governors. The Board of Trade tightened the stringency of disallowance when, beginning in 1720, it instructed royal governors to require that important colonial laws contain a "suspending clause" delaying effectiveness of the statute until after the Privy Council had reviewed it. In the most famous disallowance controversy, the Privy Council voided a Virginia statute fixing the value of tobacco paid as salaries to Anglican clergymen and in effect reducing the amount of clerical compensation. Patrick Henry, as lawyer for one vestry, denounced the disallowance as an act of tyranny. The Privy Council also ruled on disputes between governors and assemblies. Here too the most famous case was from Virginia; in 1754 the Council upheld Governor Robert Dinwiddie's claim that his royal instructions took precedence over traditional practices and powers of the House of Burgesses. During the late 1760's and early 1770's, the Privy Council adjudicated an immensely complicated dispute between New York and New Hampshire, both of which claimed possession of land that made up the future state of Vermont. Although the Council upheld New Hampshire's claim, New Yorkers went right on securing grants in the area—usually with the connivance of New York's royal governors. Finally, the Council's committee on judicial appeals heard, between 1696 and 1783, almost 1,500 appeals on decisions from colonial courts covering a wide variety of cases: white-Indian relations, church-state conflicts, vice-admiralty disputes, and all sorts of issues in criminal and civil law. Through disallowance and appellate decisions, the Privy Council, working closely with the Board of Trade, had a pervasive impact on colonial law. Its scrutiny compelled colonial statutes and judicial decisions to conform as closely as possible to the spirit of English statute law and common law. The possibility of appeal to the Privy Council made colonial legislators more polished legislative draftsmen and prompted colonial judges to model their decisions on English precedents. But the Privy Council encountered increasing difficulty in getting its rulings enforced after 1760, and the complicated, time-consuming nature of the procedure discouraged colonial claimants from appealing cases to London during the last decade of British rule in America.[15]

By far the most important agency formulating colonial policy in the first half of the eighteenth century was the Board of Trade. Created in 1696, the Lords Commissioners of Trade and Plantations, as it was officially titled, devoted much more of its attention to trade than to "plantations" (that is, colonies) and performed the valuable if unexciting task of collecting and evaluating trade statistics and a wide range of information bearing on the economy and politics of the colonies, as well as carrying out some domestic administrative duties. The board drafted instructions to royal governors, and while it had the power to advise the Crown on all royal appointments in the colonies, it effectively controlled only the seats on the royal councils. Periodically, the board took up the task of converting faltering proprietary colonies into royal possessions. Between 1624 and 1691, Virginia, Barbados, the Leeward Islands, New Hampshire, New York, Massachusetts, and Bermuda had become royal colonies. Between 1701 and 1754, under the board's direction, the Crown took over administration of New Jersey, North and South Carolina, the Bahamas, and Georgia and attempted without success to wrest control of Pennsylvania and Maryland from their proprietors. Between periods of lethargy and drift, the board bestirred itself, tried to consolidate its power and become *the* agency controlling all colonial policy and administration. But the House of Commons, still suspicious of the power of the Crown, refused to grant the board's instructions to royal governors the force of law or to punish refractory colonies with coercive legislation.

The Board of Trade did enjoy a resurgence of authority from 1748 to 1761 under the leadership of its President, the Earl of Halifax, who supervised closely the work of governors and other Crown officials. In the first seven years of his tenure on the board, Halifax laid the basis for a sweeping reorganization of colonial government. His plans had to be put aside during the Seven Years' War, when Britain needed colonial co-operation more than it did grudging obedience. Thereafter no administrator of his ability ever held a responsible position in the government of the Empire. Despite its failure to centralize the colonial administration and its eclipse after the Seven Years' War, the board had a profound effect on colonial-imperial relations. It provided employment for more than sixty years to a cluster of financial, legal, and commercial experts, and these men gradually articulated and elaborated a conception of the Empire in which the colonies were considered children of the parent state, proper subjects of subordination to British power and interests. When George III's ministers finally began to tighten imperial control after 1760, they found in the old recommendations of the Board of Trade a convincing rationale and detailed blueprint for imperial centralization.[16]

The Board of Trade's chief competitor for control of colonial policy was the British Treasury. The King's first minister was customarily first lord of the treasury—a forerunner of the modern office of prime minister. As government finance became more complicated and colonial trade burgeoned, Treasury officials moved beyond collecting taxes and auditing records and began to compute the drain that expenditures in the colonies placed on the Treasury. By the middle of the eighteenth century the Crown's operations in America were an accountant's nightmare. The postal service lost money, and customs receipts under the terms of the acts of trade did not even defray the cost of enforcement. Quitrents on land granted by the Crown were difficult to collect. Most Crown salaries and routine expenditures in the colonies were appropriated by the assemblies, over whose work the Treasury had no control whatever. Armed with voluminous figures about this fiscal chaos, Treasury officials like Thomas Whately acquired a commanding influence over British colonial policy during the 1760's.[17]

The Treasury also supervised the work of the Board of Customs Commissioners, which collected import and export duties under the Navigation Acts and inspected cargoes leaving colonial ports to determine that enumerated products went only to Britain. Understaffed and underfinanced, the board watched helplessly as an increasing volume of illegal French goods, especially smuggled molasses, filled colonial ports. The growing influence of the Treasury and the critical state of British finances after the Seven Years' War emboldened the commissioners to propose in 1763 a wholesale reform of mercantile enforcement procedures: reduction of the molasses duty to a reasonable level and then rigorous enforcement of the new tax; an array of new authority to search ships and verify the ultimate destination of enumerated goods; and use of the British Navy to eliminate smuggling. The Sugar Act of 1764 put these recommendations into effect and signaled Parliament's intention to impose new imperial control over the colonies.[18]

In addition to building and running the navy, the Admiralty Board was another official body that had important colonial responsibilities. The Sugar Act of 1764 gave the navy the impossible task of enforcing the acts of trade and suppressing smuggling. The great bulk of colonial trade was conducted legally, and such illicit French molasses and lesser amounts of Portuguese wine as reached American waters could easily be transferred to a fishing boat off the coast and unloaded in a quiet cove or inlet at night. Aggressive patrolling and random searching by British naval vessels only angered individualistic captains and merchants; when the *Gaspee,* a Royal Navy vessel officiously searching colonial ships along the Rhode Island coast, ran aground on June 9, 1772, an unidentified group of men in small boats accosted the helpless ship at midnight, shot and seriously wounded the captain, took his crew prisoners, and burned the ship to the waterline. Undermanned and plagued by deserters, the British Navy resorted everywhere to impressment of sailors. In colonial ports, especially New York and Boston, impressment incited violent resistance. The Admiralty had also operated, since 1696, eleven vice-admiralty courts in the colonies. These courts adjudicated civil disputes between sailors and captains, tried men accused of crimes on the high seas, and heard cases of alleged smuggling or illegal export of enumerated goods. Acting on complaints by customs officials, the royal attorney general for the province or the court's own advocate general conducted these prosecutions. From the beginning these courts had no juries—because juries in provincial courts refused to convict smugglers—and under the Sugar Act of 1764, vice-admiralty procedure became still more stringent. The act placed on the owner of a vessel seized by customs officials the burden of evidence proving that he had not violated the acts of trade. The Sugar Act also directed vice-admiralty judges to rule whether or not customs officials had "probable cause" for seizing a ship. If there was due cause, an acquitted defendant could still be forced to pay part of the cost of the prosecution and he could not sue the customs official for false arrest. Convicted smugglers had their entire cargo confiscated and sold at auction, with customs officials, the vice-admiralty judge, the prosecutor, the governor of the colony, and the King all receiving a share of the proceeds. Vice-admiralty judges received no regular salary and their income from fees was not considered exorbitant. In 1764 the Vice-Admiralty Court of Halifax received new authority to oversee all vice-admiralty jurisdiction in America and to interpret the new provisions of the Sugar Act. The remoteness of the court in Halifax led to its replacement in July 1768 by four regional courts, in Halifax, Boston, Philadelphia, and Charles Town; by this time it was too late to rehabilitate these tribunals. The sensational prosecutions of John Hancock and Henry Laurens in 1768, in the provincial vice-admiralty courts of Massachusetts and South Carolina respectively, raised serious constitutional and legal questions about the deprivation of jury trial, the extensive powers of judges, and the apparently cozy relationship between the judges and prosecutors in these courts.[19]

The War Office, like the Admiralty, became more deeply involved in colonial administration following the Seven Years' War. For a variety of reasons, the British Army left several thousand troops in North America after the Peace of Paris. Meant to deter Indian aggression and maintain peaceful relations between Indians and whites and also to occupy the newly and unexpectedly acquired territories of French Canada and Spanish Florida, these forces were scattered through Canada and northern New York; around New York City and neighboring New Jersey, the Ohio valley, and the Great Lakes; and through the Floridas, Georgia, and South Carolina. The colonists did not at first object to this standing army in peacetime, and the British never seriously considered the implications of leaving troops in the colonies. Parliament enacted, in 1765, legislation requiring colonies in which troops were stationed to provide barracks or quarters in private homes. Of the more than 5,000 troops in America during the mid-1760's, fewer than 200 were stationed in the more settled parts of Massachusetts, New York, New Jersey, South Carolina, and Georgia; but in all these colonies the assemblies vehemently protested the quartering requirements. All of these forces, except for those in Georgia commanded by Governor Wright, were under the command of General Thomas Gage,

Commander in Chief of British forces in North America. The resulting division of authority between Gage and the governor in each royal colony seriously weakened the authority of both army and civil authorities. Gage's men could not quell civil disorders unless invited to do so by the governor and his council; governors and councils were afraid to ask unless they knew the army had enough power and numbers to impose order with little bloodshed. During the Stamp Act crisis the army—except in Georgia—was impotent. When mob attacks against customs officials in Boston provoked the dispatch of British troops to the Massachusetts city in 1768, their military effectiveness was entirely canceled by the turbulent conditions they encountered. Insulted and abused, the army in Boston became trapped in a rising spiral of insults and heated tempers that culminated in the Boston Massacre in 1770.[20]

Finally, the Church of England was a part of the imperial bureaucracy. The legally established and predominant church in the South, and a rapidly growing and partisan denomination in the middle and New England colonies, the Anglican church in America came under the jurisdiction of the Bishop of London. Recurring proposals for the creation of an American episcopate, a bishop for the colonies, had for decades ignited arguments about the sinister political motives of the Anglican church and had kept alive the specter of a privileged church using its influence among Crown officials to undermine Congregationalist, Presbyterian, and other dissenting denominations. Although nothing ever came of the talk of an American bishop, the church's Society for the Propagation of the Gospel in Foreign Parts (known simply as the S.P.G.) appeared to have real political influence. It sent scores of missionaries to the colonies, first to Christianize the Indians, and, when that project fizzled, to establish episcopal congregations in the heartland of dissenter strength, New England and the middle colonies.[21]

While these agencies each had a share of the task of governing the Empire and day to day, in many small ways, shaped colonial policy, the ultimate determination of that policy rested in two intertwined institutions: Parliament, particularly the House of Commons, and the ministry, more specifically the small group of ministers known as the Cabinet. From the accession of the

Hanoverians to the British throne in 1713 until the 1760's, ministries and parliaments had enjoyed an era of harmony and enlarged responsibility. There were occasional fierce struggles for power and some controversial legislation, but the great controversies of the seventeenth century over church-state relations and the supremacy of Parliament had all been put to rest by 1713; only after 1815 did lower- and middle-class political leaders arise to demand a share of political power. The nation's government rested in the hands of an established and widely accepted oligarchy of landowners and professional men who had either won election to the House of Commons by a restricted and unevenly distributed electorate, inherited seats in the House of Lords, been raised to the peerage by the King, or secured executive or judicial appointments on the basis of ability and connections. The questions that agitated these men concerned patronage, foreign policy, and the periodic waging of war. Preoccupied and satisfied with this political arrangement during the reigns of George I and George II, neither parliaments nor ministries got around very often to dealing with broad issues of colonial policy. Abruptly, in the 1760's, these conditions changed and colonial policy became the most vexing concern of British politics.[22]

The House of Commons during the eighteenth century was the most splendid deliberative assembly in the history of Western man, not because it was a democratic body or a forum for great ideas or a source of enlightened laws but, rather, because it incorporated more or less harmoniously all the dominant segments of British life. Within it the ambitious and the acquisitive personalities of the time found what Sir Lewis Namier has called "a modified, socialized arena for battle, drive, and dominion." At the outset of his great work on *The Structure of Politics at the Accession of George III*, Namier describes seven categories of men who had gained access to the Commons: men born into one of the great ruling families of the realm; independent "country gentlemen," who ranked just below the great aristocratic landowners but were nevertheless the leading property owners and farmers of prosperous English counties; the ambitious professional politicians who were skilled at the management of their own and their friends' election and at the maintenance of an organization of loyal followers within the House; officeholders under the Crown who exchanged their vote in the House for lucrative government jobs, often sinecures with no duties attached; army and navy officers, civil servants, and Crown lawyers who found that a seat in the Commons was a strategic location from which to advance their own careers; merchants and bankers who sought an inside track in the pursuit of government contracts and loans; embezzlers, political hacks, and bankrupts who found immunity from prosecution and civil litigation while holding seats in the Commons. This assemblage of aristocrats, professional men, bureaucrats, political operators, and natural leaders was not organized into government and opposition parties; instead, the eighteenth-century House of Commons consisted of temporary and shifting alignments. "Placemen," or holders of Crown jobs, were the most stable element, and they constituted a relatively reliable source of votes for the ministry of the day because they owed allegiance to the King and to his ministers. If the King and his leading ministers had a falling-out, the placemen would attempt to side with the probable winner of the contest. Ministers and other factional leaders had their own personal followings, voluntary members of their faction, relatives, friends, dependents. But the "independent country gentlemen," who owed their loyalty to no man and felt assured of re-election to the House, made up a large floating vote that could not be controlled by the Crown or the leaders of factions. To govern, the King had to construct a ministry that he could respect, that had the support of a broad coalition of factional leaders, and that would not blunder so badly as to antagonize the high-minded country gentlemen. To keep a majority of the Commons in line, ministries spent a great deal of time proposing and shepherding through Parliament mundane legislation designed to satisfy particular interests: turnpike construction, licensing of public houses, trade regulations, and details of inheritance, property, and commercial law.[23]

The initiation of legislation in Parliament rested with those members of both houses who belonged to the Cabinet. This body had originated in the late seventeenth century when an intimate committee of the Privy Council was formed to deal with matters requiring the attention of a small and discreet group. Gradually, during the first half of the eighteenth century, the "cabinet council" became more and more powerful; like the Privy Council before it, this body also became too large and cumbersome. In 1757, during the Seven Years' War, an "inner" or "effective" cabinet of the most important ministers convened to deal with major questions of policy. Between 1760 and 1765 this body shrank from more than twelve to between seven and nine members and tried to exercise effective control over the formulation and implementation of policy in military, diplomatic, and colonial matters.[24] Neither the Cabinet nor its concentric circles of subministers and lesser officials were single cohesive entities. The King insisted on selecting each minister on his merits—subject to two practical limits: first, the King had to persuade the prospective member to accept his post and serve with his colleagues, and, second, the King could not afford to choose a minister who alienated any major block of votes in the Commons.

Until George III asked Lord North to head the government in 1770, he had found no single leader whom he trusted and who also commanded broad support in Parliament; and although North's ministry lasted for twelve years, it was only relatively more secure than those that preceded it. During the ministries of the 1760's, the main responsibility for determining colonial policy shifted from the old departments, boards, and committees of imperial bureaucracy into the hands of the Cabinet itself, especially the Chancellor of the Exchequer, the Secretary of State for the Southern Department, and, starting in 1768, the new post of Colonial Secretary. At long last, colonial affairs came under high-level scrutiny by the Cabinet Council and the colonial secretary's staff, called the American Department. This shift was the work of a clique of professional colonial experts who had worked as subministers at the Treasury and the Board of Trade, and after 1768 would serve in the American Department—chiefly Thomas Whately, William Knox, John Pownall, and John Robinson. These men had worked for years to master the intricacies of imperial administration and formulate new and tough colonial policies. When their patron and ally, George Grenville, became the King's first minister and chancellor of the Exchequer in 1763, they provided him with the detailed arguments and proposals he needed to tighten control over the colonies. The result of all of these developments was a new colonial policy—on which several high-ranking ministers staked their careers—prepared by a shadowy group of subministerial advisers, pilloried by an articulate but politically isolated opposition, and directed by harassed, nervous men possessing neither the time nor the temperament to listen to colonial opinion or to reflect upon the long-range impact of British policy on the health of the Empire.[25]

The effect of these centrifugal forces in British politics was to thrust men of talent and imagination to the periphery of power and influence. George Grenville became the King's first minister in 1763 because there was no one else to replace the King's close friend the Earl of Bute, who had failed utterly to win Parliamentary support. Pitt would not head a government he could not dominate, and Newcastle's price in terms of patronage was too high for the King to pay. Grenville was willing to head a ragtag coalition of remaining Parliamentary factions. From this weak base he went to work to implement the long-standing proposals of professional bureaucrats in the Treasury and Board of Trade for imperial centralization. The Sugar Act of 1764, which tightened at every level the enforcement of the acts of trade, the Currency Act of 1764, which forbade any further emissions of paper money by colonial assemblies, and the Stamp Act of 1765, which required the colonies to bear a share of the cost of running the Empire, were the heart of Grenville's program. It was coincidental that Grenville fell from power—in 1765, over a trifling dispute with George III—at the height of the Stamp Act crisis. The King had no choice but to ask Lord Rockingham to form a government. Aristocratic, haughty, and airily contemptuous of Grenville's colonial policy, the cluster of Parliamentary figures known as the Rockingham Whigs had no intention of making bargains with the King's friends or with any other Parliamentary faction in order to remain in power. Led by the brilliant young Edmund Burke, the pious and gentle Lord Dartmouth, and the constructive and generous Henry Seymour Conway, the Rockingham Whigs envisioned a general loosening of colonial policy; weakened by their own hauteur, the King's disdain, and Pitt's refusal to support them, they stayed in office only long enough to maneuver tortuously through Parliament the repeal of the Stamp Act, and only then at the cost of an accompanying Declaratory

Act affirming Parliament's power to legislate for the colonies on any subject.

If ever there was a ministry with the talent needed to reconcile the colonies to Britain, it was the Chatham ministry, formed in 1766 after Rockingham fell from power. The Earl of Chatham, as Pitt was now titled, had finally won the trust and affection of the King, by agreeing to help rid British politics of the evil influence of *party*—factions that owed their loyalty to a single leader. Consequently, Chatham, who had vociferously denounced the Stamp Act, collaborated with the King in forming a ministry that almost totally excluded the Rockingham Whigs from power. The new Secretary of State for the Southern Department was Chatham's confidant, the Earl of Shelburne. An aloof, shy intellectual, Shelburne had a vague but highly intelligent plan to harmonize the economic interests of Britain with those of the colonies. He intended to foster expansion west of the Appalachians and to reorganize the distribution of land grants and the collection of quitrents. The resulting proceeds of expanded and carefully administered land distribution would pay the soaring new costs of imperial defense, including the larger western garrisons needed under Shelburne's plan to keep the Indians at peace. Land-grant fees and quitrents would raise none of the thorny constitutional issues created by Parliamentary taxation of the colonies. Chatham's long record of sympathy for colonial attitudes and Shelburne's bold new colonial policy ought, by any calculation, to have reversed the deterioration of relations with the colonies. But neither man functioned well in the shifting, uncertain political conditions of the mid-1760's. Chatham's painful illness and virtual mental collapse made him a powerless figurehead. Moving impulsively to fill this vacuum, Chancellor of the Exchequer Charles Townshend pushed through a series of coercive measures over Shelburne's opposition: suspension of the New York Assembly for refusing to quarter British troops and the Townshend duties, new revenue-producing taxes on colonial imports. The final blow for Shelburne was the division of his cabinet post into two positions, Colonial Secretary and Secretary of State for the Southern Department. Given his choice of the two, he retained the latter title; he had given up hope of reforming colonial policy, and consequently the job went to Lord Hillsborough, an obtuse but industrious minister who spent his four years in the post scolding royal governors who showed any sign of flexibility in dealing with their assemblies. When Hillsborough stepped down in 1772, Lord North consolidated his government by giving the colonial secretaryship to Lord Dartmouth. A Rockingham Whig, Dartmouth was too gentle and politically weakened to fight for a change in colonial policy. When North pushed the Tea Act through Parliament—giving the financially shaky East India Company a monopoly on the tea trade in the colonies and thereby forcing Americans to buy taxed tea—he did not even consult Dartmouth. And when the Coercive Acts punished Massachusetts for the Boston Tea Party, Dartmouth sadly went along with the new legislation in the vague hope that it would have a sobering effect on the colonists and help produce reconciliation.[26]

The men who governed the Empire—the King and his ministers, members of Parliament, and officeholders in the imperial bureaucracy—were not unthinking automatons. They brought to their work an intelligent body of ideas and purposes. They believed in the supremacy of Parliament and, more broadly, in the need for the Crown to exercise sufficient power in the colonies to contain the natural restiveness of the people there. They believed that the colonies were a vital economic and military asset to Great Britain and, therefore, that the regulation of imperial trade, the financing of imperial government, and the preservation of colonial subordination in areas of trade and finance were ultimately the responsibility of the British government. What they lacked was a theory explaining why conflicts developed between Britain and the colonies and what limitations impinged on Britain's power to resolve those conflicts.

The sovereignty of Parliament was one of the modern triumphs of political ingenuity and intellect. A century of constitutional struggle in England between the Parliament and Stuart monarchs culminated in the Revolution of 1688, the establishment of a Protestant succession to the British throne, and the establishment of Parliamentary supremacy. Blackstone's classic treatise on English law, published during the 1760's, argued authoritatively that "no power on earth can undo" what the

Commons, Lords, and King agreed should be the law of the realm. On this issue there was no partisan disagreement; even the most stalwart defenders of colonial liberty, like Burke and Pitt, admitted Parliament's power to legislate for the colonies. "How to qualify, undermine, or reinterpret this tenet of English political theory," Bernard Bailyn writes in a crucial sentence of *The Ideological Origins of the American Revolution,* "was the central intellectual problem that confronted the leaders of the American cause. . . . It is a classic instance of the creative adjustment of ideas to reality. For if in England the concept of sovereignty was not only logical but realistic, it was far from being that in the colonies."[27] As long as Parliament left colonial policy in the hands of the Privy Council and the Board of Trade and refused to endow the royal instructions with the force of law, Parliamentary power did not disturb Americans. Once Parliament enacted into law the Treasury's program for governing the colonies—the Sugar and Currency acts of 1764 and the Stamp Act of 1765—the lines of authority and control over the colonies abruptly tightened, and further extensions of Parliamentary power through the Townshend duties and the Tea Act became almost inevitable.

The resulting controversy over Parliamentary power and colonial rights brought to the surface a long-hidden but serious disagreement about the role of the Crown itself in the colonial constitutional order. During the early seventeenth century in England there had been two rival interpretations of the power of the Crown: the early Stuarts' view that the King's *will* and volition alone guaranteed liberty and representative government, and Parliament's insistence that the power of the Crown was a *custom* in English political life that had evolved according to the needs of the kingdom in each generation. Once Parliament gained the upper hand in its struggle with the Crown following the Revolution of 1688, it no longer needed to justify its pretensions and so allowed "this conception of custom" to fall "into decay."[28] Many imperial officials continued to assume that their authority came directly from the King and that the function of royal policy was to check and oppose tendencies toward colonial autonomy. During the eighteenth century the colonists increasingly responded that local customs, practice, and precedent limited and opposed those very pretensions to supreme power. Both sides agreed that the Crown was the legitimate executive branch of colonial government and that the colonists should participate in the operation of colonial government. They disagreed about the ultimate source of executive authority, some royal officials tracing it to the will of the monarch and most colonial leaders to a compact between the Crown and the province.

A few thoughtful men within the imperial system sensed the need for a concept of empire that acknowledged forthrightly the potential for conflict between the British and the colonists. Francis Bernard composed in 1763 a series of ninety-seven propositions warning of disastrous dissidence if Britain imposed new policies on the colonies as they were then constituted. First, he pleaded, Britain needed to win the confidence and support of influential men in every province. The creation of a colonial nobility, a voluntary agreement between the colonies and Britain about a colonial contribution toward the cost of imperial defense, and a reorganization of provincial governments to make them more efficient, popular, and uniform were the preliminary steps necessary before Britain imposed new taxes and restrictions on the colonies. Bernard acknowledged the supremacy of Parliament and wanted to invigorate the authority of the Crown. He certainly expected the adoption of these recommendations to advance his own career. But he sensed as well that many colonists were ready to help improve, reform, and rationalize the machinery of government in America if only Britain would approach them in an open, respectful manner. In this way alone could the authority of Parliament and the Crown be set on a firm foundation. To Bernard's disappointment, his recommendations were ignored by officials in London.[29]

Bernard's predecessor as governor of Massachusetts, Thomas Pownall, published in 1764 a long treatise on *The Administration of the Colonies*, which he reissued and revised five times in the following decade. "A mixture of vague ideas and specific proposals, perceptiveness and obtuseness, prolix in style, . . . saved by the obvious open-mindedness of the author," as John Shy[30] describes the book, Pownall's study argued that the Empire should become a more rational enterprise in which mutual commercial prosperity rather than legality cemented the colonies

to Britain. He pleaded for British officials to approach controversies with the colonies in a conciliatory and generous frame of
mind. He skirted the vital issues of Parliament's power to tax the
colonies and the extent of the Crown's authority there. Like
Bernard, Pownall realized that the early 1760's had been the last
chance to strengthen and nourish the ties of the Empire. He
seemed to realize, with regret, that his ideas were a little too late
to alter the course of events.[31] The presence of men like Pownall
and Bernard in the imperial establishment, however, as well as
the serious efforts of men throughout the system to justify the use
of Parliamentary and prerogative power in the colonies, suggests
that British imperial thinking was not a stagnant, conventional
orthodoxy but that it was rigid, limited, and applied by men of
restricted vision and ability.

The loyalist enunciators of principle were for the most part
native American officeholders or politicians closely identified
with the interests of the Crown who tried to make the legal and
administrative machinery of the Empire function properly. They
did not all approve of every British policy, but when they spoke
of obedience and subordination they referred to legal, historical,
and constitutional ideas that held the Empire together and
necessarily circumscribed colonial liberty. They saw at close
range how the conditions of colonial politics undermined the
effectiveness of British authority. Instead of advocating loud
protests and violent resistance, they articulated an alternative
colonial response to unpopular and unwise British policies and
measures. By exploring sensitively the sources and manifestations
of colonial disobedience, the most intelligent of them brought
intellectual rigor to the task of advocating obedience and subordination. Most important, they suffered and felt lonely, impotent, isolated, and misunderstood; as they came to terms with
these sensations, they appreciated anew the weight of their
obligation to uphold British authority. These themes—knowl-
edgeability, close exposure to political change, concern with the
language of subordination, sensitivity to at least some colonial
beliefs, and a capacity to bring all of their emotional stamina to
the task at hand—were woven into the experience of the loyalist
enunciators of principle.

3

Cadwallader Colden and the Undermining of Royal Authority

ALTHOUGH British authority could not impose order or conformity on the colonies, it could regulate and accelerate economic development and form stabilizing alliances with segments of a colony's elite; or, by antagonizing important segments of a colony's society, the Crown could provoke new indigenous leadership to emerge. Whether accommodating or divisive, the power of the Crown was constantly undercut by the very complexity and increasing sophistication of American life. In no royal colony was politics so elaborate or intricate as in New York, and here, consequently, the most interesting interplay between the power of the Crown and the assertiveness of colonial leaders occurred. Two great rival factions of landowners and merchants led respectively by the Livingston and De Lancey families dominated politics. Both forces competed for control of the Assembly by seeking the support of a particularly diverse and unpredictable electorate. Tenant farmers, urban tradesmen, ethnic minorities of Dutch and German descent, and members of rival religious denominations—Anglican, Dutch Reformed, and Presbyterian—were all identifiable groups of voters. In addition to seeking control of the Assembly, the De Lancey and Livingston leaders sought to influence and manipulate successive royal governors, who from 1755 until 1776 were all British officials with scanty knowledge of the province and short terms of office. The chief demand of both factions was that the royal governors approve vast grants of land in northern New York to members of the aristocracy, who would then hold the property in hopes of making speculative profits. New York had an unusually productive and dynamic economy, thriving agriculture, internal transportation on the Hudson River, and the busy port town of New York City. The province's wealth, its culturally diverse population, its ambitious legal, merchant, and agricultural professions, and the pell-mell rush of people at all levels of society to acquire land and money created a frantic, unstable political atmosphere. Attempting to stabilize the system, New York political leaders pioneered in developing Anglo-American political alliances with strategically placed figures in London. James De Lancey excelled in this strategy and with the backing of his English patrons served successively as speaker of the Assembly, chief justice, and, from 1753 until his death in 1760, as royal governor. The power of the De Lanceys declined after James's passing. The turbulence of factional alignments in England during the 1760's prevented the De Lanceys from perpetuating their contacts in London, and the increasing influence of the Livingston group put the De Lanceys more and more on the defensive. Because the Livingstons joined in agitation against British policy after 1763, partly on grounds of principle and partly from opportunism, the De Lanceys felt it necessary to become defenders of British authority. It was within this complex milieu that Cadwallader Colden stood for more than half a century as the most stalwart and consistent defender of British authority.[1]

Colden could boast of a lifetime of accomplishment and intellectual distinction exceeded in colonial America perhaps only by that of Benjamin Franklin. Born in Scotland in 1688, he studied botany at the University of Edinburgh and medicine in London before coming to Philadelphia in 1710, and then settling in New York in 1718. During the next half century Colden became the most eminent botanist in the colonies, applying the Linnaean system of classification to American plants, and correcting several weaknesses in the Swedish system as well. He wrote a history of the Iroquois, essays on medicine, and in 1746 published an ambitious treatise in theoretical physics. This *Explication of the First Causes of Action in Matter* was a revealing document. While scientifically worthless—Colden's mathematical training was scanty and he was ignorant of the work of European physical scientists on the same problem—his book was a serious attempt to encompass all natural science and mathematics in a single, unified rational system of thought.[2] He brought to his work as a Crown official the same desire for order and system in the administration of the colonies, the same intellectual aloofness, the same serene expectation of ultimate intellectual vindication. Two minor Crown posts induced him to move from Philadelphia to New York in 1718; two years later he secured the post of surveyor general, and from 1721 to 1761 he sat on the royal Council; finally, in 1761, he became lieutenant governor and, in this capacity, served as acting governor several times before his death in 1776. Despite his years of service to the Crown, his utter devotion to the Crown's interests, and his industry and perseverance, Colden was a marginal and vulnerable figure. Like everyone in New York politics during the first half of the eighteenth century, he had a British patron, the Scottish nobleman the Marquis of Lothian. Colden's scientific publications and correspondence also gave him a scattering of other useful contacts in London. The governorship of his close ally Admiral George Clinton from 1743 to 1753 and his own tenure as acting governor in the early 1760's drew him close to the center of power in New York. Both times his attempts to humble his opponents ruined his effectiveness.

Precisely because he was so irascible and frustrated, and because his service to the Crown covered more than half a century, Colden understood the limitations that American society placed on the exercise of royal authority. As surveyor general in New York, he discovered that the landowning aristocrats evaded quitrent payments to the Crown because the exact extent and boundaries of their holdings were vague and indefinite and they successfully resisted all of his efforts to survey property lines accurately. Colden wanted to increase quitrent revenue and make the Crown independent of the Assembly for financial support. All he got for his efforts was the hostility of every major figure in the Assembly. When he next condemned the legislature, for failing to vote defense appropriations during King George's War (1744–1748), the Assembly retaliated with the unusual rebuke of branding Colden "an enemy of the province." Stung by this insult, Colden concluded that the rampant self-interest of the legislators themselves menaced the welfare of the province. He launched a fresh inquiry into the political structure of New York and discovered an intricate network of lawyers, judges, and legislators gnawing at the vital organs of the society. At the apex of this system Colden saw James De Lancey simultaneously controlling the offices in the court system, legal fees, and political preferment. Against this phalanx Governor Clinton was powerless, for all of his appointees depended on the Assembly for their salaries. Moreover, the Assembly determined the jurisdiction of particular judges; influential assemblymen could always arrange for friendly judges to be appointed in counties where they owned property or did business. There was no way the Crown could prosecute members of the aristocracy for quitrent evasion or fraudulent land acquisition.[3]

To correct this imbalance of power, Colden proposed in 1744 that all royal officials be paid by the Crown and that the office of chief justice be reserved for men who had neither family nor vested interests in New York. Officials in London ignored these recommendations, and James De Lancey's governorship, from 1753 to 1760, further eclipsed Colden's influence. Then in 1761, when De Lancey died, Colden got another chance. He became lieutenant governor and acted as governor almost continuously until 1765. Colden started, in the first place, to obey a long-ignored royal instruction that judges be appointed to serve only at the pleasure of the King and not during their good behavior. He next plunged into a protracted struggle with the Assembly over a vacancy for the office of chief justice. Colden wanted to disqualify any candidate for the post who owned property or had family connections in New York. He won initially when the Crown appointed Colden's favorite, Benjamin Pratt, of Massachusetts. But Pratt died before he could assume the office, and Robert Monckton, during his short exercise of the governorship, nominated Daniel Horsmanden, a De Lancey man, to the high bench. For his part, Colden secured an order in council from the King upholding his position on judicial tenure.[4]

Emboldened, Colden tried to break the power of the lawyers. He accused families like the Livingstons and Van Rensselaers of using legal trickery to obtain land grants and then juggling the boundaries so as to enlarge their already fraudulent holdings still more. Small farmers and Indians, Colden lamented, could not afford high-paid legal representation and were therefore victimized by the greed of the aristocracy. Colden asked the Privy Council to investigate the legality of every disputed land title in New York, a review that would have taken years to complete and had barely gotten under way when the Revolution intervened. In the meantime, Colden attacked the power of the lawyers by intervening in a routine civil suit, the case of *Forsey* v. *Cunningham,* which became a landmark in New York's legal history. At stake was the jury's award of damages in a civil suit for bodily injury suffered in a public brawl between two merchants. Colden sought to have the case referred to the Privy Council and to have the damages reduced. In so doing, Colden united the entire legal community against him. The lawyers argued that the facts of the case could not be reconsidered and that only procedural errors in the trial could be reviewed by the Privy Council. Colden insisted that a royal governor had to have the power to send any decision of a colonial court to London for review by the Privy Council. In no other way could the excessive power of lawyers and judges be curbed and the court system made into an impartial agency of the Crown. But the Privy Council in 1765 rebuffed Colden and declined to overturn the *Forsey* decision. It was a prudent decision, for in 1765 the Crown faced a far more serious crisis of authority in New York and everywhere in the colonies, resistance against the Stamp Act.[5]

Colden sensed quite correctly that the Stamp Act opposition in New York owed some of its momentum and organization to the Forsey-Cunningham fight. "The lawyers . . . have raised this seditious spirit," he wrote of the opposition to the Stamp Act; "since the [Forsey-Cunningham dispute of] last winter, infamous, scurrilous papers have been weekly published in this place in order to render me odious in the eyes of the people."[6] He had no doubt that the lawyers of the Livingston faction had organized the resistance against the Stamp Act in New York, although, in fact, William Livingston and his close ally William Smith, Jr., wanted to keep demonstrations under control and at the same time use the potential danger of violence as a means of preventing enforcement of the Stamp Act. After news of more serious violence in Boston, Newport, and Annapolis between August 14 and September 2, Colden asked General Thomas Gage to send a battalion of troops to keep peace in New York City. Gage did not have a battalion to spare and told Colden he would have to make do with the troops then stationed in Fort George, on the southern tip of Manhattan. Gage also pointedly reminded Colden that only civil authorities in New York City could make the decision to use troops against the populace, and Colden replied that in the event of general anarchy the troops should take the responsibility of firing first. Each, clearly, wanted the other to take responsibility for using military force against the crowd if the need arose. Gage, however, was legally correct as well as politically prudent. He had no power to use force to coerce the colonists except at Colden's request. For his part, Colden nearly blundered into a major blood bath. He made it clear that the stamps were going to be stored in Fort George, made ostentatious preparations to repulse any armed attack on the fort, and declared that the people should obey the act. On November 1, an enormous throng marched to the fort, sacked the house of one particularly officious and arrogant officer, and then hanged Colden in effigy "with the grossest ribaldry," as Colden described it delicately. Despite the taunts of the crowd, the troops, under strict orders from Gage, refused to be provoked. As Gage explained, he could have opened fire and killed as many as 900 of the mob, but by morning the fort would surely have been overrun by an avenging force of as many as 50,000 from New York and New Jersey. Gage took the responsibility for deciding that the stamps could not be kept secure, and Colden had no choice but to surrender them to the city government, which had no intention of allowing a single stamp to be sold.[7]

All the dangerous tendencies that Colden had diagnosed and tried to resist for more than forty years—the prominence and guile of the lawyers, the opposition of the aristocracy to any British policy that affected their interests or curbed their power, his inability to get anyone in the British government to back him in a crisis, and his own abrasive impulse to rub in the faces of a rebellious multitude the iniquity of their actions—all of this frustration and disappointment had culminated in the Stamp Act crisis. It was the sad climax of his career. Later in November, a new governor, Henry Moore, arrived, and Colden at seventy-eight returned to relative obscurity as lieutenant governor, though he would twice again serve as acting governor, in 1769–1770 and in 1771. That pathetic period in his life and the quixotic quality of his fight against the legal profession, the landed aristocracy, and the Assembly should not obscure his intelligence as an analyst of colonial politics. He lived in a political community where the governor and the Assembly were protagonists. The governor could choose to fight or to collaborate with the Assembly, and in the process the Assembly grew steadily more powerful. But behind the small stage of that struggle Colden perceived a larger and more comprehensive decline of royal authority. The exploding wealth of the province had gotten completely out of control. Compared with the seventeenth century, the mid-eighteenth century saw wealth increasing at an unbelievable rate. Far from regulating it for the public good, the Crown had been outmaneuvered by a land-hungry aristocracy that controlled both the courts and the bar and used the legal system to feed its insatiable appetite for land and political control over land acquisition. In this way, Colden concluded, private interest rather than the collective good of the province had come to dominate politics.

This frenzied race for economic, social, and political preferment constantly drew new men into the aristocracy, and this upward movement kept society even more unstable, Colden feared. Several means were available to a young man seeking to scramble to the top: marriage, the legal profession, public office, land speculation, or, most likely, some combination of these activities; and these plentiful opportunities only encouraged the corrosive greed and recklessness already rampant in the society. The "only principle of life propagated among the young people is to get money," Colden lamented in 1748, men being "esteemed only according to what they are worth, that is the money they are possessed of." When he looked out at New York he saw an open, acquisitive, rowdy, fluid, but still stratified society, with a weak executive pitted against powerful, interlocking judicial and legislative branches of government—in short, everything that he detested most. Colden further revealed the depth of his alienation from his social and political order in his utterly utopian plan, drafted in the 1730's, to revolutionize landownership in New York. Common citizens, he proposed, would be allowed up to 3,000 acres on the strict condition that they live on the land, develop it, and pay full quitrent to the Crown. A ruling class would be allowed up to 5,000 acres, and royal officials as much as 20,000 plus hereditary claim to their offices. The estate and the office would become indivisible; one could not be inherited without the other; in this way, competition for land and office would cease. What Colden wanted this scheme to accomplish was a return to a simpler society in which interlocking networks of land, office, legal skill, and social connection would not be permitted to operate to the detriment of the government and the rest of society. He owed this antique social vision to the writings of Viscount Bolingbroke, the brilliant critic of the pluralistic and commercially oriented British social order during the 1720's and 1730's. Ironically, during the 1760's and 1770's, Bolingbroke's ideas about ministerial power would provide colonial leaders with powerful arguments against the machinations of the Crown. Colden, however, had concluded that colonial liberty could survive only if a powerful executive kept private ambitions and interests in check. An integral part of his plan was, consequently, extensive and autonomous prerogative power in the hands of royal officials to enforce the law in the name of the Crown. The trouble with adaptable royal governors and distracted officials in London was that they allowed the prerogative to become one more private interest, competing with factions, professions, families, and economic groups. No one seemed to realize, Colden lamented, that the prerogative was special, that it ought to have priority over all other political influences, and that it should be entrusted only to men with no private interest to cultivate. A "patriot king" standing above classes and parties, a monarch like the one Bolingbroke envisioned, was the model of the Crown officials Colden wanted in New York. Such men had to be, like Colden, men who would sacrifice their entire careers to the interests of the Crown and thereby serve the interests of the community.[8]

4

Thomas Hutchinson and the Preservation of Royal Authority

WHERE Colden was voluble, angry, estranged from the provincial leadership of New York, and prone to blunder in political controversies, Thomas Hutchinson was austere, proud, a member of Massachusetts' mercantile and officeholding elite—an adept and resourceful politician. He served in the House of Representatives from 1739 to 1749, was once elected its speaker, and was elevated by the House to the Council, where he served from 1749 to 1766. Appointed lieutenant governor in 1758, he was acting governor from 1769 to 1771 and then royal governor until 1774. Though he was not a lawyer, his judicial service as inferior-court and county probate judge and as chief justice of Massachusetts from 1760 to 1769 was widely respected. Related by marriage to the Oliver family, Hutchinson and his brother-in-law, Peter Oliver, systematically acquired offices and influence with the Crown for their relatives and friends. Hutchinson's physical appearance was unforgettable; his steely gaze, angular cheeks, long, straight nose, and erect, rigid posture emphasized his self-assurance and flinty pride. To his friends and enemies alike these features were a kind of armor; "a solidity of judgment and great regularity of manners," wrote Peter Oliver,[1] while Mercy Otis Warren saw a "dark, intriguing, insinuating, haughty and ambitious," a man of "extreme avarice" and "Machiavellian" calculation.[2] In contrast with this forbidding image, Hutchinson's background and career were thoroughly conventional and unsinister. Except for his great-great-grandmother Anne Hutchinson, a religious schismatic in the 1630's, the Hutchinsons of Boston have been aptly described as "sedate and conscientious burgers."[3] After graduating from Harvard at the age of sixteen, Thomas entered his father's countinghouse and began his career as a merchant, a pursuit of wealth augmented in 1734 by the middling dowry that his bride, Peggy Sanford, brought to their marriage. By the early 1740's, Hutchinson's thrift, diligence, and impeccable reputation for reliability had made him one of Boston's richest merchants and afforded him the time and resources to build a lovely home on a hilltop in Milford, Massachusetts, overlooking Boston harbor.

Hutchinson's ability, integrity, and capacity for hard work naturally made him a political insider. Among the many members of Governor Shirley's broadly based coalition of supporters in the 1740's and 1750's, Hutchinson emerged as the Governor's most effective agent and spokesman. Shirley's successor, Thomas Pownall, tried during his short term as governor (1757–1760) to maintain equally friendly relations with the Hutchinson-Oliver faction and with the Otis family of Barnstable. For a time, the balancing act worked. Pownall helped Hutchinson get the lieutenant governorship, Andrew Oliver the post of secretary to the colony, and both families a batch of judicial offices. To James Otis, Sr., Pownall promised the post of chief justice as soon as it became vacant. In 1760, when the office did become available, Pownall was gone and the new Governor, Francis Bernard, refused to be bound by Pownall's promise to Otis, even though Hutchinson scrupulously reminded Bernard of Otis's claim to the post. Bernard then named Hutchinson chief justice and in so doing made the elder Otis and his son, James, Jr., implacable enemies of his administration. The first issue to come before the superior court was the legality of writs of assistance, new and sweeping search warrants in the hands of customs officials. Bernard wanted the writs upheld; James Otis, Jr., argued brilliantly before the court that they were unconstitutional. At the risk of being labeled a lackey of the Governor, Chief Justice Hutchinson, after delay and rehearing the arguments, ruled in favor of the writs. In 1762 the General Court quickly passed a bill invalidating the writs; on the advice of Hutchinson and the other justices, Bernard vetoed it. Unexpectedly and dramatically, between 1760 and 1762, Hutchinson's appointment as chief justice and his decision upholding the writs of assistance had fractured Massachusetts politics and subtly altered Hutchinson's political role. In the 1740's and 1750's he had been an ambitious and useful ally of royal governors; now he was a successful and indispensable tool of British authority in Massachusetts.[4] Aloof, seemingly haughty, utterly convinced of the rectitude and propriety of his intentions and actions, Hutchinson does not invite sympathy or understanding. To penetrate this façade, one must rely on unpromising material, scattered and elusive evidence that he was, in reality, a passionate man.

A suggestive indication of Hutchinson's emotionality was a document he wrote during the spring and early summer of 1764. It was an essay on colonial rights that he sent to Richard Jackson—an English politician, an agent for several colonies, and a bureaucratic operator with excellent connections in official London—with the suggestion that Jackson disguise its authorship and publish it as an argument against adoption of the Stamp Act. The document had limited practical value; Jackson did not publish but, rather, circulated it among politicians already sympathetic with the colonies. Hutchinson's essay was a remarkably ambitious and intelligent effort to understand what was happening to the Empire during the early stages of the Grenville ministry. It attempted, moreover, to clothe a forthright defense of colonial liberty in language that was respectful and ingratiating. Hutchinson believed to the core of his being that the only way to defend colonial liberty was to submit prudently to British authority and, without denying the subordinate status of the colonies, to expand quietly the scope of colonial autonomy. Long considered consistent and desirable strategies in Massachusetts, prudent acquiescence and the defense of liberty had become difficult goals to reconcile in 1765. Still, Hutchinson felt impelled to try.

Hutchinson, first of all, made it perfectly clear that he did not question the supremacy of Parliament over the colonies. Having said that, he proceeded to argue at some length that Parliamentary supremacy was not an unlimited sanction. Parliament was constrained by precedent and tradition from trampling the rights of Englishmen—including, specifically, the "rights" of the colonists to elect their own assemblies and to pay only those taxes imposed by their representatives. Hutchinson, moreover, neatly disposed of the conventional British argument that the colonists were "virtually represented" in Parliament and therefore had consented to the Stamp Act. Virtual representation, Hutchinson noted, was based on the notion that nine out of ten Englishmen could not vote for members of the House of Commons but were nonetheless represented in Parliament; by the same token, the colonists were also represented there. That argument would only be sufficient, he retorted, if members of Parliament represented individuals; but Parliament represented, instead, formal segments of British society—landed gentlemen or groups of merchants that had some legitimate claim to participate directly in the affairs of government. The colonies, he insisted, were not regarded in Britain as an integral part of the body politic. Hutchinson barely concealed his zeal for colonial liberty when he set forth the actual status of the colonies in a series of rhetorical questions: "Are not the colonies considered as detached and having a distinct interest from the interest of the nation? . . . Is it not a general question what can be done to make the colonies further beneficial to the nation? . . . In short, do you not consider us as your property to improve in the best way you can for your own advantage?" The way Britain conceived of the colonies, Hutchinson suggested, belied any claim that Americans were virtually represented in Parliament.

Hutchinson was incapable of sustaining his argument in defense of colonial liberty or of pushing his denunciation of British encroachments to a logical conclusion. He interlaced his contentions with concessions to the principle of colonial subordination and at one point inserted a lengthy digression on Roman colonial policy, which, in a labored way, illustrated, he said, that colonial settlers "are entitled to all the privileges they enjoyed in the mother country" consistent with the preservation of imperial authority. He devoted the last half of his treatise to an analysis of colonial history; it showed that while Britain profited from the colonies, the burden of establishing and sustaining those communities was borne by the colonists themselves. Even the vaunted military protection that Britain afforded its colonies, he observed, came only during major wars, while the colonists carried on without assistance the protracted struggle against French-supported Indian tribes. Hutchinson allowed the luxuriant and complex story of the colonists' contribution to the wealth and growth of the Empire to unfold gradually; he had little taste for turning it into a polemic. But its main points were obviously sensational; Isaac Barré, a member of Parliament, and vehement opponent of the Stamp Act, wrenched them out of context and hurled them dramatically at the Grenville ministry during Parliamentary debate. When Barré heard Charles Townshend speak of the colonists as "these Americans, children planted by our care, nourished by our indulgence, . . . protected by our arms," he thundered back, "No! your oppressions planted em. . . . They grew by your neglect. . . . They have nobly taken up arms in your defense." Barré had access to Hutchinson's essay and probably lifted these points from it. When the mob sacked Hutchinson's fine house in August 1765 because he was falsely reputed to have been an advocate of the Stamp Act, "Hutchinson must have reflected with some bitterness on the irony of his situation," for, in Edmund S. Morgan's words, "he stood in the eyes of his countrymen as a traitor, while Barré . . . basked in a shower of fulsome tributes."[5]

Hutchinson may well have known that he was cursed with prophetic insight into the nature of the conflict between Britain and the colonies. He pleaded almost pathetically with British readers of his essay on colonial rights to view the colonists with a discerning eye: "Like all the rest of the human race, [they] are of different spirits and dispositions, some more calm and moderate, others more violent and extravagant," and all prone to the "intemperate zeal, shall I say of Englishmen, in support of what . . . appears to be their rights."[6] Understanding and seeking to direct that "zeal" were the dangerous tasks that Hutchinson undertook in 1765. Accompanied only by a single sheriff, he tried to halt the attack on Andrew Oliver's house. A year earlier he had persuaded the assembly—in Massachusetts, called the General Court—to tone down a petition against the Sugar Act by substituting the more submissive word "privileges" for "rights." In private writings, including his essay on colonial rights, he declared that all British taxation—internal taxes like the Stamp Act or external ones like the sugar duties—violated colonial rights and vital interests, not merely privileges. Once the Sugar Act was law and the Stamp Act had been proposed, however, Hutchinson decided to humor British ministers who thought there was a constitutional difference between internal and external taxation of the colonies. "I am for saving as much of our privileges as we can," he wrote privately, "and if the people of England make this distinction I think it tends to strengthen us in our claim for an exemption from internal taxes. Really, there is no difference."[7] Hutchinson's private hostility to the Sugar Act and Stamp Act and his discreet silence in public about the constitutional and moral issues at stake were neither timid nor cowardly. Prudent submission to British authority, Hutchinson believed, could strengthen the hands of colonial spokesmen like himself who sought to influence British policy and enlarge the scope of colonial freedom. If his contemporaries could have trusted in Hutchinson's leadership, the Grenville ministry surely would have found him a wily adversary. Instead, the hostility and suspicion he aroused in Massachusetts reduced Hutchinson's usefulness to the Crown.

Hutchinson kept his opposition to the Stamp Act and his convictions about colonial liberty a carefully hidden secret for a number of reasons. As lieutenant governor, he bore responsibility for helping enforce the Stamp Act. Moreover, he feared that if Crown officials did not uphold British authority, popular agitation would increase in intensity. Most important, he believed that his only chance to succeed Francis Bernard as governor was to demonstrate his complete reliability as a supporter of the ministry and its policies—irrespective of his private opinions. Hutchinson's reticence, however, had deeper roots. He felt torn between his ambition to provide dramatic public leadership in Massachusetts politics and his preference for private, scholarly contemplation of public issues. During the late 1760's, from the repeal of the Stamp Act until he became acting governor in August 1769, Hutchinson spent a great deal of time thinking about the ominous conflict between British authority and colonial assertiveness. He distilled much of this reflection in two unpublished memoranda,[8] an essay on taxation and an intriguing imaginary dialogue between an Englishman and a colonist. Both cover the same ground, but the dialogue is the more interesting of the two. In it, Hutchinson has arranged British and colonial arguments in the form of a candid exchange in which each party listens intently to the other and takes full account of the other's point of view in framing his own rebuttals. Hutchinson's personal thoughts about the dialogue are difficult to ascertain; he has scrupulously refused to allow either side in the debate to triumph over the other. At some points he seems to have envisioned himself as the colonist, subjecting the views of his contemporaries to the test of informed British criticism, while elsewhere he allows the British spokesman to demolish colonial notions about disobedience and authority. Most likely, the dialogue represents the kind of discussion he yearned to have with his fellow colonists but found impossible in the contentious, brittle atmosphere of pre-Revolutionary Boston.

The most disturbing quality of the controversy over colonial rights, Hutchinson observed, was the colonists' preoccupation with the exact nature of British authority. This fixation, in British eyes, made colonial remonstrances seem "more violent and extravagant, . . . rude and indecent" than they really were. "You assumed and exercised an authority over us which we thought you had no right to do," Hutchinson's colonist declares. "We are Englishmen, and the property of Englishmen cannot be taken from them without their consent. . . . If the Parliament [can impose internal or external taxes on the colonists,] we are no better than slaves."

"Hold, my friend . . . ," Hutchinson's British advocate responds; "this dispute, like all other party disputes in the affairs of government . . . has been carried on with great zeal and warmth of temper. *This temper must subside* before there can be any room to hope for an accommodation." The British voice then predicts that if the Townshend duties were to be repealed, the colonists would claim that Britain had no right to regulate the commerce of the Empire; the colonist in the dialogue denies the charge and reiterates that America would never question the responsibility of Parliament to govern the Empire as long as it did not violate the natural rights of the colonists or transgress the traditional limits the British constitution placed on Parliamentary power. *"This,"* the British debater declares, *"is submitting to just nothing."* In order to convince the mother country of their loyalty, Hutchinson concluded in early 1769, the colonies had to make their professions of obedience unqualified and transparently sincere. Promising to obey Parliament and the Crown only as long as they did not transgress the constitutional rights of the colonists, he lamented, was a veiled way of shouting defiance.

A self-righteous, defensive posture, he argued, was a dangerous luxury. The colonists could never define the exact limits of British authority because that authority was in its nature hidden, potential, and slumbering. Precedents from the early seventeenth century—when the Stuart monarchs lost much of their prerogative power—had no necessary bearing on the eighteenth century. Contrary to popular belief, there had never been a pristine English constitution against which actions of Parliament or the Crown could be measured. By the eighteenth century Parliament had determined what the British constitution said. Hutchinson did not deny that the people could resist a government that usurped their liberty or property arbitrarily, but he contended that colonists who talked loudly about the right of revolution had not read John Locke's classic treatise on the subject very closely. Locke did not say that individuals could disobey an arbitrary government with impunity, Hutchinson claimed; the *Second Treatise on Government* only permitted the whole body of the people, acting nearly in unison, to renounce their allegiance to a ruler. After the most dispassionate examination of colonial arguments against British policy, Hutchinson's dialogue could find no definition of British authority that officials in London could possibly comprehend, much less endorse. Colonial efforts to persuade Britain to redefine the imperial relationship were, therefore, self-defeating. Hutchinson's own characterization of British authority came, significantly, not from the colonial past but from Roman history. Livy described how twelve Roman colonies had refused to pay imperial taxes during the Carthaginian war, and Hutchinson seized on the episode as an impeccable source on the constitutions of empires. After a protracted controversy, the Roman Senate had insisted that the recalcitrant colonies repay arrears in taxes, and ultimately the colonies had complied. Here was a model of imperial authority that Hutchinson could analyze and admire without reservation, one that was calculating in its use of power, capable of responding to bluster with the lofty insistence that principles were at stake, and patient enough to wait until a wayward colony worked out its own way of acquiescing. The only comparably elaborate effort to abstract a full-scale rationale for colonial policy from classical sources was a treatise by the English barrister Robert Mackintosh, who found in Tacitus and Sallust support for a repressive imperial regime, exactly the reverse of Hutchinson's view.[9]

The sad conclusion of Hutchinson's private contemplation, in the late 1760's, of the controversy between Britain and the colonies was that the gulf between their respective concepts of authority, obedience, and liberty was unbridgeable during the foreseeable future. Perhaps a generation of firm British insistence on the supremacy of Parliament and the Crown would work, as it had for Rome; perhaps the colonists would someday learn to eschew high-sounding pronouncements about constitutionality and concede British supremacy in return for a mild and mutually beneficial colonial policy. The immediate outlook, however, was bleak. Against this background, Hutchinson drafted in early 1770 and sent to Lord Hillsborough a series of proposals for coercing the colonies: Parliament should link any partial repeal of the Townshend duties to a new requirement that all assemblymen take an oath to uphold the authority of Parliament; a new royally appointed Council should be created in Massachusetts and given responsibility, with the governor, for the enforcement of law; alliances of men seeking to thwart the enforcement of British law should be declared illegal. In 1770, shortly after becoming acting governor, Hutchinson offered to resign and make room for a British official with increased power and a mandate from the Crown to restore order, and he further suggested that royal governors always be British noblemen serving terms of no more than three years in the same colony, "as in New Spain." When Hutchinson's letters containing these proposals fell into the hands of his enemies and were published in Boston in 1775, they sounded like a blueprint for tyranny and the work of a man completely hostile to Massachusetts's traditions of liberty and self-government. Hutchinson's purpose was more complex and less sinister than that.[10] He wanted Parliament in 1770 to impose just enough coercion on Massachusetts to stun the colonists and disabuse them of "loose, false, and absurd notions of . . . government, spread by designing men, [who went about] setting bounds to the supreme authority and [permitting] parts of the community or even individuals to judge when those bounds are exceeded, and to obey or disobey accordingly." Once that cluster of ideas was discredited, the colonists could get back to the task of promoting their interests and defending their liberty in a safe and proper manner. The timing and exact degree of this coercion were extremely important; Hutchinson therefore qualified his proposals. He wanted from Britain "a steady and uniform refusal to countenance" rebellious actions, "watching [for] every opportunity of exerting the authority of government as far as the temper of the people and the state of things" permit. In this way royal officials might "be able to keep off a general convulsion until" the people had had enough "of the evils of anarchy." Above all, this curtailment of colonial autonomy had to be calculated, restrained, and no more severe than was absolutely essential; Britain should act only "so far as it [was] necessary for its own authority and the general weal of the whole Empire and no farther." It was a distinction that invited misunderstanding. "I am charged with arbitrary principles," he acknowledged in 1775, "but I am as far from them as any man in the world and never wished for a greater restraint of natural liberty than is necessary to answer the end of government."[11]

"Nothing would have pleased him more," Carl Becker wrote discerningly of Hutchinson, "than that New England would have shown its emancipation from provincialism by meriting the good will of the King. His irritation with America in general and with Boston in particular was the irritation of a proud and possessive father with a beloved but wayward child who fails to do him credit in high places. It was essential to his peace of mind, such was his sense of provincial inferiority, that Americans should be more loyal than the English and royal governors should be more correct than British ministers."[12] Hutchinson's astringent contemplation of the pre-Revolutionary controversy in 1769 and 1770 was not merely prophetic and accurate; these introspective thoughts actually affected history because they shaped his conduct as governor from August 1769 until his departure for England in 1774. Two events in early March 1770 thrust him into a prominent public role; the Boston Massacre on March 5 and the convening of the General Court in Cambridge on March 15 instigated controversies that tested Hutchinson's capacity to act as he knew he should: with dignity, restraint, firmness.

Considering its complex, tumultuous consequences, the Boston Massacre had a reasonably clear-cut factual chronology. On the evening of March 5, 1770, a lone British sentry standing guard in front of the customs house on King Street "became embroiled"[13] with a crowd of rowdy young men and called for help. Captain Thomas Preston and seven soldiers marched to his rescue. The growing crowd increased in size, pressed forward, and hurled abusive language, snowballs, and pieces of ice at the line of British uniforms. In panic, some of the soldiers fired into the crowd and killed or mortally wounded five people. Within a few minutes Hutchinson heard of the shooting, strode with a companion up King Street, noticed blood on the snow, and confronted Captain Preston at the guardhouse. "How came you to fire without orders from a civil magistrate?" Hutchinson demanded. "I was obliged to, to save my sentry," the officer replied, suggesting that he could talk more openly if he and Hutchinson could have a private conference at once. Hutchinson knew that the crowd in the street was on the verge of tumult. He declined Preston's request for a conference, pushed through the crowd to the town hall, and, mounting the balcony, which overlooked the site of the shooting, spoke to the throng that had gathered. His impromptu speech probably averted a rash of new attacks on British soldiers in the town that only could have provoked a long night of bloodshed and terror. He talked of the dangers of further violence and the dire consequences if the town sank into anarchy. He promised that Captain Preston and the soldiers would be tried and, if found guilty, punished.[14]

Hutchinson realized that the presence of British troops in Boston had upset the delicate balance between order and violence in this turbulent, crowded town. Responsibility over the troops was divided between General Thomas Gage, who resided in New York, local officers, who commanded the force in Boston on a day-to-day basis, and the governor of Massachusetts, who alone could authorize the use of troops in civil disturbances. Intended to protect customs officials from harassment, the army only exacerbated tensions in Boston. When soldiers brawled in taverns and streets, patronized the newly flourishing trade of prostitution, and drilled in fashionable streets on Sunday morning, British power became a naked, immediate reality. The army quickly learned that it served best when it stayed out of sight, but, increasingly, trouble sought out the army. Town rowdies delighted in taunting the soldiers. The soldiers in turn committed minor and serious crimes and were summoned into hostile provincial courts. The incident called the Boston Massacre differed from earlier clashes only in that it caused the death of five men.[15]

On the morning of March 6, 1770, all the elements of this messy situation spilled irretrievably together: an army impotent to assert its authority in a turbulent city, a populace newly aroused by this jarring evidence of British coercive policy, a native-born royal governor who wanted to persuade his countrymen to live tranquilly under British rule. Threatening, tough-talking committees dogged the judges of the Massachusetts Superior Court, pressing them to hold trials for the British soldiers at once. Hutchinson's first task was to prevent an immediate, emotional trial that might convict the soldiers in a spasm of vengeance. Hutchinson seized the initiative and negotiated an agreement with the leaders of the town meeting to postpone the trial until August 1770, on the condition that a soldier accused of killing a young boy be tried immediately. Then he had to cajole his former colleagues on the superior court not to resign in panic. Twice, Justice Benjamin Lunde tried to resign, only to have Hutchinson persuade him "to hold his place a little longer; timid as he is [Justice Edmund] Goffe is more so, the only difference is, little matters as well as great frighten Lunde [while] Goffe appears valiant until the danger, or apprehensions of it, rise to a considerable height; after that he is more terrified than the other." Only his kinsman and successor as chief justice, Peter Oliver, was "firm" and courageous. Hutchinson next prepared for the outcome of the trial itself. He had to prevent vengeful execution of the soldiers if they were convicted and mob lynching if they were acquitted. Though he discounted rumors that the soldiers might be seized and hanged before the trial—the good chances for conviction made it unlikely that popular leaders would jeopardize the trial—he took special precautions to have the key removed from the jailhouse every night. Against the possibility that the soldiers would be convicted, Hutchinson and officials in London prepared a clever strategy. Under the plan, Hutchinson would keep the men in close custody awaiting sentencing, and by prearrangement the Crown would grant them a royal pardon. Then British troops would protect the pardoned soldiers until they could be shipped back to England. The plan nearly misfired when the superior court went on circuit in September and delayed the trial of the soldiers until later in the autumn. With stormy conditions on the north Atlantic in winter, the danger existed that the pardon would not reach Boston before the spring term of court, when sentencing would occur.

Hutchinson's sly preparations, it turned out, were unnecessary. The jury in the Massacre trial—if not deliberately packed—contained five future loyalists, several of whom had already voiced sympathy for the defendants. A vague jury-impaneling procedure allowed John Adams and Josiah Quincy, the lawyers for the defense, unusually wide latitude in rejecting prospective jurors, and the Crown, while it prosecuted the case with proper vigor, was not anxious to secure a conviction. All were acquitted of murder; three were convicted of manslaughter, asked for mercy, and were released.[16]

Although the Massacre crisis revealed Hutchinson's dexterity in a difficult situation, his character as a royal governor revealed itself more clearly in his messages to the General Court and his rebuttals to the arguments of the House of Representatives and the Council. In this highly intellectual combat, he was as constrained as ever. He avoided unnecessary quarrels with the Court, and he doubted whether his preachments to them did much good. But when the Court adopted resolutions that were clearly presumptuous and insulting to the King, Parliament, or Crown officials in Massachusetts, Hutchinson felt compelled to reply with every argument and insight at his command. Once engaged in such conflict, he seemed buoyed along by the possibility that his masterful use of the English language and his self-control in the face of insults would compel the Court to recognize its errors. His public messages were, therefore, among the most honest and revealing sources of the man.

Three days after the massacre, Hutchinson summoned the General Court to begin its next session on March 15 in Cambridge, Massachusetts, instead of the Court's traditional seat in Boston. Francis Bernard had relegated the previous session of the Court to Cambridge in rebuke for its vehement attacks on his administration and its allegations of tyranny on the part of Parliament and the Crown. Hutchinson did not want to prolong the punishment, but in December 1769, Hillsborough had instructed him to summon the Court to Cambridge unless new and unforeseen circumstances prompted him to ignore this advice. Hutchinson knew that he could not return the Court to Boston until the legislature muted its attacks on the Crown. But the House and Council, instead of subduing their criticism, charged that the removal itself was unconstitutional and in the process created an impasse that lasted for the next two years. Prudently, the Court did not deny that Hutchinson, as acting governor, had the power to call it into session and specify the meeting place; instead, the House and Council insisted that the Crown could not order Hutchinson to pick a place outside Boston. Hutchinson could remove the Court on his own initiative, but only after first seeking the advice of the legislature in the matter. Hutchinson replied that he was obligated by his oath of office and commission as lieutenant governor to obey all royal instructions, especially those regulating his normal duties as acting governor. He further claimed, correctly, that he was forbidden to show his instructions to the Court. Had they seen the instructions, the assemblymen and councillors would have known that Hutchinson had discretionary authority to return the Court to Boston whenever he saw fit. Hutchinson knew he could not use that discretion, however, until the Court stopped challenging the power of the Crown to dictate the place it assembled. The Court at first refused to transact any business in Cambridge, except the drafting of angry messages of protest to the Acting Governor. Even after it resumed routine business in April, the Court ignored Hutchinson's legislative requests on the ground that removal from its "ancient and legal seat" was an infringement on the liberty of the province and jeopardized "the very being of the Constitution" of Massachusetts.

Throughout the spring and summer of 1770, during intermittent sessions of the Court and in the pages of Boston newspapers, the controversy raged onward. The interpretation of Massachusetts's charter of 1691 was at stake as to whether the Crown could instruct the governor in the use of his powers specified in the charter. Hutchinson and Attorney General Jonathan Sewall argued that the Crown could do so because it had granted the charter to Massachusetts in the first place. As a royal grant, the charter could not be used to exclude the King's wishes from consideration by the royal governor. The General Court argued that the charter of 1691 existed for the sole purpose of providing government and preserving liberty for the people of Massachusetts and that the Crown had no business interfering in the provincial concern of deciding where the General Court would meet. The Crown could appoint and remove its royal governors, this argument ran, but it could not dictate, like a puppetmaster, how they used their powers. Thus the relatively minor dispute over the meeting place of the Court had raised in stark form one of the most important issues of the pre-Revolutionary debate: Did the legitimacy of government and the blessings of liberty come from the Crown alone or from a compact between the people and the Crown? To add urgency to this question, Samuel Adams's chilling draft of the House's message of August 1, 1770, warned that the removal of the Court from Boston was an attempt to intimidate and incapacitate the assembly at the very moment when a pattern of tyranny had appeared in customs enforcement, vice-admiralty jurisdiction, and the presence of British troops in Boston. Only a vigilant legislature stood between the people and further acts of coercion.

Hutchinson accepted the challenge to constitutional debate. The Court had reiterated one of the most hallowed tenets of New England's political theory: the ultimate obligation of the magistrate to serve the interests of the people and the duty of their representatives to thwart any magistrate who became a tool of "wicked ministers" or some other special interest. The Court's refusal to do business, according to that principle, was a legitimate way of compelling Hutchinson to reconsider the interests of the province and dissuading him from further assaults on the public good. Hutchinson, significantly, did not deny this interpretation of the compact between the people and their rulers. He complained, however, that the Court wanted to hold the Crown strictly to the terms of the compact while flouting its own contractual obligations. By calling the General Court into session, Hutchinson explained, he had met his responsibilities under the charter, and by refusing to do business the Court had violated its duty. The Court, he further argued, was presuming to be the final judge of the governor's conduct and the interests of the province. The Court was encroaching on the governor's powers when it argued that the Crown could not compel a governor to obey royal instructions. Until the Court retreated from the positions it had advanced and stopped questioning the prerogative of the Crown to instruct its governors, he would have to resist every effort to have the Court returned to Boston. If he could be convinced "that removing the Court from Boston was an encroachment upon your natural or constitutional rights," he told the Court, "I would not urge my . . . instructions to justify . . . doing it; but I must make my own reason and judgment my rule and not yours." It was a cogent argument; Hutchinson had accepted entirely the premises of New England's compact theory—that the rulers and the ruled are equally untrustworthy and both sides must appeal to the other's reason, self-interest, and ego to act with restraint and civility. Once the Court acquired the final power of review over the governor's exercise of any of the Crown's prerogative powers, Hutchinson realized, the delicate balance of power in Massachusetts would shift toward legislative domination of the executive. The dispute dragged on until June 1772, when Hutchinson and some of the leaders of the Court devised a face-saving solution by which the Court returned to Boston and neither side acknowledged defeat.[17]

Clashes between the colonists and appointees of the King and disputes over the executive power of the Crown in the colonies created many individual collisions of British authority with colonial liberty. Parliament's claim to supreme legislative authority throughout the Empire, however, challenged colonial leaders to devise a comprehensive defense of American liberty;

and the vindication of Parliamentary power became Hutchinson's most difficult task as governor. Late in 1772, the Boston town meeting directed its newly formed committee of correspondence to send every other town in Massachusetts a series of resolves complaining of Parliament's and the Crown's encroachments upon liberty. Hoping to blunt the effect of these Boston Resolves before the towns could consider them, Hutchinson challenged the General Court to repudiate the central assumption of the Boston leaders: their denial of the "supreme authority of Parliament." Neither the Massachusetts Charter nor the dictates of reason nor the rights of Englishmen, Hutchinson systematically argued, provided a shred of justification for the claim that the colonies were outside the reach of Parliament's jurisdiction. "I know of no line," he concluded, "that can be drawn between the supreme authority of Parliament and the total independence of the colonies" because "it is impossible there should be two independent legislatures in one and the same state." If the Court was not prepared to announce forthwith the province's complete autonomy and its equality with Great Britain, it had no other safe course to follow than to admit colonial dependence on the will of Parliament.

Unexpectedly confronted with Hutchinson's attack on the Boston Resolves, the House and Council squirmed uncomfortably as they drafted their answers to the Governor. Both chambers complained that it was very "difficult" to measure exactly how much autonomy the colonies possessed. The Council questioned whether any human institution was supreme and exempt from limitations on its power; the House went further and argued that both Parliament and the General Court possessed genuine legislative power because both were tied to the same King. Hutchinson replied first to the Council that the very task of reserving certain powers to the provincial assembly "evince[s] the impracticality of drawing such a [ragged, irregular] line" between the powers of two legislative bodies. The House's idea that two sovereign legislative bodies could both owe allegiance to the same monarch was more difficult to dismiss. "It took this accomplished lawyer, scholar, and politician twenty-two pages of closely wrought and learned prose," Bailyn explains, "to state his reasons for believing that the chartered authority of the

Massachusetts government" came from " 'the Crown of England' and was " 'consequently subject to the supreme authority of England,' that is, to Parliament."[18] Hutchinson's legal and historical defense in early 1773 of Parliament's supreme power over the colonies was the climax of his political career. The Boston Tea Party in December of that year, his replacement as governor by General Thomas Gage in 1774, his visit to England later in 1774, and the bitter years of exile there until his death in 1780 still lay ahead. But to isolate and vindicate single-handedly the beneficent role of the prerogative and the supremacy of Parliament had required a supreme exertion of will and intellect. Hutchinson had shed a little of his reserve and sacrificed some of his intellectual privacy. The kind of dialogue he sought with his fellow countrymen was a healing exchange, for which he once prescribed the premises. "I have laid before you what I think are the principles of your constitution," he had told the General Court in a plea for understanding; "if I am wrong . . . I wish to be convinced of my error. . . . Your objections . . . may be convincing to me, or I may be able to satisfy you of the insufficiency of them. In either case, I hope, we shall be able to put an end to those irregularities, which ever will be the portion of a government where the supreme authority is controverted."[19]

5

Jonathan Sewall and the Dilemma
of a Loyalist Lawyer

JONATHAN SEWALL was the most gifted lawyer of the late colonial period in Massachusetts. His "soft, smooth, insinuating eloquence," his friend John Adams wrote, "which glided imperceptibly into the minds of a jury, gave him as much power over that tribunal as any lawyer ought ever to possess."[1] As the royal attorney general of Massachusetts from 1767 to 1775 and a scrupulously loyal ally of Francis Bernard and Thomas Hutchinson, Jonathan Sewall was a natural and inevitable opponent of the pre-Revolutionary movement. But for all of his consistency, eminence, and distinction, he was a complex and deeply troubled man. His whole adult life had been a struggle between conflicting tendencies in his character. Though born into a distinguished New England family, he had grown up in a nearly destitute household following the financial ruin and early death of his father, an unsuccessful merchant. Relatives who recognized the boy's intellectuality helped finance his education, and he finally won two scholarships to Harvard College. A serious, bookish student, he was nevertheless twice disciplined and nearly expelled for acts of vandalism during student disorders. After college he studied law, taught school, and came to depend deeply on the friendship of two older men, a lawyer and a judge, who tutored him in law and became adopted fathers. Their companionship helped him overcome his extreme nervousness about public speaking, and, to his astonishment, he was an instant success when he first appeared in the courtroom.[2]

Maturity and success did not quiet the conflicting pressures generated by his individualism and his desire to conform to society's standards. Goaded by the need to restore his family's finances, Sewall decided to ally himself with Governor Francis Bernard. (He advised his friend John Adams to make his reputation as an opponent of British policy, confessing that he could not risk such a turbulent course of action.) With Bernard's support Sewall rose in six years from justice of the peace for Middlesex County to attorney general of the colony. Then, as prosecutor for the Crown, he clashed with customs officials who had illegally searched John Hancock's ship the *Lydia* in April 1768. He fully expected that his refusal to prosecute Hancock in this instance would cost him his job as attorney general. On May 10, 1768, determined to humiliate Hancock, the customs commissioners seized a second of his ships, named, unluckily for them, the *Liberty*. Sewall was again appalled by the flimsy case that the customs commissioners brought to him to prosecute, but the Treasury in London insisted that the prosecution proceed. The trial dragged on until March 1769, when Sewall, who also served as advocate general for the Crown in the vice-admiralty court, finally got the case dismissed—but not before Boston had been convulsed with agitation in Hancock's behalf and mob attacks on the customs commissioners had provoked the British government to send troops to that city. Sewall then received a commission as absentee judge of the Halifax Vice-Admiralty Court. He left Boston at once to journey there and turn the post over to a deputy. His involvement in the Hancock prosecution had suddenly made him a hated man and he was glad to get away. A brave and principled lawyer and prosecutor, he was galled, nevertheless, to discover that rising tensions between British officials and the townspeople of Boston had caught him in the crossfire. When the Boston Massacre occurred he had drawn up the indictments against Preston and the soldiers; but when crowds and committees began to abuse the judges who would hear the case, he had withdrawn from Boston, leaving the prosecution of the hapless soldiers to Samuel Quincy and Robert Treat Paine. His refusal to lead the prosecution of a major case without also resigning as attorney general was an unprofessional action.[3]

Sewall's dilemma was much more substantial than mere priggish reticence in the face of involvement in controversial cases like the Hancock and Massacre trials. Sewall was caught up in the transformation of the legal profession in Massachusetts that coincided with and accelerated the coming of the Revolution. Lawyers became, during the 1750's and 1760's, a closely knit professional elite, with their own intellectual leadership, social fellowship, and group *élan*. Prosperity and economic growth produced a growing volume of criminal prosecutions and civil disputes over property, inheritance, and contracts, which in turn made legal services valuable and brought lawyers into close and frequent contact with every segment of society. The law replaced the church as the primary professional route to community leadership and intellectual distinction. Massachusetts had a sophisticated court system—courts of general sessions and common pleas on the county level and, above them, the superior court, which regularly went on circuit through the province, heard appeals from the county courts, and possessed original jurisdiction in felony cases. Lawyers underwent an arduous apprenticeship of reading law under the direction of a member of the bar and undergoing an oral examination given by the leaders of the bar, often supervised by Jeremiah Gridley, the dean of Massachusetts lawyers. Gridley had an enormous influence on young lawyers in the 1750's; under his guidance, they read widely in classical, Renaissance, and Enlightenment philosophy, history, and legal theory, as well as ingesting massive doses of English common-law precedents.

For all its growing sophistication, the legal system only mirrored the society it served, and throughout the 1760's and 1770's the courts were politicized by two simultaneous pressures. From within the legal profession, lawyers like John Adams and James Otis, Jr., used common-law precedents and continental legal theory to challenge the constitutionality of new British policies: writs of assistance and other new methods of customs enforcement, Parliamentary taxation, limitations on judicial independence, and the lack of jury trials in vice-admiralty courts. To counteract this force, British officials, recognizing the crucial role of the courts, reserved every judicial post in Massachusetts for members of the politically favored Hutchinson and Oliver families and their relatives and supporters. Beginning in 1754, the Board of Trade had ordered that all judicial appointments be made subject to the pleasure of the Crown instead of during the good behavior of the appointee; judges were henceforth under notice that the Crown could order their dismissal without showing cause. By 1771 the Crown began paying the salaries of Massachusetts Superior Court judges to insulate them from popular pressures. Of the forty-seven barristers practicing in the colony in 1774, John M. Murrin shows, fifteen became ardent patriots, four reluctant patriots, nineteen avowed supporters of the Crown, eight others reluctant Tories, with the leanings of only one man unknown. Most of the patriots began their legal careers before 1740 or after 1765; most of the adherents of the Crown began their careers during the governorships of William Shirley or Francis Bernard, when opportunity seemed to beckon Crown supporters. The once closely knit fraternity of lawyers and judges in Massachusetts was polarized by these forces into two hostile camps: Tory judges and lawyers, who sought to restore order, and Whig lawyers and politicians, who wanted to use the law as a bulwark against British encroachments upon American liberty. In eight politically charged civil and criminal cases in Boston between 1769 and 1771, mob intimidation of judges and jurors compromised impartial justice.[4] During a period when lawyers were becoming the intellectual and political leaders of the province, when laymen were growing more knowledgeable about the law and juries more independent about applying popular notions of right and wrong in their deliberations, lawyers felt the strongest pressures to choose sides in the struggle between British authority and colonial autonomy.

Jonathan Sewall studied, practiced, and enforced law in Massachusetts during this period of change and ferment. His ruling in the case of the *Lydia* warned customs officials that tradition and precedent limited their powers of search and seizure. Between 1768 and 1770, while controversies about customs officials and British troops raged in Boston, Sewall went to considerable trouble in behalf of two unusual clients—Negro slaves, identified only as Margaret and James, who were probably mother and son. In separate litigations they had sued their masters for their freedom on the ground that they had been born in Massachusetts and, under its charter, were therefore free. Sewall did not establish a precedent in these actions—as early as 1766 a slave in Massachusetts had won his freedom by proving he had been born in the province—but in Margaret's case he went to a great deal of trouble to obtain depositions from distant witnesses who had known her as a girl, and he argued eloquently that slavery violated "humanity, common justice, and eternal morality."[5]

For a fastidious, enlightened man like Sewall, the tensions of the pre-Revolutionary controversy in Massachusetts were unusually painful. "He always lamented the conduct of Great Britain toward America," his friend John Adams noted, "but the society in which he lived had convinced him that all resistance was not only useless but ruinous." In response to these conflicting tensions he adopted a faintly ironic, bemused, slightly cynical attitude toward any exuberant human enterprise. Lawyers, he noted as a young man, often made a fetish out of hard work: "We toil, tug, labour, plunge, paddle, scramble, wallow" in the reading of cases, laws, and precedents "and . . . at length emerge with souls fitly enlarged and enlightened for . . . the guardianship of the lives, liberties, and properties, of our ignorant fellow men."[6] As he grew older, Sewall's sense of the absurd enabled him to look knowingly at the human limitations of men involved in the operation of the law. Perhaps to make amends for his default of duty during the Massacre trials, he engaged in a long retrospective controversy about the verdicts with Samuel Adams, in the Boston newspapers. Adams quoted from depositions, collected before the trial but not used by the prosecution, which showed that the soldiers were wanton murderers. This evidence, Sewall retorted, was tainted: "In . . . the full discovery of the whole truth, much depends upon the cross-examination of a witness. . . . If he be unused to testifying, he may, by artful interrogatories, be easily drawn, inadvertently, to give a very partial and imperfect account of the facts," and on the other hand, "if his . . . prejudices and inclinations happen to be on the side of the party who takes his testimony, tho' he is conscious that he has not declared the whole truth, yet he will readily apply this salve to his conscience, that he has answered truly all such questions as were put to him."[7] As the crisis of authority in Massachusetts deepened, Sewall analyzed it with the same realism and respect for fact but also the same sad disparagement of human folly. "I really believe," he wrote in December 1774, "the greater part of my countrymen to be well-meaning, deluded people" who "conscientiously believe it is their duty to put their lives and fortunes at hazard in defense of those rights and privileges which, they have been persuaded, the ministry have planned to deprive them of. [If] they once . . . could . . . be brought to make use of their own understanding . . . and judge for themselves the real grounds of their fears, they would be shocked at the cold steps they have been driven to take; but I despair of this."[8]

As the pre-Revolutionary movement in Massachusetts crossed the threshold from resistance to rebellion in 1775, Sewall appraised the events around him with insight as well as with withering contempt. More important than recounting the awful "scenes" of rebellion, he remarked, it was necessary to examine "the connection in which they stood to each other." It was a forbidding task, for, as Sewall explained, colonial unrest "is so truly astonishing, so entirely out of the course of nature, so repugnant to the known principles which most forceably actuate the human mind, that we must search deeper for the grand and more hidden spring." To begin with, Sewall could not minimize the extent of disaffection. "It is now become too plain to be any longer doubted," he wrote to General Frederick Haldimand, "that a union is formed by a great majority, . . . throughout this whole continent, for opposing" the authority of Parliament. The broad social base and intense commitment of the pre-Revolutionary movement, he observed, posed the most serious question. Consider, he wrote, this astonishing spectacle: a nation of property-owning, prosperous, hard-working farmers who enjoy more personal liberty and less government interference than people anywhere else in the world—"a people so situated for happiness"—suddenly "throw off their rural simplicity" and "bid open defiance to . . . the parent state . . . and rush to arms with the ferocity of savages and . . . the fiery zeal of crusaders." Certainly this strange behavior had its roots in "that ancient republican independent spirit" the Puritans had first brought to New England and in the degree of popular participation in government that had developed in colonial Massachusetts. Nourished by lenient government, this tendency to turbulence and unrest had sometimes seemed to "wither" but at other times it grew "with that luxuriance with which we now see it spread."[9] The single word *"Liberty* . . . conjured up the most horrid phantoms in the minds of the common people" and made these folk the ready prey of radical merchants and congregationalist clergy. Both groups were dissatisfied with their place in society and hungry for influence and power. The merchants were driven by "a desire of a free and unrestrained trade," and the clergy were cursed with "that restless spirit and lust of dominion which, with a melancholy notoriety, mark the character of a priesthood in all ages and nations." Dazzled by the example of these leaders, "simple and unmeaning" farmers and tradesmen with no real stake in the controversy over Parliamentary power were "hoodwinked, inflamed, and goaded on by their spiritual drivers" and "fancied they saw . . . tyranny advancing with hasty strides."[10]

"Pray reverend sir, have the Parliament any right to make laws for us, and isn't this a grievance?" asks Puff, the politician in Sewall's satirical comedy on pre-Revolutionary politics, *A Cure for the Spleen,* which illustrates this process of deluding simple folk. "Aye," responds Fillpot, the innkeeper, "there was a Boston minister and another gentleman lodged at our house last night, and they talked about this very thing and made it out clear as the sun at noon-day that the Parliament have no such right; though I did not understand them—but they argued very powerfully and proved that we ought to resist. However, I don't like taking up arms neither, that I must own."[11]

Ironically, Sewall continued, the Americans like Fillpot were not by nature violent or "warlike," but were all the more dangerous when aroused by popular excitement. "Such is the infatuation," he observed, "that like madmen, they are totally incapable of attending to the dictates of reason." Reinforcing that mania were their exaggerated affection for and trust in their new leaders. Though temporarily "buoyed up" by the initial unity of the movement, the "whole system" of Whig organization depended for direction on the leadership of "unprincipled, factious, designing men." That leadership merely capitalized on "an enthusiasm in politics, like that which religious notions inspire, that drive men on with an unnatural impetuosity that baffles and confounds all . . . rational . . . calculation."[12] Consequently, Whig leaders were able to use "popular frenzy" to "extort . . . confessions, acknowledgements, recantations, and submissions" from loyal subjects of the Crown. This method of silencing opposition, Sewall complained, was the work of "the inebriated and intoxicated devotees of rapine and licentiousness."[13]

6

Egerton Leigh:
"Downright Placeman"

"I AM a downright placeman," boasted Egerton Leigh[1] in 1773, as he spat back in the faces of his detractors the most insulting epithet in South Carolina's political vocabulary. A placeman was a British official in the colonies who depended on the income of his office for his livelihood and on its dignity for his self-importance. Since the 1750's Charles Town, South Carolina had become a dumping ground where the British government could dispose of suppliants for patronage positions. Over half the royal councillors there during the pre-Revolutionary years and all other Crown officials except Lieutenant Governor William Bull—former Speaker of the Commons House of Assembly and head of a distinguished aristocratic family—were British office seekers. These men were not entirely alien to South Carolina. Many settled there, married local women, bought property, and established families; but native South Carolinians never fully accepted most of these outsiders. To make matters worse, many placemen augmented their income by holding more than one royal appointment and appearing to be greedy plural officeholders.

Leigh was the most successful placeman. While others aspired to success and security, he obtained these goals with seeming ease. He had arrived in South Carolina in 1753, at the age of twenty, in the company of his father, Peter Leigh, the newly appointed Chief Justice of the province. In quick succession he founded a thriving law practice, was elected to the Commons House, and married Martha Bremar, the niece of wealthy merchant Henry Laurens. Leigh's wife's uncle took a liking to him; Laurens gave

Leigh the bulk of his legal business for nearly a decade and even guaranteed Leigh's credit. Leigh became the most accomplished plural officeholder in any of the colonies; between 1755 and 1765 he acquired the offices of surveyor general, royal councillor, judge of the Charles Town Vice-Admiralty Court, and royal attorney general. He bought a plantation and built in Charles Town a splendid town house, which he furnished with a library of over 800 volumes, a large organ, and a magnificent collection of paintings, including works by Veronese and Correggio. His election as Anglican vestryman, appointment as a commissioner of a local school, and elevation to the rank of deputy grand master of the province's Masonic lodge indicated his capacity for hard work and his skill in impressing influential people with his ability and charm.

Two pre-Revolutionary controversies toppled Leigh from this eminent position and drove him into a quixotic struggle against the political leaders of South Carolina. The first was his famous quarrel with his kinsman Henry Laurens following Laurens's prosecution in Leigh's vice-admiralty court in 1767 and 1768; the second was his effort as president of the Council to lead that chamber into battle against the Commons House in a dispute over the control of the purse. Leigh's troubles had begun during the Stamp Act crisis. He had defended the hated law, and the paralysis of royal government during the crisis had cut deeply into his income of official fees. Hoping to capitalize on the repeal of the act, the Commons had asked the Rockingham ministry for an inquiry into South Carolina affairs and in particular into Leigh's simultaneous occupation of four royal offices. Then, in 1767, Daniel Moore, the new customs collector in Charles Town, began a campaign of harassment—similar to the Boston customs agents' treatment of John Hancock—of local merchants and especially of Laurens. Plagued by lawsuits and abuse from the Charles Town merchant community, Moore fled to England, leaving his deputy, George Roupell, an experienced and respected Charles Town official, to handle the repercussions of his actions.

The controversy produced five sensational cases in Leigh's vice-admiralty court—"as difficult . . . as perhaps ever came before into that court in America," the *South Carolina Gazette* correctly evaluated them. First, on July 19, 1767, Leigh released from seizure the *Active,* a coastal vessel charged with failure to secure proper customs clearance. Leigh ruled that inspection of exclusively coastal shipping violated traditional interpretation of the Acts of Trade. The decision angered the Lords of the Treasury, and even before their rebuke reached him Leigh knew he must balance his decision with one supporting rigorous customs enforcement. He dismissed a suit filed against Moore by the merchants but did so only on the basis of an obscure technicality. Then, when Moore seized two of Laurens's coastal vessels, the *Wambaw* and the *Broughton Island Packet,* Leigh returned the latter ship to its owner and permitted the confiscation of the other on the ground that the *Wambaw* had not listed as cargo its salable load of ballast lumber. To soften the impact of the decision, Leigh deliberately neglected to declare that the customs officials had "probable cause" for seizing the *Broughton Island Packet.* That "oversight" permitted Laurens to sue the customs officials for civil damages in a provincial court. Unable to pay the large judgment the court awarded Laurens, Roupell—who had made the actual seizure—faced jail. In an apparent attempt to force Laurens to drop his civil claim against Roupell, customs agents seized the *Ann,* a large vessel belonging partly to Laurens, and then offered to release the *Ann* if Laurens would free Roupell from civil liability. It was to Laurens's financial advantage to settle the matter in this way, but he considered the seizure of the *Ann* a moral outrage—an act of blackmail. So it was that the case of the *Ann* came to trial in the court of vice-admiralty. As the evidence made abundantly clear, even to Leigh, Laurens had been framed. Port authorities in Charles Town had long allowed merchants to post required bond with customs officers at any time prior to sailing, though technically payment was required before loading began. The customs collector had deliberately delayed accepting Laurens's bond until loading of the *Ann* had commenced, thus giving Roupell reason to seize the ship for violation of the acts of trade. Leigh knew he would lose his judgeship if he failed to protect Roupell, so again he devised an ingenious compromise. He required Roupell to swear an archaic oath that he had not acted with malice toward Laurens; he then declared that Roupell had "probable cause" for the seizure; finally, he released the *Ann* to its owners.

Throughout the whole series of customs prosecutions in 1767 and 1768, Leigh had acted as an arbitrator between the merchants, especially Laurens, and the customs officials, especially Roupell. Considering the pressures upon him, he was reasonably even handed; but by playing this role, he antagonized both sides and made himself vulnerable. In reports to his superiors in London, Roupell mercilessly attacked Leigh as a spineless defender of royal officials; Laurens wrote a scathing exposé of Leigh's complicity in the activities of customs men.

The vice-admiralty cases thrust Leigh into the glare of publicity and accelerated the deterioration of his position in society. First, the complaints about his plural officeholding—rumbling ever since the Stamp Act crisis—now exploded. In the capacity of attorney general, he had, under pressure from Moore, advised the customs collectors that seizure of the *Broughton Island Packet* was legally justified; from his judicial seat in the vice-admiralty court, he had found the seizure improper and unwarranted; as attorney general, he felt obligated to serve as Roupell's lawyer in Laurens's civil suit for damages. Roupell complained bitterly to London that Leigh had betrayed him and that South Carolina leaders had for some time criticized Leigh's dual role as the Crown's prosecutor in provincial courts and judge in the vice-admiralty court. As a result, the Crown ordered Leigh to resign one of the two posts. The vice-admiralty judgeship was much less profitable, and Leigh chose to relinquish it. But that humiliation was only fleeting compared with the public denunciation Leigh received from Henry Laurens, who condemned the entire series of customs prosecutions against him and laid the responsibility directly on Leigh as judge. Laurens, of course, had valid grievances. Only by suing Roupell for unjustified seizure of the *Broughton Island Packet* did he recover the substantial losses from the confiscation of the *Wambaw*—a seizure upheld on the most specious of technicalities. The delay in the sailing of the *Ann* had also cost him money. However, moral principle rather than monetary loss brought Laurens to the offensive. Moore and Roupell had used trickery, deceit, blackmail, and intimidation against him; and a vice-admiralty judge, Egerton Leigh, had for the most part let them get away with these tactics. All the cases should have been dismissed, Laurens contended, and none should have been protected with a probable-cause ruling. Leigh's attempts to protect the customs officials and only afterward to do justice to the accused were intolerable and reprehensible abuses of judicial power. Most galling to Laurens had been Leigh's ingenious way of finding probable cause for the seizure of the *Ann*—a maneuver that prevented Laurens from taking this attempted extortion into a provincial court of law.

Leigh was aghast when he read Laurens's attack on his judicial ability and personal ethics. He had expected Laurens to understand the pressures he had been under as vice-admiralty judge and, as his kinsman and friend, to make the best of an awkward situation by remaining silent about the unpleasantness of the trials. Instead, Leigh felt, Laurens had attacked him when he was down and had taken advantage of his vulnerability as an unpopular Crown official. "Every man who reads his book must perceive the motive," Leigh retorted in a counterattack on Laurens entitled *The Man Unmasked*. "Under the specious show of an exalted kind of virtue, which regards no law, no friendship, no alliances, no ties of blood," Laurens was now attempting "to gain a popular name" by destroying "the fame of a man in the meridian of his days" and ruthlessly jeopardizing the livelihood of Leigh's wife, seven children, and mother-in-law.

Leigh's side of the story in *The Man Unmasked* was a skillful blend of injured innocence, invective, and self-justification. It was an extraordinarily revealing document; Leigh knew that he was a hated man in Charles Town, and, in the belief that he could alter his public image, he tried to make his pamphlet a transparently candid personal memoir. He argued that Laurens, as a legal layman, was unqualified to discuss the mysteries and technicalities of the law. Leigh pleaded that judges ought to be exempt from criticism of their decisions and that "charity" required men to trust the basic integrity of vice-admiralty judges who had the unpleasant task of confiscating whole cargoes. If he had made mistakes, Leigh confessed, they were errors of judgment and not intent. Forced to defend his own conduct, Leigh felt reduced to pleading his good intentions. For a proud and sensitive man, it was a humiliating and frustrating experience. He tried to hide the embarrassment by expounding the principles of psychology that explained his own behavior. Men were difficult to understand because they were a "mixture of so much *goodness* and so much *baseness* . . . a compound of opposite *qualities, humours,* and *inclinations."* Most observers simply counted a person's good and bad qualities and deducted one total from the other, "as we do in vulgar arithmetic." Leigh proceeded differently: "I . . . sift out . . . the first ruling principle of the man, and then . . . carry in my eye his leading passion, which I separate from the other parts of his character and then observe how far his other qualities, good and bad, are brought to support *that."* If his own words could not do it, Leigh hoped that recognition from the Crown would compel men to recognize his leading passion of service to his King and thereby dissuade them from simply compiling his alleged misdeeds. Thus, in the spring of 1771, he went to England and for nearly a year pestered the King's advisers until he was finally granted a baronetcy—the lowest rank of the nobility—and the title Sir Egerton Leigh.

Leigh's loyalty to the Crown was not his only "leading passion" to win attention in 1772. While in London he made pregnant a girl in his household named Molly Bremar, an orphan who was his own ward, his wife's sister, and also Henry Laurens's niece. The girl herself was rebellious and undisciplined and was probably not entirely innocent in the affair. The two returned separately to Charles Town, and when her time to deliver the child was near Leigh put the girl on a ship bound for England. Before it sailed, she went into labor; the captain tried to put her ashore; Leigh insisted she remain on board; and the child, born on the high seas without a midwife, died within a week. Later, in a face-to-face meeting with Laurens, Leigh admitted responsibility for the girl's pregnancy and offered financial restitution. Characteristically, Laurens refused the offer and accused Leigh of murder. The story spread throughout America, and Thomas Lynch, a South Carolina representative to the First Continental Congress in 1774, "entertained" a group of delegates "with the scandalous history of Sir Egerton Leigh—the story of his wife's sister, . . . and all that."

His reputation and career in ruins, Leigh nevertheless busied himself in 1773 with new projects to restore his power and prestige. As president of the royal Council he involved himself in a dispute that had been in progress since 1769—the Wilkes Fund controversy. The Commons House of Assembly had sent a contribution from public funds to the supporters of John Wilkes, an English radical; in retaliation, the ministry had instructed the governor to veto every appropriation bill until the Commons relinquished its sole power to transmit money out of the province. At issue was the exclusive control of the purse, which the South Carolina Commons had won in the 1720's. By 1773 the deadlock was complete. The governor would not sign a tax bill, and the Commons would not restrict its power to control public funds. On his return from England, Leigh launched a Council investigation of the province's finances—one designed to dramatize the need for a tax bill that the governor could sign. Two native South Carolinians on the Council, John and William Henry Drayton, wrote a manifesto denouncing the Council's intervention in the Wilkes Fund dispute and published it in the *South Carolina Gazette*. Infuriated at this attack, Leigh and the majority of the Council threw the printer of the *Gazette* in jail on the ground that he had violated the privileges of the Council as the upper house of the legislature. A sympathetic justice of the peace quickly released the printer from jail, and Acting Governor William Bull said nothing in defense of the Council's actions. As a result of this high-handed maneuver, the Council sank still lower in public estimation.

Leigh responded to this disaster in typical fashion. He composed a long and elegant account of the Wilkes Fund controversy and of his own role in it. He loved to replay humiliating episodes on paper and demonstrate with literary flourish that he had been right all along. This time he sent his pamphlet to London for publication, hoping it would induce the ministry to rebuke the Commons House and vindicate the Council. Like *The Man Unmasked,* Leigh's *Considerations on Certain Political Transactions in the Province of South Carolina* was a thorough treatise and at the same time a candid version of the author's image of himself. In the first place, Leigh knew what he was talking about. His service in the Commons from 1755 to 1760 had acquainted him well with the mentality of provincial legislators, and his pamphlet conceded their principal arguments. Of course, there were ample precedents, dating to the 1730's, for the Commons to have sole control of appropriations, and there were also precedents for sending money out of the province. Leigh also acknowledged that the preservation of these legislative powers instilled in the assemblymen a high degree of seriousness and purpose; "tenacious of their rights as conceived by them," the assemblymen derived a new sense of importance and confidence from their intransigence. Against this deliberate resistance, the power of the governor and the Council was utterly frustrated. Certainly the Council could not pretend to have any meaningful authority unless people freely acknowledged that it was a genuine replica of the British House of Lords. "What security can such a branch of the legislature have," Leigh asked rhetorically, "when the general opinion proclaims that a place in Council is a kind of alienation from the concerns and interest of the people?" Obviously, none. Leigh had conclusively demonstrated that the collapse of British authority in pre-Revolutionary South Carolina was not simply the result of unpopular Parliamentary taxes and executive decisions. Early in the eighteenth century South Carolinians had conceived of themselves as a separate community with its own values and interests. Unconsciously, the province's popular leaders had become so preoccupied with the virtues of their political system that they were caught in a kind of narcissistic daze: "They have brought their colony to such an outward state that they feel some *self-conceit* has crept into their hearts; then it is that men begin to give the polish to their acts and to be emulous of fame. . . . By slow and almost imperceptible degrees jealousies and distrusts have fastened themselves upon men's understandings, and the tone and temper of the people's minds have undergone some fatal changes." The very success with which South Carolinians had assumed responsibility for their own affairs, Leigh concluded, had warped their estimate of their own capacities and wisdom: "Man is not born for a series of indulgences and human nature teaches us that we cannot bear a constant tide of flattering success without becoming insolently saucy and arrogantly vain." In the process of trying to thwart South Carolina's resistance, Leigh had seen at very close range the motives and impulses that were driving a society toward a collision with British authority.

Leigh had revealed with astonishing accuracy the socially pervasive, deeply rooted, and emotionally gratifying character of resistance in South Carolina. Only in this way could he explain the utter collapse of royal authority there and the consuming hostility he had provoked when he defended the disinterestedness and benevolence of British power. South Carolina had forgotten, he argued, that its constitution—with its representative Assembly and encouragement of local leadership—was entirely *"derivative"* from the Crown and that, "without the King's grace, we are destitute of any constitution whatsoever." The genius of the British constitution, which the Crown had extended to South Carolina, was the balance between the Crown, Lords, and Commons. An essential part of the system was the duty of the Lords—and in South Carolina, the Council—to act as a *"barrier* to withstand the encroachments of the lower house." Until South Carolina returned—or was compelled to return—to this prescribed form of government, British authority would be precarious and the province itself would live in imminent danger of royal punishment. "Justice as well as prudence," Leigh pleaded with his contemporaries, "require us to yield." Prudent submission to one's political superiors had been instilled in Leigh from boyhood. As a placeman, he had learned that success depended on one's ability to impress a small group of patrons who were in a position to advance a suppliant's career. Ability, good intentions, and loyalty to one's betters were the qualities that earned success and reputation. Leigh knew that dutiful obedience would be extremely painful for South Carolinians; what he could not fully appreciate was that the province's leaders felt wedded to an entirely different set of moral imperatives—a duty to follow individual conscience before any other influence and a responsibility to preserve the integrity of the community from all external threats.[2]

7

Conclusion: Joseph Galloway and
Daniel Leonard on Principles
under Pressure

THE enunciation of the principles of imperial subordination
compelled men to reconstruct their understanding of the conflict
between British authority and colonial rights. In so doing, each
imperial apologist grappled—more closely than any official in
London—with the problem of preserving the legal and historical
bonds that connected the colonies to the mother country. The
struggle exacted from each man a high price of endurance and
self-discipline. No one gave himself so unstintingly to this work
as Joseph Galloway, of Philadelphia.

On September 8, 1774, Galloway sat on a committee of the First
Continental Congress.[1] A dizzy sequence of events had brought
the delegates to Philadelphia: the Tea Act of 1773 had provoked
a new crisis over Parliament's power to tax the colonies; on
November 27, 1773, the first shipload of newly taxed tea reached
Boston, and the outraged populace sent the five tea consignees
and four customs commissioners fleeing to Castle William in
Boston harbor for safety; Governor Hutchinson refused to issue
clearance papers for the ship to leave Boston unless the tea was
unloaded and the duty paid within twenty days of the ship's
arrival, as the law required; on December 16, 1773, the night
before the deadline expired, an unidentified band of men
boarded the ship, broke open 342 chests of tea, and dumped the
contents, valued at around £10,000, into Boston harbor. Parliament and the ministry retaliated swiftly, between March and

85

June 1774, by drafting and enacting four Coercive Acts which closed the port of Boston, suspended portions of the Massachusetts Charter of 1691, authorized the dispatch of colonial radicals to England for trial and imprisonment, and made new and more sweeping provisions for quartering British troops in the colonies. After some disagreement about the proper response, colonial leaders decided to call a congress, to meet in September 1774, to reiterate American rights and petition once more for redress of grievances.

During the tense summer months of 1774, Galloway watched these developments from the vantage point of his position as speaker of the Pennsylvania Assembly. A lawyer by profession, he had once been the most powerful figure in the politics of that proprietary colony: the manager of Benjamin Franklin's faction in the province's politics and the leader of an astute offensive in the early 1760's to reduce the power and influence of the ruling Penn family. In 1764, with Franklin, he had almost succeeded in converting Pennsylvania into a royal colony; the Assembly had requested that Britain make the change, but in the uproar over the Stamp Act the Crown shelved the proposal. Galloway saw the Crown as a more efficient and responsive ruler than the Penns, and he obviously expected royal government to advance his own career. The dispute, however, had elevated John Dickinson, another lawyer, to political prominence; without defending the proprietors, Dickinson had argued prophetically in 1764 that ominous new developments in British colonial policy made the adoption of royal government an extremely risky course for Pennsylvania to follow. Dickinson and Galloway thereafter had differed vehemently on every issue of the pre-Revolutionary controversy: the Stamp Act, the boycott against the Townshend duties, the existence of a ministerial conspiracy to undermine colonial liberty. Dickinson's *Letters of a Pennsylvania Farmer* (1767–1768) had been the most widely read and skillfully written rationale for resistance against British policy of the whole pre-Revolutionary period. Now, in 1774, Galloway decided to act with similar boldness; he would devise, and at a dramatic moment unveil, a new constitution for the British Empire. While Dickinson dominated the public meetings and the provincial congress that committed Pennsylvania to participate in the forthcoming Continental Congress, Galloway persuaded the Assembly to appoint him to, and exclude Dickinson and his friends from, the province's delegation to that congress.

The Congressional committee of which Galloway became a member had the task of defining colonial rights, and four delegates quickly crystallized the issue at hand. Richard Henry Lee, of Virginia, and John Jay, of New York, took the more radical position that the colonies were distinct political communities voluntarily associated with the British state; John Rutledge, of South Carolina, and James Duane, of New York, argued that the colonies were extensions of the British political system. Lee and Jay wanted to base colonial rights, in part, on the natural-law freedom of a people to choose their own form of government, while Rutledge and Duane considered natural law a dangerous ground and pleaded that British precedents protecting liberty only should serve as the basis for colonial remonstrance. After these differences of opinion had emerged, Galloway entered the discussion and, speaking at greater length than the others, tried to provide irrefutable support for Duane's and Rutledge's position. Congress should not base its appeals on natural law, he argued, because the colonies had been from the earliest settlement politically organized societies that had not emerged from a state of nature. Therefore, only the constitutional history of England provided a credible explanation of colonial rights. "The essence" of the constitution was the representation in Parliament of the proprietors of land in the realm and their consent to legislation binding the inhabitants of those lands. Because the first settlers in America occupied territory not so represented, no law of Parliament enacted since the establishment of the colonies necessarily bound the colonists. Even Lord North, Galloway concluded, would concede the validity of these arguments if he made an effort to inform himself of the history of the constitution. Strong language! Galloway quickly acknowledged its radical implications: "I am well aware that my arguments tend to an independency of the colonies and militate against the maxim that there must be some absolute power to draw together all the wills and strengths of the Empire."

This admission represented the crux of Galloway's problem during his direct involvement in the pre-Revolutionary debate from July 1774 to April 1775. Throughout that period he tried to sustain two distinct lines of argument containing the very contradictory implications he had confessed to the committee of Congress. Representation was the key to the imperial problem; therefore the exercise of Parliamentary jurisdiction over the colonies was a grievous anomaly that justified colonial opposition to the British policy. At the same time, the subordinate status of the colonists within the Empire sharply circumscribed the permissible limits of colonial remonstrance. He felt confident that he alone could reconcile these two truths and in so doing promote the only possible solution to the imperial controversy. "I stand here almost alone," he wrote to an English friend in August 1774, in knowing that "both countries should retreat a little and take other ground, seeing that which they are now upon is likely to prove dangerous and distressing to both." The "other ground" he had in mind was, of course, Galloway's Plan of Union, which he proposed in a lengthy and closely reasoned speech to the First Continental Congress on September 28, 1774. He envisioned the creation of an American branch of the British Parliament. Its members would be chosen by the colonial assemblies for three-year terms. All colonial legislation would require approval of both the British Parliament and the American legislature. In addition, the Crown would appoint a president general with broad executive and administrative authority. This Plan of Union would enable Parliament to retain its supremacy over the whole Empire while giving the colonists a means of consenting to its laws. It would secure for the colonists, Galloway declared, the "first and most excellent privileges of Englishmen," the representation in Parliament of the land they occupied, and their right to "participate in the supreme legislative authority" of government. Only the Plan of Union, an explicit alteration of the constitution of the Empire, he warned, could protect the colonies from the power of Parliament. The colonies were subordinate communities and their assemblies possessed circumscribed authority to deal with mundane local problems. Humble, respectful petition of Parliament and the Crown was the only solution to the colonists' plight. Denials of Parliamentary supremacy would only offend the British and jeopardize the political blessings Americans already enjoyed.

Although Congress voted six states to five to postpone consideration of Galloway's Plan of Union, the narrow margin was
misleading. There was little chance the proposal could have been
adopted. Before it would listen to Galloway's proposals, Congress
endorsed the Suffolk Resolves—which, adopted earlier in Boston,
denied that colonists were obligated to obey the Coercive Acts and
also instituted military preparations—and a nonimportation boycott on British goods. Meanwhile, Galloway's political base crumbled. In mid-October an election in Philadelphia returned
Dickinson to the Assembly; the legislators removed Galloway
as speaker and named Dickinson a delegate to Congress. The
delegates in turn expunged the Plan of Union from the Congressional journal. Embittered, Galloway published his plan and
an elaborate argument in its defense early in 1775. He reiterated
his view that British authority encroached upon American
liberty and his insistence that the colonies were an integral
part of the British state and bound to obey its laws. He condemned the arrogance of colonial leaders who misrepresented his
plan, gratified their egos by inventing new constitutional ideas,
and deluded the populace into believing it could defy the power
of Parliament. Compared with their opportunism and irresponsibility, his own leadership stood starkly contrasted. "I . . . have
laid before you the constitutional extent of Parliamentary jurisdiction," he told his readers. "I have . . . *deduced* your rights,
. . . and explained your duties. I have pointed out the mode
which . . . you ought to pursue for a restoration of those rights."
Imperious and erudite, Galloway could not understand why his
immense talents actually disqualified him from leadership during
the crisis of 1774 and 1775.

The same forces that scuttled Galloway's imaginative plan for
reconciliation—the Coercive Acts, the determination of colonial
leaders to resist further encroachments on their liberty, and the
growing conviction that the people and their representatives
alone now had the responsibility for preserving freedom—had
rendered the enunciation of principle a fruitless intellectual
exercise. In the place of traditional subordination and imperial
regulation arose a contagion of resistance and common purpose
that the enunciators of principle felt powerless to counteract.
However, they perceived acutely the internal snapping of the

cords of obedience and consent. "I have frequently heard the term patriotism mentioned," declared John Randolph, the last royal Attorney General of Virginia. "I can by no means denominate a man a patriot because he enjoys the acclamations of the people. . . . True patriotism consists not in a separate attachment to any particular branch, but in the preservation of the several parts, of government"—monarchy, aristocracy, and the people, through their representative legislature. "This vast political body, with its appendages, . . . like the earth, . . . must be preserved in its due poise or else it will tumble into ruin."[2] In a subdued lament, Daniel Leonard, of Massachusetts, projected further the deterioration of imperial institutions and authority and the rise of popular leadership:

They begin by reminding the people of the elevated rank they hold in the universe, as men; that all men by nature are equal; that kings are but the ministers of the people; that their authority is delegated to them by the people, . . . and that [the people] have a right to resume it, and place it in other hands, or keep it themselves whenever it is made use of to oppress them. Doubtless there have been instances where these principles have been inculcated to obtain a redress of real grievances, but they have been much oftener perverted to the worst of purposes. No government, however perfect in theory, is administered in perfection; the frailty of man does not admit of it. A small mistake in . . . policy, often furnishes a pretense to libel government, and persuade the people that their rulers are tyrants, and the whole government a system of oppression. Thus the seeds of sedition are usually sown and the people are led to sacrifice real liberty to licentiousness.[3]

II

The Search for Accommodation

8

William Smith, Jr., and

the Bending of

Constitutional Rules

JOURNEYING to Philadelphia in the summer of 1774 to attend the First Continental Congress, and conscious that this was a historic journey, John Adams was quick to appraise and categorize the public men he met. "Mr. William Smith, councillor at law and a councillor by mandamus," he wrote in his diary, carefully noting Smith's dual roles as adviser to the royal governor and Whiggish member of the bar, "has the character of a great lawyer, a sensible and learned man and yet a consistent, unshaken friend to his country and her liberties." Smith was, apparently, master of the occasion; on this initial and "ceremonial" meeting with Adams, he chose to relate his role during the Stamp Act crisis in New York, when he had simultaneously prevented violence and thwarted distribution of the hated stamps. The tale prompted Adams to conclude that Smith had "acted an intrepid, an honest, and a prudent part" in that crisis of liberty. Adams's encounter with Smith was a moment of symbolic importance. The two provincial lawyers had so much in common and yet were to fulfill such different destinies—Adams as a leader of the American republic, Smith as a loyalist exile—and both on this occasion revealed something about themselves. Adams exhibited his inquisitiveness, his capacity to be deeply impressed once his initial defenses had been penetrated, his eagerness, his incisive judgments of men, his consuming passion to understand and preserve liberty. Smith displayed a mastery of drawing-room conversation and a curiosity and self-consciousness about his impact on the men he encountered. Adams's own choice of words sharply etched Smith's character traits: "sensible," in eighteenth-century usage open to stimuli, active, questing, intellectually and emotionally sensitive, quickly and acutely aroused; and "learned," possessing a corpus of formal knowledge to such an extent that it disciplines the mind, beautifies the man, and distinguishes him from others.[1]

Smith's inherited position in New York society and politics required him to lead a highly compartmentalized public life, to master several tasks: royal councillor, Livingston party leader, advocate of civic improvement, scholar, and historian. Aware that his considerable abilities had their limits, and determined to attain excellence in each of his undertakings, Smith failed to integrate his various roles and to subordinate some of them to the pursuit of one primary goal. The eldest son and namesake of William Smith, Sr., he followed the pattern of his father's career: Yale, class of 1745; the New York legal profession; leadership of the Presbyterian faction in the province's political and religious quarrels; and finally, in 1767, his father's seat on the governor's Council. Gregarious and clever, principled and hungry for a career of distinction, he took up with like-minded Yale men William Livingston and John Morin Scott. Known as the Triumvirate, the three men edited and wrote in 1752 and 1753 one of the first American magazines, *The Independent Reflector,* which promoted religious dissent against Anglican influence, advocated various legal and political reforms, and closely paraphrased the anticlerical passages from the English radical publication *Cato's Letters,* by Thomas Gordon and John Trenchard. During these early years of his career, Smith also turned to historical research—the outgrowth of his early employment compiling a new edition of the province's laws—and he published in 1757 *The History of the Province of New York to 1732.* It was, L. F. S. Upton explains, a thoroughly Whiggish "story of wholly bad governors and fairly good assemblymen, royal power versus the rights of the people," warm in praise of the early Livingstons and Presbyterians. In preparation for a sequel volume, which was never written, Smith kept a diary, *Historical Memoirs* of his political experiences, covering the years 1763 to 1778. This journal is a magnificent firsthand account of Smith's experience on the royal Council from 1767 to 1776, his search in those years for a compromise in the imperial controversy, and his prolonged hesitation between 1776 and 1778 before finally casting his fortunes with the British in the War for Independence. The care he lavished on his diary indicated strongly that Smith found private contemplation a consuming and deeply gratifying occupation.[2]

The Stamp Act controversy triggered Smith's morose reappraisal of the course of colonial politics. Coming on the heels of the Sugar Act and Cadwallader Colden's vendetta against New York's lawyers, the Stamp Act seemed to many of Smith's contemporaries part of a sinister pattern to wrench control of the province's affairs out of the hands of its inhabitants. At the height of the crisis, during the first week of November 1765—while Colden, Gage, and the stamps were barricaded in Fort George—Smith helped negotiate an agreement with Colden whereby he released the stamps to the city government and ceased all attempts to enforce the act. As a member of an *ad hoc* committee, Smith refused, along with Livingston and Scott, to advocate the illegal resumption of business activity without the use of stamps on legal papers. Smith preferred the passive resistance of closing business until the act was repealed or its enforcement suspended. Identified with moderate, peaceable resistance against the Stamp Act, Smith sacrificed his reputation in New York as a defender of liberty. He scarcely noticed this reversal of his political fortunes and became, instead, deeply engrossed in a re-evaluation of the nature of the Empire and the sources of colonial disaffection and British folly. Between late 1765 and early 1767 he composed an original analysis of imperial tensions. A private manuscript that he did not publicize or even distribute widely, Smith's remarkable plan was a work of imagination and vision.

Unlike the enunciators of principle, Smith rejected the idea that immutable constitutional rules of colonial subordination and British dominance governed the Empire. "Long after the Constitution was formed," he wrote, "the Empire . . . acquired a *new, adventitious state,* and the question, therefore, is not what the Constitution was or is, but what, present circumstances considered, it ought to be." The mutual economic benefits that Britain and America gained from their relationship were the Empire's very reason for being, and recent British policies and pronouncements indicated that officials in London had lost sight of Britain's paramount national interest in maintaining colonial loyalty and affection. "Those who speak of the union between these countries barely as of importance and even of vast importance do not express themselves properly," he declared sternly; "he who knows that one third . . . of the commerce of Britain depends upon her colonies—and that if this is lost, she is ruined—will talk of the union as essential to the very existence" of Britain as a major power. The Grenville ministry had been a period of "palpable blundering." The colonies had earned, during the Seven Years' War, a generous redefinition of their place in the Empire. Instead, the ministry ignored "the vast wealth acquired from us," imposed the Stamp Act, talked of the colonies' "virtual representation" in Parliament, and revealed "an overweaning attachment to their own interests" rather than those of the whole Empire.

To halt this deterioration, Smith proposed the creation of an entirely new political structure for the Empire. "The constitution," he insisted, "(be it what it will) ought to bend, and *sooner* or *later* will bend unless it is the will of Heaven to infatuate and destroy us." His blueprint for a new imperial constitution was calculated to deal with the sources of distrust and misunderstanding on both sides of the Atlantic. "The present quarrel . . . is a disease. . . . As it spreads fast, the remedy must be speedily administered." Britain was treating the colonies like children, he explained, because its leaders were frightened by the complexity of the task of governing them and confused by the variety of political systems in different colonies and by the crude, rustic quality of much of American political life. The colonists reacted petulantly to British policy and failed to take a broad view of their problems. Smith's particular proposal was the creation of an American parliament composed of 140 delegates chosen by the assemblies of the mainland colonies, a council of twenty-four members appointed by the Crown, and a royally appointed lord lieutenant. Through their parliament, Americans would make an annual payment to the Crown toward the cost of imperial defense. "The capital advantages of this scheme," he predicted, "will be a recovery of the colonies to a firm confidence in the *justice* and *affection* of the parent state." As colonial population grew and America expanded westward, an American parliament would possess the ability to govern a large domain wisely and, in the long run, secure to Britain the immense wealth of the entire North American continent. "One cannot take the state, nature, climates, and prodigious extent of the American continent into contemplation," Smith concluded in a spectacular panorama of the future, "without high prospects in favor of the power to which it belongs. It is sufficient to be the granary of all of the rest of the British dominions. Fed by our plough Britain might attend more to the cultivation of sheep, . . . the collection of raw materials from us and by us, . . . convert her own nation, as it were, into one great town of manufacturers, undersell every other nation in Europe and exalt and maintain her supremacy until heaven blots out the empires of the world."[3]

In contrast to his scholarly detachment as a student of imperial structure and theory, Smith's love of maneuver and intrigue in the governor's Council from 1767 to 1776 also shaped his search for accommodation between Britain and the colonies. Smith's tenure on the Council did not begin auspiciously; power and success in that body lay with those who could win the ear and confidence of royal governors, and Smith found the Council dominated by his enemies from the De Lancey faction and by Anglicans and merchants; he was the only lawyer and one of two Presbyterians. Smith brought to this intimate if prickly company a number of personal qualities that, even as they were caricatured by his bitter enemy, Thomas Jones, made him a formidable figure: "an artful, close, designing man, with a good share of understanding, and well read in the law; a fluent, easy speaker with . . . unbounded . . . ambition, hypocrisy and craft; a most profound dissembler [with] a smooth, glib, oily tongue, . . . a steady demure, puritanical countenance; a noted flatterer, a great sycophant. . . ."[4]

Smith brought these capabilities into full play during a protracted controversy between 1769 and 1772 over the distribution of land west of the Connecticut River—the future state of Vermont.[5] Both New York and New Hampshire claimed the right to grant land in the area. Like everyone else in the New York aristocracy, Smith and his Livingston-faction friends had invested heavily in land speculation in the disputed territory—known at the time as "the New Hampshire Grants." In 1767, during the early stages of the struggle between the two colonies, New Hampshire had won an important victory when the Crown ordered New York to stop granting land in the disputed area. But the Council advised Governor Dunmore (1770–1771) to ignore the ban and continue issuing land patents in the New Hampshire Grants. Governors earned a fee, paid by the grantee, every time they distributed land; and there was strong economic motive for the Council, composed of land speculators, and governors in collusion to disregard royal instructions restricting land grants. For reasons that are not at all clear, Smith alone in the Council opposed this business to the extent of advocating the cancellation of grants in which he and William Livingston had a financial interest. In short, he insisted on legality even at the jeopardy of his own economic interests. Smith, already wealthy, obviously enjoyed placing principle above self-interest and indulging in "the contemporary fetish for personal independence"[6] and public virtue not uncommon in the eighteenth century. He was also engaged in an elaborate gamble; he seemed to have judged that the Crown would ultimately validate the New York claims and therefore deemed it prudent to abstain from gobbling land in the disputed area before final adjudication of the controversy. He found the issue a tempting way of reminding each royal governor that a cozy relationship with the De Lancey councillors conflicted with his duty to serve the Crown. Insisting on the suspension of land distribution in the New Hampshire Grants was an ingenious opening wedge in his campaign to displace the rest of the Council as chief adviser to the governor.

The Earl of Dunmore ignored Smith's objections and approved grants in defiance of the royal instructions. But in Dunmore's successor, Governor William Tryon (1771–1776), Smith found a man who would listen to him. At first Tryon followed the advice of the majority of the Council and persisted in approving the illegal grants—even after a letter from Lord Hillsborough explicitly prohibited continuation of the practice.

The majority of councillors adopted the tactic of silence whenever an application for one of the illegal grants came before the Governor. Tryon "does not see that the Council stand off giving him advice," Smith lamented, "and yet lead him to break [the instruction]. . . . How shameful of the Council thus to mislead him! [They] get an advantage over him for they can complain of his breach, though he leaves them clear by [not] exacting a minute of their advice." Gradually Tryon seemed to become aware of the depth of Smith's objections to the grants. Early in 1772 he spoke to Smith after one heated meeting of the Council and indicated his willingness to reconsider the problem. "The governor stopped me when we broke up and said 'well we have broke the ice,'" and asked Smith to prepare a memorandum on the problem of the New Hampshire Grants.[7]

Smith seized on Tryon's wish for advice and friendship. By early March 1772, he believed his patient talks with the Governor had yielded results. He described an angry meeting of the Council in which Tryon unexpectedly refused to accede to any more pressure over the New Hampshire Grants. A new batch of petitions had arrived, and, according to Smith's account, Tryon had asked whether he should apply the royal instruction strictly or loosely. Suspecting nothing, several councillors routinely suggested loose construction. Then, Smith noted with gratification, Tryon launched into an angry diatribe, conveyed "great earnestness, and trembled. 'I mean, gentlemen, to preserve my independency. I will be your independent governor. I mean to consult the interest of the province, but being the King's servant I must have an eye to his command.'" Then, changing his tone from anger to pathetic pleading, Tryon continued, "I don't ask your advice as a Council, but as friends. Pay no regard to my interest in granting lands." Finally, he snatched an abstract of his instructions in one hand and the petitions in the other and threatened to throw the petitions into the fire if the Council "think it would be safest to grant precisely according to the instructions." This tirade, delivered "with great vehemence," Smith noted with satisfaction, left the Council "prodigiously confused." But it gave Smith a sense of real accomplishment. The next day he talked to Tryon, and when asked for his reaction to the previous night's events Smith adroitly encouraged the Governor to persist in his independent course. "I now see the good effect of my opposition to the late New Hampshire grants," Smith rejoiced. "Those who consented to that dangerous step to please [Tryon] he must now think meanly of, and suspect their integrity." At the next Council meeting Smith pointedly praised Tryon's "candor and courage." When one councillor agreed, Smith turned to another and "asked if the governor did not shine at the last Council. He assented freely." Smith reveled in this kind of tactical maneuver. Assessing his achievement and plotting his next step, he observed in a revealing confession of strategy: "I shall feed this spirit to disentangle [Tryon] from fear of Council and Assembly."[8]

News of the Tea Act in October 1773 created a new crisis of authority in America and provided Smith with a mandate to guide Tryon's hand through an unusually difficult period. "I suppose," he predicted, "we shall repeat all the confusions of 1765 and 1766. . . . Our domestic parties will probably die and be swallowed up in general opposition to the Parliamentary project." He advised Tryon to bring ashore the newly taxed East India Company tea and to store it under guard. Even as he gave Tryon this recommendation the Sons of Liberty tried to enlist Smith's support in canceling the landing of the tea; overestimating his influence with them, Smith argued that Tryon, who would soon visit London, should not be humiliated on the eve of his departure. Hearing of a mass meeting to discuss the issue, Smith struggled strenuously to arrange for the Governor to address the crowd. But the Governor did not attend, and his representative, New York City Mayor Whitehead Hicks, did not ask for a resolution in support of storing the tea. "The fortunate moment," Smith lamented, "had been lost." All this maneuvering became academic when news of the Boston Tea Party reached New York on December 21, 1773, forcing Tryon to abandon any plans to unload tea there. Smith analyzed the Governor's situation with customary delicacy: "It must mortify Tryon, who has spoken vauntingly and wrote assuring government of the landing" of the tea, now to have to retreat; "he must be hurt at being obliged to drop his high tone." But Smith was even more acutely aware of his own predicament. "How dangerous it is to give private advice," he complained; "Tryon will think I animated him at the last Council to render him unpopular."[9]

In 1774, unsuccessful in his efforts to engineer a solution to the tea crisis in New York—as he believed he had done during the Stamp Act tumult in November 1765—Smith watched from the periphery of public life as the colony agreed to participate in the First Continental Congress. He found increasingly little audience for his belief in a passive yet calculated style of resistance. "We should do nothing," he pleaded with Alexander McDougall, a leader of the Sons of Liberty, "but complain and teach the [British] nation to relieve us for fear of weening us quite off." Withdrawn and moody, Smith nonetheless realized that something specific was required. By the time of the Second Continental Congress, in May 1775, he had developed a comprehensive rationale for dealing with the crisis, and he wrote to friends in the New York delegation instructing them imperiously on how Congress should conduct itself. "The present [is] the moment in which the greatest blessings may be secured to our country," he told Philip Schuyler. The ministry's last hope had been to divide the colonies, and since that had failed it now faced the alternatives of conciliation or losing office. "Could you wish for a better opportunity to negotiate?" he asked. "You have the ball at your feet. For Heaven's sake don't slip so fair a prospect." To Lewis Morris he spelled out the ground rules Congress should follow. "In times of heat, a wise man will set a double guard upon his steps to avoid a precipitation," he warned in urging caution and careful consideration of all public statements. Indeed, the very unity of the colonists—so important in strengthening their negotiating position—"is in some degree to be suspected from its tendency to inspire an improvident confidence." Therefore Smith urged Congress to proceed with caution, to prod the ministry tentatively, and to take care not to overextend itself. Not only the approach but also the presentation of the substance of the colonial position required such self-conscious tactics. To deny Parliament "the last whole legislative authority" would require more "prowess than prudence." But, on the other hand, to insist "that an authority to tax us was not requisite to maintaining the legislative supremacy of the nation" would be a moderate, realistic contention.[10]

Smith wanted Congress to construct a verbal formula that would convince Britain of "her folly in contending for what she does not really want *and cannot execute*" while at the same time covering an American retreat from extreme claims to virtual independence from Parliament's theoretical jurisdiction. A petition to the Crown, it should begin with a declaration of loyalty to remove suspicion that the colonies sought independence, dwell on the advantages of the existing union, deplore the sad consequences of any dissolution of that connection, and then, "without a word about rights, . . . proceed to state the line of conduct that will calm the stormy, troubled sea of discontent." That conduct included the establishment of a "general convention" in America representing all the colonies and empowered to raise taxes by any means it chose. Annually it would present a "gift" to Britain toward the cost of imperial defense, and Whitehall would submit to the convention accounts of how the money was spent. "This course of negotiating will feel the pulse and try the sincerity of the ministry," Smith predicted.

This clinical concept of tactics came from Smith's years of experience in the closed arena of the Council chamber. His advice to say nothing about colonial rights in the petition while simultaneously pleading against the expediency of Parliamentary taxation revealed his continuing conviction that the mechanisms of the Empire were more important than general statements about constitutional rights. Specific reform of these mechanisms was a manageable task; the debate over colonial rights and British prerogatives was a corrosive, futile exercise. "The present is the precise moment for attempting this good work. The door is open for treating with decency [and] without offense to the pride of either party." For his own part, Smith began to circulate his plan for an American parliament. On July 4, 1775, he sent a copy to General Frederick Haldimand, who forwarded the manuscript to Lord Dartmouth. Smith's brother James had given Dartmouth a copy of the same document six years earlier, and two other of Smith's contacts submitted their copies of the plan to Dartmouth. At the first false rumor that the ministry was considering a proposal for reconciliation, Smith excitedly leaped to the conclusion that his proposals were "the ground work" of an imminent British initiative.[11]

However, the British made no move, the colonists squared off on opposite sides of the issues, and Smith found himself with few allies on either shore of the Atlantic. Although he was a gregarious man, Smith enjoyed solitude. The loneliness of holding a position that men around him rejected consoled his intellectual pride. On February 12, 1776, at Simmon's Tavern, he met Alexander McDougall, who summoned Smith to an upstairs room and after many "expressions of friendship" confided that independence was now a practical possibility. Smith warily interpreted this confidence as "a design of rendering me an instrument for urging the governor and captains to leave the port [of New York]." Accordingly, he phrased his answer with deliberate care. Independence, he cautioned McDougall, was extremely risky because the economic distress accompanying it would probably cause "the populace [to] turn their wrath upon Congress and seek peace in their own way." He hoped his reply would dissociate him tactfully from any of McDougall's schemes, but he went away from the encounter deeply disturbed. Two days later, at a Council meeting, Attorney General John Tabor Kempe insisted that a conspiracy to declare New York independent had already been laid. Despite his suspicions that this charge contained some truth, Smith heatedly rejected Kempe's insinuation that New York had no legitimate cause for grievance. "I grew warm in the debates upon this subject," he recorded, and he blamed Britain for refusing to "give up the claim of taxing the colonies." At this point, Tryon, who had kept quiet during Smith's outburst, "catched fire . . . and said he was sorry to hear an officer of the government say so." Smith now felt the loneliness of a moderate in a polarized argument. More than mere moderation, however, contributed to his predicament. Intellectual tenacity and the serenity of knowing that his analysis of the imperial crisis was more sophisticated than the one-dimensional views of a Kempe or a McDougall were the factors that prevented this otherwise crafty, adaptable man from choosing a comfortable allegiance.[12]

Increasingly introspective and moody, he returned instinctively to pondering the mechanisms of the Empire and the way their atrophied condition had placed him in limbo. "The clouds grow very dark. My hopes for conciliatory negotiation almost fail me," he wrote in his diary on June 8, 1776, when he heard that

Hessian troops had been dispatched to America and that Virginia had voted for independence. Bewilderment settled over his diary as he recorded "my thoughts for my own conduct at this melancholy hour of approaching distress." The long, revealing entry that followed, however, had much less to do with his conduct than with the roots of his melancholy anticipations. First, he listed theoretical considerations: nations have the right to frame governments and to make treason a high crime; the colonies derived their political order from Parliament as well as the Crown, and therefore the compact involved the colonists and the whole British nation. "Neither of the contracting parties may dissolve this compact as long as their joint aim in the union, to wit, their mutual prosperity, can be attained by it." The crux of the constitutional dilemma lay in the fact that "no provision was made for constituting an impartial judge between them. Their controversies are therefore to be decided by negotiation . . . or on an appeal to the Lord of Hosts by battle." The question of which side was right or wrong was less important than the absence of machinery to resolve the disputes inevitable in any society of men.

Against this background Smith surveyed the controversy and reiterated his opposition to colonial intransigence. He began by indicting British colonial policy: the Stamp Act had arrogantly assumed that Britain could dispose of the colonists' property at its pleasure; the Townshend duties and other trade restrictions had undermined colonial institutions and violated cherished customs; the Coercive Acts were a reprehensible attempt to subjugate the colonies. However, these abuses, he explained, only increased the colonists' obligation to seek a negotiated settlement. For war, the only alternative to negotiation, was evil; and "the principle that evil may be done that good may come of it is beyond all controversy a satanical maxim." Smith was no believer in passive submission to those in political authority, but his persistent search for a behind-the-scenes role as political analyst and manipulator had exhausted itself. He could only hope that somewhere other politicians would sense the needs of the situation. "I persuade myself," he told the inquisitive Haverstraw Committee of Safety on July 4, 1776, "that Great Britain will discern the propriety of negotiating for a pacification."[13]

9

The Political Culture of
the American Colonies

THE American colonies were not only part of a legal and administrative Empire; they also possessed their own "political culture, . . . the assumptions, expectations, patterns of response, and clusters of information relevant to the conduct of political affairs."[1] Pre-Revolutionary America had an especially subtle and complex set of unwritten rules and implicit tendencies.

The most pervasive influence on the conduct of politics was the very structure of society itself: conspicuous aristocratic elites of landowners, merchants, and lawyers amid a common citizenry overwhelmingly composed of self-sustaining property-owning farmers and tradesmen and, predominantly in the coastal South, a large population of Negro slaves. The organization of the governing elite varied from one colony to another. In South Carolina, a class of planter-merchants moved between low-country plantations and Charles Town town houses; in Virginia, members of the plantation-owning aristocracy cared primarily for the county in which each lived but gathered annually in Williamsburg for the meeting of the House of Burgesses; in Pennsylvania, the Quaker merchant grandees, who had controlled the province's politics during the late seventeenth and early eighteenth centuries, had been forced to retire from politics by their own religious aversion to military action against hostile Indians and by the competition of newly emergent merchants and lawyers from outside the Quaker community, who themselves split into proprietary and antiproprietary parties; in New York, shifting alliances generally organized around the rival Presbyterian Livingston and Anglican De Lancey families competed for patronage and land grants, and struggled to determine the role of the Anglican church in the administration of King's College; in Connecticut, the Great Awakening split the colony's leadership into an "Old Light," conservative, established faction and a "New Light," revivalist, newly rich group; in Rhode Island, the Samuel Ward faction of Newport and the Stephen Hopkins faction of Providence pitted two heterogeneous alliances of town and rural politicians against each other in an evenly matched, intensely competitive contest for elective office; in Massachusetts, highly autonomous towns, with their own political leadership, formed one broad level of political activity, while the great families of the province competed at a higher level for leadership in the assembly and council (in a manner that foreshadowed the future federal division between state and national government); in contrast, New Hampshire, under the Wentworths, achieved an integrated and harmonious fusion of provincial and town leadership.[2]

Within this richly variegated political scene, certain common tendencies prevailed. Property ownership conferred a voice in the political process, and by the third quarter of the eighteenth century a majority of white adult male citizens owned enough taxable property to vote in New England town meetings and in elections of representatives to the lower houses of the colonial assemblies in every colony. Contemporaries described the political system as "democratic," but by "democracy" they did not refer primarily to the widespread exercise of voting; they meant, rather, that theirs was a balanced political order in which popular participation *and* monarchical administration *and* aristocratic leadership all complemented and held each other in delicate tension—like an earthly trinity. Of course, this model, based on the English constitution, did not exactly fit the colonies. Royal officials did not have the prestige of the King; the colonial aristocracy was not a titled nobility set apart by law and tradition from the commoners; only the assemblies, which thought of themselves as little Houses of Commons, even approached the ideal of the English constitution. From the earliest period of colonial history—when the King granted charters to colonial organizers and governments—a two-level constitutional arrangement in the colonies, between the rulers and the ruled, tended to supplant the threefold division of the classical English constitution. This model of "magistrates" and "the people" was more applicable to colonial politics. It outlined the operation of a political process called "deference," which was the very core of political reality in early America. A deferential society was one in which the citizenry voluntarily and instinctively acknowledged the superior political ability of an educated and wealthy social elite. Eighteenth-century Americans used their widespread voting power to elect to public office men from a relative handful of wealthy, well-established, respected families. Ingrained in the fabric of colonial society was the assumption, Jack P. Greene writes, "that merit was very often, though by no means always, associated with wealth and social position; that men of merit were obliged to use their talents for the benefit of the public; and that deference to them was the implicit duty of the rest of society. All society was therefore divided among the rulers and the ruled, and the rulers, including the representatives of the people, were not the tools of the people but their political superiors." This public philosophy was sternly utilitarian in its determination to conserve society's resources of talent. "To make the representative nothing more than the obedient lackey of his constituents," Richard Buel, Jr., explains in his reconstruction of colonial democratic thought, "was [considered] the height of folly because it threatened to deprive society of the benefit of its most talented personnel."[3]

These patterns of political activity and conceptions of the nature of politics frequently shifted and subtly changed during the eighteenth century. Of the many unsettling forces that kept politics in flux, the most fundamental was the burgeoning economic growth of the colonies during the fifty years following the Peace of Utrecht in 1713. Between 1700 and 1750 the volume of colonial imports from England increased four and one-half times, and from 1697 to 1775 the value of colonial exports to the mother country grew sevenfold. Closely associated with this commercial explosion was the rapid growth of Philadelphia, Boston, New York, and Charles Town, which tripled in population between 1713 and 1763, as well as the emergence of many secondary ports and inland towns. Increasingly elaborate systems of distribution and marketing, and the flow of money and credit, became bonds that consolidated communities and adjacent rural areas into viable economic regions. The nearly continuous state of war and military preparation from 1740 to 1761 accelerated economic growth still more, and military contracts became a major means for young merchant firms to acquire highly profitable business. In South Carolina, fabulous profits from the export of rice and the import of slaves created other new fortunes. Illicit as well as legal trade with the West Indies augmented many others. Families that struck just the right combination of political manipulation, money management and capital accumulation, market analysis, and luck earned bountiful new wealth. The result of this economic boom was to make politics—and everything else in colonial life—much more competitive. Through taxation, land distribution, civil law, and inspection of exports, colonial governments closely regulated the economy, and politically influential merchants and landowners reaped the greatest benefits. A sharp depression of trade after the Seven Years' War—which the Sugar Act, the Currency Act of 1764, and the Stamp Act seriously exacerbated—did not dampen the merchants' acquisitiveness and ambition, but this period of adversity following a long stretch of prosperity made many merchants more politically conscious of British power and policy. In some colonies—New York, Pennsylvania, Rhode Island, Massachusetts—it fragmented the merchant community into various competing firms and groups of firms, while in others—New Hampshire, South Carolina, Georgia—relatively cohesive merchant communities exuberantly shared the seemingly limitless bounty of rising commerce. Everywhere, except for the cluster of alien Scottish merchants in Norfolk, Virginia, and Cross Creek, North Carolina, intermarriage with landed and professional families and land speculation operated to draw successful merchants into the social elite of each colony. Those with government contracts or other connections with imperial officials tended to become supporters of British authority during the pre-Revolutionary controversy, but on the whole merchants exhibited as full a spectrum of political viewpoints as did the rest of the community.[4]

Because merchants needed a wide range of accurate information about political and social conditions throughout the Empire, they encouraged the spread of a kind of intelligent empirical learning and thereby helped raise the level of public discourse. Newspapers became highly sensitive to their interests and knowledge. Full of advertisements, price lists, shipping announcements, as well as news of government and politics, colonial newspapers became an important business enterprise in their own right and the most widely read printed material in the colonies. The newspapers created and reinforced "significant changes in the colonists' perceptions and attitudes toward their community," Richard Merritt has written in a quantitative study of seven of these journals. Between the late 1730's and the early 1770's, he finds, there was a sixfold increase in references to events in other parts of America and a corresponding decline in British coverage. The discovery of America by the colonial newspaper over this forty-year period ran in cycles. Britain's wars with France periodically restored the mother country to a dominant place in public prints, but with peace came still higher levels of awareness of the problems of other colonies. The Stamp Act crisis, far from *creating* colonial union, only *accelerated* the spread of well-established American attention patterns in the colonial press.[5]

After economic expansion, the most powerful force capable of disturbing political affairs in mid-eighteenth-century America was the religious revivalism generated by the Great Awakening of the late 1730's and early 1740's. The most tumultuous event of the entire colonial period, the Awakening, like the Revolution, revealed a crisis of authority in American society. For more than a century, Congregational clergy in New England—as well as Dutch Reformed and Presbyterian in the middle colonies—had occupied a special place of status and influence in the community. During the early decades of the eighteenth century, that leadership had become more formal and brittle. The established social elite and a wider circle of older and more settled families of the community often dominated the congregational life and made churches into respectable, stabilizing, and prosperous social institutions. But an increasingly large majority of the population was outside the reach of the church; as the population grew and the economy expanded, an accompanying rise of crime, sexual offenses, quarrels over property and money, and physical violence created the impression that the old values of religion, piety, obedience to the law, and respect for a moral code were about to disappear. Alarmed by the declining influence of the church, and at the same time seeking to please a conservative and economically privileged laity, the clergy had become Arminian in their theology and preaching—that is, they stressed the rationalist idea that men were not innately evil, that good works were an intrinsic part of achieving salvation, and that a benevolent God bestowed upon men the freedom to choose to live in a state of grace. The Great Awakening was a rebellion against that *status quo* in church organization and theology. It insisted that men were thoroughly sinful, capricious, self-destructive, and self-deluding and that only a cleansing and purging experience of salvation could cut through the crust of complacency.

Although the Great Awakening was conducted by a wide variety of clergymen with different approaches and emphases, the Reverend Jonathan Edwards, of Northampton, Massachusetts, was one who sought not only religious conversion but political and social transformation as well. Edwards, the most distinguished intellectual of the entire colonial period of American history, had read and thoroughly understood the ideas of John Locke about human psychology and had completely reordered his understanding of reality in the light of Locke's writing. Thus, Edwards declared that there are no innate ideas, that all knowledge, including divine inspiration, comes through the senses, that words conveying sound, light, touch, taste, and smell are only devices to penetrate the mind and there to ignite the emotions of love, trust, hate, envy, fear, or desire that are intrinsic to the personality. This psychological understanding required that preaching take seriously the needs of the listener and convey the sound, smell, feel, and taste of unregenerate sinners suffering in Hell. Edwards rightly believed that the new kind of religious experience aroused by this preaching would shake New England towns to their foundations. Churches, families, and whole communities split into "New Light" Christians, who were enthralled by revivalism, and "Old Lights," who shuddered at the spectacle. Although the Awakening cut across economic class lines, many of the Old Lights were the established and prosperous leaders of society who found in traditional worship and church life reassuring stability, calm, and decorum.[6]

One of the beliefs that sustained the preachers and congregations of the Awakening was the expectation that ecstatic revival and conversion would fuse the people of America into a new fellowship of pious, joyful, self-disciplined, self-sacrificing, and democratic people and that this particular version of the millennium was at hand. These preachers therefore defined American national identity in moral and spiritual terms a generation before the leaders of the Revolution and the new nation did so in political and constitutional terms. In many cases the evangelical clergy during the 1760's and 1770's argued that this millennial vision could only be realized by a people who resisted British encroachments on their liberty. They saw in hostile British policy God's punishment of a whole people for its sin. They believed that repentance, a Spartan moral life, and political activism in the defense of liberty each were integral qualities of Christian living. Some Old Lights also condemned British measures and even preached the duty of Christians to resist oppression; but theological rationalists, for the most part, found the emotions generated by the pre-Revolutionary controversy as bewildering as those that had characterized revivalism in the 1740's.[7] No simple formula equating Calvinism with Whiggery and rationalism with Toryism can explain the relationship of the Awakening to the Revolution. In many ways, however, Calvinism and revivalism loosened the constraints against political radicalism, while Arminianism and rationalism frowned upon excessive enthusiasm in politics and religion.[8]

For all the difficult readjustments required by the Great Awakening and economic expansion, these two forces were the foremost nationalizing tendencies at work in American society before the onset of the pre-Revolutionary controversies in the 1760's. In addition to these positive developments, colonial society contained disruptive and regressive tendencies that also shaped the colonial political culture. Of these, the most highly focused were provocations of mob violence. Mobs in colonial America were, in many cases, positive attempts by the community to settle problems that local or provincial government seemed unable or unwilling to resolve. During an outbreak of uncontrolled crime in the South Carolina back country in 1759 and 1760, when the provincial government could not provide enough courts and sheriffs to protect citizens in the area, prominent property owners formed the first vigilante mobs, which captured suspected outlaws and "shredded the flesh of miscreants in orgiastic flogging sessions while fiddles played."[9] In North Carolina and Pennsylvania, frontier farmers with grievances against eastern-dominated assemblies rose in armed though short-lived rebellion. In Northern port towns, gangs of sailors banded together to resist impressment into the British Navy, and their courage won the sympathy of juries, which refused to convict rioting sailors, and of lawyers like John Adams, who successfully argued in 1769 that the killing of a British naval officer by a sailor resisting illegal impressment was justifiable homicide. Because mobs often possessed their own internal leadership, they drew members and sympathizers not only from waterfront rabble but also from more respectable levels of society; because they frequently championed some valid public cause, eighteenth-century Americans believed that mobs were "symptoms of a strong and healthy constitution" and an integral check against oppressive or incompetent government. Colonial leaders had institutionalized the mob without actually condoning violence and had assigned it a special function to perform in the defense of liberty. But in the process, they shifted part of the initiative in colonial politics to the hands of political figures who, like the Sons of Liberty in New York, had a special talent for mobilizing and directing public disorders.[10]

The most deeply disturbing and potentially volatile feature of colonial society was, of course, the institution of Negro slavery. Although slavery as a labor system was restricted to Maryland, Virginia, the Carolinas, and Georgia, it was not finally abolished in the North until the 1780's, and New England merchants throughout the colonial period remained deeply involved in the lucrative slave trade. "It is clear," Donald L. Robinson concludes, "that the American economy in all sections rested substantially on slavery and its fruits."[11] Added to such benefits as land and British markets and credits, the exploitation of thousands of slaves created immense wealth for the plantation-owning aristocracy of the Southern colonies. The fear of slave uprising was one of the strongest bonds uniting the ruling elite and the rest of the white population into a homogeneous community, especially in South Carolina, where, in lowland areas, the proportion of slaves to whites ran as high as seven to one.[12] Fear of black insurrection, which would annihilate the white population's "lives, liberties, properties, and every other human blessing,"[13] as one Virginian put it, amounted to an obsession throughout the seventeenth and eighteenth centuries. The slave trade—the most difficult, expensive, but profitable cargo in all colonial commerce—provided invaluable experience as well as huge profits for numerous colonial merchants, and the legal regimentation of both slaves and free blacks posed a similar challenge to the ingenuity of colonial legislators. Slavery also posed a challenge to conscience and political realism. As early as the 1750's, Quaker abolitionists like John Woolman forced their sect to come to terms with this moral problem and after a painful struggle committed the Friends to uncompromising condemnation of Negro slavery.[14] It was no coincidence that the pamphlet literature of the pre-Revolutionary controversy repeatedly used the words "slave" and "slavery" to describe the impact of British authority on the colonial subject. "With grief, . . . anguish, . . . shame, . . . [and] indignation," Josiah Quincy, Jr., declared in 1774, "we are slaves" to "British oppressors." Most colonial writers refused to admit the glaring inconsistency between the enslavement of blacks in America and the defense of political liberty for white Americans. But some did; James Otis, Jr., declared that "all men . . . white or black" were "born free" and that the institution of slavery discredited the defense of colonial liberty.[15] (During the early years of the republic other voices—some of them Southern—would echo Otis's indictment of slavery, until the first decade of the nineteenth century, when fear of black rebellion caused a return in the South to the rigid defense of slavery and of Negro inferiority.) Within the context of colonial politics, slavery quietly contaminated the colonists' self-image as an especially virtuous people.

Economic expansion, religious revivalism, mob violence, and slavery were not congruent kinds of disorienting influences, nor did they form a coherent pattern. In some ways they had a benign effect on colonial society: racial fears drew the Southern white community into a more unified body; mobs became almost public agencies supplementing the machinery of government and providing sophisticated political training for leaders at lower levels of the social scale; the Great Awakening split churches and denominations but went on to create a strong sense of a new communion among revivalist churches throughout America. These turbulent forces—in some ways disruptive and in others consolidating—did not drastically alter the nature of colonial politics during the first six decades of the eighteenth century. The pressure they exerted on the conduct of public affairs, however, and the many specific changes they caused may well indicate that colonial politics was still young, impressionable, and lacking an authoritative character and a fully developed public philosophy. Such a conjecture would help explain the colonists' voracious appetite for political concepts that would enable them to control and direct their destiny and their rapid consumption of ideas about politics, history, law, ethics, and constitutionalism.

The deepest cause of this appetite was the colonists' unfulfilled quest for a sense of identity during the first three-quarters of the eighteenth century. Their pragmatic, optimistic, innovative, exuberant qualities during that period represented only a part of the social character of colonial Americans. For all their achievements, the colonists had failed to develop a satisfactory set of ideals with which to evaluate their deeds and hopes. In the absence of intrinsic American values, they relied on two contrasting external models of desirable societies. The first and oldest of these prototypes was the heroic struggle of the first-generation seventeenth-century settlers in each colony, and the second was the grandeur of eighteenth-century England. "So compelling were these models that they inhibited the colonists from fully adjusting to conditions of life in America," Jack P. Greene writes in an important recent exploration of early American anxiety.[16] As long as the colonists had fixations with the first generation of colonial settlement and with the cultural superiority of the mother country, Greene suggests, they could not fully comprehend their own qualities, needs, weaknesses, and capabilities. In every important respect, thoughtful colonists believed they had fallen short of achieving the high standards of the first settlers, who seemed to have been pious, uncontaminated by greed, willing to endure hardship to tame the wilderness—the very embodiment of fortitude. Perhaps because the colonists could never return to the simpler and morally austere world of John Winthrop, Thomas Hooker, or William Penn, they imitated certain attractive values of recent and contemporary English history: landed aristocrats styled themselves after the English landed gentry; wealthy families spent more than they could afford on imported English clothing, furniture, books, and carriages; politicians steeped themselves in the history of Parliament's victory over the Crown in the seventeenth century and cultivated useful political contacts in London. The most ardent colonial students of the history of liberty—men like Benjamin Rush, John Adams, John Dickinson, and Charles Carroll—expressed a powerful love-hate attitude toward British society. They were deeply impressed by the vitality and sophistication of life in London, the long tradition of British law—Rush "felt as if [he] walked on sacred ground" when he first visited Parliament—and British learning and scholarship, but at the same time repelled by what Adams called the "luxury, effeminacy, and venality" of public life, by the bribery in elections, and by the drunkenness and squalor of the urban poor.[17]

The fascination with which educated colonials fixed upon the founding of the colonies and the nature of British culture made them extraordinarily avid readers of history. They regarded historical writing as the most practical and gratifying reading matter. Historical books occupied a large and conspicuous place in every institutional or private colonial library. Busy and industrious men took the trouble to read these books because they believed, with James Burgh, a notable English historical writer of the time, that "history [is] an inexhaustible mine out of which political knowledge is to be brought up."[18] Accordingly, the historians best known in the colonies were a small cluster who chronicled the rise of political liberty in England, analyzed the subtle and sinister tactics of kings and courtiers who tried to usurp power from Parliament and the people, championed religious toleration (at least for Protestants), boasted that theirs was a rational and empirical study of politics, and called themselves "real Whigs." The earliest and probably most influential of these historians was Viscount Robert Molesworth, an Anglo-Irish nobleman and Protestant who fled to Denmark during the reign of James II and returned there as diplomatic envoy for William III following the Revolution of 1688. There he wrote a book that electrified English politics, even though it bore the unpolemical title *An Account of Denmark as it was in the Year 1692*. The story of the slow destruction of freedom in Denmark by a clique of privileged figures, *An Account of Denmark* was really an indictment of England's failure to reform its institutions following the Revolution of 1688. The Danes lost their liberty, Molesworth contended, because they tolerated a standing army in time of peace, because the monarchy undermined the independence of Parliament, because the nobility did not resist the ambitions of the King, and because a state church imposed stifling religious and political orthodoxy on the people. These were vital issues in England during the late seventeenth and early eighteenth centuries, and Molesworth's book therefore helped inspire a radical critique of English politics and society. During the early eighteenth century, Anglican Bishop Benjamin Hoadly not only repudiated the Church of England's pretensions to spiritual and political authority but also emphasized the most libertarian and rational implications of Shaftesbury's and Molesworth's Whig philosophy. During the 1720's and 1730's, John Trenchard and Thomas Gordon, in *Cato's Letters* and *The Independent Whig*, berated high-church Anglicans and Catholics alike, condemned the greed and arrogance of Robert Walpole's government, and, utilizing a wide variety of historical examples, chiefly classical and seventeenth-century English, constructed a history of liberty that emphasized the equality of man and the tendency of government to trample on human rights. Next in importance was Paul de Rapin de Thoyras, an exiled French Huguenot, whose massive *History of England* (1725–1731) and shorter *Dissertation on the . . . Whigs and Tories* (1717) popularized the notion that Saxon England had been a free and open society upon which the Norman Conquest of 1066 had imposed an alien and authoritarian constitution; he interpreted subsequent English history in the light of that development. Finally, on the very eve of the American Revolution, the obscure English schoolmaster James Burgh published his *Political Disquisitions* (1774) and brought the ideas of his predecessors to bear on the political problems of the reign of George III. Burgh denounced the unrepresentative nature of the House of Commons, saw in the policies of George III's ministers a conspiracy to subvert English liberty, and championed the cause of the American colonies. This band of English radical historians, from Molesworth to Burgh, strongly reinforced the predisposition of educated colonists to think of politics as constant struggle between good and evil, to exult in the remembrance of the Magna Carta, the Petition of Right, the Long Parliament, and the Revolution of 1688, and to search continually for the location of power in a community and the available restraints against its abuse.[19]

Drawing heavily on this Whiggish interpretation of English history, and applying it directly to the problem of political behavior, a body of English writings called "the Country Ideology"[20] propounded, during the late seventeenth and early eighteenth centuries, a fully developed political philosophy. Its writers were highly educated and intellectually resourceful men who had been excluded from public life by the fierce jealousies and animosities of the age. Distinguishing themselves from the "Court Party" of royal, ministerial, and Parliamentary insiders, the "Country Party" theorists proclaimed that the integrity of the individual transcended the claims of parties and institutions. The Country Ideology condemned the tendency of factions and governments to compromise the independence of the individual; it saw in the power of governments and institutions an amoral and potentially destructive force; it celebrated the virtue and benevolence of the unfettered individual but at the same time agonized over the frailty of man and the ease with which ignorance, complacency, greed, bigotry, or vanity seduced man's civic responsibility. Their solution to this moral dilemma—the virtue of the individual and the ease with which he was corrupted—was to advocate the constant enlargement and preservation of liberty. "Liberty," Trenchard and Gordon wrote, "is the inalienable right of all mankind, . . . the power which every man has over his actions and his right to enjoy the fruit of his labour, art, and industry." Subject only to the limitation that he not harm his fellow men, "every man is sole lord and arbiter of his own private actions and property." Understandably, then, "liberty naturally [drew] new men to it as well as increase[d] the old stock" and promoted "a due distribution of property and an equal distribution of justice."[21] Though these ideas aroused excitement in Britain from time to time, they were relatively harmless, and the men who propagated them had not the remotest chance of acquiring political power. But when the writings of the Country Ideology reached the American colonies during the 1730's, 1740's, and 1750's, powerful figures in colonial politics read and absorbed them. In colonies where bitter factional struggles ensued—especially in New York between the dominant De Lancey faction and the opposition Livingston alliance, and in Massachusetts between the powerful interests supporting Governor William Shirley and their vocally resentful critics—the political opposition hurled quotations and concepts from the Country Ideology at their entrenched adversaries. In such instances, the Country Ideology was a catalyst of political disruption. In South Carolina, however, the same ideas helped sustain a prolonged political calm; starting in the late 1740's, the leaders of that colony coalesced into a united front, decided they could not afford factional disruption, and used the Country Ideology to define the duty of every citizen to act according to his conscience and private judgment rather than yield to the pressures of any interest group or institution.[22]

In contrast with the Country Ideology, an imported and exotic political influence on the politics of mid-eighteenth-century America, seventeenth-century Puritanism was an indigenous American legacy from which the colonists derived a similarly important set of predispositions. The Puritan Ethic was the religious idea that every man receives a divine calling to do a particular work in the world, to practice thrift, prudence, and self-control in his stewardship of the wealth God has enabled him to acquire, and, indeed, to treat all of life in the same manner by purging himself of complacency, sloth, and social indifference. The Great Awakening drastically altered the function and structure of the Puritan Ethic. By freeing men from guilt about their sins and from "all anxious fears and distresses" with a single cleansing experience of conversion that bathed the recipient in "sweet solace, rest, and joy of spirit,"[23] the Awakening gave fresh purpose and confidence to newly emergent landowners and merchants and thereby unshackled their acquisitiveness. But the Awakening did not condone materialism; it rather stressed that man's emotions and self-consciousness were gifts to be used with the same responsibility and strictness that the older version of the ethic had applied to material possessions. When the colonists imposed a nonimportation boycott on British goods during the Stamp Act, Townshend duties, and Coercive Acts crises, they often believed that this self-denial would purge their society of complacency, selfishness, and other sins unworthy of a people struggling for liberty. "We may talk and boast of liberty," declared a writer who signed his name "Frugality," in 1774, "but, after all, only the industrious and frugal . . . will be free."[24] When the Reverend David Caldwell rallied his Guilford County, North Carolina parishioners to support the Revolutionary movement in 1775, he preached on "The Character and Doom of the Sluggard":[25] the tendency of moral, political, personal slothfulness to paralyze a man's spirit even in time of public and religious crisis.

This political culture—this rich but chaotic aggregation of animal impulses, social aspirations, intellectual devices, and moral and psychological assumptions—propelled the colonists into resistance and finally revolution. The process was neither consistent nor uniform, but, as Edmund Burke perceived in 1769, by the time "the Americans have made a discovery, or think they have made one, that we mean to oppress them, [and] we [British] have made a discovery, or think we have made one, that they intend to rise in rebellion," both sides were locked on a collision course. "We do not know how to advance," Burke explained prophetically, and "they do not know how to retreat."[26] The advocates of accommodation in the pre-Revolutionary controversy surely would have agreed with Burke that they did not know how to retreat, much less how to induce their more zealous contemporaries to do so. They had tried to teach a lesson and develop a capability they did not understand themselves.

10

Three Accommodating Royal Governors: William Franklin, William Bull, and John Wentworth

THE most knowledgeable and politically sophisticated loyalist advocates of accommodation were those native American royal governors who favored an unrestrictive and loosely defined British regime over the American colonies: John Wentworth, of New Hampshire, William Franklin, of New Jersey, and Lieutenant Governor William Bull, of South Carolina. Critical of much of British colonial policy during the pre-Revolutionary controversy, and unusually aware of the risks involved in imposing Parliamentary or royal decisions on the colonists—and also acutely aware that either coercion or rebellion would ruin their own careers—the conciliatory royal governors tried to interpret colonial sensitivities for British officials. In this respect they differed from principled royal governors like Hutchinson and Wright, who, while they opposed Parliamentary taxation of the colonies, considered their first duty the explanation and interpretation of British policy and intentions to their fellow colonists.

The illegitimate son of Benjamin Franklin, William Franklin lacked the charm, literary brilliance, and intellectual virtuosity that characterized his famous parent. A man of average intelligence, quiet and diffident in manner, lacking commanding personal presence, Franklin nonetheless struggled within himself to understand his strengths, overcome his limitations, and accurately appraise the situations in which he found himself.[1] "I have had a difficult part to manage," he explained to his father during the Stamp Act crisis, to "steer clear of giving any umbrage to the people here and of embarrassing myself with the ministry."[2] Those understated words almost prophetically described his entire governorship of New Jersey, which lasted from 1763 to 1776. Franklin had become governor amid fortunate circumstances. Formed in 1702 when the Crown took over the two proprietary colonies of East and West Jersey, the colony was a cohesive social and political community that was, however, experiencing several potentially serious internal stresses. The governing elite, a tightly knit group of Anglican lawyers, merchants, and officeholders living in the East Jersey port town of Perth Amboy, dominated the Council and other strategic royal offices; their power, however, was never so extensive that they could impose their will on the General Assembly or on the aristocracy in West Jersey. Economic opportunity among farmers and tradesmen abounded, and most property owners possessed the voting franchise, although entry into the aristocracy was extremely difficult. Provincial government, in any event, had relatively little impact on the day-to-day life of the province; instead, religious and ethnic antagonisms between settlers of English, Scotch-Irish, and Dutch ancestry, intense localism, rivalry between East and West Jersey, and tension between tenants and landowners in some areas were the political concerns of most people. Dominated by New York to the northeast and Philadelphia to the southwest, New Jersey never became an arena of great political struggle. In spite of its fragmented character, the province was capable of attaining an unusual degree of stability. In fact, New Jersey realized its potential for unity at about the time Franklin became governor. Prior to Franklin, the colony had seen a succession of three ineffective governors in five years. It had been wracked for a decade by a controversy over who should become chief justice, and in 1764 that struggle ended happily with the appointment of Frederick Smyth, a man of considerable stature, who also became Franklin's closest adviser. Though his father's influence got him the job at the comparatively young age of thirty-three and the appointment was widely criticized, Franklin received a warm reception when he arrived in the province in February 1763. During the next two years his conciliatory and co-operative dealings with the Assembly added enormously to his popularity.[3]

The Stamp Act crisis threw into high relief these contours of political development in New Jersey. The initial response of the province was remarkably mild. The Assembly declined to appoint delegates to the proposed Stamp Act Congress. New Jersey's designated stamp distributor, William Coxe, went all through the summer of 1765 without encountering any overt hostility concerning his acceptance of the sensitive post, and on August 27 he posted the required £2,000 bond guaranteeing his performance of his duties. News of violence against stamp distributors in other provinces and a single—perhaps bogus—report in a New York newspaper about planned reprisals against him frightened Coxe so badly that on September 2, 1765, he abruptly resigned his post and forfeited his bond. Suddenly Franklin's problems became more difficult. He lacked the authority to name a successor to Coxe, and consequently there was no way for him to administer the Stamp Act when it went into effect on November 1, 1765. Troops were available in New York to keep order in New Jersey, but the Council recommended not bringing them into the province lest their appearance provoke violence. With no place to store the stamps safely, Franklin prevailed on the commander of a British warship to take temporary custody of the stamped paper. News of violence and protest in other colonies filtered into New Jersey in early autumn 1765 and aroused previously dormant hostility against the act.[4] The spread of resistance in neighboring provinces provoked a newly emerged anti-Stamp Act leader, Richard Stockton, to complain that New Jersey looked "like a speckled bird among our sister colonies" in her acquiescent reaction to the act. Stockton then implored Speaker of the Assembly Robert Ogden to ask the Governor to reconvene the legislature for the purpose of naming delegates to the Stamp Act Congress.[5] Franklin obligingly let it be known that he was willing to accede to such a request. Ogden still delayed, and only after being hanged in effigy and denounced widely did he take the extraordinary step of summoning an extralegal rump of the Assembly to name unofficial delegates to the congress. Franklin could have dissolved the Assembly, then

only prorogued, and denied the illegal meeting a shred of legitimacy, but he refrained from doing so, he told the Lords of
Trade, because it would "have thrown the province into the
utmost confusion." He restricted himself to "expressing my disapprobation of their conduct in pretty strong terms, lest they
should . . . make it a precedent for such . . . meetings."[6] The
example of opposition to the Stamp Act set in neighboring
provinces and by the Stamp Act Congress prompted the New
Jersey Assembly to adopt its own Stamp Act Resolves in late
November. In part a duplication of the resolves of the recent
congress, the New Jersey remonstrance added a number of special
assertions: an attack on vice-admiralty courts; a plea for freedom
of the press; and, significantly, in resolve number eleven, a condemnation of violence and a call for moderation. Responding to
these resolves, Franklin criticized the assemblymen for having *"a
greater regard to popularity than to their own judgment,"* and
then, paraphrasing their own eleventh resolve, he asked their
"utmost endeavours to calm and heal all animosities and divisions, to support the authority of government, and to preserve
the peace and good order of the province."[7] Like James Wright
in Georgia, Franklin capitalized on his province's abhorrence of
immoderate political agitation.

For all Franklin's efforts to avert violence in New Jersey, the
contagion of resistance in other colonies was so strong that, as
one observer accurately noted, people "of all ranks and orders" in
New Jersey became "ripe for violence and confusion." Throughout the colony, royal officials were abused and effigies hanged.
Franklin warily watched the conduct of other governors, and his
observations on their behavior sharply expressed his own modest
and adaptable—if somewhat anguished—political style. Cadwallader Colden's and Francis Bernard's "unnecessary officiousness"
only "made matters worse," he wrote; "for any man to set himself
up as an advocate of the Stamp Act is a mere piece of quixotism
and can answer no good purpose." When his father's enemies
accused him of trying to sabotage New Jersey's participation in
the Stamp Act Congress, William Franklin published a detailed
rebuttal of the charges in which he strongly implied his sympathy
with colonial resentment of the act.[8] Looking back on this tactical retreat the following spring, he compared his conduct with

Thomas Hutchinson's. Hutchinson knew perfectly well that his enemies had spread false rumors about his advocacy of the Stamp Act, Franklin explained to his father, "but he thought it beneath him to take any pains to undeceive the people," who, in their fury, wrecked his house. Franklin disavowed such pride: "On the whole I am of opinion that it is best . . . for a man to lower himself a little rather than to let others lower him."[9]

Franklin's lack of pretense and refusal to indulge in self-deception were the products of his determined effort to succeed as governor in spite of his political inexperience and lack of personal political authority. But he learned politics quickly and became an extraordinarily deft and accomplished imperial intermediary, pleading his province's case to officials in London. When the Assembly evaded strict compliance with the Quartering Act in 1767, Franklin explained to Hillsborough that the legislators did not deny their obligation to provide barracks for British troops, "but they insist on doing it in their own manner, as has been heretofore customary in this province."[10] When Franklin permitted the New Jersey Assembly to consider the Massachusetts Circular Letter, which denounced the Townshend duties, Hillsborough issued him a scathing rebuke. Franklin responded in kind, and his angry and detailed retort to Hillsborough went to the heart of the problem of conciliating the colonists and persuading them to respect British authority. Accused by the Colonial Secretary of allowing the Assembly to "draw into question the power and authority of Parliament," Franklin bluntly replied that "the right of Parliament to lay taxes on the colonies is not questioned by the Assembly of New Jersey alone, but by every other house on the continent." The Declaratory Act of 1766, asserting Parliament's power to impose any law on the colonies, and now the Townshend duties, Franklin continued, had done incalculable psychological damage: "Men's minds are soured, a sullen discontent prevails, and, in my opinion, no force on earth is sufficient to make the assemblies acknowledge . . . that Parliament has any right to impose taxes on America." To Hillsborough's rebuke that he should have prorogued or dissolved the Assembly rather than let it consider the Massachusetts Circular Letter, Franklin replied that the legislature was at that time debating a new currency bill and he did not want to disrupt that delicate and complex business with an abusive attack on the Massachusetts epistle. Instead, he had privately persuaded the assemblymen to draft a petition to the Crown that was "as humble and diffident as the nature of the case would admit." More fundamentally, he imperiously lectured Hillsborough, "petitioning the King is generally deemed an inherent right of the subject, provided the language is decent. . . . Had I attempted to hinder the Assembly from exercising this supposed right, . . . I [would] have been . . . accused here of an unwarrantable stretch of power." Franklin fully expected to be fired for his outspoken reply to Hillsborough; but—probably because the British government faced more serious problems in other colonies—he kept his job.[11]

Agitation over the Townshend duties coincided with a serious shortage of currency in New Jersey, and together the two conditions engendered an ominous mixture of economic stagnation and political frustration. In 1768 Franklin approved a new provincial currency act that technically violated Parliament's Currency Act of 1764 by making public bills of credit legal tender. Franklin implored the Privy Council to approve the act on the ground that New Jersey desperately needed the additional source of exchange; in May 1769 the Privy Council disallowed the statute but, impressed with Franklin's arguments, hinted that an amended version which did not make the bills of credit legal tender would win approval. Franklin then persuaded an angry and resentful legislature to enact a new currency bill along those lines. Despite all his efforts and his father's lobbying in behalf of New Jersey in London, the Privy Council, in 1770, inexplicably disallowed the revised statute as well. Franklin was furious; he had staked his whole reputation in New Jersey on winning approval of legislation to relieve New Jersey's dire shortage of money.[12] If they had deliberately tried, British officials could not have found a better means of damaging respect for imperial authority in New Jersey. His capacity to conciliate the Assembly drastically weakened, Governor Franklin drifted helplessly toward the final collision between British authority and colonial resistance in 1774 and 1775. "It is not for me to decide on the particular merits of the dispute between Great Britain and her colonies, nor do I mean to censure those who conceived themselves aggrieved,"[13] he told the General Assembly in January 1775, as he opened an appeal for peaceful petition and eventual reconciliation.

The New Jersey Revolutionary Provincial Congress ordered Franklin arrested in June 1776, and officials sent him to Connecticut for confinement a few weeks later. Handed over to the British in a prisoner exchange in 1778, he spent the remainder of the war in New York City, where he served from 1780 to 1782 as president of the Board of Associated Loyalists, an abortive organization that tried to organize a campaign of guerrilla resistance against the patriots in the middle states. In 1784 he pleaded with his father for understanding in a passage that exactly expresses his self-awareness, modesty, and candor: "I can with confidence appeal not only to you but to my God that I have uniformly acted from a strong sense of what I conceived my duty to my King and regard to my country required. If I have been mistaken I cannot help it. It is an error of judgment that the maturest reflection I am capable of cannot rectify, and I verily believe were the same circumstances to happen again tomorrow my conduct would be exactly similar."[14]

William Bull II, of South Carolina, practiced the conciliatory techniques that Franklin struggled arduously to develop in New Jersey with apparent ease and grace. One of the most attractive personalities of the entire period, Bull was an immensely wealthy planter whose career duplicated that of his father, William Bull I. Both were leaders of the Commons House of Assembly and went on to service on the Council and finally the office of lieutenant governor. The younger Bull was also speaker of the Commons from 1740 to 1742, 1744 to 1747, and 1748 to 1749; during frequent intervals between royal governors he served as acting governor, from 1760 to 1761, from 1764 to 1766, in 1768, from 1769 to 1771, and from 1773 to 1775. He remained aloof from the alien placemen like Egerton Leigh, and when war came in 1775 most South Carolina loyalists suspected, incorrectly, that he was secretly in league with the patriots. Although he chose to go to England during the War of Independence, he was the only South Carolina Crown official who was not banished and whose estate was not confiscated by the new state government.[15]

Bull's experience in the Commons House, his wealth and his prestige with the planter elite, and above all his imperturbability freed him from a defensive, legalistic outlook during the pre-Revolutionary period. "I am endeavouring to sow the seeds of such future benefits to Great Britain and this province as will ripen into perfection as soon as the genial warmth of restored confidence and affection . . . shall break forth upon us," he explained to Hillsborough in 1770. Bull was the very embodiment of "genial warmth"; he understood better than anyone else that the disputes over Parliamentary power and the conduct of British placemen in the province from the Stamp Act onward had poisoned relations with the mother country; he was determined to use all of his influence to avoid a direct clash between Britain and the leaders of the province; most important, he knew that he could play only a marginal part. He did not have the power to overawe the Commons House, and he was not going to squander the influence he did possess in futile denunciations of the Assembly's actions. "I thought it prudent to be silent," he wrote of his role when the Commons House denounced the Townshend duties. "The sovereign authority of the British Parliament did not stand in need of the feeble voice of an American governor to support its rights," he explained, thinly veiling his contempt for the contentious function Hillsborough wanted royal governors to serve. "Reviving disputes now on such subjects would only serve to produce fruitless altercation and render the minds of people . . . more irritated" and thereby jeopardize "the restoration of mutual confidence and affection between the mother country and her colonies."[16]

The basis of Bull's conciliatory approach was his understanding of the disposition of power in South Carolina and the processes that governed its use. Colonies, he stressed, might appear stable and wealthy, but the appearance was misleading. The growth of the colonies had been nourished by British "indulgences" like the encouragement of self-government and religious diversity and the fostering of rapid economic development. The very success of this process made the colonies luxuriant, unpredictable societies with expansive goals and impatient temperaments. The initiative and expectation of the "democratical" branch of government had outstripped the power of the Crown.

Despite the attempt of leaders in South Carolina to model their
government on the British constitution, the smallest differences
between the British model and provincial practice caused serious
reverberations. In South Carolina, Bull stressed, the treasurer
was not an officer in the executive branch but, rather, a creature
of the Assembly. That fact alone prevented Bull from stopping the
dispatch of the Wilkes Fund contribution to England. Another
intangible peculiarity in South Carolina society that impinged
on the governor's power was the unanimity with which the
members of the Commons House preferred to act. Even "moderate members" who would have opposed the Wilkes Fund contribution if they had known the significance of the action before it
was sent "are nevertheless averse to rescind or censure it, as is the
common disposition of all popular assemblies. They adhere to
resolutions once made."[17]

Bull seemed to sense that Crown officials in London were
incapable of sympathizing with, much less understanding, his
low-keyed and imperturbable attitude toward political conflict.
When he occasionally deigned to defend his approach, he
couched his explanations in language that was both supremely
self-assured and impeccably correct. "I have always conceived it
to be my duty," he wrote to an enraged Hillsborough at the start
of the Wilkes Fund controversy, "to make my representation of
our affairs . . . consistent with the whole truth of their state."
Surely, he twitted Hillsborough, "his Majesty's Ministers expect"
to be given all the facts, even unpleasant ones.[18] Near the end of
the Stamp Act crisis, Bull wrote an even more explicit justification. Blaming "suspense with regards to the Stamp Act" for
paralyzing the machinery of royal government throughout
America, he reminded the Board of Trade of the "virtues" of
mild and generous government: "I have thought it my duty
upon all occasions to conduct myself with as much lenity, moderation, and indulgence as could consist with the positive injunction of the law, . . . a humble imitation of those royal virtues
which reflect so much lustre on our gracious sovereign and diffuse
so much happiness on the subject."[19]

The intricate web of family, bureaucratic, economic, and
political relationships that had made the Wentworths a uniquely

powerful, influential, and wealthy family during the time of Benning Wentworth was just beginning to disintegrate when his nephew John Wentworth succeeded him as governor of New Hampshire in 1767. In many ways, of course, John Wentworth preserved and enhanced his family's position in New Hampshire. He was an intimate friend of Lord Rockingham and of several important figures in Rockingham's faction. In 1766 he succeeded his uncle Benning as surveyor of the King's Forests in North America—a highly strategic position from which to promote the family's extensive trade in masts and lumber. He was even more generous than Benning in creating new towns and recruiting supporters by dispensing land grants in these new communities. He staunchly supported the Anglican church and the activities of the S.P.G. in New Hampshire—which provided another source of political leverage in London. John Wentworth brought unusual insight and ability and a cool head to the difficult task of royal governor. He understood that the prosperity, expansion, and harmony of the province were essential to his family's future security; he accommodated himself gracefully to a gradual decline in his personal political power as the newer towns of the province became more assertive. Throughout his governorship he maintained unusually amicable relations with the House of Representatives.

These achievements, however, could not offset what Jere Daniell calls "two processes, independent in origin but mutually reinforcing in impact," that "undermined the political position of family-dominated oligarchy" in New Hampshire.[20] The first of these was the erosion of the sources of Wentworth's political power. The Wentworths' network of contacts in England was the last of the Anglo-American political alliances to survive; it too began to crumble in the late 1760's. John Thomlinson, Benning Wentworth's man in London, died in 1759, and the family never found a personal representative of like stature to take his place. During his visit to England between 1763 and 1765, John Wentworth assiduously cultivated the Rockingham Whigs; he formed a close friendship with Barlow Trecothick, Rockingham's most energetic and resourceful political operative and a man well qualified to succeed Thomlinson in the crucial business of securing mast contracts for New Hampshire producers. Rockingham's fall from power in 1776 and the subsequent collapse of his faction's influence almost ruined Wentworth's carefully cultivated contacts, and Trecothick found representing Wentworth interests an increasingly difficult and unrewarding occupation. In a crisis, to be sure, Wentworth's friends could still come to his rescue. (In the early 1770's a disgruntled former merchant and councillor named Peter Livius, who had lived in Portsmouth, New Hampshire during the 1760's and had there developed a fierce antagonism to Wentworth, brought charges of misconduct against the Governor in London and even persuaded the Board of Trade to recommend Wentworth's dismissal. Rockingham himself organized a "massive effort" of behind-the-scenes lobbying to prevail on the Privy Council to retain Wentworth.) But the Governor had already lost the power to influence the patronage decisions and naval-mast purchases that had once been the foundation of the family's political power in New Hampshire. As governor, he advocated the construction of a new road system to unite more closely the colony; he proposed the creation of new western counties with control over their own court systems, although he and the Council would appoint the judges; he generously supported the founding of Dartmouth College, a project of New Light Congregational evangelicals. These enlightened policies did not restore his control over the province. Instead, the decline of his political leverage, the depression in the mast trade, the influx of settlers from Massachusetts, Connecticut, and Rhode Island who looked with suspicion on the old aristocracy around Portsmouth, and the soaring demands for land and jobs from his old political supporters tied Wentworth's hands and prevented him from stemming the decline of the family's power.

The pre-Revolutionary controversy in New England, with its escalating protest of Parliamentary taxation, British troops in Boston, and customs enforcement, was the second dimension of Wentworth's dilemma. However much Wentworth personally disliked these policies, he had to defend them. The nonimportation movement following the passage of the Townshend duties and a few incidents of mob violence in New Hampshire inevitably tarnished Wentworth's reputation as the leader of a harmonious royal province and lessened the prestige of all Crown officials. During the Stamp Act crisis, Wentworth's uncle, Benning, had refused to co-operate in any way with a particularly officious stamp distributor and had secretly encouraged New Hampshire's protests against the act. Ironically, Benning's prudent course of action in 1765 complicated John Wentworth's position following passage of the Townshend duties, for, as Jere Daniell explains, "the new governor was in no position to alienate a ministry [in colonial affairs now dominated by Townshend and Hillsborough] in which Rockingham and Trecothick had little influence." Underestimating the opposition to the Townshend duties in New Hampshire, John Wentworth opposed any official petition from the New Hampshire Assembly for repeal and in the process only provoked individual towns to denounce the duties and condemn the Governor and his allies for their apparent insensitivity.[21]

In fact, Wentworth was extraordinarily sensitive to the dynamics of the pre-Revolutionary movement. Like Wright in Georgia and Franklin in New Jersey, Wentworth knew that smaller and relatively tranquil colonies could not withstand the intrusion of external political forces. Parliamentary taxation and other forms of tightened imperial control, coupled with the example of resistance in neighboring Massachusetts, spread tremors through the structure of New Hampshire politics. "The death of five men killed by the troops at Boston in March . . . has spread a flame like wildfire," he reported to Hillsborough in April 1770. "It is impossible to describe the unhappy effect it has produced": renewed opposition to customs enforcement and allegations that the Townshend duties would "absorb the property and destroy the lives of the people."[22] Wentworth particularly resented the tactless and heavy-handed conduct of the new American Board of Customs Commissioners, established, with headquarters in Boston, in 1767 as a part of intensified customs enforcement. He found commissioners "absurd, inflammatory, and contumacious" and declared that "all the paper imported since their arrival would not suffice to record their arrogance and unavailing management."[23] The commissioners never consulted him before prosecuting New Hampshire merchants, and in twenty-nine of every thirty prosecutions they failed to secure convictions.[24] When he signed a law changing the valuation of coins in the province and the Privy Council readily disallowed it on specious technical grounds, Wentworth—like Franklin in a similar situation—exploded in anger: "Good God! what governor will not rather throw this province into confusion rather than risk any measure not verbatim instructed" for him to approve.[25]

Wentworth carefully distinguished between the emotions and vivid rhetoric of colonial protests and the underlying constitutional principles of liberty that colonial leaders felt compelled to defend. These principles, Wentworth warned in 1769, "were infinitely more likely to get rooted than all the former noise and clamor"[26] of the Stamp Act and Townshend duties crises. "I think the temper of this continent seems to abate," he explained in a perceptive assessment of one of those periods of calm that fell between the explosive events of the pre-Revolutionary years, "but it subsides into such opinions as are much to be regretted by Great Britain," lingering suspicions that Britain was "determined to oppress them by power without even an inquiry into right or expediency."[27] "All the warm politics that have lately fermented in the other colonies are now at a stand, waiting for some measures from home [Britain] either to heal or inflame as it may happen."[28] Unless British officials rid themselves of "injudicious hauteur which too often aggravates the conduct of power in this country," colonial cynicism and resentment would continue to mount. The colonies, he concluded, were "a country . . . most easy to be governed by moderation or distracted by violence." Wentworth found the process by which violence engulfed moderation entirely understandable. In the emotionally charged atmosphere prevailing a few days before he fled Portsmouth in June 1775, Wentworth explained that "a general spirit of jealousy, alarm, and apprehension have either banished sober reason or blinded the judgment of men, . . . and . . . people in a fit of despair seem to have lost all sight of any possible alternative but slavery or civil war and abandon hope that there is yet remaining a possibility of reconciliation with the mother country."[29] Wentworth's purpose in defining the nature of revolutionary contagion was to impress upon the Assembly its duty to practice moderation; the aim proved futile, but Wentworth's comprehension of revolutionary psychology was nonetheless penetrating and detached.

John Wentworth's sensitivity and intelligence—as well as the position and role he inherited from his uncle Benning—help explain his conciliatory conduct during the pre-Revolutionary controversy. Additional crucial ingredients were his qualities of unusual serenity and authentic civility. During his exile in England during the War for Independence, he made a trip to Paris and there, coming out of a theater box, almost bumped into his Harvard classmate John Adams. Adams at once thought to himself, "We belonged to two different nations at war with each other and consequently we were enemies," and stood there in embarrassed silence, but Wentworth without hesitation asked about mutual friends in America, inquired about Benjamin Franklin's health, and invited Adams to visit him. "Not an indelicate expression to us or our country or our [French] ally escaped him," Adams noted, deeply impressed; "his whole behavior was that of an accomplished gentleman."[30] The evidence of Wentworth's conduct throughout his adult life supports Adams's impression of his character. His highly integrated and stable personality enabled Wentworth to become an accommodating loyalist and at the same time to believe in strict principles of colonial subordination. Joseph Galloway wanted to be a man of accommodation as well as an enunciator of principle, but his vanity and insecurity undermined his search for conciliation and made him cling all the more tightly to strict definitions of liberty and subordination. In contrast, Wentworth could move easily from one stance to another. Though he never publicly defended Parliamentary taxation, and though he called the stamp tax "this *cursed act*,"[31] he privately believed that such laws were entirely constitutional.[32] Without a trace of ambivalence, he ordered a militia company to prepare to fire on a hostile mob of men "and then to take what prisoners was possible to hang up the next day by a trial at law." He then waited in the freezing night air while "scouts" carried word of this threat to "the insurgents, . . . whose fears of the gallows magnified our numbers to more than a regiment and . . . disheartened the poor mob."[33] The exercise of authority caused Wentworth no inner qualms. In November 1771, when sailors and waterfront laborers surrounded a government witness in a customs prosecution, Wentworth saved the man from violence and averted a riot when he "walked unattended and publicly" into the "midst" of the crowd; it at once became "quiet and submissive."[34] From tests of that kind Wentworth learned to understand "the genius of the people": that "candor and reason are more necessary than troops and ships to govern them [and that] much depends upon acting with spirit upon the occasion."[35]

11

Daniel Dulany and the Difficulty of Maintaining a Balanced Political Order

LIKE John Wentworth, Daniel Dulany, of Maryland, inherited enormous power, influence, and wealth in a relatively small and self-contained province where those assets were magnified in scale. Also like Wentworth, this inheritance gave Dulany an independence of mind that made him a powerful critic of British policy but also kept him aloof from his contemporaries. While Wentworth's position deteriorated gradually during the early 1770's, Dulany's plummeted more drastically during those years. His father, Daniel Dulany the elder, had arrived in Maryland in 1703, a penniless indentured servant who had studied law in Dublin and had come to work as legal clerk for a Maryland lawyer. His apprenticeship prepared him for admission to the bar in 1709. Law was the most strategic of all paths to social mobility, and to it the elder Dulany added land speculation, iron manufacturing, moneylending, an opportune marriage, and the acquisition of political office. He intended that his namesake build on this foundation, and Daniel the younger received the best education available, at Eton; Clare College, Cambridge; and the Middle Temple in London.[1] Concerned broadly with philosophy and history, "the law of nature and nations,"[2] he studied with such distinction that he was given the unusual honor for a colonial student of being called to the English bar. "A man of great parts, of general knowledge, indisputably the best lawyer on this continent," his enemy Charles Carroll called him, and "a very entertaining companion when he pleases." Dulany did not always "please" to ingratiate himself and often appeared to be "very vain and proud and designing, . . . [and] . . . overscrupulous"[3] in his choice of political tactics.

Dulany's apparent hauteur was the outward manifestation of his private struggle to apply himself to the stewardship of the exalted place in Maryland society and politics that his father had prepared for him and his younger brother, Walter. On his return to Maryland in 1747 from years of study in England, Daniel took over management of the family's extensive landholdings in the recently established county of Frederick, began law practice in the bustling new settlement there, and, in 1749, won election to the Assembly. When Daniel Dulany the elder died in 1753, Daniel the younger secured his father's lucrative post as recorder of the town of Annapolis, and in 1755—after resisting the Proprietor's efforts to satisfy him with lesser posts—won appointment to the Council. Unwilling to be subservient to the Proprietary Governor, Horatio Sharpe, Dulany spent the two years from 1761 to 1763 in England mending political relationships with Cecilius Calvert, secretary to and uncle of the last Lord Baltimore. Dulany used all of his charm and ability to secure numerous offices in Maryland for his relatives and friends. When he returned to Maryland, Dulany found, at the age of forty-one, that he had attained all the goals he had hoped to reach when he launched his political and legal career sixteen years earlier.[4] To Governor Sharpe's dismay, by 1764 Dulany had become "rather fond of being thought a patriot councillor," as likely to support popular groups as to uphold the policies of proprietary officials.[5] "The role in which Dulany cast himself," his biographer writes, "was not unusual for a man who has attained a station in the world fundamentally to his liking. He was to be a balance in the world of strife and commotion, a judicious arbitrator when disputes arose, an adviser above party and, as far as possible, above contention."[6]

In the long run, this role proved increasingly difficult and finally impossible to play, because it presupposed that the balance of power between popular and proprietary interests in Maryland would remain constant and it required that Dulany's reputation and influence would continue undiminished. For the immediate future, Dulany's assets—legal and historical acumen, understanding of the language of English officials, and self-assurance—enabled him to play a prominent part in rallying colonial opposition to the Stamp Act. Dulany's fame as a hero of the Stamp Act crisis rested on the popularity of his pamphlet, *Considerations on the Propriety of Imposing Taxes in the British Colonies for the Purpose of Raising a Revenue.* . . . Neither graceful in style nor electrifying in its impact on the reader, the pamphlet was, nevertheless, unique. It called attention to Grenville's tactic of sponsoring the publication in England of authoritative constitutional treatises upholding the constitutionality of the Stamp Act and other measures curbing colonial autonomy. Sensitive to the atmosphere of English politics and society, as few other colonists could be, Dulany obtained copies of Soame Jenyns's *Objections to the Taxation of Our American Colonies . . . Considered,* Thomas Whately's *The Regulations Lately Made Concerning the Colonies . . .* , and William Knox's *The Claim of the Colonies to an Exemption from Internal Taxes . . . Examined* and at once spotted in them a design to discredit in advance any arguments the colonists or their English sympathizers might raise against Parliament's power to impose the Stamp Act. At the heart of Jenyns's and Whately's argument was the claim that the colonies were "virtually represented" in Parliament and had therefore implicitly consented to the Stamp Act.[7] A product of the intrigue and manipulation that characterized British politics in the 1760's, the concept of virtual representation was too clever and slick to command the respect of informed, thoughtful men, as Hutchinson privately demonstrated. It was, however, an ingenious attempt to by-pass entirely the subject of colonial rights or the constitutional nature of the Empire. Unless they refuted the virtual-representation argument, colonial writers would have difficulty even raising these broader issues. "It is an essential principle of the English constitution that the subject shall not be taxed without his consent," Dulany began his demolition of the principle of virtual representation. While, admittedly, residents of England were disenfranchised and yet also represented in Parliament, "the situation of [these] nonelectors" had to be considered: "their capacity to become electors [at some future time], their inseparable connection with those who are electors, [and] their security against oppression resulting from this connection" placed disenfranchised Englishmen in a fundamentally different position from the American colonists. "There is not," Dulany explained, "that intimate and inseparable relation between electors of Great Britain and *inhabitants of the colonies* which must inevitably involve both in the same taxation; on the contrary, not a single actual elector in England might be immediately affected . . . by . . . taxation in America," but the colonists "might be oppressed in a thousand shapes without any sympathy or . . . alarm" arising among British voters.

Having established that the notion of colonial virtual representation "consists of facts not true and of conclusions inadmissible," Dulany proceeded to elaborate his own view of the nature of the Empire. Prohibition of Parliament's power to tax the colonies, he argued, did not make the colonies less subordinate to Great Britain. Although Britain, of course, had the legitimate power to perpetuate colonial subordination, Dulany denied that Britain could use its legitimate authority to seize property and by "degrees" to confiscate "everything" the colonists owned. "There may very well exist a *dependence* and *inferiority*," he argued, "without absolute *vassalage* and *slavery*." This distinction between subordination and tyranny, like its underlying premise that the power to tax was unnecessary for the preservation of British authority, papered over an immense chasm between British and American constitutional thinking concerning the indivisibility of sovereignty. Like most other colonial leaders during the Stamp Act crisis, Dulany had little desire to expose the gap or even to admit its existence. "His aim was to create grounds for mediation," Bernard Bailyn explains. "Deeply committed to the maintenance of the imperial *status quo,* he had no desire to follow the implications of his own arguments." Dulany wanted the colonists to protest the Stamp Act by making their own clothing, thus eliminating the demand for British garments—making "linsey-woolsey . . . the symbol of dignity, the badge of virtue"—and producing "a legal, orderly, and prudent resentment . . . expressed in a zealous and vigorous industry." No British critic could slander such a strategy, he promised, and by adopting it the colonists would make it easier for Britain to acknowledge the error of the Stamp Act.[8]

For rather complic ted reasons, Dulany retreated during the late 1760's and early 1770's from his bold defense of colonial liberty. He took no part in the protest of the Townshend duties and by 1774 was completely estranged from the leadership of the pre-Revolutionary movement in Maryland. His conduct as viewed from several perspectives was quite understandable. After 1769, one line of reasoning explains, he became increasingly involved in defending the policies of Proprietary Governor Robert Eden. At the same time, Eden's antiproprietary opponents, led by Charles Carroll and William Paca, linked their opposition to the power of the Proprietor to protests of the policies of Parliament and the Crown. The arguments that antiproprietary politicians in Maryland had long used against the proprietor and his appointees acquired fresh cogency when directed against the British government. Committed by self-interest and friendship to perpetuating the power of the proprietary establishment, Dulany apparently could not help but oppose the entire pre-Revolutionary movement. Another explanation of Dulany's drift toward loyalism interprets the moderation and restraint of his attack on the Stamp Act as a foreshadowing of his later attitudes. Both explanations contain a good deal of truth, but they imply that Dulany was the victim of his own ideas, that moderation or self-interest governed his behavior mechanically. If any political ideas controlled him, they were his Whiggish view of society, in which the constituent elements of society make up a static equilibrium, and his resulting distrust of ambitious, expanding concentrations of power. In the late 1760's and early 1770's a complex series of political changes unique to Maryland rendered Dulany's highly intelligent, if conventional, political perception hazardous and unreliable.

Although the fourth most populous of the thirteen colonies, Maryland was an unusually self-contained province with an apparently orderly, compact social and political order. Commercially overshadowed by Philadelphia to the north, and economically and socially eclipsed by Virginia to the south, Maryland had a stable, prosperous agricultural economy in which commerce was becoming increasingly important. Proprietary government had retarded Maryland's political development. The Calvert family, which had lost control of the colony to the Crown in 1689 during an anti-Catholic uprising, regained possession in 1715, when Lord Baltimore and most of his family became Anglicans. Until the end of the colonial period, the fifth and sixth Lords Baltimore governed the province like a feudal barony. Though the proprietors were English, many of their appointees to political positions were relatives of the Calvert family. Quitrents, provincial taxes on tobacco, and fees for the performance of government functions provided the lord proprietor with the income for running the provincial government and a sizable profit as well. High-Church Anglicans, the lord proprietors regarded the appointment of Anglican clergymen in the province as their personal prerogative. Annapolis, the provincial capital, with its handsome mansions built by provincial officials and planters related by marriage to the Calverts, reflected the opulence of the proprietary establishment. Twenty-five years of royal rule before 1715 had created a powerful royal government in Maryland; the proprietors retained this centralization, assumed the same powers the Crown exercised in royal colonies in the early eighteenth century, and through the use of instructions to their governors kept a tight rein on land grants, patronage, and relations with the Assembly. Unlike royal colonies in the mid-eighteenth century, in which the power of the Crown and its executive receded, proprietary Maryland remained rigidly governed and closely administered by proprietary officials. The Assembly, elected by only 40 per cent of the adult white male population, contained vocal antiproprietary spokesmen, but as a body it never acquired the stature or leverage enjoyed by the Virginia House of Burgesses or the Pennsylvania Assembly, the latter having steadily eroded the authority of America's other pre-Revolutionary proprietary family, the Penns. The proprietors shrewdly undercut popular opposition by appointing members of the wealthy Lloyd family to the Council in an effort to neutralize, if not entirely conciliate, this potential group of opponents. Similarly, Daniel Dulany the elder, at first an enemy of the proprietors, found collaboration with the Calverts the most prudent and advantageous political course. His sons began their political careers in the Assembly as supporters of the proprietary governor. Daniel the younger's ultimate goal, achieved by the early 1760's, was, of course, to have enough power to be independent of both the proprietary governor and his enemies in the Assembly.

This history of proprietary dominance climaxed in a bitter controversy in the early 1770's over clerical salaries and bureaucratic fees. First, Lord Baltimore had enraged the province by appointing notoriously incompetent Anglican clergymen to the most lucrative parishes. Then, it was generally agreed by everyone that the fees charged by proprietary officials for the exercise of their offices had become, in a period of declining tobacco prices, exorbitantly high. In 1770, finally, the expiration of the province's important tobacco-inspection law gave the Assembly a chance to insert into the new act a steep reduction of official fees and clerical salaries, both of which were paid in tobacco. The Council rejected the new inspection act on the ground that its reduction of fees was too drastic. The resulting impasse brought the conduct of government to a halt, and Governor Eden responded by issuing a proclamation setting a maximum ceiling on the level of fees—ostensibly to prohibit excessive fees, but in fact to usurp the Assembly's sole control over money bills. The controversy raged until 1773, when both the popular and proprietary factions acknowledged a stalemate and arranged a compromise. The Assembly gave way on official fees, the Governor on clerical salaries.

In retrospect, the controversy was a mild prelude to the violent overthrow of both proprietary and British rule in 1775. At the time, however, it was a terrifying struggle. The antiproprietary party really believed that Governor Eden and his cohorts intended to bend the province's populace to their will by insisting on control over fees and clerical salaries. The men around the Governor, Dulany most prominent among them, saw in the newly invigorated antiproprietary leadership a movement to destroy the proprietary rule and with it their own privileged position in Maryland society. Moreover, the last Lord Baltimore died in 1771, and in the aftermath of his death Governor Eden waited two years before calling a new election—a period of waiting that heightened the public's anxiety. For many years public sentiment, even to the degree that it was reflected in the

Assembly, had been a stabilizing influence in Maryland politics, because both the proprietary party and its foes enjoyed elements of popular electoral support. The Stamp Act and Townshend duties crises threatened to upset this balance. Extralegal associations led by prominent antiproprietary figures enforced nonimportation and in the process brought dormant political energies to life. The archaic role of the absentee proprietor became vulnerable, despite his shrewd use of power, not so much because he was identified with British policy but because the antiauthoritarian arguments long used ineffectively against the proprietor could by the late 1760's justify overt opposition to British authority. That convergence of antiproprietary and anti-Parliamentary sentiment and action explained the unprecedented intensity of the struggle over fees and salaries.[9]

Dulany became the Proprietary Governor's foremost advocate in this controversy. A prolonged newspaper debate in 1773 with Charles Carroll, a wealthy Roman Catholic aristocrat and rising popular leader, forced Dulany to abandon his lofty position as independent statesman and to defend candidly his now vulnerable pretensions to political leadership. Although Dulany and Carroll were strikingly different personalities, they knew each other well and had a great deal in common. Trained in French Jesuit seminaries as well as the English Inns of Court, Carroll was steeped in the French Enlightenment and seventeenth-century English Parliamentary writing. From their first meeting in London, he and Dulany disliked each other. Their two families shared an interest in an ironworks and often disagreed about its management. In 1768, when Carroll married a nineteen-year-old girl who was not competent to sign the complicated legal papers involved in the marriage settlement, he asked the Assembly to pass a special act validating the marital arrangement; Councillor Dulany unsuccessfully objected to the use of public law for this private purpose and deepened the rift between himself and Carroll. As the debate over Governor Eden's proclamation on official fees became more bitter, Dulany attempted to lure the Governor's enemies into open debate. He composed a dialogue between two antagonists in the controversy: "First Citizen," who argued against the Governor's action, and "Second Citizen," who adroitly rebutted these contentions.[10]

What clearly bothered Dulany was the widespread assumption that a man could not preserve his intellectual and political independence and still support the proprietary party. "You brand every man with the odious appellations of court-hireling and sycophant who dares to exercise his own judgment, in opposition to yours, and that of your party," Second Citizen lashes out at his accuser. "Is it not the most criminal and unpardonable arrogance thus to strike at the public reputation" of a man? Carroll accepted the challenge and took the pseudonym "First Citizen" in replying to these charges; Dulany, in turn, styled himself "Antilon"—a misspelling of the Spanish word *antillon,* a plaster that draws out poison.[11]

The resulting exchange of letters between First Citizen and Antilon in the *Maryland Gazette* ran from January to July 1773. This exhausting examination of the controversy over the legality and constitutionality of the Governor's proclamation on fees injected bitter invective into an erudite debate about seventeenth-century precedents concerning the fiscal powers of the Crown. "Inveterate malice, destitute of proofs," Dulany said of Carroll's motives, "has invented falsehood for incorrigible folly to adopt, and indurated impudence to propagate." Carroll pictured Dulany as "dismayed, trembling, and aghast, . . . skulking behind the strong rampart of governor and council, . . . chin deep in precedents, [a man whose talents were like] a jewel buried in a dunghill."[12] Dulany presented the strongest possible case for Eden's proclamation setting fees. When the old tobacco-inspection law expired, the Governor had no choice but to act; his proclamation prevented proprietary officials from charging excessive fees; the Governor's right to regulate fees had ample precedent in both English and Maryland law and practice; his actions directly affected only proprietary officials and did not impinge on the freedom of any other citizen; the proclamation did not institute a fully developed fee schedule and therefore was no usurpation of the Assembly's traditional right to devise such a schedule; finally, Dulany contended, fees were not taxes and the Assembly had no exclusive power to determine their level.

The debate was inconclusive because Carroll was interested not in these legalistic matters but, rather, in broad constitutional and philosophical issues. The benign motivation of the proprietary government—or any government, for that matter—was a myth: "Our constitution is founded on jealousy and suspicion; its true spirit and full vigor cannot be preserved without the most watchful care and strictest vigilance . . . over the conduct of administration. . . . The pursuits of government in the enlargement of its powers and its encroachments on liberty are steady, patient, uniform, and gradual."[13] In the light of these principles, opposition to the fee proclamation was imperative. Eden's actions corresponded exactly to Charles I's extortion of ship money, Carroll declared, referring to the King's effort in 1635 to collect funds for naval building from inland counties without Parliamentary authorization. When John Hampden defied the King over ship money and forced a famous test case, the judges upheld the King; but the injustice and unpopularity of the decision did much to discredit Charles I and his advisers, and subsequent constitutional developments in seventeenth-century England vindicated Hampden's stand. In this complex and important episode, Dulany and Carroll each found ample precedent to defend their positions. Carroll, however, turned this digression into history to his advantage. He surveyed the long course of English constitutional development and ransacked it for evidence of abuse and greed by officials of the Crown.

Dulany was simply not prepared to construct so extensive a justification for the power and dignity of the proprietary government in Maryland, and he was not accustomed to having his reputation as a legal scholar publicly challenged. Dulany's whole approach to politics—his sensitive appraisal of the British presumptions behind the Stamp Act, his conciliatory recommendations concerning resistance against the act, his desire to exert independent political influence for stability in Maryland—was made possible by his wealth, knowledge, and intimate involvement in Maryland society. At the same time, these qualifications for leadership inhibited Dulany by burdening him with the heavy responsibility to act with uncommon wisdom and independent judgment. The emergence of newly competitive, contentious antiproprietary leadership in the early 1770's endangered his isomorphic relationship with Maryland's social and political order. "I have often lamented that *electioneering*, as it is called, should be so ruinous to private attachments and good fellowship

and should generate such black blood in society as it does. . . .
Those who administer this cruel distemper, whether they lurk in
secret or act openly, have much to answer for. We frequently see
the bonds of nature torn asunder. . . . Confederated bands of
politicians, hackneyed in their trade, . . . have availed themselves without remorse of the avowed rawness, simplicity, and
vanity of youth to accomplish their purposes, though they divided a house against itself and kindled the inextinguishable
flames of hatred and animosity."[14]

Dulany's was a remarkably accurate commentary on the violent and radical proclivities in Maryland that the controversy
over official fees had helped arouse. Although the dispute ended
with a moderate compromise, the proprietary establishment possessed a shell of its former authority. A deceptive calm fell over
the province from midsummer 1773 until the following spring,
when news of the Coercive Acts ignited the combustible political
situation that Dulany had described so vividly a year earlier. The
Popular Party, through an extralegal convention elected in June
1774, dominated the province and supported the edicts of the
First Continental Congress. The first violation in Maryland of
Congress's nonimportation boycott occurred on October 14, 1774,
when the *Peggy Stewart,* owned by Dulany's friend Anthony
Stewart, entered Annapolis harbor carrying a load of tea. Stewart
paid the tax required by the Tea Act, and an enraged crowd, led
by Charles Carroll, seized the ship and burned it to the waterline. In the months that followed, mobs expelled royal customs
officials from the province and Governor Eden's power and
influence completely evaporated. Dulany found himself isolated
and immobilized. His friendship with Anthony Stewart accelerated his estrangement from the pre-Revolutionary movement.[15]
But for reasons of both prudence and conviction, he stopped
short of becoming an outright loyalist. As he told the Anne
Arundel County Revolutionary Committee on January 16, 1775,
"I do not assume any pretention to control the opinion of
others, but I claim the right of judging freely and of acting freely
according to my judgment. . . . As a member of the Council, I
have taken an oath to support the rights and authorities of
government . . . and therefore any assistance, directly or indi-
rectly in the execution of the proposed measure [raising funds

for a revolutionary militia] would be, I think, a violation of my oath. I act upon my own judgment and avow it, and no more censure others . . . who may think and act differently . . . *than I would creep for shelter under their conduct.*"[16] It was a fitting final statement of a political creed that Dulany followed for more than a quarter of a century.

12

Two Accommodating Clergymen: William Smith and Andrew Eliot

THE search for accommodation appealed strongly to rationalist clergy—especially Anglican and Old Light Congregationalist—who did not believe in the depravity of man or in the transcendent need for the colonists to confess humbly to God their collective and individual sins. The rationalist Old Light Congregationalists, to be sure, did form the vanguard of protest against proposals for an Anglican bishop in the colonies and other Anglican attempts to secure what seemed to them a privileged place in colonial society. The Old Light Congregationalists, moreover, did emphasize in their political writing the ideas of John Locke about a compact between the ruler and the ruled; Jonathan Mayhew, the leading Boston rationalist Congregationalist clergyman of the 1750's and early 1760's, carried this Lockean belief to its logical and intended conclusion when, in 1750, he condemned the Anglican doctrine of unlimited submission to constituted authority in a sermon that contributed some key ideas to later Revolutionary ideology. For the most part, however, the rationalists resisted the idea that Parliament and the ministry were irredeemably corrupt, and consequently they urged Americans to seek redress of grievances through a reasoned appeal to British self-interest and generosity. This cautious proclivity among the rationalist clergy did not mean that their theology was necessarily hostile to the defense of colonial liberty. But it did mean that these men were especially receptive to impulses of prudence and restraint and were impelled to elaborate strategies for conciliation with Britain in the years 1774 and 1775. Openness of mind and yearning for conciliation became an increasingly heavy burden as the pre-Revolutionary controversy progressed. Attempting to alleviate their discomfiture without sacrificing their beliefs, the more conservative of the accommodating rationalist clergy found themselves caught in an ill-defined but nonetheless excruciating dilemma.

In June 1775 the Reverend William Smith presided over the composition of a letter, from six Philadelphia Anglican clergymen to the Bishop of London, that identified the stresses and anxieties inherent in a moderate, accommodating perception of the imperial crisis. "We sit down under deep affliction of mind to address your Lordship on a subject in which the very existence of our Church in America seems to be interested." For over a year they had observed strict public silence on the issues of British policy and colonial rights while privately praying for the emergence of a spirit of reconciliation: "We have spared no means in our power for advancing such a spirit *so far as our private influence and advice could extend.*" After a year of keeping "our pulpits wholly clear of anything bordering on this contest" and thereby avoiding the unfair suspicion that "we were opposed to the interests of the country in which we live," this strategy had played itself out. "The time is now come . . . when our silence would be misconstrued and when we are called upon to take a public part." Congress had forced this decision upon them by setting aside July 20, 1775, as a day of prayer and fasting. Anglican sermons on that day would have to invoke God's blessing on the struggle to preserve colonial liberty and by implication express disloyal sentiments toward the mother country. Acknowledging that "our complying may perhaps be interpreted to our disadvantage in the parent state," the letter moved gingerly past this problem to explain that refusal to pray for the colonial cause would be considered a hostile action, one "inconsistent with our characters as ministers of the gospel of peace." As a result of these pressures, Smith and his colleagues had decided to preach prescribed sermons that would be at least nominally sympathetic with the defense of colonial rights and critical of British attempts to tax the colonies and govern them more closely.[1] Composing such a sermon, he realized, posed new and difficult problems. As he had admitted a week previously in his famous *Sermon on the Present Situation of American Affairs,* preached to a newly formed militia battalion, "to draw the line and say where submission ends and resistance begins is not the province of ministers of Christ. . . . Pulpit casuistry is too feeble to direct or control here."[2] "The people will feel and judge for themselves in matters affecting their own civil happiness," he explained bluntly; any Anglican attempts to endorse "what they think would be a slavish resignation of their rights . . . would be destructive to ourselves, as well as to the Church of which we are ministers."[3]

Smith brought an unusually rich experience in dodging personal criticism to the difficult task of advocating accommodation in 1775. A man of immense intellectual and professional promise, he was also insufferably vain, drunken, profane, abusive, and greedy. Born and educated in Scotland, he had come to Long Island as a schoolmaster in 1751. Two years later his ideas on educational theory, stressing practical vocational as well as traditional curriculum, caught the attention of Benjamin Franklin. After returning to England and being ordained an Anglican clergyman, Smith decided to settle in Philadelphia, where he became rector of the Academy and, in 1755, provost of the new College of Philadelphia. There he influenced a remarkable group of students who later attained distinction—notably, Francis Hopkinson, the writer, Benjamin West, the painter, and John Morgan, a noted physician.[4] In the pulpit he was, according to Benjamin Rush, "solemn, eloquent, and expressive to a high degree." An accomplished poet and astronomer as well, Smith devoted much of his energy to highhanded tactics in land speculation, to acrimonious quarrels with almost everyone he knew— including his benefactor, Franklin—and to the bottle. "It was a favorite maxim with him," explained Rush, "that to gain mankind it was necessary not to respect them."[5] During the Seven Years' War, Smith had gotten into a great deal of trouble with his attacks on the pacifist Quaker majority in the Pennsylvania Assembly, calling it "a factious cabal, effectively promoting the French interest";[6] and for more than a decade thereafter he avoided political controversy. He privately condemned the Stamp Act as "greatly mistaken" and "contrary to the . . . inherent rights of Englishmen"[7] and in 1766 publicly congratulated the student winners of an essay contest who had written on

"The Reciprocal Advantages of a Perpetual Union between Great Britain and her Colonies" for their treatment of a "truly delicate and difficult subject." "At a time when fatal misunderstanding had untwisted the cords of union and . . . too much inflamed . . . the minds of so many," he noted with approval, his students had balanced their condemnation of the Stamp Act with praise for Britain's other colonial and commercial policies. They had behaved, he concluded, like "true *sons of liberty,* . . . neither betraying her sacred cause . . . nor degenerating into *licentiousness.*"[8]

That ideal of a balance between virtuous defense of liberty and licentious troublemaking governed Smith's conduct as he was drawn into public life from May to July 1774, when Philadelphia became aroused with news of the Coercive Acts. He served with John Dickinson on a committee that drafted a reply to Boston's plea for assistance. The committee called exemption from Parliamentary taxation *"a right from which we can never recede"*; however, it also urged Boston to act with "firmness, prudence, and moderation," suggested restitution for the destroyed tea, declined for the time being to endorse nonimportation, but did support the idea of a general colonial congress to petition the Crown for redress of grievances. Smith rightly guessed that Boston found the letter "too cold in the cause."[9] A few weeks later, his address to a public meeting set forth the limitations that he felt the colonists should place on their own actions during the imperial crisis. "Everything that may inflame and mislead the passions should be cast behind us," he declared. Haste, internal dissension, or "even too severe a recapitulation of past grievances" would impair the colonial cause. Instead, discussion should remain in general terms in order to maintain unanimity and prevent the intrusion of "party distinctions." Smith abhorred the notion of little knots of men operating within a larger group to secure ends of their own. His tactics were obvious: to keep the machinery of remonstrance in moderate, self-controlled hands. But beneath this conscious purpose was a feeling about how groups of men ought to behave. The function of this particular assembly, he had explained in his meticulously circuitous manner, was not to protest but "to devise . . . ways and means upon a constitutional ground" for restoring harmony with the mother country. The scene of such delicate deliberation ought to remain free from contention and what he called "party strife," organized and concerted political activity by anyone other than the appointed representatives of the entire meeting. "Whenever party distinctions begin to operate we shall give cause of triumph to those who may [want] . . . to abridge our native rights."[10]

His *Sermon on the Present Situation of American Affairs* reiterated the path he hoped to follow: to avoid the extremes of "licentious opposition" to legitimate British interests on one hand and a "passive surrender" of colonial rights on the other. He based his sermon on the account in Joshua of the dispute between the tribes of Reuben and Gad and the related tribe of Manasseh. Manasseh had decided to settle on the eastern side of the Jordan, and its people understood that in so doing they forfeited the opportunity of worshiping at the High Altar of Gilead in Shiloh, which all acknowledged was a holy place. With no thought of irreverence, they built an altar in their new homeland. But "the zealots of that day scrupled not to declare them *rebels* against the living God" and of "setting up an altar against His holy altar." Civil war threatened until Manasseh sent an emissary named Phineas to confront the leaders of the older tribes. Far from challenging the sanctity of the high temple, Phineas pleaded, his people sought only to honor Jehovah with a small tabernacle of their own and to remind themselves of their common religious heritage with Reuben and Gad. "This noble defense," Smith exulted, "wrought an immediate reconciliation." No passage of scripture, he declared, applied more aptly to the present dispute between Britain and its colonies. He then proceeded to explicate the lesson: the nature of the compact between parent state and departing settlers; the advantages and hazards of settling a remote land, far from the seat of government; the possibilities for misunderstanding between the older and newer communities; and the unfortunate opportunity for contentious people in both communities to stir up trouble. "So far you see the parallel holds good," he concluded. "But what *high altars* have we built to alarm the British Israel?" The glory of British society, he answered, was its tradition of political and religious liberty; "with these principles and these views . . . we thought it our duty to build up American altars, or *constitutions,* as nearly as we could, upon the great British model." Colonial assemblies, laws, and courts emulated British examples. So the issue stood. Britain, like Reuben and Gad, had accused the colonies of refusing to pay "homage at the great altar" of the British Empire, and the colonists had replied that the attempt to tax them violated the constitution, that their resistance was an act of devotion to the higher law of constitutional liberty.

"Here the weight of my subject almost overcomes me," Smith admitted. No American Phineas had arisen to proclaim the purity of colonial claims; no inspired plan of reconciliation emerged from the babble of dissension. In such a void what guidance did the church offer? Beyond counseling restraint and moderation, Smith explained, it could only follow events. "A continued submission to violence," he concluded, "is no tenet of our Church." Anglicanism did embrace a historical and religious rationale for limited, calculated resistance. Historically, the church had preached the resolution of conflict, he explained, but not to the point of "crying 'peace, peace,' when there is no peace." The English bishops of 1687, who had defied the authority of James II, had set an example for Anglicans to follow when conscience conflicted with political allegiance. If Smith's listeners would consult their consciences while "engaged in . . . the grandest of struggles, . . . contending for *what you conceive to be* your constitutional rights," they would surely realize that their ultimate goal was reconciliation and the discovery of "the terms upon which this country may be perpetually united to the parent state."[11] That perception of the colonists' duty, he stressed in his sermon on the official day for prayer and fasting, July 20, 1775, could only remain sharp if the people forswore the sins that invariably tempted men during periods of political tumult: "turbulent desires," "secret views of fostering party strife," "impatience with lawful government." Wanting the colonists to act nearly in unison instead of yielding piecemeal to the leadership of factions and zealots, Smith even conceded in the spring of 1776 that independence could be achieved in a legitimate fashion. "When it shall clearly appear that we can no longer stand upon this ground, when we shall be generally convinced by better arguments than declamations and abuse of all things venerable and ancient that future connection with *Great Britain* is neither possible nor safe," he declared, "then we shall be fully united and prepared at every risk to pursue whatever measures the sense of the community, fairly collected, shall think necessary to adopt."[12]

Influenced by their conception of sin, rationalist clergy brooded obsessively on the excesses committed by unreflective men in a time of turbulence. This viewpoint directly contradicted the Calvinist belief that men were innately evil, that British ministers had given way entirely to the rule of their own vicious passions, and that Americans could not resist tyranny unless they first purged themselves of guilt by confessing to God their materialism, greed, self-centeredness, and complacency. "Into what fatal policy has the [British] nation been impelled," exclaimed the Calvinist preacher and President of Harvard, Samuel Langdon, on May 31, 1775, "by its own public vices to wage a cruel war with its own children in these colonies only to gratify the lust of power and the demands of extravagance! . . . But, alas! have not the sins of America . . . had a hand in bringing down upon us the righteous judgments of Heaven? Wherefore is all this evil come upon us? Is it not because we have forsaken the Lord? . . . It becomes us to humble ourselves under his mighty hand, that he may exalt us in due time."[13]

Although the rationalist clergy found elements of this theological-political explanation acceptable, they could not embrace it wholeheartedly. None struggled more earnestly to resolve this problem of religious identity than the Reverend Andrew Eliot, minister of the New North Church in Boston. As one of Massachusetts's most influential Congregationalist clergymen, he was invited to preach the election sermon at the opening of the General Court in May 1765, before Governor Bernard and the members of the Council and House. It was a ritual event, but one that everyone took quite seriously.[14] Traditionally, the election sermons in Massachusetts elegantly reiterated the principles of compact government: the sinful nature of subjects and sovereigns and the consequent need for a political order that enabled the rulers and the ruled to check each other. Eliot's election sermon, delivered against the ominous backdrop of the opening weeks of the Stamp Act crisis, adhered faithfully to this format. But it contained an unmistakable undertone of reservation. Eliot's description of good magistrates depicted men whose wisdom, piety, political skill, and firmness should prevent them from becoming tyrannical, inconsistent, or weak. The magistrate might sin, Eliot conceded, but the provocation to sin was the troublesome conduct of other men rather than any inner character flaws of the ruler himself. "The rulers of a people are seldom so happy as to please all who are under their authority. They have often personal enemies, or crafty and ambitious men will find fault with government. . . . They . . . need to be wise as serpents, as well as harmless as doves, to counterwork the machinations of such men." Even men defending their legitimate rights were exposed to moral peril! "To touch [people's] liberties is to touch the apple of their eye; every attempt alarms them, makes them jealous of further designs, and often throws them into the arms of factious demagogues, who hate government and are ever watching for opportunities to embarrass public measures and to introduce anarchy and tyranny." Eliot found none of this quickening tendency toward evil in the behavior of British rulers. "I am far from impeaching the justice of the British Parliament," he declared. "If any acts have passed which seem hard on the colonies, we ought to suppose they are not owing to any design formed against them, but to mistakes and misrepresentations." In contrast with this generally equivocal treatment of liberty and authority, Eliot's insertion of a standard New England justification for resisting tyranny reverberated like breaking glass in an empty church: "Where men . . . pervert their power to tyrannical purposes, submission . . . is a crime, . . . an offense against the state, . . . against mankind, . . . against God."[15] Eliot's reluctance to denounce British policy emphatically and his unwillingness to affirm the depravity of rulers and ruled with equal severity sprang from what Bernard Bailyn calls his "broadly reasonable, tolerant, instinctively cautious, and indecisive"[16] temperament. Theological beliefs and clerical duties were the most important factors in shaping his character.

Central to everything he did as a clergyman and a political thinker were Eliot's gravitation toward Arminianism and yet his lingering reluctance to repudiate Calvinism entirely. His ordination sermon in 1742 acknowledged and then evaded the great theological issue of the day: the Great Awakening's insistence on the absolute necessity of a regenerating conversion experience. Eliot admitted that a clergyman "who has never felt the power of divine truths upon his own soul" could not lead others to experience that reality, but then he added that a "sovereign God" could make use of unregenerate clergymen if He chose to do so. His only published "jeremiad" against *"impiety,* . . . neglect of *family religion,* . . . profanity, . . . intemperance, . . . gaming, excessive drinking, *uncleanness,* . . . *lying* or *speaking falsely"* assured his fashionable congregation that he was "not charging" them "with the crimes I have mentioned" and softened the impact of his indictment by warning that "we are in danger of becoming very soon *an evil* and *adulterous generation."* Invited in 1771 to contribute to a distinguished lecture series on "Natural Religion," Eliot undertook to demonstrate the existence of God and of religion and to discuss the character of natural religion. He disposed of the issues of God and religion by quoting from the most eminent eighteenth-century Christian apologists. The conflict between God's omnipotence and man's free will troubled him deeply, and he dealt with the issue by quoting John Locke's words: "I cannot have a clearer perception of any thing, than that I am free: yet I cannot make freedom in man consistent with omnipotence . . . in God, though I am fully persuaded of both . . . truths. . . . Therefore I have long since left off consideration of the question." The idea of "natural religion" provided, for Eliot at least, some light on the problem. "God having made us . . . intelligent, rational creatures, . . . there arise certain . . . obligations which constitute the law of nature. . . . To obey a law which results . . . from the nature He has given to men, is . . . natural religion." While he affirmed the benevolence of God and the natural goodness of man, Eliot carefully admitted that "man, through inattention and corruption, or some other cause, if left to himself, would certainly attain to very little knowledge of God or his duty." Revelation and instruction, he admitted, had to supplement men's natural capacity to love and obey God.[17]

An unusual intellectual and emotional experience between 1766 and 1775 forced Eliot to apply his reasonable, benevolent, conventional ideas and predispositions to the task of defining and preserving colonial liberty and determining his own political conduct. His election sermon of 1765 caught the attention of three English intellectuals and religious dissenters, Thomas Hollis, his heir, Thomas Brand, and Archdeacon William Blackburne. Hollis initiated a correspondence, believing Eliot a promising channel for disseminating Hollis's conviction that liberty throughout the world was gravely threatened by the evil designs of Roman Catholics, high Anglicans, and virtually all the men around George III. Eliot found their letters flattering and entrancing. These English radicals described a conspiracy by evil ministers to destroy liberty in Britain and throughout the Empire; they saw a current revival of the seventeenth-century Stuart and high-Anglican machinations against representative government and religious toleration; and, most important to Hollis, they sought to counteract these evils by circulating throughout the world the writings of the great seventeenth-century and early-eighteenth-century libertarian publicists: Algernon Sidney, John Milton, John Trenchard, and Robert Molesworth, who believed that "good learning . . . is a great antidote against tyranny."[18]

Eliot, already vaguely familiar with these ideas, found his sudden immersion in them a bracing experience. Seeing British politics through their eyes convinced Eliot that Crown officials in London and Boston "are governed by private views and the spirit of party. Few have any regard to the good of the public. Men are patriots till they get in place [that is, public office], and then are!!!—anything." Eliot quickly mastered the rhetoric and concepts of Hollis's radical critique of English politics and applied his new insights to colonial affairs. If Britain succeeded in taxing the colonists, a resulting bureaucracy, "a parcel of pitiful sycophants, court parasites, and hungry dependents" living in "luxury and extravagance," would fasten itself to colonial society. If the British began to pay a royal salary to the governor and judges in Massachusetts, "we shall have needy, *poor* lawyers from England, *Scotland,* or some tools of [the Crown] of our own, placed on the bench, . . . and our governors will be men who, having answered the ends of some minister, will be sent here for a reward of their despicable services; these [officials], being hackneyed in the paths of deceit and avarice, will be fit tools to enslave and oppress an honest people." Of the news that troops were being sent to Boston, he wrote to Hollis bitterly: "To have a standing army! Good God! what can be worse to a people who have tasted the sweets of liberty!" The Boston Massacre confirmed his belief in "the impossibility of our living in peace with a standing army," a subject on which he found "Trenchard's history of standing armies . . . excellent."[19]

Yet even in the congenial setting of this correspondence with Hollis and his circle, Eliot's optimistic view of human nature blunted his newly found radicalism. "Places, pensions, and salaries bias men without their knowing it, and human nature is too easily warped by interest, connections, etc.," he wrote, simultaneously acknowledging human weakness but shifting the blame for sin away from the psyche of the individual and toward external influences. *"For his own sake, . . .* I never . . . desired to see [Hutchinson] governor, lest it should destroy his comfort and affect the purity of his heart." The very intensity of his own condemnation of British policy seemed to unnerve Eliot and force him to revert to an ambivalent view of the conflict between the mother country and the colonies. "There is something to me absolutely absurd and irrational," he thundered to Blackburne, "in [the proposition] that because our fathers were born in England six or seven generations ago . . . therefore we are obliged in conscience to be subject to the authority there in all generations to come, altho that authority be ever so tyrannical and oppressive." Just three sentences later this melancholy train of thought led Eliot to predict regretfully that "the moment the colonies are disconnected from Great Britain there will be the most terrible convulsions within each government and great contentions with one another."[20] These dire apprehensions heightened, and in his description of military preparations in Massachusetts in February 1775 he drew into focus all the elements of his experience during the preceding decade:

We are preparing for war . . . to fight with whom? Not with France and Spain, whom we have been used to think our natural enemies, but with Great Britain—our parent country. . . . My heart recoils—my flesh trembles at the thought. . . . I have ever wished for moderate counsels and temperate measures on both sides. But I can have very little influence on men or measures anywhere. Pride and passion, avarice and a lust of domination have an uncontrolled sway. In a good measure sequestered from the great world, unconnected with parties, I endeavor to attend the duties of my station and enjoy myself never more than when I can find time for reading and contemplation in my own study. I can there wish and pray for better times, which I see no prospect of without some remarkable interposition of divine providence. . . . I am distressed for my country, in which I include Great Britain. I should fear a disconnection with it as one of the greatest evils.[21]

13

The Rejection of Political Values:
Samuel Quincy and Robert Beverley

THE most pervasive sentiments in the pre-Revolutionary search for accommodation were apolitical resentment of and bewilderment about the disruptive intrusion of politics into the lives of individuals, families, and communities. "We are all, as it were, on the wing, not yet ready for flight, but anxious for the event," Samuel Quincy remarked to his brother, Josiah, in 1768, describing the anxiety he felt about British-colonial relations.[1] Both brothers were lawyers; Samuel, ten years the elder, who had begun legal practice in 1758 and gravitated easily into the pool of lawyers allied to Governors Shirley and Bernard, was genial and apparently pleased with himself; Josiah, who started practice in 1766, intense, idealistic, introspective, had completely internalized the ideology of colonial resistance and perceived events in terms of a grim moral struggle between American virtue and British tyranny.[2] They pleaded opposing cases in the Boston Massacre trials: Samuel, because he was closely allied to the Crown, substituted for absent Attorney General Sewall and prosecuted Captain Preston and the seven soldiers; Josiah, because he was a Whig, joined John Adams in defending Preston and the soldiers. For both brothers it was an unpleasant task carrying heavy responsibilities. Samuel had to show that the Crown would prosecute lawbreakers vigorously—even if they happened to be British troops and their victims rebellious rabble. Josiah had to convince the jury that as Bostonians and Americans they had a civic duty to acquit soldiers who had been victims of mob violence. In a sense, both succeeded. What set Samuel's usually hearty disposition on edge in 1768 was the roar of political agitation against the Townshend duties and other British measures. "The increasing zeal for liberty, or mobism, call it what you please," offended Samuel Quincy, and the prospect of an unending contagion of unrest upset him still more. Even in Britain disgusting political opportunism seemed rampant. "Behold a favourite [the Earl of Bute, George III's hated adviser] perpetrating his wicked schemes by all the sly maneuvers of state. . . . Behold a Wilkes, . . . supported even to frenzy by his idolizing adherents," Quincy lamented. "What is to be expected? . . . what is not to be feared? A favourite of the Crown on one hand, a favourite of the people on the other." In Britain, public licentiousness and official mendacity were the symptoms of political ferment that Samuel Quincy perceived and detested.[3] By 1774, the political and personal rift between the brothers was deep. Samuel attributed his refusal to support colonial resistance to a dislike of "the subject of politics," with its provocation of men's "fiercer passions." He was conscious of the qualities of temperament that distinguished himself from Josiah. "A love of ease and retirement (tho' not idle nor unemployed in the valuable purposes of life) " was his own "predominant passion," while in Josiah he saw "zeal and fervor of imagination, strength of genius and love of glory" and a desire to gain "fame through the turmoils of *public action.*" To judge by appearances, he admitted, Josiah was the more public-spirited man, but Samuel pleaded with his brother to look beyond these factors of his personality and judge whether, at heart, Samuel was a man of integrity and virtue.[4]

No critic of colonial resistance expressed more fully this dislike of political controversy than Robert Beverley, of Virginia. One of the wealthiest planters in Virginia and son-in-law of Landon Carter, a formidable defender of colonial liberty, Beverley was one of a handful of Virginia aristocrats who shunned the political duties in county government and in the House of Burgesses that their contemporaries took so seriously. Perhaps his ten formative years (1751–1761) of English education deprived him of the camaraderie of his fellow planters. He impressed them—especially his Carter in-laws—as insecure and unfriendly. When Beverley dutifully tried to discuss politics with his father-in-law, all he got for his trouble was Carter's cruel ridicule. Self-conscious and embarrassed during the pre-Revolutionary controversy, Beverley described and understood the swirling currents that disrupted his own life and examined with clinical care the breakdown of his own composure.[5]

"At present the country is in a most unhappy state of anarchy and misrule," Beverley wrote to John Backhouse, of Liverpool, in July 1775; "all I can do is to remain . . . a sorrowful spectator of these tumultuous times." He hoped he could remain a static observer on the fringe of Virginia's intense political activity and enjoy the tranquillity he would find in neutrality. From that vantage point, however, he could not avoid making occasional comments on politics, and the hostility that these aroused spurred him to defend himself and extend his criticism of Whig tactics. His aloofness and political naïveté as well as his compulsiveness tended to hide another side of his introspective personality—his acute curiosity about the consequences of emotionalism and agitation on the conduct of politically active Virginians in 1774 and 1775. "In the ardour of commotions," he observed, "the passions become so inflamed and the tempers so much prejudiced, that frequently measures of the most salutary nature are rejected as the effects of pusillanimity or treachery." Beverley was not only isolated and immobilized by that turmoil, but he also understood how anxiety and stress among Virginia's ruling elite could accelerate the pace of events and limit the options open to political leaders. Certainly he believed that his reason and judgment had revealed to him an atmosphere in which those rational tools were of little use. While that assessment may have been a subtle and even sophisticated one, Beverley himself was not the kind of facile thinker who could pursue the implications of this sobering insight. He preferred, instead, to make a virtue of indecision. "In all combustions of this kind," he predicted, "the impartial world will find errors and faults on both sides."

Nothing soothed Beverley's anxiety more than finding equivalent injustice in both British and colonial conduct. At the outset of a long letter to William Fitzhugh in July 1775, he put the best possible face on colonial grievances. He acknowledged the colonies' exemption from British taxation. He conceded that the operation of vice-admiralty courts as well as the penal provisions of the Coercive Acts infringed on the right of trial by a jury of

a defendant's own peers. He condemned the suspension of the
New York Assembly in 1767. But here his concession to the Whig
position ended. The Boston Tea Party, he feared, had fatally
compromised the integrity of colonial principles. In discussing
the tumult in Boston, he brooded over the excesses of both sides.
Avoiding the obvious issue of authority versus disobedience, he
weighed instead a variety of extenuating circumstances that
suggested to him that both sides were wrong yet each had some
justification for its actions. Clearly, Boston had the right to
oppose implementation of the Tea Act, but the violent destruction of the tea itself did not sound to him like a deed motivated
by patriotism. Because many men there stood to lose money
under the East India Company's monopoly, he queried Fitzhugh:
"Let me ask how far the destruction of the tea was influenced by
virtuous principles." The ministry, he cautioned, ought first to
have asked for restitution for the tea before considering harsher
penalties. Thus torn, he could only "lament that this unnatural
civil war took rise from such a cause."

However, because the crisis in Boston did exist and did involve
Virginians, Beverley sought pretexts that would justify continued
submission. Virginia could not complain too loudly about the
treatment of Boston, he suggested incorrectly, because it had
"beheld with silence and unconcern" the suspension of the New
York Assembly in 1767 and thereby compromised its capacity to
defend the preservation of Massachusetts's representative institutions. Nor, he added, could the colonies claim that the colonial
charters protected their assemblies from arbitrary suspension.
Charter rights seemed to him conditional on good behavior.
Quickly retreating from such a positive statement, he doubted
whether the destruction of the tea in itself merited so severe a
penalty. Still, he went on, the people of Massachusetts had only
themselves to blame because "their constitution . . . rests so
entirely with the people that they are perpetually engaged in
tumults and cabals."

Patriot agitators and the emotional quality of their appeals
alarmed Beverley much more than the underlying constitutional
issues of the pre-Revolutionary crisis. Demagoguery provided
him with a phenomenon he could analyze endlessly, pass judgment upon, and blame for all public disorder. The tone of

patriot polemics explained to his satisfaction why a constitutional dispute had grown into an emotional contagion endangering his society. At the outset of the controversy each side, he believed, had nervously exaggerated its claims. "Extravagant encomiums" and "illiberal abuse" at once became the medium of discussion. Agitators quickly took advantage of the situation and perpetuated the use of emotional and ill-considered rhetoric. Caught in a trap of their own making, responsible colonial leaders could not retreat or compromise without arousing cries of cowardice or treachery. The tone of patriot propaganda also suggested several concrete consequences of the controversy. The functioning of the British constitution, Beverley explained, depended on men's restraint and willingness to forgo personal advantage when they engaged in politics. The militant tone of patriot appeals suggested to him that "ambition, corruption, [and] faction" had seriously blemished the operation of the constitution in Virginia. Emotional rhetoric, moreover, foreclosed the possibility of reconciliation because it artificially inflated men's estimates of their own power and exaggerated the rightness of their position. Under its influence, Beverley's acquaintances simply would not listen to his arguments about the true interest of the colonies. Finally, emotional Whig arguments only needlessly antagonized British officials. Virginian attacks on Lord Dunmore illustrated this danger. Conceding that Dunmore was a bad governor and ignorant of the colony's interests and rights, Beverley argued that vilifying him served no useful purpose. "May it not be presumed . . . that he has met with some unmerited, illiberal treatment? If he has, resentment is natural to all men, and most probably he may be supposed to retaliate."

The alacrity with which patriot agitators exploited their advantages—such as Dunmore's indiscretions—excited Beverley's curiosity about their motives. "I have long apprehended," he told Fitzhugh, "that we have some men amongst us who, from the beginning, have been artfully endeavouring to blow up the seeds of dissatisfaction that they might gradually and wickedly prepare the minds of men for a change of government." These militants, he suspected, had no concrete program. Instead, they felt only a vague anticipation that a republic might be more congenial to their restless temperaments than the ordered society of a limited monarchy. Patriot leaders therefore recognized no debt to what Beverley considered the province's traditions of law enforcement, and their committees of safety in many instances "tyrannized over the liberty of mankind, and trampled upon the very appearance of humanity and justice." Still more suggestive about the motives of agitation, in Beverley's eyes, were the conduct of colonial printers in publishing anti-British tracts and their ambition to "flatter our prejudices and fascinate our understandings." Typically, he came to no definite conclusions about the motives of agitators. Their conduct suggested to him their lack of appreciation of colonial political traditions, their inability to select concrete goals, and their willingness to undermine the liberties of their critics. Unable to proceed beyond these indefinite suggestions about their motives, he relied on the imagery of disease to satisfy his desire for explanation. He returned repeatedly to the "inflamed" condition of their minds and those of their converts.

In Beverley's eyes, the resort to emotional persuasion and the encouragement of intimidation made the colonial defense of liberty ambiguous. Throughout the controversy that ambiguity made him feel more comfortable in his own precarious neutrality. Even when he tried to put the best possible face on the colonists' cause, in a letter to an English merchant in September 1774, he underlined its ambiguity. "I profess myself strongly for moderate though not submissive measures," he explained. The colonists wanted "liberty, not licentiousness [or] independence." If pushed too far they might try to develop their own manufacturing capacity, but such austerity would be unpleasant. "I would not have you infer from hence that this measure is the object of our choice," he cautioned his correspondent. "It is a step which cruelty, injustice, and necessity have driven us to." Quickly he qualified himself: "Independence we desire not, as we are conscious it must be as serious to ourselves as to you, and must involve us in endless misery." In this light he reassured the merchant about the purposes of the nonimportation association initiated by the First Continental Congress. It was not an act of defiance, but a safety valve, "a means of extricating many people from their present distresses." Beverley's inability to take a resolute position on the validity of colonial grievances or the propriety of nonimportation was rooted in his yearning for repose.

"Little more is required," he declared, "to bring this dreadful dispute to a fortunate and honorable issue . . . than to consider ourselves as members of the British Empire." Only tactics "of the negative cast," he warned Fitzhugh, could serve the cause of liberty.

Throughout the year of crisis in Virginia, roughly between the summers of 1774 and 1775, Beverley tried to find something constructive to say. When he did so he moved erratically from one suggestion to another, uncertain of his facts or their meanings to politically conscious Virginians. He praised the period of relative calm during Lord Botetourt's term as governor (1768–1770) and deduced from that example an argument for restraint in dealing with Britain. He dwelled on a host of dangers created by the controversy. As an alternative, he proposed a scheme of negotiated reconciliation that seemed to him to go to the heart of the imperial problem. His compulsion to speak on these issues, if even to a small audience of other planters, occurred in fits and starts during his period of general avoidance of political activity. The process became all the more painful as his relations with Landon Carter continued to deteriorate. "I heard perhaps a pretended excuse from Blandfield [Beverley's estate] for its coolness to Sabine Hall," Carter wrote in his diary in August 1775. "It seems the conceited wise one attempted, in his trammeled way of condemning, all measures publicly fallen upon to support our liberties."

To Carter's astonishment, Beverley saw no oppressive pattern in recent British policy and he separated Virginia's political interests in the controversy from those of other colonies. No British encroachment had occurred in Virginia, he declared, since 1770, when Parliament had partially repealed the Townshend duties. So restricted was his definition of a British encroachment that he saw no danger to Virginia's liberty in the Tea Act or Coercive Acts. Having disposed of more recent developments, he turned to consider Lord Botetourt's term as royal governor and depicted it as a happy interlude during which discontent evaporated. Citing two pieces of evidence that seemed to him conclusive, he recalled Botetourt's speech announcing partial repeal of the Townshend duties and the Burgesses' conciliatory reply. He also called attention to the statue the Burgesses had purchased to honor Botetourt. These considerations, he concluded, "ought in some measure to have restrained our passion for laying aside government." These suggestions revealed Beverley's skepticism about the cumulative dangers of British policies and about the durability of colonial unity. He therefore feared that colonial retaliation would jeopardize colonial interests, especially Virginia's, far more than a continuation of these present difficulties. Nonimportation, for example, was particularly dangerous. British merchants, he warned, would consider an embargo not as a temporary delay in the payment of planter debts but as an absolute repudiation of those obligations; nonimportation would not only destroy the planters' credit standing but would also needlessly ruin "nine-tenths of the persons engaged in this trade." Finally, it would not deprive the British Treasury of needed revenues because Parliament had enacted the Tea Act "more . . . as a precedent" than as a revenue measure.

As an alternative to these precipitate actions, Beverley proposed a plan of negotiated reconciliation that constituted his most forthright contribution to the pre-Revolutionary debate and the furthermost extent of his reluctant participation in it. In the summer of 1774 he had presented a version of his plan to a meeting of freeholders in Essex County. The colonies, he urged, should send to London a delegation of prominent colonists with mercantile experience that would reiterate colonial opposition to Parliamentary taxation but temper this stand with the offer of an annual contribution to the cost of imperial defense. The negotiators should reaffirm colonial sympathy for the plight of Boston and request repeal of the Coercive Acts. If the ministry did not respond sympathetically to these suggestions, they should appeal directly to the British electorate. The Essex freeholders declined to endorse Beverley's proposals; in Landon Carter's view, they found them "too round about and too passive for people infringed in their common right." Beverley's hopes declined even more when the First Continental Congress showed no more interest in reconciliation. Congress's action was all the more tragic for Beverley because he felt "fully persuaded that the ministry and nation . . . are cordially disposed to accommodate the matter." Britain, he argued, had made a meaningful gesture in the form of Lord North's plan of conciliation. Conceding the unpopularity of North's proposal, he characteristically declared, "I do not by any means approve it, but am sincerely concerned it was not made use of for the purpose of opening a negotiation."

The failure of the colonies to seek reconciliation rendered Beverley's sole concrete suggestion meaningless. His halting retreat into isolation left a trail of warnings about the consequences of independence, but primarily he nursed personal grievances against men who had ostracized him. Acknowledging his ignorance of what colonial leaders were actually doing, he felt that his disregard of tactical considerations gave him a clearer vision of larger problems. "Take it from me," he told Fitzhugh, "though [I am] no *adept in politics,* as my present character will plainly evince, . . . America can enjoy no solid or even tolerable advantages from an independence." The colonies, he asserted, could only prosper in close commercial relationship with Britain; they needed British protection from European powers; they possessed neither the technical skills nor the resources to wage war against Britain. The disunity of the colonies and their proliferation of political systems, religious groups, and ways of life all undermined their apparent unity. "It is true indeed that there seems to be a union of sorts at present, but . . . only in appearance. Ambition, resentment, and interest have united us for a moment." But inevitable disagreements about taxes, the autonomy of the states, the powers of the central government, and the conduct of foreign policy would surely tear apart any American union. In the face of these perils, negotiations with the British ministry seemed a mild ordeal. Regretting the unwillingness of the House of Burgesses to seek reconciliation, Beverley condemned the representatives for jeopardizing the safety of their constituents. Had the responsibility been his, Beverley declared, "I would scrupulously have kept the claims and grievances of the people in view, and would in an ingenuous and declaratory style have laid them before the Crown." Nothing more complicated seemed necessary. "These [grievances] would have been attended to, and no exception could have been made to the propriety or legality of the petition."

As his hopes for negotiation and restraint crumbled, Beverley could only ponder his own position. The hostility with which other planters regarded his neutrality and criticism of Whig tactics caused him unrelenting pain. "I want only to vindicate myself in the estimate of my friends," he told Fitzhugh, "from the cruel suspicion of being unfriendly to my country." He encountered that suspicion in what seemed to him bizarre forms. Men suspected him of seeking special favors from Governor Dunmore, he complained, and even of aspiring to a position in the royal government. All he desired, he replied, was to be left alone to tend his plantations and enjoy the companionship of his family. That privacy was, for Beverley, his "constitutional liberty." Though resisting bitterness, he occasionally burst out in resentment before lapsing into despondency. "You seem surprised," he told Fitzhugh, "that I should conceive I have been ill-treated by my quondam friends. But I tell you I have been, and by some nearly allied to me—or mine." He wished his tormentors well in their political ambition but questioned whether they would find inner satisfaction. What hurt him was not their disagreement with his views but their inability to separate personal regard from public differences. "It is astonishing," he complained, "that men cannot differ in political opinions without unhinging their former intimacies." In his complete withdrawal from the issues of the pre-Revolutionary debate, he could define his feelings about events only in terms of the damage men had done to his self-esteem. Tolerance and relaxed discussion had always been an essential feature of gentry society, he reflected. Men had an obligation to state their views candidly and temperately. In his limited participation in political discussion he believed he had always done so.

The apprehension he felt but could not fully express impelled him in July 1775 to state in conceptual terms his perception of what had happened to political discourse: "I do not esteem a man a jot the less for differing with me in opinion; 'til of late it was common to do so. But by some strange metamorphosis or other, this contrariety of opinions is denied." *"Some strange metamorphosis or other"*—this comment came close to expressing the essence of his view of the Revolution. Because he perceived no difference between ordinary discussion and intense political strife, he could not realize that for his contemporaries the pre-Revolutionary debate had passed the stage of a conversation between gentlemen. Driven by events he profoundly misunderstood, he tried to acquiesce gracefully. "I have found the torrent strong, and therefore shall not oppose it," he wrote, concluding his apologia to Fitzhugh. "The die is cast; I must await the event with melancholy concern." To the end he kept his fundamental commitment clearly in view. "I have always endeavored to avoid any side but that of reason and justice," he wrote in a perceptive summary of his conduct. "I have ever disliked the idea of being thought a party man."

14

The Quakers and Reconciliation

THE Quakers conducted the most strenuous and conscientious and the only truly collective pursuit of reconciliation in the pre-Revolutionary period.[1] A very few Friends were forthright apologists for British policy[2] and a small minority active participants in colonial resistance;[3] the great majority of the sect and virtually all its leadership were genuine pacifists, who looked upon any overt involvement in the imperial controversy as a provocation of armed conflict and hence a betrayal of Quaker belief. "The divine principle of grace and truth which we profess," declared the January 1775 Philadelphia Meeting for Suffering—an aptly named body of leading Friends assembled to deal with emergencies in the relations of Quakers to society—"leads all who attend to its dictates to demean themselves as peaceable subjects and to discountenance and avoid every measure tending to excite disaffection to the King as supreme magistrate or to the legal authorities of government." The meeting utterly condemned "the spirit and temper" of recent political statements advocating resistance against British authority because such agitated, militant sentiments "disqualify [men], in these times of difficulty" from "wise and judicious consideration" and distract them from the work of "reconciling differences or obtaining the redress of grievances."[4]

The pre-Revolutionary controversy, from which the Quakers conscientiously abstained, was only one segment of a prolonged crisis of conscience and identity facing the Society of Friends between the 1750's and 1780's. From the earliest Quaker settlement of Pennsylvania in the 1680's, the Friends had sought to be a fellowship apart from the world and a political force applying Quaker doctrines to the government of the colony. "Make outward plantations in America," George Fox, the founder of the denomination, beseeched the first Quaker emigrants to Pennsylvania in 1682, but "keep your own plantations in your hearts and with the spirit and power of God, that your own vines and lilies be not hurt."[5] For seventy years, prominent Pennsylvania Friends cultivated both the inner plantation of the spirit and the outer plantation of provincial affairs. The Quaker merchants of Philadelphia built a powerful political organization that dominated the Assembly and opposed the policies of proprietary governors and officials, who, after William Penn's death in 1718, were either Anglicans or nominal Quakers. In order to obtain and consolidate political power, the Quaker politicians compromised their strict pacifism and agreed to the indirect use of public funds for military defense. Suddenly, in 1755, this uneasy compromise collapsed. First, a revival movement within the church revitalized Quaker beliefs in strict pacifism, complete reliance on God's direction in place of prudent otherworldly instincts, an uncompromising witness against slavery and other forms of human degradation, and introspective and highly mystical meditation. Second, an outbreak of savage Indian warfare on the eve of the great war with France provoked the Proprietary Governor and his Council to declare war on the Indians and offer a bounty for both male and female Indian scalps. Rather than acquiesce in this barbarous practice, the leading Quaker politicians, who had previously supported defense expenditures, withdrew from the Assembly.[6] Freed from the political necessity of compromising with non-Quakers over issues like military spending, the leaders of the sect could turn their full energies to the work of tightening lax discipline and exploring afresh the inner plantation of Quaker meditation—"a time of inward waiting," as one Quaker described it, when "the humbling divine presence, . . . felt in reverent profound silence, . . . [and] the gentle operation of divine power caused an inward trembling" and "in language intelligible to the inward man, . . . the voice of the holy one of Israel said 'gather thyself from all the cumbers of the world and be thou weaned from the popularity, love, and friendship thereof.' "[7]

The withdrawal from politics and reawakening of spiritual sensitivity by the Pennsylvania Quakers did not resolve the ambivalent relationship of the church to society. Was its witness against war a proper goad to the consciences of men outside the Quaker fellowship, or was it sinful involvement "with the things of this world and the unsettled state thereof" that diverted the believer from the cultivation of the spirit? During the Stamp Act crisis, the Friends who opposed the tax on constitutional grounds could still agree with the apolitical purists in the church that the proper conduct was to "stand still and be quiet" during the "violent ferment" of the period. Quaker merchants prominently supported nonimportation as a means of resisting the Townshend duties in 1769 because this tactic was a passive and nonviolent form of resistance. When enforcement of the boycott fell into the hands of extralegal committees and uproarious public meetings, however, the Philadelphia Yearly Meeting warned that even the most peaceable participation in nonimportation brought Quakers into the spell of "the subtle wiles and allurements of the adversary [the Devil], who is endeavouring to rend and divide by drawing the unwary into practices inconsistent with our holy profession." The phraseology "drawing the unwary" into improper political conduct implied, Richard Bauman notes, that the Quakers were still a people set apart from the sinful world, and it ignored the clear evidence that some Quakers had overtly engaged in pre-Revolutionary protest.[8]

When the passage of the Coercive Acts in 1774 brought on a new crisis in relations with the mother country, this split in the Quaker community became visible. Eleven prominent Philadelphia Quakers accepted invitations to join the Philadelphia Committee of Correspondence, which, in principle at least, sympathized with Boston's plight and condemned the Coercive Acts. By 1774, however, control of the church was entirely in the hands of new leaders who shunned all participation in politics and were firmly convinced that the Quakers could no longer pretend to exercise a moderating influence on the conduct of non-Quaker political leaders. After spending "a considerable time" discussing "the fluctuating state of people's minds under the situation of public affairs," the Philadelphia Meeting of Sufferings, on June 16, 1774, concluded that "it would be safest and most consistent for us as a religious society to keep as much as possible from mixing with the people in their human policy and contrivance and to forbear meeting in their public consultations, as snares and danger may arise from meetings of that kind, however well-disposed particulars may be to mitigate and soften the violent disposition."[9]

There was a faintly sanctimonious tone in these official Quaker pronouncements of pacifism and neutrality during the pre-Revolutionary crisis of 1774 and 1775 that would have simply been irritating had this stance not been based on profound commitment to nonviolence and if the Friends had not been sincerely struggling to find a way to participate in their society without losing the capacity to make moral judgments and abstain from evil social practices. Moses Brown, Quaker merchant of Providence, Rhode Island, bore witness to these same beliefs in a more appealing and less strident fashion. A member of the old and wealthy Rhode Island merchant family, Moses was converted to Quakerism in 1773, at the age of thirty-four, after five years of depression and deepening introspection. Illness had triggered this "journey through the wilderness," and the death of his wife brought it to a final crisis. Already a successful and hard-driving partner in the firm of Nicholas Brown and Company and an astute and public-spirited politician, Moses now turned his energies to the pursuit of Quaker goals, in particular the unsuccessful but skillfully conducted campaign to outlaw the slave trade in Rhode Island in 1774.[10]

Two overlapping but contrasting obligations bore down upon Moses Brown as he attempted to cope with the pre-Revolutionary crisis in 1775. In the first place, he felt a duty to preserve the unity of the Quaker community by following the example of John and Israel Pemberton in Pennsylvania, who exhibited not the slightest sympathy for the colonial cause lest they appear unneutral. Accordingly, he publicly urged Rhode Island to seek "accommodation of the unhappy differences subsisting between the two countries." However, it was the arrest of his brother John Brown and the seizure of John's ship in Newport harbor by a British naval officer, Captain James Wallace, in April, that gave Moses a more specific reason for advocating reconciliation. He persuaded Rhode Island leaders to refrain from hostile actions against the British until he could negotiate his brother's freedom. Journeying to Boston, where John was being held, Moses worked out an agreement with General Thomas Gage for his brother's release and the return of his ship; in the bargain the brothers jointly pledged that John Brown would ask the Rhode Island Assembly to support a negotiated settlement of colonial differences with Britain. John made the required speech to the Assembly, but the legislators rejected his advice; and when Captain Wallace seized another one of his ships John Brown considered his obligation to his former captors ended and again became a leading organizer of resistance in Rhode Island.

Moses Brown played the roles of ostentatious pacifist and opportunistic organizer of his brother's rescue with some distaste. "My religious principles, thou art, I presume, sensible," he explained to James Warren, prominent Massachusetts patriot, "does not admit of my interfering in war, but my love for my country and sense of our just rights is not thereby abated"; his prominent opposition to the Stamp Act and Townshend duties, he wanted to make clear, had not "abated" simply because of his conversion to Quakerism.[11] "I am [conscious] of having as great a regard for my country's rights, liberty, [and] happiness as the most sanguine Whig," he declared in a plea to his brother to remain neutral and adhere to the spirit of their agreement with Gage. "I am clear of having entered into any engagements but such as, if pursued by all, would . . . effect the happiness of both countries." It was not easy, he told John, to endure "the torrents of censure so prevalent against . . . moderate men that don't run with the tide." The demands of conscience were, however, infinitely stronger than his concern for his reputation: "Were I to go to work to please these people, I must do things worse than anything charged on me . . . to the loss of a quiet and peaceful mind."[12]

15

Conclusion: The Uses of Reason in Political Upheaval

THE search for accommodation reflected the ordeal of men who wanted to find practical ways of reconciling colonial liberty with the maintenance of British authority. As events swept past them, they tried to adjust their thinking to rapidly changing conditions and gauge the dynamics of the imperial controversy in order to find standards of analysis and conduct that they and their fellow men could use in a dispute in which both sides seemed to be wrong, misguided, or lost.[1]

The threatening polarization of British policy and colonial response provoked and fueled the search for accommodation. "Affairs are now brought to a crisis," wrote Edward Burd, of Pennsylvania, in July 1774, in a typical discovery of this fact. "The Parliament of Great Britain claim and have endeavored to enforce the right of taxing America," while the colonists deny "that such a right exists and [are] determined to oppose the execution of it to blood. If they both persist in a determined resolution of this kind, wretched will be the situation of us both." Repeatedly these diagnoses of British and colonial folly sprang from the sense of helplessness and foreboding each man felt. The entire range of advantages that accrued to the colonists from their "connection with Great Britain," including the British legal and religious heritage, a supply of British products, the protection of the fleet and army, and the role of the Crown as mediator of colonial disputes, had "sheltered" the colonies from the "machinations of all the powers of Europe," declared another Pennsylvanian; "no wonder, therefore, we look forward with horror to those convulsions which must attend ([for] ages hence) our separation from that country." But it was equally unthinkable, the writer continued, to acquiesce further to British directives. The colonists had to find a way to weather "the storms of British vengeance and tyranny." Britain's insistence on its power to tax the colonists, wrote Richard Wells, in June 1774, was "so unjust, so unnatural, and absurd that . . . every American . . . must unite in opposing it," but "to oppose force to force is what the heart of every American must revolt at." The real danger was that "the base profligacy of a ministry abandoned to every principle of virtue and raging for despotism" would "tempt" the colonists and British brothers "to sheave the sword into each other's bowels." There must be, Wells pleaded, "surer, safer ways to end the controversy." The alternatives of submission and rebellion repeatedly provoked an unstable mixture of urgent alarm and bewilderment. "What are we to do! Tamely to give up our rights and suffer to be taxed at the will of persons at such a distance . . . is to consent to be slaves. . . . How dreadful the thought of a contest with the parent country," the Reverend Andrew Eliot sadly declared. A considerable feat of imagination was needed to conceive of a resolution of the imperial impasse that would escape the twin evils of submission and bloody conflict. "May the cloud which hangs over Great Britain and the colonies," declared the proposer of a toast at a Philadelphia banquet for Congressional delegates, in September 1774, "burst *only* on the heads of the present ministry." Few sober men thought the explosion could be so neatly deflected.[2]

The looming poles of submission and rebellion raised discomforting questions about the mentality of the British ministry and the colonists' capacity to respond intelligently to hostile British policies. "I am not a malcontent," declared Eliot, "but . . . I see nothing but little, mean, sinister views in those who have direction of your public affairs." Their stubborn legalistic view of the colonies, Eliot feared, would only ignite the passions of volatile men, whose rash actions, in turn, would provoke even harsher British reactions. "There are men with you and men with us," he shuddered, "who regard no consequence if they can gratify their passions." Lenient, mild, healing measures alone, he stressed, would disarm the rash and impetuous. As the controversy moved toward its conclusion, the men of accommodation increasingly realized that only colonial exertion could guide British policy back into reasonable channels. Americans must avoid "abject servility" and "unbecoming petulancy" in order to disarm hostile British intentions, advised a Philadelphian in January 1775. "We must have the strictest guard on our passions," urged Richard Wells, in order to keep the initiative and respond to British provocations with calm deliberation. Governor Tryon, of New York, understood the moderate dilemma. "The American friends of government," he explained in August 1775, "consider themselves between Scylla and Charybdis, that is the head of Parliamentary taxation and the tyranny of their present [Revolutionary] masters; would the first principle be put out of the way, his Majesty would probably see America put on a less determined complexion."[3]

The search for a viable alternative to the awful choice between submission and Revolutionary tyranny began with an evaluation of the location and function of reason in politics. For the rationalist clergy of New England, reason meant many things: it was the opposite of evangelical enthusiasm and pietistic fervor; it motivated restraint and self-discipline and thereby encouraged the spread and practice of true religion; most important, reason taught the rationalist clergy that men were not fundamentally sinful in their nature. Elements of this intellectual position permeated widely the search for accommodation in the pre-Revolutionary debate.

The strongest imperative behind this search for reason was the need to locate and localize the human evil manifested by British policy and colonial disobedience. Both the colonies and mother country were victims of "the grand enemy of mankind," who uses "every opportunity to raise up heats and animosities, to stir up depraved passions . . . to do his destructive work. . . . The heads and rulers of societies are men of like passions and infirmities with their subjects." Above all, the rationalist clergy stressed, evil circulated through society and tempted men, rather than springing internally from their very natures. George III was therefore "a prince, whose goodness of soul and unsuspecting heart, unfortunately for his people, have unwarily betrayed him into the ensnaring measures of designing men." On this assumption that rulers were good men and subject to external temptation the rationalist search for accommodation built its case for restraint and prudence. Rulers, the Reverend John Tucker declared, had the same interests in the welfare of the community as the people; "they are both parts of the same body, their true interests are interwoven, and their happiness inseparable." This mutuality of interest made resistance to tyranny a formalized and restricted activity. The people had a right and a duty to oppose tyranny, the Reverend Gad Hitchcock announced in 1774, but only as a means of appealing to the ruler's prudence and good sense. Given the opportunity of responding to the protests of the community, any ruler would prefer to base his power on "the surest foundation," the esteem and respect of the people. Self-interest alone assured the success of remonstrance. By institutionalizing resistance in this way and making it a means of communication with the ruler, the rationalists acted on their assumption that men were basically good and reasonable.[4]

An additional justification for applying reason to the imperial controversy was the need for a workable program of action. Only positive, identifiable deeds could break down the polarization of political hostility and stem the rising tide of blind emotion. "Such is the violence of our disputing parties, that whoever differs from either is immediately stigmatized as a *Whig* or a *Tory*," both "terms of disgrace," a Massachusetts "Moderate Man" announced. "To moderate these party heats, to draw that zeal into a channel where it would really be serviceable, is the duty of every member of the community." This channeling of human energy, Eliot believed, required the utmost discrimination. "Perhaps," he suggested, "it might be as well not to dispute in such strong terms the legal right of Parliament. This is a point that cannot easily be settled, and had therefore best be touched very gently." There were other ways of exerting political muscle, Jeremy Belknap agreed. Britain could not understand that "force could not generate submission," nor could the colonists sense that "resistance could not enervate force." Neither could respect the other's "strengths and resources" because each side perceived only the other's weaknesses and folly. The task of reasonable men was to find an alternative strategy that did not pit British force against colonial recalcitrance. Paine Wingate, of New Hampshire, wanted the colonists to "press on" in the controversy with Britain but to use "healing" measures as a means of securing "the restoration of our invaded rights." Nonimportation, he suggested, would enable Britain to estimate the annual value of colonial trade to the mother country; the colonies should seize the initiative by making an estimate of their own and then proposing it as the basis for computing a voluntary colonial contribution toward the cost of running the Empire. Any conciliatory gesture, Wingate felt, would delay the impending collision. "Time," he assured, "performs miracles. If we could only while away the time" for as much as a year, circumstances might change and new possibilities arise. "If we would not be so needlessly irritating" to the British, "I doubt not our deliverance will come."[5]

No matter how concrete and forceful, programs for securing accommodation crumbled in the face of growing intransigence on both sides and were reduced to pleas for time and the arrival of unforeseen good fortune. "Does not that man deserve to be heard with candour," asked "A Philadelphian," "who desires not to counteract the general sentiments of his countrymen, but thinks it a duty . . . to guard against an evil which may . . . destroy the hope of every virtuous patriot . . ., [for] lasting and happy union . . . between the mother country and her colonies?" Nathaniel Peaslee Sargeant, of Haverhill, Massachusetts, wanted the colonists to turn Lord North's peace proposal of 1775 to their own advantage by accepting it as a basis for negotiation. North had proposed repeal of tea duties if the colonies would agree to a perpetual contribution to the British Treasury. Sargeant eagerly examined the possible colonial responses to this proposal. By praising it, the colonists could make North a political hero in England and give him a freer hand to pursue reconciliation. If they rejected the plan, North would be able to point to the "apparent fairness" of the proposals as a means of uniting British opinion against the Americans. A still more delicate maneuver, Sargeant envisioned, would be an offer to contribute to the British a sum slightly less than the cost of colonial defense rather than a vague proposal to pay some undesignated amount in lieu of taxes. Such a shrewd tactic would serve to "embarrass him in his policy with safety to ourselves." The essential aim, Sargeant explained, was to make Lord North appear to extract concessions from America, while in fact the colonies were giving up very little and gaining, in the bargain, a perpetual exemption from Parliamentary taxation. But to humiliate him by wrecking his peace initiative would, in actuality, free North to coerce the colonists. "He, as a politician, ought to keep his arm extended over us. The honor of government likewise requires . . . that it might appear . . . they compelled us to take their terms. I think he clearly proves in his *speech* that a people may with dignity recede from some of their claims. . . . If we don't get all we asked for *before,* won't such an accommodation secure to us something worth all our trouble and expense?"[6]

For all its ingenuity, the search for accommodation failed to find a way of utilizing reason to solve the pre-Revolutionary crisis; but as the advocates of accommodation wrestled with this problem they sought for a secure point of departure in their thinking: an ultimate source of moral and political authority. They found this source of authority by locating the central elements of their anxiety. "The Americans are no idiots," J. J. Zubly wrote in a public appeal to Lord Dartmouth. "Oppression will make wise men mad, but oppressors in the end frequently find they are not wise men; *there may be resources even in despair* sufficient to render any set of men strong enough" to resist tyranny. The ominous prospect that "we must either submit to *slavery* or defend our liberties by our own sword," the Reverend Simeon Howard complained, was all the more painful because "everything belonging to the present state [of affairs] is uncertain and fluctuating." For the Reverend David Hall, Congregationalist clergyman, "the disputes between the nation and her colonies" made the early 1770's "an evil, dark, and doubtful day," not because colonial liberty was in jeopardy but because God was displeased with his people. Andrew Eliot could only pray that, "amidst all the fears, dangers, and anxieties" of "the present troubles," he would grow more deeply committed to serving his "heavenly Father."[7]

A sense of humility and skepticism about the righteousness of political judgments, the advocates of accommodation believed, was the first obligation of men facing difficult political decisions. "We would fain obey our superiors, yet we cannot think of giving up our . . . rights," declared J. J. Zubly in a now familiar reiteration of the apparent alternatives available in 1775. "We would express duty, respect, and obedience to the king as supreme, and yet we wish not to strengthen the hands of tyranny nor call oppression lawful." In this "delicate situation," Zubly asserted, coming to the crux of the problem, men should heed the scriptural injunction " 'so speak ye, and so do, as they that shall be judged by the law of liberty.' " That liberty was the freedom given to believers to act as moral men, not in fear of punishment or under coercion from other men but, rather, in the confidence that God alone, on the day of judgment, would weigh the deeds of men and in the meantime guide but not dictate how they should behave. This expectation of final judgment should "make us act with prudence, justice, and moderation." The Christian law of liberty, Zubly explained, meant that conscience alone governed men in dealings with their political rulers; it forbade men from giving unquestioning obedience to their government; it condemned arbitrary uses of governmental power; it assured rulers and ruled alike that God would ultimately judge their actions and intentions. Because the purpose of Christianity was to "regulate our desires and restrain our passions" by teaching men humility, the most valuable benefit derived from the law of liberty was the extraordinary self-consciousness it implanted in men. God will not judge a man from "external appearance" or even by his "own opinion of himself" but, rather, "by his inward reality . . . ; God judges men according to their invisible spring," their innermost instincts and desires. "Let me entreat you, gentlemen," Zubly implored the Georgia Assembly in early 1775, "think coolly and act deliberately; rash counsels are seldom good ones. Ministerial rashness and American rashness can only be productive of untoward compounds. . . . Let neither the frowns of tyranny nor the pleasure of popularity sway you from what you clearly apprehend just and right. . . . Endeavour to act like freemen, like loyal subjects, like real Christians, and you will '. . . be judged by the law of liberty.' Act conscientiously, and with a view to God, then commit your ways to God, leave the event with God, and you will have great reason to hope that the event will be just, honourable, and happy."[8]

That hope, Zubly knew, was a slender one. But it was also the only possible one men could properly embrace. "Never let us lose

. . . sight that our interest lies in a perpetual connection with our mother country," he told the Georgia Assembly in the spring of 1775; rather, "let us convince our enemies that the struggles of America have not their rise in a desire of independency, . . . that to the wish of a perpetual connection" we add only "that we may be virtuous and free." By the time he had prepared the sermon for publication in September 1775, he noted, "a British ministry . . . [had] wasted British blood and treasure to alienate America and Great Britain; the breach is growing wider and wider." The only moral he could draw was the urgent need to find some grounds for reconciliation. The quest for accommodation had to seek continually for finer distinctions between the righteous defense of liberty and immoral recklessness. Simeon Howard constructed a lengthy catalogue of tests to distinguish between the two kinds of resistance. Any governmental action that made men timid and complacent was oppressive and required vigorous and outspoken denunciation. The happiness of future generations was the responsibility of the living. Men could recognize in themselves the quality of "truest fortitude" when their political conduct merited "the favor of God" by its discipline, vitality, and concern for the good of the community. Candor, sincerity, and idealism distinguished good from evil in political struggles. *"Designedly* to spread false alarms, to fill the minds of people with groundless prejudices against their rulers, . . . to stir up faction and encourage opposition to *good* government are things highly criminal," Howard concluded; "but to show people their real danger, point out the source of it, and exhort them to such exertions as are necessary to avoid it are acts of benevolence." With this kind of aesthetic judgment about the ugliness of selfish political ambition and the beauty of controlled protest by the whole community, the rationalist clergy pronounced the duty of Christian men in the last stages of the pre-Revolutionary controversy.[9]

In the final analysis, the quest for accommodation reflected a peculiar perception of the function of politics in American society. Acts of organized resistance and protest against British policy and authority, these men believed, varied widely in propriety and legitimacy; invariably, however, resistance was closely related to some form of political enthusiasm, rivalry, or maneuver. "Our own provincial politics," New York moderate John Jones wrote to James Duane in December 1775, is "a subject . . . I never troubled my head with, till it was connected with the general interests of America in the present unhappy and deplorable contest." The practice of his friends in the Livingston faction of distributing militia posts only to their own political supporters almost turned Jones speechless with "honest rage" provoked by "Whig and Tory" alike. "Would to heaven," he exclaimed, "I could throw a veil over this nakedness of my countrymen." For many colonists, the pre-Revolutionary debate thrust politics into their experience for the first time and upset the equilibrium of their values. An obscure New Englander named Gill "contemplated the scenes of oppressions, hardships, and miseries" caused by the "struggles of many with the rod of arbitrary power." The whole enterprise seemed to him misguided because of the "ignorance of multitudes" and their lack of a "clear gospel vision." Political alignments of all kinds, he lamented, channeled "the pride, the extreme selfishness, the narrowness, and bigotry of the human heart"; these, he explained, "are the sources of my apprehension." The intensity of pre-Revolutionary protest disturbed him most because it substituted "a fiery zeal and a cold charity" for the example of "the meek and lowly Jesus." Gill felt torn by this "apprehension" because he respected "the cause," which some call "liberty" and others decry as "anarchy or rebellion or faction." The colonists, he conceded, had a duty to preserve their rights against the "ravages of tyranny," but he was still disturbed by "unwarrantable measures" and "low means" used in that defense of liberty. On balance, he concluded, only a "fool" would expect "large bodies of men (as are at this day engaged in the controversy)" to make only "wise speeches, wise determinations, and wise actions." "Errors of judgment" and "imprudence of conduct" were inevitable, if lamentable, and brought the whole cause of liberty into disrepute. If Gill's ambivalence makes his openness and candor difficult to recognize, it also underlines the dilemma: "I can live on as friendly terms with an Episcopalian as a Congregationalist; a Tory (as they're called) as a Whig; a disciple of . . . Arminius as of Calvin. Yet in my heart I am inclined to the doctrines of Calvin, the principles of true Whigism, and the model of the Congregational Churches."[10]

"True Whigism"! The term implied a conscious intellectual and emotional effort to return to a pure source of political values and to refurbish a once proud historical orthodoxy. "I am a Whig of the old stamp," William Smith, Jr., said at a Christmas Day dinner in 1777 during a discussion of the virtues and hazards of republican government; "no roundhead," he explained, referring to Puritan insurgents in the English Civil War, but rather more like "one of King William's Whigs, for liberty and the constitution."[11] When the advocates of accommodation appealed to the English Whig tradition of liberty and constitutional government they were striving to occupy a position of detachment from which they could study the prevailing tumult. William Samuel Johnson, of Connecticut, had struggled to maintain just such a balance between his commitment to colonial liberty and his preference for order and civility. As a member of the Stamp Act Congress in 1765 he had drafted the key document that labeled all Parliamentary taxation—both internal taxes like the Stamp Act and external revenue-producing duties on trade—denials of the "reasonable measure of civil liberty" belonging to the colonists as "freemen and British subjects." Accordingly, he strongly opposed the Townshend duties. "The principle on which they are founded, alone, is worth contesting," he declared, because "a tax of a penny is equally a tax as one of a pound; if they have a constitutional right to impose the first they may the last." He served as Connecticut's colonial agent in London from 1766 to 1771 and during that period became increasingly adamant in his insistence that even token Parliamentary taxation would destroy colonial liberty. Johnson could not move from that position to the slightly more advanced one of advocating resistance against British encroachments. A devout Anglican, he was the son of the Reverend Samuel Johnson, President of King's College in New York City and the most prominent colonial Anglican clergyman until his death in 1772. But more than filial obedience constrained him. "The ill-advised measures that have been taken with respect to the colonies have weakened the connection between the two countries but have not yet broken it;

a little wisdom and a little shrewdness might yet set all right again," he wrote, expressing his deep yearning for a peaceful resolution of the conflict between British authority and colonial rights. Johnson had no illusions. "In every light the prospect is melancholy," he wrote in July 1774. "Will no hand be stretched forth to prevent these two countries, perhaps the finest in the universe, from . . . injuring each other?" Despite his close connections with the leaders of the pre-Revolutionary movement in Connecticut, Johnson withdrew into isolation in 1775 and, like Daniel Dulany, became a neutral because he was "convinced that I could not join in war against England and much less . . . against my own country."[12]

Carl Becker noted a similar "preciseness, . . . awareness of small matters, . . . [and] rigidity" in the personality of another of these introspective accommodating loyalists, Peter Van Schaack, "that made it [difficult] for him to associate with others in a common cause." As late as the spring of 1774, Van Schaack, a New York lawyer, believed that the colonies should prepare for war with Britain unless Parliament renounced any right to tax America. Only dire consequences, he predicted, would "compel" the British to alter their colonial policy. By early 1775, however, the colonists were not simply defending their rights; rather, they had recklessly accused the British of "a design of subverting the constitution and enslaving America." British violations of colonial liberty were still a serious matter, he believed, but did not yet amount to systematic tyranny. Colonial resistance, on the other hand, had taken on an ominous quality: "The present situation of affairs—committees, remonstrances, addresses to the people, pretending dangers of impending slavery . . . —cannot fail to remind us of those unhappy times which blackened the annals of English history [referring to the English Civil War of the 1640's]. May God avert similar calamities."[13] Retiring to his country home at Kinderhook in January 1776, Van Schaack read and reread John Locke's *Two Treatises on Government* and wrote this private statement of political conscience. Dealing firmly and deliberately with many of the conflicting truths and values sensed by the advocates of accommodation, it deserves to be quoted here at length:

The only foundation of all legitimate governments is certainly a compact between the rulers and the people, containing mutual conditions, and equally obligatory on both the contracting parties. No question can therefore exist, at this enlightened day, about the lawfulness of resistance, in cases of gross and palpable infractions on the part of the governing power. It is impossible, however, clearly to ascertain every case which shall effect a dissolution of this contract; for these, though always tacitly implied, are never expressly declared, in any form of government.

As a man is bound by the sacred ties of conscience, to yield obedience to every act of the legislature so long as the government exists, so, on the other hand, he owes it to the cause of liberty, to resist the invasion of those rights, which, being inherent and inalienable, could not be surrendered at the institution of the civil society of which he is a member. In times of civil commotions, therefore, an investigation of those rights, which will necessarily infer an inquiry into the nature of government, becomes the indispensable duty of every man. . . .

Our reasonings must resolve into one or the other of the following three grounds, and our right of resistance must be founded upon either the first or third of them; for either, first, we owe no obedience to any acts of Parliament; or, secondly, we are bound by all acts to which British subjects in Great Britain would, if passed with respect to them, owe obedience; or, thirdly, we are subordinate in a certain degree, or, in other words, certain acts may be valid in Britain which are not so here.

Upon the first point I am exceedingly clear in my mind, for I consider the Colonies as members of the British empire, and subordinate to the Parliament. But, with regard to the second and third, I am not so clear. The necessity of a supreme power in every state strikes me very forcibly; at the same time, I foresee the destructive consequences of a right in Parliament to bind us in all cases whatsoever. To obviate the ill effects of either extreme, some middle way should be found out, by which the benefits to the empire should be secured arising from the doctrine of a supreme power, while the abuses of that power to the prejudice of the colonists should be guarded against; and this, I hope, will be the happy effect of the present struggle. . . . I cannot see any principle of regard for my country which will authorize me in taking up arms, as absolute *dependence* and *independence* are two extremes which I would avoid; for, should we succeed in the latter, we shall still be in a sea of uncertainty, and have to fight among ourselves for that constitution we aim at.

There are many very weighty reasons besides the above to restrain a man from taking up arms, but some of them are of too delicate a nature to be put upon paper; however, it may be proper to mention what does *not* restrain *me.* It is not from apprehension of the consequences should America be subdued, or the hopes of any favor from government, both which I disclaim; nor is it from any disparagement of the cause my countrymen are engaged in, or a desire of obstructing the present measures. . . . It is a question of morality and religion in which a man cannot conscientiously take an active part without being convinced in his own mind of the justice of the cause; . . . whatever disagreeable consequences may follow from dissenting from the general voice, yet I cannot but remember that I am to render an account of my conduct before a more awful tribunal, where no man can be justified who stands accused by his own conscience of taking part in measures which, through the distress and bloodshed of his fellow-creatures, may precipitate his country into ruin.[14]

III

The Appeal to Doctrine

16

Samuel Peters and the Social Origins of Tory Doctrine

ON August 29, 1774, the Reverend Samuel Peters rose in the Hebron, Connecticut town meeting to oppose a motion branding the Boston Port Act "unconstitutional, oppressive, and tyrannical."[1] Hebron lay just east of the Connecticut River Valley in a region as staunchly Congregationalist, self-governing, and hostile to British authority as any part of New England, and Peters had never disguised his opinion that eastern Connecticut society verged on anarchy. Yet Peters proved a wily antagonist for the Sons of Liberty, who were busily promoting the campaign in Connecticut against the Coercive Acts. Peters demanded that copies of the Boston Port Act and the Magna Carta be read to the meeting before a vote was taken "to inform us what is constitutional and what is not." Caught off guard, the Sons of Liberty moved their next proposal, that Hebron contribute to the relief of poor people in Boston. Again Peters rose to speak. A person, he insisted, should neither "be marked as a Tory nor liable to tar and feathers" simply because he refused to "give to [the] Boston poor." "Should this town vote to give to the poor of Boston the very record will be an everlasting proof against us that we are rebels to the law of the kingdom." Boston fully deserved "the rod for their riotous conduct." Hebron would incur grave risks if the town should "meddle" in "other men's matters. . . . We may with as much propriety," he thundered, "vote convicts free." The meeting adjourned without reaching a decision.

Five days later, on Sunday morning, September 4, rumors reached Hebron that fighting had broken out in Boston, that General Gage was slaughtering old men and babies. "To arms, to

191

arms," the messenger shouted outside the church. Peters at once tried to calm his stunned parishioners: "Keep your seats. The report is not true. General Gage is a good man who would not hurt old men and babes nor fire on the town of Boston." Even if bloodshed has occurred, "you must not take up arms against General Gage. It is high treason to levy war against him." Peters's admonitions subdued the town's Anglicans, but a large body of other men—"Puritans (alias) Sons of Liberty," he called them—"set off for Boston," carrying their guns and "cursing General Gage, King George 3rd, Lord North" and Anglican clergy and hierarchy "who teach nonresistance." The next day, when they returned, having discovered that the rumors of fighting in Boston were false, a crowd of several hundred armed men from neighboring towns converged on Peters's house. Exactly what happened next is unclear. There was "a violent affray,"[2] probably consisting of pushing, shoving, and angry verbal exchanges, that forced Peters to leave his house and comply with the crowd's wishes. Trying to get control of the situation, an impromptu committee drew up charges against Peters and read them to him when he came out to face the crowd. The indictment charged him with writing articles for the New London newspaper that contained "a doctrine destructive to the liberties of America," using his influence in the Hebron town meeting to thwart resolutions supporting the people of Boston, and, finally, telling people on the previous Sunday that it was treason to take up arms against General Gage, that Gage was a good man— sentiments "contrary to the general opinion" and "inimical to our liberties both civil and religious." Peters readily admitted doing all these things. Satisfied with this admission, the committee told Peters that he had "sufficiently cleared himself," but the crowd demanded abject submission. Shouting that Peters was "a Tory rebel, a Roman Catholic, a tool of tyranny" who should be hanged in effigy at "the liberty pole and tarred and feathered," they forced him to ride to the village green and there sign an outrageous statement affirming that George III had "forfeited his Kingdom," that North, Gage, and the Anglican bishops were "tyrants," and that in America "only the voice of the people" could limit men's liberty. "The voice of the people" had an unforgettably ugly sound to Peters as he stood in the middle of the Hebron town common that September day in 1774, for as the proceeding ended the cries of the crowd mounted: "Liberty. Destroy the badge of Babylon, those rags of popery—damnation to the church—the King is a fool and a Roman devil." "You have done enough," Peters shouted back; "you have forfeited your lives and property to the laws of God and man." "Damn your soul," shouted back a Mr. Payne, a neighbor of Governor Jonathan Trumbull; "your patience is founded on hopes of getting redress for these things, but you will get none, for the Governor told us, this day, to come and give it to you. So he will not help you." A few days later Peters slipped out of Hebron, eluded the surveillance of the Sons of Liberty, who intended to harass him, and traveled to Boston to seek the protection of the British Army.[3]

The raw tempers exhibited in Hebron's confrontation with Samuel Peters exposed a serious cleavage in Connecticut's homogeneous social order. In the strongly Congregationalist colony, the Church of England had grown steadily during the eighteenth century. Almost nonexistent before 1700, its original brave members, during the first two decades of the century, were subject to heavy fines and even imprisonment for refusing to pay taxes for the support of the established Congregationalist churches. The Anglicans made a break-through in 1722 when three brilliant young Congregationalist clergymen, Timothy Cutler, Rector of Yale College, Daniel Brown, a tutor at Yale, and Samuel Johnson, a former Yale tutor, renounced their denominational affiliation and journeyed to England to seek ordination in the Church of England. Supported by S.P.G. missionaries, the Anglicans established forty-five new churches in Connecticut between 1723 and 1770—all but one in towns with existing Congregationalist churches. Between 1701 and 1739 the number of confirmed Anglicans in the colony rose from 150 to more than 2,000.

Legal discrimination receded but never disappeared. In 1727 the Assembly allowed towns with resident Anglican clergymen to turn church-support taxes paid by Anglicans over to the support of their own church, but in towns with no resident clergyman Anglicans continued to pay taxes for the support of the Congregationalist meeting. The Great Awakening in Connecticut gave the Anglican church a fresh mission. Its clergy resolutely opposed the tide of ecstatic religious experience. As every town split into

New Light and Old Light Congregationalist factions, which quarreled furiously about the nature of conversion and forms of worship, the Church of England provided an attractive alternative to "peaceable souls" who admired the dignity of its liturgy and the internal harmony produced by its hierarchical polity and administration. By exploiting the schism within Congregationalism, Anglicans aroused intensified hostility from both factions of the dominant church. Old Lights resented the Anglicans' ability to attract theologically rationalist and conservative members, while the New Lights detested Anglicanism's Arminian theology and apparent trappings of Catholicism. The one vital issue on which Old and New Lights could agree was their opposition to the establishment of Anglican bishops in America. As the Revolution approached, Anglican clergy who defended British authority bore the brunt of popular fury. In this charter colony there were almost no royal officials to hate; moreover, the Old Light faction in Connecticut politics, which mildly favored obedience to British measures, fell from power in 1765, a casualty of the Stamp Act crisis. The New Light leaders who led the colony into the Revolution also governed it for a decade before independence. And so it was that Anglican clergymen became scapegoats for popular mobs in 1774 and 1775.[4]

None of these tangible grounds for conflict, however, fully explained the ferocious animosity that came to the surface in confrontations between Anglicans and their critics in Connecticut. For all its boast of being a "land of steady habits," Connecticut went through a painful transformation during the first half of the eighteenth century. Throughout the seventeenth century the colony's leaders had created and sustained a tightly knit social order. Men were to obey and respect their superiors; the leaders of society were to merit their position by public-spirited dedication; the material greed of individuals was never to be allowed to supersede the good of the whole community, but work, enterprise, and the advancement of one's family were to provide a legitimate channel for human energy and desire. Every sanction of religion, law, and tradition supported that public philosophy. Between 1700 and 1750 this vital credo became slightly anachronistic. Burgeoning population growth—from 30,000 in 1701 to 130,000 in 1756—made Connecticut one of the most densely populated colonies in America. With more people came such bountiful economic opportunity that the small, exclusive economic and political elite inherited from the previous century was overwhelmed by a new breed of talented, intensely competitive, successful leaders. The Great Awakening released the pent-up conflicts between tradition and change in Connecticut. The revival taught men that acquisitiveness was not a sin and that men who rapturously embraced conversion could in the process also enjoy material success.[5]

The triumph of this individualistic, emotional, and volatile collective style in Connecticut was not complete or entirely satisfying to anyone. As thoughtful men looked at their society in the 1760's—at its partisan division between New and Old Light factions, its fragmented religious and political leadership, its ambiguous relationship to the British Empire—they searched for the means to make it whole and seamless once more. The Old Lights in the 1760's wanted provincial government to become more responsive to the economic needs of the people and thereby to give men a stronger rational reason to obey and respect authority. The New Lights rejected this appeal to rational self-interest and declared that nothing less than a complete experience of repentance and new spiritual life would enable men to rectify the flaws in government and society. The Connecticut Anglican clergy, likewise, joined in this search for a new social order. Yearning ideally for the appointment of American bishops and the replacement of Connecticut's charter government with a royal administration, and, at the very least, urging parishioners to obey hated British laws like the Stamp Act, the Anglican clergy argued that royal and Anglican authority could provide the healing, disinterested, benevolent leadership that Connecticut badly needed. "All three of these proposals—the Anglican, the New Divinity, and the rationalist—retained to a large degree the spirit of the older [seventeenth-century] conception of the social order," Richard L. Bushman explains. "The purpose of all three was to keep peace and order in society and to restrain human wilfulness." The three groups of religious leaders shared a common anxiety about the maintenance of social order and the difficulty of inculcating and rewarding virtuous public conduct. The extreme antipathy between Anglicans and their detractors existed, in part, because both sides shared a desire to see Connecticut fulfill its apparent potential and become a land of pious, harmonious, and prosperous towns.[6] The idealistic opponents of the pre-Revolutionary movement—those who saw only outrage and blasphemy in colonial assertions of right and threats of resistance—were not simple-minded reactionaries. They shared a vision of what American society might become once rancor, contention, incoherent social arrangements, and ambiguity concerning the location of authority were expunged. Admirers of reason, harmony, and order, the doctrinaire Tories felt a mission to become educators and intellectual systematizers. In this sense they were an integral part and product of the flourishing intellectual life of the eighteenth century.

17

Formal Thought in
Late Colonial Culture

THE American Revolution not only ruptured the institutions and legal obligations of the Empire and transformed an already agitated political culture; the transformation of American society in the eighteenth century that culminated in the Revolution also raised serious philosophical questions about human existence, knowledge, and destiny.

Late colonial intellectual life was, of course, part of the Enlightenment—that eighteenth-century movement of Western thought which sought to liberate man from custom, superstition, and ignorance. The "Enlightenment" is a term frequently misused. It was not a monolithic orthodoxy of reason, progress, and human perfectability; nor was it consistently anticlerical, politically radical, or scientific; nor can it be neatly distinguished from the thought of the seventeenth century which preceded it or that of the nineteenth century which followed. Historians now define the Enlightenment as the work of a "band," or "family," of particular intellectuals throughout Europe and America who were aware of each other's work and felt a strong sense of kinship. Peter Gay has called them "a loose, informal, wholly unorganized coalition of cultural critics, religious skeptics, and political reformers," whose writings projected "a vastly ambitious program . . . of secularism, humanity, cosmopolitanism, and freedom . . . of moral man to make his way in the world."[1] Spanning three generations, the Enlightenment was rooted in Isaac Newton's discoveries in physics and John Locke's in psychology and gained momentum as men like Montesquieu and Voltaire undertook the vast reorganization of knowledge in the light of Locke and Newton; it reached a peak of excitement in the middle of the eighteenth century, when thinkers like Diderot and Rousseau, in Gay's words, "fused the fashionable anticlericalism and scientific speculation of the first generation into a coherent world view"; finally, during the last quarter of the century, the writers of the Enlightenment—Burke, Hume, Adam Smith, and Goethe, among others—moved in many new directions, either building ambitious new philosophical systems, advocating particular social, economic, and political reforms, or anticipating the romanticism of the nineteenth century.[2] "Made up of as many fiercely independent virtuosos as it was," Leonard Krieger observes, "the movement was organized in no definite institution and subscribed to no universal doctrine, but it did develop a real if intangible supranational identity in which its members came to participate and which took on a life of its own."[3] In that spirit, Enlightenment writers appealed to ancient Greece and Rome for literary and aesthetic models. They reluctantly admired the philosophical and ethical achievements of medieval and Renaissance Christianity and as the eighteenth century progressed increasingly preferred to embrace deism. Most significantly, they perceived and proclaimed the arrival of a secular, rational, individualistic world that had been approaching since the Renaissance—a world of science and advancing scientific knowledge where intelligent men sought to apply reason and experience to the solution of human problems and the attainment of individual goals.

The literature of the Enlightenment was fashionable in the colonies. Most well-educated men claimed familiarity with Rousseau's social contract, Locke's political theory, Montesquieu's separation of powers, or Puffendorf's and Vattel's legal philosophy. Beneath this superficial veneer of popular discourse, the American reception of the Enlightenment was selective and eclectic. The most distinguished and original eighteenth-century intellectual activity in the colonies was scientific. At the very time that a fraternity of Swedish, Dutch, and English botanists were collaborating to develop a new system of plant classification, colonial botanists like Peter Collison, of Philadelphia, Cadwallader Colden, of New York, and Alexander Garden, of Charles Town, South Carolina, won international recognition for their work on American plants. Colonial physicians, some trained in Edinburgh or Leyden, brought the most advanced medical practices to America—notably, inoculation against smallpox. Benjamin Franklin's experiments in electricity were famous partly because Franklin was the great popularizer and organizer of scientific activity in the British colonies and a founder in 1768 of the American Philosophical Society for Promoting Useful Knowledge, which provided recognition and publicity to scientific activity. Next to science, legal thought absorbed the highest concentration of Enlightenment ideas. At a time when law supplanted the ministry as the prime professional route to community leadership, lawyers read widely in European legal and political theory, constitutional and political history, and formal philosophy in an effort to acquire authoritative knowledge to use in the courtroom. Enlightenment ideas enabled several of the more intelligent and speculative religious leaders to adapt worship and theology to new social conditions. Jonathan Edwards, as stated earlier, derived his original concept of conversion and regeneration from his understanding of Locke's psychology; among Anglicans, Samuel Johnson, the first President of King's College, attempted a grand synthesis of Anglican theology and secular academic knowledge. Finally, the most far-reaching colonial application of Enlightenment ideas was the attempt by leaders of the Revolution, especially James Madison and John Adams, to devise a science of politics—an integrated and systematic synthesis of all historical knowledge and philosophical insight concerning the sources and uses of political power.[4]

Enlightenment ideas did not in themselves effect direct changes in the outlook and thinking of colonial readers. Other elements of the social and political culture were also at work. The frustrations of trying to civilize and tame a harsh environment, the power of religious conviction, anxiety about slavery, white-Indian relations, and commonplace political controversies and economic activities helped determine colonial thought. The competition between these influences acted as a kind of filter through which only the most compelling and usable European Enlightenment ideas could pass. Amid this babble of ideas and theories, it was remarkable that any elements of Enlightenment thought survived. Part of the explanation lay in the fact that the mid-eighteenth century in America was an era of great candor, in which men took seriously their own public pronouncements as well as those of their adversaries. As a result of this interplay between formal ideas and less fully articulated attitudes—and also as a consequence of the high seriousness with which men approached intellectual discussion—several peculiar offshoots and ancillary branches of Enlightenment thought had extraordinary impact on educated American readers.

John Locke (1632–1704) was no offshoot figure in the Enlightenment; however, the immense popularity and reputation he enjoyed in the colonies and the central place that some of his ideas occupied in colonial thought separated his work from that of other European intellectuals and endowed his ideas with special meaning in America. Born into a modest though well-connected middle-class English family, he was educated at Christ Church, Oxford, where he studied medicine and read widely in philosophy, politics, and history. From 1666 to 1683 he served as secretary, physician, and adviser to Anthony Ashley Cooper, first Earl of Shaftesbury, the leader of a shadowy opposition to Charles II and, from 1679 to 1683, organizer of the abortive but masterfully directed movement to have Parliament exclude James, Duke of York, from succession to the throne. From Shaftesbury's household, Locke moved easily into service of the Whig magnates who overthrew James II in 1688 and summoned William and Mary to the throne. During the early stages of the Exclusion crisis, and in close collaboration with Shaftesbury, Locke wrote *Two Treatises on Government,* which declared that government was a compact between rulers and subjects and that men possessed a moral right to overthrow a ruler who arbitrarily deprived his subjects of their liberty. Published in 1690, Locke's *Two Treatises on Government* appeared to have been a clever after-the-fact justification of the Revolution of 1688. In reality, Locke composed them during the early stages of the Exclusion crisis, around 1680 and 1681. At a moment when political and religious liberty in England was in apparent jeopardy, Locke walked an excruciatingly narrow line between advocating treason and merely defending Parliamentary government and the existing social order. This circumstance alone may account for the qualities of elegance, delicacy, and boldness that characterize

Locke's *Two Treatises on Government.* Locke did not believe that man's reason and intellect made possible the compact between the ruler and his subjects. He shared the contemporary Calvinist fear of the irrationality and violence of the mass of the populace. "But," as John Dunn explains, "he understood his society well enough to know that the threat of anarchy came not from their determined and indomitable willfulness but from the destruction of the elementary security of their joyless lives. What really threatened the fabric of seventeenth-century English society was not the exuberant self-will of the consciously exploited but the sheer panic of the starving and helpless." For Locke, the frailty of human nature, the fact that men could learn only slowly through their senses, made necessary a compact theory of government that men could at least begin to understand and that, all the while, would protect them from bewildering and arbitrary deprivations of liberty.[5]

Deeply grounded in his work on the psychology of learning—which proclaimed that all knowledge is transmitted to the mind by the senses and which denied the existence of innate ideas—Locke's political theory was an important step in the gradual separation of political thought from theology that had been taking place ever since the late Middle Ages. However, the rise of the modern monarchy during the sixteenth and seventeenth centuries had created the need for a highly mystical and theological political theory of order and obedience that would buttress the claims of kings to the absolute obedience of their subjects. Sir Robert Filmer (158?–1653) had written the most elaborate rationale for this position by arguing that all creation was patriarchal: God, the Father of mankind, prescribed the authority of kings to rule the people at His behest, and kings upheld the authority of fathers to rule their children. Published posthumously in 1680, during the Exclusion controversy, Filmer's writings seemed to Locke a dangerous and reprehensible attempt to obliterate freedom and endow royal tyranny with theological sanction, all the more offensive to Locke, a devout Anglican. His *Two Treatises on Government* not only tried to demolish Filmer's argument favoring the divine right of kings; Locke's *Two Treatises* also wrestled with the intellectual problem that would dominate the next two centuries: the kind of autonomy men should enjoy in a secular and individualistic society. Locke declared that no man was born with any inherent right to control the life of another. While membership in a civil society imposed restraints on the freedom of each individual, those restraints were legitimate only if expressed in laws and could never be imposed at the whim of a particular ruler.[6]

American readers selected what they thought they needed from Locke, just as they did with the larger body of Enlightenment writing. A few colonial intellectuals—Jonathan Edwards, Cotton Mather, Samuel Johnson, for example—read his *Essay Concerning Human Understanding, Thoughts on Education,* and *The Reasonableness of Christianity* closely and in agreement or disagreement took seriously his ideas about the mind and knowledge. In contrast, numerous colonists who claimed to have read his *Two Treatises on Government* usually attributed to Locke what was also a commonplace tenet of New England Puritanism: that government rests on a social covenant between subject and magistrate; but they overlooked Locke's delicate and difficult criteria for determining whether the magistrate had broken a compact with his subjects. (The few colonists who struggled with Locke's distinctive ideas in the *Two Treatises*—notably Peter Van Schaack on the eve of independence—found it a sobering and humbling experience.) [7] By attacking Filmer and the philosophy of order and obedience so effectively, Locke extended the evil reputation of patriarchal political theory into the eighteenth century. In response to Locke, Charles Leslie, an early-eighteenth-century English theorist, resurrected Filmer's reactionary royalist position and perpetuated still further the class of patriarchal and compact theories. Replying to Bishop Benjamin Hoadly in 1711, Leslie sought to demolish in one "finishing stroke" the notion that liberty was a natural right of men: "The sum of the matter betwixt Mr. *Hoadly* and me is this. I think it most natural that *authority* should *descend* . . . from *superiour* to *inferiour,* from *God* to *fathers* and *kings* and from *kings* and *fathers* to *sons* and *servants.* But Mr. *Hoadly* would have it *ascend* from sons to fathers, from *subjects* to *sovereigns,* nay to *God* Himself. . . . The [natural rights] *argument* does naturally carry it all that way. For if *authority* does *ascend,* it must *ascend* to the *height.*"[8] When the doctrinaire American Tories echoed Filmer's and Leslie's ideas in 1774 and 1775 and intimated their yearning for an organic and authoritarian society, they touched a delicate nerve in the American consciousness.[9] Locke had long since shown that the compact theory of government offered security to the anxious while encouraging the more speculative citizen to criticize and rationally evaluate the performance of his rulers. By comparison, a philosophy of order and obedience seemed sterile, fearful, and pointless. By implanting that contrast so deeply in colonial thought, Locke exercised his most pointed influence on the ideology of the American Revolution.

Next to Locke's curious penetration into the colonists' intellectual awareness, the most concentrated transmission of Enlightenment ideas was a body of Scottish philosophy that flourished during the second and third quarters of the eighteenth century. Francis Hutcheson, Adam Ferguson, Thomas Reid, and others provided the colonists with a welcome method of theorizing, in concrete terms, about man, society, and human knowledge. These men have a peculiar relationship to the Enlightenment. Their abstract ideas about the mind refuted the radical empiricism of Scotland's most famous Enlightenment philosopher, David Hume—who, incidentally, enjoyed little popularity in America but exerted a powerful influence on the thinking of the few American readers, notably James Madison, patient and sophisticated enough to appreciate his complex ideas.[10] It is not altogether clear why Scotland and America came to have such an intellectual affinity in the pre-Revolutionary era. Newly growing trade with Glasgow and the University of Edinburgh's attraction for a few colonial students provided an impetus. More fundamentally, Bernard Bailyn and John Clive have suggested, Scotland and America were both England's "cultural provinces," feeling intellectually and aesthetically inferior to England and especially to London, and were both places where middle-class professional men hungry for distinction and recognition made up the intellectual leadership.[11] The pivotal figure in the Scottish renaissance of the mid-eighteenth century was Francis Hutcheson, an Irish Protestant who taught philosophy at Glasgow University from 1730 until his death in 1746 and emancipated a whole generation of Scottish students from the restricted outlook that then characterized the Presbyterian Church of Scotland. Hutcheson pioneered in the study of the functioning of the mind that a century and a half later took the name "psychology." Though he accepted and incorporated Locke's findings on sensory learning, Hutcheson pressed the inquiry forward into regions where most Enlightenment scholars did not want to venture. He concentrated on perception, the process by which the mind structures and arranges the sense impressions it receives. Hutcheson argued that during perception the mind activates certain moral intuitions of benevolence, sociability, and civic responsibility that are not unlike innate ideas. In this way Hutcheson came to hold an optimistic view of human nature—a view that permeated much of the European Enlightenment. But he gained this faith in man after a different intellectual pilgrimage than that of most Enlightenment thinkers: a peculiarly analytical exploration into the working of the mind. Through a complicated analysis of human "understanding," "will," and "disposition," Hutcheson and his followers reorganized human knowledge of man and society into a new discipline called "moral philosophy."[12] It was the integrated study of the contemporary disciplines of history, ethics, sociology, and psychology and the humanist implications of natural science and mathematics. A compelling program for educational reform, moral philosophy became the heart of American higher education from the 1750's until the mid-nineteenth century.[13] The most concrete utilization of Scottish moral philosophy in the politics of the American Revolution was Jefferson's reliance in drafting the Declaration of Independence on a new system of rhetoric and persuasion developed by a Scottish teacher, William Duncan. In Duncan's deductive argumentation, the major and minor premises both contained within themselves *self-evident* moral convictions that were designed simultaneously to activate the conscience and secure rational agreement. Jefferson's great preamble on the right of revolution, though based externally on Locke's contract theory, used Duncan's rhetorical devices in every phrase.[14]

American public philosophy on the eve of the Revolution was an eclectic mixture of assumptions: a vaguely Lockean notion about the contractual basis of government fortified by a Calvinist distrust of human nature; a belief that under favorable conditions the mind and personality could generate virtue in men's public conduct; and an admiration of balance and symmetry in political and social arrangements like the harmony that existed in nature. Thomas Paine's pamphlet *Common Sense,* published in January 1776, confronted this philosophical orientation with a severe challenge. Paine was an itinerant English radical who arrived in Philadelphia in the autumn of 1774 and wrote a breathtakingly direct justification for American independence. Unencumbered by the legal, historical, and theological premises that the leaders of colonial resistance had laboriously converted into a radical ideology, Paine declared that men were naturally good and pure and that "government, like dress, is the badge of lost innocence."[15] Unlike colonial leaders who believed that only wicked ministers had corrupted the British constitution and perverted the benevolent role of a limited monarch, Paine condemned all monarchy and hereditary privilege as vile usurpation of authority that belonged to the people themselves. Once the colonists threw off the yoke of monarchy, he assured his readers, harmonious republican government would spring naturally into life. The timing of Paine's appeal immensely increased its impact. It came two months after news that the King had rejected the Continental Congress's final appeal for reconciliation and only weeks after Governor Dunmore in Virginia had tried to put down rebellion by force only to be driven from the mainland. In the face of these bewildering events, Paine provided American readers with a program of action and a flattering social philosophy of republican purity and vigor. *Common Sense* became the most widely read of the more than 400 pamphlets of the pre-Revolutionary controversy. To Whigs like John Adams, *Common Sense* threatened to cause anarchy because it "was so democratical, without any restraint or even an attempt at any equilibrium or counterpoise. . . . It must produce confusion and every evil work."[16]

The two outstanding loyalist rebuttals to *Common Sense,* pamphlets by James Chalmers, of Maryland, and Charles Inglis, of New York, endorsed some Enlightenment ideas and accepted as axiomatic an empirical and critical approach to the study of human behavior. Chalmers delighted in exposing Paine's ignorance of modern history and thought. He used quotations from

Rousseau and Montesquieu to demonstrate that only time, experience, and slow development could create effective, responsive governments and legal systems. He ridiculed Paine's stereotyped portraits of a decadent, oppressive English society, of European powers eager and ready to assist the colonies, and of America teeming with economic resources and military and naval manpower, and endowed with a sense of mission unknown to the world since the journey of the Old Testament Jews to the promised land. The children of Israel, he argued, knew suffering, homelessness, and bickering following their revolt against Egyptian authority. Considering that Negro slaves, Quakers, and other religious pacifists would not fight for independence, Chalmers believed that Paine vastly overestimated American manpower. Enthusiastic patriotism counted little in the military equation, Chalmers insisted, citing the "slaughter" of fervent Scottish Presbyterian rebels by Cromwell's calculating Scottish supporters in 1648. The French and Spanish monarchs would jeopardize their very existence if they supported the cause of American independence, "which, inspiring their own subjects with a relish for liberty, might eventually shake their own arbitrary thrones." Chalmers cited David Hume to show that most people were incapable of thinking with discrimination about the policies of kings and governments: "The cruel unrelenting tyrant, Philip II of Spain, with his infernal inquisition was not more detested by the people of the Netherlands than was the humane Charles with his inoffensive liturgy by his mutinous subjects." Therefore, Chalmers concluded, the state of mind of discontented, aggrieved people rather than the actual severity of oppression was the root cause of rebellion. Charles Inglis declared that Paine's utopian faith in human goodness was as simple and crude in its way as Hobbes's view that only force and violence could induce men to live under a government. Paine's contempt for the British constitution allowed Inglis to invoke the Whig interpretation of the Revolution of 1688, which, he correctly insisted, had transformed that constitution by limiting the power of the Crown and guaranteeing the liberties of the subjects. Paine's boyish intensity reminded Inglis of Bishop Berkeley's warning: when "I see a man rage, rail, and rave, I suspect his patriotism." To counter Paine's dogmatic rejection of all monarchy and aristocracy, Inglis pointed out that both James Harrington and Algernon Sidney—the influential seventeenth-century theorists of republican government—had conceded that pure republican government, devoid of hereditary privileges, was a practical impossibility. The heart of the conflict, Inglis declared, was the meaning of the term "constitution," and his definition of the word at least conceded the Enlightenment claim that power ought to be regulated and the security and interests of the subject protected: a "constitution . . . is, as I conceive, *that assemblage of laws, customs, and institutions which form the general system according to which the several powers of the state are distributed and their respective rights are secured to the different members of the community.*"[17]

18

Colonial Anglicanism

ON the whole, then, formal thought played a conciliatory role in colonial America by providing with regard to the relationship of man to society a common pool of insights from which most participants drew arguments and assumptions. In some respects, however, abstract ideas did exert a polarizing influence. Paine's *Common Sense* was the expression of a previously unarticulated radical idealism; moreover, some Anglican clergy constructed their own version of social reality, which served as a kind of armor protecting the Church of England and its mission from what they regarded as a hostile American environment. Though the predominant and nominally established church in the Southern colonies, its clergy there were dominated by wealthy planter lay vestries, and, except for quarrels over clerical salaries in Virginia in 1759 and Maryland between 1770 and 1773, the Anglican church had played little part in Southern politics since the early eighteenth century. In New Jersey, New York, and Connecticut, however, more argumentative and aggressive Anglican clergy had become involved in and often fomented a series of rancorous controversies with dissenters. A bitter struggle in New York during the 1750's over the extent of Anglican control of the newly established King's College exposed the underlying issue: whether a powerful and influential Anglican church was compatible with religious liberty. In 1767 the most outspoken high-Anglican leader, the Reverend Thomas Bradbury Chandler, of New Jersey, organized a concerted public campaign to pressure the British government to allow the appointment of an American bishop.[1] The ensuing furor lasted for three years and served only to rekindle and fan dissenter fears of an Anglican plot to become the privileged and dominant colonial church. "We firmly believe," Chandler candidly explained in a letter to the English hierarchy, "that [the British government's] best security in the colonies does and must always arise from the principles of submission and loyalty taught by the Church. The clergy . . . are constantly instilling these great principles into the people." That the ministry did not approve creation of an American episcopate —the "most reasonable request" that the colonial church had ever made of the British government—was to Chandler simply inexplicable.[2] Already embroiled in the difficulties of enforcing the Townshend duties and tightening executive control of the Empire, the ministry had no desire to create a new grievance in the colonies. This ministerial coolness toward the demands of the Anglicans was well-founded. As William Smith, Jr., accurately observed in the mid-1750's, *"the body of the people are for an equal, universal toleration of protestants and utterly averse to any kind of ecclesiastical establishment.* The dissenters . . . are all jealous of the episcopal party, being apprehensive that the countenance they have from home will foment a *lust for dominion* and enable them, in the process, to subjugate and oppress their fellow subjects."[3]

The colonial Anglican church in reality was much more varied and adaptable an institution than its polemical defenders or opponents ever realized. It was the second largest denomination in the colonies throughout the colonial period, and during the decade from 1760 to 1770 nearly tripled its earlier rate of increase in the first half of the century. Only Congregationalists and Baptists enjoyed a larger increase in the number of new churches during the 1760's. Likewise, in the 1760's, there was a dramatic upsurge in the number of colonial candidates for Anglican ordination, even though this process required an expensive trip to London. Clerical salaries increased sharply during the pre-Revolutionary period (1760–1775) and the proportion of clergymen born and educated in the colonies began to outstrip those with English backgrounds. Anglican clergy came not only from the Reverend William Smith's College of Philadelphia and the Anglican-dominated King's College in New York but also from Yale, Harvard, William and Mary, and Princeton.[4] The pre-Revolutionary Anglican church not only expanded dramatically; it also touched every stratum of colonial society. It was not only the church of the Wentworths in New Hampshire, the De Lanceys in New York, and the planter elite throughout the South; the majority of Anglicans in many of the colonies were humble folk with little property and meager income. Even in the wealthy, elite Boston churches, King's Chapel and Trinity, which boasted as members some of the city's wealthiest merchants, 66 per cent of the parishioners owned so little property that they fell in the lower two-thirds of the city's economic scale. The 15 per cent of Christ Church who ranked in the upper third of Boston's property owners included many ordinary folk—several shopkeepers, sea captains, and an assortment of artisans. Outside of major port towns, Anglican clergy, usually S.P.G. missionaries, regularly reported that their parishioners were poor, struggling farmers.[5]

Only partially adapted to the demands of the colonial environment, and pushed into a defensive position by the strength of dissenting denominations and the appeal of Calvinist theology, the colonial Anglican church nevertheless harbored and disseminated positive and attractive values. Anglicans insisted that the only form of church government sanctioned by God was the apostolic succession of the bishops, which from the first apostles through the present hierarchy of the church constituted a seamless web of legitimate ecclesiastical authority. Anglicans also believed that the *Book of Common Prayer* empowered men to worship with a freedom and reverence attainable through no other liturgy or religious form. Together, these two fundamentals of Anglicanism served to protect the sanctity of religion from profane abuse. "You have cast off the original government which Christ, or at least his apostles under the guidance of the Holy Spirit, established in his church, . . . as is evident . . . in the many disorders, contentions, and confusions which you miserably see and feel abounding and daily increasing among you," the Reverend Samuel Johnson, of Stratford, Connecticut, taunted his Congregationalist critics in 1733. "In the Church of England," he told his parishioners, "worship consists in a most serious and solemn address to the great creator, preserver, and governor of the world, testifying from the bottom of our hearts our dependence upon . . . and submission to Him, praising Him for everything we enjoy, praying to Him for whatsoever we want, and devoting ourselves . . . to his service." Such an embracing experience, Johnson argued, required form and practice: "How can a worshipping assembly, jointly and with one heart and soul and with a full assurance of faith, offer up their prayers and praises to God, unless they have properly a Common Prayer and are beforehand satisfied that what is to be offered is both agreeable to the will of God and suitable to their common necessities and occasions?"[6] There was nothing in this body of belief inimical to religious liberty in the colonies or intrinsically incompatible with colonial values and moral imperatives; moreover, as Jack M. Sosin cogently argues, even the English hierarchy had developed by the 1760's some appreciation of the sensitivities of colonial dissenters.[7] But colonial Anglicanism's emphasis on form and tradition, and the very vitality of its ministry in the colonies, made the absorption of the Anglican church into colonial culture a difficult and complex process.

Part of the interaction between Anglicanism and colonial society occurred in the classroom. The S.P.G. employed both lay catechists, who could assist in conducting services, and less well paid pedagogues to conduct classes in reading, handwriting, numbers, and, where dissenters did not object, the rudiments of Anglican belief. Ordained Society missionaries also often augmented their slender incomes by taking in students. The entire educational enterprise was directed from London, and hence it was never effectively supervised. Low stipends, a heavy work load, and the necessity of sending tedious attendance and curricular reports to the secretary of the S.P.G. in London accounted for the uneven quality of instruction in S.P.G. schools. But it was an audacious and pioneering educational effort. The S.P.G. brought instruction to thousands of students, including, between 1704 and 1718, more than 200 slave children at the Negro Catechetical School in New York run by Elias Neau, a remarkable humanitarian and resourceful French-born lay catechist.[8] The S.P.G. sent to its teachers in America thousands of Bibles as well as other books, pamphlets, devotional writings, and the annual sermons preached on the anniversary of the founding of the Society. S.P.G. sermons and other publications written in England by men with scant personal knowledge of colonial conditions prescribed the rules that were supposed to govern the colonial social order. "The S.P.G. task," John Calam explains, "was to adjust the conditions of American colonial life to fit the Society pattern rather than the other way round."[9] These writings lauded the mercantilist theory of the Empire, justifying British profit, riches, and wealth and rationalizing colonial toil, servitude, and labor. S.P.G. anniversary sermons spoke approvingly of rank, order, and subservience in human affairs, and they held that Anglican worship and church government were the necessary antidotes to faction, enthusiasm, ungovernable behavior, and uncivilized manners. The S.P.G. widely disseminated the popular Anglican behavior manual, *The Whole Duty of Man,* which dwelt repeatedly on the necessity of class distinctions, urged children to dress and act according to their station in life, and vindicated the values of obedience, duty, and respect for one's spiritual, parental, and political superiors.[10] The very quantity, elegance, and handsome physical appearance of S.P.G. publications must have made this literature at least a subtle influence on the social outlook of colonial Anglicanism, and this writing certainly influenced the dissenters' image of the Church of England.

This emphasis on decorum and order ran counter to much of what Anglican clergy discovered as they tried to serve a larger segment of American society. Charles Woodmason, a prosperous Charles Town layman who chose to take holy orders, served for five years in the harsh South Carolina back country, and genuinely cared for the welfare of the people he knew there, catalogued what he regarded as the offenses against true religion and piety. Even in Anglican churches people arrived late and carelessly dressed for worship; they passed around cups and slurped punch during the service, and petitioned in jest that marriage banns be proclaimed. Woodmason described "lascivious" baptismal ceremonies in mountain streams among Baptists, and Presbyterians "howling, ranting, crying, dancing, skipping, laughing, and rejoicing" during communion services. From all dissenters, Woodmason complained, came slanders labeling "the Church of England a rotten foundation" whose "liturgy and discipline" were "chaff and stubble," whose "sacraments" were "carnal ordinances," and whose "ministers" were "children of Hell." Woodmason discovered alarming signs of degeneration in the back country—widespread theft, assault, bigamy, and illegitimacy. These were, of course, the very crimes that appeared

rampant in colonial society whenever growing population spread
into new regions and the restraints that operated in more static
and tightly knit communities ceased to function. Like the Congregationalists' laments over sin and moral decline in New
England during the late seventeenth and early eighteenth centuries, Woodmason's sermons in the South Carolina back country
attributed crime and sin solely to the absence of piety and
reverence. Understandably, he also associated sexual laxity with
disrespect for Anglican forms and practices. "Some of our qualm-
ish neighbors, whose consciences keep them in perpetual dis-
quiet, cannot bear the thought (without shuddering and
sweating) of bowing at the name of Jesus," he declared, "but
their tender consciences will never upbraid them . . . for bowing down upon a strumpet and committing fornication. . . .
Others, whose consciences torment . . . them for having made
use of a prayer printed upon a page, make no scruple of promising marriage to a young ignorant maiden, then debauching her
. . . and . . . abandoning her as a wanton hussey."[11]

During the first half of the eighteenth century, Anglican clergy
increasingly conceived their duty to be the eradication of irrational religion and social libertinism through a patient and calm
appeal to men's reason and to their instinctive fondness of order.
A flourishing Church of England in South Carolina would
"reclaim vice and immorality, remove ignorance, enthusiasm,
prejudice, and every cause of schism and dissension," declared the
Anglican clergy of that colony in 1722; because "all differences in
religion would be composed in the bosom of the Church,"
Anglicanism in South Carolina would promote "solid virtue and
piety, . . . knowledge, sound doctrine, catholic unity, and uni-
formity," and make the colony "a pattern to all . . . the British
colonies in America."[12] This comprehensive and integrated program sought to Anglicize the colonies religiously and culturally
and extirpate religious enthusiasm and other barbarian tendencies. In order to think in those terms, colonial Anglican
clergymen may well have needed a substantial body of formal
inquiry into human nature, social and educational theory, and
ethics and morality.

The Reverend Samuel Johnson devoted his life's work to the
construction of such a philosophy, and although few contempo-

raries understood his more advanced and complicated ideas, the rudiments of Johnson's thought imparted an authentic intellectual sophistication and self-confidence to a generation of Anglican clergymen in the middle and New England colonies. He was the Anglican counterpart of his Yale classmate and teaching colleague Jonathan Edwards. Johnson's philosophical writing, based largely on George Berkeley's idealism, was a major American effort to explain the nature of knowledge and the relationship of man to the world of ideas, and to buttress a theology of rational religion. Johnson wholeheartedly embraced Berkeley's fundamental contention that physical matter did not exist, that, instead, only ideas made up reality. Rejecting Locke's contention that ideas could enter the mind only through the senses, Berkeley and Johnson held that sense impressions were just another set of abstract ideas. Men, they insisted, perceived truth only in the form of spiritual intuitions. The immense advantage of this philosophy, for Johnson, was the ease with which it proved the existence of God. Ideas, he explained, "must derive to us from an Almighty, intelligent active cause, exhibiting them to us, impressing our minds with them, or producing them in us." Because reality consisted of ideas, and because God was the instigator and sustainer of all thought that occurred in the human mind, Johnson reasoned, the operation of the mind intimately connected men to their Maker. Just as sense impressions were the foundation of Locke's psychology, the perception of rationally comprehensible spiritual truths was the basis of Johnson's. It was a philosophy rich with religious implications. Because he believed that the human mind could grasp only ideas about particular individuals and specific attributes of God, Johnson urged men to curb their curiosity about human nature and the mysteries of salvation. Nothing disrupted Christian unity so much as uncontrolled speculation about sin and God's wrath, Johnson contended, and nothing blocked the transmission of divine inspiration so much as an elaborate theology of human depravity and divine intervention like Calvinism.[13]

Johnson's philosophy of idealism sought to bring coherence to the confusing intellectual life of mid-eighteenth-century America. Like Edwards, Johnson sought to revitalize American Christianity by synthesizing Enlightenment ideas about the mind with older Puritan doctrines about the omnipotence of God and the primacy of religious values. Edwards had used Lockean psychology to precipitate and justify a passionate religious experience: sinners visualizing the heat, roar, sulphurous odors, and fiery glow of Hell and converts discovering the sweet, soothing, melodious sensations of salvation. Johnson, in contrast, believed in a God who "condescended to accommodate himself to the low capacities of mankind, . . . to wean and disengage us from fleeting and sensible things and low animal pursuits and gratifications . . . and engage our attention to spiritual, eternal, and immutable things, the objects of reason and faith."[14] Thus, only God decided what the mind of the believer needed to receive, and therefore Anglicans stressed "the necessity of restraining our curiosity within proper bounds" and shunning men's morbid fascination with the depth of their own depravity.[15]

The uproar over proposals for bishops in the colonies, the deep-seated suspicion that Anglicans wanted to destroy religious liberty in America, and the allegation that Anglicans preached unlimited submission to constituted authority obscured the authentic political implications of Anglican preaching and belief. Colonial Anglicanism was profoundly apolitical. It taught that human nature disqualified man from joining responsibly in collective political movements. "When men once engage in strife and contention, they cannot tell where they stop or what pitch they shall carry it to," the Reverend Edward Bass told his parishioners in Newburyport, Massachusetts. Even "harmless and innocent or at least not very bad" political activities should be shunned, he warned, because men "cannot certainly tell what their future conduct will be or how mischievous. They know not what circumstances may happen in the course of contention—nor how their passions may be raised and enflamed."[16] These human imperfections made "the great blessing of stable times" a moral necessity, declared the Reverend Henry Caner, of Boston, who sounded a muted but unmistakable note of alarm in a sermon celebrating the Peace of Paris in 1763. The treaty, he noted gratefully, "promise[s] all reasonable security against foreign violence and . . . leave[s] no just occasion to faction or dissension at home." But the preservation of that harmony, Caner warned, would require constant vigilance. "An impartial administration of justice and a disinterested distribution of rewards will go a great way in preventing any inbred disturbance," he explained deliberately, before turning to the darker side of the picture. "At least they will so far suppress the seeds of faction and disorder that [these forces] will not come to maturity or acquire strength enough to endanger the peace and quiet of the state." The danger of dissatisfaction and discontent, Caner argued, was always at work, ready to enlarge its scope and engulf the unwary. "The prosperity of a nation"—by which Caner clearly meant its vitality and harmony and not just economic abundance—"requires . . . rulers [who] are wise, just, prudent and tender of the liberties, . . . privileges, and happiness of the people."

Without this enlightened, calculating governmental approach to society, he warned, the cluster of prevailing public attitudes about obedience and order would surely begin to come apart. Only "when the subjects are quiet and peaceable and obedient to their rulers, content with their respective stations, reverent to the laws, and cheerfully ready" to serve in war "when . . . called upon by their superiors" is society truly stable and safe from the threat of internal disputes. Caner shrewdly sensed the interdependence of these components of civic acquiescence, and he realized that flaws existed in even the most secure political systems: "Every government will have some discontented spirits . . . and every prince must expect some subjects of less loyalty and attachment than might be wished."[17]

Because Anglicanism often seemed to reject Calvinism's belief in the depravity of man, many Anglican clergy brought the full force of their concern about evil to bear on the sins of "wrath, malice, envy, impatience, revenge." These sins, Edward Bass argued, both destroyed the individual's peace of mind and "naturally draw upon us the hatred and contempt of others." This cycle of hostility, guilt, and estrangement became self-perpetuating: "Any of these passions is enough to render a man uneasy to himself and make his conversation troublesome to all about him." A man who surrendered to the passions of "anger and impatience" exposed his "weak and impotent mind" and lived in ceaseless fear that others had seen his weaknesses and held him in "secret contempt." Shame and self-hatred, Bass warned, were the final consequences of intemperate behavior.

"After men have forfeited their natural modesty, they are apt by degrees to grow profligate and desperate. If a man gives way but a little to his own vicious inclinations, they will soon get head of him and no man knows how far they will hurry him at last."[18]

The task of religion, therefore, Anglican clergy apparently believed, was to implore men to curb their resentments and animosities lest they infect society with rancor and turbulence. "We are partakers of each other's sins," Bass warned; sinful and undisciplined men made up a "society of vice," a network of greed, cruelty, and weakness that continually assaulted the virtuous and honorable. "As . . . members of society," Bass pointedly observed, "we are all obliged in point of honour, interest, and conscience to maintain its security, promote its welfare, and guard it against any factious designs or seditious conspiracies." Only by conscious and deliberate actions in support of constituted authority, colonial Anglicans emphasized, could men insulate themselves from the prevailing ingratitude and discontent that all human beings were prone to feel from time to time. "If the supreme power of any state, through want of due information or attention, should adopt measures that are wrong and oppressive," Thomas Bradbury Chandler declared in a masterful summary of high-Anglican political belief, "the subjects may complain and remonstrate against them in a respectful manner, but they are bound by the laws of heaven and earth not to behave undutifully" or, still worse, "insolently" or "rebelliously." "The bands of society would be dissolved, the harmony of the world confounded, and the order of nature subverted," Chandler warned, "if reverence, respect, and obedience might be refused to those whom the constitution has vested with the highest authority. *The ill-consequences of open disrespect to government are so great that no misconduct by the administration can justify or excuse it.*"[19]

19

Jonathan Boucher and
the Nature of Authority

ON the morning of Thursday, July 20, 1775, the day set apart for worship and prayer by a resolution of the Second Continental Congress, the Anglican clergyman the Reverend Jonathan Boucher gathered up the pages of his carefully prepared sermon and left his house to conduct special services of prayer and fasting at his parish church, Queen Anne's, near Annapolis, Maryland. He knew that his presence there would be deeply resented by the Whig leadership of the parish, but Boucher was stunned to find "not less than 200 armed men" crowded into the church and determined to prevent him from preaching. He sent word to the leader of the crowd that the pulpit was his by right and that at the risk of his life he intended to occupy it that morning. For the preceding six months, Boucher's curate, a Whig named Walter Harrison, had conducted services in the parish while Boucher had withdrawn to serve in the less hostile parish where his wife's uncle was rector, though even there his advocacy of "peaceableness" gave offense and he began the practice of placing "a pair of loaded pistols" on the cushioned seat of the pulpit. He had chosen the official day of prayer and fasting in behalf of the colonial cause to return to Queen Anne's because Curate Harrison was "promoting factious" activities in support of colonial resistance and because it "was a day of great expectation," when his sermon would receive the widest hearing. Governor Eden himself had urged Boucher to "make a point of appearing in [his] own pulpit" on that day.

Boucher entered the church, immediately whispered to Harrison that he intended to preach that day, and told him "at his peril, not to attempt to dispossess me." Taking no chances, he took a seat closer than Harrison's to the pulpit, and "at the proper time, with my sermon in one hand and a loaded pistol in the other, like Nehemiah, I prepared to ascend the steps of the pulpit." Before he could reach them a friend named David Crawford leaped from a front pew and wrestled Boucher away from the pulpit stairs; as the two men panted and struggled behind the pulpit Crawford managed to tell Boucher that he knew of at least twenty men in the church under orders to shoot him if he tried to preach. Two more men joined Crawford in keeping Boucher from entering the pulpit despite his pleas that, as he later recalled, "once to flinch was forever to invite danger." Efforts to restrain Boucher succeeded momentarily; his "well wishers, however, prevailed—by force rather than by persuasion." The brief struggle brought the congregation to an uproar. Some shouted that Boucher should be expelled and others that he should be allowed to preach. The leader of the armed men in the church, Osborne Sprigg, led a group toward the front of the church and they surrounded Boucher and his defenders. Boucher suddenly pushed forward and, "seizing Sprigg . . . by the collar" and placing "my cocked pistol" at his head, "assur[ed] him that if any violence was offered to me I would instantly blow his brains out." Pulling the hapless Sprigg by the collar and keeping his gun pointed at Sprigg's head, Boucher led a strangely subdued procession out of the church until he reached his horse, mounted it, and rode away unmolested. The following Sunday he returned to the church, shouted down his detractors, and preached his sermon against participation in rebellion. After the service he placed his back against a pillar and began to "bawl and . . . harangue" in a manner he thought his detractors would understand.[1]

Boucher was not the only Anglican cleric to preach obedience and loyalty to hostile audiences in 1775 in the face of invective and threats of violence, although his rough response was unusually forceful. What made him unique among the doctrinaire Tories was his insight into the nature of the pre-Revolutionary movement, his strategy for denouncing it, and his sense of moral and intellectual authority. Born in 1738 in Cumberland County, England, into a once prominent family that had fallen on hard times, Boucher watched his debt-ridden parents struggle to maintain the family just above the level of poverty. His father, who managed an alehouse and conducted a local school, taught Jonathan to read English and Latin before he was six, and thereafter Boucher received a spotty education between long periods of work as an agricultural laborer. At sixteen, he found a meager post as a schoolmaster, which he left to study mathematics and surveying, and finally, at eighteen, his father found him a job as "usher"—a sort of tutor and minor functionary—in a school run by the Reverend John James, in the town of St. Bees. James and his young wife, only a few years older than Boucher, became his benefactors and intimates. John James rigorously expanded and supplemented Boucher's irregular educational background, and Ann James sympathized with his cycles of youthful depression and excitement. They encouraged him to accept, in 1759, a position as private tutor to the sons of a Virginia merchant, John Younger. In 1761 the nearby Anglican parish of Hanover became vacant when its rector, Boucher's acquaintance the Reverend Isaac Giberne, moved to another post. Invited to replace Giberne, he returned to England to receive ordination and in 1762 assumed his new duties. After a year he secured the more comfortable parish of St. Mary's in Caroline County, Virginia, and in 1770, after three years of tireless supplication, prominent Maryland friends acquired for Boucher the lucrative parish of St. Anne's, near Annapolis, where he met leaders of the proprietary party. In November 1771 he moved to the prestigious parish of Queen Anne's in Prince George's County, also near Annapolis.[2]

Boucher was a resourceful and energetic young man. During his rising clerical career he augmented his slender income by operating a boarding school that eventually grew to an enrollment of thirty students, among them George Washington's stepson, Jackie Custis. Faced with Presbyterian and Baptist dissent in Virginia, Boucher counterattacked by preaching eloquently on the superior virtues of the Church of England and by patiently counseling parishioners who had strayed from the Anglican fold. When a dissenting clergyman challenged him to debate, Boucher sent instead "one David Barksdale, a carpenter in my parish who had a good front and a voluble tongue." "This method of treating [dissenting] preachers with well judged ridicule and contempt and their followers with gentleness, persuasion, and attention," he concluded, "is a good one." Boucher's most significant achievement was his pioneering work in educating Negro slaves in St. Mary's parish, Virginia. His predecessor in the parish had recoiled from "the great fatigue and disagreeableness" of instructing slaves, "on the pretense," Boucher noted curtly, "that the poor creatures were so extremely ignorant." Boucher taught several of the most promising slaves to read and then, using them as assistants, began large-scale Sunday-afternoon instruction of blacks in the rudiments of Christianity. He baptized several hundred adult slaves, and at one time more than a thousand received instruction. Thirteen slaves were regular communicants in his church at St. Mary's parish, and Boucher concluded that blacks were "as well informed, as orderly, and as regularly pious as country people usually are, even in England."[3] As early as 1763, Boucher declared that slavery in the mainland English colonies was rooted in the fear and apprehension of white men. "In some respects I hope it [slavery] is on a better footing than it . . . is anywhere else," he told his parishioners; "but it is surely worse in this [respect] . . . ; here, in one sense, it can never end. An African slave, even when made free and supposing him to be possessed of talents and of virtue, can never in these colonies be quite on terms of equality with a free white man. Nature has placed insuperable barriers in his way."[4]

His energy and versatility during the 1760's in part reflected the fact that he was a newcomer and bachelor, free from the responsibilities and restraints of supporting a family. In turn, however, his restlessness perpetuated itself and kept him in a state of anxious uncertainty. His first year in St. Mary's parish, Virginia, during 1763, nearly shattered his composure and purposefulness. He fell "too often . . . to hard drinking," and his avid reading in the rationalist Anglican philosophy of Dr. Samuel Clarke shook his belief in the doctrine of the Trinity. For months he could not bring himself to pronounce the Athanasian Creed, and, deeply disturbed by his theological doubts, he considered abandoning the priesthood. The trouble, he later realized, was that he had no ecclesiastical superiors or intellectual colleagues to whom he could turn for counsel. It was probably just as well, for Boucher's solitary efforts to re-establish his own faith involved rigorous self-examination. "My ruling passion was, if possible, to see to the bottom of things, and it was this, I suppose, which led me first to addict myself" to a rational explanation of theology. Sustained reading and meditation finally persuaded him "to submit my understanding to the obedience of faith."[5] However, Boucher never sacrificed Samuel Clarke's prominent teaching: that religious conviction can never be instilled by coercion, fear, or manipulation. Grounded in this advanced Enlightenment idea, and in the face of virulent anti-Catholic sentiment among his Virginia parishioners, Boucher defended the right of Catholics to freedom of conscience.[6] This unpopular viewpoint only further isolated Boucher and prolonged his loneliness. "I am not yet a married man and speak with much sincere grief of heart that I do not know when I shall be," he confessed to John James in 1767; "I am said to be unsettled, so giddy and fickle, that the dear amiable girl I have fixed my affections upon frankly declares she dares not venture to engage with me."[7] Finally, in 1772, at the age of thirty-four, he married Nelly Addison, then thirty-three, niece of his patron in Maryland, the wealthy and influential Anglican clergyman Henry Addison. The relationship brought Boucher the kind of warmth he had longed for ever since leaving St. Bees. "Mr. Addison . . . is my James in America," Boucher exulted to John James.[8] In addition, the marriage strengthened ties he had already made with the Dulanys, for his wife's uncle Henry Addison was married to Rachel, Daniel Dulany's sister.

With the support of a wealthy family and a long-awaited degree of personal intimacy and security, Boucher's life suddenly coalesced, and he found himself performing an important social role. As chaplain to the Maryland Assembly, he became a confidant of Governor Eden. He may have exaggerated when he claimed that "the management of the Assembly was left very much to me," but his wit and intelligence made him a useful political figure.[9] During the controversy over official fees and clerical salaries from 1770 to 1773, Boucher led the campaign to block any reduction of the salaries of Anglican clergy. Because the Tobacco Inspection Act, setting the level of clerical salaries, had expired, he argued that the terms of a more generous 1702 salary act automatically came into force, a claim that, if sus-

tained, would have raised clerical salaries by one-third. Samuel
Chase and William Paca, antiproprietary leaders, denounced
Anglican efforts to secure higher salaries and declared that in any
event vestries possessed legal authority to determine the level of
clerical compensation. Boucher cleverly demonstrated that the
1702 act, which Paca and Chase denounced as invalid, gave
vestries whatever legal standing they possessed. "UNCHARITABLE
PRIEST!" Paca and Chase blurted in outrage at finding the
ground of their argument cut from under them, "tell us what
passion dictated your resentment against us? Was it a laudable
zeal for the public welfare or was it revenge?"[10]

What "passion" indeed had transformed Boucher from a fastidious clergyman and educator into a frighteningly incisive
polemicist? This is the central question about his character and
career. Boucher came to America a bright, alert, highly impressionable young man, proud, eager to ingratiate, a little insecure.
The transit from Cumberland County, England to Port Royal,
Virginia had wrenched him from the first secure and really
gratifying relationship he had ever known. He pleaded with
John and Ann James to send letters on every ship bound for
Virginia, for he confessed, "I know how little I am able to bear
interruptions" in communication with them. But "there is a rule
I must insist upon your always observing," his intense peremp-
tory letter continued, "that is that you drop all reserve. I have
often found you too gentle in rebuke. Be so much my friend as to
be in appearance my enemy: trust me, I'll look upon it as the
greatest instance of your regard for me." Rushing onward,
Boucher admitted the motive for this demand for greater intimacy. "I was told the day I left England of some, who by artful
insinuations, have endeavoured to lessen your esteem for me.
. . . Though you were generous enough to conceal it from me,
[the rumor] has given me prodigious uneasiness." Virginia was a
barren environment. During his two years as a tutor, he later
reflected, "I did not form a single friendship on which I can now
look back with much approbation." His letters to John James
accented his sense of dislocation: "The hotness of the weather,
Sir, has so prodigious an influence on the [human] constitution
that it fevers the blood and sets all the animal spirits in an
uproar. . . . Hence we think and act tumultuously and all in a

flutter and are strangers to that cool steadiness which you in England justly value yourselves upon." Though he called the Virginians "we," Boucher felt awkward and out of place as he tried to adapt himself to the bawdy tone of their society. "[Self-] interest and good manners force me into companies where too often libertinism is the reigning topic; What shall I say? I blush to own it, but I'm not content with being a mere cypher. Judge me not too rashly; I have not yet joined in anything my reason opposed, but in a start of glee have been disposed to waver." Torn between a sense of propriety and the pull of impulse, he recognized that he was projecting a disagreeable image. "Stunned and stupefied" by Americans' coarse "manners," and naturally "sheepish" himself, Boucher felt that people looked on him as "a stingy milksop . . . unaccountably splenetic and grave," in a word, "dull."[11] After a year and a half of tutoring Virginia merchant Younger's four sons, Boucher decided to explore a career as a merchant himself and with Younger's encouragement went to work for a Captain Dixon, a sixty-year-old widower. Unexpectedly, the job entailed helping to arrange and promote Dixon's courtship of a wealthy and attractive widow. The position ended abruptly when Dixon asked Boucher, "after much *humming* and *haing*," to admit paternity of one of Dixon's illegitimate children and accept as payment a lucrative commercial position. Boucher refused. His career as a clerk in shambles, he leaped at the opportunity in 1762 to take Anglican orders and fill the vacant rectorship in Hanover, Virginia.[12]

His work as Anglican parson in Virginia and Maryland brought Boucher a measure of self-confidence and stability, but he remained an innocent, vulnerable man with a vivid dramatic imagination. Experiences and sensations amazed, outraged, chagrined, or delighted him, and this lack of protective emotional covering made him self-conscious, candid, perceptive, but also moody, naïve, and unpredictable. His ability to form strong friendships and also to provoke bitter hostility never ceased to amaze Boucher. One of his enemies was the Reverend Isaac Giberne, his predecessor as rector of Hanover parish. As a newcomer to Virginia trying to ingratiate himself, Boucher entertained high-spirited companions by publicly ridiculing Giberne's intellectual pretensions. During Boucher's return to Eng-

land to receive ordination, Giberne and Captain Dixon assiduously spread the word to Boucher's new parishioners that he
was a disreputable person. Their campaign of vilification was
well advanced when Boucher returned from England in July
1762. Their criticism, Boucher later admitted, was not entirely
unjustified, for he realized that his statements about both Giberne and Dixon had been imprudent and gratuitous. He
preached his first sermon in Virginia on the text from Psalms
"They have spoken against me . . ." and appealed to his new
parishioners to suspend judgment until he could "disprove all
the vile calumnies that had been so industriously propagated
against me during my absence." To his surprise, a man named
Thornton came to Boucher's defense and discredited Giberne's
allegations, and Boucher himself took pains to apologize to
Captain Dixon.[13] "Curse on poverty," he wrote to John James;
"it dooms me to receive favours from those I cannot esteem. I
must knuckle to Captain Dixon who most cowardly gave me up
and joined to tear me to pieces." Boucher's sense of himself as a
protagonist capable of turning reverses in fortune to his own
advantage became a deeply implanted trait of his character.
"There is a kind of magic elasticity in injured innocence," he
said of himself, "which like some creeping plants, the more they
are trampled upon the more vigorous do they rise and flourish."[14]

The "magic elasticity" of temperament—a blend of resilience,
astringency, and patience in the face of economic vicissitudes—
enabled Boucher to adapt to his insecure position as an Anglican
clergyman in Virginia and Maryland, but it also created within
him several acute stresses. He knew that scholarship, hard work,
eloquence, and piety were prerequisites for success but would
avail him little unless he also cultivated well-placed patrons,
practiced discreet opportunism, and was very lucky. Unable to
hold these demands in equilibrium, Boucher had, understandably, a mercurial emotional life. Despite his industry and perseverance, Boucher felt the "irresistibly insinuating and invei-
gling . . . allurement of indolence." "Old and young," he later
boasted, "I was naturally lazy and hated work." He argued good-
naturedly with John James about the virtues of ambition.
"There is only one way to get over this [anxiety about the
future]," he admitted, "and that, . . . as you have often told

me, . . . is by making a fortune here to retire with; and yet it is not very likely I shall ever do this effectually." Whether from "indolence," "vanity," or *"too much virtue,"* he felt ill-equipped to practice what he scornfully called "the principles of the art of thriving." Thus inhibited, Boucher must have projected just the proper degree of independence and acerbity to make a favorable impression on powerful Anglican laymen and clergy in Virginia and Maryland.[15]

His letters to George Washington concerning Jackie Custis's education blended reassuring interest in the young man's progress with an intellectual authority bordering on arrogance. Projecting from his own abrupt and difficult adolescence, Boucher lectured Washington on the principles of character formation. By attending a school with other boys, Jackie would become "inured to combat those little oppositions and collisions of interest which resemble in miniature the contests which happen in the great school in the world." "When we speak of a well educated man," Boucher continued, "we seldom mean more than that he has been well instructed in the languages which are avenues to knowledge. But surely this is but a partial and imperfect account of it; . . . the aim of education should not only be to form wise and good men, not only to cultivate the understanding, but to expand the heart, to meliorate the temper, and *fix the generous purpose in the glowing breast.*" He found Jackie "teeming with all the softer virtues"; though graced with the "harmlessness of a dove," the boy needed to acquire as well "the wisdom of the serpent," said Boucher. "How will you forgive me should I suffer him to lose in gentleness, simplicity, and inoffensiveness as much as he gains in address, prudence, and resolution?" he asked rhetorically. "This is a dilemma by no means so easily avoided in practice as . . . in theory." A year and a half later, Boucher found himself facing an altogether different dilemma with Custis. "I never did in my life know a youth so exceedingly indolent or so surprisingly voluptuous. . . . There is a period in life when these passions will wage war with reason. . . . The system we set out with, that of tender persuasion, must be pursued. . . . I consider his rising passions as some little streamlet, swelling by successive showers into a . . . torrent. You will

in vain oppose its course by dams. . . . The only certain means
. . . is to lead it gently along a variety of channels, lessening its
force by dividing it." Boucher's remarkably assured and analytical appraisal of Washington's stepson suggests that he regarded
his own attainment of adulthood as a struggle between competing character traits over which he had enjoyed little control. He
seemed to regard maturity and self-mastery as fortuitous attain-
ments for which an individual deserved little credit.[16]

Inclined to view men's success, good fortune, and even virtue
as the products of circumstances beyond their control or comprehension, Boucher plunged into the heady Anglicized environment of the proprietary society without timidity or hesitation.
He became a close friend of Governor Eden, whose intellect,
warmth, and generosity more than offset, in Boucher's estimation, his dissolute personal habits. Boucher joined and rose to
prominence in the elite Homony Club of Annapolis, a jolly
assemblage of wealthy and highly placed Maryland gentlemen
that split apart after 1773 with political dissension. Most of all,
Boucher cherished his association—first of friendship and then of
marriage—with the Addison and Dulany families. He unhesitatingly stepped forth between 1772 and 1774 as the spokesman for
proprietary and Anglican privilege.[17]

Boucher's political sermons in 1774 and 1775 cast in elegant
prose his reaction as an Anglican cleric, proprietary publicist,
and Addison kinsman to the eruption of a rebellion in Maryland. More clearly than any other writer of the era, Boucher
understood what Bailyn calls "the threat to the traditional
ordering of human relations implicit in Revolutionary thought."[18]
At the heart of colonial discontent Boucher perceived a series
of unexamined propositions: that government existed only to
serve the needs of men, that government rested upon a compact
by which the people consented to the disciplines of living in a
civil order, and, finally, "that the whole human race is born equal
and that no man is naturally inferior or in any respect subject to
another." The justification for a free and egalitarian society,
Boucher scornfully observed, was shot through with fantasy, con-
tradiction, and logical inconsistency. Men obviously were not
equal in their abilities, capacities, or virtue. Because God in-

tended that men should be social creatures and live under fair and just government, the Creator necessarily prescribed that there must be "some relative inferiority and superiority" among men. No musical instrument composed of equal and identical "chords, keys, or pipes" could produce harmony. A world of equal citizens would not only be a bedlam of discord; it would also be terrifyingly insecure and unstable. "The same principle of equality that exempts [a man] from being governed without his own consent, clearly entitles him to recall and resume that consent whenever he sees fit; and he alone has a right to judge when and for what reasons it may be resumed." When Boucher drew this staccato of objections to a conclusion, he did not prophesy a Hobbesian jungle of human violence; rather, he predicted, in remarkably subdued terms, a social and political order in which men would constantly re-examine and readjust the purposes and goals of their society and seek to renew their collective willingness to pursue those goals. In such a social order, he speculated, the authority of government and the obligations of citizens would always be a little tentative and uncertain: "Any attempt to introduce this fantastic scheme [of equality and consent] into practice would reduce the whole business of social life to the wearisome, confused, and useless task of mankind's first expressing and then withdrawing their consent to an endless succession of schemes of government. Governments, though always forming, would never be completely formed. . . . The majority today might be the minority tomorrow and . . . that which is now fixed might and would be soon unfixed." It is not entirely clear what Boucher meant by this statement, for a few pages later he predicted that republicanism would lead to "perpetual dissensions and contests" ultimately "rendering the world . . . [a] field of blood." But the restraint and specificity of most of his language foresaw the political machination and intense partisanship that in fact have become the hallmark of democratic politics.[19]

To justify his audacious repudiation of personal liberty and government by consent, Boucher utilized elements of the sixteenth- and early-seventeenth-century philosophy of order and obedience. "When man was made, his Maker did not turn him adrift into a shoreless sea without star or compass to steer by," he explained, establishing impeccable precedent for his theory of the origin of government; "as soon as there were some to be governed, there were also some to govern, and the first man, by virtue of his paternal claim, . . . was first invested with the power of government." "All subsequent governments" derived their legitimacy from Adam's authority as the first human father. God, as Creator, never ceased controlling and sanctioning this arrangement; therefore, "kings and princes" derived their authority "from God, the source and origin of all power," rather than from "any supposed consent or suffrage of men." This "patriarchal scheme" of government, Boucher contended, was the only political theory that adequately protected men from chaos and the disintegration of authority; patriarchal theory was the only explanation of government in harmony with the Christian concept of a benevolent, protecting Creator. Boucher found it inconceivable that "an all-wise and all-merciful Creator, . . . having formed creatures capable of order and rule, [would] turn them loose into the world under the guidance only of their own unruly wills. . . . His purpose, from the first, no doubt, was that men should live *godly and sober lives.*" Drawing judiciously on Filmer and other authorities, Boucher constructed a comprehensive justification for political subservence. No authority, he argued, was so understanding and properly restrained as that exercised by a loving father over obedient children or a pious king over loyal subjects.[20]

In the most original and humane portions of his political thought Boucher argued, however, that the subject was no helpless automaton. Rather, he was an individual with responsible choices to make—choices that would bring into play all of man's emotional and intellectual resources. Obedience and submission demanded a high degree of self-consciousness and self-awareness. "A non-resisting spirit never made any man a bad subject [that is, a bad citizen or member of society]. . . . If men of such mild and yielding tempers have shown less ardour than many others do in the pursuit of liberty, . . . it can only be for this reason: that they think it precisely that kind of liberty which has so often set the world in an uproar and that . . . it would be better for the world if [uproarious movements to defend liberty] were never heard of." Because the Bible did not deal explicitly with the duties of subjects, the problems of civil obligation required the most scrupulous study. Boucher boldly chose as the text for his sermon on obedience in July 1775 the verse Galatians 5:1, which inspired so many pre-Revolutionary sermons on the duty of Christians to resist tyranny: "Stand fast therefore in the liberty wherewith Christ has made us free." After objecting that "the liberty here spoke of . . . meant a freedom from sin" that "cannot, without infinite perversion and torture, be made to refer to any other kind of liberty," Boucher went further and acknowledged that the concept of Christian freedom was an appealing and suggestive tenet. God's purpose was to make men "more *free* in the *inner man*, . . . endowed with greater firmness of mind in the cause of truth against the terrors and allurements of the world," and capable of controlling "the natural temper and bias of the human mind to be impatient under restraint." "However humiliating such acquiescence [to constituted authority] may seem to men of warm and eager minds," he concluded, "the wisdom of God, in having made it our duty, is manifest." The denial of one's own natural unruly spirit and the acceptance of a divine order in human affairs requiring men to obey those in authority, Boucher insisted, were in reality the only means to achieve liberty. "Liberty is not the setting at naught and despising established laws—much less the making of our own wills the rule of our own actions— . . . but it is being governed by the law and the law only. . . . To pursue liberty in any manner not warranted by law, whatever the pretext may be, is clearly hostile to liberty, and those persons who thus promise you liberty are themselves servants of corruption." The ability to resist this kind of temptation constituted, for Boucher, true liberty. Freedom was hence a state of mind, a degree of wisdom and sophistication, a willingness and ability to direct energy into undisruptive channels. Thus equipped, men could recognize the dangers in the superficially attractive idea that "the end of government is the common good of mankind," for they would recognize that the common good was a "vague and loose" idea about which men could never fully agree and that they could never properly understand. Likewise, men had to resist the temptation to consider themselves heirs to a theoretical compact between ruler and ruled. This "visionary idea" and "utopian fiction" required that men believe without evidence that at the end of "some fabulous age of gold" men had grown tired of roaming the forests like wild animals and during some "lucid interval of reason and reflection had set together in a spacious plain" and placed political authority in the hands of some of their number. Even if such a farfetched event actually occurred, Boucher declared, it did not create a compact limiting the power of the ruler; the very act of bestowing authority on a ruler established, for all time and beyond any possibility of recall, his superiority and his subjects' inferiority.[21]

Boucher was not simply a harsh reactionary occupying the extreme right wing on the ideological spectrum of the pre-Revolutionary period—a kind of Tory counterpart to Tom Paine. Boucher's "high Toryism," Michael D. Clark argues, "seems to have been the result of his temperament, his serious acceptance of Anglican theology, and a strong admixture of chance which more than anything else placed him in a position which required him to define his political philosophy in a certain way."[22] The rapid shifts of role and fortune in his career, his remarkable escape from an obscure and humble childhood, and his unvarnished reaction to new experiences made him exceptionally self-conscious and prevented him from lapsing into a familiar and benumbing routine of thought and attitude. Boucher's vivid, almost unfiltered perception of pre-Revolutionary ideology and his image of himself as a man of unpredictable dramatic impulses combined to make him a polemicist for an antique philosophy of order and obedience. Early in 1775 a "blacksmith, . . . a stoutish fellow," tried to provoke Boucher to a fist fight. Boucher, whose wife was present, tried to shame the man into desisting. As soon as he realized that violence was unavoidable, Boucher began to picture in his mind the advantages of a single surprise punch. Though he had never hit a man with his fist, Boucher threw a clumsy "lucky blow" that sent the blacksmith sprawling.[23]

Boucher approached other confrontations in 1774 and 1775 in the same open, spontaneous fashion. "The ground I have taken, I am aware, is deemed untenable," he admitted in his sermon on obedience, acknowledging the vast gulf between his conception of an organic society and the loosely knit individualism that most educated colonists embraced; "but, having just gone over that ground with great care, I feel a becoming confidence that I shall not be driven from it." Having chosen to defend an elaborate, demanding philosophical position, he felt conscious of no inconsistency between this stand and his mildly Whiggish reaction to the British measures in the 1760's. He had branded the Stamp Act "oppressive, impolitic, and illegal" and had praised Virginia's resolves against the Townshend duties as "the most warrantable, generous, and manly that history can produce."[24] As late as 1774, he conceded that British colonial policy had been inconsistent, often unfair, and dangerously insensitive to colonial petitions for redress. Looming above this background of imperial incompetence, the contagion of colonial resistance and hostility threatened to engulf and destroy all civilized and rational communication between colonists and the mother country. "If through the degeneracy or the imperfection of all political wisdom, . . . she now seems to us no longer just or generous, let us in common candor hope and believe that she neither can nor will persist in a temper . . . unnatural to her."[25] Boucher learned, however, that the judgmental way Americans regarded British policy was too deeply instilled by decades of mild rule and social development to be eradicated by any appeal to prudence or restraint. "Civil broils are the luxuriant offspring of the best formed governments, as hurricanes are of the finest climates," he wrote in January 1776, shortly after fleeing the colonies. He analyzed the political process behind this figure of speech: "Early prejudices, fostered by education and confirmed by religion, all conspire to cherish republicanism. Their schools, academies, or colleges seem . . . to have been instituted for that end; all their students are orators, philosophers, or statesmen [who] . . . harangue plausibly. . . . The multitude will ever be wrought on by public speaking; in America, literally and truly, all power flows from the people."[26] Because Boucher was sensitive to the influence of oratory in the colonies, to the intellectual respectability of republican ideas, and to the popular sources of political authority, he conceived of himself as a contentious figure thrust by circumstances into Maryland politics at the very moment when the opposing forces of authority and rebellion were closely matched and the outcome of the contest still in doubt. His duty was clear: the vindication of an "ancient, honorable, moribund philosophy"[27] of order and obedience was an impulse that swept him free of the protective moorings of prudence, self-preservation, or inertia.

20

Peter Oliver and the Horror
of Rebellion

WHEN Peter Oliver graduated from Harvard in 1730, his name stood at the head of the class because among his classmates he came from the most socially august family. He was related to some of the most powerful and wealthy families in New England. His uncle Jonathan Belcher, Governor of Massachusetts from 1730 to 1741 and of New Jersey from 1747 to 1757, had amassed enormous wealth and political influence throughout the Empire. Peter Oliver's father was pious, scrupulously honest and diligent, and a very successful merchant, and Peter's elder brother, Andrew, became influential in his own right. In alliance with Andrew's brother-in-law, Thomas Hutchinson, the Oliver family would acquire strategic political offices at every level of Massachusetts government. Both Peter and Andrew served in the House of Representatives, the lower chamber of the General Court, and both were elevated by the lower house to seats on the Council—Andrew in 1743 and Peter in 1759—though both were defeated for re-election in 1766 in the aftermath of the Stamp Act crisis. Andrew also held the influential position of secretary to the province from 1755 to 1770, and in 1771 he succeeded Hutchinson as lieutenant governor. Office was their public duty and usually a burdensome expense, but it also brought the Oliver family tangible advantages: military contracts in time of war, numerous local offices for family and allies, and, in the 1740's and 1750's, a strategic position from which to oppose inflationary money schemes.

A combination of business acumen and political influence enabled Peter and Andrew to triple the value of their inheritance by the eve of the Revolution. Peter did so through diverse activities in commerce, farming, and iron manufacturing. In Middleborough, Massachusetts, where his foundry was located, he built a magnificent home and estate. This hard-working, energetic, curious man developed an impenetrable shell of intellectual certainty. "There was only one man in Middleborough," Clifford K. Shipton writes, "who would express a contrary opinion if [Oliver] had already stated his views on a subject." Oliver unhesitatingly formed strong opinions and acted upon them. He built an advanced iron-slitting mill by using an industrial spy disguised as an idiot to study the only comparable facility in the colonies; the British Society for Promoting Agriculture recognized his work on scientific farming; a staunch Congregationalist, he favored a new form of hymn singing described by unappreciative church members as "bawling in the gallery with the boys"; he used a divining rod to locate mineral deposits, collected hundreds of historical documents, and wrote creditable poetry. Without formal legal training, he became a popular and respected jurist—Plymouth County justice of the peace from 1744 to 1747, judge of the court of common pleas from 1747 to 1756, and, finally, a seat on the Massachusetts Superior Court. When the court went on circuit from one county seat to another, Shipton relates, Oliver traveled "in a coach emblazoned with his arms and accompanied by postillions and outriders in scarlet livery." In 1772, on Governor Hutchinson's recommendation, he became chief justice of the superior court.[1] His ostentation was neither defensive nor anachronistic. Massachusetts society in the middle of the eighteenth century expected a segment of its elite to amass a disproportionate share of power and influence, to protect their elitist economic interests, and to gratify expensive tastes in houses, furnishings, and entertainment. Oliver's contemporaries believed, Robert Zemsky explains, that their political system was "an eminently reasonable amalgam of royal prerogative, popular expression, and conservative control." Men like Andrew and Peter Oliver, with vast ability, contact with royal officials, and great wealth, still occupied a privileged and respected position in society. The abrupt increase in the power and influence of the Oliver-Hutchinson alignment under the administration of Governor Francis Bernard, however, made the

Oliver family in the early 1760's unusually vulnerable to hostility and resentment; Andrew Oliver's appointment as stamp distributor in 1765 provoked an eruption of these feelings when the mob broke into his house and smashed everything breakable in sight. Peter Oliver responded to the violence against the Stamp Act with bluff good humor; he spent most of the crisis sequestered in Middleborough, cultivating his potatoes, he said, and he jokingly asked Hutchinson to remind King George that, during the riots, officers of the Crown had taken refuge in his Boston pigeon house. "If I am not a man of the first consequence," he wrote in mock defense of his loyal position during the Stamp Act troubles, "there is no man of consequence at all. I expect a very great reward for my services."[2] The next ten years destroyed Peter Oliver's imperturbability. He became one of the most bitter and intransigent critics of the pre-Revolutionary movement. Later, during his exile in England, he wrote *The Origin and Progress of the American Rebellion,* a craftsmanlike and often brilliant polemic about revolution in Massachusetts.

The events that thrust Peter Oliver into the vortex of conflict in Massachusetts began with the Boston Massacre trials, over which he presided as superior-court justice. He was the only member of the court, in Hutchinson's opinion, who refused to be intimidated by hostile Boston crowds demanding the conviction and execution of the soldiers. Oliver's conduct of the case and his thorough summation of the evidence in his instructions to the jurors did almost as much as John Adams's defense of the soldiers to win acquittals for Preston and all but two of his men. The case made both British officials and Massachusetts popular leaders still more keenly aware that judges occupied the most politically sensitive positions in Massachusetts. In 1772 the Crown decided to use some of the revenue from the Townshend duties to pay the salaries of Massachusetts judges. The new practice became known in early 1773, when Oliver drew only half of his provincial salary because he expected the British Treasury to augment his judicial income substantially. Oliver tried to allay criticisms of his new salary by proposing what seemed to him a reasonable compromise to a group of assemblymen. If the General Court would compensate him for the £2,000 of his own money he had expended as judge in the service of the province,

Oliver would seek the King's permission to decline the Crown grant or he would resign from the bench. Privately the legislators told Oliver to accept the Crown salary and remain chief justice.

Throughout the summer of 1773, however, protests against the Crown salaries mounted, and other judges discreetly refused to accept the new stipends. Peter Oliver stood alone in refusing to surrender his salary. Jurors in Boston and Worcester in August and September 1773 dramatically refused to serve if Oliver was on the bench. In early 1774 the House of Representatives resolved that Oliver should be removed from his office because his acceptance of a Crown salary was "contrary to the usage and custom of the . . . Superior Court, . . . contrary to the plain sense and meaning of the . . . Charter [which allowed the General Court to pay the salaries of Crown officials], and against the known constitution of this province." Most damning of all was the fact that the salary was tainted money, "revenue unjustly and unconstitutionally levied and extorted from the inhabitants of the American colonies." Oliver's insensitivity to this constitutional issue—his willingness to become a beneficiary of Parliamentary taxation and his close attachment to the British Crown —"hath an obvious and direct tendency to the perversion of law and justice in the . . . Superior Court," the House concluded. The House forbade Oliver to continue sitting as judge, on February 24, 1774, voted ninety-two to eight to impeach him for accepting a Crown salary, and asked the Council and the Governor to remove the Chief Justice from office. Hutchinson declared that he had no power to remove a royal appointee and refused to convey the House's resolution to the Crown. In March 1774 Peter Oliver's brother, Lieutenant Governor Andrew Oliver, died. In vain, Hutchinson asked popular leaders to promise the Chief Justice safe-conduct to attend the funeral in Boston; Oliver dared not appear, and other mourners marched to the cemetery amid jeers and insults. Had Oliver remained in seclusion in Middleborough after these incidents, he might have avoided further trouble. Instead, he took his place on the bench when the superior court met in Charles Town in April 1774. The grand jurors denounced Oliver for "sitting as Chief Justice . . . while he himself lies under impeachment for high crimes and misdemeanors." In May, Oliver asked his fellow judge Edmund Trowbridge whether the rest of the superior court would support him by rebuking and fining obstreperous jurors. Trowbridge avoided a direct answer but advised Oliver for his own safety to stay away when the court next sat in Plymouth. Oliver complied, but he insisted on presiding over the Boston session of the court, which convened on August 30. A crowd of more than a thousand surrounded the courthouse, restrained only by the presence of British troops under the command of the new royal Governor, General Thomas Gage. Oliver and the other judges took their places in the tense courtroom; the jurors predictably refused to serve as long as Oliver was present; the judges filed out of the building to the hisses of the populace. Oliver had become by this point the symbol of all that was unbending, privileged, and haughty in British officialdom. Crowds repeatedly stopped his carriage, blocked the shipment of any of his possessions from Middleborough to Boston, and in November even dragged him bodily from the Boston courtroom. Characteristically, he returned to the bench the next day under armed guard. But with Boston under virtual martial law and the rest of Massachusetts in rebellious defiance, the work of the superior court came to an end in February 1775. Peter Oliver remained in the besieged city for more than a year, buried his wife there in March 1775, served on Gage's new royally appointed Council, and sailed first to Halifax and then to London when the British evacuated Boston in March 1776.[3]

Oliver's *Origin and Progress of the American Rebellion,* a most important document which languished in manuscript until it was published in 1961, reveals how much he had learned and suffered from the experience. "Any reader of Oliver's account of Massachusetts' revolutionary politics," the editors of his history emphasize, "will recognize that Oliver had suffered a traumatic experience. His descriptions of the leaders of the patriot party" were "unforgiving and bitter." He depicted James Otis, Jr., as a brilliant intellect but drunken, wildly ambitious, often irrational, and the first avowed enemy of royal government, the first to foment actual resistance against British authority by deluding the simple. Oliver cast Samuel Adams as the Devil constantly whispering flattery to his Eve, the egotistical and stupid John Hancock. "Mr. Hancock . . . was as closely attached to the hindermost part of Mr. Adams as the rattles are affixed to the tail of the rattlesnake," Oliver remarked, switching to a still more demeaning figure of speech. The son of a meagerly paid parson, Hancock had inherited a fabulously rich mercantile business from his uncle. "His understanding was of the dwarf size," Oliver explained, "but his ambition, upon the accession to so great an estate, was . . . gigantic." Capitalizing on this fact, Samuel Adams exercised an almost hypnotic influence over Hancock; and whenever the merchant showed signs of thinking for himself, "Adams, like the cuddlefish [i.e., octopus] would discharge his muddy liquid and darken the water to such a hue that [Hancock] was lost . . . in the cloudy vortex." Oliver's most bitter attacks fell upon the Congregationalist clergymen who sanctioned resistance against British authority and lent a sanctimonious air to the proceeding. He called them "Mr. *Otis's* black regiment, . . . a set of very weak men" who flocked to the ministry to avoid menial labor. Mounted in the pulpit, they "acquired a supreme self-importance which was too apparent in their manners." They were, in Oliver's estimation, intellectual frauds and the "few" intelligent and learned clergy were, in most cases, "tinctured with republicanism." At the root of the problem was the fact that the Boston churches, instead of prescribing moral values, responded to the demands of the people. "The town of Boston, being the metropolis, . . . was also the metropolis of sedition, and hence it was that their clergy, being dependent on the people for . . . daily bread [and] having frequent intercourse with the people, imbibed their principles."[4]

Oliver's little sketch of the black regiment skittering around the streets of Boston, obsequiously currying favor with the populace, and embracing the lowest common denominator of political opinion was not merely a literary device. Word pictures were Oliver's method of analyzing political processes. Oliver was asking some of the most serious and important questions that have ever been raised about the American Revolution: Why did revolt occur in the most mildly governed of colonial empires? What mixture of impulse, calculation, and contagion made particular Americans act as they did between 1760 and 1776? What processes converted disaffection into rebellion? Intimately involved with the events he was describing, and passionately subjective in his interpretation, Oliver seized upon pictorial description as a means of making his indictment persuasive. Pen sketches, figures of speech, and little dramatizations were his hypotheses—imaginative windows to the interior of tumultuous events. "As for the people in general," he wrote in a sharply etched example of this method, "they were like the mobility of all countries, perfect machines, wound up by any hand who might first take the winch. They were like the poor Negro boy, who in the time of the late Stamp Act was bid by his master to fetch something from his barn, but did not move at the command. His master spoke to him with severity and asked him why he did not go as he was bid? The poor wretch replied with tears in his eyes, 'me fraid Massah Tamp he catch me.' Thus the common people had had that act . . . dressed up by their seditious leaders either with raw head and bloody bones or with horns, tails, and cloven feet." In this one passage, Oliver had fused three images: the winch-operated machine, the pathetic fear of the black boy, and the popular representation of British laws as ghoulish figures. To these he added a fourth picture: "As for men of sense who could see through the delusion, it would have been imprudent . . . to have interposed; for the government was in the hands of the mob . . . and it was in vain to combat *a whirlwind or a hurricane.*"[5]

The allusions to which Oliver turned most often in the last resort, therefore, came from his extensive knowledge of natural science. Anxious to protect illicit profits from smuggling, merchants denounced the Navigation Acts as a threat to "liberty"—a word with a "magic . . . sound" that "echoed through the interior parts of the country and the deluded vulgar were charmed with it; like the poor harmless squirrel that runs into the mouth of the *rattlesnake* the fascination in the word *liberty* threw the people into the harpy claws of their destroyers, and for what? [Nothing] but to gratify the artful smugglers in carrying on their contraband tea trade with the Dutch." Dr. Samuel Cooper, the most sophisticated of the radical clergymen, in Oliver's estimation, had a "tongue" of "butter and oil but under it was the poison of asps," and when the Boston rabble gathered to conspire acts of lawlessness "the serpentine Dr. Cooper presided." Former Massachusetts Governor Thomas Pownall (1757–

1760), the philosophical English gentleman who sympathized with some colonial grievances, was a "venemous animal, . . . a vermin" who "gnawed and poisoned" the British nation "almost to death." News of William Pitt's declaration in the House of Commons in 1765, "I rejoice that America hath resisted," was "like an electric shock" that "instantaneously pervaded the whole American continent." Indeed, Oliver summed up the difference between the British and colonial political cultures when he described the Crown's removal of unpopular royal governors in the early eighteenth century as "a stimulus to the itch of complaining" that spurred popular politicians to tireless campaigns of opposition. In responding to such ceaseless energy and opportunism, lamentably, "the springs of the English government too often lost their elasticity." British reluctance to punish colonial radicals who broke the law provoked Oliver to repeat the image: "A law without penalties, or . . . penalties not exacted is similar to a clock whose machinery hath no weight to set the wheels in motion or a watch whose spring hath lost its elasticity." The images of the "itch" for power and recognition and of the slack "spring" of weakened imperial authority suggested that British conduct could be explained in predictable mechanical terms, while a mysterious physiological process lay at the core of colonial discontent. Oliver's description of brutish, painful, uncontrollable natural processes expressed his conviction that just below the surface of human civility were ferocious and destructive animal passions capable of causing "anarchy and every species of confusion" if ever unleashed in sufficient quantity.[6]

To account for the awesome power and unnatural pattern of colonial aggression, Oliver employed two symbolic representations, the hydra and the volcano. Oliver used the hydra, the horrible nine-headed serpent of Greek mythology, to depict the early colonial critics of the Stamp Act, men like Otis and Dulany, a group "whose every factious mouth vomited out curses against *Great Britain.*" Massachusetts "was the *volcano* from whence issues all the smoke, flame, and lava which . . . enveloped the whole British American continent." The hydra brought sedition into the open: the volcano of Massachusetts's example ignited insurrection from New Hampshire to Georgia. Between 1776 and

1779, haunted by these perceptions, Oliver flirted with the macabre. *"Rebellion is as the sin of witchcraft,"* he declared in his last published writing in America, in January 1776. "It is so my countrymen! in a double sense; for in the first place, no person but one who was bewitched would run the risk of engaging in a rebellion; and in the next place, . . . as witchcraft is renouncing the authority of *God Almighty* and applying to the Devil, so rebellion is withdrawing allegiance from a lawful sovereign, overturning his government and laws, and joining a power inimical to him."[7] On March 27, 1776, as the British were evacuating Boston, Oliver sailed for England and wrote, as the ship pulled away from the coast of his native Massachusetts: "Here I took my leave of that once happy country, where peace and plenty reigned uncontrolled, till that infernal hydra rebellion, with its hundred heads, had devoured its happiness, spread desolation over its fertile fields, and ravaged the peaceful mansions of its inhabitants." He reached London on June 23, thankful to "be protected from the harpy claws of that rebellion which is now tearing out its own bowels in America, as well as destroying all who in any degree oppose its progress."[8]

The opportunity to travel widely in England and the difficult work of arranging his affairs reactivated Oliver's energy and curiosity; his diary of his travels sparkles with acute observations and descriptions. But occasionally his growing preoccupation with death asserted itself. On October 26, 1776, he visited a church in Grantham, and after studying the external architecture carefully, he descended into the cellar, where he found thousands of skulls and other human bones from some ancient burial stacked neatly in ghastly piles. On the wall was a sign bearing the words "Such as *I* am, such you must be; such as *you* are, I was like to thee; pray remember the sexton, 1710." Oliver almost trembled with anger as he wrote his denunciation of the sexton, who sixty-six years earlier "monopolized the profits of exhibiting these ruins to humanity. . . . I dare say he gained more from the dead than from the living for he appeared so much of a skeleton himself that he was fitted to make his own contribution to those heaps of mortality." The following June found Oliver standing in Westminster Abbey, transfixed with the "venerable and solemn effect" of entering this "repository of the dead," with its graves of so many famous and forgotten men. He could not help murmuring to himself, *"Such as you are, such I must be."*[9] It was as if the horror of the American Revolution had impressed upon Oliver that death was every man's companion and that agitation and discontent deprived innocent and guilty alike of irreplaceable moments of life.

21

Samuel Seabury and the Perception
of Political Truth

THE ability to articulate the sensations of outrage and horror and to channel this emotional energy into vigorous action during the confused and agitated period in late 1774 and early 1775 was the peculiar talent of the Reverend Samuel Seabury, Jr., of Westchester, New York. His father, Samuel Seabury, Sr., had been among the pioneers of New England Anglicanism who had followed the example of Samuel Johnson and left the Congregationalist church to seek Anglican ordination. In 1743 the elder Seabury moved from New London, Connecticut to Hempstead, New York, on Long Island. Samuel, Jr., graduated from Yale in 1748 and studied medicine at Edinburgh before obtaining Anglican ordination and an appointment as an S.P.G. missionary in 1753. Difficulty and frustration beset the first twelve years of Seabury's ministry. The S.P.G. sent him first to serve a scattering of Anglican churches around New Brunswick, New Jersey, a stronghold of Presbyterian and Dutch Reformed denominations. He gladly escaped to the more familiar setting of Jamaica, New York, on Long Island, in 1757, only to find the parish infested with Quakers, who encouraged "a general indifference to all religion" by their disregard for formal worship and institutional religious activity. The scandalous conduct of an Anglican clergyman in Westchester who was charged with drunkenness and a sexual assault on the son of the church warden in 1765 created a vacancy in the reasonably comfortable and congenial parish to which Seabury moved in 1766. There he operated a school and settled into an uneventful parish ministry. "Though I think appearances are somewhat mended since I have been in this mission," he wrote of his first five years in the town of West-chester, "yet my success has not been equal to my first expecta-tions. I find it very difficult to convince people that religion is a matter of any importance."[1]

Never "an eminently successful parish priest," his most recent biographer writes, Seabury nonetheless had unusual qualities of intellect and judgment that impressed his fellow churchmen. During the 1750's and 1760's, his friends Thomas Bradbury Chandler, John Inglis, and Myles Cooper invited Seabury to join in their campaign to defend high Anglicanism from virulent public attacks by dissenters. Despite his impeccable credentials and connections as the son of a famous Anglican clergyman, a protégé of Samuel Johnson, and an intimate of Chandler, Cooper, and Inglis, Seabury remained on the fringe of this clique of high-Anglican leaders. Lethargy and despondency aggravated by financial anxiety periodically beset him, and he came to despise controversies with dissenters. After completing a reply to a particularly obnoxious dissenting publication, Seabury com-plained that "I am tired and beat out. Had I suspected that there was so much nonsense, so much trifling, so much falsehood in the way, I believe I never should have meddled with him. It is the worst, the most disagreeable task I ever undertook. Tis like suing a beggar, or shearing a hog, or fighting a skunk." When Chandler proposed that Seabury apply his great intellectual and scholarly talents to the task of writing a complete refutation to Jonathan Edwards's *Freedom of the Will,* he found Seabury too "dull and inactive" to undertake the assignment. There was a quality of reticence and irresolution that kept Seabury from moving into the vanguard of leadership among the high Angli-cans during the 1760's and early 1770's.[2] New York's participa-tion in the First Continental Congress and Congress's imposition of nonimportation in the autumn of 1774, however, created just the impetus needed to thrust Seabury into action.

Seabury's *Letters of a Westchester Farmer* was the most comprehensive and sustained polemical effort by any doctrinaire Tory to repudiate the pre-Revolutionary movement, demolish its constitutional arguments, discredit its methods of protest, and expose its coercive tactics and presumptions. In the first letter, *Free Thoughts on the Proceedings of the Congress . . . ,* dated

245

November 16, 1774, Seabury condemned Congress's imposition of nonimportation on the colonies and the extralegal methods of its enforcement. *The Congress Canvassed; or an examination into the Conduct of the Delegates, Addressed to the Merchants of New York,* completed eight days later, focused on the Tea Act and denied that the duty on tea was a deprivation of liberty. After Alexander Hamilton, then a student at King's College, responded anonymously to *Free Thoughts* in *A Full Vindication of the Measures of the Congress . . .* (New York, 1774), Seabury defended his position in *A View of the Controversy,* dated December 24, 1774. On January 17, 1775, he completed *An Alarm to the Legislature,* the shortest of the four pamphlets and a concise summary of his argument. The fifth letter of a Westchester farmer, *The Republican Dissected . . . ,* responding to Hamilton's *The Farmer Refuted . . .* (New York, 1775), was advertised on April 20, 1775, but never appeared, and its publication was probably suppressed.

The *Westchester Farmer* certainly provoked the New York Whigs' consternation. The most striking quality of the pamphlets was Seabury's colorful denunciation of violence. "Do as you please," he taunted his readers who would acquiesce to enforcement of the 1774 nonimportation boycott on British goods; "if you like it better, choose your committee or suffer it to be chosen by a half dozen fools in your neighborhood—open your doors to them—let them examine your tea-cannisters and molasses-jugs, and your wives' and daughters' petty coats—bow and cringe and tremble and quake—fall down and worship our sovereign lord the mob. . . . Should any pragmatical committee-gentleman come to my house and give himself airs, I shall show him the door, and if he does not soon take himself away, a good hickory cudgel shall teach him better manners." In contrast with most Revolutionary pamphleteers, who were caught up in the seriousness and complexity of the debate, Seabury managed to overcome his distaste for controversy and compose some superbly insulting retorts. "Do you think, sir," he asked Hamilton, "that Great Britain is like an old, wrinkled, withered, worn-out hag, whom every jackanape that truants along the street may insult with impunity? You will find her a vigorous matron, just approaching green old age, and with spirit sufficient to chastise her undutiful and rebellious subjects." In recalling the hopes of moderate men that the First Continental Congress would seek reconciliation, Seabury used a series of images that mocked the Congress and its admirers and then injected a note of terror into the jocular scene: "Like the country people in the fable, we stood all attentive to the *throes* and *pangs* of the labouring mountain, . . . with the expectation of some mighty matter to be produced at birth. I would to God that our expectations, like theirs, had ended in laughter and merriment; but alas the labour of the Congress produced, not a silly mouse to make us laugh, but a venomous brood of scorpions to sting us to death."[3]

While Seabury's surprising talent for vituperation may account for the contemporary notoriety of the *Letters of a Westchester Farmer*, his chief concern in these pamphlets was to understand, explain, and ultimately influence the mental processes that operated in men as they came under the influence of seditious teachings. He was deeply interested in the psychology of perception. Possibly it dated to his training in medicine; certainly Samuel Johnson's writings must have strongly encouraged his speculation about the mind. Seabury's most systematic statement on the subject was a sermon on II Timothy 3:16 ("All scripture is given by inspiration of God"), preached first in Trinity Church, New York, in 1773. Dealing with "the proper use of human reason" in the search for spiritual guidance, Seabury defined reason as the capacity of the mind to connect, relate, and recognize individual pieces of observation and experience. He believed that reason was a tool rather than a source of wisdom in its own right; no amount of rational inquiry could reveal to man the world of the spirit or the nature of God. Rather, Seabury declared, echoing Samuel Johnson, such knowledge came through man's "internal sense, a quick sensibility of good and evil . . . which in conjunction with his reason makes him capable of religion and moral obligation." Because false insights would be "contrary to our reason," while true intuition would be "above its reach," Seabury argued that man could use reason to verify "the credibility" of his spiritual insights. Nature was full of evidence corroborating the immortality of the soul and sovereignty of God. Trouble arose when men's minds acquired "vicious affections" or "warped prejudices" that prevented them from performing the task of verification. In religion, prejudice produced the evil of dogmatic theology, and Seabury condemned the "system-makers and commentators" who conjured up such doctrines as salvation by election, salvation without good works, and original sin, doctrines that, in his view, contradicted man's instinctive knowledge of God's love and justice and were therefore contrary to reason. To prevent such a corruption of the mind, constant mental discipline was required because, he concluded, "this [uncorrupted] knowledge of God will not terminate in an inactive, speculative faith nor in the vain pride of disputation" but, rather, would "descend deep into the heart, and . . . subdue and regulate the lusts and passions."[4]

In the political contention of the pre-Revolutionary period, Seabury wanted reason to permeate men's consciousness to "subdue and regulate" their passions. He knew that process of emotional pacification was enormously difficult. In 1769 he lamented that "politics engross almost everybody and leave little or no room for more serious or important reflection."[5] By 1774 this preoccupation had become dangerously perverse: "A kind of sullen, sulky obstinacy takes possession of us" during a period of discontent. "Preposterous pride! It defeats the end it aims at. It degrades instead of exalting our characters" and destroys the ability "to learn prudence from our own misconduct."[6] The absolutely crucial element in eluding this infection, Seabury maintained, was to avoid overtaxing the capacity of the mind at the very outset of any thought about politics. Men must refrain from asking long-range questions about the equity, tendency, and implications of British policy that called for conjectural and emotion-tinged answers. Instead, they must ask limited questions concerning problems close at hand and readily observable. "What must be the case," he asked the New York Assembly in January 1775, "when all proper and moderate measures are *rejected* and not even the *appearance* of decency is regarded, when nothing seems to be consulted but how to perplex, irritate, and affront the *British ministry, Parliament, Nation, and King?*"[7]

The process of asking limited questions about immediately observable conditions—such as the effects on society of political acrimony and upheaval—should, according to Seabury, have protected moderate men from unwitting complicity in rebellion.

The tumultuous way New York's delegates to the First Continental Congress had been selected, for example, tainted that colony's participation in the Congress. Even New York's moderate delegates compromised themselves by agreeing to serve in an illegitimate body. They sat helpless as more radical and uninhibited delegates endorsed the Suffolk Resolves and imposed nonimportation on the colonies. "All the insidious arts that evil-minded and designing men can make use of," he warned the New York assemblymen, now operated to lure well-meaning, moderate men *"away* from *rectitude of conduct."* The only way to participate in colonial remonstrance without giving the initiative to "evil-minded . . . designing men," Seabury concluded, was to "try [a closely controlled] experiment: . . . only show your willingness towards accommodation by acknowledging the supreme legislative authority of Great Britain and I dare confidently pronounce the attainment of whatever you, with propriety, can ask and the LEGISLATURE OF GREAT BRITAIN [can], with *honour, concede."* That extremely narrow ground for political change within the Empire, between what "propriety" permitted the colonists to ask and "honour" allowed Britain to give, was exactly the scope of political change that Seabury believed men had the capacity and the moral right to pursue.[8]

Alexander Hamilton's *Full Vindication of the Measures of the Congress* enabled Seabury to amplify his views on the perversion of thought processes in the pre-Revolutionary controversy. Hamilton was a prime example of the problem, but he was intelligent enough to be at least partially conscious of his own deceit. "You felt, Sir, the force of the stubborn facts . . . in the *Free Thoughts.* You perceived the ground on which the decrees of the Congress were founded to be hollow. . . . You had no remedy but *artifice, sophistry, misrepresentation,* and *abuse."* So emboldened, Seabury denied that his attacks on Congress were "presumptuous," as Hamilton had charged. Public criticism of legislative bodies was a normal practice. Surely the patriots indulged in it; "does not every pidler in politics, who calls himself a *son of liberty,* take the licence of censuring . . . the conduct of the *King,* the *Lords,* and the *Commons,* the supreme sovereign authority of the whole British Empire?" Though simply claiming a similar privilege to attack members of Congress,

Seabury did impose a restriction on his invective, confining his scrutiny to "their public conduct as *delegates*." Thus limiting the discussion to manageable bounds, he took up Hamilton's first broadside, the contention that since the New York delegates to Congress represented the entire province, all its citizens owed loyal support to Congress. Seabury quoted Hamilton's words and then feigned a long pause. "I have looked at this paragraph at least ten times, and every time with astonishment. It is so superlatively arrogant and impudent, that I confess myself at a loss what to say to it." Even if his highest hopes had been well-founded and the New York delegates had attempted to moderate the resolutions of Congress, Seabury exclaimed, they still forfeited his respect by acquiescing in the radical measures that Congress adopted. Moderate and obedient New Yorkers certainly had not been faithfully represented in Congress. "Evil communications corrupt good manners," Seabury concluded; "let no man hereafter trust himself at a Philadelphia Congress!"[9]

Trying to get at the root of Hamilton's technique of deception, Seabury delved into semantics. Hamilton, he conceded, had gone to needless lengths to prove that liberty was a good thing and slavery bad. Even granting this claim, he asked, by what logic could Hamilton associate liberty only with the aims of Congress and slavery exclusively with British policy? Potentially both Congress and Parliament could either impose slavery or preserve liberty, and he knew of no reason to suppose that liberty under Parliament was not preferable to liberty under Congress. As a practical matter, Congress's nonimportation association deprived men throughout the colonies of their liberty to conduct their own business. Hamilton not only attributed capricious meanings to words, Seabury continued, but he mixed together contradictory concepts. When he spoke of the colonies as autonomous societies, Seabury corrected him: "It is an impropriety of speech to talk of an independent colony. The words *independency* and *colony* convey contradictory meanings." Such semantic sophistry, Seabury continued, led Hamilton to erroneous conclusions about the right of the colonies to legislate for themselves. "Legislation is not an inherent right of the colonies," Seabury argued, because the Roman colonies never possessed such a power. Hamilton's contention that Parliament could not legislate for the colonies,

Seabury declared, "has arisen from an artful change of terms." He then proceeded to restore the words "representative," "colony," "Parliament," and "legislation" to their correct meanings in a rather crude restatement of the doctrine of virtual representation.[10]

Gathering momentum, the remainder of *A View of the Controversy* made a comprehensive and inflexible case against colonial claims: the limited extent of colonial charters, the colonies' obligation and ability to pay British taxes, the subordination of the assemblies, the illegitimacy of Congress as a representative body, the prudence of placating Parliament, the beneficial character of the Navigation Acts, the economic advantages of staying within the Empire, Britain's obvious ability to crush colonial rebellion, and, finally, the reasonableness of customs duties and the Quebec Act. Seabury managed, in the midst of this immense constitutional and political argument, to relate it all to his central concern. "That you will perceive the force of this reasoning," he told Hamilton, "I cannot pretend to say. A person diseased with the jaundice sees no colour but yellow. Party heat, *the fever of liberty, may . . . vitiate the mind,* as much as . . . jaundice does the eyes." Colonial unrest seemed to him an interplay between blind impulse and inflamed emotion—a downward spiral toward rebellion that reversed the operation of human perception, prevented prudent self-correction, and destroyed the use of reason as a tool in the consideration of human affairs.[11]

Seabury's pamphlets may have had some effect on the New York Assembly, which in February 1775 refused to endorse the work of the First Continental Congress and then petitioned Parliament and the King for a settlement of the imperial controversy. Rebuffed by the Assembly, the New York Whigs called for a provincial convention to name delegates to the Second Continental Congress and direct New York's defiance of British authority. Seabury participated prominently in an impromptu meeting of between 300 and 400 Westchester County loyalists opposed to further complicity in colonial resistance, probably the largest spontaneous political gathering by loyalists in the entire pre-Revolutionary period. On November 22, 1775, a company of about forty armed men came to his home while he was conducting grammar-school classes, seized him, and took him to the town of East Chester. There another fifty men, led by the prominent New York Son of Liberty, Colonel Isaac Sears, joined Seabury's captors and took him to New Haven, Connecticut, where he was held prisoner for seven weeks. His captors in New Haven tried to get him to admit writing the *Letters of a Westchester Farmer;* Seabury refused to affirm or deny the charge and finally secured permission to appeal to the Connecticut General Assembly for release. Apparently tired of holding him, his guards let Seabury slip away from the house where he had been held and return to New York. In December 1776 he looked back on the upheaval he had experienced during the preceding two and a half years and succinctly reiterated the role he had sought to play: "When the present unnatural rebellion was first beginning, I foresaw evidently what was coming on the country, and I exerted myself to stem the torrent of popular clamor, to recall the people to the use of their reason, and to retain them in their loyalty and allegiance."[12]

22

Myles Cooper and the Civilizing
of American Society

THE Reverend Myles Cooper, Samuel Johnson's successor as president of King's College from 1763 to 1775, made the most sophisticated effort to elevate high-Anglican political thought to the level of a viable intellectual position. A graduate of Queen's College, Oxford, who had emigrated to the colonies in 1762, Cooper endeavored to transform King's into a kind of American Oxford—an institution that would be a bulwark of academic excellence and political conservatism. In 1767 he added a medical school modeled on Oxford's. He used the device of honorary degrees to bestow the college's recognition on outspoken Anglican clergy and on laymen active in the support of British authority. Of twenty-nine honorary doctorates between 1765 and 1774, four went to Anglican members of the school's new medical faculty; Governor Tryon and his secretary were both recipients; and twenty-two of the remaining twenty-three degrees were bestowed on prominent Anglican clergymen.

Cooper, moreover, dominated the board of governors and set in motion a long-term plan to transform King's College into a university with a royal charter, regius professorships, and close ties to the Anglican hierarchy in England. On October 12, 1771, at Cooper's instigation, the governors dispatched a battery of lengthy petitions to the King, Lords North and Hillsborough, and the Archbishops of York and Canterbury. These flowery memorials depicted King's College as a beleaguered outpost of Anglican orthodoxy and loyalty to the Crown and predicted that nothing less than substantial financial support from the Crown and parent church would enable the college to "become the

happy means of increasing learning, virtue, and piety; of diffus-
ing the principles of loyalty and of affection to the constitution;
and of perpetuating . . . the union between Great Britain and
her colonies." Cooper then sailed to England and spent several
months seeking financial support for King's, including endow-
ments for two or three regius professorships, the establishment of
an American episcopate, and an expanded Anglican missionary
program among the Iroquois. He got no support for Indian
missions or an American bishop, but he did secure remission of
quitrents on church property, a grant of 20,000 acres, and a gift of
books from the Clarendon Press at Oxford. He did not press for
approval of a university charter, however, until 1774, when the
governors completed their draft. It was, David C. Humphrey
declares, "an incredible document." Although vesting internal
control in the hands of faculties of each of its constituent colleges
and over-all governance in a large board of regents, real power
would have resided in a university senate. This would have
replaced the college's existing committee of visitation, composed
of New York City Anglican clergy and laity and already controlled by Cooper's allies. In the transition from college to
university, his control of the institution would have remained
undiminished.[1]

The onslaught of the Revolution aborted the plan for a King's
University in New York City, but Cooper's ambitious plans for
the institution were nevertheless significant. To Cooper, King's
College was locked in grim warfare with a numerous, aggressive,
fanatical foe. "We have enemies in abundance—that is every
dissenter of high principles upon the [American] continent is
our enemy," he wrote to Jonathan Boucher in 1770. "Many of
their missionaries from the northern into the southern provinces,
make it their business, nay, have it in charge from their masters,
to decry this institution by all *possible* means *because* they are
convinced from its very constitution (being in the hands only of
Churchmen [Anglican clergy]) they are convinced that it must
eventually prove one of the firmest supporters of the Church of
England in America. Hence there arose an opposition coeval
with the College itself, or rather with the very first mention of an
institution so circumstanced," Cooper noted, remembering the
bitter controversy in New York over the founding of the college,

"which hath continued without interruption to this very day, with much resentment, inveteracy, and malice."[2]

Cooper's remedy for these symptoms of social disorganization was a powerful Anglican mission in America, complete with a resident bishop, close control over the education and doctrinal fidelity of the clergy, and an Anglican university so prestigious and influential that it would knit believers into a cohesive and confident social alignment. The happy results of this transformation would be harmony and unity, a symmetrical social order, and an esthetically pleasing dignity in the conduct of government and the practice of religion. Once men began to taste this superior style of life, Cooper felt certain, they would in increasing numbers turn their backs on the contentious, emotional, and individualistic values that had dominated eighteenth-century American society.[3] In the course of a lengthy newspaper controversy in 1768 and 1769 between "The American Whig," written principally by William Livingston, and "A Whip for the American Whig," by Cooper, Charles Inglis, and others, Cooper explained the process by which Anglicanism might civilize and cultivate society. "Religion," he postulated, "is so confessedly advantageous to society that every reasonable man must endeavour to advance it," if only for the secular motive of "increasing the happiness of the society of which he is a member." Because the "advantages of honesty and obedience to government" do not automatically "restrain the sallies of ambition or the unresisted desire of unlimited freedom," only the prospect of ultimate divine judgment—"rewards" for "virtue and punishment of vice"—can insure the operation of "that *order* and *harmony* so requisite to the just motion in the springs of every political system."[4]

Cooper utilized the resources of Enlightenment philosophy in the "Whip" essays, depicting the political system as a natural phenomenon with qualities of order and harmony and conditions of health or disease. He conceived of political acquiescence as an attitude of mind requiring certain predispositions and assumptions. He knew that human institutions had to be rationally adapted to the natural scheme of things. Because religion was an intrinsic part of the process of allegiance and obedience, Cooper explained, the Crown had an entirely legitimate reason to enter into a "union" with the Church of England. The King's position as head and protector of the church, Cooper argued, "is a prerogative right in itself and advantageous to the state. Tis a just privilege resulting from the alliance between church and state. The civil magistrate, for the benefit of the commonwealth, desired an union between it and the Church. To effect this, the Church deprived herself of her natural independency and relied on the protection of the state, which was due to her for the advantages it would receive from her influence in its favour." The King's ecclesiastical power guaranteed that Anglican doctrines would not be "corrupted" and that the church would continue to be "serviceable" to the King. The Anglican establishment, moreover, kept the power of church and state in admirable equilibrium—another Enlightenment value—by preventing the King from arbitrarily manipulating the clergy and the church from treating rulers like puppets; it was a "conditional subordinancy." Finally, "this prerogative" by which the King was head of the church "tends . . . to create a reverence and veneration for the Prince, as head of two bodies united, as defender of their religious as well as civil privileges: a reverence extremely well adapted to engage his subjects to a ready and cheerful obedience." It was to this calling that Myles Cooper responded: the creation of visible institutional symbols of order and hierarchy in human affairs.[5]

23

Conclusion: The Anatomy
of Tory Doctrine

THE appeal to doctrine expressed the total antipathy to popular political activity and expressions of discontent felt by a small but articulate segment of colonial society. Less well informed about constitutional technicalities than the enunciators of principle, and far less open-minded and sensitive to political subtleties than the advocates of accommodation, the doctrinaire Tories perceived the intolerant, violent, outraged quality of the pre-Revolutionary movement in all its fury. They believed with total conviction that colonial resistance was morally wrong and esthetically abhorrent. Like a Picasso painting, their harsh, judgmental, and sometimes distorted portrayal revealed truths about the pre-Revolutionary impulse that more objective contemporary accounts did not comprehend. The Reverend John Wiswall, a native American, a Harvard graduate, and a respected S.P.G. missionary in Falmouth, Massachusetts, strove to avoid offending the town's Whig leaders during the tense period from the summer of 1774 to the spring of 1775. But his friendship with British naval officers whose ships operated from Falmouth harbor and his insistence on praying, according to Anglican liturgy, that God protect his parishioners " 'from all sedition, privy conspiracy, and rebellion' " gradually exposed him to "the malice and rage of a lawless rabble." On May 9, 1775, "a company of banditti" surrounded Wiswall and a British naval officer, Lieutenant Henry Mowat, and held them at gun point for more than three hours. After a hearing before the Falmouth selectmen, the two men were released from captivity but confined to the limits of the town. Mowat fled to his ship, H.M.S. *Canceaux*. After enduring further hostile interrogation before a local investigating committee, Wiswall also took refuge on the *Canceaux,* which took him to safety in Boston. Falmouth officials allowed Wiswall's wife and three children to gather a few possessions and join him there. The whole family immediately came down with a violent intestinal disorder that was widespread in the besieged port town, and his wife and only daughter died. Before he and his two sons sailed for England in January 1776, Wiswall tried to grasp what had happened to him during the previous year and a half as "a discontent bordering on madness," spread like "leaven" from one town to another in Massachusetts.[1] Only "the God who stilleth the raging of the sea, the noise of the waves, and the *madness* of the people" could "restore peace, order, and government to this distracted continent," for, he concluded, American society was "too free and happy" ever "to be contented with its happiness."[2] It was a remarkable insight, all the more because Wiswall used the term "happiness" in the same way Jefferson employed it a few months later in the Declaration of Independence, to refer to the almost painful state of expectancy that political liberty conferred upon a people. "A cruel and relentless mob, [of] several thousands, have rose in arms at a time with the most hostile intentions against those who hold a place in government, nay, to such a pitch of madness have the people arrived that we are now forbidden not only to speak but to think," wrote the Reverend William Clark, S.P.G. missionary in Dedham, Massachusetts, in October 1774, describing the ecstatic frenzy that carried men along and that they sought desperately to keep alive by humiliating and silencing the opposition.[3]

Sustaining this unnatural state of outrage, Thomas Bradbury Chandler exclaimed, was a kind of mass emotional illness that produced destructive, cruel, and vicious behavior. Chandler counterattacked by composing a series of one hundred questions designed to strip from the American position every shred of intellectual pretension. Ponderous and cumbersome, Chandler's questions nevertheless identified with unusual forcefulness the philosophical issues raised by the pre-Revolutionary debate: "Whether Great Britain bears not a relationship to these colonies similar to that of a parent to children?"; "Whether . . . plain facts [and] general and established principles" or "the opinions of empirics" should influence colonial thought?; "Whether . . . partial construction and remote inferences" on the meaning of ancient colonial charters were "valid either in law or equity?"; and, most important, "Whether some degree of respect be not always due from inferiors to superiors?" Chandler's formulations explicitly assumed that the colonists were suffering from a strange collective disorder, and his questions were laced with judgmental phraseology about the malady. "Bigotry and intolerance in politics," he declared, were "as absurd . . . and as destructive to society as bigotry and intolerance in matters of religion." "By refusing to hear or see what is offered on the side of government," he charged, "many of the colonists betray . . . fear" of the "weakness" of their "cause." As a result of their inability to consider both sides in the controversy openly, men gave themselves to a "feverish kind" of "language . . . attended with an irregular high pulse, and . . . dangerous swelling and inflammation . . . occasioned in great measure by their own *imprudence* and *intemperance.*" Thus afflicted, groups of men slandered and abused the opponents of colonial resistance and committed acts no "less disgusting and shocking to the genuine feelings of the *moral sense*" than the same actions would be if perpetrated by one human being against his neighbor. Chandler's sense of moral outrage, however, did not delude him into regarding American behavior as a mere aberration; one of his closing questions, implicitly acknowledging the extent and depth of discontent, asked "whether . . . the supreme governor of the world . . . has given any dispensation to the body of the people, under any government, to refuse *honor* or *custom* or *tribute* to whom they are *due;* to contract habits of thinking and *speaking evil of dignities,* and to weaken the natural principle of respect for those in authority?"[4]

The sources of this blasphemous presumption, the doctrinaire Tories declared, lay everywhere in colonial life and society. Henry Caner believed that any signs of moderation on the part of royal officials encouraged "the invidious designs of those who would interrupt the harmony and peace of government." "Bad men," he warned, "are made worse by forbearance." Fearful respect for the power of government, he explained, was not easy to instill. "Our sons of violence affect to appear unconcerned" about the punishment they might receive "and strive to keep alive the flame they have kindled among the ignorant, impiously asserting that God will show his power in their defense." If the Crown would authorize Gage to arrest and punish the leaders of resistance, "the troubles . . . will soon be composed." But any "modesty or timidity" on Gage's part would only cause "the insolence of our sovereign lords the people" to "increase till it becomes inexorable."[5] Nowhere was that insolence more blatant, wrote another Tory polemicist, than when it prompted unschooled common citizens to make public pronouncements about the history of the British constitution. A satirical drama, *The Debates at the Robin-Hood Society,* depicted this activity in an exchange among the characters Mr. Moderator, Mr. Make-do-all, and Mr. Smart Cock concerning the significance of the English Revolution of 1688:

Mr. Moderator [reading the draft of a colonial remonstrance]: 'Resolved that we will acknowledge . . . and will bear faith and true allegiance to his most sacred majesty King George, the third, our most gracious sovereign and rightful lord . . .'

Mr. Make-do-all: Mr. Moderator, I rise for to *purropose* an amendment; which is, *for* to put it 'liege' at least (you might indeed add 'lawful') , the more we *purropose,* the more the world will think us in earnest. A little tau-tau-tology is of no consequence in these times.

Mr. Moderator: A very good hint, sir; you know I am a lover of *professions.* '. . . gracious sovereign and rightful liege lord, that we will upon the true revolution principles . . .'

Mr. Smart Cock: 'Revolution *principles!*' what's that, what's that? Explain the term, if you please, Mr. Moderator.

Mr. Moderator: Why gentlemen, *revolution principles* means 'to be quiet as long as we think it our interest to be so; but the moment we imagine ourselves otherwise, to make all the bustle and confusion in our power.'

Mr. Smart Cock: Very well, very well; I'm satisfied; that is my sentiment. Ah! Mr. Silver Tongue [the author of the resolves], *larning* is better than house and land. I never knew so fine a thing could be said in two words before. Ay, ay! use him well whilst he behaves well; the first wry face he makes, let him feel his masters, the way I serve Cuff [Mr. Smart Cock's Negro slave]. Go on.[6]

The Triumph of the Whigs, a high-spirited parody of the patriot movement in New York, published in 1775, taunted Americans for the slippery, almost giddy way they manipulated the word "revolution": "Rouse, therefore, my friends! Support the Congress and assert your *native* rights of doing as you please. Your only danger will arise from . . . failing. . . . In that case you will indeed be *rebels* and may chance to be hanged. But if you *succeed,* it will only be a *revolution,* and you will be justified before God and man. Nothing . . . was wanting to make Lucifer's rebellion in Heaven *a glorious revolution* but success."[7]

The most scathing Tory polemic on the sources of colonial discontent was a sermon delivered by S.P.G. missionary the Reverend Samuel Andrews in Wallingford, Connecticut, on July 20, 1775, the day prescribed by Congress for services of prayer and fasting. He chose as his text Amos 5:21: "I hate, I despise your feast days, and I will not smell in your solemn assemblies." Mocking the ritual of formal, collective repentance and prayer for forgiveness, Andrews warned that an "unruly," "vindictive," "ungodly spirit with those who happen to differ with us in things civil or religious" utterly destroyed the worshipers' claims of penitence. Amos expressly condemned those who *"drew nigh to God . . . while their hearts were removed far from him."* The very act of confession and petition for forgiveness imposed a heavy responsibility on men to make certain that theirs was "real grief and sorrow for sin" and that they had done everything within their power to abstain from boastful, angry, cruel, or disruptive behavior. Scripture required the most severe renunciation of malice, illtemper, judgment against neighbors, or divisiveness, Andrews insisted, before men could be certain that God would not be angered by their prayers for forgiveness. "Only . . . if we . . . repent . . . of our vileness, as a people and reform our manners—live in strict piety towards God and charity towards men, and perform all the duties of our stations as good Christians and faithful subjects, without controversy—[will] our 'light break forth as the morning . . . and the glory of the Lord be our reward.'" There could be no hidden reservations, no inten. to resume public contention after the appeal for forgiveness, he continued, for *"if we . . .* attend this fast with a proper temper," worshipers must necessarily declare "an unshaken . . . resolution" to adopt "a total reformation of manners in things we have done amiss." Finally, Andrews warned, the penitents must sacrifice all claims to wisdom. They must not expect God to rescue them immediately from their distresses. "God, for wise reasons known only to His infinite mind, may delay the salvation of a people for a time, even though they should repent of their sins," while all the time "our miseries are accumulating, our distresses increasing, and our punishments growing." Because "'charity . . . beareth all things, believeth all things, and hopeth all things,'" he explained, Christians should not expect unpopular British measures to disappear suddenly. Indeed, the severity of the crisis in relations between Britain and the colonies, making "the clouds grow blacker and heavier" with "no signs of an accommodation . . . to be seen," was fresh evidence that Americans had not yet humbled themselves and made themselves ready to receive divine assistance.

Then, in a remarkable change of tone, Andrews conceded that the spirit of resistance to British authority, which he had been denouncing, was a natural and appealing mode of thought and feeling. "I know there are many who talk a language different from me in these matters; they are extremely confident of success, and brand [those] who show the least diffidence . . . as enemies or cowards. Now they are girding on the harness. . . . But in my opinion such confidence is an ill omen of success. However just it may be to struggle for our rights when they are invaded and however strong and well prepared for war we may be, . . . yet we are to consider that the battle is the Lord's and that it is alike easy with Him to save or to punish [the] many or [the] few. I am not so much afraid of the power of England as I am of the sins of America."[8] By acknowledging that fundamental differences in "language" divided the contending sides in the pre-Revolutionary controversy, and by realizing that the dynamic sense of "girding" for battle sustained the spirit of resistance, Andrews brought sharply into focus the Tory perception of the conflict. Other doctrinaire Tories confirmed this insight and groped for words to express the emotional state that gave patriots their sense of power. Myles Cooper wrote of

Men deprived, who quit their sphere
without remorse or shame or fear,
and boldly rush, they know not where

> seduced alas! by fond applause,
> of gaping mobs and loud huzzas,
> unconscious all of nobler aims,
> than sordid self or vulgar fame;
> men undefined by any rules
> ambiguous things, half knaves half fools,
> whom God denied the talents great
> required to make a fool complete;
> whom nature formed, vile paltry fools,
> absurder much than downright fools.[9]

Chandler noted more tangible but no less powerful influences when he attributed discontent to the "sort of persons . . . who derive their importance, their high titles, and offices from the present confusion."[10] The "present confusion" was so pervasive and complex that it seemed to accelerate as it spread. "It is the prevailing rage of the present times," explained a Massachusetts loyalist broadside in March 1775, "for people of all ranks, orders and professions to form associations and erect themselves into what they call Congresses and committees, . . . under the pretext of redressing grievances, . . . [but in reality] tending to the subversion of all order and good government and the total abolition of law and justice. . . . Much private property has been destroyed; the most daring piracies and robberies have been perpetrated in the face of open day. . . . The pulpit and press are become subservient to the infernal schemes of these diabolic assemblies and are used as the great engines to destroy the peace and tranquility of this devoted nation."[11]

However contagious and gratifying the spirit of rebellion might have been, the doctrinaire Tories knew it was shallow and transparently fraudulent. None stripped away its façade more savagely than the wife in an imaginary marital quarrel entitled *A Dialogue between a Southern Delegate and his Spouse on his Return from the Grand Continental Congress:*

Wife: Mark me Sir, you'll repent of't, as sure as you're there.

Husband: Pray, for God's sake, my dear, be a little discreet;
As I hope to be sav'd, you'll alarm the whole street;
Don't delight so in scolding yourself out of breath;
To the neighbors 'tis sport, but to me it is death. . . .

Wife: Call the doctor! by this unusual palaver,
   I fear thou'st been bit, you so foam and so slaver:
   Alas! never, ah! never, elect him again;
   This pride of delegation, turns many a brain.

Husband: You mistook me, my dear, I did not pretend,
   Every measure of Congress, right or wrong, to defend. . . .
   Nice discussions, a wise man will ever decline,
   When his head and his heart are o'er heated with wine;

   Men, when drunk, are all heroes, all prudent, all gallant. . . .
   But grant their resolves were more absurd than they are,
   Could you really expect your meek husband would dare
   Oppose such a torrent, when it's very well known,
   He dares not to say to your face, his soul is his own.

Wife: God bless us, and keep us! why, my dearest, till now,
   I ne'er heard you so wise, or so witty, I vow;
   I protest this same Congress's a very fine school;
   A man comes back a *Chatham,* who goes there a fool.

Husband: You're afraid to hear all, but for once I will speak,
   Wherever I am known, I am called *Jerry Sneak;*
   I bear, for all that, with your caprice, and tricks,
   But prithee, dear, dabble not in our politics.

Wife: Prithee! ha, ha, ha, prithee! my senator grave!
   Sir! I'll make you repent of that speech, to your grave. . . .

Husband: That horse-laugh is all feign'd, with much better grace,
   You know Ma'm, you cou'd hit me a slap in the face;
   Consider, my dear, you're a woman of fashion,
   'Tis really indecent to be in such passion;
   Mind thy household affairs, teach thy children to read,
   And never, dear, with politics, trouble thy head. . . .

Wife: I have said it, my Dear, and I'll say it again,
   That your famous Congress were a strange set of men:
   To you, my dear love, I may be sometimes too pert,
   But then, you know well, dear, it is but for a spirt. . . .
   I defy you, to say now; but can't for your life,
   That I'm not, at the bottom, a very good wife:
   Could I see you in prison, or hang'd, without pain?
   Then, pray, have not I reason enough to complain?

Husband: Psha! for God's sake, what hazard of that do I run?

Wife: Psha, on, but beware, dear, that you are not undone;
'Twou'd soon break my heart, tho' we do now and then jar,
Were you ruin'd, or taken, or killed in war. . . .
To your mighty high Congress, the members were sent,
To lay all our complaints, before Parliament;

Usurpation rear'd its head, from that fatal hour,
You resolv'd, you enacted, like a sovereign pow'r. . . .
Instead of addresses, fram'd in truth, and on reason,
They breathe nothing, but insult, rebellion, and treason. . . .
When I think how these things must infallibly end,
I am distracted with fear, and my hair stands on end.

Husband: You've been heating your brain, with romances and plays,
Such rant, and bombast, I never heard in my days. . . .

Wife: Whilst you are in danger, by your good leave, my dear,
Both by night and by day, I will ring in your ear,
Make your peace, fear the King; the Parliament fear.
Oh! my country! remember that a woman unknown,
Cry'd aloud, like *Cassandra,* in oracular tone,
Repent! or you are forever, forever undone.[12]

IV

Loyalists and Political Cohesion
in New England

24

Loyalists on the Threshold of Revolution: Allies of the Crown and Massachusetts's Reaction to the Coercive Acts

WHEN Governor Thomas Gage tried to implement the Massachusetts Government Act during the summer of 1774, he tore the fabric of society and politics in the Bay Colony. The most constitutionally far-reaching of the Coercive Acts, this statute effectively gutted the Massachusetts royal Charter of 1691. It replaced the Council elected by the House with one appointed by the Crown, gave the governor sole power to name and remove judicial and administrative officers in the colony, vested the summoning of juries in the hands of royally appointed county sheriffs, and prohibited the towns from holding more than a single annual town meeting. The closing of the port of Boston until the city paid for the destroyed tea, the appointment of General Gage as governor of the province, and the Massachusetts Government Act, taken together, evoked a pattern of resistance that plunged the colony into revolution.

Because Boston's leaders were overwhelmed with problems created by the blockade, the initiative for action during the summer of 1774 passed to the town meetings. To direct and co-ordinate their response to the Coercive Acts, town meetings within ten of the colony's fifteen largest counties co-operated in summoning county conventions, which met between July and September 1774. Although stressing the imperative need for order, the county conventions were, in Gage's eyes, insurrectionary assemblies because they claimed that ultimate authority rested with the people and because several conventions called on the people to obey only those royal officials appointed before implementation of the Massachusetts Government Act. In retaliation, Gage refused to call the General Court into session in September; ninety members assembled illegally on September 28, and after waiting for the Governor to administer oaths of office and present his message, they voted to constitute themselves as a provincial Congress, to convene in Concord on October 5. The provincial Congress hesitated, however, to seize political power. It did not pass legislation; it assumed that the charter of 1691 was still in effect and required only the repeal of the Coercive Acts to function again; it acted only as a link between Massachusetts and the Continental Congress in Philadelphia. The provincial Congress did, however, co-ordinate the mustering and supplying of town militia companies, and it did ask the Second Continental Congress for authority to create a new government. In June 1775 Congress merely recommended that Massachusetts hold elections for a new legislature under the old charter. Because that document was for all practical purposes defunct, the new General Court would hold only *de facto* power until the adoption of a new state constitution in 1780. What was certain in 1775 was that ultimate authority rested with the people and could be exercised through the instrument of the town meeting.

Many processes operated during this delicate transition, between the summer of 1774 and the summer of 1779. Overshadowing all else was the realization that the Coercive Acts were an "unparalleled usurpation of unconstitutional power" that, unchallenged, annihilated political liberty in America. But also at work was a widespread aversion to precipitate action. The Massachusetts towns wanted to work out a united and deliberate response to British policy, and they wanted Massachusetts to secure the widest possible support from other colonies. They were averse to any form of resistance that might "breed a discord among the inhabitants"; they felt a responsibility "to use the utmost [of their] influence in suppressing all riotous and disorderly proceedings in our respective towns"; and they were at first leery of harassing timid or even downright obstructive citizens. In the summer of 1774 one town refused to release publicly the names of those opposed to the nonimportation covenant because of its "expectation of our uniting to a man and the great reluctance we have in holding up to the world a brother, a fellow townsman as an enemy to his country."[1]

This aversion to violence and intimidation did not mean Massachusetts leaders were afraid to use such tactics but that they would employ them only as a last resort, with high seriousness and in the name of the whole body of the people. The Whigs in Massachusetts reserved violence and intimidation for one purpose during the last half of 1774: dissuading supporters of the Crown from accepting or holding offices under the Massachusetts Government Act. Only in the city of Boston, blockaded by the British Navy and patrolled by British troops, were Governor Gage and his circle of allies safe. Elsewhere, allies of the Crown, often officials in county government, found themselves looked upon as agents of an alien and illegitimate power. Even their horrified complaints revealed the complex structure of the long-pent-up anger and tough communal self-discipline that made up resistance in Massachusetts. "Never was a time when such numbers of *wise* and *good men, as well as others,* were so infatuated, 'til the present," wrote one Hampshire County man to Gage on August 10, 1774. "An enthusiastic frenzy and surprising madness obtains everywhere; nothing said in the coolest manner avails, but rather irritates. Indeed whoever proposes pacific measures is considered as an enemy to his country, and threatened with ruin. The source of all this your Excellency will easily conceive, and from whence propagated. The fences of law are broken down, and without your Excellency's aid, our lives as well as property will be much endangered."[2] What was the nature of the "frenzy" that engulfed supporters of the Crown and infected alike "wise and good men" as well as the multitude? Part of the answer lay in the testimony of the victims. Officials of the Crown were not the primary evil; rather, the influence that had to be expelled was the operation of the Massachusetts Government Act itself. Accordingly, the mobs that threatened Crown officials with violence possessed an internal structure of restraining leadership that might not control them but did have some room for maneuver, some capacity to stir up and calm down the body of men.

Usually there was a number of the better educated and well-to-do scattered through a crowd. At their most effective level of operation, gatherings could at one minute threaten and vilify and at the next cajole and flatter.[3]

Such was the crowd of some 4,000 people who came to the home of Lieutenant Governor Thomas Oliver on September 2, 1774. It had been a long day for the Lieutenant Governor, who was no kin to Peter and Andrew Oliver but, rather, a wealthy Cambridge, Massachusetts landowner, and who, unlike the politically prominent Olivers, enjoyed widespread popularity and respect. He had been appointed lieutenant governor under the Massachusetts Government Act, had taken the oath of office on August 8, 1774, and had automatically become a member of the hated Mandamus, or appointed, Council. Alone among the new royal appointees, he did not move for safety into Boston in the summer of 1774. He felt little hesitation on September 2 in meeting with a large crowd of "land owners from neighboring towns" who came to Cambridge to complain about the Coercive Acts. "Thoroughly persuaded they would do no harm," Oliver tried as tactfully as possible to induce the people to return quietly to their homes. "They respectfully answered they came peaceably to enquire why they had been deprived of their rights and privileges." Oliver archly "addressed them upon the impropriety of such embodied multitudes" of protesting subjects and lectured them on the fallacies of their specific complaints against the Crown. Apparently mollified, the crowd moved on to the Cambridge common, where a false rumor circulated that British troops were marching toward Cambridge to disperse the assembled citizens. Oliver went to the common and was besieged with requests that he prevent the arrival of the troops. Under pressure to respond, he drafted a message to Gage reporting the rumor and urging that no troops be dispatched lest they provoke "the most violent consequences." The leaders of the crowd thanked Oliver for his intervention, but as he was leaving they asked him to hear one further request: "How happy I should make them if I would quit the [Mandamus Council] board." Two mandamus councillors had resigned that very day, from the steps of the Cambridge Courthouse. "I told them I considered it as very ungrateful treatment to mention the thing to me," but he did concede he would seriously consider resigning if the whole province asked him to do so. It was a well-mannered crowd, and Oliver felt he had satisfied their objections.

Nonetheless, he noticed more and more people, including some "of a lower class," filling the streets in the late afternoon and therefore decided to take his family to Boston for safety. Just before he could leave his house, some 4,000 people, a quarter of them armed, gathered outside in the street. Ominous but still quiet, they stood there while a committee of five walked to the front door, knocked, and were received inside—because, Oliver noted, they had "a decent appearance." "The people," one of the five informed Oliver, did not approve the lenient treatment the Lieutenant Governor had received from crowds earlier in the day and now demanded his resignation from the Mandamus Council. The five men brought with them a resignation statement for Oliver to sign. Oliver refused. The delegation warned him to consider "the consequences of an enraged people." At this point Oliver could hear footsteps in the yard and see faces pressed against the windows. From farther away in the crowd he could hear voices "swearing they would have my blood." He could also hear his wife and children in the next room, by this time frantic with fear. "I found myself giving way. . . . I cast about to find some means of preserving my reputation. I proposed that the people should take me by force, but [the committee] urged the danger of such an expedient. I told them I would take the risk, but they would not consent. Reduced to this extremity I took up the paper and casting my eyes over it with a hurry of mind and conflict of passion, I wrote underneath the following words: 'My house being surrounded with four thousand people, in compliance with their commands I sign my name.' " The committee left the house and read Oliver's grudging agreement to resign. Some in the crowd shouted disapproval. Messages came back to the house telling Oliver that he must write a more gracious and explicit resignation statement. Oliver grimly replied that the mob would have to kill him; he would not change the statement. "The more respectable farmers," as Oliver described them, "used all their endeavours to reconcile the rest and finally prevailed, . . . marched off in their several companies, wishing me well and cautioning me not to break my promise." Oliver and his family went immediately to Boston, and the next day he reassumed his posts as lieutenant governor and mandamus councillor. Making a promise to the crowd in Cambridge one day and breaking it in safety in Boston the next troubled him, even though he knew that an oath extracted by intimidation carried neither moral nor legal weight. "A hard alternative 'tis true; but still I had it in my power either to die or to make the promise. I chose to live."[4]

Others also chose to live. On August 5, 1774, three Berkshire County men, William Williams, Israel Stoddard, and Woodbridge Little, found themselves suddenly surrounded by a crowd of over one hundred that questioned the trio "in a tumultuous manner" about their political views. (Williams and Stoddard were, respectively, son and son-in-law of Israel Williams, the most wealthy and powerful of the "River Gods," the aristocratic great landowners of western Massachusetts and staunch allies of Hutchinson and the Crown.) Was it not true that the three men had tried to "disunite the people" by opposing agitation against the Coercive Acts? Was it not true that "in general" the three "were enemies to the constitution of this province, Tories, etc.?" They could only reply that they were "utterly averse" to riotous "combinations" but quite willing to "use salutary and lawful measures" to secure redress of the province's grievances. The crowd wanted to know if any of the three had received commissions from the Crown under the Massachusetts Government Act. They answered they had not. The leaders of the crowd then presented a paper for the three to sign. They asked for time to consider it. When the crowd became impatient, they asked what alternative they had to signing. The leaders implied increasing verbal abuse and possibly physical attack. "We judged that we had nothing to expect but severity and violence," they concluded, "unless we somehow appeased them." After two hours of haggling they managed to persuade the crowd to accept changes in wording that reduced the statement to four "senseless and unnecessary propositions": that the acts of Parliament were unconstitutional (the three took comfort in the fact that they mentioned no specific laws and did not know at that point whether all of the Coercive Acts had received the royal assent); that resistance against those acts was just and reasonable; that the three would not support the enforcement of the Coercive Acts;

and, finally, that they would not speak in opposition to those who did protest.[5]

In total, eighteen of the thirty-seven men named mandamus councillors in Massachusetts under the Massachusetts Government Act resigned by the end of the summer or refused to serve at all. Timothy Ruggles, of Hardwick in Worcester County, received his appointment in early August. A crowd led by local militia and commanded by Ruggles's brother, Benjamin, momentarily blocked the Old Furnace Bridge when the old man, riding a fine black horse, left for Boston. "With the greatest anxiety of mind for your safety," Councillor Daniel Oliver, who later resigned his seat, wrote to Ruggles on August 19, 1774, "I set down to inform you that the spirits of the people in this and the neighboring towns . . . are worked up to such a pitch of resentment and rage . . . that you must not attribute it to pusillanimity in me when I advise you if you value the preservation of your life not to return home at present; I mean at least if you have accepted any appointment under the Crown in consequence of the late Acts of Parliament; for the people are determined not to submit to them, and to run all hazards to avoid it. There are those here who I am satisfied thirst for your blood and they have enough influence over others to put them upon spilling it. High threats continue that you shall never pass the great bridge alive, and all unite in the opinion that you will not be able to do it. I really think it will be the highest act of rashness in you to attempt it at present." The townspeople seized all the guns in Ruggles's home, poisoned his best English stallion, and put his son Timothy under house arrest. They imprisoned other suspected Crown sympathizers and gave them no more than a ration of bread and water.[6]

On August 25, 1774, messages circulated from Worcester, Massachusetts inviting inhabitants of the surrounding area to assemble in the town on the following day. The crowd began to form at seven in the morning, and by nine there were more than 2,000 parading in military ranks on the town common. Led by the militia officers present, the crowd elected a large committee, which in turn appointed a smaller "subcommittee" to "wait upon" Worcester's most powerful and wealthy citizen, Timothy Paine, an appointee to the Mandamus Council. All this Paine watched from his window. He had known throughout the night that the gathering had been summoned. He saw the subcommittee walk to his house, noticed that it contained three members of the last House of Representatives, and, after inquiring whether they intended to do him bodily harm, admitted the men into his home. "They then informed me of their business, that they were a committee chosen by a large body of people assembled on the common to wait upon me to resign my seat at the Council board. I endeavoured to convince them of the ill consequences that would ensue upon the measures they were taking, that instead of having their grievances redressed, . . . they were pursuing steps that would tend to the ruin of the province. But all to no purpose. They insisted that the measures were peaceable, that nothing would satisfy the assembly unless I resigned, and that they would not answer for the consequences if I did not." Paine felt he had no alternative but to comply, and he and the committee haggled over the terms of a resignation statement, Paine preferring language that made the coercion manifest, the committee seeking some degree of contrition. The compromise wording held that "my appointment was without my solicitation and am very sorry I accepted and thereby given any uneasiness to the people of the county from whom I have received many favors. . . . I . . . will not take a seat . . . unless it is agreeable to the Charter of this province." The subcommittee then insisted that Paine come to the common and read his resignation. He first refused and secured a pledge that "I should meet with no insult" except that he must walk bareheaded through the crowd.[7]

"Thus, sir, you see an open opposition has taken place," Paine wrote to Gage. "I dread the consequence of enforcing [the Coercive Acts] by a military power; the people's spirits are so raised they seem determined to risk their lives and everything dear to them in the opposition." The people *"seem* determined" to risk all! The scene, as Paine portrayed it, was strangely subdued, as though the solemnity of the occasion affected everyone present: the size of the crowd insuring an overwhelming impression; men marching to or from the encounter in military rank under militia officers; the election of a committee responsible to the whole body of the assembled people; the apprehension of the leaders that violence *might* ensue if the offending councillor did not resign. There seemed to be safety and self-control in numbers; the larger the crowd, the greater the chance that verbal abuse and intimidation would suffice. Yet never could the victim be allowed to believe that the gathering and the threat of physical violence were a charade. Most important, all of these confrontations focused on the Massachusetts Government Act, the attack upon the charter, as the evil to be opposed; always the victim was given the opportunity to stand with the community simply by dissociating himself in some limited fashion from what Parliament, the Crown, and General Gage were doing to the province.

When the crowd dispersed, Paine heard some men shouting that they would next visit Councillor Daniel Murray in nearby Rutland, Massachusetts, and on schedule the following day some 1,500 men carrying heavy clubs and firearms assembled in front of Murray's home. Murray had already received verbal reports of the previous day's events on the Worcester common, and the committee elected by the crowd followed the same procedure, except that they insisted on a perfunctory search of his house and simply gave him an ultimatum to resign within two weeks. As with Paine, Murray's attempt to reason with the people made a much deeper impression on him than on his listeners. "Tell them the consequences of their proceedings will be rebellion, confiscation, and death and it only serves as oil to increase the flame; they can draw no consequence to be equally dreadful to a free people (as they say) like that of being made slaves, and this is not the language of the common people only, you may be assured," Murray wrote the same day to Gage; "those that have heretofore in life sustained the fairest characters in every respect are the warmest in this matter." What also impressed Murray deeply was the fact that 1,500 people could assemble on his land, threaten to destroy all his property, and then "disperse without doing the least damage to any part of the estate."[8] Murray soon took refuge in Boston.

In the Connecticut River Valley, in western Massachusetts, popular fury swirled around Israel Williams, his son Israel, Jr., and two fellow River Gods, John Worthington and Oliver Partridge. A fifth dominant member of this regional aristocracy, Joseph Hawley, was a vociferous Whig. Williams and

Worthington had declined to accept appointment as mandamus councillors, but neither of them had made his refusal public. Only a few days after his son's and son-in-law's interrogation by a crowd, Williams himself was seized in Chesterfield, Massachusetts and forced to sign some sort of "covenant." He had no sooner gotten back to his home in Hatfield than Israel Stoddard's wife, Williams's daughter, had a miscarriage as a result of her husband's ordeal and lingered near death. Williams traveled at once to Pittsfield, to his daughter's bedside, and this public appearance incited another confrontation with the mob. In another carefully phrased statement, its leaders accused Williams of maintaining personal belief in Parliament's power to tax the colonists without their consent. "From *a man of your place and of your ability and influence,* we conceive [such an attitude] . . . dangerous . . . to the liberties and privileges of this people." They extracted from him a statement that the Coercive Acts were unconstitutional and could properly be opposed, and he agreed to decline a Council seat. In spite of very heavy pressure, he refused to leave his position as inferior-court judge. He made the one concession only because the mob was within earshot of his daughter's bed and tumult might hasten her death. The next day, Partridge and Worthington were summoned to a session of the county convention in Hadley, called to discuss the Massachusetts Government Act. According to one observer, Worthington tried to "harangue" the convention "in mitigation of his conduct," but the very "sight of him flashed lightning from their eyes" and "he was soon obliged to desist. The people were not to be dallied with. Nothing would satisfy them but a recantation of his address to Governor Gage." Accustomed to the awe and deference of valley folk, the River God had experienced an immense drop in status. On August 30, 1774, another mob prevented Williams from opening the court of general sessions at Springfield. In early February 1775 yet another crowd dragged both Israels, junior and senior, to Hatfield, confined them in a smokehouse overnight, stopped up the chimney so that the pair nearly suffocated, and in the morning forced them to sign a new pledge not to oppose measures of the Continental Congress or to correspond with the British. "Have you made Murray look less big, or smoked old Williams to a Whig?" celebrated John Trumbull in *M'Fingal*.[9]

Intimidation of mandamus councillors and other allies of the Crown in the last half of 1774 was not an exuberantly spontaneous enterprise. Successful mobs needed educated leadership, planning, and publicity. To secure their goals, they had to express the authentic sentiments of the entire community. Lacking any of these elements, a demonstration of force was not likely to succeed. News reached Deerfield, Massachusetts, on September 5, 1774, that an immense rabble, "all the western world," was coming to "mob Colonel [William] Williams." Nearly 150 sympathetic neighbors gathered to resist, and they easily surrounded and disarmed the band of some fifty disorganized marchers who straggled into town the next day. These people were so disoriented that they agreed to sign a "covenant" disavowing "mobbing" and to write affidavits confessing their guilt in the affair. An unverified tale related that in January 1775, when another hostile crowd came to William Williams's house, "a window opened and Seth Catlin [one of the Williams's cronies] appeared, musket in hand, threatening to blow a lane through them if they advanced another step. The crowd knew him too well to doubt his meaning and a parley was called. A committee of the mob was admitted and for an hour the questions at issue were debated. Meanwhile the committee was well plied with a hot, strong flip, . . . declared themselves well satisfied, went out, and reported to their constituents that Mr. Williams was a good patriot and had given Christian satisfaction." The rank and file of the crowd disputed the findings of the committee, but Seth Catlin and his musket finally induced the quarrelsome intruders to disperse.[10]

The British evacuation of Boston in March 1776 was the most massive and traumatic experience that befell the New England loyalists. Several hundred supporters of the Crown had fled to Boston in late 1774 and early 1775, enduring the deprivations of the blockade in order to obtain the protection of British troops. When Gage's successor, General William Howe, in consultation with Colonial Secretary George Germain, decided that Boston could not be defended, the loyalists received only a few days' notice that the British Army was leaving. Gathering whatever personal property they could carry, a thousand loyalists crowded onto ships and sailed with the army to Halifax, Nova Scotia. There they found food and rent quintupled in price. Soldiers and sailors stole their possessions. Most exiles made their way to England within a few weeks. But the dislocation of evacuation paled in comparison to the outrage they felt toward their contemporaries in Massachusetts. "I found I could not remain in Boston and trust my person with a set of lawless rebels whose actions have disgraced human nature and have treated all the King's loyal subjects that have fallen into their hands with great cruelty," explained one of the evacuees, Sylvester Gardiner, a wealthy physician from Cambridge, Massachusetts. "I don't believe," he exclaimed, "there ever was a people in any age or part of the world that enjoyed so much liberty as the people of America did under the mild, indulgent government (God bless it) of England and never was a people under a worse state of tyranny than they are at present."[11] Peter Oliver, Jr., vented his dismay and frustration much more directly: "All we poor refugees must be made good our losses and damage. Hanging people won't pay me for what I have suffered. Nothing short of forfeited estates will answer. And after damages are sufficiently compensated, then hang all the Massachusetts rebels by the dozens, if you please." Three years later, the same moral outrage and cry for vengeance motivated the confiscation of the estates of those Crown supporters who departed with the British. "Shall those traitors who first conspired the ruin of our liberties, . . . who basely forsook their country in her distress and sought protection from the enemy . . . , shall these wretches have their estates reserved for them and restored at the conclusion of this glorious struggle?" Samuel Adams demanded indignantly in 1778. Significantly, the seizure of property in Suffolk County, Massachusetts—and probably elsewhere in New England as well—was not particularly motivated by the state's need for revenue, nor was there public clamor to distribute confiscated property to an acquisitive multitude. Instead, the Massachusetts legislature confiscated these estates so that the loyalists' creditors could recover just debts.[12]

25

Initial Abuse of the Loyalists in Connecticut, Rhode Island, and New Hampshire

IN 1774 and 1775, Connecticut, like western Massachusetts, was a rural society structured politically and socially around its towns —units whose boundaries extended into the surrounding-countryside and united an agricultural people through the institutions of the church and town meetings, and through local merchants, courts, and lawyers. But the approaching confrontation with British authority did not disrupt the existing balance of political power in Connecticut as it did in Massachusetts. For not only was Connecticut a charter colony with no royal governor or establishment of Crown officeholders, but also, more important, the decisive seizure of power by the men who would lead Connecticut into the Revolution had occurred in 1766 rather than 1774. Then the New Light faction in the province's religious controversies had used the Stamp Act crisis to discredit their Old Light and conservative opponents and to seize control of the Assembly, Council, and governorship. By 1774, the New Light faction enjoyed an unassailable political ascendancy in the colony. Former Governor Thomas Fitch, the last Old Light with the personal following and ability to lead a credible opposition, died, and other prominent defenders of British authority—men like Jared Ingersoll and Benjamin Gale—abruptly acquiesced. Only 6 per cent of the adult males voted in 1774 for avowedly Tory candidates. Though leaderless, unorganized, and politically impotent, the presence of some 2,000 to 2,500 active, identifiable loyalists temporarily convulsed the province at the outbreak of hostilities. Concentrated in Fairfield County, where they constituted a quarter of the population, and also present in disturbing numbers in New Haven, these loyalists and their detractors revealed vividly the specific rents revolution tore in the fabric of Connecticut society during 1775 and 1776.

The loyalist opponents of resistance in Connecticut in 1775 were predominantly Anglicans. While they represented all levels of the province's society, the great majority of those apart from Anglican clergy were "moderately prosperous farmers" and a small number of artisans—hatters, weavers, cobblers, blacksmiths, and the like—among the more successful craftsmen. Several Anglican clergymen preached and talked openly against the sin of rebellion. Others admitted to patriot committees that they could not support colonial resistance. In two Fairfield County towns, Newtown and Ridgefield, a majority of the voters in the town meetings repudiated the proceedings of the Continental Congress and affirmed their loyalty to the Crown, and in Litchfield and Fairfield counties several informal Tory meetings occurred.[1] An S.P.G. missionary, the Reverend Richard Mansfield, appealed to Governor William Tryon, of New York, to send troops to protect loyal British subjects in Derby.[2] In New Haven, Joshua Chandler, close friend of Old Light leader Jared Ingersoll and open defender of British authority, secured the chairmanship of the town's committee of correspondence. These scattered overt actions in turn provided committees of inspection and informal bands of men throughout the province with concrete evidence of a serious internal threat to liberty. Consequent fear of subversion intensified the effort to purge enemies of resistance from the militia and local offices, to disarm suspected persons, and to subject the unpopular to various indignities. A mob dragged Samuel Jarvis, his wife, and four children from their house without warning in the middle of the night, stripped them naked, ferried them across Long Island Sound, and forced them to wade ashore in water "almost up to their middles." William Davies was tarred, feathered, and beaten with muskets. The most vociferous Anglican clergyman, Samuel Peters, as already discussed, fled in fear of serious physical violence. Peter Guire had the initials "G.R." branded on his forehead.[3] Peter Oliver included this word-of-mouth report in the appendix to his history of the Revolution: "A parish clerk of an Episcopal Church at East Haddam in Connecticut, a man of 70 years of age, was taken out of his bed in a cold night, and beat against his hearth by men who held him by his arms and legs. He was then laid across his horse, without his clothes, and drove to a considerable distance in that naked condition. His nephew Dr. Abner Beebe, a physician, complained of the bad usage of his uncle, and spoke very freely in favor of government; for which he was assaulted by a mob, stripped naked, and hot pitch was poured upon him, which blistered his skin. He was then carried to an hog sty and rubbed over with hog's dung. They threw the hog's dung in his face, and rammed some of it down his throat; and in that condition exposed to a company of women. His house was attacked, his windows broke, when one of his children was sick, and a child of his went into distraction upon this treatment. His gristmill was broke, and persons prevented from grinding at it, and from having any connections with him."[4] Although closely knit communities, where tensions had no other outlet, were prone to this sort of violence, Dr. Beebe's treatment was exceptional. Usually the abuse was verbal, and often the victims were disoriented and upset, as was Nathaniel Guyer, who explained that "many of the good people" of Connecticut "were confused and distracted to know their duty in the great controversy."[5]

The suppression of the loyalists in Rhode Island was at once easier and more complicated than in Connecticut or Massachusetts. Even more than in Fairfield County, Connecticut, the Rhode Island loyalists were concentrated geographically in Newport, while the dominant sources of political power in the province lay inland, especially in the rival commercial center of Providence. Like Connecticut, Rhode Island was a charter colony with no royal governor, but, unlike its neighbor, the province had in Newport a wealthy clique of Anglican merchants and British customs and vice-admiralty officials. Ever since the early 1760's they had ostentatiously banded together in contempt for the colony's autonomy and its unique charter rights. However weak and ineffectual this clique had become by 1775, its very presence had frightening potential; on the eve of independence that threat nearly plunged the colony back into the bitter factional turmoil that had characterized much of its earlier politics, in the 1750's and 1760's.

The election of Governor Joseph Wanton in 1769 and his re-election every spring through 1775 caused a subsidence of bitter factional strife between the parties led by Samuel Ward, of Newport, and Stephen Hopkins, of Providence. The stakes of power in those struggles had been patronage and tax policy—both vital advantages to the rival Newport and Providence economies. But both parties were united in their opposition to British encroachments like the Sugar and Stamp acts and especially to the strong-arm methods of enforcing those laws practiced by the British Navy, which patrolled Narragansett Sound. Hopkins's alliance with the Wanton faction of Newport finally defeated Samuel Ward in 1770. In the aftermath of the burning of the British ship *Gaspee* by unidentified Rhode Islanders in 1772 and the uproar over the Townshend duties between 1768 and 1770, the voters were probably glad to support a stable and steady administration. The news of fighting at Lexington and Concord, which reached Rhode Island the day after Wanton's sixth consecutive re-election, in 1775, undercut this stability, for he opposed the Assembly's desire to send troops to the defense of the Massachusetts patriots and he argued that a confrontation with Britain could only mean suspension of the Rhode Island Charter. Abruptly the alignment of politics shifted, and the Ward and Hopkins factions coalesced. Wanton was forced by the Assembly to resign; Ward and Hopkins were sent together to represent the colony at the First and Second Continental Congresses.[6]

The ejection of Wanton from the governorship and the defeat of his son as a Providence deputy in the Assembly the previous year, amid charges that he was "a flaming tory" who "stood ready for preferment" if the British intervened in Rhode Island affairs, effectively demolished the political power of those in the colony who favored a mild response to British policy in 1775. But the upheaval raised fears in the province that the Newport Tories were poised for a counterattack, that they would use the crisis as an opportunity to mislead the populace and seize political power in the 1776 elections. The state of undeclared war with Britain lent credence to those fears, for Captain James Wallace, aboard the Royal Navy man-of-war *Rose* and commanding ten other vessels, controlled Narragansett Sound and had the town of Newport at his mercy. Cutting the town off from commerce by sea, Wallace reduced Newport to near famine and put the town in a state of genuine panic. He demanded and secured an agreement in the autumn of 1775 with the town's officials to supply his ships with beef and beer; in return, he would cease harassing fishing and coastal shipping. Newport had no alternative but to comply with his terms, and the resulting truce encouraged Tories in the town to seek alliances with fearful moderates in preparation for the next election. The fear that the Tories would dominate the town meetings that conducted the spring elections grew into the specter of a Tory political revival that might even gain legal control of the government and repudiate Rhode Island's participation in the Continental Congress. Already the province's patriots had been forced to ignore Congress's directives for disarming Tories in dealing with the disaffected in Newport, and by neutralizing patriot activity in that town Captain Wallace had seriously reduced the province's support of the Continental Army. Moreover, prominent Newport Tories regularly visited the *Rose,* where Wallace wined and dined them luxuriously.[7]

The specter of Tory resurgence in a colony where these men had always been ineffectual pariahs provoked retaliation against them in the spring of 1776. The chief instruments were informal bands of patriots and town meetings, both of which dealt directly with disaffected persons. In early 1775 a crowd on Block Island informed one suspect that unless he renounced his support of British authority he would be publicly coated with "fish-gurry." In September 1774, inferior-court Judge Stephen Arnold was hanged in effigy in East Greenwich for "industriously propagating principles unfriendly to American liberty." When the Judge and his friends tried to avenge the insult, mayhem nearly occurred. Only the prompt arrival of militia prevented bloodshed and prompted Arnold to apologize for participating in an unlawful assembly and to declare himself a friend to his country's liberty. In South Kingstown the town meeting voted to hold in the "utmost contempt" anyone who sold supplies to the "enemies of American liberty." The October 1775 meeting of the Assembly enacted successive laws prohibiting citizens of the province from acting as pilots for the British, communicating with British officers, or aiding the enemy in any manner. First the Assembly imposed a twelve-month prison term and £500 fine on offenders and then increased this penalty to forfeiture of all property in the province. The Assembly specifically confiscated the Rhode Island estates of Massachusetts royal officials Thomas Hutchinson and Isaac Royall. The thrust of this policy was to isolate and punish the scattering of loyalists outside Newport and to serve as a warning to those within the town.[8] Taking no chances, the Assembly further permitted Newport freemen who had left the town for their own safety to cast absentee ballots in the spring election. Patriot leaders made much of the danger that Newport was on the verge of electing "a set of deputies inimical to the liberties of this country," and the combined effect of these actions was to secure the election of two Whigs and another man, whose sentiments were not identifiable, to represent Newport in the next Assembly. Tensions then relaxed somewhat. A Test Act in 1776 imposed an oath to support the Revolutionary cause on all officeholders except Quakers. Only seventeen civil and militia officials refused to subscribe to the new test, and those from Newport were ordered to take up residence in inland towns. By the end of 1776 all of them had petitioned successfully to return to Newport.[9]

General Nathanael Greene concluded that his native Rhode Island possessed "only a shadow" of the "disaffection" that existed in other states. British occupation of Newport from December 1776 until October 1779 did not seriously increase the danger loyalist subversion or the intensity of the government's suppression of suspected persons. Because Newport was isolated on the southern tip of Aquidneck Island, the General Assembly responded simply by moving twenty-one suspicious families who were caught corresponding with the British to inland towns. A writer in January 1778 declared that it was "high time that a decisive line of separation be drawn between those miscreants and the friends to the country," but stronger political forces in the state favored a lax attitude toward those merely suspected of disaffection. With Nathanael Greene, the General Assembly favored "a happy medium between too great severity and too much indulgence." When the British evacuated Newport, only forty-five loyalists from Aquidneck Island went with them.[10]

The suppression of loyalist disaffection in New Hampshire was carried on with less severity than in southern New England. Wentworth had been powerless to prevent the election of a provincial Congress that met in the summer of 1774 to name delegates to the First Continental Congress, and the few brave stalwarts who tried to interfere with the election of a second congress, in the autumn of 1774, faced threats of mob violence unless they recanted their opposition. When General Gage asked Wentworth to recruit carpenters in New Hampshire to build barracks in Boston, an angry crowd threatened to pillage the estate of the Governor's hiring agent unless he apologized for assisting the British Army. In December rumors from Massachusetts that British regulars would soon occupy Fort William and Mary, near Portsmouth, provoked a force of 400 men led by John Sullivan to strip the fort of some of its cannon. When Wentworth called on the militia to repulse the looting, its officers simply refused to obey. These outbursts of violent protest soon precipitated a counterreaction in New Hampshire; the fear that British troops would come to the province provoked towns simultaneously to make military preparations and organize patrols guarding against impulsive acts of violence. From November 1774 until the following summer, county government also became a Revolutionary yet still moderating force. The normal county courts of general session, composed of justices of the peace, began to coordinate town-level resistance to royal authority while at the same time condemning "licentious attacks" on individuals and their property and preventing counties from "declining into a state of nature" as British authority collapsed and men's passions waxed. The third Hillsborough County Congress, on May 24, 1775, singled out Sheriff Benjamin Whiting, of Hollis, a stalwart of the Crown, for condemnation. The Congress heard sworn statements that Whiting had called patriot leader John Sullivan "a damned perjured villain . . . and a damned rebel [who] deserved to be hanged" and that he had predicted that an overwhelming British force would soon arrive in the colonies and had threatened that those who did not seek pardon for their role in the rebellion "would be deemed rebels and suffer death jointly."[11]

Although a few self-appointed bands of men had begun roaming the countryside in the fall of 1774, looking for supporters of the Crown to harass, town meetings took steps to discipline such lawless conduct and also to ban "swearing, loitering, fighting, and name-calling," which might precipitate wider disorders. As late as April 20, 1775, the Portsmouth town meeting voted to protect Governor Wentworth and his family from insults.[12] Wentworth's young wife, Frances, accused the rebellious populace only of extreme naïveté, and she perceived in their behavior a strangely impressive solidarity: "The people are content to die. It is past example or even credit should I attempt to paint their enthusiastic passion. From the old and decrepit to the youngest prattler, they cry for liberty. They desert the true cause [of liberty] only by their excess. . . . Though many wise and rational men among us are as high as possible in support of the rights of the people, yet the popular clan, from want of education, fly into riots and unpardonable conduct."

She wrote those words sometime on June 13, 1775. That evening Frances Wentworth and her husband tasted riot and unpardonable conduct. The crowd learned that Governor Wentworth's dinner guest that evening was John Fenton, a crony of the Governor's and a particularly obnoxious plural officeholder from Grafton County. Following Lexington and Concord, Fenton had lectured his neighbors to stay on their farms and mind their own business. Wentworth had illegally extended representation in the Assembly to Fenton's town in order to get him elected. Before the legislators disqualified Fenton from membership, he disrupted their proceedings by urging them to endorse Lord North's conciliatory proposals. On the evening of his expulsion from the Assembly, as Fenton and Wentworth sat talking after dinner, the two men heard a crowd gathering in the street outside demanding Fenton's surrender. Wentworth at first refused to acknowledge the demands, but when the people began beating on the sides of the house with clubs and next aimed a cannon at the front door, Fenton allowed himself to be taken prisoner. The crowd forced him to walk the fifteen miles from Portsmouth to Exeter, where two weeks later he was officially labeled "not a friend to this country" and allowed to leave the province. After the "rabble" and their prisoner left the street in front of the Governor's residence, Wentworth, his wife, and his five-month-old son boarded a small boat in Portsmouth harbor and sought refuge in Castle William, a fortification guarded by a British warship, the *Scarborough*. There rumor reached them that when the crowd had returned and found the Governor fled some swore in frustration that they wished they "could get the governor's fat child, . . . split him down the back and broil him." While Frances Wentworth realized there were many respectable people in the popular movement determined to repudiate that kind of talk, these threats terrified her and impressed upon her Britain's inability to protect the safety of servants of the Crown.[13]

Wentworth's flight actually facilitated a bloodless transfer of authority from the Crown to New Hampshire's provincial congresses. Wentworth's closest associate, Chief Justice and Provincial Secretary Theodore Atkinson, limited himself to token resistance when the provincial Congress demanded that he turn over the royal government's records. "I have, gentlemen, no thought of maintaining the security of the records in my custody by force. This I know would have no good effect. My aim is only to remove the grounds of complaint that may be entered against me for either neglect or malpractice. . . . The difficulties and, may I say the distresses, in the province and indeed of the whole continent," Atkinson said of his own sense of responsibility, "are such that every cause of additional perplexity need be avoided."[14] The same sense of prudence prompted many servants of the Crown to acquiesce in the face of the Revolution. The Attorney General, three of six customs officers, nineteen of twenty-four judges, including the Chief Justice of the superior court, two of five clerks of court, fourteen of twenty county officials, and twelve of twenty militia officers supported the Revolution.[15] Of course, those closely identified with Wentworth also sank into political obscurity along with several of Wentworth's most outspoken political opponents. In their place emerged a new set of leaders who had been active in the five provincial congresses that had met between 1774 and 1776; the most important among them was Meshech Weare, of Hamilton Falls. A superior court judge since 1747 and a member of the Assembly until 1755, a militia officer, lawyer, and active Old Light Congregationalist, Weare was over sixty years of age when the Revolution began. Elected to the first provincial Congress, he had been jeered at as a Tory when he argued in the Congress for prudence and moderation. These were the very traits that had prompted Revolutionary New Hampshire to entrust him with three major offices: president of the Council, chief justice, and chairman of the committee of safety.[16] On April 12, 1776, the committee of safety, under Weare's leadership, undertook an ambitious attempt to determine the amount of loyalist support in the province. It issued to the towns an "association test" obligating signers to participate "to the utmost of our power at the risk of our lives and fortunes with arms [to] oppose the hostile proceedings of the British fleets and armies against the united American colonies." The process of administering the association test and returning names of signers and nonsigners to the provincial committee of safety accelerated the process, already well under way, of identifying and exposing the remaining opposition to the Revolution. Of approximately 150 towns in the province, the returns of the test from 87 survive in provincial records. These towns probably had a population of about 50,000, or 66 per cent of the total of the new state. These returns showed 8,567 signers and 781 nonsigners, of whom 131 were identified as religious pacifists. The test gave an inexact measure of the extent of loyalist affiliation in the spring of 1776; it obligated the signer to military service and not just sympathy with the colonial cause.[17]

The association test did help to institute the pattern of New Hampshire's control of Revolutionary disaffection: vigorous provincial leadership by Meshech Weare and the New Hampshire Committee of Safety, scrutiny of individuals at the local level by town committees of safety, and adjudication of the more difficult cases by a legislative committee of the whole house, which Weare also chaired. On January 15, 1776, prior to the association test, the Londonderry Committee of Safety notified the newly established legislature that Adam Stuart, missing from the town and presumed living in Cambridge, Massachusetts, was under suspicion of being unfriendly to the colonial cause. With the complaint came sworn statements that Stuart had announced "he would fight under the colors of King George" and that British soldiers "were more expert and better disciplined and more used to fighting than the undisciplined country[men]" of New Hampshire. "The whole of his conversation was on the dark side of our unhappy difference with our mother country," explained another witness, "all of which gave me ground to conclude him inimical to his country." Meshech Weare's provincial committee of safety voted only to deny Stuart the "full liberty of a true friend of this country" and sent warnings about the man to Massachusetts officials. In the spring of 1776, in a similarly moderate manner, a committee of the whole house allowed three inimical men to leave the province unmolested and even paid one man £20 expense money for his journey to the West Indies. On June 19, 1776, it heard complaints submitted by several town committees of safety against two pairs of brothers, Thomas and Samuel Cummings and Leonard and Benjamin Whiting, who were represented by counsel and released on grounds of insufficient evidence.[18]

Responsibility for detecting and controlling disaffection rested increasingly with the town committees of safety. Only problems they could not satisfactorily handle went before the legislature's committee of the whole house. Meshech Weare was not anxious to start an aggressive campaign to uncover and harass the disaffected, although town officials readily believed that harsh retribution against them would both gratify the public and eliminate instability in the new regime. A group of Portsmouth petitioners "who are zealous in the grand cause now in contest with Great Britain" complained in May 1777 that they had "waited . . . for a long time" for the legislature to adopt "some mode of procedure against those abandoned wretches well known by the name of tories who have too long infested this town and state." While some were in the town jail, other notorious suspects, through influence and bribery, walked free. The petition complained of the counterfeiting of provincial currency by British sympathizers, but its actual frustration was that the government did not resort to summary deportation and even execution of all "vile traitors." In December 1776 the Claremont Committee of Safety wanted the legislature to take effective action against the many professed "neuters" within that town, who were actually Anglicans who ignored religious fast days in support of the American cause. The target of their complaint was a particularly resourceful Anglican clergyman, the Reverend Ranna Cossitt, who enjoyed enough local support that Claremont officials could not keep him in confinement. Cossitt freely admitted in 1775 that "I believe the American colonies, in their dispute with Great Britain . . . are unjust but will not take up arms" on either side. "I mean to be on the side of the administration, and I had as leave any person call me a damned Tory as not, and take it as an affront if people don't call me a Tory, for I verily believe the British troops will overcome by the greatness of their power and the justice of their cause." Cossitt probably knew of the location of "Tory Hole," a hiding place in a swamp near Claremont where loyalist refugees bound for Canada hid and met with sympathizers. Local officials never succeeded in locating the spot or in suppressing the activities of these loyalists.[19]

Much of the alleged loyalist activity that towns tried to discover and punish consisted simply of disrespectful conversation and correspondence. Oliver Parker was jailed for composing "a recipe to make a whig: Take of conspiracy and the root of pride three handfuls, two of ambition and vain glory. Pound them in the mortar of faction and discord. Boil it in 3 quarts of dissembling tears and a little New England rum over the fire of sedition until you find the scum of falsehood to rise to the top. Then strain it through the cloth of rebellion, put it into the bottle of envy, stop it with the cork of malice . . ." and so on until the mixture has been made into pills, swallowed at bedtime, and the "next day . . . you will be thinking how to cozzen, cheat, lie, and get drunk, abuse the minister of the gospel, cut the throats of all honest men, and plunder the nation."[20] This explicit version of Revolutionary zeal, depicting a wide range of familiar antisocial behavior, apparently touched a delicate nerve and probably expressed the opposite of the kind of public conduct New Hampshire patriots wanted to encourage.

Indicative of the random and incomplete suppression of disaffection in New England was the treatment of Asa Porter, a prominent and unusual figure in the frontier town of Haverhill, New Hampshire.[21] A prosperous farmer and merchant, Porter was a compulsive talker and schemer who apparently spent July and August 1776 advocating that a delegation of citizens from

Haverhill and other nearby towns travel to Canada and invite General Burgoyne to send troops into the valley to protect the area from Indian attacks. As rumors of Porter's remarks spread, John Hurd, Chairman of the Haverhill Committee of Safety, made Porter's arrest and conviction an obsessive personal goal. Hurd's star witness was a young man named Daniel Hall, who had infiltrated Porter's circle and had seen Porter organize a network of trusted allies in the Connecticut Valley who would cooperate with the British troops when they occupied the region. Porter kept postponing actual execution of his appeal to Burgoyne, and on August 5, 1776, with plans for the mission to Canada still hanging fire, Hall slipped away from Porter's farm and told his story to the Haverhill Committee of Safety. Two days later Porter was under arrest and Hurd had sent a full report of the conspiracy to Meshech Weare. Porter turned out to be a well-connected, resourceful, and slippery suspect. His friends in Haverhill blocked for nearly two weeks his transfer to Exeter for trial, and during this period he collected a mass of evidence in his own defense—affidavits impugning the reliability of Daniel Hall and explaining away his alleged remarks about inviting British troops into the area. Nevertheless, by August 19, 1776, Porter was in jail in Exeter.

The jurisdiction of the New Hampshire legislature to punish Porter's alleged offenses was the central issue in his defense. He complained that his words about sending an appeal to Burgoyne had been "inadvertently spoken" in a moment of "crisis" and that Hurd's witnesses quoted these remarks out of context. But fundamentally he appealed that "it doth not consist with the liberties of the people that the same body which hath the power of making laws should also have the power of executing the laws or determining the causes [that is, cases] of individuals." Porter's appeal showed that he was not only resourceful and well connected but that he was also an adroit constitutional theorist. He sensed that Revolutionary constitutionalism did not require a strict separation between the legislative branch on one hand and the executive and judicial on the other.[22] The legislature, he argued, was arrogating to itself a host of executive and judicial functions: determining what treason was before passing a law defining the crime, examining the facts in a criminal prosecution before formal charges had been presented, and denying the right of trial by jury. These were steps that made the "lives, liberties, and property of the people" dependent "solely on the will of the legislative body" and therefore represented the first stage in "the establishment of the most despotic tyranny." Although Porter's challenge to the Assembly's jurisdiction to try him was fruitless, his case continued to vex the legislature. His petitions and appeals consumed a great deal of the Assembly's time, and he apparently had enough political influence to win repeated paroles from confinement although he consistently violated the conditions of his release.

Hurd and his allies on the Haverhill Committee of Safety were furious with the state committee of safety for its leniency. What galled Hurd was Porter's refusal to "go to Exeter" and "make any acknowledgement or accommodation with the Assembly." Porter refused to concede any wrongdoing, even as a way of clearing his name. It was the result, Hurd fumed, of "his natural willful and obstinate temper which I well know." " 'There is a kind of bastard generosity,' " Hurd quoted from Thomas Paine's *American Crisis,* in a revealing postscript to a letter to a friend about Porter's case, " 'which is as fatal to society on one hand as the want of true generosity on the other; a lax manner in administering justice, falsely termed moderation, has a tendency to dispirit public virtue and promote the growth of public evils.' " Those words depicted accurately the fragmentary and incomplete suppression of disaffection in New Hampshire. The precious quality of public virtue, Hurd and Paine feared, might easily dissipate if scoundrels like Porter could slip in and out of captivity. The extralegal attempts to prosecute Porter were offset by the laxity of his punishment. Moreover, the weakness of New Hampshire loyalism reflected the lethargy or fearfulness of most of its potential adherents. As Hurd himself admitted two months after Porter's first arrest, "We have had no more difficulty among the Tory gentry here since the removal of Colonel Porter. Not one of them dare make a stir."

26

Committees of Safety
and the Control of Disaffection

LOCAL committees of correspondence, inspection, and safety in many Massachusetts, Connecticut, and New Hampshire towns were, after mob threats and protests, a second line of defense against disloyalty and disaffection in 1775 and 1776. These bodies, created by the vote of town meetings, had originated in 1773, when the Boston town meeting's Committee of Correspondence had sent a circular letter to the towns of the province stating its grievances against British policy and inviting discussion and exchange of views on the subject. The resulting network of communication continued to function in 1774 and 1775 as fresh crises erupted. It acted as the link between the hastily organized executive branches of the Revolutionary state governments, conveying their recommendations and providing information. Elected by the voters in town meetings, these committees helped provide a legitimacy during the transition period between 1774 and 1776, when bodies like the Massachusetts provincial Congress were still uncertain of their authority and permanence.

The defection and control of disaffection and subversion, then, were only part of the committees' functions, but the exercise of this power was especially important as a model of the relationship between the individual and society during the highly controlled upheaval that Revolution brought to New England from 1775 to 1777. A special convention of the committees of safety for the towns of Petersham, Athol, Templeton, and Hutchinson, on July 12, 1776, took on its own initiative the steps that effectively isolated and immobilized potential New England loyalists. It voted, first, not to release suspected persons already in custody and to bar others in the town of Petersham from public worship; those defying this ban would be confined "until our political troubles are at an end"—itself an interesting tentative definition of the early stages of the Revolutionary struggle. Because Aaron Whitney had already publicly defied and insulted the Petersham committee, he was to be disarmed and forbidden from attending meetings of three or more persons. Finally, the committees surveyed the recent history of their work. On the previous February 25, twelve committees had met in Petersham to investigate Joshua Willard, William Barrow, Ebenezer Bragg, and others who "had entered into a covenant . . . utterly subversive of our natural and chartered rights," armed themselves, and tried to intimidate David Stone, an already timid patriot. Some of those men, the committees noted with satisfaction, had already made peace with the Petersham committee.[1]

The committees sensed quickly that they were subject to conflicting demands. Called upon to weigh fragmentary evidence about suspected Tories, they also had to assess and reflect community sentiment about the disaffected. The painstaking care with which the committees described these responsibilities suggests that they did not want to become imprisoned by the sentiments of their constituents or dominated by every rumor or accusation about Tory activity. Nathaniel Brinley, of Framingham, Massachusetts, found himself in jail in the summer of 1776 for having signed an address of welcome to General Gage two years earlier. After he posted bond to live peaceably and not aid the enemy, a court paroled him. The town committee, however, required further that he work for John Fisk and remain at all times within twenty rods of Fisk's house. The committee admitted that these restrictions violated a resolution of the General Court encouraging parole of co-operative prisoners. In Brinley's case, the committee explained, leniency was "impracticable . . . as the people take him for a very villain." And with good reason, the committee continued; Brinley had a long record of behavior, attitudes, and statements hostile to the American cause—openly predicting British victory in 1775 and ominously taking his family to the safety of Boston before the outbreak of fighting at Lexington in April 1775. "Nothing . . . in his conduct or dis-

position" suggested "the least contrition," the committee explained. This failure to accuse him of actual subversion and the
attempt to explain without endorsing the town's hostile attitude were underscored by the committee's inclusion, without
comment, of Brinley's defense in its records: "He says he is a
gentleman and has done nothing to forfeit that character."[2]
Artemas Ward, of Shrewsbury, Massachusetts, the only Worcester
County justice of the peace not aligned with the Crown in early
1774, complained that committees easily succumbed to community pressures and jailed prominent suspects unnecessarily simply
"to appease the irritated minds of some people."[3]

In its interrogation of the Anglican cleric Jacob Bailey between May and December 1776, the Pownallboro, Massachusetts
Committee of Correspondence felt pulled in different directions
by the bitter antagonism toward Bailey on the part of the committee chairman, Colonel Charles Cushing, and by the more
phlegmatic attitude of its other three members. "As there are
diverse parts of your conduct within this time of public calamity
exceptionable as unfriendly to the rights and liberties of America
and . . . grievous to the good people of this town, particularly a
neglect to read proclamations issued by authority of the Colony
and the Continental Congress," the committee's summons to
Bailey ponderously explained, "the committee of correspondence
of this town will meet at the courthouse in Pownallboro . . .
where they will hear you in your defense . . . that they may act
thereon consistent [with] the *cause of freedom, the peace of the
town, and no injury to you if friendly to the united colonies.*" It
was an accurate enumeration of the conflicting pressures the committee felt and a descending list of its priorities. Bailey met with
the committee and endured two hours of "very critical and severe"
interrogation, but the strongest allegation against him was for
"speaking disrespectfully of Mr. [John] Hancock." The labored
reasoning of the committee's findings suggested how uncomfortable they felt about their encounter with a respected Anglican
cleric: "Jacob Bailey has in divers instances since the year 1774
discovered an undue attachment to the authority claimed by
Great Britain over the united colonies and thereby he has given
great reason to believe that he does not wish success to their
struggles for freedom." Specifically, he had refused to read proc-

lamations calling for prayer and fasting issued by the Continental Congresses—behavior that "virtually denied their authority." The committee required Bailey to post bond guaranteeing
his good behavior and future appearance before the Massachusetts
General Court. Summoned before a town meeting to respond to
these restrictions and "called upon with an imperious tone of
voice" by Colonel Charles Cushing, Bailey reported that "I modestly desired to be excused" from posting the bond, "whereupon
the Colonel (being surrounded by his constituents) fell immediately into a violent passion, abused me with the most illiberal and
virulent language and having worked himself into a perfect frenzy
stamped on the floor and smote on the table and exclaimed 'now
for it, gentlemen,' as if he meant to excite the people to tear me
to pieces." Instead, the crowd remained relatively friendly and
several men even volunteered to post his bond.

The following October the committee again summoned Bailey,
to explain why he had not publicly read the Declaration of
Independence. Bailey gave the committee a scrupulously worded
statement: "I was very unwilling to give any offense by refusing
to read the Declaration," and "neither was I desirous of bringing
myself into any further trouble. But when I came seriously to
examine the solemn oaths I had taken" when ordained as an
Anglican cleric, "I found I could not comply without offering
great violence to my conscience. I concluded that nothing more
could be expected [of me] than passive obedience and non-resist-
ance, and if an active compliance was required, I must persist in
my refusal and patiently submit to the penalty, resolving with
the Apostle that it is my duty to obey God rather than man."
The "most eminent writers" Bailey could find all concurred that
an oath was "sacred" and a man should endure any penalty
imposed by society rather than break an oath. "I have lived a
considerable time in the world and have passed through a variety
of scenes," Bailey concluded, "without heretofore being considered a seditious, obstinate, or injurious person," and many of
his neighbors could testify that he was "sober, peaceable, and
inoffensive." Had he, Bailey asked, borne arms for Britain,
spoken publicly in defense of Parliament, discouraged men from
enlisting in American forces, communicated with British officials,
or "aided, abetted, or assisted those (who are styled) the invaders

of America? What is my crime? Is it those connections I cannot dissolve? I am criminal only for . . . choosing to suffer the penalty . . . to an order of council than to feel the eternal reproaches of a guilty conscience." The only reply was Colonel Cushing's explanation that oaths taken before 1760 were sworn to George II and were not binding under his successor, especially after the present King had "broken his coronation oath" and "absolved his subjects from their allegiance."[4] Bailey remained in Pownallboro until 1779, when he fled to Nova Scotia.

In addition to weighing community sentiment and identifying genuine disaffection, the committees had to determine the degree of repression needed to deal with potential British sympathizers. The committees of inspection of Georgetown and Woolwich in the district of Maine (then part of Massachusetts) went to considerable trouble considering how to deal with Edward Perry, a lumberman under contract to provide masts to the royal navy yard in Halifax, Nova Scotia. In April 1775 the committee seized a large supply of Perry's masts and required him to post bond of £2,000 in provincial currency as a guarantee that he would not fulfill his contract to send the masts to the British. "The unfortunate temper of the times," the large bond he had posted, and the threat of violence against his employees prevented him from doing any further business with the British or, for that matter, conducting any other business. The situation was likewise unsatisfactory to the local committees of inspection. Having secured Perry's bond, they argued, there was no practical means of getting the masts out of Perry's possession or taking further punitive action against him. In the meantime, two reputable citizens had posted bond for Perry and could ill afford to wait indefinitely for restitution of their bond money. The committees strongly hinted that the provincial Congress, which had originally ordered the steps taken to halt Perry's trade with the British, should permit the bonds to be refunded. Perry also petitioned along the same lines and asked, as well, for release from confinement. There is no record of the Congress's action on canceling the bond, but its resolution on Perry's petition for release recognized the practical problems of dealing with a disaffected person. It noted his "close connection with and dependence on persons employed by the Crown" in his lumber business, an activity "contrary to the known sentiments of this people." Having defined with some delicacy the extent of his disaffection, the Congress ordered him removed to an inland town. He was sent to Sturbridge, where in March 1776 he persuaded the town's selectmen to allow him to attend to business affairs in Portsmouth, New Hampshire, his former home, a request they found "reasonable" but lacked authority to grant. Again the provincial Congress had to resolve the matter and voted to allow Perry three months to go to Portsmouth and settle his affairs.[5]

In dealing with these day-to-day problems, the committees became the primary custodians of public virtue in the midst of uncertainty and anxiety. They had the responsibility to explore the twilight zone between wholehearted support of the American cause and overt identification with the British. This job consisted of determining degrees of disaffected behavior and constructing viable standards against which to judge such conduct. In the process, the committees had to define the Revolution at certain times in 1775 and 1776. Because their definitions centered around the body of the people as a collective entity and the beliefs that bound it together, the committees worked on the basis of certain assumptions about the nature of the community and its relationship to the principles of the Revolution. As the committees probed the gray area between conformity and disaffection, they sought first to define the potential extent of a suspect's disaffection at a particular time and then to establish the maximum provable misconduct of the individual in question. "Whereas Josiah Martin, under guard, has been brought before this Committee," the Massachusetts provincial Congress's Committee of Safety declared on May 11, 1775, "respecting his appearing in favour of . . . the tyrannical designs of administration for enslaving this province," the members resolved that Martin's conduct had only been "unfriendly to his country . . . in some instances." Because of his promise to "stand forth for the defense of his country," he merited no further "insult or injury" so long as he did not again try to enter Boston.[6] The Groton, Massachusetts committee investigated a complaint by the committee of Townshend about a man "who called himself James Ford" and concluded "upon the whole that he is a bad man and that it is not consistent with the safety of the country for him to travel by different names."[7] The Northboro, Massachusetts committee delayed granting Ebenezer Cutler permission to go to Boston in May 1775 because he "appears to us to be an avowed enemy to his country," having "set at naught and despised all the resolutions of the Continental and Provincial Congresses," and "appeared in the eyes of the public" to favor British policy.[8] But the eyes of the public did not always govern committees of safety. The provincial committee of safety ruled on May 19, 1775, that although "some persons have hinted that Samuel Barrett has in some instances been unfriendly to his country," the evidence indicated his active support of "the rights and liberties" of America. The same committee received accusations from the Sudbury, Massachusetts committee that Ezra Taylor had suspiciously "tarried" in Boston after the outbreak of fighting at Lexington and dismissed him with the verbal admonition to return to Sudbury and stay there.[9] The Farmington, Connecticut Committee of Inspection investigated reports that militia officer Thomas Brooks was "unfriendly to the constitutional rights of America in June 1776!" Brooks freely admitted that he "could not satisfy himself that the colonies were justified in their present measures and that he could not join them to take up arms." Such "principles and temper," the committee voted, disqualified him from holding a militia office, and it recommended that the General Assembly strip him of that office.[10] Committees repeatedly used the formula of stating the furthest extent of suspicion brought to their attention before indicating that the evidence demonstrated a specific and less serious infraction.

The most fascinating tasks of the committees were defining the moral relationship between the community and the accused loyalist and if possible eliciting from the suspect statements of guilt and penitence that further clarified that relationship. First, the interrogation of a suspected inimical person attempted to establish the limits of the committee's inquiry into the conduct of an individual, to narrow as much as possible the grounds of the investigation, in an implicit appeal to the accused to acknowledge the legitimacy of the proceeding against him. The target for investigation was not the defendant but the British government, and therefore the committee's job was to describe the elaborate linkage that could conceivably connect the accused to British policy. The investigation in Medway, Massachusetts on June 5, 1775, of Elisha Adams, Timothy Hammant, and Jonathan Cutler opened with this cumbersome declaration of purpose: to establish the danger of "the people of this province yielding or being forced to the obedience of the late acts of the British Parliament for altering the constitution" of Massachusetts, "and to inquire into the grounds of suspicion and jealousy prevailing relative to [the defendants] being unfriendly and inimical to the just rights and liberties of America and the measures adopted for the recovery and preservation of the rights, liberties, and constitution thereof." Starting with this rambling yet capsule statement of the entire Revolutionary crisis in 1775, the preamble to the proceedings swiftly narrowed its focus to the still general "suspicions and jealousies" concerning the accused men's stand on two broad but more specific issues. The committee put to each of the accused five questions clearly designed to extricate him from "suspicions and jealousies": Did he regard all acts of Parliament binding on America? Were the Coercive Acts unjustifiable? Should the acts be obeyed either voluntarily or under coercion? Did he think the British regarded him as a supporter of royal authority? Would he "adhere" to the recommendations of the Continental and provincial Congresses? Each man gave the expected correct answers. The questions called for simple yes or no replies instead of demanding awkward explanations of complex constitutional issues. The expected answers committed each man, however, to support the full range of Revolutionary positions and therefore precluded his later backsliding into opposition on any particular issue. In short, the committee sought to persuade suspected opponents of resistance to endorse a body of principles that united them with the rest of the community. To make this relationship explicit, each of the three men composed, probably with assistance, a statement affirming that he found it impossible to live in a society where he was under suspicion and he therefore accepted the committee's suggestion that he repudiate the Coercive Acts and promise to obey the provincial and Continental Congresses. The committee also allowed the men to retain that portion of their "unfriendly" opinions which did not directly contradict their newly voiced support for colonial resistance, for each still insisted that "I cannot see any reason nor justice in any of the riotous actions in the later times" and then promised "to exert myself in a just, constitutional way and manner in the recovery and preservation of the rights, liberties, and constitution" of Massachusetts and America. One of the three added that he could not bear arms because the shedding of blood was against his conscience, and another said he was sorry he had made a baseless prediction of a race riot in Boston and explained that there was no sinister meaning to the fact that he had sold his horse two days before Lexington and Concord. Their restoration to the community was complete.[11]

A distant reflection of this kind of interrogation by a committee of safety came from the little community of New England settlers in Sunbury County, Nova Scotia. There a committee of safety petitioned the Massachusetts legislature in May 1776 to join the Revolutionary cause and affiliate itself politically with Massachusetts. Receiving no answer to this request, the committee sent in September 1776 a new appeal and with it an example of the interrogation procedure that it had adopted for dealing with suspected British sympathizers and that had been modeled as closely as possible on procedures it understood to be in use in Massachusetts. This highly stylized and self-conscious document revealed in its distortions and contrived appearance the technique of exposing the evil of Toryism without destroying the self-respect of the suspect, the peeling away of thin layers of misguided belief in an effort to isolate and excise specific tendencies. Because "the disputes between Great Britain and America are so fully known . . . and understood by you," the committee told James Simonds, James White, and Garvas Say, "to say anything upon that subject would be needless. Likewise the proceedings of the inhabitants of this [region] you have been made acquainted with. Neither have you declared against them. This conduct of yours gives uneasiness to many . . . who think you stand ready to be reconciled to the strongest party. . . ." Therefore, the committee asked for an explicit answer and studiously explained that if "you will perhaps say that you are determined to stand neutral, . . . this will not be a satisfactory answer." The committee then suggested that the three men had in fact already decided which side in the War for American

Independence was likely to win and that such an expectation was in itself an unneutral action. "He must be a slothful man who chooses or desires a thing may come to pass and yet shall use no measures, direct or indirect, to accomplish his desire." Having exposed human proclivities for partisanship in that general way, the interrogation then shifted tack. "We don't mean to prescribe rules binding on the consciences of men nor yet urge any person into measures contrary to his inclination. All we request of you is a plain declaration of your sentiments." An evasive reply from Simonds prompted the committee to ostracize him.[12]

The committees of safety sought to be the custodians of civic virtue and to design their interrogations so as to include within the protective bounds of the community all who could be persuaded to renounce the smallest necessary portion of pro-British sentiment. In May 1775 the Massachusetts provincial Congress's Committee of Safety published six recantations of Marblehead men who had signed a farewell address to Thomas Hutchinson a year earlier. These confessions were models of the penitence expected of suspects appearing before Revolutionary committees. Each man, using somewhat different wording but following a prescribed format, placed himself in a repentant, isolated position in relation to the town of Marblehead. Each depicted the sin of applauding Hutchinson as an unintentional but genuine threat to the safety of the community. They pleaded that the address had been a naïve means of winning the favor of the Crown for the town. Each spoke of the collective hostility of the community as a cleansing force that, if they would avail themselves of it, would purge them of their irresponsibility and restore them to the confidence of the community. "I supposed . . . an address to Governor Hutchinson . . . would answer a good purpose and be generally adopted," explained Richard Reed, one of the six. "Being now convinced from further attention to the matter as well as the public opinion that it will greatly injure the cause of America, I do now publicly declare that I had no such design and therefore renounce the said address in every respect and am heartily sorry that I ever signed it and hope to be forgiven by my town and my countrymen."[13] This sense of estrangement from the community and the candid desire to end it were frequently expressed, doubtless at the invitation of committees, and served to define the moral and inclusive character of a community in crisis. "As my comfort does so much depend on the regard and good will of those among whom I live," explained Enoch Bartlett, of Haverhill, Massachusetts, "I hereby give under my hand . . . that I will not buy or sell tea or act in any public" manner "contrary to the minds of the people in general . . . and will yet hope that all my errors in judgment or conduct will meet with their forgiveness and favour which I humbly ask."[14]

27

The Courts and Legal Control
of the Disaffected

DURING the Revolution, New England's court system and law-enforcement machinery sought to prosecute and punish those who illegally obstructed the American cause. A highly developed court system that had evolved during the colonial period remained completely intact under new state government, except for the flight of loyalist judges in Massachusetts and New Hampshire. The maintenance of procedure in loyalist cases and the development of an effective judicial attack on disaffection were two critical tests of the maturity and vigor of these courts. The basis for these prosecutions was the Continental Congress's resolution of June 24, 1775, which defined the levying of war against the "united colonies," being adherent to "the King of Great Britain," or "giving him aid and comfort" as "treason." The resolution authorized the Revolutionary legislatures to "pass laws for punishing such persons." Some legislatures simply enacted into their own law the English common-law definition of treason: attempting to overthrow the government by force or giving aid and comfort to the enemy. Most went further and specified treasonable acts: joining the enemy or inducing others to do so, supplying the enemy with arms or other supplies, conducting subversive correspondence with the British. Some included conspiracy against the Revolutionary regime as treason. Only one state, New Hampshire, late in the war, made personal belief in British authority treasonable. In addition, states outlawed a wide range of activities that were less than treasonable: acknowledging the sovereignty of the King, discouraging men from enlisting, advising submission to the British Army, undermining patriot morale, counterfeiting. These offenses usually incurred fines and imprisonment.[1]

Prosecution often began when a justice of the peace received a complaint against a suspected inimical person. The justice of the peace would then collect sworn statements from as many witnesses as possible; if the suspect had not fled to British protection, he would be taken into custody and ordered held for trial. On April 14, 1777, Constable Ebenezer Whitney, of Norwalk, delivered Thaddeus Bennet, of Danbury, to Justice of the Peace Thaddeus Betts, of Fairfield, Connecticut. Evidence and witnesses were presented, and Betts began a lengthy interrogation of Bennet. The suspect admitted that he had served in a loyalist regiment of the British Army commanded by Jabez Lockwood. But he denied that he had recruited some fifteen other Connecticut men for the British Army. "How do you exculpate yourself?" asked Justice of the Peace Betts. "It appeared afterwards that . . . Lockwood never was properly enlisted," and therefore Bennet believed he had not acted in an official capacity in rounding up his little band of volunteers. Betts concluded that this technicality scarcely altered Bennet's guilt and ordered him held for trial before the Connecticut Superior Court. He then computed the costs of the prosecution: the charge for the writ originally authorizing the constable to arrest Bennet, another fee to cover the cost of his forthcoming trial, a third to Betts himself for issuing a "mittimus," or ruling that the defendant should be held for trial, a fee for the constable, and the expenses of two witnesses he had brought with him. Three weeks later Whitney returned to Justice of the Peace Betts with John Cannon, who had returned home in haste and stealth, which had aroused the constable's suspicion. When searched Cannon was discovered with a letter of safe-conduct through British lines signed by William Franklin, a prisoner in Middletown. This time the costs included fees for the writ ordering Cannon's arrest, the cost of his trial, another fee for the "recognizance," or order that he post money promising to appear before the justice of the peace, and the constable's fee.[2]

The hearing before the justice of the peace apparently took the place of a grand-jury proceeding and determined whether there was sufficient evidence to hold the accused for trial. It also determined whether a crime had actually been committed and whether a state court had jurisdiction. On May 11, 1778, Thaddeus Betts interrogated David McKinsey concerning a constable's complaint that he had committed high treason by joining the British Army in October 1776. McKinsey freely admitted that he had enlisted, that he had recruited others, and that he would do so again. "By perpetrating that very crime," McKinsey "claimed the privilege of a Briton and an exemption from the penalty of that act." Betts recorded that he "judged him worthy of trial" and denied bail. Two days later a Norwalk constable reported to Betts that Sturgis Burr had, on April 20, 1777, gone illegally to Long Island carrying a gun and had there given intelligence to the British. He was arrested trying to slip back into Connecticut and was brought before Betts, where he confessed he had gone armed to Long Island and was ordered held without bail.[3]

Justices of the peace served other functions vital to the control of disaffection. They received sworn statements testifying to the innocence of suspected persons. Elisha Smith and Elnathan Mitchell went to Justice of the Peace Increase Mosely, of Woodbury, Connecticut, on May 6, 1777, to testify that the wife of departed Tory John Davis was "a steady and true and faithful friend to the American states in opposition to her husband, who has been of quite a different character." A year later, when her husband deserted the British Army, he surrendered to three justices of the peace in Derby and confessed his guilt so convincingly that they successfully petitioned the General Assembly to grant him a pardon. In Massachusetts, three or more justices of the peace sat together as a court of special sessions. In Suffolk County, in June 1777, four J.P.'s ordered that Congregationalist minister Mather Byles be put on a guard ship in Boston harbor and from there transferred to the first ship that would transport him to the West Indies or Europe. A special court of sessions held in Boston on July 1, 1777, to deal with several accused loyalists, including the Anglican clergyman Edward Winslow, of Braintree, was dissolved because of irregularities concerning its composition, and cases before it were dismissed. At Great Barrington, in December 1777, the trial of John Burghardt began with the reading of a resolution of the town meeting accusing him of trying "to counter the united struggles" of the American states. Other evidence, unspecified in the court record, was presented, and the jury found him guilty. The J.P.'s ordered him banished to the West Indies or Europe. J.P.'s in such trials also had extensive powers to instruct jurors. In the trial of John Stetson, of Scituate, Massachusetts, the jury found that his presence in the province was "not now dangerous, by which verdict," the defendant later explained, "he conceived that he was legally acquitted." But the presiding J.P.'s told the jury that they were not satisfied with this verdict. The jury then ruled that Stetson had once, presumably in 1776, "counteracted" the American cause and was to that extent guilty. In vain did the defendant plead that he had only opposed the taking up of arms and merely preferred "to see all things done decently and in order" but did not favor British victory in the war.[4]

These proceedings often left suspects bewildered about their plight as defendants. Prince Barker, of Pembroke, Massachusetts, a Quaker convicted of inimical behavior, later explained that his "religious persuasion . . . forbids his taking an active part in military operations" but he had said nothing at his trial because "a consciousness of his own rectitude prevented his employing those means to establish his innocence." Jov[?]tt Bullough was quoted at his trial as condemning the American cause in "heinous" terms; he wrote from a guard ship in Boston harbor: "I made no defense at all for myself, knowing within myself that I never spoke them words so I was resolved to take the event of the trial, let the consequence be what it would."[5]

By far the most common penalty inflicted by New England courts was to require the convicted defendant to post bond guaranteeing that he would live peaceably within the boundaries of his town, or in some cases of another town, and subject himself to the scrutiny of the selectmen. Thomas Williams, "laborer," of Boston, was convicted of "contriving and desiring to discourage divers of the people of this state from supporting the Declaration of Independency of the United States" by publicly drinking a toast to the King, assembling a group of armed men with him, and announcing, " 'I am enlisting men for the King,' meaning George the third, King of Great Britain; 'in six weeks time this town will be overcome and will be in the hands of the King's troops. . . . The time will come when the streets of Boston will run with blood.' " Williams further boasted that he was " 'bound for Providence and thence to Halifax' " to join the King's forces. Found guilty, he was required by the court to post £100 bond guaranteeing his good behavior. In some cases the terms of parole were laid down by the justices of the peace and in others by the committees of safety, higher courts, or the Assembly itself. The Connecticut Council of War insisted that J. Montfort Brown promise not to bear arms or give intelligence to the British, and to attest that while a prisoner of the Council he had been "kindly treated." Brown refused to sign the parole but gave his oral word to abide by it, insisting that the word of a "gentleman" should be sufficient. Early in the war, a common penalty in Massachusetts was banishment aboard a ship bound for the West Indies or Europe. The Massachusetts Superior Court, which found John Pell guilty of "enticing" Asa Hiccock and Eli Lyon to enlist in the British Army, sentenced him to sit for an hour in the pillory in both Springfield and Northampton, serve a year in jail, and pay the costs of his prosecution. But eleven other defendants, accused of going to Albany County, in New York, in August 1777, allegedly to join Burgoyne, won acquittals from the jury. Attorney General Robert Treat Paine, however, moved successfully that the men post from £400 to £600 bonds securing their good behavior. In Windham County, Connecticut, one of the few loyalist prosecutions in that eastern Connecticut county accused William Walton of telling Ezra Brownel, a blacksmith and army contractor, that he "hoped and wished and would use his endeavour that the British troops . . . might . . . prevail over America." Pleading guilty, Walton was fined £15 and posted an unspecified bond guaranteeing his good conduct.[6]

Prison terms for convicted inimical persons were rarely longer than two years and usually only a few months in actual length. In the first place, New England states lacked prison facilities. Two jails in Connecticut, at Hartford and Litchfield, held many of that state's prisoners, and they were only makeshift structures. In Boston, guard ships in the harbor provided better security for convicted men awaiting transfer to vessels that would take them into banishment—perhaps accounting for the common use of that penalty in Boston. One such convict complained that "he has been so long subject to the miseries necessarily attendant on the marine prison" that he pleaded with the Board of War to order his immediate banishment. In many parts of New England jails were little used, as in Worcester, where in June 1776 the jail contained only three prisoners: one breaker of the peace, another man who had attempted to flee to the British Army, and a third who had refused to join the Continental Army. In January 1779 the Connecticut Assembly resolved to parole all Tory prisoners from Hartford and Windham counties who would agree to perform supervised labor for the state. Prisoners seeking release from captivity frequently argued that cold, bad food, and filthy conditions were ruining their health. One Tory prisoner in Middlesex County jail, in Concord, Massachusetts, argued that "long imprisonment . . . in great degree defeats the end of the penal law as through length of time the prisoner and the crime with which he is charged are forgotten by the public." Because "the horrors of confinement and distress and anxious concerns of his family make your petitioner's situation truly pitiable and though he is conscious of no guilt, yet his circumstances operate a heavy punishment on him especially as he has not the consolation of knowing at what given hour his sufferings may come to a period." The most notorious jail during the Revolution was Connecticut's maximum-security prison, Newgate, in the town of Simsbury. The prison consisted of several dank rooms underground in what had formerly been a lead mine. Near the entrance to the main shaft were several small wooden buildings. Between 1773 and the end of the Revolution these structures burned down three times. Half of the prison's inmates during the war years escaped. One mass breakout occurred on May 18, 1781, when a prisoner's wife appeared at the iron gate in the passageway into the prison; as the guards opened the hatch, several prisoners overpowered them, seized their muskets, and killed six other guards in a gun battle within the prison. Six guards and a larger number of prisoners were seriously wounded in the fighting before the insurgents overwhelmed the guards and the majority escaped.[7]

28

"A Melancholy Condition": New England Loyalists' Perception of the Revolution

THE nature and danger of loyalist disaffection in New England perplexed not only courts and committees but also the loyalists themselves. They struggled to understand what was happening to them and to the society in which they lived. It was a difficult task, for, as Paul H. Smith has noted, the Revolution was "too large an event for most persons to comprehend in its entirety" and was therefore "perceived in terms of immediate commonplace local issues." "For many," he suggests, "the issue of their allegiance was never perceived as a matter upon which they might exercise some meaningful choice." Many loyalists seemed aware of the awesome scope of the Revolution and the relative puniness of their own situation; by this awareness, moreover, they gave some structure and pattern to what was happening to them. They struggled to discover where they stood in relation to an overwhelming event, to impose order on the confusion surrounding them, and to ascertain the causes of their dilemma. This effort by loyalists who wrote about their experiences most often explored one or more of three preoccupations: first, the external pressures, influences, and circumstances that led men, often unwittingly, into disaffection and inimical conduct; second and more important, the interior and private dilemmas of a loyalist, his emotional and mental vulnerability during a time of upheaval; third and most often, the gap between the loyalists' personal definitions of illegal conduct and the public, official standards of behavior that they found they had unknowingly violated. "To the honneur . . . ," a prisoner wrote painfully, and then started again: "To the honourable, the General Assembly of the State of Connecticut, the petition of Ephraim Hawley to your oneurs. I being in a mallon colly condission in Hartford gold [jail], I beg and pray that your oneurs would consider me and set me free and I will dow all that lies in my power for the good of my country and I will be faithful in the service. God save the Congress and if I have done amis I am sorry for it." Even this touching declaration revealed the complexities of a loyalist's perception of his relationship to Revolutionary authority. The Connecticut Anglican cleric Richard Mansfield drafted in 1777 a bitter "Catechism" of patriot belief, which further illustrates this desire to give structure and pattern to loyalist fears and apprehensions:

Question: What is a Tory?
Answer: A Tory is nowadays one that is a friend to government, keeps his oath to be true to the King and his lawful successor.
Question: What rule have you to know what makes a Tory which is sufficient to punish him as such?
Answer: The infallible rule is by his frequent citing texts of scripture to prove that kings are God's ministers and the like. . . .
Question: But do you not use arguments . . . to convert them to be Whigs?
Answer: None but such as these, viz., . . . if the Tories don't join us and fight with us, they will not be a whit better off than we at the last if the King's forces overcome them. . . .
Question: What are the special benefits that accompany and flow from anarchy, pulpit drummers [i.e., dissenting clergy], and independency?
Answer: They are these: the pleasure of punishing Tories; the free enjoyment of all false doctrine, heresy, and schism; hardness of heart; contempt of God's word and commandments; privy conspiracy and rebellion.[1]

Allowing for the special pleading and self-justification of accused loyalists, the writings and statements of these men still form a coherent, believable body of evidence. Repeatedly they emphasized that an unlucky combination of circumstances trapped them into committing or appearing to commit illegal deeds. A convicted Connecticut loyalist, John Baker, had been "warmly engaged" in the patriot cause until he decided that he was in danger of offending his father-in-law, who "possessed . . . a very considerable estate" and "was greatly inclined to favor the interest of Great Britain in opposition to the independence of America." Only his need for the inheritance in order to support his family "induced him to favour Britain" and at the same time provoke his neighbors, who "abused him and called him an enemy to his country." After that sequence of events he "inadvertently" visited Long Island, fell into patriot hands, and found himself in the Hartford jail. Titus Butler, of Connecticut, had answered the Lexington alarm and served in the Canadian campaign in 1775 and 1776, but when he returned home his neighbors falsely impugned his loyalty and he was fined. Then, "in this moment of despondency and despair," he went illegally to Long Island. He did nothing to help the British but was nonetheless captured by a patriot raiding party and jailed. Stephen Gorham, of Fairfield, Connecticut, described himself as "one of those unhappy persons" who refused to take up arms in 1775 "against the (then) parent state." The anger of his neighbors drove Gorham to Long Island; once there, he felt guilty about "quitting his friends and neighbors" and voluntarily returned, stood trial, and served a prison term. Then, on his release, he was arrested and jailed again without a hearing or a specific charge. Stephen Parker, of Massachusetts, went to Philadelphia on business in 1776, but, unable to find credit there to finance his purchases and destitute, he found room on a ship sailing to Nova Scotia. When he finally reached Massachusetts, authorities jailed him for fleeing to a British territory. "Ignorance, inadvertence, and absolute necessity were the sole cause of my setting foot in . . . Nova Scotia," he explained. Thomas Osbourn, of Connecticut, likewise took a business trip to Long Island, in 1776, where the British captured him. He returned to New Haven, and while he was enjoying a drink at Captain Thatcher's tavern, a local committee accused him of trading with the enemy. He denied knowing whether the tar and hemp he had sold a man on Long Island had gone to the British. William Mitchell, who had served as commissary in the Continental Army in 1775 and 1776, "was . . . unfortunately . . . in the pasture between . . . eight and nine . . . at night" when "I

was accosted by seven men who after what resistance I could make
. . . cocked two pistols and swore they would shoot me if I did
not go with them." Taken to New York and imprisoned by the
British, he escaped and returned to Middletown, where Connecticut officials put him in jail.[2]

External pressures and circumstances during the Revolution
often seemed to magnify simple human weakness and misjudg-
ment. Judah and Benjamin Leaming had served under General
Arnold in Quebec but failed to answer the Danbury alarm in
1777 because they resented neighbors who had not served at all
and who should have taken their turn first. This objection only
made the Leamings targets for "unreasonable jealousy," and the
Farmington Committee of Safety ordered them jailed. The failure to respond to the Danbury alarm provoked the Farmington
Committee of Inspection to restrict the movements of seventeen
other men "upon mere suspicion only that they were not in favor
of American measures." Three young men in New Town, Fairfield County, Connecticut signed British enlistment papers in
August 1776 after a loyalist recruiter "persuaded" them "that the
country would be conquered and . . . being on that side" they
"would be safe." Only the fortunate intervention of one boy's
father dissuaded officials from this "unjustifiable proceeding."
Prosper Brown confessed that he fled to the British fleet after
having a "controversy with one Obadiah Wright," by way of
"retaliation upon said Wright." He returned to Connecticut in
April 1781 with a Tory raiding party only for the purpose of
taking his wife and child to Long Island. He was captured and
convicted of inimical conduct.[3] Repeatedly loyalists felt victimized by bad luck, errors of their own judgment, and a resulting cycle of terrible consequences. This preoccupation was more
than self-pity; it is substantial evidence that the line between
inimical and loyal Americans was a ragged one in which confusion, simple error, or accident often determined the safety or
danger of confused and vulnerable men.

Even more striking among loyalist attempts to find structure in
these experiences was their depiction of their mental and emotional habits. Again, these testimonies emphasize the concatena-
tion of circumstances and actions that cast them into inimical
behavior; in addition, they depict the inner turmoil and tensions

that those circumstances activated or enlarged. "Being a young man and the more liable to be impressed, and living toward the western limits of this state, where a great diversity of sentiments prevailed about the contest between Great Britain and America," David Washburn felt that he had been ill equipped to evaluate "which was in the right and which in the wrong" and was therefore "persuaded" that Great Britain "still ought to have the rule." Agitated, frightened, and intimidated by an argument in which he felt himself outclassed, Washburn did not feel able to resist inducements to join British forces on Long Island. He felt suspended "between hope and fear" when he illegally fled Connecticut. Samuel Roberts explained that he had been "bred from the cradle under the influence of the Episcopal clergyman" in New Town, Connecticut and when the Revolution began he was both "unacquainted with politics" and surrounded solely with Tory acquaintances. "In the year 1776" he "did as almost every ignorant man generally does, swim with the tide or current near him." John Jennings, of Sandwich, Massachusetts, stressed this sense of inner vulnerability. He had refused to take the oath of allegiance "for want of time" to consider it and because "his passions" had been "unduly excited by reason of his being particularly complained of." Nathan Turrill, age seventeen, of Fairfield County, Connecticut, was "unhappily . . . too much under the influence of certain evil minded and inimical persons," who persuaded him to flee to Long Island. There he found himself "plied with threats and lucrative offers" to join the British Army. This sense of being caught between conflicting poles of hope and fear, safety and danger, "the threatenings of some and the allurements of others," was a recurring theme in loyalist testimony.[4]

The tension and internal pressure also had a dynamic character, pulling men into a spiral of fear and away from the resources of habit and reason. John McKee had come to Connecticut from England in 1766, married into a "respectable" family, established a business, and at the outset of the Revolution "formed his opinion in favour of the colonies." He had answered the Lexington alarm. Then, in the spring of 1776, this protective shield of associations and opinions had been pierced by more specific fears. Tory leaders began to "beguile and terrify" him with warnings that British troops invading Connecticut "would be very numerous and like a flood bear down and sweep away all opposition." McKee learned that because he was not a native American "he would be a particular mark for British vengeance." His "only method for . . . escape . . . was to slack his zeal in the American cause" and, specifically, to cease supporting the disarming of "Tories." The cumulative effect of these "insinuations, . . . cloaked under the artful mask of personal friendship, flung" McKee "into the utmost perplexity of mind." Similarly, Nathan Daton, of New Milford, Connecticut, had taken "an active part" against British "tyranny" until Washington's retreat from New York City in late 1776 "filled" him "with gloomy apprehensions." In this "perplexing anxiety of mind," he was misled by evil counselors using "the stratagem of magnifying the dangers of his country." Solomon Ferris's "penury and consequent gloomy state of mind" and his "apparent backwardness" combined to make him vulnerable to the advice of his "ill-chosen companion" to join in kidnaping and robbing Connecticut patriots and to forget entirely his "sense of the obligations of moral nature." Ashbel Humphrey, of Goshen, Connecticut, believed that his stubborn and abrasive personality was his undoing, for he could not "disguise" his "doubts and his fears" or curb his tongue about the propriety and legality of declaring independence. As a result, he was "flung into the hands of the committees" and ostracized by his neighbors. These "too hasty measures . . . almost brought him to the borders of despair" after the theft of his mare and then his cow. Only then did he flee to the woods and live as a fugitive.[5]

The most compelling loyalist attempts to explain and organize their experiences and sensations sought to define the point at which they had become disaffected from the Revolution. "Scruples of conscience, not corruption of heart" prompted the Reverend Edward Winslow, an Anglican from Braintree, Massachusetts, to oppose the Revolution. The claims of conscience were clear-cut for Winslow: "An early and steady prepossession in favour of that constitution under which he has so long acted and from which he has received so many real favours . . . must bind him to gratitude and affection." Hopestill Capen felt himself in solitary estrangement from those who "say that the voice of the people is the voice of God. In this I must dissent from them, let it offend who it will because we are assured in the Scriptures that the voice of great multitudes with their boldest assertions have in the end proved . . . altogether false . . . while the sayings of those who were few in number and were looked on by the great and wise men of this world to be foolish, poor, ignorant, base, and . . . petulant fellows . . . were taught by the God of Heaven." This claim of conscience and Capen's reliance on Old Testament prophecy established the clear-cut gulf between him and his accusers. Other loyalists tried to define simultaneously the precise grounds of their disaffection and the limits they placed on their opposition to the Revolution. "We . . . entertained sentiments variant from those of our fellow countrymen" on only one issue, explained Jonathan Hicks and Josiah Jones, of Concord, Massachusetts; that was "in supposing it inexpedient and unsafe for us to bear arms against the power of Great Britain." Beyond that, they fully sympathized with the "cause in which this people are so seriously engaged" and would comply with every measure of the Massachusetts provincial Congress "so far at least as in no degree to counteract their resolutions."[6]

Andrew Leet, of Guilford, Connecticut, struggled to maintain a sense of perspective in his definition of loyal behavior. "From the beginning of the present controversy," he explained, he had "esteemed it his duty to take no active part in it by taking up arms" because "he was born under allegiance to the King . . . and never in his best judgment and conscience considered it justifiable to renounce that allegiance." This analysis, he stressed, was a product of his "most mature deliberation and thorough examination into the merits of the dispute," and if it was "erroneous" it was still an honest act and not the result of any "spirit of perverseness or ill will." Like Hicks and Jones, Leet renounced any "disposition to counteract the doings of those who are engaged in the controversy." Similarly, Leet reiterated that he did not question the motives of the supporters of the Revolution. They ought to respect "the most sacred idea of . . . liberty (viz) liberty of conscience," he said. He was careful not to say that the Revolution was "unjust" but only that his participation in it would be "unjustifiable." Jacob Bull, of New Milford, Connecticut, struggled to contrast his apparently inimical conduct with the innocence of his intentions. "I did not make any escape for to hurt the state nor any of my neighbors," he protested, in explanation of his breaking out of jail. He promised to take an oath of loyalty to the American cause, to report all "plots and conspiracies," but he insisted that "I am not willing to take up arms to kill anybody for I think it is not right." In some cases loyalists frankly admitted that the line between inimical and lawful conduct had to be determined by the state. Hopestill Capen's wife asked the General Court to "grant her . . . husband as much lenity as your honors may think consistent with the safety of the state." William Apthorp faced deportation to Nova Scotia because he went to England in 1775 but "without any design of aiding the foes to America"; he had never been "a tory." Yet he admitted that "the safety of the state . . . is and ought to be the supreme law . . . in such times as these" and asked only that this "vigilant jealousy . . . be exerted with as little injury as possible."[7]

At the other end of the spectrum were the loyalists who insisted that they alone could determine whether they had crossed the line into disaffection. Samuel Mather declared that he went to England during the Revolution to claim an allowance due him from the British government for his long service to the Crown. That action, he declared, was "wholly abstracted from any idea or intention of being concerned in the dispute at that time subsisting between Great Britain and the colonies." Similarly, Isaac Royall did not regard his exile in England as evidence of disloyalty to the American cause. He left in April 1775 only because the "prevailing tumults and commotions" were too much for his precarious health. Other loyalists acknowledged that they had violated the rules of the Revolutionary states but pointed to mitigating circumstances. Darling Whelply and William Peck, of Greenwich, Connecticut, fled to New York in 1777 because they found their state dominated by "the prevailing principle . . . that those who did not unite in the common cause were to be treated as enemies." They went to New York only to seek work and physical safety and later went to Long Island, where work was more plentiful and where they could support their families. There a patriot raiding party from Connecticut plundered and terrorized them. Only to secure "reparation" for this "injury" did the two men join a retaliatory Tory raiding party which attacked the Connecticut coast. Convicted of high treason, the two men appealed to the General Assembly. Whelply declared that from his "heart" he did "detest this evil practice of plundering and captivating peaceable inhabitants" and asked the legislature to "make great allowance for his misconception of his rights." This definition of loyalist disaffection impressed the Assembly, for both houses voted to release Whelply from imprisonment. Robert Cutts Shannon, of New Hampshire, located the line between disaffection and legal conduct not in the conduct of the accused loyalist but in the confused and turbulent passions of patriot leaders. Speaking for nine imprisoned loyalists, he condemned the prevailing rationale for suppressing the disaffected. "It is said if we were permitted our liberty, the people would commit outrages upon us. This we declare to be an infamous falsehood, contrived probably by infamous men who would gladly attribute to the people at large the same malicious sentiments that they find lurking within their own breasts." Imprudent outbursts like Shannon's and obsequious confessions of guilt like those of Whelply and Peck contained a like candor concerning their plight and a similar inquisitiveness about its causes.[8]

The most striking attempts by loyalist and patriot alike to define disaffection occurred when the loyalists used provocative language about the Revolution and in so doing fell afoul of the law. Abusive, defiant, treasonous words, whether shouted foolishly in public or muttered indiscreetly in private, were taken as matters of grave importance. Many Tories who spoke in this fashion seemed fully conscious of the risks they were taking, and patriot committees and courts regarded these words as the most precise evidence of the state of mind of a disaffected person. Provocative anti-Revolutionary language and official responses to it constitute a dramatic dialogue on the issues of the Revolution and the emotional context created by those issues.

Patriot officials were acutely aware that irresponsible public statements could cause panic, undermine already shaky morale, and disrupt normal political processes. But their fears were not merely pragmatic. Wicked language implied hidden dissatisfaction in the body politic. Men rash enough to expose their seditious opinions must feel impelled to do so by devilish beliefs of imponderable magnitude. When Henry Stone and Ebenezer Tisdale, of Stoughton and Stoughtonham, Massachusetts, spread reports that the Southern states had abandoned the American cause, that Connecticut was on the verge of following suit, and that "General Washington had turned devil," the two towns' committees of safety considered the rumors a grave threat to the security of the area. There was no suggestion that these men were Tories; they were, however, dangerous loudmouths and rumor-mongers and thus appropriate targets for committees of safety.[9]

Open and forthright Tory language implied that the speaker possessed dangerous boldness and self-confidence. New Hampshire militia captain Nathaniel Odiorne "frequented" Stavers's tavern, a notorious Tory gathering place, to collect evidence against the customers. Without hiding his rank in the Revolutionary forces, he jollied his Tory drinking companions into promising—probably in an unroarious scene—that if he would side with them they would "recommend him as an object of favor" when General Howe crushed the Revolution, which he would surely do following the capture of Philadelphia. Jonathan Warner told another New Hampshire officer, Captain Samuel Dalling, that Howe had entered Philadelphia and that the war was nearly over. Dalling replied that rumors of this kind were illegal and that Warner could only protect himself by revealing the source of the report. "You may be damned," Warner exploded, " 'tis high time for people to speak their minds. They have been long enough restrained." The selectmen of Cambridge instituted criminal proceedings in 1777 against Samuel Teagers on charges of "being inimical to the liberties of America" and "counter[acting] the united struggles of this and the United States for the preservation of their rights and privileges." Teagers was accused of saying he would "travel fifty miles to blow out the brains of Samuel Adams and John Hancock," he "hoped to see the hills covered with the dead bodies of rebels," and "many like expressions."[10]

Even ironic, veiled Tory language was relatively forthright, and patriot witnesses of such talk proceeded without much fuss to describe its manifest meaning. Samuel Goodrich, of Middletown, Connecticut, testified that he heard the suspected Tory

Abner Camp express "extravagant" praise to Continental money "which from his air and manner I judged to be ironical, calculated to show his contemp thereof." Frustrated at getting Oliver Parker to confess his Tory sympathies openly, New Hampshire Whig Isaac Temple "challenged him to tell of one action he had done or one word he had ever said that would affront the greatest tory in the province. . . . Parker made this reply that he never had nor never intended to affront a tory," thus amply confirming Temple's experience that "I have never heard nor seen him do the least in the cause of liberty." These verbal clashes were part of the raw edge of hostility between Whigs and Tories. Intimate and familiar with each other, they collided directly, lacking the protective padding of traditional estrangement or aloofness.[11]

Tory language cut most deeply into the consciousness of Revolutionary New England when it identified and directly challenged central tenets of Whig belief. *"I scruple your authority. I defy your authority,"* declared Lewis Allen, a Shrewsbury, Massachusetts goldsmith, when Justice of the Peace Samuel Crosby attempted to arrest him. For both men, the meaning of Crosby's "authority" was of paramount importance, and the J.P. carefully asked whether it was Crosby's personal authority to make arrests that Allen called into question. "I do not scruple that. . . . I scruple the authority that gave you" your "commission" as a law officer. Pressed still further to explain himself, Allen drove his complaint to its seditious conclusion: all of your "authority, even to Congress, is a bubble." John Gallespie, of Cohasset, Massachusetts, "maliciously, wickedly, and presumptuously" disturbed "peace, good order, and government" when he told his angry customers, "Damn your Congress; . . . go to your damned Congress to change your money." Ephraim Whitney, a physician in Petersham, Massachusetts, struck more directly at the source of his troubles: "I do not care anything for your law. Your law is treason and your government is treason. . . . I have no money, no stock. I will go to gaol and rot. I am not going to pay money to support rebellion." James Hewit, of Great Barrington, Massachusetts, publicly declared that he wished all the American troops in an engagement at New London, Connecticut "had been killed, and cut to pieces, and broiled. . . . Damn the rebels. I would cut them into hunks, broil them on the coals, and eat them." The most thoroughgoing attempt to confound the doctrines of the Revolution came in Ezra Houghton's trial, in Worcester, Massachusetts, on a charge of counterfeiting. He was accused of boasting: "It would be a capital stroke if we could destroy the currency"; the judge asked him if he thought counterfeiting was morally justifiable. "No, when it is done on a selfish principle to build a man up, but when it is done on a more noble principle with a view to bring the war to an end and to prevent the effusion of human blood, he did not," the court clerk recorded, "view it so bad." *"We are all, as it were, a wheel,"* he concluded ominously; *"your spoke . . . is up now but it will soon be down."*[12]

Abusive Tory language was usually less dramatic and more often expressed fragments of immediate anger, frustration, or outrage that characterized relations between isolated loyalists and their neighbors. "It has been to me a great cross that I have been so contrary to people in general," confessed Benjamin Whitcher, in New Hampshire, after asserting that "King George . . . has always sufficiently protected . . . his [Whitcher's] interest and . . . that he always looked on the people in Boston as the aggressors and to blame in destroying [the tea] as they did." Adam Stuart offended his Londonderry, New Hampshire neighbors by dwelling always in his "conversation . . . on the dark side of our unhappy difference with our mother country" and by predicting certain defeat for this "undisciplined country." Such hostile sentiments lay close to the surface and were readily exposed in the face of equally hostile questions like those posed to the Lincoln, Massachusetts merchant Abiel Wood, who wanted to sell timber to the British Army in Boston in June 1775. Challenged by town officials to cease this commerce, Wood quickly revealed the basis of his actions: "The devil made . . . Handcock [*sic*] and Adams . . . believe that one of them should be a king" and "another a governor and that they should be in some great places of honour and profit. . . . Their view was to stir up the people to sedition in order to accomplish their designs." Seth Fogg, of Rockingham, New Hampshire, "in an unguarded hour and . . . being irritated by being called an enemy to his country, . . . spoke unadvisedly and said many things which, on . . . reflection, he should not have said: [for example] there are no laws but the king's laws" and "this is King George's dominion and he will soon make you know it." These sporadic exchanges of insults were, however, a serious business. One produced a civil suit between a seaman, Stanislaus Crowley, and Captain John Grimes, of the Massachusetts privateer *Minerva*. Grimes put Crowley in irons for, among other things, calling the officers of the ship "a parcel of damned yankee, Indian buggers" and threatening to get "satisfaction for the ill-usage" he had received if the ship fell into the hands of the British Navy.[13]

These verbal exchanges identified and brought into focus the many varieties of incidental conflicts that the Revolution created as it cut across an already closely knit, complex, and argumentative society. And these uses of acrid language indicated the extent as well as the limits of social cleavage and disunity. The care that justices of the peace and clerks of court took to preserve a man's exact words was an effort to distinguish between the irritating and the illegal. The prosecution of Sheriff Eleazer Fitch, of Windham, Connecticut, was unusual, considering the political standing of the defendant, but typical in the fullness and detail of the indictment. Throughout 1775 and 1776 Fitch paraded his "contempt" and "ridicule" for the Revolutionary effort. He openly declared that "it was in vain for . . . united states to make any defense against the power and force of Great Britain." He tried to dissuade his neighbor, Abner Robinson, from raising a company for the Continental Army. A month later he strutted around the parade ground near the Windham County courthouse in the presence of Robinson's troops shouting, "Damn them. I wish they . . . never would get back again." When a group of British prisoners was brought to his jail for custody, Fitch refused to take charge of the captives. He shouted for all to hear that "it was a damned trick" for prisoners of war to be sent to his jail. The officer in charge told Fitch that he was under orders from the governor and the Council of State to place the prisoners in Fitch's custody and that if Fitch did not cooperate he would lose his commission to hold his office. The Sheriff told the officer that "the Governor and Council might take his Commission and wipe their damned asses with it." These statements in sworn affidavits then accompanied Fitch's indictment, and on March 3, 1778, he stood trial in the Connecticut Superior Court for inimical behavior. He pleaded not guilty and was acquitted,[14] perhaps because of his local prominence and because in staunchly patriot eastern Connecticut his erratic behavior created no real public danger.

29

The Breakdown of Cohesion: Social
Flaws and Flourishing Disaffection
in Revolutionary New England

THE pattern of overwhelming surveillance and interrogation of loyalists and neutralists in New England and the scrupulous attempts to win them back into political conformity did not function uniformly, and in several dramatic cases these techniques of social control labored heavily.

Along Fairfield County's coast on Long Island Sound and its common border with Westchester County, New York, order partially disintegrated, under the pressure of war, from 1777 until 1782. There were three British invasions of the state: Danbury in 1777; New Haven, Norwalk, and Fairfield in 1779; and New London in 1781. Rampant illicit trade with the enemy on Long Island and in New York City, vigilante Tory raiding parties from Long Island, retaliatory patriot raiding from Connecticut against Long Island, streams of embittered Tory refugees from Connecticut, and patriots driven from their homes on Long Island were further blows to social and political stability. Together, these events seriously weakened the social order and created a milieu of random violence in which many Connecticut loyalists and Whigs lived during the Revolution.

Fueling this process of social disorganization was illicit trade. From 1777 onward a staggering flow of agricultural produce illegally crossed Long Island Sound or traveled overland through Westchester County to New York City. The presence of the British Army in New York City created an abnormally hungry market and acted as a centrifugal force pulling apart the bonds of civil society in adjacent parts of Connecticut. "Large and weekly supplies of fresh provisions are brought into [New] York . . . from Connecticut," reported one patriot officer held prisoner in New York City; "the most common conveyance is by water. . . . The supplies are from those who live on the Sound." The illicit commerce "is now in everybody's mouth," reported another eyewitness, and despite severe penalties enacted by the Connecticut legislature "the diabolic trade still stalks on with gigantic pace" conducted by men "who are . . . well known."[1] Tory ships bound for Long Island regularly slipped out of Black Rock and New Field harbors near Fairfield, Connecticut, carrying supplies and men seeking the protection of the British forces on Long Island. Lloyd's Neck, a British post on Long Island, became a notorious rendezvous for illicit trade from Connecticut. Whaleboats hired by the Connecticut government to suppress this traffic often engaged in it. Long Island suppliers of the British Army often paid for agricultural goods from Connecticut by arranging for their stores to be robbed of manufactured goods that later mysteriously appeared in Connecticut. A thriving illicit traffic in beef developed along the New York border, where farmers routinely reported large "thefts" of cattle but replaced their losses with cash purchases of more livestock. The dealers who drove these cattle across the border into New York became known as "cowboys." In addition to massive illicit trade, the border with New York also swarmed with "skinners," outlaws who raided adherents of both sides in the Revolution and took advantage of the general collapse of law enforcement in the area.[2]

British invasions of the state and Tory raiding parties along the Connecticut coast enlarged the pattern of social disorganization. Major Richard Rogers, British soldier of fortune and hero of the Seven Years' War, recruited and led one of the first loyalist companies during the autumn of 1776 and early months of 1777. He assembled in the Queen's Rangers some 500 Tory refugees from Westchester County, New York and Fairfield County, Connecticut. During October and November of 1776 the Queen's Rangers became the most feared British unit on Long Island Sound, striking the Connecticut coast almost at will and threatening the security of patriot families in Greenwich, Stamford, and Norwalk. On one raid in late October against Bedford, New York, Rogers contacted and escorted to safety on Long Island more than 120 Connecticut loyalist refugees. A month later Rogers's men captured the celebrated patriot spy Nathan Hale. From December 1776 until February 1777, Rogers operated against New York towns. Then there occurred a reorganization of loyalist armed forces in America, placing the Rangers under British Inspector General Alexander Innes. Innes strongly disapproved of Rogers's practice of promoting into officer ranks old comrades from the Seven Years' War who lacked the proper gentility and breeding to qualify as British officers.[3] Another terrorizing figure in southwest Connecticut was Moses Dunbar. Born in Wallingford, Connecticut, in 1746, he grew up in a small community of Anglicans in Bristol, Connecticut, and came under the influence of an Anglican cleric, the Reverend James Nichols. Though he attempted to remain neutral in 1775, a mob forced Dunbar to sign an oath, and in May 1776 a still-suspicious committee of safety briefly imprisoned him. His wife had recently died, and on his release he fled to Long Island and joined Colonel Edmund Fanning's loyalist regiment. Returning secretly to Connecticut to remarry, he was captured and tried for treason, specifically for accepting a commission as captain in a loyalist force and for recruiting other Connecticut men to join it. Convicted and sentenced to death, he escaped from the Hartford jail only to be recaptured and hanged in the presence of a large crowd in Hartford on March 19, 1777. Dunbar was the only loyalist executed in Connecticut, and his punishment served chiefly as a warning to other loyalists tempted to join British forces on Long Island.[4]

Even more disruptive than British military attacks on Connecticut was what one early historian of the port of New London called "the inveterate system of smuggling, marauding, plundering, and kidnaping" that festered along both sides of Long Island Sound during the War for Independence. The property of farmers in the region, the essential element in a secure social order there, suddenly became perilously insecure. Near midnight on August 14, 1780, for example, two boatloads of marauding Tories landed at Miller's Place, on the Connecticut coast near

Fairfield. One boatload of men went to Captain Ebenezer Miller's home and demanded that he surrender his weapons. The family obeyed the order, but when Miller's son opened an upstairs window the Tories shot and killed him. The other party went to Andrew Miller's home, and, according to a witness, when Miller opened the door "one of the party struck him with the breech of his gun, broke the bone over his eye, tore his eye all to pieces, broke his cheek bone, and left him for dead." The same night two other parties seized Gilbert Flint, of Oyster Bay, New York, and hanged him by the neck until he was almost dead. "There's not a night but that they are over if boats can cross," complained one Fairfield County resident; "people can't ride the roads but what they are robbed."[5]

Connecticut retaliated by commissioning privateers to raid Long Island for the purpose of recovering stolen property. Obviously, such groups were not going to be scrupulous about whom they plundered. When one of their victims, William Scudder, sued in Connecticut courts for recovery of property seized by these groups, the judges ruled such seizures legal. General Samuel Holden Parsons, of Connecticut, was scandalized. "No civilized nation," he wrote to John Jay, "ever avowed the practice of plundering the inhabitants of the nation they were contending with" so long as they "remained in their own business and were not found in arms." Violations of "civilized" warfare abounded. "The scandalous savage conduct of the Britons in their late descent on the coast," Parsons complained of Tryon's raid on Danbury, "exceeds description." Some of Parsons's troops had their heads blown off their corpses after they were dead and one soldier who surrendered and gave up his gun was stabbed with a bayonet.[6]

The cumulative effect of this contagion of violence and retaliation in southwestern Connecticut was a growing fear that it might dissolve the bands of civil order. John Mackay, of Greenwich, complained to Governor Jonathan Trumbull about "the newly invented mode of retaliation (as it is called) practiced in this town and places adjacent by mobs, who in defiance of law and authority assemble and seize the property of their neighbors on the pretext of their being Tories and to replace what the enemy has taken from others, but who in fact convert such property chiefly to their own use." Mackay wrote of a band of some fifty men, led by a Captain Lockwood and Jonathan Waring, of Stamford, that had visited the homes of alleged loyalists in Greenwich, taken a great quantity of utensils and livestock—much of it stolen from innocent women and children—and sold it for personal profit at an auction in Stamford. "Those who were thus plundered have taken the oath of fidelity to the State, and although that alone is not an infallible mark of friendship" and although many victims were wives and children of men who had gone to fight for the British, Mackay concluded, "yet *these* people have not committed any overt acts (that I know of) whereby their estates became forfeit, and even [if] the case were otherwise, . . . the community and not individuals ought to be benefited by such forfeitures."[7] For Ashbel Humphrey, of Goshen, Connecticut, his first contact with this incipient anarchy was a shattering ordeal for which none of his previous experiences and misfortunes equipped him. Humphrey had been unable to support his fellow countrymen in "the capital article of their independency," and the Goshen Committee of Safety had ordered the public to refuse to do business with him. Finally, in September 1780, he fled to Long Island, where "in expectation of finding an asylum for himself and his family" he found "himself and [his] sons plunged amidst a *host* of *murderers, thieves, robbers,* and *blasphemers* at the port at Lloyd's Neck." The sight was so frightening that he returned to face imprisonment in Connecticut.[8]

Nowhere in New England was the social and political order so tangled and full of internal stresses as in the territory that became the state of Vermont, known from 1763 to 1777 simply as the New Hampshire Grants. Situated roughly between the Connecticut River Valley and Lake Champlain, the region had been contested between New York and New Hampshire, and land speculators from both coveted the territory. In the early 1770's Yankee settlers were led by three remarkable brothers, Ethan, Ira, and Levi Allen, who had migrated from Connecticut into the New Hampshire Grants in the late 1760's, bought large amounts of land, and established lucrative commerce with Quebec. The Allens built an alliance between Yankee speculators and settlers who resented New York's political control over the grants.[9]

A number of circumstances—the protracted and unresolved dispute between New York and New Hampshire; the sudden rise of the Allen family, with their appetite for power and wealth and their commensurate talent and resourcefulness; the newness of the towns in the grants; the variety of geographic, family, religious, and personal affiliations that Yankee and New Yorker settlers brought to the region; and the control by wealthy Yorkers of county courts—made Vermont an unstable, malleable, unpredictable political setting during the 1770's. The Revolutionary crisis of 1774 gave the Allens an unexpected opportunity. Conservative New York settlers at first dominated county conventions summoned to protest the Coercive Acts, but in early 1775 the Yorkers lost control of the situation and by March 1775 were forced to flee from the territory. As British authority collapsed throughout New England, New York's control of the New Hampshire Grants vanished with it. Ethan and Ira Allen led the creation of an independent Vermont in 1777, and the first action of the new government was the confiscation of loyalist estates; in the process, all absentee New Yorkers, patriot and loyalist alike, had their titles to Vermont property invalidated. One of the victims was their brother, Levi, who had moved to Dutchess County, New York, early in the War for Independence to conduct a lucrative trade with the British. In part motivated by a family quarrel over land and money, Ethan himself initiated confiscation proceedings against his brother. The popular support behind colonial resistance in 1775 and the confiscation of loyalist property from 1778 to 1780 were bound up in the impulse to expel New York influence and establish Vermont's independence under the leadership of the Allens. The same instinct for regional survival almost swung Vermont back into the British Empire. After New York blocked Vermont's bid for recognition by the Continental Congress, the Allens began to negotiate with General Haldimand, in Quebec, for British recognition of Vermont's independence in return for the state's withdrawal from the Revolution. British defeat at Yorktown seriously complicated the negotiations, but the Allens and Haldimand resumed their discussions until Lord Shelburne replaced Lord North and called them to a halt in 1782. Ethan and Ira Allen did not present themselves to the British as potential loyalists in the Haldimand negotiations. They simply explained that a loose association with Canada was the best way of securing their original aim of Vermont's territorial integrity and political survival. However, the desperate venture of the Haldimand negotiations did cast them into alliance with many loyalists and neutralists who were British sympathizers and who had remained in Vermont and avoided prosecution by discreet political inactivity and were led by Justus Sherwood, an agent of Yorker interests.[10]

The precarious military balance in Vermont and northern New York during the summer of 1777—during the opening stages of the campaign that climaxed at Saratoga in October—created many shades of loyalist and patriot activity and excruciating choices for civilians, especially in the town of Castleton, twelve miles southeast of Fort Ticonderoga. Castleton was the home of Sylvanus Ewarts, the brother-in-law of Ira Allen's closest political lieutenant, Thomas Chittenden. On July 6, 1775, the Americans abandoned Fort Ticonderoga, leaving Castleton defenseless. The same day Justus Sherwood led a band of loyalists and Indians on a raid against Whigs in the town. On July 10 Burgoyne occupied Castleton and issued a proclamation for residents of the area to support British forces or face "devastation, famine, and every concomitant horror." Those who preferred to aid the British surreptitiously were permitted to put a piece of paper in their hats and wear their shirts outside their coats as evidence of their compliance with Burgoyne's demands. In return, he promised civilian supporters a profitable business in farm produce and protection from rebel forces. Four hundred local residents complied with Burgoyne's request, but one German soldier estimated that two-thirds of the town secretly retained their allegiance to the Revolutionary movement and stayed in the area only to spy on genuine loyalists. "Very few," he wrote, consent to "take the oath of allegiance," and "a number agree to neutrality perhaps because of our proximity and their property." This apprehension was justified. A month later Burgoyne dispatched his Hessian subordinate, Colonel Baum, with 800 British, German, and loyalist troops and Indians to destroy a supposed store of rebel arms in southern Vermont. Burgoyne's intelligence claimed that numerous loyalists lived in the area. Near Bennington Baum's force stumbled, instead, into an ambush by an unexpectedly large force of 1,500 New Hampshire militia led by Colonel John Stark. Baum was so bewildered that he assumed that the band of shirt-sleeved farmers approaching his rear were loyalist reinforcements. Baum died leading his men in "a desperate sabre charge." Burgoyne lost 900 men at Bennington and its immediate aftermath, half of them regulars, and found himself desperately outnumbered and weakened on the eve of the Battle of Saratoga.[11]

As the British threat in southern Vermont suddenly receded after Bennington, the Vermont government took little action against most Castleton residents who had agreed to support Burgoyne. Sylvanus Ewarts, however, was another matter. He and three kinsmen had enthusiastically procured goods and horses and recruited labor to help clear roads for the British. All four were declared traitors and had their property seized. Even in Ewarts's case the line between accuser and accused was very thin. Two of the five members of the confiscation board were related by marriage to Ewarts and a third was a family friend from Salisbury, Vermont. The board did confiscate all of his property, but the governor and Council returned to his sons, Eli and Timothy, who were patriots, 120 acres they had given the state of Vermont only six days earlier in payment of a debt their father owed the state. Timothy and Eli were permitted to purchase other confiscated property; and a notoriously pro-British resident, Zadock Remington, succeeded in purchasing a part interest in the most valuable of Ewarts's confiscated properties—a mill lot and water rights to the flow of Lake Bomoseen.[12]

The abruptness with which war had descended on this Yankee wilderness during the summer of 1777 cast men of identical social and political backgrounds on opposite sides and created many shades and degrees of complicity with the British. Vermont society had not coalesced in the way that older New England communities had done, and it was a highly fluid amalgam of Yankee and Yorker influences, in which Yorker-loyalist activity was difficult to suppress and in which the struggle for political advantage among prominent Yankee landowners was a stronger force than the desire to support the American cause in the War for Independence. Zadock Wright, of the Connecticut River Valley town of Hartland, Vermont, was a characteristic product of this shifting and unrefined political environment. Wright was born into a prominent Northfield, Massachusetts family in 1736. With his brothers, Amasa and Moses, Zadock fought against the Indians and the French throughout the Seven Years' War, and in 1761 the three brothers joined with other veterans of those campaigns as charter founders of the town of Hartland, established by Oliver Willard under a grant from Governor Benning Wentworth, of New Hampshire. With a secure place among the insiders who had originally settled Hartland, Wright held a variety of profitable local offices between 1768 and 1776: overseer of highways, overseer of the poor, commissioner to lay out highways, assessor, constable, town clerk, county supervisor, and treasurer. In 1772, probably as a reward for his support of New York's claim to jurisdiction in the New Hampshire Grants region, Governor Tryon appointed Wright justice of the peace in Cumberland County, one of the three counties New York had created in the disputed region.

Allied to the Crown and removed from office by the upheaval of 1775, Wright became a company commander in the Queen's Loyal Rangers, a loyalist force organized by John Peters. Peters was a Yankee speculator and plural officeholder in Moortown, in the New Hampshire Grants. Peters's father was a Whig and his four uncles were Tories; he had tried to remain neutral in 1775, but mobs had harassed him unmercifully and he had fled to Canada in January 1776. Commissioned by General Guy Carleton to raise a loyalist regiment, Peters accompanied Burgoyne to New York State and organized loyalist volunteers from the region, Zadock Wright among them, into the Queen's Rangers. The regiment suffered heavy losses at Bennington and Saratoga. Captured in 1778, while secretly visiting his home in Hartland, and sent to Massachusetts for imprisonment, Wright was transferred to Albany and paroled. There he was converted to the Shaker sect, which preached pacifism and the rejection of secular authority; after the war he settled in Enfield, New Hampshire, and became a prominent Shaker layman.[13]

The War for Independence created a complex set of dilemmas

for American Quakers. The way in which New England Quakers dealt with issues of military service and taxation foreshadowed the entire adjustment of the Society of Friends to life in a new American Republic. Led by Moses Brown, the New England Friends sought to achieve a practical compromise between the demands of conscience and the actual exigencies of the time, between church government that imposed discipline on its members and one that responded to the concerns of its constituents. The first step was thoroughly conventional: the establishment of the New England Meeting for Sufferings, on June 9, 1775, modeled on the Philadelphia Meeting for Sufferings, which had dealt with the legal and financial needs of pacifists and brought relief to other victims of war since 1756. Between December 1775 and January 1777, using funds contributed largely by Philadelphia Quakers, Brown and his co-workers assisted more than 5,000 destitute Boston-area residents whose incomes had been cut off by the commencement of hostilities. Unwittingly, Brown enlarged the scope of Quaker humanitarianism. In the past, Quakers had channeled direct economic relief only to the poor within their membership. Whatever the New England Meeting for Sufferings sacrificed in exclusivism, it regained in publicly demonstrating a viable service for the sect to perform in Revolutionary America.[14]

Throughout the early years of the War for Independence, the New England Friends continued to seek a moderate means of practicing pacifism without appearing to be openly hostile to the Revolutionary cause, and to maintain the unity of the fellowship without becoming narrowly exclusive. The New England Quakers agreed that they should not accept paper money issued by the Continental Congress or by Revolutionary state governments because the issuance of this money was a means of financing the war. But, under Moses Brown's guidance, monthly and yearly meetings imposed no arbitrary prohibitions on transactions payable in the new currency and left the matter, instead, to the conscience of each individual. Open dissension arose over payment of taxes. Some purists wanted to refuse any tax payments to new state governments on the ground that support of a Revolutionary regime was as evil as complicity in warfare, while a strong minority argued that Quakers had a responsibility to contribute to the costs of government even if by so doing they inadvertently contributed to the support of military activity as well. Trying to mediate between the two camps, Brown believed that on the issue of paying taxes members should be answerable only to their consciences and should be disciplined only for unauthorized public statements on matters that weakened Quaker solidarity. The longer the war lasted, the stronger became the influence of doctrinaire Friends, and Brown only narrowly prevented the adoption in New England in 1780 of a rule making nonpayment of taxes mandatory.[15]

On the island of Nantucket, Quakers actually made up a majority of the population. Under the leadership of William Rotch, a wealthy Quaker shipowner and whaler, the people of the island tried to observe strict neutrality. Except for a few irrepressible patriots, the bulk of the non-Quaker majority agreed that abstention from the war was the only safe course to follow for an island community completely vulnerable to attack by the British Navy. In 1764 Rotch had received a shipment of muskets, complete with bayonets, from a merchant in Boston in partial payment for a bad business debt. He had sold the muskets to customers who wanted to shoot waterfowl but had refused on conscience to traffic in bayonets, which could only be used against other human beings. During the War for Independence, word of his pile of rusty bayonets reached the mainland, and repeatedly customers came to Nantucket and pressed Rotch to sell the weapons. His refusals provoked "a great noise in the country and my life was threatened. I would gladly have beaten them into 'pruning hooks' but took the first opportunity of throwing them into the sea." Massachusetts merchants refused to do business with the Nantucket Friends, and the commerce of the island stagnated. Tory privateers commissioned by the British in New York City took misguided vengeance by raiding Nantucket several times and seizing one of Rotch's ships. Meanwhile, the American Navy seized as prizes of war several of his whaling vessels.[16]

It was conscription into the army that most brutally violated Quaker conscience. The Quakers believed in "the precepts of Christ as set forth . . . in the New Testament, . . . *that we should love our enemies*, . . . that *we war not after the flesh and that we fight not with flesh and blood,* [and] . . . *that the weapons of our warfare are not carnal but spiritual,* . . . [and] that wars and strifes came from the lust . . . of carnal men, but Christians, those that are truly saints, have crucified the flesh with the infection of lusts." In spite of the fact that the New England states tried to respect the Quakers' pacifism in the operation of military conscription, the search for military man-power kept Quakers in jeopardy. In Rhode Island, all men became eligible for conscription; after induction had occurred, regimental officers submitted to town officials the names of that town's Quaker conscripts eligible for exemption. The towns then bore the responsibility of hiring substitutes and confiscating a portion of the exempted Quaker's property to pay the cost of the hireling. In retaliation against this cumbersome system of harassment, Quaker monthly meetings ceased helping authori-ties identify Quaker conscripts who claimed exemption from military service. In 1779 Massachusetts adopted a similar formula. Tireless lobbying by monthly meetings and the New England Meeting for Sufferings in behalf of Quakers conscripted under the new law secured some relief, in one instance persuading a committee of the General Court to rule that a group of Quaker conscripts from Barnstable County "are not proper subjects for the draft." The most significant efforts by Quaker meetings were to sensitize harried provincial officials to the mo-tives and scruples of the sect. "Not out of obstinacy or in con-tempt of authority," explained petitions from Yarmouth and Sandwich, Massachusetts, seeking exemption from military serv-ice, "but really and singly from a conscientious scruple that wars and learning war and bloodshed is against the command of Christ . . . we submit [our case] to your consideration with pleasing hopes that you in your wisdom will find out some way for our relief."[17]

Just as the Revolution cast the Quakers into serious danger, it also exacerbated tensions between another zealous sect, the Bap-tists, and the predominantly Congregationalist political leader-ship of the region. Some of the most exuberant New Light clergy and laity had entirely rejected the authority of the established Congregationalist church and affiliated with the Baptists, who were a small cluster of churches founded by a variety of Puritan schismatics between 1630 and 1650. The influx of the evangelical and pietistic newcomers, called Separate-Baptists, caused a burgeoning growth of the Baptist denomination from eleven churches in Connecticut and Massachusetts in 1740 to fifty-five in 1770. Led by a remarkable clergyman, the Reverend Isaac Backus, the Separate-Baptists demanded abolition of taxes to support the established Congregationalist church, and they spurned an elaborate compromise under which Baptists holding certificates of church membership were exempt from religious taxes. When the General Court failed to meet their demands in 1771, the Baptists, with Hutchinson's shrewd encouragement, appealed to the Crown for relief. In October 1774 Backus and other Baptist leaders took their case to the Continental Congress in Philadelphia. At a private meeting with a group of delegates, including those from Massachusetts, Backus argued for "the liberty of worshipping God according to our consciences" without "being obliged to support the ministry we cannot attend." John Adams replied that the establishment of Congregationalism in Massachusetts was "but a very slender one, hardly to be called an establishment," and Robert Treat Paine blamed the whole dispute on the Baptists' obstinate refusal to certify their members for tax-exemption purposes. "It is absolutely a point of conscience with me," Backus retorted; "I cannot give in the certificates they require without implicitly acknowledging that power in man which I believe belongs to God." The clash between Paine and Backus was revealing. As William G. McLoughlin explains, "Most people in Boston who had little contact with the Baptists simply could not comprehend that level of radical pietism which considered even the giving of a certificate as 'a point of conscience.'" There was an immense barrier of misunderstanding between the Baptists and the Congregationalists. "In truth," observed Ezra Stiles in 1774, "the Baptists intend to avail themselves of this opportunity to complain to England of persecution because they hate Congregationalists who they know are hated by the King, ministry, and Parliament"—a staggering misrepresentation of the Baptists' motives. Backus was simply incapable of such sophisticated opportunism. He was too parochial to comprehend that for his contemporaries the dispute with Britain had engulfed all other considerations. Retrospectively, in

1783 he claimed early conversion to the cause of colonial liberty, and though he was sincere, his choice of words revealed how difficult it had been for him to identify emotionally with colonial resistance: "About the time of the Stamp Act I perceived . . . that there could be no neuters among us and . . . took some pains to inform myself as to the real merits of the cause for I was sensible that bad men and bad actions were to be expected on both sides of the question in this sinful world." Although Backus and the overwhelming majority of his followers supported the Revolution wholeheartedly once hostilities began, lingering traces of the suspicion against colonial resistance continued in the denomination. On June 26, 1778, a hostile throng disrupted an outdoor Baptist service in Pepperell, Massachusetts on the pretext that the meeting was a "Tory plan" and "work of the devil."[18]

A group of Sandamanians in Danbury, Connecticut, members of a tiny pietistic and pacifist sect, exhibited the same touching simplicity. One of their leaders, Comfort Benedict, had been drafted in 1777. He had appealed to General Israel Putnam, who "could do no more than commiserate" over his plight, and so Benedict fled to New York. When he returned in 1779 the Fairfield County Superior Court sentenced him to prison. In 1780 he and nineteen other members of his church, unwittingly confessing their continued allegiance to the King and depicting their experience accurately, petitioned Governor Jonathan Trumbull: "Your petitioners have uniformly professed and avowed loyalty and subjection to the King during the present war. . . . In consequence of it many have suffered much, . . . though they have at all times behaved peaceably . . . and most of them have paid fines without murmuring for not going into the war which they look upon as unjust. They are now drafted and understand no fine can excuse them. . . . They declare it to be utterly against their conscience to take up arms against the King and . . . have been frequently told that if they would remain quietly at home, . . . they might be suffered to remain in peace—which is all they desire."[19]

30

Barnstable, Massachusetts:

A Divided Community

THE Revolution and the specter of Tory disaffection were not restricted to Hutchinson's and Wentworth's allies or to atypical fringe areas like Vermont or Fairfield County, Connecticut. The strain of Revolution on society sapped the resources, energy, and emotional endurance of the close-knit and outwardly secure town of Barnstable, Massachusetts, and in the process revealed a special sort of tendency toward loyalty to Britain and against Revolution.

Barnstable was a secure, stable, prosperous, conservative community on the southern coast of Cape Cod.[1] Several spasms of change during the colonial period—the land-bank speculation of the 1740's and the revivalism of the Great Awakening—had passed by, scarcely touching the life of the town because it had a stable and well-integrated economy of agriculture, coastal shipping, and fishing and because it enjoyed a modestly favorable position in Massachusetts politics. Barnstable owed both blessings to the famous Otis family, which had immigrated to New England around 1630 as obscure and relatively humble folk. Ever since 1692, when Barnstable in the Old Plymouth Colony became a part of Massachusetts Bay, the Otises and the town had prospered together. John Otis III (1657–1727), head of the third generation of the family in America, turned from farming and land speculation to shipping and commerce. The decline in the old Plymouth families left a void of leadership into which John Otis moved, acquiring local judicial offices. These posts, in turn, helped him acquire the capital necessary for his mercantile ventures, for he learned inside the court system the techniques of civil debt recovery. He mastered the use of the courts to both

harry debtors and postpone the claims of creditors, and this short-
term debt advantage gained for him the money he needed to
become an ascendant merchant. The quest for political power
also made Otis a representative to the Massachusetts General
Court and brought him contacts in Boston through whom he
could expand his commercial activity. John Otis III's son, James
Otis, Sr., built upon his legacy of property, position, and influence and became by the 1750's one of Massachusetts's leading
political figures and a close ally of royal governors William
Shirley and Thomas Pownall. Like his father and grandfather,
James, Sr., tripled the value of his inheritance during his lifetime
and planned carefully for his sons to reach, with his guidance
and sponsorship, a new plateau of power and wealth in Massachusetts. James Otis, Jr., the favored and eldest son, would study
law and specialize in provincial politics; Samuel Allyn Otis
would manage the family's overseas trade and interests in Boston; Joseph Otis, the youngest, would direct the family's multifaceted property holdings and economic activities in Barnstable.

The whole scheme and the family's carefully husbanded position nearly unraveled during the Revolutionary era. James Otis,
Jr.'s brilliant attacks on the Sugar and Stamp acts in 1764 and
1765 made him the spokesman for Boston radicals, friends he did
not need in his quest for political power, and the bitter enemy of
Governor Francis Bernard, an enemy who still had the ability to
wreck his career. Worse still, Otis was a brilliant student of legal
and political theory, and his arguments against the Stamp Act
rested on an ingenious attempt to acknowledge the supremacy of
Parliament over the colonies and deny the constitutionality of its
most recent legislation. Friends and foes alike misunderstood
him, and the brilliant but incompatible traits that impelled him
to write pamphlets and to be a popular leader as well as the
steward of the family's interests drove James, Jr., to periodic
insanity before 1770. Then Samuel Allyn Otis, frightened by the
probably disastrous effect of political upheaval on commerce,
abandoned politics altogether and during the early 1770's carved
out for himself the most cautious, prudent niche possible short of
supporting Hutchinson, thereby incurring the wrath of the community. During the Revolution he worked hard for the American

cause but felt uneasy and out of place among the newly rich merchants who emerged after 1776. It remained for the father, James, Sr., who was seventy-four when independence came and still had two active years of life ahead of him, and Joseph, the youngest son, to shore up the family's interests and political strength in Barnstable during the War for Independence.

James Otis, Sr., knew instinctively that Barnstable hated the British colonial policy of the 1760's in its own private way. The town abhorred arbitrary changes in its dealings with the outside world, whether imposed from London or Boston. James, Sr., knew, as John J. Waters writes, that the town "had its own mores, . . . its own understanding of an absolute natural law which bound it as surely as did the sea, the eternal low hills, and its salt marshes."[2] Though the inhabitants of the town differed over the issue of independence, Otis also knew that the preponderance were men who would not "make a leap" before they got "to the hedge." When the town meeting voted on independence on June 25, 1776, the result vindicated the elder Otis's judgment—thirty in favor, thirty-five against, sixty-five abstaining. On the other hand, Joseph Otis, a strong supporter of independence, was infuriated. The father's shrewdness and the son's anger would both be needed in the years ahead.

During the months of crisis in 1776, James, Sr., drew on a lifetime of experience to keep Barnstable from tearing apart and, in the process, destroying the Otis family's last base of power and influence. As a local judge, he tried to open the inferior court in 1774 after the new coercive Administration of Justice Act had packed the superior court with prerogative-minded judges. Otis assured the crowd demanding the closing of the court that he stood with them in defending the "old charter." He defended Tory widow Abigail Freeman when another crowd tarred and feathered her in March 1776. He supported the creation of the Massachusetts provincial Congress in 1775, and when independence came he helped enlarge the minority that had openly supported it in June 1776 to a majority willing to support the war effort.

If the patriarch, James Otis, Sr., could hold Barnstable together during the crises of 1775 and 1776, it was the son Joseph who succeeded in committing the entire resources of the divided town to the war effort in 1776 and 1777. Joseph was the heir to three generations of Otis toil in the town; he alone had his hands on all the levers of economic and political power. First, through family connections, relatives, and friends, he had direct influence over the entire network of the town's economy—fishing, whaling, agriculture, local commerce. His brother Samuel, an official of the Massachusetts war department, depended on Joseph for such scarce commodities as salt. The family's long political dominance enabled Joseph to collect the particular wartime offices that complemented his commercial leadership of the military effort: muster master of militia, brigadier general of the county militia, customs collector, clerk of the inferior court, and representative to the General Assembly. This "fusion" of "commercial, commissary, military, fiscal, and political functions in one person" meant that divided and fearful Barnstable would become a stalwart supplier of revenue, men, and material to the war effort; it was the logical outcome of the Otises' industry and ascendency in the town. The town and family, like the rest of the new nation, paid a high price for this concentration of effort and leadership. By 1778, inflation, British naval control of Narragansett Bay, lack of troops to defend against the threatened British invasion of Cape Cod, and shortages of everything, including food, had revived the large loyalist part in Barnstable, again under the influence of a man as skillful, ambitious, egocentric, and socially secure, in Barnstable at least, as any Otis: Edward Bacon.[3]

Edward Bacon (1714–1783) knew the Otises well. He and James, Sr., had been political allies and then political enemies for nearly two decades. Bacon had started his political career in Barnstable, in 1756, in the most expedient manner possible, by winning James, Sr.'s sponsorship. Otis had persuaded Governor Shirley to give Bacon a militia post, and a year later Otis arranged for Bacon to succeed him as representative to the House of Representatives—the elder Otis had declined re-election in anticipation of being elevated by the House to the Council. Now at the pinnacle of his ascendency, Otis narrowly overestimated the extent of his reach. First, he had a minor but awkward quarrel with Shirley's successor, Thomas Pownall. He was thus a little vulnerable when it became clear to everyone that the

Council seat he coveted would go instead to his old neighbor and friend Silvanus Bourn. Otis chose Bacon to manage his campaign for election to the Council in the House, and when Bourn was chosen and Otis was not, Otis concluded that Bacon had not tried very hard in his behalf. Otis got his revenge in 1760 when he ran again for the House and displaced Bacon. The House elected him speaker, and his political fortunes seemed again secure. But they were not. The new Governor, Francis Bernard, regarded Otis as an ambitious schemer and, though it had not seemed to matter much at the time, Otis had made a bitter enemy of Edward Bacon.

When Bacon rallied nearly half of Barnstable to oppose independence—and thereby to humiliate Joseph Otis—in June 1776, he did not act merely out of revenge, nor was he a supporter of British authority. His motives were more complex. As a figure whose impact and successes were limited to a single town, his political capacity was shaped entirely by the nature of that community. Barnstable was an integral, tightly interwoven community that simply could not tolerate rampant political factionalism. The stresses of rival, open, hostile factions could tear directly at the delicate pattern of personal, family, and communal relationships that bound the town into an organic, interdependent whole. Disagreements existed and could not be suppressed; but they would produce unbearable rancor if allowed to foment visible political parties. The personal influence of individual leaders and the weight of tradition both militated against factionalism.

The choice between submission to the Coercive Acts and armed resistance against Gage's troops in Boston had severely tested this antifactional, communal tradition in 1775 and early 1776. But the refusal of half the Barnstable voters to vote one way or the other on the issue of independence revealed the weight of tradition and the extent to which a crisis strengthened it, for the crisis also forced Joseph Otis and Edward Bacon to become factional leaders without factions to lead. Each man wanted to rally not a faction of followers but, rather, the preponderant will of the community. Barnstable clearly preferred that kind of political contest. What the Revolution did was to increase the influence and pressure that both Otis and Bacon were able to exert. Instead of making one weaker and the other stronger, the crisis of 1776 increased the offensive power of both and set them on a collision course.

Otis's strength derived from his family's three generations of penetration into Barnstable's economic, political, and social order and the family's capacity in both success and adversity to work steadily and hard at the tasks of economic and political leadership. Bacon's strength began where Otis's first ebbed: among the many in the town who resented the family's wealth and success, distrusted James, Jr.'s past identification with the Boston radicals, and in a typical eighteenth-century manner co-alesced instinctively against those in power. Moreover, Bacon was supported by an unwritten but sacred tenet of the town's consti-tution—which the Otises fully understood and accepted—that the interests of the town transcended the glory of its leading family, that the Otises needed Barnstable as much as the town needed them. Bacon's supporters were as varied and numerous as the sources of Joseph Otis's authority. They were the small farmers and merchants who feared British naval retaliation on coastal towns that strongly supported the American cause, the citizens of modest means who suffered most from inflation and the deprecia-tion of continental currency, and men who fell afoul of Otis's vigorous efforts to collect taxes or his effective surveillance of smuggling and sale of contraband goods to the British. As war eroded Barnstable's fragile consensus and death claimed James, Sr., in 1778, Bacon became the natural beneficiary of local sources of opposition. Because much of it resided in the humbler strata of the town—small farmers and tradesmen—he had fewer rivals for leadership.

His opposition stance had consisted of a series of negative posi-tions. Bacon and his allies had shrewdly characterized their de-fense of community interests and their fight with Otis and his supporters in unpretentious moral terms. As soon as the town meeting of June 26, 1776, had voted not to instruct the town's representatives to support independence, Otis and twenty-three other residents sent a protest to the *Boston Gazette* condemning the arguments used by Bacon's supporters in the town meeting and lamenting that "the cause of liberty is treated with such indignity by some of the inhabitants of the town of Barnstable."

Bacon's ally Sturgis Gorham objected to this "protest" and complained that it falsely painted the majority in the Barnstable town meeting as "absolutely" opposed to independence. This inference was false and the record of the debate at the town meeting would prove it false. Not so, responded Otis; "there was a long debate about declaring Independency. One said, 'It was down right rebellion'; another staunch friend of Governor Hutchinson said 'our trade was as free as if we were independent' and these [speakers] were violently against the motion" to support independence. By disclosing such rascality, Otis complained, he had also "opened upon me the throats of deep mouthed mastiffs as well as . . . the barking of lesser curs." Gorham replied that Otis could protect himself from the dogs and public ridicule if he would cease fabricating accounts of what was said in town meetings and attributing cowardice to his opponents, and would acknowledge humbly that the town meeting of July 23, 1776, had already censured Otis for his attacks. Bacon and allies like Gorham could rally those who resented Otis's articulate use of language, his access to an audience outside Barnstable, and his willingness to scold his neighbors in public. Bacon's faction could focus and manipulate these dislikes and characterize Otis's rough tactics and impatience as attacks on the interests of the community.[4]

Bacon's speech in his own defense, written just before the House voted his expulsion, set forth his creed as an opposition figure. He could not believe, he declared, that the House would expel a man who had behaved like "a genuine Englishman" by speaking his own mind in a time of crisis. He accepted without reservation the notion that all citizens of Massachusetts ought to obey the government of that state and be loyal to it. But at the same time "each individual may with modesty and candor and decency endeavour to convince the majority of their mistake, always guarding against everything that may have a tendency to break or disturb the public peace and tranquillity or endanger the safety of the state." If he had ever exceeded this conscientious role, it was because "some sudden ebullition of the mind" occurred after "cruel and insulting treatment from those persons, their connections, and abettors who for years before the present unhappy war have seemed to bear the most settled malice and ill will against me."[5]

The greater Otis's successes in these measures and the higher his prestige with state leaders in Boston in 1778 and 1779, the firmer became Bacon's hold on the recalcitrant anti-Otis faction. Increasingly, Otis had the administrative power and money, and Bacon the majority of voters in town meetings. In a fine gesture of defiance, the town elected Bacon, along with Joseph Otis, as a representative to the House of Representatives in 1778 and 1779, and as a delegate to the 1780 Constitutional Convention. Otis countered in 1778 by asking the House to deny Bacon a seat. The town meeting branded this action as interference in its right to select its own representatives and Otis's attack on Bacon "wrong and perjurious." Ultimately, Otis succeeded. After Bacon's re-election in 1779, the House permitted Otis to present formal charges of Toryism against Bacon and voted ninety-five to five to expel him. His ascendency was over; in 1780 he tried and failed to get the Barnstable church to rebuke Otis and his allies.

Bacon's abrupt political demise should not disguise the fact that he represented a peculiar kind of opposition to the Revolution. "He said he was a Tory, but not an enemy to his country," testified Lot Crowell, a hostile but reliable witness. It was a perceptive self-appraisal. By "an enemy to his country," Massachusetts citizens probably meant one who favored enforcement of the Coercive Acts or was a creature of the Hutchinson organization. There is no evidence that Bacon was a loyalist in either of these senses. He accepted the label reluctantly. He probably meant that he was a "Tory" only in the specially qualified sense that he was proud of the opprobrium heaped upon him by Joseph Otis; and he undoubtedly intended the phrase "not an enemy to his country" to strip the term "Tory" of much of its conventional meaning. In what sense, then, was he a Tory? Why did he use and earn the label at all? Again, Lot Crowell's testimony went to the core of Bacon's behavior: "He said he was determined not to go to fight, but if they [the British] landed and come to destroy his house he did not know what he should do." The double negatives in that declaration of intention marked Bacon as a local man of opposition, an essential creature of eighteenth-century local politics. He voiced local, insular opposition to change and to the outside world; but England and New England were societies consisting of discrete, self-conscious, stratified local communities and superior institutions as well—like the House of Commons and Whitehall, in the mother country, and the General Court, the Continental Congress, and the Continental Army, in the colonies. There was an ingrained, unavoidable tension between those local elites who also had a place in the national or state scene and the local elites whose horizons were limited to the immediate community. Often the two sets of political leaders coexisted, co-operated, or complemented one another. The opportunities for the two to coalesce or conflict were simultaneous. This was the configuration of the Otis-Bacon competition.[6]

The same kind of isolation and exclusiveness appeared in another town in the southern part of the province, Freetown, Massachusetts. The majority of the members of the Congregationalist Church in Freetown were loyalists, and on February 24, 1776, they dismissed the Reverend Silas Brett for "repeated disappointments" as a clergyman and for his "sectarian principles" in the "public disputes of the country in which Freetown has had an unhappy share." Colonel Thomas Gilbert, a member of the Freetown church, organized one of the earliest loyalist regiments in New England, Gilbert's Rangers, in December 1774. On December 11 of that year he and Brett clashed in a meeting of the congregation on whether or not to hold services of prayer and fasting for the colonial cause. After an acrimonious debate, Gilbert called for a vote; Brett countered with a demand for a show of hands rather than a voice vote. Brett could not tell which side had the majority, but before he could call for a count of hands the distraught parishioners dispersed—without waiting for the benediction.[7]

Quite a different pattern appeared in the western Massachusetts town of Deerfield, in Hampshire County. Approximately fifty men in the town were identified as loyalists during the Revolution. Out of a total population of some 800, this number represented a strong minority movement of opposition to the Revolution. A recent occupational and economic analysis of the rival sides in Revolutionary Deerfield reveals that landowners and men with agrarian interests became Whigs, while men engaged in commerce and trade became Tories. This alignment brought major landowners and small farmers together in support of the Revolution, just as it placed wealthy merchants and humble artisans, tavernkeepers, and others engaged in nonagricultural business in opposition to the Revolution. The ten men with the most taxable income split almost evenly between Whigs and Tories, while of the ten with the most personal property, seven were Tories and three were Whigs. For nearly a generation before the Revolution, Deerfield's commercial elite had monopolized local government and held the appointive offices of sheriff, judges of the court of common pleas, and justices of the peace. Political allies of Israel Williams, men like Jonathan Ashley, benefited from Williams's influence with Hutchinson and Bernard. The commercial elite's standing with the voters, however, suffered badly during the decade following the Stamp Act crisis. The great majority of selectmen prior to 1750 were men who later became loyalists; during the 1760's the balance steadily tilted from a small majority of future Tories to a small majority of future Whigs; between 1771 and 1775 a substantial majority were identifiable opponents of British policy. Growing in population and prosperity between 1750 and 1775, the farmers in Deerfield were on the verge of displacing the old commercial families as community leaders and holders of political power. The collapse of British authority in 1775 and 1776 simply brought the process to an abrupt completion.[8]

V

Loyalists and Cultural Pluralism
in the Middle States

31

War Comes to the Middle States

AT four o'clock in the morning of August 22, 1776, following a night of "thunder, lightning, and prodigious heavy rain,"[1] General William Howe dispatched 15,000 British regulars from a staging area on Staten Island to Long Island, where three days later they were reinforced with 5,000 Hessians. The combined force outnumbered Washington's untested Continental Army by nearly two to one. Completely outmaneuvering the rebel force, Howe's enveloping attack killed, wounded, or captured over 1,000 of Washington's soldiers and drove the rest into an indefensible position in Brooklyn. On August 29, instead of destroying the American Army in one crushing engagement, Howe allowed Washington to escape during a providential fog to Manhattan. While the British commander paused to hold an abortive peace conference with several members of the Continental Congress on Staten Island, on September 11 his brother, Admiral Richard Howe, and his second-in-command, General Henry Clinton, appraised Washington's meager defenses. General Howe methodically occupied New York City and, disregarding Clinton's recommendation for an immediate and vigorous offensive, waited until October 10 to occupy the northern end of Manhattan Island, and until October 18 to cross the East River and take possession of Throgg's Neck and Pell's Point. Ten more days of cautious movement northward brought him to within a few miles of Washington's lines. He attacked the Americans' weak right flank, forcing Washington to retreat to higher ground. Howe was poised for a decisive attack when a sudden rain spoiled his ammunition, and he chose instead to turn south and lay devastating siege to rebel-held Fort Washington, on the Hudson River. Washington then slipped across the Hudson; his force straggled through New Jersey and thence to safety across the Delaware River, in Pennsylvania. Howe's pursuing force occupied large areas of New Jersey. For his part, William Howe found winter quarters in New York City quite satisfying; he spent a good deal of time consorting with the blonde, blue-eyed Betsy Loring, whose obliging husband, Joshua Loring, held a profitable post as British commissary of prisoners.[2]

William Howe's refusal to move aggressively against the American Army between August 25 and November 1, 1776, ruined any chance the British had of crushing the rebellion quickly. His lackadaisical temperament and self-indulgent life style certainly contributed to this crucial failure of execution, but the underlying causes of Howe's languid movement in late 1776 formed a complex web of calculation and circumstances. William Howe and the war he was about to direct were both creatures of the British ministry. By the end of 1774, the ministry had come to realize that further coercive measures would be needed to subject the colonies to the supreme authority of Parliament, but while two ministers, Alexander Wedderburn and Edward Thurlow, and George III himself were anxious to get started, Lord North, head of the ministry, and his stepbrother, Lord Dartmouth, Colonial Secretary, still hoped for a settlement of the imperial dispute. "Temperamentally addicted to compromise," Ira D. Gruber writes, "North was one of those fat, amiable men who hate trouble,"[3] while Dartmouth bore strong moral scruples against coercive measures. Both men went along with laws restraining most colonial commerce until resistance should cease and with plans to send reinforcements to Gage in Boston; however, they realized by July 1775 that all Britain could do immediately was instruct the navy to enforce the Restraining Acts and prepare to send a large store of weapons to the belligerent Governor Martin in North Carolina. Dartmouth was at home in Staffordshire when the last reconciliation petition, the Second Continental Congress's "Olive Branch Petition," reached London. Its stiff terms for peace enraged the King, who ordered immediate publication of a royal proclamation declaring the colonies in a state of rebellion and announcing the government's determination to suppress it. With preparations for war in full swing, North again weakly applied a brake in September 1775;

in the face of strong Parliamentary opposition to any softening of policy, he proposed sending, with the armed forces, commissioners empowered to make minor concessions to those colonies that would lay down their arms—"any colony," North's ally William Eden cynically but shrewdly noted, "which fear, interest, fickleness, or duty might bring to submission." In November a complex patronage deal brought about what North, Dartmouth, Lord George Germain, and the King all desired: Dartmouth's appointment as lord privy seal and his release from responsibility for a military policy he detested, and Germain's elevation to colonial secretary, with full power to plan and execute the suppression of colonial rebellion. Amid all this activity no one paid much attention to the growing evidence from America that resistance was not limited to Boston and to cliques of ambitious and unrepresentative politicians elsewhere in the colonies, and no one acknowledged even stronger indications that the colonists were unexpectedly competent soldiers. In the tortuous process by which the ministry had become committed to war in America, there was no point at which the King, North, Germain, or Parliament was disposed to discuss rationally Britain's liabilities and the colonies' potential assets. North had to keep his Parliamentary majority pacified; Dartmouth and North had to keep the door for conciliation open a crack; the King, Thurlow, and Wedderburn had to rouse a lethargic bureaucracy to action; Germain had to gather support for his appointment to the ministry. Anyone who had raised searching questions at this point would have committed political suicide, and therefore only political outcasts like the Earl of Chatham, who in 1775 rediscovered his old sympathy for a mild colonial policy, objected to preparations for war.[4]

There was a scattering of figures in the political establishment who were disturbed by the shortsightedness and lack of candor that characterized the ministry's decision to suppress the colonial rebellion. Politically unrelated, unco-ordinated, and possessing only marginal influence, these men nonetheless sought to "deflect" the government from its determination to force the colonists to acknowledge the supremacy of Parliament. In 1775 the most important of these figures were the brothers Howe—Admiral Richard and General William. Richard was the more responsible and diligent of the two. An ally of Pitt and member of Parliament, he had used political and family connections to advance his naval career, but he was also a superb officer and seaman. Like Dartmouth and other British "doves," he believed vaguely in Parliamentary supremacy but recoiled from the folly of insisting on explicit colonial acknowledgment of that authority. He played an important secondary role in the abortive negotiations between Benjamin Franklin and some friends of Lord Dartmouth in January 1775, when he tried unsuccessfully to persuade both Franklin and the ministry to narrow the area of disagreement between them. William's career in the army paralleled his brother's. An able commander with a conspicuous record of bravery in the Seven Years' War, William had also served in Parliament. He lacked only Richard's stern sense of duty. To curry favor with the voters in 1774 he condemned the Massachusetts Government Act and promised not to serve in the colonies; nonetheless, ambitious for the post of commander of the British Army in America, he secretly volunteered to go to Boston as Gage's second-in-command. Once William Howe was there, Gage ordered him to lead the disastrous attack on Bunker Hill on June 17, 1775; in September he realized his ambition to replace Gage, and the following March his troops evacuated Boston and sailed to Halifax, from whence, in the summer of 1776, he sailed for Staten Island. Meanwhile, in early 1776, North patiently executed a maneuver to keep Germain's war plans on a short leash: the appointment of Admiral Richard Howe as commander of the fleet in an expedition to America *and* as peace commissioner. His power on the ascent, Germain shrewdly agreed to North's plan but insisted that Howe be shorn of any authority to make meaningful concessions to the Americans. Howe's instructions allowed him only to grant pardons to rebels who came forward and took an oath of allegiance to the Crown. After entire provinces had surrendered to the British, Howe could promise an exemption from Parliamentary taxation in exchange for a colonial pledge to contribute an annual sum to the imperial treasury.[5]

Entangled in the political and bureaucratic web of ministerial politics, Richard Howe could not exert himself strenuously to secure flexible and realistic terms of negotiation. Germain knew, even if North did not, that Howe's instructions required a humiliating submission from American leaders. From the time of Richard Howe's arrival off Staten Island on June 12, 1776, he sought to arrange a conference with American leaders. His publication of a declaration of an appeal for conciliation did hearten conservatives in the Congress, and it put Congressional opponents of any reconciliation on the defensive. When a delegation from Congress consisting of Benjamin Franklin, John Adams, and Edward Rutledge dined with Howe, on September 11, on "good claret, bread, cold ham, tongue, and mutton," they soon discovered that he had no authority even to discuss repeal of offensive British statutes until the Americans surrendered and dismantled their new machinery of government. The meeting abruptly ended. "They met; they talked; they parted," noted Howe's secretary, Ambrose Serle; "and now nothing remains but to fight it out."[6]

Sophisticated and persistent, the Howes did not believe that the choice between conciliation and war was so clear-cut. Instead of abandoning conciliation and unleashing the full force of available military power, they tried the middle path of psychological warfare. As soon as he reached Staten Island, General William Howe issued orders forbidding on pain of death any plundering that might alienate uncommitted colonists. While Germain assumed that the great majority of colonists were loyalists anxious for restoration of British authority, the Howes knew that sympathy and support for the Revolution ran much stronger than outright loyalist sentiment. With some justification, they also hoped for the existence of a large reservoir of men who preferred a fair constitutional settlement of the imperial dispute to armed conflict. Loyalist emissaries made their way to William Howe's Staten Island headquarters in early July 1776, but he soon learned to discount their estimates of loyalist support in New York, New Jersey, and Connecticut. Word of the Declaration of Independence and its reception further dampened his optimism about reconciliation. He paid more heed to the testimony of deserters from Washington's forces on the size and deployment of rebel forces and decided to postpone an attack until reinforcements arrived. Vastly preferring to use their immense military power as an inducement for negotiations, the

Howes put aside plans for a decisive military encounter. William feared that heavy casualties would deprive him of room to maneuver, and Richard wanted additional ships and port facilities before undertaking offensive operations. Both men believed that savage attacks against the rebels would alienate the moderate and uncommitted colonists. Even after attempts at negotiation floundered and Admiral Howe reluctantly concluded that only bloodshed would compel the colonists to negotiation, Professor Gruber explains, "he was anxious that the war be restricted as much as possible and probably helped persuade his brother to modify his strategy accordingly." Washington's escape from the threat of total defeat in Brooklyn had been a bad piece of luck, but thereafter General Howe's deliberate flanking movement, forcing Washington without a battle to withdraw from Manhattan and then from the province of New York altogether, was intentional. Howe assumed, Gruber writes, that this strategy would "create the impression of British invincibility and make conciliation more attractive—all without risking heavier losses and without further alienating the colonists. . . ." The lost opportunity to win an early military victory, Gruber concludes, did not "trouble the Howes. . . . Temporarily they were willing to subordinate all else to their hopes of finding a permanent reconciliation—to their dreams of a triumphal return to England as saviors of the Empire."[7]

It was also an enlightened dream. The Howes knew that Germain's assumptions about the Revolution bordered on fantasy. They fully realized that the great majority of colonists were not loyalists, that colonial grievances had not been fabricated by a handful of discontented and pernicious men, and that the colonies would never again be governable until Britain dramatically abandoned restrictive policies and fired the imaginations of the Americans with the advantages of their attachment to the mother country. They saw military victory as one integral part of a larger effort to re-educate Americans that would include, first, generous terms for reconciliation; then, the steady occupation of as much territory as possible, forcing Washington into unseemly retreat and demonstrating the futility of further resistance; next, sharp but limited engagements with those rebel troops who did not flee; and finally, as the colonists abandoned resistance, the immediate lifting of restraints on colonial trade and the satisfaction of those specific grievances that could be alleviated without jeopardizing Parliamentary authority. What doomed this intelligent plan was that the early stages of hostilities—from Lexington Green to the occupation of New York City—unleashed within American society powerful antagonistic forces that the Howes could not foresee or calculate.

32

The Loyalists and Revolutionary
Turmoil in New Jersey

AFTER his well-managed occupation of New York City, William Howe's occupation of New Jersey threw the province into chaos; it thrust into view the state's Revolutionary leadership and its large loyalist population and initiated bloody internecine combat. In line with Howe's aim of expanding the area under British control, British troops occupied Burlington, Bordentown, and Trenton, on the Delaware River, as well as Princeton and New Brunswick. Howe sent Cornwallis in chase of Washington, but the cold wet weather of November 1776 was an inauspicious season for grim pursuit. Howe was briefly tempted in early December to catch his prey at Trenton, but again Washington responded quickly to Howe's movements and whisked his force across the river into Pennsylvania. Howe paused and issued another proclamation promising pardon to defectors from the rebel cause. His timing was good. "The state is totally deranged without government or officers, civil or military, in it that will act with any spirit," General Alexander McDougall declared. "Many of them have gone to the enemy for protection, others are out of the state, and the few that remain are mostly indecisive in their conduct." Initially this process of disintegration worked to Howe's advantage. Samuel Tucker, a staunch leader of the pre-Revolutionary movement and first President of the New Jersey provincial Congress, fled his home in Trenton just ahead of advancing British troops and hid in the countryside for three days before trying to slip back to visit his sick wife. A band of Tory insurgents caught and held him for three days. While a captive, he learned that British troops had broken into his house and confiscated his hidden cache of public funds and all his valuable personal possessions. Desperate to recover his coach, horse, cows, silver plate, and money, he turned himself over to General Howe and took the oath. The British returned to him only a few mortgages and bonds, and he gained, as well, the disgrace of being one of the first prominent Whigs to defect from the American cause. Richard Stockton, leading opponent of British authority since 1765 and signer of the Declaration of Independence, fell into British hands and suffered such brutal treatment that he signed Howe's oath and pledged to refrain from any further political activity. News of his apostasy spread rapidly, and although Stockton reaffirmed his allegiance to the Revolutionary government of New Jersey in 1777, the disgrace prevented him from holding any office. He suffered a complete physical collapse and had no sooner begun to recover in 1779 when he was stricken with a fatal cancer. Howe sought to multiply the psychological impact of these defections by holding frequent public drills of occupying British forces and by paying generous prices to loyalist farmers who brought goods to a procurement center at Bordentown. By spring, some 2,700 New Jersey residents had signed Howe's oath and received pardon.[1]

But more than canceling the success of Howe's scheme were the widespread looting and indiscriminate assault of private citizens by British and Hessian troops. The effect was reported by the prominent New Jersey loyalist Stephen Kemble, a man who had served under both Howe and Gage in the Seven Years' War, had later become Gage's brother-in-law, was appointed deputy adjutant general for the British Army in North America in 1772, and had taken part in the seizure of New York in 1776. "The country [around New York City] is all this time unmercifully pillaged by our troops, Hessians in particular," he lamented in his diary on November 2, 1776. "No wonder if the country people refuse to join us." General William Howe's strict orders against looting and pillaging of any kind did little good with his own troops and none with the Hessians. "November 7. All quiet. 8 or 10 of our people taken for marauding," Kemble noted. "Scandalous behavior for British troops, and the Hessians outrageously licentious and cruel to such a degree as to threaten with death all [who] dare obstruct them in their depredations. Shudder for Jersey, the

Army thought to move there shortly," he concluded in despair. Kemble's apprehensions were justified. General Charles Cornwallis was far less vigorous than Howe had been in forbidding plundering. As his forces moved across New Jersey they seized livestock and produce without ceremony and looted fine homes along the way of silver plate, jewelry, clothing, horses, wine, books, plaster-of-Paris busts, warming pans, and even "a large mahogany case of wax works." British officers vied with each other to furnish field headquarters with the fine mahogany furniture of the region. Uncomfortable in the New Jersey winter, troops appropriated all available firewood and destroyed farm buildings for more fuel. Numerous reports of rape and killing by British and Hessian troops appear to have been grossly exaggerated, but the offenses that did occur further fanned abhorrence of the British occupiers during the winter of 1776–77, when patriot morale was at its lowest ebb and the machinery of Revolutionary government in New Jersey in near ruin.[2]

A strong contributing factor to this violent polarization of New Jersey society was the organization of the New Jersey Volunteers, one of the largest of the loyalist provincial forces. Commanded by Brigadier General Courtland Skinner and organized in September 1776, the New Jersey Volunteers ultimately enlisted at least 2,450 men, of whom the great majority were natives of the province. The best available projections from these enlistment figures strongly suggest that Skinner's men came from a pool of some 13,000 "potentially active loyalists," who, with their families, made up more than 35 per cent of New Jersey's population.[3] Skinner's background illustrates the dramatic collapse of social stability in New Jersey during Howe's occupation. The heir to old proprietary land grants in East Jersey, a wealthy lawyer, and a member of the clique of privileged allies of the Crown in the port town of Perth Amboy, Skinner had shared at the same time Governor William Franklin's deep aversion to British colonial policy in the 1760's. Discreet "ambiguous utterances" had saved him from condemnation by a Revolutionary committee in September 1775. But in December he had imprudently written to his brother, serving in the British Army, that he feared popular leaders wanted to form a republic at the risk of plunging the country into civil strife. "A few regiments and fleets . . . will set us right; at least"—anticipating General Howe's theory of pacification—"bring us to our senses and support the friends of government." The letter fell into Whig hands, and Skinner, leaving his wife and children behind, fled to a British man-of-war only a day ahead of the provincial soldiers who came to arrest him.

Skinner's force, organized at various times into as many as six battalions of 200 to 500 men each, and commanded by a heavy complement of officers, suffered a very high attrition rate. Unwilling to serve regular terms of duty or conform to discipline, the men gladly received royal arms and ammunition with which to loot, pillage, or settle private scores.[4] From Monmouth and Sussex counties—both adjacent to Howe's area of occupation—recruits for the Crown's forces came in large numbers, and many farmers found it prudent to contribute their best hogs and cattle for the table of British officers. Howe appointed several prominent local supporters—John Taylor, of Middletown, John Lawrence and his son Elisha, of Upper Freehold, and John Wardell, of Shrewsbury—as commissioners to administer oaths of allegiance to defecting patriots. They posted notices ordering all able-bodied men between the ages of sixteen and fifty capable of military service to come to the town of Freehold, on December 30, to take the oath; they further ordered the Monmouth County militia to muster in support of the Crown. In Bergen County, in the northeastern corner of the state, newly armed bands of loyalists roamed the countryside disarming, looting, and terrorizing Whigs. The southern part of the state, however, possessed fewer recruits for such vengeful activity. Large numbers of Quakers remained aloof from the struggle, and many Whigs, considering the cause hopeless, hid in the woods or remained at home and ceased all activity that the British might construe as hostile. The Reverend Nicholas Collin observed that people were afraid to visit church because the British would seize the opportunity to confiscate their horses and enlist the men into loyalist armed forces. In this tense atmosphere old feuds and antagonisms were rekindled. "What does the whigs think now?" loyalist William Dansors taunted Catherine Cox; her father, Dansors gloated, could no longer "let his tongue run" and "old Chamberlin" would not get away very long with hiding his son from loyalist militia recruiters. "I don't want to hurt anybody," he boasted; "I have authority to do it [that is, cause the punishment and even execution of recalcitrant Whigs] and it must be done."[5]

Nowhere were these intimate, corrosive community tensions so strong as in the Hackensack Valley (Bergen County), where the Dutch settlers had split during the Great Awakening into two rival religious factions; the Coetus party, which was ecumenical and embraced the values of colonial society, and the Conferentie party, which retained ties with the parent church in Holland and fiercely resisted innovations in worship or church polity. During the War for Independence the Coetus clergy and laymen played a leading role in sustaining resistance against the British, while most Conferentie leaders became loyalists. Deeply rooted in the same communities and intimately related to each other, neither of the two factions found it easy to embrace loyalist or patriot allegiances.[6] In May 1775 the membership of the Bergen County Committee of Safety reflected a wide spectrum of viewpoints on the dispute with Britain. While most of its members were cautious moderates, it did elect as chairman a "dour" but intense Whig, John Fell, and its most outspoken member was Peter Zabriskie, a fiery Coetus leader. Reflecting this mixed composition, the committee justified military preparations in the county on the ground that "the present struggle for liberty" might deteriorate into "anarchy and confusion . . . unless regular steps are taken to preserve regularity and unanimity among us." The proclamation balanced its condemnation of British policy with its concern for "the preservation of peace and good order and the safety of individuals and security of private property,"[7] in a sincere effort to minimize their Conferentie neighbors' hostility. There was a large and well-led segment of the county that opposed any involvement in the Revolutionary movement. One of the leaders of these people was Daniel Isaac Brown, of Hackensack, a lawyer, the son of an Anglican clergyman, and an extremely ambitious man. Committed patriots and loyalists alike regarded him with suspicion. In 1775 he publicly endorsed colonial resistance while privately organizing potential loyalists in Bergen County. Significantly, his leadership exactly suited the troubled members of the Conferentie clergy and laity. "Brown and his friends," Adrian C. Leiby explains, "played shrewdly upon the fears of many conservative Dutchmen that the Hackensack Valley faced the danger of lawless mobs if its patriot leaders were given full power; they worked hard to take advantage of the political sentiment for the county's long-time political figures; and they never neglected a word where it would do the most good to keep alive the twenty-year-old hatred of the conservative Conferentie church people for their Coetus enemies. No one could be sure their efforts were in vain." Brown and his allies packed the Hackensack Courthouse with their supporters on September 21, 1775, and won complete control of the Bergen County Committee of Observation and Correspondence, expelling Peter Zabriskie. Brown replaced John Fell as chairman.[8]

Conferentie clergymen strongly influenced this mixture of neutralist and outright loyalist response to the Revolutionary crisis of 1775 and 1776. The Reverend Warmoldus Kuypers, Adrian Leiby explains, "was the very embodiment of a neutral: a corpulent Dutchman directly out of [*Deitrich*] *Knickerbocker's History of New York*, not half as ardent in the church wars as his congregations [and seemingly] indifferent to the political fires that burned around him at the outset of the war." Simply because the Reverend Benjamin Van der Linde, of Paramus, hated Coetus theologian John Henry Goetschius, he condemned all the political activity of the Coetus party. The one really outspoken Tory among the Conferentie clergy was the Reverend Garret Leydecker. Leydecker had begun his career as a student of Goetschius's and then had broken with the Coetus faction to study with John Ritzema—"the most reactionary minister of the entire Conferentie" wing of the Dutch Reformed church. Indeed, his student Leydecker was the only native American ever ordained by the Conferentie wing of the Dutch Reformed church. Throughout the pre-Revolutionary period, Leydecker had preached submission to royal authority as fervently as any high Anglican. Alienated from colonial politics and occasionally overtly pro-British, the Conferentie churchmen exercised a powerful restraining influence on the Revolutionary movement in northern New Jersey.[9]

This religious exclusiveness compounded broader cultural divisions. In neighboring Tappan, New York, Dutchmen in the militia proved so difficult to work with that the widely respected militia officer Colonel Abraham Lent resigned in protest of the unco-operative conduct of Dutch-speaking soldiers, who "are prejudiced against me." Dutch patriot leader John Haring tried to smooth over the dispute by explaining to New York Whig officials, on May 28, 1776, that Lent had always been unusually "punctual" in obeying orders from his superiors "and he consequently expected that those under his command should obey him." But in 1776 Lent's Orangetown regiment was "chiefly composed of such as know but little English and nothing of military affairs; wherefore, I must impute their backwardness and delays to ignorance and ill-founded jealousies of being imposed upon by their commanders and not to disaffection." The New York provincial Congress concluded, on June 30, 1776, that some of the Dutch-speaking militia in Captain Arie Blauvelt's regiment "are notoriously disaffected" and should be disarmed immediately. Almost every Dutch family in Tappan had been split by the Coetus-Conferentie conflict. Though leaders in both factions tried to avoid an open rupture of the Dutch community along patriot-loyalist lines, each side, Adrian Leiby concludes, could not help seeing "the conflict in simple terms of the wickedness of the other." A number of prominent Bergen County Dutch, led by Daniel Isaac Brown's political associate Abraham Van Buskirk, became officers in the New Jersey Volunteers in late 1776 and officiously busied themselves with the administration of occupied New Jersey under the British. Van Buskirk had been an apparently moderate Whig when he served on the Bergen County Committee of Correspondence and then in the provincial Congress in May 1775. He later claimed that he had begun sometime in 1775 to send intelligence to Governor Tryon in New York and that Tryon had asked him to remain an ostensible Whig sympathizer. Early in 1776 he took to the woods, where he hid until Howe's army arrived. He recruited more than one hundred German settlers for the greencoated Volunteers from the district of northwestern New Jersey known as Ramapo, and he directed the British Army to the homes of scores of patriot leaders marked for arrest. Daniel Isaac Brown, meanwhile, basked in his new importance and loudly boasted that he had been secretly consorting with Governor Tryon throughout the period from June 1775 to the following summer.[10]

As with Fairfield County, Connecticut, proximity to the British stronghold in New York City made northern New Jersey a highly unstable social setting during the War for Independence, with raiding and plundering frequent occurrences. Two weeks after the British had arrived in December 1776, Samuel and Jacobus Peek ran out of Whigs to harass in Schraalenburgh, New Jersey; they collected a force of Tories, British soldiers, and camp followers and marched the eight miles north to Tappan, New York. There they cut down the liberty pole and captured one patriot militia lieutenant, two oxen, and one horse before the militia in the area forced the disorganized band to retreat to New Jersey. British officers in the area felt powerless to halt the Peeks' rampage but were appalled by their random cruelty toward and plundering of disarmed and defenseless Whig families. Others shared the notoriety. Gabriel Van Norden, of Steenrapier, the most prominent New Jersey loyalist not in the uniform of the Volunteers, and Andrew Van Buskirk, Abraham's brother, aroused widespread hostility for their attacks on Whigs and the seizure of property.

Thus, the stage was set for a decisive turn of events, when the British garrisons suddenly withdrew their support from many of the state's loyalists early in the new year. Unwilling to continue his offensive in the bitter winter weather, and stung by Washington's brilliant victories over the Hessians at Trenton on December 26, 1776, and over Cornwallis at Princeton on January 3, 1777, Howe relinquished all the territory he had gained in New Jersey except Perth Amboy and New Brunswick. The retreat left Bergen County loyalists vulnerable to retaliation. The first patriot force to enter Schraalenburgh after the British retreat, the New York Rangers, led by Captain Robert Johnston, went on a rampage on January 3, 1777. They looted loyalist David Peek's tannery without realizing that the 400 pounds of pelts they had confiscated belonged to Peek's customers, many of them neutralists leaning toward the Whig side. They also stole ten hogsheads of rum, gin, and brandy belonging to Cornelius Cooper, of Kinderkamack, a "zealous" patriot. Illicit trade between Bergen

County and nearby New York City sustained loyalist disaffection after British military control in New Jersey had receded. Eight Jersey farmers—Casparus Westervelt, Cornelius and Derick Banta, Derick Brinkerhoff, John Paulison, Lawrence Van Horn, Martin Roelefson, and Michael Demott—brought fat cattle to market in New York City and unhesitatingly took the oath of allegiance to George III, which was a conditon of doing business.[11]

Though the Dutch farmers in northwestern New Jersey called Bergen County "neutral ground" on which they simply wanted to live in peace after British evacuation of the region, the area became a grim twilight zone of random violence and increasing insecurity. In January 1778 a patriot militia officer sent Abraham Brouwer, an active Coetus churchman, and John Lozier to guard the road near Paulis Hook, on the Hudson, directly across the river from New York City. It was a dangerous assignment, and the two must have been nervous when they intercepted John Richards, a loyalist refugee from New Jersey living in New York City, who had returned to visit his family, reportedly sick with smallpox. Scoffing at Richards's story, Lozier climbed aboard Richards's wagon, Brouwer followed on horseback, and they set out for the nearest militia headquarters. During the ride, Richards grabbed for Lozier's gun and Brouwer galloped up in time to shoot the prisoner and kill him. When news of the killing reached New York City, the Jersey loyalist community there was enraged. The popular version of the event cast Brouwer and Lozier as murdering thieves. Richards's friends had warned him not to make the trip, but he had assured them that his former neighbors in Bergen County would not interfere with a mission of mercy. A reward for the capture of the two militiamen prompted the Jersey loyalist exile Wiert Banta to undertake a daring raid on February 5, 1778, into the Jersey neutral ground; Banta captured Brouwer alive and brought him back to face murder charges in New York City. Lozier was captured on March 27. To the disgust of New York loyalists, General Henry Clinton declined to hang the men, probably fearing Whig retaliation against British prisoners. The loyalist jailers in New York City, however, got revenge by subjecting the two infamous prisoners to incredible abuse and virtual starvation. News of this alleged mistreatment spread throughout New Jersey, and the patriot Commissary of Prisoners, Elisha Boudinot, retaliated by placing prisoners in his custody in chains and reducing their diet to bread and water. Clinton had little patience with abuse of prisoners of war, and he ordered the two men exchanged.[12] Bergen County's proximity to New York City, the inability of either Britain or the New Jersey government to bring security to the region, illicit trade, internecine violence, and the rewards reaped by men who secretly promised their loyalty to both sides fueled a corrosive civil war that raged for years through a society of Dutch families and communities once bound together by ties of kinship, religion, and common belief in submission to constituted authority.

33

<hr/>

New York City, 1776–1780:
Loyalist Sanctuary or Trap?

WHEN British policymakers thought about the loyalists at all during the early stages of the War for Independence, their assumptions predisposed them to one of two commonly held views. The North ministry was led by men who accepted the dubious proposition that most of the colonists were at heart loyalist sympathizers who would return America to obedience once a British Army crushed the rash and ill-considered rebel force. On the other hand, a few military leaders who had experience in America adopted the more sophisticated and realistic view that, however widespread the patriot movement might be, the majority was still uncommitted and could be won back to obedience by applying steady military pressure. The first assumption was not only incorrect but also dangerous, for it dissuaded the British from early and thorough mobilization of loyalist forces; an overwhelmingly loyal populace would mobilize itself as soon as the military balance shifted decisively in favor of the British—or so official reasoning seemed to run. The second assumption, as William Howe's experiences in 1776 and 1777 demonstrated, could not be tested because the British never gained the kind of momentum necessary to attract a growing stream of loyalist adherents to the British side. Instead, British successes in New Jersey in early 1777—and later in South Carolina, in 1780—produced sudden freshets of loyalist military activity that galvanized dispirited Whigs to action and then left aggressive loyalists exposed and vulnerable to Whig retaliation.

Both assumptions, however, confirmed British officials in their view that New York City should be the hub of British operations in America. It was ideally located as a base for offensive movements that would cut New England off from the other colonies; it provided the major port facility needed for landing and supplying the British Army; and there was ample superficial evidence that the province of New York was at least evenly divided between Whigs and Tories, because in 1775 politics in the colony had become sharply polarized into broad but distinct alignments bearing those labels. Following the January elections, the De Lancey faction and its supporters in the Assembly rallied against the Revolutionary movement, defeating three crucial Whig resolutions, one endorsing the work of the First Continental Congress, another seeking approval of nonimportation, and a third calling for selection of delegates to the Second Continental Congress. In several rural counties, Tories succeeded in scuttling committees created to enforce nonimportation. New York City, moreover, was a source of pervasive royal influence. There the British Army in America, which had extensive purchasing power, maintained its headquarters; speculators in the New Hampshire Grants expected the royal Governor's help in their struggle to confirm Yorker land claims in the region; and James Rivington's *New York Gazetteer* was the most aggressive and lively pro-British newspaper in America.

These indications of Tory strength in New York were highly misleading. That colony's relatively slow and equivocal response to the Coercive Acts and the nonimportation association resulted from the division of Whig leadership between the Livingston faction and the Sons of Liberty, and from the immense difficulties in unifying and mobilizing sentiment in a culturally pluralistic society like New York. Most important, the figures with the greatest public stature in the Whig movement—chiefly the leaders of the Livingston faction—were wealthy and deliberate men who refused to be stampeded into overt resistance.

Nevertheless, the collapse of royal authority played itself out at a deliberate pace. Governor Tryon retreated for safety to the British warship *Duchess of Gordon* in New York harbor, where he continued to hold Council meetings. He was powerless to protect outspoken defenders of British authority, several of whom the Sons of Liberty, led by Isaac Sears, rounded up and sent to Connecticut for confinement in the Simsbury mines. By

February 1776, the arrival of Continental troops in the city and British warships in the harbor had turned New York City into an armed camp. Troops found barracks where they could, some in magnificent homes of departed wealthy loyalists. British warships moved out of New York harbor and out of range of fire from the shore. On March 16, 1776, Tryon sent a message to the populace assuring them that "a door is still open to such honest but deluded people as shall avail themselves of the justice and benevolence which the supreme legislature has held out to them of being restored to the King's grace and peace." He promised loyalists who persevered assurance of British support. This imprudent proclamation, Thomas J. Wertenbaker observes, did much more harm than good. It provoked a renewed campaign of intimidation against suspected loyalists that "threatened to snap completely the already attenuated link between the province and the old government." During the last desperate weeks before British occupation of the city, suspected loyalists endured repeated indignities at the hands of mobs. On June 10, 1776, the Moravian clergyman the Reverend Gustavus Shewkirk, a loyalist, saw a crowd that "carried and hauled" several suspects through the streets of the city; each victim held a lighted candle directly aloft and was told that if he slackened his pace or lowered the candle the flame would be pushed into his face. At every corner the procession stopped and a crier shouted the names of the victims; the crowd gave three loud "huzzas" and then proceeded again. The area around New York suddenly swarmed with British collaborators recruiting troops to serve with the British Army and secretly shipping supplies to the British ships at the Narrows of New York harbor. No amount of intimidation and harassment seemed to stem the pro-British activity. Several prominent New York politicians were forced to flee, including Assemblyman John Walton and Councillor John Henry Cruger, who hid in a barn outside the city to avoid arrest and abuse. Augustus Van Cortlandt concealed himself in a cowshed. Theophilus Hardenbrook, after being beaten by a mob, lived in the woods and in old barns and houses around Bloomingdale. A rumor swept the city of a Tory plot to blow up the powder magazine, spike the city's cannon, and turn the city over to the British without a fight. Mayor David Mathews, a strong supporter of British authority; a gunsmith named Gilbert Forbes; Thomas Hickey, one of Washington's bodyguards; William Green, a drummer in the Continental Army; and James Johnson, a fifer, were arrested as conspirators in the plan. There was little direct evidence against Mathews, and he was sent to Litchfield, Connecticut for imprisonment. A few months later he escaped and returned to British-occupied New York City. Forbes and Green confessed their roles in the plot, and on June 28, 1776, in a field near Bowery Lane, Thomas Hickey, the last of the accused, was hanged in the presence of some 20,000 spectators. Both those loyalists who had remained in the city and those who had fled and returned after the British capture in September found their experiences during 1776 thoroughly disorienting. Compounding their shock, a fire of undetermined origin broke out on the night of September 21, 1776, and destroyed nearly 500 houses and businesses, temporarily shattering the economy and vastly complicating the work of finding quarters for British troops and loyalist refugees who began to stream into the city from nearby areas of Connecticut, New York, and New Jersey.

General James Robertson, British Commandant of New York City, executed his duties with impressive efficiency. He ended vandalizing and looting by British soldiers and protected loyalists from unauthorized seizure of their homes by British troops. Every house deserted by fleeing rebels had the letters "G.R." painted on the door to designate that the building had been forfeited to the Crown. Slowly, Robertson located cramped quarters for British and Hessian troops and wives and children of British officers who had joined them in New York City—some 2,500 dependents by 1779. Warehouses were converted to handle British war supplies; churches were used as hospitals; and prisons had to be improvised in empty buildings and ships in the harbor. Housing for returning loyalists and refugees remained the most pressing problem in occupied New York City. Most rented rooms cost four times their prewar amounts. In November 1777 many people were forced to vacate these dwellings when fresh arrivals of British troops needed more barracks. General Robertson appointed a city vestry to care for the poor and destitute, administer the homes of departed rebels that the army had not occupied, and provide for essential city services such as street lighting and cleaning. The vestry wanted the occupants of houses abandoned by the rebels to pay rent to the vestry. Though opposed to levying city taxes, General Clinton did consent to rent collection from those using the property of departed rebels. By rigorous collection of these levies and by rent control, the vestry managed by 1778 to stabilize the cost of housing and halt the most serious profiteering by landlords. There were constant complaints from residents of the city about the rudeness of British soldiers and the greed of employees of the barracks board, who commandeered comfortable quarters for themselves. Not until 1780 did the army develop machinery to regulate and prevent abuses in its occupancy of private homes. Moreover, the army was supposed to pay loyalists for the use of their homes but regularly neglected these obligations. Loyalists in turn were not above falsely claiming ownership of buildings used by the British. In spite of General Robertson's tireless efforts to be fair, the shortage of housing and the absence of a court system to settle disputes over housing created persistent friction between loyalist inhabitants and the British Army.[1]

The second most serious problem in occupied New York City was the plight of the destitute. The vestry used the funds it collected from occupiers of rebel property to provide relief to the large number of people without housing or employment. An almshouse provided shelter and food for 300 people dislocated by the fire of September 1776. The vestry, however, did not begin to have enough funds to meet the needs of the helpless. Wealthy loyalists, British officers, and Anglican clergymen organized a charity drive on Christmas Eve 1777 for the benefit of forty widows and housekeepers. An improved long-term solution to these fiscal problems was the assignment of fines collected for the vestry by the board of police—another administrative agency appointed by General Robertson. The police levied fines against those who violated military regulations, anyone who sold flour above price ceilings, watchmen who slept on duty, bakers who sold underweight loaves of bread, and cartmen who charged excessive rates. The police also collected large sums for tavern licenses and ferry rents. Lotteries and benefit dramatic performances also augmented the vestry's resources.[2]

Everyone in the city suffered from irregular supplies of food and firewood. Neither the British nor the Americans occupied Long Island, but the British had outposts at Lloyd's Neck and the Americans could not prevent farmers on the island from selling produce to the British. That source met only a fraction of the city's needs. The British fleet brought food supplies from England, but delays and spoilage made the victualing board an inadequate source of food. British foraging parties never developed the kinds of systematic and rigorous tactics needed to secure more than a fraction of the cattle, sheep, and hogs available in adjacent rebel-controlled areas. Perhaps the large volume of illicit trade in agricultural commodities from Connecticut, New York, and New Jersey prevented the need for forcible seizure of livestock. But all of these sources were still insufficient to meet civilian demand because the army enjoyed priority in food acquisition. To alleviate this problem, the army rigidly controlled the prices paid farmers in areas neighboring New York City. Farmers in sections controlled by the British retaliated by withholding goods and hiding crops from army purchasing agents. The army in turn became increasingly dependent on expensive imported goods from England as a medium of exchange. As a result, food prices climbed steadily during the war, the quality of produce declined, and graft in the victualing service became scandalous. For all but British officers and the very well-to-do, life in occupied New York became increasingly difficult and unhealthy. Restraints on commerce compounded these difficulties. Under the Prohibitory Act of 1776, New York City could not export goods to any other province and could import goods only from Great Britain. Only the army's spending kept the money supply from drying up altogether on this one-way commercial avenue. Merchants indulged in profiteering at the expense of the British Army and justified themselves on the ground that military purchasing officers extorted graft from them. A spiral of recriminations between the army and the merchants resulted. Nevertheless, the volume of British imports rose steadily during the war. New York depended entirely on British suppliers for all manner of consumer goods. Textiles, paper, ink, rope, canvas, ivory combs, china, hats, knives, blankets, saddles, sealing wax, and rugs did a brisk business.

General Howe appointed Andrew Elliot superintendent of

exports and imports for the port of New York. Elliot, the son of a Scottish official, had grown up in Philadelphia, married into wealth, established himself as a New York merchant, and held, from 1764 to 1776, the post of receiver general and collector for the port of New York. He also served as head of the board of police in occupied New York City. Elliot was the most important loyalist during the first half of British occupation of New York City. A civilian, he was responsible for the enforcement of detailed regulations and procedures preventing the illegal re-export of goods to other parts of the rebelling colonies. With his cronies former Mayor David Mathews and Police Magistrate Peter Dubois, Elliot monopolized political influence and authority in New York during the first half of the war. As prominent members of the board of police, the trio was responsible for a wide range of governmental functions: "suppression of vice and licentiousness," support of the poor, direction of the night watch, regulation of ferries, and maintenance of the "economy, peace, and good order of the city."[3]

This patchwork of administrative agencies under the control of the British Army was wholly unsatisfactory as a means of restoring confidence in British rule. The Carlisle Commission in 1778 listened to the complaints of prominent loyalists in the city and recommended that civil government be restored. That action, the commissioners argued, would encourage loyalists in other provinces, normalize relations between soldiers and civilians, help eliminate illicit trade with patriot-held areas, and greatly stimulate the economic life of the city. As a transitional expedient, the commissioners urged the creation of a board presided over by the British commander in America and the ranking admiral in America and including such prominent loyalist counselors as Andrew Elliot, John Tabor Kempe, William Smith, Jr., Josiah Martin, William Franklin, and Frederick Smythe, former Chief Justice of New Jersey. This board would possess power to declare portions of New York at peace, whereupon Assembly elections would be held and civil courts reopened. The commission specifically recommended that William Smith, Jr., be named chief justice of New York in anticipation of the return to civil government in the province. Two years elapsed, however, before Smith's appointment arrived, in March 1780, and because civil government was never restored the office remained inactive.[4]

Symptomatic of the difficulties of establishing broad political support for British rule in occupied New York was William Smith, Jr.'s wary, circuitous route from neutralist to loyalist, from a political loner with suspiciously recent ties to the Livingston faction to a still aloof but imperturbable adviser to General Henry Clinton. The Reverend John Vardill sensed the irony and difficulty of this situation when he advised the British officials to try to recruit Smith for the British cause because he "has more influence over the rebels in the province than any other person. . . . He is subtle, cool, and persuasive [and] may be secured by an application to *his ambition.*" The accuracy of Vardill's cynical comment and the twisted course of Smith's conduct from 1776 to 1780 were important because they reflected on the integrity and authenticity of Smith's Whiggish loyalist beliefs. If Smith was ultimately an opportunist, then his finely drawn statements of civic conscience in 1775 and 1776 did nothing more than postpone for two years his conversion to the British cause in the war; but if a consistent political creed did underlie his wartime writings and actions, then his efforts to implement his Whiggish ideas about liberty and empire marked him as a truly tragic figure.[5]

Smith maintained his contacts with the Revolutionary regime in New York State until 1778. Asked to comment on the New York Constitution, he observed that "the essential properties of civil governments are power in the magistracy to protect all the [social] orders who live under it in every enjoyment not repugnant to the general felicity and the establishment of that power, free from the arbitrary exertions of the few or the capricious wantonness of the multitude." It was a prescription for republican government identical to the views espoused by moderate nationalists—like Smith's friend William Samuel Johnson—a decade later, during the drafting and ratification of the federal Constitution. While Connecticut could afford to tolerate Johnson's dissociation from the Revolution, New York, with its large loyalist minority and a metropolis occupied by the British, could

377

not let such matters rest. In 1776 Smith had secured parole to live on Livingston Manor, but he avoided taking an oath to abide by parole terms. He declined to take the required oath of allegiance in 1777, and he depended on his old protégé, Governor George Clinton, for protection. In June 1777 the New York Committee of Safety listened sympathetically to him for more than an hour while he explained why he still considered himself a subject of the King and thought independence unjustified. Smith's views on independence and allegiance to the Crown were, however, strangely elastic. Independence, he explained to the committee, "was . . . destructive of the interests of the colonies." "Independency," he told James Duane, *"was our first object and should have been our last."* Neither statement suggests that he regarded separation as morally wrong or intrinsically abhorrent. He expressed the same sense of being unable to move beyond a carefully nurtured, somewhat scholarly position in his memorable self-characterization, on Christmas Day 1777, as "a Whig of the old stamp . . . one of King William's Whigs, for liberty and the constitution." He also came to distrust his capacity to sustain a position of neutrality. His country home at Haverstraw was plundered; a newspaper article bearing his name urged a massive British invasion of the colonies, though he claimed it was a forgery; and, finally, an invitation to testify before the New York Commission for Detecting Conspiracies prompted Smith to ask Governor George Clinton, on June 7, 1778, for permission to go to New York City. There he conferred with the visiting Carlisle Commission, and to one of its members, William Eden, the interview confirmed Smith's reputation for both ability and duplicity: "a lawyer of great intrigue and subtlety, . . . an independent republican in church and state, in his heat . . . avaricious and ambitious," Eden noted; Smith was the kind of man who would "prefer certain [that is, sure] gratifications to speculative pursuits. Few men so able, if he could be trusted."[6]

With characteristic adroitness, Smith began to explore the avenues of influence open to him in occupied New York City, at the same time preserving his intellectual and personal aloofness. He persuaded the Carlisle Commission to recommend him for the post of chief justice once civil government in New York was restored, and although the office was never activated, Smith, as an exile in London, demanded that the British government compensate him for unpaid judicial salary. He frequently visited Henry Clinton and tried to maneuver the General just as he had royal governors before 1776. In 1779 he had a report that General Philip Schuyler was about to defect to the British, and he urged Clinton to seize the opportunity to annihilate Washington's army. Watching Clinton's expression closely, "I discerned both firmness and diffidence in his conversation. . . . He smiled and was pleased, encouraged and discouraged by turns. In short I perceived the necessity for everything that had a tendency to animate him." Instead of succeeding in animating Clinton, Smith found himself enmeshed in the General's bitter quarrels with Admiral Marriot Arbuthnot. "Artful and proud and fearless of everybody (the government excepted, with whom he relies on the interest of his friends)," Clinton appeared to Smith nothing but "an arrant blockhead." Smith's assessment of Clinton corresponded with that of most intelligent observers, but the General probably had good reason to disregard Smith's military advice. For as time passed Smith became increasingly dogmatic about the ease of defeating the American Army if only the British would strike boldly. His isolation in New York City and his preoccupation with salvaging some benefit from his outright support of the British cause seriously affected his judgment, and Smith, who earlier in his career had shown some capacity for introspection and self-criticism, could not understand what was happening to himself. He busily organized an elaborate intelligence system and had paid couriers bringing him a mass of messages and information on conditions in rebel territory.[7]

His most ambitious activity began in 1780, when he volunteered to represent Clinton in the secret Haldimand negotiations between the British and the leaders of Vermont. Smith's investments in the New Hampshire Grants and his curious principled opposition to New York's pre-Revolutionary policy in the region made him extremely knowledgeable about Vermont, and he still had good contacts there. His fondness for secret maneuver, moreover, predisposed him to admire the Allens' gamble. He recommended to Clinton that Britain recognize Vermont's independence and thereby exacerbate the hostility between the state of New York and Vermont, as well as make Vermont more dependent on the British for protection. Smith appeared to be hedging his speculative interests in Vermont land; if the British won the war his land titles would be validated, and if not an independent Vermont would ally itself with Quebec and Smith's interests would still be protected. Such a conjecture explains why Smith, in early 1782, leaked news of the Haldimand negotiations to the New York Revolutionary government, thus scuttling the whole secret affair. As L. F. S. Upton reconstructs the story, Smith did so because Vermont had already invalidated his claims there, while his old friends in New York had thus far delayed seizure of Smith's New York properties. His role in the risky Haldimand negotiations certainly indicated that Smith's absorption in the intricacies and intrigues of occupied New York City and in the shadowy world of spies and military intelligence had seriously affected his judgment and made him a liability for the British.

This pathetic chapter in his career, however, did not destroy Smith's claim to a kind of integrity and consistency as a political thinker and operator. His biographer, L. F. S. Upton, has probably come as close as any historian using conventional methods can to identifying a coherent pattern in Smith's life and to reconciling his devious actions with his great capacity for reflection and courage. "It would be simple," Upton writes, "to present Smith as a politician with his eye on the main chance, using his considerable legal skills to advance himself," or "to interpret his every move in the light of a determination to hold on to his investment at all costs. . . . But such an approach can be only a partial explanation. . . . He never ceased being a dissenter," and "as he grew older and wealthier this dissent had the virtue of presenting him with a choice: to acknowledge his acquired position as conservative or to rely on his past as a 'popular' politician. Smith had no intention of giving up the luxury of choice." Although "his intelligence was of the highest order, . . . his career was one of potential rather than actual achievement. . . . He was incapable of steering a straightforward course, and surrounded every act with so many reservations and calculations that he rendered himself impotent in practical politics." A child of the eighteenth century, Smith believed that he could contain within himself, in equilibrium and fruitful tension, concern for the "common weal," a subtle and shrewd defense of his own interests, grandiose constitutional schemes and political maneuvers, and carefully circumscribed personal risks and involvements.[8]

34

Political and Social Alignments
in Revolutionary Pennsylvania

REVOLUTIONARY politics in 1776 obliterated traditional political alignments in Pennsylvania and, to an extent unknown in other states, thrust new men into positions of power. Although Joseph Galloway's political enemies, led by John Dickinson, Thomas Mifflin, and Charles Thomson, had gained control of the Assembly and of Pennsylvania's delegation to the Continental Congress in late 1774 and early 1775, they discovered by the end of 1775 that their triumph was transitory. Their constituency and base of support were, to be sure, much broader than Galloway's had been in the 1760's; but years of jockeying for position among the Penn family, the Galloway-Franklin faction, the Dickinson antiproprietary party, German and Scotch-Irish ethnic groups, and Anglican, Presbyterian, and Quaker denominational blocks had prevented Pennsylvania from developing strong provincial leadership. By early 1776 fervent Whigs like Dickinson and James Wilson opposed immediate independence but supported military preparations by the colonists. This ambivalent stance represented, in a loose manner unique to Pennsylvania, a wide spectrum of opinion, including the views of moderate Anglicans like Jacob Duche and William Smith, the Quaker establishment, wealthy Philadelphia merchants who had much to lose from disruption of commerce, German pietist groups, and the Penn family. The lack of coalescence and consensus among these groups, however, made the moderate Whigs' leadership precarious and vulnerable to challenges from hitherto obscure political figures—Christopher Marshall, Timothy Matlack, George Bryan, James Cannon, Thomas

Paine—who strongly supported independence, hoped to vault into power over the heads of Pennsylvania's cautious leadership, and came to be known as radical constitutionalists. Paine's *Common Sense* gave focus and direction in other colonies to already rising sentiment for independence and provoked an orthodox Whig constitutionalist like John Adams to publish his own theories of government at an opportune time. In Pennsylvania the pamphlet helped ignite an insurgent movement against the power of familiar Whig leaders. In February 1776 the radicals gained control of the Philadelphia Committee of Inspection, which demanded that the Assembly grant fair representation to western counties and threatened to call a convention that might well have usurped the authority of the legislature. With John Adams acting as intermediary, the Assembly created new western legislative districts and agreed to mobilization of the province for war but balked at endorsing independence or rescinding its previous motion against separation from Britain. Vigorous and diverse, the opponents of independence won a surprisingly strong victory in Assembly elections on May 1, 1776. The supporters of independence then turned to the Continental Congress for support. It passed a resolution calling for the formation of representative governments in each colony, and then, to make it clear that Pennsylvania's old proprietary government did not qualify, Congress approved by a narrow vote of six states to four a preamble declaring that all governments deriving their authority from the Crown "should be totally suppressed." In vain, James Wilson warned that "if this preamble passes there will be an instant dissolution of every kind of authority" and that "the people will instantly be in a state of nature." On May 20, with Congressional sanction, the new leadership called a mass meeting in Philadelphia that summoned a constitutional convention and denied the Assembly any role in the creation of a new government. All the Assembly could do was withdraw the instructions prohibiting its delegates from supporting independence.[1]

The Pennsylvania Constitutional Convention deliberated from July 16 to September 28, 1776, and drafted a document that departed radically from the notions of constitutionalism prevailing in the other Revolutionary states. It created a unicameral legislature subject only to the restraint of a Council of Censors, to meet every seven years and review the constitutionality of laws, and to a provision suspending the operation of laws until they were printed and available to the public; it gave the right to vote to all taxpayers, and, while this provision did not provide for manhood suffrage, it did, in J. R. Pole's fine phrase, "sweep away the basic economic presumption that the ownership of a specified amount of property was an essential guarantee of political competence." It created a weak Executive Council and a still more insecure judiciary. All local officials were to be popularly elected. These innovations reflected a heady ideology of antagonism to aristocracy, to concentrations of wealth, and to presumptions to gentility and rank—ideas that filled the pamphlets and newspaper writings of Pennsylvania's new political leadership. Not surprisingly, the convention was excessively sensitive to criticism and opposition. The eclipse of the old proprietary Assembly forced the convention to assume quasi-legislative authority, and it sometimes used this power capriciously, levying heavy fines on those who did not associate with the Revolutionary movement for reasons of conscience, virtually suspending freedom of speech, and requiring as a condition for voting acceptance of the new constitution.[2]

The new government that assumed power under the Constitution of 1776 possessed a dangerously small base of popular support, and it faced the overwhelming difficulties of preparing the state for war and maintaining internal security. Lawyers at first boycotted the courts in protest of the new constitution. Most moderate constitutionalists refused to hold office under the new administration, although two prominent moderates did accept high office in the government—Thomas McKean, who agreed to serve as the first chief justice, and Thomas Wharton, who was elected by the Council and Assembly to the position of president of the Council. Militia enlistment languished. Dependent on the Continental Congress for prestige and recognition, and fearful of imminent British invasion, the government of Pennsylvania felt beset by obstruction and apathy. In June 1777 the Assembly struck back with a test oath, imposed on all white male inhabitants, renouncing fidelity to George III, swearing allegiance to Pennsylvania as an independent state, and promising to expose all conspiracies against the United States. Those refusing to take the oath suffered heavy disqualifications; they could not vote or hold office, serve on juries, bring actions in civil courts, purchase or sell real estate, or, at the discretion of local officials, own firearms. The test oath of 1777 deepened the divisions within the state; it was anathema to Pennsylvania's large population of religious pacifists.[3]

Consequently, the most visible groups in Pennsylvania suffered first for their refusal to support the Revolution. The Mennonites were willing to sell grain to the Continental Army, to supply teamsters and wagons to the government on request, and to pay commutation fees in lieu of military service. But they refused to take the compulsory oath of allegiance to the state imposed in June 1777, and they refused to pay special war taxes. They objected not only because it was an oath—a mere affirmation would have satisfied the law—but also because it required renunciation of their allegiance to the King and affirmative endorsement of authorities in Philadelphia whom they had no reason to respect or support. Moreover, the oath implied their endorsement of the warfare necessary for the establishment of the new government. They had always been, the Mennonites declared in 1776, "a defenseless people and could neither institute nor destroy any government." A Lancaster County militia officer recommended a new oath for the Mennonites that expressly excused them from condoning military activity. "They say, a good many at least, that they would affirm to be faithful subjects to the state [and] endeavor nothing to its hurt" so long as these actions were consistent "with their principles against bearing arms; to require them to do more, they say, is persecution." Mennonites living in large settlements suffered only small fines for refusing the test oath, but in areas where they were in the minority retribution was severe. "All of their personal estate," wrote eleven Mennonite farmers from Upper Saucon, Pennsylvania, "even their beds, bedding, linen, Bibles, and books were taken from them and sold by the sheriff. . . . From some of them all their provisions were taken and not even a morsel of bread left them for their children. . . . As all their iron stoves were taken from them, . . . they were deprived of every means of keeping their children warm in the approaching winter, especially at nights, being obliged to lie on the floor without any beds. . . . Some of the men's wives were pregnant and near the time of deliverance, which makes their case the more distressing." This punishment occurred in spite of pleas of the men's non-pacifist neighbors, who explained quizzically that the Mennonites' "present blindness to their own essential interests proceeds from an unhappy bias in their education and not from any disaffection to the present government." One prominent Mennonite clergyman, Bishop Christian Funk, advocated paying taxes levied by the state for military expenditures on the ground that "were Christ here, he would say, give unto *Congress* that which belongs to congress, and to God what is God's." Funk was expelled from the church and a small group of supporters followed him; it was the first schism in the Pennsylvania Mennonite church. For most Mennonites, arrests, fines, and seizures of property, Peter Brock concludes, were "not too onerous. . . . The main strain was psychological: with the passing of the old tolerant regime of colonial times, uncertainty seized the Mennonites regarding their future under the rule of new and possibly unsympathetic masters." Following the war, some of them emigrated to the Canadian wilderness for sanctuary.[4]

The Brethren, Dunkers, and Schwenkfelders suffered similar pressures. In 1776 the Ephrata community of Brethren simply declared their neutrality on the ground that they were subject to a higher magistrate "and consequently emancipated from the civil government." Though opposed to both military service and oaths of allegiance, the Brethren were far less strict in enforcing these prohibitions and ruled that the payment of fines in lieu of military service "would not be deemed so sinful" as actually bearing arms if it was done under "compulsion" and not "voluntarily." The Schwenkfelders adapted themselves to the conditions of war still more adroitly. Two of their leaders, the Reverend Christopher Schultz and his cousin David Schultze, actively supported the war but insisted upon respect for the pacifist convictions of the majority of the sect. The church established a charitable fund to pay fines for nonparticipation in the militia. It was not military service but oaths or affirmations of allegiance that caused the greatest friction between pietist sects and the Revolutionary government. From the viewpoint of the government, the oath contained nothing offensive to tender consciences:

"I renounce and refuse all allegiance to George the Third, King of Great Britain, his heirs and successors, and . . . I will be faithful and bear true allegiance to the commonwealth of Pennsylvania as a free and independent state" and will do nothing injurious or prejudicial to its "freedom and independence." Germans, however, had no experience with oaths of allegiance and notions of contract between ruler and ruled that might be abrogated for cause. "They were inclined," Henry J. Young explains, "to consider a promissory oath as definitive as any other. . . . So long as the King claimed their allegiance, old oaths were hard to repudiate." In one dramatic case in Northampton County, in the summer of 1777, a Schwenkfelder boy too young to be liable for military service had been fined for failure to serve in the militia. The boy's father, George Kriebel, tried to testify in his son's behalf, but the court held him incompetent to testify on the ground that he had not sworn allegiance to the state. Kriebel avoided affirming allegiance to the King and went so far as promising to be "true to the state as much as were in my power in paying any lawful taxes or other charges and in carting [goods for the army] and anything they should want except in bearing arms which was against my conscience." The court forgot about the boy and prosecuted the father on the spot for refusing to abjure allegiance to the King. Kriebel persisted in his refusal on two grounds: first, he had taken an oath of allegiance to the King when he was naturalized, and, second, the outcome of the war was still in doubt and it was not yet clear "upon what side God almighty would bestow the victory." As opportunistic and equivocal as the reasons appear, they represented an important pietist belief and one that distinguished these pacifists from the Quakers: the assurance that divine providence ultimately controlled the military struggle and that men could not alter oaths of allegiance until God had granted victory and spiritual legitimacy to one side or the other.[5]

The most serious conflict between the government of Pennsylvania and pacifist citizens, of course, involved the Quakers. The Philadelphia Quakers were too wealthy and influential a group to be ignored by Revolutionary leaders. Quaker aversion to even indirect and innocuous complicity with the war effort was both ingenious and scrupulous, but there were just enough wealthy

Quakers who were outright British sympathizers to taint the neutrality of the whole sect. The Philadelphia Meeting for Suffering called on Friends in the city "with Christian fortitude and firmness" to "withstand and refuse to submit to the arbitrary injunctions and ordinances of men who assume to themselves the power of compelling others . . . to join in carrying on war by imposing tests not warranted by the precepts of Christ . . . or the laws of the happy constitution under which [the Friends had] long enjoyed tranquillity and peace"—language that came perilously close to being unneutral. Influential delegates to the Continental Congress, meeting in Philadelphia prior to Howe's occupation of the city in September 1777, were understandably distraught at the collapse of resistance in Pennsylvania and insisted that Pennsylvania officials take action against the Quaker leaders. These factors rendered the Society of Friends unusually vulnerable to persecution. In the summer of 1777 Congress asked officials in Pennsylvania and Delaware to arrest and disarm all persons who were "notoriously disaffected" and to search the homes of those "who have not manifested their attachment to the American cause." Although Congress did not specify the Quakers as targets for this campaign, the Supreme Executive Council of Pennsylvania considered the Friends a prime source of disaffection and proper subjects for harassment. In late August, Congress received documents, purporting to be the records of a Spanktown Yearly Meeting, that implicated Quakers as spies for the British Army. No Quaker meeting existed in Spanktown, an obscure settlement in eastern New Jersey, nor had any Quaker gathering ever occurred there, and the documents were almost certainly a forgery.[6]

Accordingly, Congress asked Pennsylvania officials to arrest eleven prominent Quakers—including James, Israel, and John Pemberton, Henry Drinker, Samuel Thomas Fisher, and Thomas Wharton—and to add to the list other names of persons "inimically disposed toward the American states." All were to have their homes searched for incriminating documents. By August 31, 1777, more than forty persons were under arrest. "About 11 o'clock our new-made council sent some of their deputies to many of the inhabitants whom they suspected of toryism, and without any regular warrant or any written paper mentioning their crime or telling them of it in any way, committed them to confinement, and among their number was my dear husband," Sara Logan Fisher, wife of Thomas Fisher, recorded in her diary. "Three men came for him and offered him his parole to confine himself as a prisoner to his own house, which he refused signing. They then told him he must go with them and be confined to the [Masonic] Lodge. He refused going until he had seen the warrant. Upon which they read over a paper which they called one, which was an order from the Congress, recommending to the Executive Council to fall upon some measure to take up all persons who had by their conduct or otherwise shown themselves enemies to the United States." No incriminating papers were found in the homes of the men. In vain they demanded a hearing and protested that the Supreme Executive Council had arrogated to itself "authority not grounded in law or reason" in its arbitrary arrest of "peaceable men" who "have never bore arms." Both Congress and the Supreme Executive Council avoided taking responsibility for the detainment. Congress finally recommended that Pennsylvania officials deport the prisoners to confinement in Virginia. The Council first ordered militia to transport twenty unrepentant prisoners to Reading. A judge then ordered their release on a writ of habeas corpus, but a special ex post facto law denied the group the protection of habeas corpus. After a few days the group was taken to Winchester, Virginia, arriving there on September 29, 1777, just three days after the British had occupied Philadelphia. There they lived under lenient confinement until sympathy for the exiles persuaded the Supreme Executive Council to return them to Lancaster, Pennsylvania and release them.[7]

Release from exile did not end the ordeal for these prominent Quakers. Henry Drinker suffered imprisonment in October 1779 because, he wrote, he had been "endeavoring steadily to adhere to what I believed to be my Christian duty in refusing to join in any of the prevailing seditions and tumults." Pennsylvania officials charged Samuel R. Fisher with sending intelligence to the British, and when the jury returned a verdict of not guilty the judge ordered them to reconsider; after an hour and a half of further deliberation they found him guilty. Fisher declared that he would rather lose all his property than violate the "Friends' principles against putting down and setting up governments and the promotion of war in the land." The very severity and injustice of this deprivation of the Quakers' civil liberties may have helped Philadelphia members of the sect realize that symbolic pacifist gestures did not project an effective witness of Quaker abhorrence of war. The very unsettled nature of Pennsylvania during the War for Independence forced the sect to tighten its organization, intensify its humanitarian activities, and maintain its contacts with Quakers in England and elsewhere in America. The horrors of the war prompted the Quakers to blame this calamity on the sins of slavery and drunkenness, by which Americans had forfeited God's protection and benevolence. In these ways—and without making a conscious decision to alter the nature of their fellowship—the sect managed during the War for Independence to adapt itself more fully to the realities of American life. By ceasing to claim that its beliefs set it morally apart from the rest of society, and by asserting, instead, that the Friends were another Protestant denomination, which preserved a particular religious heritage and provided a home for those born into that faith or those attracted by its teaching, Sydney V. James concludes, "the Quakers had found a way to reconcile their beliefs with the pluralism of the American religious scene."[8]

The British occupied Philadelphia from September 26, 1777, until June 18, 1778—by far the shortest British occupation of a major American city during the entire War for Independence. (They held New York from September 1776 until November 1783, Newport, Rhode Island from December 1776 until October 1779, Savannah from December 1778 until July 1782, and Charles Town from May 1780 until December 1782.) The invasion of Pennsylvania in 1777 and the abrupt decision to abandon the state the following spring marked the first great crisis of British strategy and execution in the American war. Howe's leisurely offensive into Pennsylvania was a temporary victory because it occurred at the very time when he should have been making every effort to support Burgoyne's advance from Canada down the Hudson valley. A consequence of Saratoga and the subsequent French alliance, the decision to abandon Philadelphia signaled a major shift in British strategy. After Saratoga the British effort to defeat the American rebels became less a matter of offensive warfare and more a test of will and determination. The administration of occupied Philadelphia reflected this shift. In New York City, Joseph Galloway had for the previous year strongly advocated an invasion of Pennsylvania and had assured Howe that the great majority of the province supported the British cause. Galloway knew, however, that loyal sentiment would have to be nurtured and mobilized, and he struggled to provide leadership and encouragement to British sympathizers. "When I returned to Philadelphia" with Howe's army, "the numerous inhabitants who remained there almost unanimously [demanded] to know whether they were to be governed by military law or restored to their civil rights." Moreover, he found them "still wishing that the wisdom of Parliament would propose some system of government" that would eliminate colonial grievances about taxation and other infringements. "To convince them that Great Britain meant to do what was right, I prevailed on the General to establish a civil police in that city. It gave general satisfaction because it was esteemed a prelude" to an early restoration of civil government and a wholesale reformation of the constitution of the Empire. On December 4, 1777, Howe complied and named Galloway "Superintendent of the Police in the city and its environs and Superintendent of Imports and Exports to and from Philadelphia." It was the same post held in New York City by Andrew Elliot, and it was not at all intended to serve as a transitional agency inaugurating prompt return to civil government. Elliot, in New York, and Galloway, in Philadelphia, were adjuncts of the military, and their primary responsibility was the suppression of illicit trade between merchants in these garrison towns and agents for the Revolutionary governments. They were to make monthly reports on all arriving vessels and cargoes, report all seizures of illicit goods to military authorities, and sell all confiscated goods at public auction. Informers were to be paid from the proceeds. Because of the danger of fire, duplicate records were to be maintained and regular tabulations of trade figures reported to the British commander. Galloway and Elliot shared primary responsibility for regulating British trade for the entire region of the middle states. Galloway insisted that Howe grant to both himself and Elliot wide discretionary power to inspect military as well as private shipping. He sought to expand his position into that of a powerful administrative overseer of British policy in Philadelphia preparatory to the resumption of civil government. Galloway easily elbowed aside the pre-Revolutionary customs inspector for Philadelphia, John Patterson, who felt entitled to the inspectorship of customs and shipping.[9]

Galloway astutely judged that constitutional and administrative reform of the Empire should go "hand in hand" with the prosecution of the war against the rebels. "The offer of . . . a system of polity, . . . to the people of America, . . . a settled constitution between the two countries . . . I have always thought should have attended the British arms from the beginning." As late as the spring of 1779, he argued, such British assurances would "have been productive of the most beneficial consequences by removing all fears and jealousies from the minds of the people." The restoration of civil government within a redefined imperial relationship, Galloway declared, would "be equally effectual with the power of arms in suppressing the rebellion and finally restoring the peace." Given these expectations, he conceived of his role as superintendent of police more as that of a long-range constitutional theorist than that of a mere overseer of policy subordinate to the British commander. Galloway had assumed that Howe's transports would approach Philadelphia by way of the Delaware River, but when the expedition reached the mouth of the river on July 30, 1777, General Howe decided, on the basis of unsubstantiated supposition, that this route would be too dangerous, and he took the longer route to the northern tip of Chesapeake Bay, thus losing another month of time. Galloway had already gone to the trouble of hiring loyalist pilots familiar with the river to accompany Howe and help guide ships up the Delaware River to a landing point near New Castle. James Molesworth, one of the pilots Galloway had hired, was captured and hanged by the patriots. When Howe abandoned the Delaware route without even testing rebel defenses, after Galloway had "risked his neck and the necks of several of his friends to make possible the passing . . . on the Delaware," John M. Coleman shows, the proud Pennsylvania loyalist concluded that the British commander was an irresolute fool.[10]

This hardening of his already haughty and self-confident out-look prompted Galloway to assume the duties of political over-lord of the Pennsylvania campaign as soon as the troops landed, on August 25, at Head of Elk, at the northern end of Chesa-peake Bay. He hired intelligence agents, organized efforts at supply operations, and ordered Cornwallis to destroy a bridge the rebels had built across the Schuylkill River. Loyalists who helped prevent the burning of Philadelphia by retreating rebels received rewards for their courage from Galloway. He sought lucrative governmental positions for other conspicuous loyalists, like Anthony Yeldall, a self-styled "practitioner of physic and surgery," who busied himself with disarming "the disaffected" as British troops entered the city and prepared a list of rebels and their properties for the use of General Howe. Galloway employed a force of nearly eighty spies, who fanned out into the Pennsyl-vania countryside, and a staff of police magistrates, including Samuel Shoemaker, former Mayor of Philadelphia; Daniel Coxe, former owner of the old proprietary land grants in New Jersey and member of the Assembly there; and John Potts, former Judge of Common Pleas in Philadelphia. Abel Evans, former clerk of the Assembly under Galloway, became clerk of police. All were men of stature and ability who had sacrificed much by remaining loyal to the Crown from 1775 to 1777.[11]

Galloway promptly forged his subordinates into an effective and adaptable administrative agency. His deputy inspector of prohibited goods, Enoch Story, for example, boasted that he had "conducted the Army into Philadelphia, attested [to the loyalty of] the recruits, superintended the return of [loyalist] inhabitants and [recovery of] their property, . . . [made] desig-nations . . . respecting their political principles," and served as acting collector of customs prior to Galloway's appointment. Gal-loway also confiscated arms from "suspected persons," secured blankets for British soldiers wounded at the Battle of German-town—Washington's unsuccessful attempt to dislodge Howe on October 4, 1777—assisted the barracksmaster in obtaining rum, molasses, salt, and medicines, compiled weekly lists of defectors from the American Army, administered oaths of allegiance, and handled financial accounts involving transactions between civil-ians and the British government. The day before his appointment as superintendent of police, Galloway negotiated with the managers of a hospital that had formerly been used by the Continental Congress and that still housed several patients. "Representing it to be a charitable institution entirely independent and unconnected with the military hospital," the directors asked Galloway for permission to continue to operate the facility. They promised to keep their patients confined to a garret and a new building and open the main part of the hospital to injured British troops. Galloway rejected the proposal. The hospital was to pass entirely into his control, though the former directors might apply to him for permission to admit civilian patients. Galloway also took charge of foraging operations and preparation of maps and up-to-date guides to nearby parts of Pennsylvania.

Galloway's personal corps of loyalist troops did conduct a wide range of irregular raids in Pennsylvania during the winter of 1777–78, seizing rebel provisions and supplies bound for Valley Forge, capturing many supporters of the Revolution within a thirty-mile radius of Philadelphia, and collecting military intelligence. When Cornwallis had failed for six weeks to erect batteries on Mud Island in the Delaware River because tides kept washing over the foundations, Galloway organized and supervised a crew that built batteries there in less than a week, to the astonishment of the army's chief engineer. Galloway also conducted a census of the entire population of the city, designating the loyalty or disaffection of every inhabitant. He designed a campaign of newspaper proclamations urging voluntary restrictions on price increases, which prevented the kind of inflation rampant in occupied New York City in spite of that city's efforts at mandatory price-fixing. Other proclamations issued by Galloway dealt with law enforcement, curfew hours, punishment of disorderly conduct, limitations on cutting of wood, regulation of ferryboats, maintenance of chimneys, disposal of rubbish, operation of a night watch, supervision of wharves, markets, and butcher shops, registration of horses, carts, and wagons, licences for draymen and porters, donations for the poor, and forage and pasturage for the King's horses. Galloway's tireless initiatives indicated his determination to enlarge the scope and impact of the responsibilities Howe had assigned him. He wanted his governance of the city to become a rallying point for loyal

sentiment in Pennsylvania and to demonstrate that strong, determined, and effective administration, in conjunction with military victory, could break the back of resistance. Most important,
Galloway wanted to demonstrate to the British government that
loyalist officials like himself were competent to restore civil
government and to effect the reformation of imperial organization outlined in his Plan of Union.[12]

Trade and prosperity revived dramatically in occupied Philadelphia. Wealthy loyalist exiles returned to the city and together
with British officers created a brilliant social scene. Theaters
reopened and balls, concerts, and parties filled the calendar—all
suggesting that British sympathizers were anxious to reassure
themselves that the war was nearly over and the unpleasantness
of the recent past a thing to be forgotten. There was a sudden
demand for all sorts of expensive consumer goods. Tench Coxe, a
young merchant who was barely twenty at the start of the
Revolution and who had wavered between support of colonial
resistance and opposition to the use of force, fled to New York
City to seek British protection in December 1776. There he
formed a commercial alliance with long-time family friend and
New York loyalist merchant Edward Goold, under which Goold
would supply him with goods once he was able to re-establish his
mercantile business in Philadelphia. Coxe returned to the city
with Howe's army and within a month advertised for sale
"counter cotton panes, pearl necklaces, brocades, satin knee
garters, and a few boxes of Keyser's pills," useful in treating
venereal disease, rheumatism, asthma, dropsy, and apoplexy.
Coxe's New York suppliers shipped him these goods on a 5-per-
cent-commission basis, another clear indication that loyalists in
both cities expected the British to succeed in restoring British
authority to Pennsylvania. Although Coxe found it prudent to
avoid open collaboration with British officials, he secured their
help in gaining a relaxation of the sale of imported goods in
Pennsylvania and also in receiving permission to trade directly
with the West Indies.[13]

Certain events, however, frustrated Galloway's initially successful attempt to convert Philadelphia into a showplace of benevolent, vigorous, confident reimposition of royal authority. Howe,
for example, vetoed his scheme to kidnap the Revolutionary

governor and Council of New Jersey. When news came that Philadelphia was to be abruptly abandoned to the Americans the loyalist community asked permission to negotiate directly with General Washington for their safety. "Mr. Galloway, on the part of the principal persons of the town asks permission to make terms with Washington," Henry Clinton noted when he arrived in Philadelphia in May 1778 to take command from William Howe. Clinton denied the request, even though Howe had been inclined to grant it. "Half of the garrison of New York are provincials," he observed, and they might "be tempted" by such a spectacle into "betraying the post" and making their own peace with New York rebels. Oblivious to the fact that withdrawal from Philadelphia had been forced on the British government by the American victory at Saratoga and the subsequent French alliance, Galloway urged Clinton to remain in the city. Clinton could only reply that the decision to depart was irrevocable. Both Galloway's staggering accomplishments during his eight months as a loyalist administrator and his stubborn refusal to admit the deterioration of Britain's strategic position in 1778 reflected his grim determination to reverse his humiliation at the First Continental Congress and to repair the British Empire with the same remedy he had proposed in 1774—benevolent, energetic royal government and enlightened constitutional restructuring. As the Reverend John Vardill, New York loyalist, perceptively advised British officials in 1778, Galloway "is a man of integrity, much esteemed by the people, and possessed of improved understanding; but he is too fond of *system* and his natural warmth of temper, inflamed by the oppressions and indignities he has suffered, will render you cautious of trusting his representations. You will, however, find him too valuable to be neglected." On exactly such strengths and weaknesses rested Britain's best hope of restoring royal authority and civil government in the middle colonies.[14]

35

The Suppression of the Loyalists
in Pennsylvania, Delaware,
and New Jersey

THE treatment of loyalists in Pennsylvania reflected the peculiar array of political divisions in the state. Pennsylvania's broad moderation and reasonableness and its debilitating history of proprietary-antiproprietary political infighting had impeded the province's willingness to support independence and had created a crisis of leadership in 1776, as pressures to sever ties with Britain became irresistible. Into this vacuum the radical constitutionalists had moved. The very narrowness of the radicals' base of support enabled the moderate Whigs to continue to exercise an influence on the conduct of government. Some of the legislation dealing with disaffection was humane and some was vindictive, and the pattern of enforcement oscillated between preserving social harmony and exacting revenge. The two tendencies seemed to converge and to reinforce one another. "On the Tories, . . . I am for the general line of lenity and forgiveness, making as little sacrifice to the passions and prejudices of the populace as possible," wrote General John Armstrong; he also opposed "condemning men [who] differ only with us in mere political sentiments without . . . the least actual opposition or . . . aid to our enemies, yet [I] *am of opinion that a few examples ought to be made of the more atrocious.*"[1] Pennsylvania policy alternated between lenience for British sympathizers and harsh retribution for a selected number of notorious loyalists. Even though the humbling of the Penn family was a high priority for the radical Whigs, the Divesting Act, which the legislature adopted in 1779, was remarkably mild and generous. It left the Penns' personal estates untouched and compensated the family with £130,000 sterling for its loss of public domain.

The oscillating pattern began in the autumn of 1775, when a group of English-born residents of Philadelphia, led by Dr. John Kearsley and Leonard Snowden, were caught transmitting intelligence to the British ministry. Until that occurrence, no one in the Whig camp had seriously expected any Pennsylvanians to conspire in inviting the British Army to invade the province. Congress swiftly recommended that provincial assemblies and committees of safety arrest and hold persons "whose going at large may endanger the safety of the colony or the liberties of America." Kearsley and his friends were soon seized by extralegal committees and held in various county jails as prisoners of the Continental Congress itself. These jails were filthy, dilapidated structures, where Kearsley died and Snowden went mad. In response to Congress's recommendation in June 1776 that states make treason a crime, the Pennsylvania Constitutional Convention on September 5, 1776, assuming legislative authority, enacted a rather conventional statute defining treason as the levying of war against Pennsylvania, the adherence to the King, or the aiding and comforting of the British by any inhabitant or voluntary resident of the state. Furthermore, concealing knowledge of traitorous actions or aiding persons involved in them was the lesser crime of "misprision of treason." The lack of a court system at this early stage in the state's independence, however, prevented this moderate law from ever being enforced. A less-restrained ordinance against "seditious utterances" allowed justices of the peace to jail without jury trial or bail persons who spoke or wrote in opposition to the work of Congress and were deemed to possess dangerous influence. On the last day of its corporate existence, September 26, 1776, the old provincial Assembly presumed to nullify this statute, and no prosecutions occurred under it.[2]

Goaded by their inability to command broad public support, the radical Whigs looked for scapegoats. In November 1776 a group of partisans launched a vigilante campaign, breaking into homes and seizing and jailing suspected loyalists. On November

25 the radicals prevailed on Thomas McKean, respected Revolutionary leader, to preside over a hearing for the suspects held in the Indian Queen Tavern. The house searches had turned up no documentary evidence, and the only evidence presented at the hearing was testimony that the suspects had been overheard singing "God Save the King" at private social gatherings. Support for the drive against suspected loyalists dissipated, and by the middle of September 1777 the Council of Safety had paroled all but one of the victims of the November raids. Even this rather weak drive against British sympathizers, however, altered the precarious balance in Pennsylvania between tendencies of toleration and vengeance; Christian Huck, a young conservative lawyer, heard a report that more than 200 prominent people, many of them kinsmen of the Allen family, would soon be arrested and imprisoned or banished to North Carolina. John, Andrew, and William Allen and their cousins Tench Coxe and Edward Shippen, along with Huck, fled to New Jersey to seek the protection of the British Army. Galloway also chose this moment to flee to New York. Other men on the list went into hiding. "The significant result of this flare-up," Henry J. Young writes, "was that some of the ablest men in the state were alienated" from the new government by the actions of "an irresponsible minority." "What [men like the Allens, Huck, and Coxe] had claimed was only the right of neutrality, and by more tolerant treatment they might in time have been won over by the revolutionists."[3] For during the first year of the Revolution, Thomas McKean declared as chief justice in 1781, "Pennsylvania was not a nation at war with another nation, but a country in a state of *civil war*," and men then had a moral right to choose which allegiance to declare. McKean apparently soon regretted his involvement in the harassment of harmless British supporters in Philadelphia in November 1776. He epitomized the state's paradoxical tolerance of political diversity and its impulse to create categories of civic purity and impurity.[4]

The moderates reasserted themselves when the legislature created a legal system for the state in January and February 1777. It declared English common law binding in Pennsylvania so far as it did not conflict with the creation of republican government and the defense of independence, and it replaced the treason ordinance of 1776 with a new statute—one in some ways more restrained and in others more repressive than the earlier law. Probably working in consultation with delegates to the Continental Congress from several other states, authors of the act designated seven offenses as high treason, punishable by death, forfeiture of all property, and disinheritance of the traitor's family: accepting a commission from the British, levying war, enlisting in the King's service, recruiting others to enlist, furnishing arms or supplies to the enemy, corresponding with British officials, or giving them intelligence. Replacing the seditious-utterances ordinances of 1776, the new treason law defined the lesser offense of misprision of treason as speaking or writing against military preparedness, attempting to send intelligence to the British, attempting to incite others to submit to British authority, discouraging men from enlisting in the American forces, "stirring up tumults or disposing people to favor the enemy, opposing or endeavoring to prevent . . . revolutionary measures." The punishment for these crimes was imprisonment for the duration of the war and forfeiture of half of one's estate. Offsetting the harshness of the sentences for treason and misprision of treason was the specificity of the offenses themselves, which tended to limit prosecution to these precise actions. The "humane" 1776 ordinance, Professor Young suggests, was designed to impose uniform punishment on all traitors, while the harsher but more specific 1777 statute was designed to single out only the most dangerous and notorious offenders.[5]

While the Pennsylvania government languished in exile in Lancaster during the British occupation of Philadelphia from September 1777 to June 1778, the legislature created, in March 1778, a more drastic weapon—a confiscation act providing for bills of attainder. This legislation named particular loyalists who had joined the British and gave them until April 21, 1778, to surrender themselves and stand trial for treason. For failing to comply they would automatically suffer forfeiture of all property, disinheritance of themselves and their heirs, and—in the event of their capture—hanging. Furthermore, the law authorized the new Council of Safety to proclaim bills of attainder against additional loyalists. The council appointed agents to manage estates forfeited under bills of attainder, and eight separate proclamations between 1778 and 1781 invoked the penalties on nearly 500 persons—80 per cent of them in 1778 during and immediately following British occupation of Philadelphia. The sheer volume of treason convictions under the Act of Attainder meant that some innocent people lost their estates on flimsy and unsubstantiated evidence, although 386 of the 500 persons named failed to appear within the time limits set by the attainder proclamations because they had fled to the protection of the British. Of the 113 who did surrender, less than twenty ever came to trial, because there was insufficient evidence to warrant prosecution. Of sixteen who stood trial, only three were convicted. One of these was judged insane and pardoned, while two others, John Roberts and Abraham Carlisle, were hanged. Tench Coxe, who remained in Philadelphia after the British departed to care for his dying wife, escaped conviction by taking an oath of allegiance.[6]

The regular criminal code served better than the law of treason in punishing Pennsylvania loyalists. The most dangerous figures were not men who had fled to the British and could be handled by attainder prosecutions that confiscated their property; on the contrary, they were gangs of outlaws who aided the British and also enriched themselves in the process. James Fitzpatrick was a guerrilla fighter and loyalist partisan who plundered scores of Whig homes until captured in 1778, convicted of burglary and larceny, and executed—the first Pennsylvania loyalist put to death by civil officials. William Rankin's Associated Loyalists hired the gang led by James Nugent, Christopher Shockey, and Henry Trout to distribute counterfeit money and commit robberies in Pennsylvania; but four of the gang were captured and hanged in 1779, two for passing counterfeit bills and two for stealing a bottle of yeast valued at three pence. James Roberts, who served as a courier between General Clinton and loyalist partisans, was executed for using counterfeit currency. Execution was not a normal punishment for these crimes; it was simply easier to convict loyalists of robbery and counterfeiting than of actual treason, and to impose the death penalty for the lesser offense. Another means of heightening the severity of the law in loyalist prosecutions was withdrawal of the right of pleading benefit of clergy in cases of counterfeiting. Benefit of clergy derived its name from a law of the Middle Ages, when members of religious orders were exempt from trial in civil courts; by the eighteenth century it had become a plea-swapping device by which the defendant in effect entered a guilty plea and was assured of a light sentence—usually brief imprisonment and having his hand branded so that he could not repeat the plea in any trial for a future offense. Schemes of currency debasement were the most widespread form of subversion, so withdrawal of benefit of clergy in counterfeiting cases made many more loyalists subject to capital punishment. Forty-eight men were hanged in Pennsylvania during the War for Independence for offenses other than treason. Of twenty-two men tried for counterfeiting in Pennsylvania between 1779 and 1782, eleven were convicted and five hanged. Abijah Wright, captured trying to kidnap a man for the British, was convicted of burglary and executed. James Sutton, who led a mutiny on a Whig privateer, was executed as a pirate; Thomas Wilkinson, also sentenced to death for piracy, escaped the hangman only because of an error in his trial.[7] The most famous loyalist "guerrilla" band in Pennsylvania was composed of at least three brothers: Aaron, Moses, and Levi Doan. The Doans were not just a criminal gang taking advantage of war conditions but loyalist partisans, whose daring robberies, which commenced as early as 1777, became increasingly flamboyant between 1781 and 1784.[8]

The struggle to suppress disaffection in New Jersey coincided from 1777 until 1782 with the state's effort to establish a viable government under the shadow of the British Army's mighty garrison in New York City. The British had invaded New Jersey during the autumn of 1776, and this brief occupation had shattered the coherence of the Revolutionary government. When Howe temporarily withdrew the last of his forces from the state in June 1777, in preparation for the invasion of Pennsylvania, the patriots' chief concern was preventing the sizable loyalist minority from operating openly and inviting the British troops to return. Although the new state preserved its provincial court system, the legal initiative rested with a new body, the Council of Safety, created early in 1777 to provide executive leadership to a weak government. Composed of twelve members chosen by the legislature, the Council included Attorney General William

Paterson. The Council had the power to imprison those suspected of active disloyalty, and, according to Richard C. Haskett,
it "became a powerful agency of indictment." When existing
courts and grand juries slackened in their efforts to detect and
punish conspiracies, the Council would "descend upon a
county," order arrests, hear witnesses, jail suspicious figures, and
even transport them to safer prisons elsewhere in the state. In a
single day of such emergency proceedings in Morristown, in July
1777, the Council ordered the arrest of forty-eight persons. This
rough but effective means of indicting suspected loyalists gave
New Jersey an unusually strong hand in its subsequent prosecutions because William Paterson served as the leader of the
Council in these inquisitorial matters and also as prosecuting
attorney when the cases came to court.[9]

Even with the impetus that Council of Safety investigations
and indictments gave to suppression of loyalist activity, the court
system barely managed to function during 1777 and 1778. Many
court officials had little training; constables tried to protect their
own insecure positions by creating as little stir as possible;
periodic incursions by the New Jersey Volunteers or British
troops often forced cancellation of court sessions; communications between judges and the Assembly broke down, so that
judges dismissed cases because they had not received copies of the
laws that the defendants in their courts had supposedly violated.
Nevertheless, under Paterson's relentless prodding, the courts
vindicated the state's capacity to exact support for the Revolution from its citizens. Normally, the most serious sanction was
confiscation of the estates of those who had left their homes and
had presumably joined the King's forces. The use of seditious
language was the next most serious violation of state law and
periodically provoked a rash of prosecutions intended as a warning to covert opponents of the Revolution who tested the new
government with abusive language and whispered subversion.
The most widespread form of resistance was simply refusing
militia service—an action that did not necessarily spring from
disloyal motives but that had to be punished in order to maintain the vitality of the legal system.[10]

New Jersey government sought to penetrate and overcome the
kind of covert, sullen, unco-operative disaffection that did not

necessarily produce overt acts of disloyalty but that encouraged disrespect and mocked the capacity of the government to exercise its authority. One of the functions of law enforcement seemed to be to identify and expose men with these attitudes—to clarify and make explicit the relationship between the state and its shadowy internal opponents. Constable William Tatem reported his chance meeting with a suspicious figure named Joseph Cogil. Their conversation reveals the kinds of tensions that existed at the local level between Revolutionary government and disaffected individuals. According to Constable Tatem, Cogil demanded to know "what authority I had to summon men to court. It being always the sheriff's business, I told him I had an order from the sheriff to summon such a number of men of my own town to come to court; he then insisted on seeing my order, and if I did not show it to him he would not obey. I then took the order out of my pocket and read it to him," including the part "which mentioned the name of the Chief Justice by whose order the Court was called. He . . . replied he did not care for the Chief Justice nor none of the rest of the devils, that the Presbyterians were striving to get the rule into their own hands and that he would never be subject to a Presbyterian government, that he was as good a Whig as ever sat upon a pot till independency was declared but that the war would not be over the next summer, that a great many of the soldiers had come home [deserted], that the next summer the English would be here, and that George would have the rule." It was a curiously intimate exchange for constable and suspect, suggesting that these conflicts over authority lay close to the surface of everyday life; and after asking Tatem to lend him money to cover his expenses as a defendant, Cogil went peaceably to court.[11]

Loyalist disaffection in Delaware was, paradoxically, weaker and yet more widespread than in New Jersey. This small, rural charter colony, ruled by the Penns and closely tied to Pennsylvania during the colonial period, had not been a particularly politicized society until the Revolutionary crises of 1775 and 1776 forced men to choose sides and compete for power. Thomas Robinson, in southernmost Sussex County, was the most active loyalist in the state. He claimed to have obtained 5,000 signatures on a petition opposing independence in 1776, while a rival petition favoring the break with England attracted only 300 names. While the Assembly, dominated by the northern and middle counties of New Castle and Kent, supported the Continental Congress and created a new government, large crowds in Sussex County during the first election under the new regime tore down liberty poles, cheered the name of the King, and drove known Whigs away from polling places with stout hickory clubs. The loyalist revival reached into the northern counties as well, and the first new legislature under independence was, ironically, dominated by men opposed to the Revolution or at least unwilling to allow Delaware's leading Whigs and delegates to Congress—Caesar Rodney and Thomas McKean—to continue to represent the state. Only in New Castle County were the judges, named by the legislature, Whigs; in Sussex and Kent they were almost all notorious supporters of British authority. As militia commander in Kent and part of Sussex County, Caesar Rodney launched a campaign to seize known loyalists in the southern part of the state, but trading by sea with the British in New York continued unabated.[12]

Howe's invasion of Pennsylvania in early September 1777 had the effect of bringing enthusiastic loyalists into the open and then exposing far more of them to Whig retaliation than the British Army could possibly protect—a phenomenon repeatedly duplicated elsewhere with the appearance of British troops during the later stages of the war. The Sussex County loyalists had expected Howe to sail his invasion force up the Delaware River; they planned to help secure control of the state as the British ships arrived, and they contributed several knowledgeable river pilots to Howe's force. Thomas Robinson, on board one of the British vessels en route to the Chesapeake, pleaded with Howe to land 500 soldiers at the mouth of the Delaware and promised that such a force would attract 5,000 loyalists to arms. When Howe's men landed some weeks later at Head of Elk in Maryland instead, Delaware loyalists had to move northward to aid the British offensive. British troops occupied Wilmington briefly, seizing the governmental archives and doing considerable damage to farms and buildings in the area. A number of New Castle County loyalists managed to elude officials and join Howe's forces. But Howe's choice of the Chesapeake instead of the Delaware River as the water route for his invasion had the effect of by-passing Delaware and depriving the considerable majority of Sussex County loyalists of an opportunity to flock to the royal standard and throw the weight of their numbers into the struggle for control of the entire state. There were many rumors of conspiracies and probably active planning of loyalist risings late in the summer of 1777, but none actually occurred. "Thus passed," Harold B. Hancock observes, "the most favorable opportunity for a successful insurrection."[13]

The decline of loyalist fortunes in Delaware the following winter was dramatic. A British officer stationed in New Castle in October 1777 had noted that the people of Delaware "are certainly well-affected in general and have brought us large supplies of everything wanted." The dockets of New Castle County courts the following winter were crammed with prosecutions of people who sold goods to the British. William Foot, of Wilmington, admitted selling meat to the British and declared that if the American Army starved, it was no concern of his. William Hazlet, in October 1777, had warned people of British military invincibility and referred "in a laughing manner" to the rebels "making old Miller . . . a general." The wealthiest loyalist in the state, and apparently one of the most energetic, was Joshua North. Taken before the president of the state, John McKinly, on September 1, 1777, and accused of discouraging enlistment in the American Army, he was released because he and McKinly were relatives. He fled to Philadelphia but returned to New Castle in December; facing charges that he had given information that helped the British capture three Continental soldiers during the occupation of Wilmington, he fled again to Philadelphia. After British withdrawal from the city, North was arrested and returned to Delaware, where he served nine weeks in jail before securing release on £3,000 bail. He decided to join the British Army in Georgia and rode overland on horseback during the winter of 1778–79, sleeping on the ground and providing British troops with useful intelligence prior to the American siege of Savannah in 1779. The surprising numerical strength of the Delaware loyalists and the ease with which a weak Revolutionary government controlled them derived from the essential moderation of both groups and from the readiness of Pennsylvania and Maryland to send troops into the state when rumors of loyalist insurrections abounded. It was possible for a loyalist to remain in Delaware as late as June 1778 "without trimming," Joseph Galloway later explained. "They were a moderate people in the Delaware government. There was throughout the war a majority in favor of retaining their allegiance, but [Delaware] was a small [state], surrounded by larger ones and incapable of acting of itself." Galloway's estimates of loyalist strength, usually absurdly high, were in the case of Delaware probably reasonably accurate.[14]

36

Whig Containment of
Loyalist Activity in
New York State

IT may never be known how many loyalists there were in New York State during the War for Independence. Moreover, the lines between patriotism and disaffection were more indistinct and shifting than anywhere else in Revolutionary America. A Long Island innkeeper spoke for many when, being asked if he was Whig or Tory, he replied, "I told him I was for peace." Nevertheless, there appear to have been a significantly higher proportion of loyalists in New York than in any other state. The presence of the British in New York City, the large number of recent immigrants from Britain, the relatively sharp cultural, economic, and political divisions within the society, and the military threat posed by Burgoyne's invasion stimulated types of behavior that Whigs considered dangerous or suspicious. Baltus Vankleek, a witness told New York officials in an attempt to cast a sufficiently wide net, "is an equivocal character. All of [his] connections are equivocal," and, specifically, when Dutchess County voters met to decide whether or not to create a committee of safety, Vankleek "was of that party which voted against the committee."[1]

New York's machinery for "detecting and defeating conspiracies" was centralized, thorough, and moderate, indicating the Whig leadership's political competence and sensitivity to the stresses and heterogeneity of their society. It was the product of a surprisingly short period of trial and error. On June 16, 1776, the provincial Convention defined citizenship and treason. Everyone living in the state owed it allegiance; anyone making war against it, adhering to the King, or giving aid to its enemies was guilty of treason and subject to the death penalty. The Convention instructed county committees of safety to arrest not only traitors but also all those "whose going at large at this critical time" appeared "dangerous to the liberties of the state." Faced with imminent British attack, Washington asked the committee in New York City to remove "all equivocal and suspicious persons" for detention in Connecticut, though he also requested that their property be protected and that they be well treated. On August 7 the provincial Convention dismissed the committee that had been coordinating this activity throughout the state and appointed committees of its own members to hear charges against suspected persons and to decide whether or not to banish them to Connecticut. As the number of suspects grew, the Convention decided to establish new and effective machinery, and on September 21, 1776, it appointed a Committee and Commission for Detecting and Defeating Conspiracies. This consisted of seven men and became the keystone in a network of inquisitorial and quasi-judicial bodies that operated throughout the state. It had the power to arrest and seize evidence. Troops were placed at its disposal, as well as generous funds from the state treasurer. The chairman and two members made up a quorum. It controlled and directed all antisubversive activity within the state, including that of county committees. As the Committee and Commission became active, the older county-level organizations atrophied, and the state body replaced them with its own district-level boards. The most common penalty inflicted by the Committee and Commission was exile to a neighboring state, where the accused would live under surveillance. These prisoners had to pay the expenses of their transportation from the state or risk being jailed along with those persons regarded as unusually dangerous. Less offensive persons of doubtful allegiance were paroled on condition that they post bond guaranteeing their good behavior, or were allowed to move to New York City, where they could do less mischief than living on parole in patriot-held territory.[2]

From the outset, the Committee and Commission tried to act

in the most moderate and inoffensive manner still consistent with rigor and vigilance. It sought medical aid for sick prisoners and detainees, ordered gentle treatment of women and children, fed destitute suspects, and allowed the dependents of loyalists to join fathers and husbands who had been exiled or sent to New York City. The Committee and Commission became more concerned with identifying persons of doubtful loyalty than with punishment or harassment. Early in 1777 the provincial Convention ordered the Commission to administer an oath to all suspected persons pledging their obedience to the laws of the state and their willingness to reveal any conspiracies against the American cause. Those taking the oath would be relieved of suspicion and all disabilities; those refusing would have six days to either change their minds or move to New York City; those refusing to take the oath and to move to New York City would be regarded as "open enemies of this state"; and those who did not appear before the commissioners would be seen "as having gone over to the enemy" and would forfeit their property to the state.[3]

When necessary, the Commission moved with speed and energy. It frequently voted expenditures for blacksmiths to make manacles and handcuffs—an indication that numerous suspects came before the Commission in chains. On December 26, 1776, it "resolved that Enoch Crosby, assuming the name of [blank] do forthwith repair to Mount Ephraim and use his utmost art to discover the designs, places or resort, and route of certain disaffected persons in that quarter who have formed a design of joining the enemy." The Commission provided Crosby with papers allowing him to move freely in areas where suspicious movements were under close surveillance and with other papers identifying him as a British agent; it also voted him wages and funds to cover his expenses. Within ninety days Crosby provided the Commission with details of several loyalist recruiting operations—their organizers and leaders and the names of men who intended to join the King's forces. The Commission also created an adequate bureaucracy. To house prisoners, it established a number of prison ships on the Hudson, to which the most dangerous suspects were sent at their own expense. A warden, a victualer (food-supply officer), a commissary, and a clerk were named to administer these temporary prisons. At first, prisoners the state could not handle were sent to Hartford, Connecticut for confinement, but in January 1778 the Commission brought all its prisoners back from Hartford, reconsidered their cases, released some, and kept others in confinement in New York jails. Because there were no courts, the death penalty for treason, established in 1776, was not imposed. Therefore, in 1777, the provincial Convention authorized military court-martial proceedings at the discretion of the Continental Army, with the limitation that the Convention must approve impositions of the death penalty. In April 1777 court-martial trials occurred in Albany, Orange, Dutchess, and Ulster counties; as a result of these trials, the Convention approved, on April 29, 1777, three executions for spying, though it later commuted one of the death sentences. On May 3 court-martial trials sentenced fourteen to death, imprisoned one, and acquitted five others. The Convention upheld twelve of these death sentences. Commissioners sent to investigate rumors of loyalist uprisings on Livingston Manor and in Albany County rounded up seventeen alleged conspirators, but a court-martial released all but two of them. On May 29, 1777, John Jay proposed the creation and operation of civil courts to try cases of treason, insurrection, illegal assembly, broken oaths of allegiance, and other political offenses in order "to awe the disaffected." Although such a court met in Tryon County, courts-martial continued to be the primary means of imposing penalties for treason. The Commission for Detecting Conspiracies enlarged and expanded its operations. It moved around the state and between 1776 and 1779 tried more than a thousand cases. Over 600 defendants were paroled on bail, a smaller number closely confined, a few released on pledge of good behavior, and many dismissed after taking an oath of allegiance. After July 1778, administration of an oath became the primary means of resolving these cases. By this time the number of loyalists and suspects who had not already gone to New York City or taken Revolutionary oaths was down to a manageable figure.[4]

Two cases illustrated the work of the Commission. One of the earliest concerned the activities of David Akins, blacksmith from Fredericksburgh, New York. Akins said he had traveled to Westchester, New York, late in November 1776 in an unsuccessful effort to collect a debt. Rogers's Rangers captured him while he was sleeping at a cousin's home and took him to a nearby fort, where "a major whose name he has forgot" threatened to charge him as a spy because he carried a pass from the rebel government. In return for release, another British officer, Archibald Campbell, asked Akins to carry certain papers promising British protection to five loyalists living in his neighborhood. He agreed, and Campbell gave Akins six protection papers—one for himself and one each for Malcom Morrison, John Kain, Alexander Kidd, Matthew Paterson, and Charles Collins. Akins returned home and sought out Morrison, "who appeared much pleased" and paid Akins for bringing him the document. Kain, however, was "shy about it" and leery of accepting the document but finally agreed. Akins became nervous when he learned that Morrison had sent a little girl to the home of Lemuel Wilmot, a notorious loyalist who had already "gone over to the enemy," to show Wilmot's wife the protection document as a reassurance that there were loyalists in the neighborhood to look after her. Akins told Kain that "Morrison had divulged the affair of the protection." To protect Akins from further implication in the matter, Kain suggested that he "would fall out with" Akins "but that he must not mind it" and that both men should burn their protection documents. Akins was shaken by all of this stealthy business, and he told his story to the Commission, which administered an oath of allegiance and discharged him. Akins's testimony gave the commission plenty of leads to pursue. It ordered Kain's arrest and confronted him with at least the gist of Akins's allegations. Kain admitted receiving a British protection document from Akins but declared that after showing it to his wife, who was "much dissatisfied at his having [it]," he burned the incriminating document. Kain denied soliciting it, assumed that the British had been given his name by his brother, who "he thinks is with the enemy," and declared himself "friendly to the measures America is pursuing." Kain added that "he and Akins have been upon very bad terms for a long time." Extending their inquiry into the matter, the commissioners interrogated Malcom Morrison's friend Roswell Wilcox. Wilcox admitted that as he and Morrison had stood in front of the fireplace in William Paterson's house on the previous Tuesday, "Morrison asked him in a whisper whether, if the regular [British] Army was to come, . . .

he shouldn't want a protection." Wilcox concurred but then, realizing the implications of such a remark, decided to leave. Morrison followed him outside and persuaded him to come back inside to a "back room," where he showed him a "printed paper" that "purported to be an order from the Commander in Chief of the British army to all his officers, soldiers, and others not to molest or injure . . . Morrison in his person or property." Wilcox angrily told Morrison that such a document was dangerous to possess, for it would obligate its holder to fight for the British; Morrison replied that "the meaning of the . . . protection was to save his property from plunder." Because Morrison was "in liquor," Wilcox told him they would discuss it further in the morning. The next day he told Morrison that he was very disturbed about the British document, and Morrison responded that he "wished he had never seen it." Wilcox further told the Commission that Akins was no innocent victim and that in Fredericksburg he "is generally reputed to be very disaffected to the American cause." Akins allegedly had admitted to Wilcox that he signed the Continental Association in 1775 to protect himself from Whig retaliation; "his moral character is very suspicious and questionable," Wilcox concluded. Arrested by the Commission, Matthew Paterson admitted that Akins had offered him a protection document but he had refused to accept it.[5]

On September 9, 1777, a different case of subversion unfolded in testimony before the commission. "Jack (a Negro belonging to Hendrick Freligh) . . . saith [the transcript recorded] that on the morning after the burning of his master's barn, Teunis Peer" came to the Freligh farm; and after commiserating with Freligh, Peer "winked" at Jack and indicated he wanted to talk to him. As soon as the two got behind a haystack, Peer said to him, " 'Now this barn is burnt; 'tis a pity but Captain Sheldon's barn [will be] burnt tonight also. . . . That would scare them' (meaning the Whigs), he understood" Peer to imply. Peer then asked Jack to carry a load of burning coals the following night and "throw it on the thatched roof of . . . Sheldon's barn." Peer explained he could not do it himself because he was "too near a neighbor" of Sheldon's. Jack refused and told Peer that if he wanted someone to burn down Captain Sheldon's barn he should "do it himself." Apparently caught off guard by the slave's impertinence, Peer assured Jack that he only meant that if Jack saw fit to do so "it would be best." Before they parted, Freligh's nephew Jacob Freligh happened upon them. Peer told him "that he had best go away from his uncle." For although "a great accident had happened," Peer warned that he would be "damned if that would be all, for a worse thing woud befall his uncle." Despite Peer's threat to make "a great disturbance" if Jack revealed their conversation, Jack told Freligh and Sheldon the whole story. Freligh told Jack to pretend to go along with Peer's plot. When Jack went to Peer's home and said he was ready to burn Sheldon's barn, Peer replied that he was afraid of being incriminated; he denied having asked Jack the previous day to burn Sheldon's barn but told Jack "he might use his own pleasure" about committing the act. Sometime after all this transpired, Jack, the slave, became involved in inimical conduct. A group of eighteen or nineteen loyalist refugees hiding in the woods, including several relatives of the Freligh family, persuaded him to keep them supplied with provisions. Young Jacob Freligh's affidavit to the commission reporting Jack's involvement with the fugitives led to the slave's arrest and to his testimony implicating Teunis Peer. Jack was imprisoned aboard a prison ship in the Hudson from September 10 to October 2, 1777, and then returned to his master.[6]

37

Tenant–Landlord Conflict and
Revolutionary Schism in
the Hudson Valley

COMPLICATING and intensifying the Revolutionary struggle
at the local level in New York's Hudson Valley was the deeply
rooted divergence of interest between aristocratic landlords and
their tenants. Except for New York, sections of New Jersey where
aggrieved tenants had rioted against landlords in 1747, and
portions of Virginia, agricultural tenantry was relatively uncommon in the American colonies. In New York the great majority of
the rural population consisted of tenant farmers. The landlord-
tenant relationship had not been a one-sided exploitation of the
poor by the rich. The landlords were not a homogeneous interest
group. Some were simply land speculators of the kind Cadwallader Colden detested; others were land developers who built
towns, established farms and stores in previously undeveloped
tracts of land and attracted settlers more easily with leases than
with sale of land; and the majority of Hudson Valley grandees
combined rental of portions of land on their vast country estates
with mercantile or legal careers and political activity in New
York City. There was always much more land suitable for cultivation than there was available farm labor to develop it, and
therefore landlords competed fiercely for tenants, offering low
rent, sometimes deferring rental payments until a tenant had
established himself, and often providing free houses, tools, building materials, and supplies. The profit margin on agricultural
rentals remained relatively low, although the long-term specu-

lative advantages were considerably higher. The political role of tenants demonstrated their rising status; many qualified to vote in Assembly elections, and on some manors all adult male inhabitants voted on local government issues. Members of the aristocracy frequently bemoaned their inability to influence tenant voting.[1]

This amount of democracy and opportunity, according to Patricia U. Bonomi, made the land system of colonial New York something other than the "feudal" relationship of landlord and tenant, as some historians have portrayed it. Nevertheless, she makes clear, the interests of the two groups diverged so sharply that unusually strong social stress developed. In the northern New York frontier and on the western side of the Hudson Valley, ever-plentiful land kept the system open and fluid. But between the Hudson and New York's border with Connecticut and Massachusetts, where the largest and oldest estates were situated, all arable land was under lease and cultivation. In this region conflict between settlers with New England backgrounds and their aristocratic landlords was endemic. The immediate issues were, first, alienation fees, which landlords charged tenants who sold leasing rights, called "quarter-sales" because they often absorbed 25 per cent of the proceeds of the transaction, and, second, leases-at-will instead of long-term freehold leases. These points of dispute, all of which made the landlords edgy, were of several kinds: Colden's hostility to the great landowners, boundary disputes with the neighboring New England states, and unresolved litigation about old Indian claims. In this mood, the landlords clashed with squatters from the New England states; bands of undisciplined Yankee settlers forcibly resisted the landlords' efforts to burn down their cabins and drive them out of the province. The "infection" of illegal squatting Yankees soon inspired the formerly contented Dutch and German tenants to complain about their treatment at the hands of the landlords. There were serious clashes between landlords and Yankee settlers between 1740 and 1757; and in May 1766 a full-scale tenant insurrection erupted, initially in Dutchess County, involving both Yankee intruders and legitimate tenants who were allegedly "seduced" by the New Englanders. Inspired by the example of the New York Sons of Liberty during the Stamp Act crisis, mobs of several hundred men—some organized into military companies with elected judicial tribunals—briefly occupied parts of Dutchess County and the Livingston Manor and kept up a running battle with provincial officials until a fully mobilized militia restored order by the end of the summer. More than sixty men were indicted, pleaded guilty, and received fines, imprisonment, or pillorying; their leader in Dutchess County, a New Englander, William Prendergast, was convicted of high treason and sentenced to death. In a prudent gesture, however, New York officials successfully secured his pardon from the Crown. These tensions were by no means dissipated, and they exercised a stubborn and complicated influence on Revolutionary politics in New York after independence. Where landlords were loyalists who had fled to British protection in New York City and finally into exile in England, the tenants had a chance to benefit from the confiscation of the estate; in one dramatic case, in which the landlords, the Livingston family, were leading patriots, tenants concluded that their only hope lay in an insurrection in support of the British. The largest estate in the province, Philipsburgh Manor, in Westchester County, illustrated the operation of these social tensions even in a setting almost devoid of conflict and rancor.[2]

In 1775, the Philipsburgh Manor had more than 270 tenant farmers occupying lots that averaged 200 acres. Merchants and artisans usually farmed as well, and all the inhabitants of the manor were tenants. When Frederick Philipse, the third lord of the manor, inherited the enormous estate in 1751, he persuaded his tenants to accept a modest increase in rents in return for a promise not to raise them again during his lifetime. Yonkers, the center of the estate, consisted of the Philipse family's imposing mansion, a church, two mills, a tavern, and a fishhouse. There were smaller villages at Tarrytown and Dobbs Ferry. In contrast with neighboring Cortlandt Manor, where some farmers owned their own land and many heirs of the family owned parcels of property, Philipsburgh remained the sole possession of the head of the family. Tenant families on the estate had lived there for generations; they were free to divide or sell their leases or to sublease, and the lord of the manor assisted in making improvements on the land at reasonable terms.[3] Philipse's tenants were content; and, moreover, because he held undisputed title to the manor, they were more secure than tenants on many estates where legal squabbles over property rights and inheritance jeopardized the positions of leaseholders. Although they were technically tenants-at-will, with no legally assured security of tenure, there was considerable legal opinion in New York that Philipse's custom of not evicting tenants amounted to legal protection against eviction. When tenants sold lease rights to land on which they had made improvements, Philipse received one-third of the proceeds of the first sale and one-sixth on all subsequent sales, marginally more generous than the hated "quarter-sale" requirements. Yet this evidence of Philipse's liberality and conscientious concern for the well-being of his tenants subtly underscored the divergence between his interests and those of his tenants. When the loyalist claims commissioners in London, seeking in 1784 to ascertain his losses in the Revolution, asked him whether he had possessed "absolute" title to Philipsburgh Manor before the Revolution, he responded, according to the third-person record of the testimony, that "he does not well know how to give a regular answer. In some sense it might be said not . . . and yet he certainly must look on him[self] as the proprietor. He could not turn off a tenant because he did not like his face but he had at the same time the power of raising their rents, which was tantamount to it." Apparently his pledge in 1751 not to raise rents again in his lifetime was an obligation of personal honor and not a legal impediment. Nor did it preclude his requesting his tenants to accept an interim rent increase, for he told the claims commissioners that "he had it in agitation to have raised the rents about the time of the troubles commencing" in 1775 and 1776. The purpose of Philipse's testimony about his harmonious relationship with his tenants was to show that the level of their rent and obligations did not gauge the full value of the confiscated estate for which he was seeking compensation. Nonetheless, his phraseology clearly indicated his paternalistic view of his role in society. "The rents were very regularly paid every year," he testified. "They were rather acknowledgments than rents. He should [that is, could] have doubled his rents with great ease."[4]

Philipse had served for thirty years as a Westchester County representative to the Assembly and in 1775 had worked hard to dissociate the Assembly from the proceedings of the Continental Congress. In 1776 a band of armed Whigs captured him, took him to Connecticut, and put him to work. But, by his own admission, he was well treated. After six months New York officials paroled him to go to New York City. The British occupied his manor and turned his mansion at Yonkers into a military headquarters. After British evacuation in 1783, New York State confiscated nearly the entire estate and sold it. Under the terms of a 1779 statute, tenants on the manor—both Philipse's own tenants in 1776 and those who purchased leases from pre-Revolutionary occupants during the war—had pre-emptive, or first refusal, rights to purchase the land they occupied if they could prove that they had taken an "active and decided part" in the Revolution and could summon the endorsement of twelve "reputable inhabitants of the county, of known and undoubted attachment to the American cause." The requirement that twelve known patriots attest to a tenant's loyalty indicated that the state had no ready and reliable way to determine how most of the population had behaved during the War for Independence. In Westchester County, near or inside British lines, Beatrice G. Reubens explains, a tenant "might find it extremely difficult to obtain twelve references," and in 1785 the legislature exempted those people from that requirement who could pay for their estates in cash. Others had paid a third down and received a 7-per-cent mortgage on the balance. Although confiscated loyalist estates, especially those contiguous to urban areas, fell into the hands of the *nouveaux riches*, businessmen who had prospered during the War for Independence, the effect in Philipsburgh was relatively leveling and democratic. "The immediate effect of the sale by the state," Beatrice Reubens concludes, "was to displace one wealthy and powerful landlord who had ruled over 50,000 acres and more than 270 tenants and to install 287 independent owners with an average holding of 174 acres. Moreover, at least 194 of the new owners, or well over two-thirds of the total, bought farms they had previously worked as tenants or inherited from tenants."[5]

If Philipsburgh Manor represented in subdued and unspectacular terms the cleavage of tenant and landlord in Revolutionary New York, the struggle on Livingston Manor, in Albany County, gave full vent to bitter antagonisms and social tensions. Together, various branches of the Livingston family owned 160,000 acres in Albany County—an area bounded by Dutchess County on the south, Massachusetts and Connecticut on the east, and the Hudson River on the west. During the tenant riots of 1766, more than 200 armed tenants had, according to one observer, "turned levellers" and "marched to murder the lord of the manor and level his house unless he would sign leases for them agreeable to their form." "After independence," Staughton Lynd writes, in one of the most compelling of his studies of Revolutionary radicalism, "Livingston Manor became a microcosm of the struggle over who should rule at home. The landlords were the traditional leaders of the anti-British party in the state; the tenants were New York's most obdurate malcontents. Where landlords were Tories, as in neighboring Dutchess County, tenant uprisings could be harnessed to the Revolution, . . . but on Livingston Manor, where the landlords were prominent Whigs, the tenants became vigorous Tories."[6] This configuration appeared early in the final stages of the pre-Revolutionary crisis. In July 1775, Robert R. Livingston reminded his friend John Jay that "I told you sometime before I left you that many of our tenants here refused to sign the association and resolved to stand by the King, as they called it, in hopes that if he succeeded they should have their lands." The fact that two Livingstons held commissions in the Continental Army had "frighted" the tenants away from outright loyalism and toward neutrality; "they assert that they cannot engage in the controversy since, as their leases [are] not for lives, their families must want when they are killed. To deprive them of all excuse, my father has declared to them a new lease shall be given to the family of every man who is killed in the service." Now, Livingston complained bitterly, the tenants had the presumption to petition the provincial Convention in a complaint "replete with falsehoods and charges injurious" to the Livingston family. From another part of the manor, Henry Livingston bluntly concurred: "The tenants here are great villains. Some of them are resolved to take advantage of the times and make their landlords give them leases forever." The tenants were serious about capitalizing on their new opportunity. The

Committee of Safety of Livingston Manor compiled considerable
evidence of tenant disaffection from the Revolutionary cause: a
threat by one man to shoot his captain if he was forced to join
the American Army, another who predicted that celebrations
would greet the arrival of British troops, and word of a mysterious "King's book" in which tenants had signed their pledges to
fight for the royal cause. In the autumn of 1776 reports reached
the manor that 400 loyalists had taken up arms, and the following spring came news that desertions had crippled the militia.[7]

Rumors in 1777 of Burgoyne's attempted drive through New
York State from Canada galvanized the tenant insurgents. "Almost everybody in the upper manor [of the Livingston do-
mains], particularly in the eastern part of it," the Commission
for Detecting Conspiracies reported to the provincial Congress in
May 1777, "appears to have engaged with the enemy, first by
taking an oath of secrecy and then by an oath of allegiance to the
King of Great Britain; it appears to have been their design to
have waited till the enemy came up, when they were to rise and
take the Whigs prisoners." The price of this collaboration, according to William Smith, Jr., who was in seclusion on the manor,
was "pay from the time of the juncture" with British troops and
"200 acres of land" for each man. The whole enterprise depended on the accuracy of rumors of Burgoyne's movements.
Early in May 1777, when it became known that bands of tenants
were collecting arms and preparing to fight, Burgoyne was still in
Canada. The tenants were poorly armed and, despite the theft of
several hundred pounds of powder from the Livingston mill at
Rhinebeck, were poorly supplied with ball and powder. The
Livingstons mobilized dependable Dutchess County and New
England militiamen, who quickly dispersed the conspirators after
brief skirmishes in which six tenants were killed and hundreds
arrested. "If you give anything by compulsions of this sort," the
elder Robert Livingston had told his son at the time of the 1766
tenant rising, "you must give up everything"; the Livingstons
did not need to fret very long over how they should respond to a
tenant conspiracy, and their swift response overwhelmed the
tenants. Nevertheless, the experience left Robert Livingston un-
nerved. William Smith, Jr., coolly noted the effect on his kinsman and former ally: "He did not utter a sentiment which he

did not contradict . . . except his execrations upon his tenants. His fears have driven him to temerity. He exclaims against setting up any government at this juncture. . . . Poor gentleman, he says his tenants owe him £10,000. He can't bear the thought that his indulgences show he has no influence over them—much less that they are in such a temper as to prevent him from riding about his own Manor—and, seeing no safety but in their expulsion, hints his wishes that they may all be hanged and their children starved." Though there were rumors of plans to hang the leaders of the conspiracy, no executions were reported. But the Livingstons and their Albany County neighbors the Van Rensselaers did maintain their estates and imposed "prolonged, antiquated, and degrading leasehold tenures affecting 260,000 persons and 1,800,000 acres" until the mid-nineteenth century, when fresh agrarian violence finally did away with agricultural tenancy in New York.[8]

In Dutchess County, situated between Philipsburgh and Livingston manors, the struggle between landlords and tenants became more protracted, more complex, and more political. The Revolution divided the aristocracy in the county. In the northern part, the Whig Beekman and Livingston families dominated; the major landowners in the south were Philip Philipse, Beverley Robinson, and Roger Morris, all of whom became loyalists; and the middle of the county, where tenantry was weaker, was dominated by "a rising middle-class of freeholders which disliked the domination of the landed aristocracy." Led by aggressive and newly emergent politicians like Dirck Brinckerhoff and Melancton Smith, this segment of the county strongly supported the Revolution and also capitalized on its opportunities during the war to gain power and influence at the expense of the Whig aristocracy. James Duane had predicted such a contest in 1775, when he stressed the importance of aristocratic control of the militia: "We must think in time of the means of assuring the reins of government when these commotions shall subside. Licentiousness is the natural object of a civil war [here Duane crossed out "war" and substituted "discord"] and it can only be guarded against by placing the command of the troops in the hands of men of property and rank, who, by that means, will preserve the same authority over the minds of the people which they enjoyed in the time of tranquillity." The maintenance of stability was by no means that simple. Inflation, depreciated currency, food shortages, and low pay for soldiers bore down inexorably on the populace. Revolutionary committees reconstituted themselves in 1779 to detect and punish persons charging exorbitant prices, and in the wake of that agitation came demands to sell confiscated loyalist estates in Dutchess County to former tenants. Loyalists in New York City circulated promises that the Crown would confiscate rebel estates and give the land to the tenants after defeating the rebels, and middle-class Whigs in the county responded by pledging former loyalist estates to tenants who supported the Revolution. In 1779 the state seized the vast estates of Roger Morris and Beverly Robinson in southern Dutchess County and placed the property in the hands of sequestration commissioners. These officials, in turn, leased the land to refugees who had fled from British-occupied areas adjacent to New York City and in the process evicted former tenants still occupying their old farms. In February and March 1780 the New York Assembly voted to sell confiscated loyalist property. Of 496 forfeited lots of land sold under this law, 455 were in southern Dutchess County and 414 came from the former estates of Beverly Robinson and Roger Morris. There were 401 purchasers of these 455 units of land, which by law could not exceed 500 acres each. Probably a majority of the former tenants secured ownership of the land they had previously rented, although a large number were dispossessed by other successful bidders for the property. The Livingstons vehemently opposed this disposition of confiscated land. Brinckerhoff, the new champion of the middling elements of the county, led the legislative fight for the sale of the land. During the 1780's, however, most of the purchasers of these farms fell behind in their payments and lost possession of the land. A good deal of tenancy survived the Revolution in southern Dutchess County, though not in the form of the leases-by-will of the pre-Revolutionary period. The structure of society after the Revolution did not differ radically from that of the colonial era, but, as Lynd argues, the "brief hour of domination over Dutchess politics" that antilandlord spokesmen enjoyed in 1780 "foreshadowed the decline of the aristocracy in the politics of New York a generation later."[9]

38

Iroquois Adherence to the Crown

INDIAN tribes constituted a tempting source of military strength and a delicate problem in diplomacy for the British at the outset of the war. The energetic and impartial work of the Crown's two superintendents for Indian affairs—John Stuart for the southern and Sir William Johnson for the northern tribes—in fostering trade and protecting Indian lands from illegal land-grabbing had created a reservoir of good will for the British. To the extent that a large portion of the Iroquois nation looked on the Crown as protector and benefactor and fought for the British in the War for Independence out of moral obligation as well as self-interest, these Indians were loyalists and subjects as well as independent military allies.[1]

The six tribes of the Iroquois Confederacy—Mohawks, Oneidas, Onondagas, Cayugas, Senecas, and, after 1722, Tuscaroras—situated in a large area from southern Ontario to northeastern Pennsylvania and between the Adirondacks and Lake Erie, had a peculiar relationship to white America.[2] The Mohawks tended to favor the British and the Senecas the French, but not until it was clear that the British were winning the Seven Years' War did the Iroquois Confederacy give the British substantial military support in the successful assault on French-held Fort Niagara, and then only the Mohawks participated directly in combat. Throughout the first three-quarters of the eighteenth century, the Iroquois' primary political and diplomatic goals were preserving access to their vast hunting lands west of the Appalachians and securing the support of the British Crown against white land speculators and settlers who sought to infringe on their territory. In addition to mutually advantageous military alliances, the advanced Iroquois appreciated the technological advantages that muskets, farming tools, and brass kettles brought to their economy and social development. Dependence on these goods led the Iroquois to neglect the older hunting skills but also conferred upon them military superiority over rival tribes.

The most remarkable feature of this relationship was the Iroquois' adroitness at defining and pursuing their own interests even while being drawn ever deeper into involvement with white society. Both facilitating and capitalizing on Iroquois statecraft, Sir William Johnson sought to harmonize Iroquois interests with those of the Crown and succeeded in constructing a durable relationship of mutual respect between the British government and Iroquois leadership. Johnson's career—even in the acquisitive and burgeoning atmosphere of New York society—was singularly spectacular. Born in Ireland in 1715, he emigrated to Boston in 1737 and the next year moved to the Mohawk Valley in New York to manage the property of his uncle, who had married into the De Lancey family. As an Indian trader, land speculator, agent for the British government, and militia officer, he became deeply involved in the life of the Mohawks. He learned their language, was inducted into their tribe, received vast gifts of Indian land, and used all of his influence to prevent the encroachment of white speculators into Iroquois territory. In 1768, after years of maneuvering, he persuaded the British government to guarantee, in the Treaty of Fort Stanwix, Indian possession of land west of the old Proclamation Line of 1763 in return for cession of a vast area east of that line. To Indian and white settlers alike on his estate in the Mohawk Valley, Johnson was an indulgent and baronial overlord, who expected only loyalty in return for loans, gifts, and protection.

When Sir William Johnson died in July 1774, Iroquois adherence to the Crown was a substantial but elusive alignment. During the pre-Revolutionary period, New England missionaries, led by the Reverend Samuel Kirkland, had won considerable influence among the Oneidas. But the continued designs on Indian land by speculators from Virginia to Connecticut profoundly alarmed Indian tribes, especially the Iroquois. Johnson himself died during a conference at Johnson Hall at which Iroquois leaders were strenuously protesting illegal white settlement in violation of the Treaty of Fort Stanwix. The chiefs pressed Johnson to explain why Governor Dunmore, in Virginia, was actively encouraging Virginian settlement in Shawnee land in the Ohio Valley. Johnson could only urge patience and plead with the Iroquois to honor their obligations to the King by remaining at peace. If they resorted to the warpath in support of the Shawnees, he argued, they would only provoke devastating retaliation. Already enfeebled with illness, Johnson collapsed after delivering an impassioned two-hour oration to the Iroquois. Prior to his death, Johnson had already recommended his nephew and son-in-law, Guy Johnson, to succeed him as Indian superintendent for the northern district. After the burial, Guy Johnson concluded the conference and reaffirmed his uncle's advice to the Iroquois leaders.

The formal opening of offensive operations against the American rebels, occurring when Howe captured New York City in September 1776, finally placed irresistible pressures on traditional Iroquois neutrality, which in turn affected the position and subsequent fortunes of loyalists in upstate New York. In late July 1776 Guy Johnson returned from a visit to England, accompanied by Joseph Brant, a young Mohawk leader who had been well educated by Anglican and Congregationalist missionaries. Brant expected to accompany Howe on a victorious offensive up the Hudson Valley and into Iroquois country, and when it became apparent that Howe envisioned no such operation Brant asked permission to travel secretly into Iroquois country and mobilize the Six Nations. The cautious Howe was skeptical, but with Henry Clinton's endorsement Brant won permission to undertake the venture. Guy Johnson gave Brant oral instructions to enlist the Indians in the King's service, and at the end of November 1776, together with Gilbert Tice, a Mohawk Valley loyalist, Brant embarked on a dangerous mission through patriot-held territory. Brant and Tice returned home to find the Iroquois deeply divided and uncertain whether to remain neutral, support the British, or aid the Americans. Brant continued on to Niagara, where he reported to Colonel John Butler, prominent western New York landowner and supporter of the Crown, who in Guy Johnson's absence was acting Indian superintendent. Butler paid little attention to Brant's account of events in New York City and did nothing to further Brant's attempts to mobilize a loyalist insurgent force in western New York. Guy Johnson's precaution in not giving Brant written orders in turn gave Butler a pretext to question Brant's authority.

Throughout the next year John Butler impeded Brant's efforts to undertake widespread Indian attacks on patriot settlers. In part, Butler was following orders from General Guy Carleton, in Canada, who wanted to restrict the Indians to movements closely co-ordinated with those of British regulars. Most likely, Butler also resented Brant's obvious independence and sense of leadership, and he may have looked on Brant as an agent of his rivals, Guy Johnson and Sir William's son Sir John Johnson. In any event, Butler's condescending treatment of Brant and lack of co-operation probably prevented the rapid mobilization of Iroquois warriors. The occupation of Fort Stanwix by the American general Philip Schuyler, his appeal for Indian friendship, and his distribution of a barrel of rum to each Iroquois tribe in the autumn of 1776 encouraged Iroquois neutrality. A devastating epidemic that swept through the Onondaga tribe during the next winter further inhibited mobilization of Iroquois in support of the British. Throughout the spring and summer of 1777 John Butler implored Iroquois warriors to support the British cause, but little tangible aid materialized until British regulars appeared on the New York frontier. On July 6, 1777, a dispatch from Carleton informed Butler that a diversionary expedition supporting Burgoyne and led by Lieutenant Colonel Barry St. Leger would sweep through the Mohawk Valley, capture Fort Stanwix, and rendezvous with Burgoyne at Albany.[3] On the eve of this ambitious offensive, however, the split between Brant and Butler deepened. Butler recruited Iroquois by inviting great numbers of them to share in the distribution of lavish gifts and rum, and only after the wild celebration did he ask for warriors to fight; Brant, on the other hand, quietly recruited a small, disciplined force.

As an exercise in co-operation between Indians, white loyalists, and the British Army, the St. Leger offensive was a failure. Hungry and ill-clad because John Butler had failed to provide any supplies except a "vast" quantity of rum, Brant's 300 Mohawks and Butler's 200 Senecas made up more than a third of the 1,400-man force that marched from Oswego, on Lake Ontario, toward Fort Stanwix in late July and early August 1777. En route, a force of Indians and loyalists under the command of Sir John Johnson, in the Battle of Oriskany, ambushed and brutally mutilated a force of American reinforcements headed for Fort Stanwix and burned a neutral Oneida settlement in the process. That episode finally destroyed what little was left of Iroquois unity and neutrality. The Oneidas gave their support to the patriots, and a debilitating and savage civil war within the Confederacy commenced. Then the siege of Fort Stanwix failed, and as St. Leger's troops retreated toward Oswego some of the Indians who had served under the British plundered and assaulted British and loyalist troops, turning the flight into a bloody nightmare. The Oneidas and Americans exacted swift vengeance on the Mohawks. Every Mohawk settlement suffered when raiding parties destroyed their food and dwellings.

The over-all deterioration of British strength in northern New York in the autumn of 1777 further debilitated the Iroquois capacity to fight effectively. About a quarter of Colonel Baum's force at Bennington were Indians, who deserted him when it became apparent that defeat was inevitable. Indians were likewise of little value to the British in the Battle of Saratoga. In four months, therefore, from July to October 1777, the entry of large numbers of Mohawks and Senecas into the war against the Americans had shattered Iroquois unity and unleashed destructive Indian and white reprisals against the pro-British Indian settlements in the Mohawk Valley.

During 1778 the Iroquois tribes allied with the British staged a remarkable recovery from the debacles of the St. Leger, Burgoyne, and Baum offensives. Mary Brant, Joseph's sister and at one time Sir William Johnson's housekeeper and mistress, emerged as a crucial leader of the Iroquois in late 1777. Following the retreat from Fort Stanwix, she persuaded other Iroquois leaders not to withdraw from the war and to honor their lifelong friendships with agents of the British Crown, especially Sir William Johnson. John Butler mended his relationship with the Brants. By the summer of 1778, Indian and loyalist raiding parties led by Joseph Brant, John Butler, and a brilliant half-white half-Indian named Cornplanter were laying waste to Whig settlements in the Mohawk Valley and the Wyoming Valley, in northeastern Pennsylvania. At the close of this campaign, John Butler entrusted a final raid against the Mohawk Valley town of Cherry Valley to his vain and rash son Walter. "What young Butler lacked in experience," Barbara Graymont observes, "he made up for in hauteur. The Indians were not impressed."[4] He stripped Brant of command of the Indians serving with Butler's Rangers and provoked the best Indian warriors to depart. Brant was among the 320 Indians who embarked for the attack on Cherry Valley, but he had no command authority except personal influence over thirty Mohawks in the expedition. Although Butler's force overwhelmed the poorly defended settlement at Cherry Valley, the Indians burned loyalist and patriot farms alike. Butler lost all control over the Indians, and they went on a rampage of killing women and children. A number of patriot survivors credited Joseph Brant with saving their lives.

The cycle of retaliation and vengeance continued to decimate Iroquois society. An expedition commanded by General John Sullivan marched through Iroquois country during the summer of 1779 destroying crops and burning settlements. After Sullivan departed, the pro-British tribes and loyalists, now commanded by Sir John Johnson, spent the bitterly cold winter of 1779–80 preparing for another offensive. The spring and summer of 1780 witnessed a campaign of burning and pillaging of patriot and Oneida settlements. But the war on the New York frontier had, by this time, ceased to affect the course of the conflict. When Cornwallis's surrender at Yorktown effectively ended the struggle, Brant's warriors were still anxious to continue the fighting, and they were also still dependent on British war supplies. The Iroquois, Brant complained to John Johnson, were "between two hells": Americans invading their lands and British looking suspiciously as though they were trying to liquidate their obligations to the Indians. "I beg you don't tell us to 'go hunt deer and [make] yourselves shoes' [and assure us] we shall soon forget the war," Brant told Johnson, "for we have gone too far that way already against the rebels to be doing other things."[5] Britain, however, had gone too far toward a peace settlement with the Americans to defend the rights of its Indian allies. The Peace of

Paris granted to the United States all the territory to the Mississippi, land that the British had pledged to the Iroquois in perpetuity in the Treaty of Fort Stanwix. Brant, who had no trouble reading signs, led more than 1,800 Mohawks and other Indians who had supported the British in the Revolution to a new reservation in Ontario.

39

The Revolution and
Cultural Integration

THE middle states were an inviting battleground for the British in 1776 and 1777. New York City and Philadelphia fell easily into their hands. Cities provided two essential assets: refuges for loyalists who had fled from the countryside and secure headquarters for military operations. Social and political divisions in New York, Pennsylvania, Delaware, and New Jersey prompted large minorities of the populations there to adhere to the Crown. Yet Britain failed to capitalize on these assets and by early 1778 had to abandon hope of restoring royal authority in the middle states. During the first two years of the war, Britain had never assigned a very high priority, in terms of money, manpower, or planning, to mobilizing loyalist support or to feeding the antagonisms felt by many groups in this region toward the Revolutionary leaders. Germain and North, who should have set these priorities, never comprehended the administrative and political difficulties of simultaneously conducting military operations and regaining actual control of the civil order. Generals Howe and Clinton, though they agreed on little else, both ignored the self-seeking and unrealistic advice tendered them by prominent loyalists. The isolated examples of concerted loyalist activity to support the British Army—Galloway's corps of civil administrators in occupied Philadelphia and John Butler's and John Johnson's leadership of Indians and white loyalists in the Mohawk Valley—could not stem the deterioration of Britain's position in 1777, once Howe had failed to crush Washington and Burgoyne had stumbled into defeat. In any event, it was not lack of leadership and initiative alone that hobbled the loyalists.

Pacification in the middle states failed because the war aggravated social instability. Violence, cruelty, property destruction, and economic dislocation caused by both sides mocked Britain's efforts to institute order and security even in areas where the Crown enjoyed relative military superiority. To the extent that loyalist leaders relied on terror as an instrument of policy or means of revenge, they hastened their own defeat.

Yet an even more enlightened and adroit approach to the war and to the use of the loyalists would have encountered a further overwhelming obstacle. Those social groups that experienced the highest incidence of loyalist affiliation, William H. Nelson suggests in his astute chapter on "The Tory Rank and File," had "but one thing in common: they represented conscious minorities, people who felt weak and threatened, . . . [who] were in one way or another more afraid of America than they were of Britain [and] had interests they felt needed protection from an American majority."[1] Pietist and pacifist sects resisted being sucked into a political movement and a military conflict that violated their creed and invaded their privacy; Anglicans and conservative Dutch Reformed churches valued their ties with parent religious bodies in Europe and sensed that the ecumenical tendency of colonial religious life served to enervate those ecclesiastical ties; a few slaves and free blacks in New York worked for the British in hope of thereby winning or maintaining their freedom; tenant farmers on the Livingston estates sought British aid in securing liberal leases; settlers in the Mohawk Valley and elsewhere in western New York engaged in the Indian trade depended on the good will of the Indians and on the assistance of the Indian Superintendent and his agents; and, finally, numerous British immigrants who had come to New York between 1760 and 1774 and had been wholly immersed in the struggle for economic and social advancement as farmers or craftsmen instinctively thought of themselves as subjects and beneficiaries of the Crown.

The most suggestive insights now available into the structure and mentality of one of these defensive groups appear in Alice P. Kenney's model study of Dutch settlers in the upper Hudson Valley during the Revolution.[2] In contrast with the Hackensack Valley Dutch, who had been split by the Great Awakening into evangelical and traditionalist factions, the Albany-region Dutch immigrants retained a high degree of cultural and religious cohesion until the eve of independence. Unlike the situation in New York City, where prominent Dutch-descended families became Anglicans and where the Presbyterians far exceeded the Dutch Reformed in numbers and influence, in Albany the Dutch maintained their own churches. The Dutch Reformed Church was by far the largest and most prestigious in Albany, and in surrounding Albany County eighteen other Dutch Reformed congregations flourished and retained the Dutch language in liturgy and preaching.

The distinctive spelling of Dutch names makes it possible to examine the role of this large, self-conscious ethnic group in the Revolution. The Dutch made up between 30 and 40 per cent of the county's population, and in the county as a whole 32 per cent of those arrested for disloyal activity were of Dutch extraction. Even though the division between loyalists and patriots in Albany County sometimes seemed to run along ethnic lines, other, stronger motives and influences decisively shaped the choice of affiliation of the Dutch in the Revolution. In the Schenectady district, the Dutch were the oldest settlers in an area that had become increasingly dominated by Sir William Johnson. His Indian allies and fervently loyal tenants—recently arrived Scottish and English immigrants—resented the numerically and economically dominant Dutch landowners. Traditionally hostile to Indians and resentful of Johnson's Indian policies, the Schenectady Dutch looked to the patriots to defend them from the pro-British Mohawks once the War for Independence commenced. In the protected Kinderhook district the Dutch were the local elite, and the other inhabitants of the district were humble and recently settled New Englanders. The Dutch leaders there were parochial men who seldom traveled outside their community and felt little stake in the issues of the imperial controversy. During the early years of the War for Independence, they preferred to remain neutral until forced to take a side; when they had to choose, insularity and a simplistic form of self-interest dictated loyalty to the Crown. In the three largest estates in the district—Livingston Manor and the east and west districts of Rensselaerswyck—the large number of loyalists of Dutch descent reflected the familiar hostility of tenants toward aristocratic Whig land-lords. Here, in the autumn of 1776, Dutch tenants participated prominently in an abortive armed insurrection against the Revolutionary county government. John Van den Bergh expressed the prevailing sentiment of other Rensselaerswyck Dutch when he testified that "the people he met are friends to the country, but . . . they won't fight if they can help it; . . . the reason for not fighting for the country is, that they will not be against the King." "Friends to the country" but "not . . . against the King" neatly captured the essence of Dutch loyalism.

Finally, in the town of Albany, politics pitted two distinct and hostile factions against each other. A ruling party, led by Stephen De Lancey and Abraham and Henry Cuyler, and allied with the downstate politics of the Anglicans and the De Lanceys, controlled town government and rich local patronage. A British military post, located in Albany since the Seven Years' War, enriched local contractors who were the allies of the ruling faction. Successive royal governors appointed members of this faction to provincial offices in the area. Their opponents included several wealthy Dutch families whose members held several seats on the Common Council—the Schuylers, Van Schaicks, Ten Broecks, and Gansevoorts. Sir William Johnson had always considered the old Dutch families in Albany his bitter political enemies, and as he grew more powerful over the years he relentlessly attacked the Dutch party in Albany and sought allies among newcomers with English surnames. Although Cuyler was a Dutch name, Mayor Abraham Cuyler and his brother Henry were staunch Anglicans by the pre-Revolutionary period. The ruling Anglican faction became vociferous and energetic loyalists, and the Dutch Reformed congregation found ample revenge by becoming prominent Whigs. Ethnic factors, therefore, came into play only when activated by stronger motives and antagonisms intrinsic to the society of the upper Hudson—resentment of Sir William Johnson and his heirs in the Mohawk Valley, the insularity of the Kinderhook Dutch elite, the tenant hostility to aristocratic landlords on the Livingston and Rensselaerswyck estates, and court-versus-opposition factions in Albany politics.

The Dutch in the upper Hudson had maintained, along with church and language, a set of values that were distinctively collective and social rather than individualistic. The Dutch family was an institution primarily designed to bring its members security and opportunity; "it was taken for granted that wealth would be accumulated by families rather than by individuals, and would be convertible into both power and prestige which would be shared by all the members of the family."[3] The Revolution forced these families to accept new and unfamiliar political and military responsibilities. It brought the non-Dutch world and the world beyond the Hudson Valley much closer to the Albany Dutch. "The deeply political nature of the Revolution," Alice Kenney writes, "made politics loom larger to the Albany County Dutchman than ever before. . . . Whether he lived in the city or the country, [he] was confronted by the economic upheaval which only total war and imminent invasion can produce. . . . Whoever he was, whether patriot or Tory, he endured the distrust and coldness of some of his neighbors and the straining or breaking of ties of family and friendship. . . . No matter what his politics, the life of the Albany County Dutchman would never be the same." Soon the English language was used in Dutch church services and Dutch culture became increasingly submerged in the English-speaking ways of New York in the new republic. Because the Revolution split the Albany Dutch into loyalist and patriot camps, it intruded more deeply into the life of the group than any previous external force and made the Dutch vulnerable to assimilation.[4]

VI

Loyalists and Territorial Control

in the South

40

Test of Strength: North Carolina

Loyalists and the Coming

of War to the South

LATE winter and early spring of 1775 was a season of ominous calm in the British Empire in America. Dartmouth's orders to Gage to use force against the Massachusetts "rabble," issued on January 27, reached Boston on April 14 and were implemented five days later with the march of British troops to Lexington and Concord. Not until early June did news of the fighting there get back to London. As these events transpired, Governor Josiah Martin, of North Carolina, labored with furious determination to thwart the spread of rebellion in his province. On March 15, 1775, he issued a stern denunciation of North Carolina's projected second provincial Congress and warned that "all such meetings, cabals, and illegal proceedings . . . can only tend to introduce disorder and anarchy . . . and . . . involve this province in confusion, disgrace, and ruin." The proclamation was well timed and surprisingly effective. Nine of thirty-five counties refused to send delegates, whereas only five had failed to do so for the first provincial Congress, in August 1774. Within a few weeks Martin received loyal petitions bearing more than 500 signatures and protesting, in the words of an Anson County writer, "the wicked experiment of a most profligate and abandoned republican faction," which imperiled "the general repose and tranquillity of his Majesty's subjects on this continent." By the middle of May he had received more than 1,400 signatures on petitions vindicating British authority. In addition to these allies, Martin felt certain he could count on several thousand recent Scottish immigrants to the colony to join in the defense of the Crown. Dartmouth encouraged him to organize these supporters and "to lead the people forth against any rebellious attempts to disturb the public peace."[1]

Although these good omens filled Martin's dispatches to London, they constituted only one of several influences leading the ministry to believe that the Southern colonies contained large numbers of loyal subjects and that the war should commence with an expedition to the Carolinas. Governors Dunmore, in Virginia, and William Campbell, in South Carolina, also indicated that the revolt was the work of a small minority and that loyal subjects would assert themselves as soon as Britain took firm action against the "disturbers of the public peace." In Boston, General Gage independently began preparations to exploit British strength among loyal colonists in the South. Through the efforts of a Scottish officer, Lieutenant Colonel Allen McLean, Gage sent recruiting officers among recently arrived Scottish immigrants in several colonies. John Connolly, British Governor at Fort Pitt, told Dunmore he would volunteer to organize an ambitious uprising of loyalists and Indians in the Ohio Valley. Dunmore sent Connolly to Boston in September 1775 to consult with Gage, who approved the plan and asked Governor Guy Carleton, in Canada, and Indian Superintendent Guy Johnson to co-ordinate their activities with Connolly's projected uprising. Connolly, however, was captured in November, and his conspiracy was uncovered while he was en route to Pittsburgh. Gage's reports on the mobilization of loyalists in many parts of America reinforced the ministry's eagerness to achieve a quick victory in the Southern colonies.[2]

In mid-September the ministry replaced Gage with William Howe as commander of the British Army in America and ordered an expedition to the Southern colonies. The King personally drafted orders stressing that the expedition was "to land first in [North Carolina] . . . to call forth those who may have a sense of the duty they owe their mother country, to restore British government in that province, and to leave a battalion of Provincials formed from the back[-country] settlers under the command of the governor," and then to proceed to South Carolina or

Virginia and repeat the process. Dartmouth underscored the dependence of the expedition on vigorous loyalist support in the South. "In truth," he wrote to Howe, "the whole success of the measure . . . depends so much upon a considerable number of the inhabitants taking up arms in support of government." On January 6, 1776, Howe gave command of the Southern expedition to Henry Clinton, who was to sail from Boston with a small force and rendezvous at the mouth of the Cape Fear River, in North Carolina, with five regiments of British regulars who were scheduled to have sailed from Ireland in early December. Though he was not responsible for all these decisions, Martin apparently believed that his letters to London and the personal lobbying of his emissary to the ministry—a West Indies customs official named Alexander Schaw—had caused the expedition to be undertaken. He fully expected that the arrival of British troops would rally loyalists to assert themselves against the rebellion, restoring British authority in the Carolinas and holding the rebels in Virginia in "awe." Martin asked Dartmouth to restore his commission in the British Army—which he had sold in 1769—so that he could command the operation.[3]

Although Martin was blustering and overconfident, his assessment of the divisions within North Carolina in late 1775 and early 1776 was not entirely inaccurate. In constructing a network of organization, the provincial Congresses in 1774 and 1775 had started from scratch. Previously there had been only pockets of opposition to British policy in the plantation counties bordering the coast, in the Neuse and Roanoke valleys, and, in the west, in Mecklenburg and Rowan counties. But the majority of the white population of the province lived in a neutral belt composed of Scottish settlers in Cumberland County, on upper Cape Fear, and in Anson, Guilford, and Surry counties, where there were many German communities and where Piedmont farmers felt little kinship with low-country planters in the east. The difficulty of extending effective control over this large region was the first challenge facing Revolutionary leaders. By the time Martin denounced the calling of a second provincial Congress, the process of creating a cohesive opposition movement had just begun. Under the general supervision of a provincial committee of correspondence, only six committees to enforce the First Continental Congress's nonimportation agreement came into being in the early winter of 1774—three in the port towns of Wilmington, New Bern, and Edenton, and in Rowan, Halifax, and Pitt counties. The town committees functioned best, auctioning off confiscated British imports and sending the proceeds to the relief of Boston. The committees shifted their attention to price control—punishing profiteering—and then to denunciations of luxuries and horseracing. In July 1775 the Wilmington committee publicly condemned James Clardy for saying "in derision" that these were "fine times when the country was to be governed by committees" and for "falsely and maliciously" spreading the rumor that 50,000 Russian Cossacks were on their way to America as British mercenaries. By the spring of 1775 rumors that Martin would try to foment a slave insurrection and incite Indians to attack the frontier provoked the committees of safety to become military organizations. In May 1775 Abner Nash and the New Bern committee demanded that Martin surrender the cannon from the governor's palace, but Martin had already spirited the guns away. Sending his pregnant wife to New York for safety, Martin left New Bern on May 24 for the protection of Fort Johnston at the mouth of Cape Fear. In mid-July he fled to the British warship *Cruzier*.[4]

Although organizational momentum lay with provincial Congresses and the committees of safety and Martin enjoyed a shrinking ring of security and control, turbulent and shifting forces throughout 1774 and 1775 continued to jeopardize the Revolutionary movement in North Carolina. The population of the province grew from some 70,000 in 1750 to roughly 180,000 in 1770. Much of this increase came from an enormous influx of Scotch-Irish and German—especially Moravian—settlers in the western part of the province and Scottish Highlanders concentrated in Cumberland and Anson counties, in the upper Cape Fear River Valley.[5] Furthermore, the Regulator wars from 1769 to 1771 had united Piedmont farmers against the coastal plantation aristocracy; while there is little evidence that the Regulators became loyalists in 1775 in any significant numbers, the groups of Crown supporters who appeared in Guilford and Rowan counties gave the region the label "Regulator country." Moravians were politically neutral for religious pacifist reasons. Since

1771 Martin had assiduously courted former Regulators and Highland Scots with equitable land-granting policies. Both factors weighed heavily on the side of the Crown. Moreover, two Scottish officers, Lieutenant Colonel Donald McDonald and Captain Donald McLeod, sent by Gage and McLean, arrived in North Carolina in June 1775 and convinced the New Bern Committee of Safety that they had come to recover from wounds suffered at Bunker Hill and to visit relatives. The 10,000 Highland Scots in the province were not a cohesive political force in 1774. Scots had rioted against the Stamp Act in 1765, and a Scottish leader, Farquard Campbell, was in the vanguard of Revolutionary leadership. The most recent arrivals knew nothing of the controversy between Britain and the colony; they benefited most from Martin's generous land-granting policies and in return readily renewed their oaths of allegiance to the Crown. Scottish merchants in Cross Creek suffered badly when committees of safety seized their shipments of imports in 1774. Naturally, they resented such treatment. Martin counted on these centrifugal forces to weaken the movement of resistance.[6]

These sources of strength for the Crown placed a heavy burden on the committee of safety operating jointly in the town of Wilmington and in New Hanover County. Although Wilmington was nominally the home of nearby planters active in the Revolutionary movement—notably Cornelius Harnett, John Ashe, and James Moore—the town's mercantile elite was more or less openly hostile to the movement. Perhaps three-quarters of Wilmington's forty-four merchants objected to some of the proceedings of the provincial Congresses. Twenty-two became outright loyalists, served in the British Army, or fled to England, and eleven others managed to remain neutral but behaved suspiciously. The nonmercantile population in Wilmington also included at least sixty professional people loyal to the Crown, and during the war as many as 300 local residents were "disaffected." The slack behavior of the Wilmington committee in 1775 and 1776 was not merely a temporary lapse in Revolutionary zeal. In June 1775 several Highland Scottish leaders traveled openly through the town without any interference on their way to consult with Governor Martin at Fort Johnston. A number of men condemned by the committee suffered no serious consequences and were able to join

Governor Martin's loyalist forces, and other notorious Crown sympathizers remained at large as late as February 1776. Martin's intermediary with loyal Highland Scots was Alexander McLean, who had arrived in Wilmington in February 1775 and married a local girl. McLean must have had many friends in the Wilmington area, for he operated easily as courier between Martin and back-country loyalists.[7]

On January 3, 1776, dispatches from Germain reached the *Cruzier* notifying the Governor that Clinton's expedition would arrive at the mouth of the Cape Fear to discharge the royal troops. Martin set in motion plans for a Tory rising to coincide with the British arrival. On January 15, 1776, he issued a ringing proclamation calling all loyal subjects to rally to the defense of the Crown. He sent Alexander McLean to Cumberland County to summon Highland chieftains and Piedmont loyalist leaders from "Regulator country" and to instruct them to reach the coast no later than February 15 and to occupy Wilmington by February 25. Major difficulties beset the assembling of this back-country Tory force. McLean met with Scottish leaders and four other loyalist leaders in Cross Creek on February 5. The Scots had suddenly grown wary and did not want to march until March 1, unless prior word came that the British fleet had arrived. Impatiently, the Piedmont loyalist leaders urged immediate mobilization—with or without the Highlanders' participation—and boasted they could raise more than 3,000 troops. Already, they declared, an advance loyalist force of 500 men had gathered, waiting only for the order to march. McLean dispatched Captain McLeod to lead the 500 volunteers to Cross Creek. McLeod found them a belligerent and undisciplined lot who got drunk on the rum with which he treated them and fled at the first rumor that a hostile Whig force was approaching. McLeod desperately appealed for help to the four loyalist leaders who had promised to raise more than 3,000 men, only to find that they too had gone into hiding. In Yadkin County outspoken loyalists had been forced to flee their homes, and loyalist forces from Guilford and Surry counties had been attacked and seven of their leaders jailed in Halifax. Thomas Rutherford, a member of the first provincial Congress, who had defected to the Crown, promised to bring 500 recruits to Cross Creek but had no success. Another prominent back-country loyalist, Dr. John Pyle, managed to bring some forty men to the rendezvous. Indicative of the highly fluid lines of allegiance, patriot Scottish leader Farquard Campbell visited both the loyalist and Whig encampments in February and, apparently scenting loyalist victory, joined McDonald's force. By February 15—only a week behind schedule— 1,400 loyalist volunteers had assembled at Cross Creek. Probably two-thirds were Highland Scots. Only 520 had guns, but Colonel McDonald quickly organized a raiding party, which scoured the local countryside and obtained 130 more firearms.[8]

The existence of this Tory force spurred the North Carolina Revolutionary militia to vigorous preparation, but the Whigs also faced serious problems in their efforts to gather intelligence and to assemble and move troops. In mid-February Colonel James Moore commanded 1,100 men near Cross Creek. After exchanging challenges and messages with Colonel McDonald on February 19 and 20, Moore was tricked by McDonald into expecting a frontal attack; while the Whigs took defensive positions, the Tory force slipped away to the east and successfully ferried across the Cape Fear River at Campbelltown. Moore reacted quickly. He sent reinforcements and information about the enemy force to Colonel Richard Caswell, who commanded another Whig force somewhere between Cross Creek and Wilmington. Approaching the Black River on February 23, the Tories captured a Whig scouting party and learned that Caswell was only four miles ahead, on the other side of the Black River. A diversionary group playing bagpipes and shooting muskets across the river kept Caswell's attention while the main Tory force built a temporary bridge four miles upstream and resumed the march toward the coast. The Whigs again reacted quickly; James Moore was the first to learn that McDonald had evaded Caswell at Black River, and he ordered Caswell to take up new defensive positions at the Moore's Creek bridge, where he joined another Whig force, commanded by Colonel Alexander Lillington, on February 26.[9]

The Moore's Creek bridge provided the best defensive position yet available to McDonald's antagonists: "a narrow bridge in an area that was more swamp than dry land," relates Hugh F. Rankin, foremost authority on the campaign. "At the bridge site the stream is about fifty feet wide with a depth of five feet. . . . Here the creek crawls through the marsh in a series of twisting loops. Beneath the dank waters lay a bottom miry with the accumulation of years of swamp wastes. The bridge itself was located on a sand bar, the highest point in the area." First on the scene, Lillington's men fortified the knoll directly across the bridge and then ripped up most of the planks and greased the log runners. A few hours after Caswell reached the location, the Tory force arrived. James Hepburn, McDonald's secretary, issued Caswell a futile ultimatum to surrender. McDonald, an elderly man now near collapse from exhaustion, did not want to attack Caswell, but younger Scottish officers felt emboldened. At a council of war their views prevailed, and attack was set for dawn of February 27. There were only enough arms for 500 of the force, which now numbered 1,600. Passing the word to attack with the cry "King George and broadswords," the Highland Scots in the forefront of the attack party hurried forward to the scream of bagpipes and beat of drums. As McLeod, in the lead, tried to make his way across the slippery log runners, Caswell's cannons, "Old Mother Covington and her daughters," and muskets poured a murderous fire on the advancing Tories. For a few minutes the Scots returned fire, but two back-country loyalist leaders, James Cotton, of Anson County, and Thomas Rutherford, led their followers into hectic flight.[10]

When Clinton arrived at the mouth of Cape Fear on March 12, 1776, he learned of the disaster. Germain's reinforcements for the Cape Fear landing had not yet finished crossing the Atlantic. Clinton therefore concluded that no offensive in the South could succeed until the British controlled a major port. He sailed southward to launch a futile attack near Charles Town. Apparently, Martin realized that mobilization of the loyalists would require British military control of a strategic area, for he warned Clinton shortly before Moore's Creek that the number of volunteers in the Tory uprising might fall below initial expectations. When Clinton discovered the extent of royal weakness in North Carolina, he abandoned any idea of landing troops there and decided to seize Sullivan's Island, near Charles Town, as a sanctuary for South Carolina loyalists and a base for further operations, rather than try to capture Charles Town itself. When he failed to gain even that limited objective, the patriots wrongly congratulated themselves on having repulsed a wholesale British attack on Charles Town.[11]

41

Low Country Unity and Back Country Civil War in South Carolina

1775-1776

ALTHOUGH South Carolina Whig leadership was far more cohesive and vigorous than that of its northern neighbor, and the newly arrived Governor, Sir William Campbell, had less opportunity to engage in the kind of intrigue that occupied Josiah Martin, the South Carolina back country produced a more dangerous loyalist insurrection than the Tory rising of 1776 in North Carolina. In South Carolina, as in Virginia and North Carolina, pockets of loyalists thwarted Whig efforts to capitalize on the initial collapse of royal government and extend their control throughout the territory of the province.

The Whigs moved quickly in Charles Town and the low country to assert control. In January 1775 the first provincial Congress adopted the Continental nonimportation and exportation agreement and established local enforcement committees; it also urged citizens to practice the use of firearms. Reacting to news of Lexington and Concord and other reports of British determination to use military force to subdue the colonists, the second provincial Congress, in June 1775, raised 1,500 special troops, authorized issuance of new currency, created a Council of State, with extensive executive powers, and proclaimed an "Association" of South Carolinians "to go forth and sacrifice our lives and fortunes" in the defense of liberty. "They then ordered a committee of 26 inhabitants . . . to carry this Association round the town and neighborhood and report all who refused to sign it," observed Alexander Innes, Lord North's intelligence agent in Charles Town. "Many subscribe with great reluctance, but the dread of the terrible consequences both to their persons and properties that may follow a refusal operates so strongly that . . . few dare refuse."[1] Often threats were unnecessary. Dr. George Milligen, surgeon to the royal garrison and a Charles Town resident since 1749, reported that "the people were made to believe that His Majesty's ministers and other servants" had "instigated slaves to rebel against their masters. . . . Reports were daily circulated that the Negroes of this plantation had refused to work, that in another they had obtained arms and were gone into the woods, and that others had actually murdered their masters; . . . all [were] without foundation . . . [but] credited by the ignorant and unwary [and] strong as proofs of scripture writ . . . to keep up their fears and distractions of mind." A free black man, Thomas Jeremiah, stood trial for allegedly advising slaves to abandon their masters and seek British protection as soon as the Royal Army arrived. Ignoring Governor Campbell's strenuous objections, the General Committee hanged and burned Jeremiah on August 18, 1775.[2] James Dealy and Laughlin Martin, accused of denouncing the committee of correspondence and boasting that Catholics, slaves, and Indians would soon be armed and used to crush resistance, were tarred and feathered. In August a British soldier who had spoken disrespectfully of the colonial cause was tarred and feathered and paraded through Charles Town as a warning to other servants of the Crown. A crowd of more than 400 people so abused and frightened Dr. Milligen that he fled for protection to the British warship *Tamar*. A month later the British garrison covertly withdrew to Fort Johnston, in the harbor, and Governor Campbell himself took refuge on the *Tamar*.[3]

Yet for all their success in isolating and overawing opponents of the Revolutionary movement, and in spite of the brilliant leadership of men like Henry Laurens, William Henry Drayton, and Christopher Gadsden, the power the Whigs possessed in South Carolina in late 1775 was fragile. The powerful merchant Henry Laurens had voiced the anxieties of many members of the Charles Town elite when he protested against the clause in the Association labeling nonsigners "inimical to the liberty of the colonies."[4] The South Carolina political and economic elite valued unity and consensus above all other social achievements. Fearful of the huge slave population and frontier Indian attacks, detesting British placemen, whose loyalties belonged to the Crown, euphoric and yet also wary about the soaring economic prosperity of the colony, the South Carolina elite believed that their liberty from British oppression depended upon maintaining a common front toward all external forces. These men came to pride themselves on their complete integrity and lack of obligation to British officialdom. An undivided allegiance to both conscience *and* the public good meant that factionalism was frowned upon and that no one could initiate an internal political dispute unless he could first demonstrate that the common good of the whole community was involved in the controversy. In the interests of this unity, groups of merchants and artisans who asserted their interests had won integral places within the political structure of South Carolina politics. When Charles Town merchant Robert Smythe had returned from a trip to London in February 1775 bringing with him two race horses, which under nonimportation could not enter the province, the local enforcement committee made an exception to the policy. Aroused at this apparent favoritism and weakening of nonimportation, and electrified by the oratory of William Henry Drayton, an ambitious, impulsive politician, protestors browbeat the General Committee into reversing its earlier decision by a vote of thirty-five to thirty-four.[5] In April 1775 the General Committee had ordered seizure of all arms and gunpowder in the province, and five members of the Congress, headed by William Henry Drayton, stole 800 guns, 200 cutlasses, and 1,600 pounds of powder from under Lieutenant Governor Bull's nose.[6] Not everyone agreed that military resistance was prudent. "The opulent and sensible," Alexander Innes observed, with only a degree of exaggeration, "wish to avoid such desperate measures until they hear from the Continental Congress, . . . but they are powerfully opposed by a numerous body of the low and ignorant, led by a few desperate incendiaries who have nothing to lose, and some hot headed young men of fortune whom it will be difficult to restrain."[7]

Fearful that the British would exploit this new rift, the General Committee strained to obtain unanimous support for the Association; the committee members could understand and condone Lieutenant Governor Bull's refusal to sign, but they could not accept the opposition of the only other native South Carolinian, William Wragg. Summoned before the committee on July 22, 1775, to explain his opposition to the province's course of action, Wragg reminded the interrogators of the value the province had come to place on the inviolability of individual conscience: "Men may entertain different thoughts with regard to the welfare of the province, but he must be . . . the most consummate of all blockheads who having an interest in [that welfare] could wish any misfortune to befall it or that [the province] should be deprived of its just rights and privileges. I should look upon myself with the greatest abhorrence—and ought to be treated with the utmost detestation—if I was capable upon any considerations of subscribing to an opinion contrary to the dictates of my judgment." Wragg refused to subscribe to the Association, "first, . . . because it enjoins an implicit obedience to every proceeding, however partial, however injurious, nay how sanguinary it may be. It obliges . . . acquiescence in an approbation of any future act" that the provincial Congress may take to resist British authority. "Second, it is illegal, for no oath can be imposed . . . but by authority of the common law or by Act of Parliament," and, "third, if taken it would be totally inefficacious," for no oath can be valid unless the "obligation" it imposes is "lawful." The whole business of securing signatures to a declaration like the Association, Wragg explained, was self-defeating. "Instead of promoting unity of spirit in the bond of peace," he declared, "you are enforcing unity of opinion in the bond of ignorance or unity of practice in the bond of hypocrisy." Wragg claimed nothing less for himself than the ultimate responsibility for determining his destiny—nothing less than the province demanded from Great Britain. "He must be a very weak or a very wicked man and know little of me," Wragg softly mocked his inquisitors, who knew his prickly independence all too well, "who thinks me capable of surrendering my judgment, my honor, and my conscience upon any considerations whatever." The committee debated Wragg's case for two days before voting him "inimical to the cause of liberty," requiring him to surrender his arms, and confining him to his house. In September 1775 he was expelled from Charles Town to his plantation on the Ashley River and in 1777, when he refused to abjure allegiance to George III, expelled from the province. En route to exile in England he died in a shipwreck.[8]

The adherence of the back country to the Revolutionary cause posed vastly more difficult problems for the already divided leadership in Charles Town. Reports of back country apathy exacerbated this indecision. On June 23, 1775, the provincial Congress's Council of Safety decided to send commissioners, led by William Henry Drayton and the Reverend William Tennent, a Charles Town Congregationalist clergyman who might have influence with dissenters, to the back country to explain the controversy between the colonies and the mother country and emphasize the "necessity of a general union in order to preserve themselves and their children from slavery." The Drayton-Tennent mission sought to persuade the back country people that they had a vital stake in the defense of colonial liberty. Throughout early August the commissioners moved inland. At a German settlement on the Saluda River not a single person signed the Association. With justifiable pride, a supporter of the Crown later reported: "Tennent and Drayton [did] not experienc[e] that success in their political mission they had flattered themselves with and which the partial accounts from time to time transmitted by the country delegates to the Committee in Charlestown had given them reason to expect. In meeting a general and spirited opposition from the inhabitants, whom we had previously prepared [for] the reception of these incendiaries," the commissioners were "stung with disappointment, . . . apprehending, I imagine, their reputation and influence might suffer."[9]

Behind this sudden demonstration of defiance against low country patriot leadership was one of Governor William Campbell's few initiatives in the Revolutionary crisis. He had arrived in Charles Town on June 18, 1775, and found royal authority virtually at an end; but he did succeed in corresponding with sympathizers of the Crown in the Camden and Ninety-Six districts. They replied that he should issue a "Counter-Association" of loyalty to the Crown and circulate it in competition with the Whig Association. Campbell concluded that he could not risk the public defiance of Whig leaders, but even his surreptitious encouragement to back-country supporters was enough to spur them to action. Militia Colonel Thomas Fletchall, for one, sidestepped a council of safety directive to muster his regiment and secure their assent to the Association. It was read to every company, he reported, and not "one man signed it." Instead, he allowed his men to draft "a paper of their own resolutions." Drafted on July 13, 1775, by Joseph Robinson, these resolves denied that the King had forfeited the colonists' allegiance or violated the British constitution. While the signers refused to bear arms against the King, they asked to be left in peace by South Carolinians who disagreed with them. Reprimanded by the council of safety, Fletchall noncommittally wrote to Laurens that his men had refused to sign the Association and it "was out of my power to compel them to do so." The council of safety then ordered Major James Mayson to take two troops of militia, under captains Moses Kirkland and John Caldwell, to occupy Fort Charlotte, on the Savannah River above Augusta. Leaving Caldwell and his men in possession of the fort, Mayson and Kirkland marched to the Ninety-Six courthouse to seize a supply of powder and shot. Kirkland, "a thoroughgoing opportunist," who was disgruntled that he had not received a more prestigious command, changed sides. He arrested Mayson and appealed to Fletchall, whose loyalist militia was then mustering nearby, for assistance. Still preferring to appear uncommitted in the contest, Fletchall did not act. But his aggressive subordinates, Joseph Robinson and Patrick Cunningham, did respond. On July 17, 1775, they jailed Mayson and seized the ammunition in his possession. When word reached Governor Campbell, he cautiously instructed Fletchall to recapture and hold Fort Charlotte and seek assistance from Alexander Cameron, British Indian agent. Still immobilized by his humiliating position, Campbell, curiously, advised Fletchall to accomplish all this without unduly antagonizing Whig leadership in Charles Town. Had Campbell risked capture in July 1775 in an effort to slip into the back country and take personal command of the growing loyalist force there, he might have rallied a more potent Tory rising than the one Josiah Martin engineered from the *Cruzier* the following February. "Thus in the latter part of July 1775," Gary D. Olson concludes, "the loyalists held a favorable position in the South Carolina back country. Kirkland's defection, together with the seizure of the powder and humiliation of Mayson at Ninety-Six, swelled the ranks of the Tories between the Saluda and Savannah rivers. Even people from across the Savannah in Georgia were signing Robinson's Counter-Association."[10]

This loyalist ascendency in the South Carolina back country affected neighboring Georgia. The Georgia Sons of Liberty, who had been active in the back country during the Stamp Act crisis, mobilized again but succeeded only in enlarging the scope of the conflict between adherents of the Crown and the patriot movement. A band of nearly one hundred armed men visited the plantation of Thomas Brown, a recent immigrant from England, who had purchased 5,600 acres in newly ceded Creek and Cherokee land in the autumn of 1774. They demanded that Brown sign "an Association" that, he later reported, "implied his renunciation of the allegiance to the British government." Brown stoutly refused, and most of the intruders departed. But those who remained threatened to arrest Brown and take him to Augusta if he persisted in his refusal. At this, Brown retreated into his house and armed himself. One of the Sons of Liberty got into the house and struck Brown over the head with a rifle barrel. By Brown's account, they dragged him five miles from his house, tied him to a tree, and "applied burning torches . . . to the soles of his feet." According to one Whig version, Brown "consented voluntarily to swear that he repented of his past conduct" and promised to "do all in his power to discountenance the proceedings of . . . Fletchall's party . . . in the Ninety-Six district of South Carolina." This done, a friend brought Brown a horse, and one of his guards allowed him to escape to Fletchall's force in South Carolina. The mistreatment and release of Thomas Brown brought to the loyalists in the Southern back country one of their ablest leaders. In the short time he had been in Georgia, Brown's ability and forcefulness must have attracted attention, for rumor quickly spread that Brown and Thomas Fletchall were leading 1,000 men into Georgia to take revenge on Whigs in the area. In early August 1775 Georgia officials labeled Brown "inimical to the rights and liberties of America" and called on "all good men" to treat him accordingly. Actually, Brown spent August 1775 in South Carolina collaborating with Robert Cunningham and Joseph Robinson in an effort to undermine the Tennent-Drayton mission. At King's Creek, on the Enoree River, Brown and Cunningham interrupted Drayton's oration to a large audience. Brown read "An Address of the people of Great Britain to the inhabitants of America," which Governor Campbell had transmitted for Fletchall to use in just such a situation. It argued the futility of armed resistance against British might, the damage to American trade that a suspension of commerce would mean, and the ease with which differences between the colonies and the mother country could be resolved. Exploiting the back-country suspicion of the wealthy, adroit Charles Town bar, the address declared that "it is hard that the charge of our intending to enslave you should come oftenest from the mouths of those lawyers who in your southern provinces, at least, have long made you slaves to themselves." No one in the audience signed the Association, and a week later, when people gathered to elect delegates to the provincial Congress, Brown, Cunningham, and Kirkland persuaded them to scrub the election.[11]

When Drayton and the other commissioners finally met with Thomas Fletchall on August 17, 1775, and tried to persuade him to support "the Association," they found that Thomas Brown had become the spokesman for back country loyalist leaders. Brown's abusive tongue nearly provoked Drayton to a duel. But it was Fletchall that the commissioners needed, and he remained noncommittal. "These men," Drayton appraised Brown, Cunningham, and Robinson, "manage Fletchall as they please when they have him to themselves." The commissioners did appoint a new militia commander, Captain Ezekiel Polk, to replace Fletchall, but only 250 of the 1,000 men Fletchall had summoned to muster in July responded to Polk's muster orders on August 23, 1775. Drayton debated Brown and Kirkland before the assembled militiamen, but only seventy new signers of the Association came forward.[12]

Drayton's perseverance, however, was justified. The back country leadership was divided. Fletchall did not want to run the risk of outright defiance of the province's patriot leaders. Cunningham and Robinson each had their own followings of back country men, and Brown possessed immense drive and forcefulness; but they needed the support of the prominent Fletchall to sustain opposition. A "very corpulent" figure, who weighed more than 280 pounds, Fletchall apparently wanted to wait until British troops arrived in the back country to declare openly his allegiance to the Crown. To speed that day, Brown, Cunningham, Kirkland, and Robinson laid plans to capture Fort Charlotte, but Drayton learned of the plan, publicly denounced anyone who joined Moses Kirkland in arms, and ordered the powder supply at Fort Charlotte moved to another location. This setback meant that the loyalist leaders woud have to ask for Campbell's assistance. Kirkland took their appeal to the Governor, aboard the *Tamar*. Campbell then sent Kirkland by sea to Boston to tell Gage that "arms, ammunition, and a few experienced officers" sent to the South Carolina back country would bring 4,000 loyalists to arms and subdue the Southern colonies. Unluckily for the loyalists, the patriots captured the ship carrying Kirkland and his messages to Gage.[13]

Meanwhile, Drayton began to take the offensive. He ordered the arrest of several loyalist leaders in the Ninety-Six district, although Robert Cunningham escaped. He then led patriot militia into Fletchall's district, in the upper Saluda, only to find himself facing 1,200 men recruited by Brown and Cunningham. Drayton decided to dissuade the enemy force from fighting. "We abhor the idea of compelling any person to associate with us," he told the loyalist force; "we only with sorrow declare that any who will not associate with us . . . cannot . . . be considered . . . friendly." Drayton also circulated rumors that reinforcements were on their way to attack the loyalists from the rear and to burn their homes. The ploy worked. The loyalist force declined to fight. To Brown's and Cunningham's disgust, Fletchall decided to negotiate with Drayton. The result was the "Treaty of Ninety-Six," signed on September 16, 1775, in which the loyalists declared that they refused to sign the Association only because they wanted to live in peace, promised not to aid or support the British Army, and pledged to allow the provincial Congress to punish its opponents in South Carolina. Nonsigners of the Association could return to their homes and live there unmolested. Those who did not agree to the treaty would not enjoy its benefits. Brown and Cunningham were furious with Fletchall, but the agreement was in keeping with Governor Campbell's desire to avoid open fighting until British forces arrived. Drayton and the other commissioners returned to Charles Town, the back country pacified—for the moment.[14]

The truce soon collapsed. Drayton craftily wrote to Robert Cunningham on September 21, 1775, asking if he felt bound by the Treaty of Ninety-Six. Cunningham fell into the trap, responding to Drayton that he could not be bound by an agreement that was "false and disgraceful from beginning to end." With this incriminating evidence, the council of safety sent an armed company, in disguise, which arrested Cunningham and returned him to Charles Town for trial. In retaliation, Cunningham's brother Patrick led an uprising on November 3, 1775, that captured a shipment of gunpowder that the council of safety had sent to the Cherokee Indians as a good-will gesture. By coincidence, the council's agent to the Cherokees, Richard Pearis, chose this moment to defect to the loyalists. Pearis made the sensational claim that the gunpowder was intended for use in a general Indian uprising against back country loyalists. In response, Major Andrew Williamson raised 550 men to march into the Ninety-Six district to "retake that ammunition and bring those people to justice." Claiming that the Whigs had broken the Treaty of Ninety-Six, and playing skillfully on rumors of imminent Indian attacks against the loyalists, Joseph Robinson and Patrick Cunningham raised 2,000 men to oppose Williamson. After three days of sporadic fighting, both sides agreed to a truce of twenty-one days. By the time it ended many of the loyalists had gone into hiding, while new recruits swelled the Whig force, now commanded by Colonel Richard Richardson, to more than 4,000. A blizzard gave the renewed fighting the name "the snow campaign," during which the dispirited loyalists were easily rounded up. The council of safety released all of them except the two Cunninghams, Richard Pearis, and some others, who were held until the British attack near Charles Town in June 1776 failed. Those who surrendered voluntarily were released after receiving mild reprimands.[15]

42

Loyalists and the Security

of the Revolutionary Movement

in Virginia

IN contrast with the loyalist partisans in the two Carolinas, who offered a genuine threat to the survival of the Revolution in 1775 and 1776, the supporters of the Crown in Virginia possessed neither the numbers nor the leadership to jeopardize the existence of the Revolutionary movement there. Consisting of a handful of Anglican clergymen, the members of a moribund Royal Council, and several hundred Scottish merchants, and led by an erratic and ill-tempered governor, Lord Dunmore, the adherents of the Crown were not a very formidable coalition. Rather thar heir numbers or aggressiveness, it was the nature of the Revolution in this province that made sympathizers of the Crown a vexing problem to the Whig leadership. The planter elite prided itself on its political sophistication, administrative skill, and intellectual curiosity. Simply owning plantations and slaves, Edmund Randolph observed, "begat a pride which nourished a quick and acute sense of the rights of freemen," while the intense conviviality of Virginians at social and public gatherings stimulated "a certain fluency of speech which . . . pushed into motion many adventurous doctrines" and created lively interest in political theory.[1] Virginia, therefore, possessed the leadership, ideology, and temper to move unhesitatingly from remonstrance to resistance and finally to independence, war, and the formation of a new government. Utilizing these capabilities and resources meant extending the reach of their political power a short but crucial distance. Between the enforcement of nonimportation in December 1774 and the adoption of a new state constitution in June 1776, the leaders of Virginia had to create insurrectionary machinery capable of supplanting and resisting the authority of the royal governor, seize and keep the initiative in the uncertain task of supporting the Continental Congress at the provincial level, and formulate a constitution that reflected the virtue of the people and the energy of their leaders. The potential loyalists in Virginia, by their very presence, complicated the delicate task of effecting a new constitutional order.[2]

In the planters' eyes, the Scottish merchants in the province were outsiders who were perfectly willing to stand by and watch American liberty vanish. They were "suspicious friends at best," one Virginian observed, "by habit attached to traffic, by mutual interest induced to pursue it." Although Virginia planters perceived of the Scottish merchants, who had settled in increasing numbers between 1750 and 1770, as parasitic middlemen, the newcomers provided the planters valuable economic service. Instead of exporting tobacco on consignment to English merchants, the standard method until the early eighteenth century, the planters could sell their crops to Scottish merchants in Virginia, who shipped the tobacco to Glasgow and operated chains of stores in newer western counties. Backed by the resources of Glasgow banks, the Scottish traders in Virginia offered planters a new source of credit and a different market for their tobacco— alternatives to the old system of selling the crop on consignment and then borrowing against the next year's crop to purchase English consumer goods. Shipping costs to Glasgow were lower, and Scottish merchants on the scene in Virginia were more efficient and enterprising than the London merchants who had handled Virginia accounts. Their very distinctiveness as businessmen, however, kept the Scottish merchants in Virginia aware of the differences between themselves and their clients. To be on their guard was a professional imperative. "I hope you'll be careful to be obliging . . . to the gentlemen in shipping the cargo," Neil Jamieson advised his nephew in 1767; "don't by any means stand on trifles to carry any dispute. To be obliging and good natured always gains friends and esteem. . . . Be not too prone to passion, weigh a matter closely before you dispute, and even if you are right, do not glory too much." Another advised his store manager to avoid "too great an intimacy" with customers, especially visiting planters in their homes, lest they "take liberties at the store." While prudential ethics of this sort were common to all economic relationships in colonial America, in Virginia these apprehensions were part of a real estrangement between planters and Scottish merchants.[3]

Furthermore, in 1768, when a number of the Scottish Norfolk merchants had volunteered to have their families inoculated against smallpox, virulent anti-inoculation rioters smashed windows in the homes of the physicians in Norfolk who had introduced the new medical practice. The following spring, while the House of Burgesses considered anti-inoculation legislation, a mob broke the windows in the home of Cornelius Calvert, the proinoculation Mayor of Norfolk. Many of the victims in these disturbances had been prominently identified as supporters of British authority during the recent Stamp Act crisis, while the attackers were high-tempered anti-Stamp Act activists. This curious clash between medical advancement and superstition in Virginia deepened the suspicion between the Norfolk Scottish and native Virginian communities.[4]

The Continental Congress's boycott on commerce with Britain brought these tensions in Virginia into the open. Continental nonexportation began on December 1, 1774, and nonimportation on September 10, 1775. "Why should the entire brunt of the attempt to coerce the government fall on us?" one Norfolk merchant complained; "it is well enough for the planters to talk about boycotting the English manufacturers, for they can make out with the goods they have on hand. But for the trader it means going out of business." "Everything is managed by committee," another Norfolk Scot complained, in a graphic depiction of Revolutionary enforcement, "settling and pricing goods, imprinting books, forcing some to sign scandalous concessions, and by such bullying conduct they expect to bring the government to their own terms." In reality, the Virginia committees of safety were far less concerned with punishing the mother country than with fashioning a moderate, effective, calculated mode of supporting colonial resistance. By the end of 1774, committees of safety were operating in thirty-three counties and three towns in the Tidewater region, where most commercial activity occurred and where the boycott would have to be most effective. County government in this area ranked among the most experienced and proficient local administration in all colonial America. When some of the committees grew to more than fifty members and proved cumbersome, the Virginia Revolutionary Convention quickly responded with legislation standardizing the size of a committee at twenty-one "of the most discreet, fit, and able men" and allowing for this group to appoint as many subcommittees as were needed to police each of the commercial districts within its jurisdiction. The committees at once encountered a rash of perplexing specific cases in which fairness to individuals conflicted with the public need for uniform and undeviating enforcement. Early in 1775, Captain John Sampson's ship, *Elizabeth*, from Bristol, arrived at Norfolk to unload salt and take on a cargo of lumber. The Norfolk committee allowed him to leave the salt in a warehouse and to make repairs on his ship; when Sampson tried to load the lumber and sail from the colony, the committee ordered him to explain his conduct and Sampson fled to a British warship. He was then branded an enemy and citizens were requested to break all connections with him. Seeking to move deliberately yet vigorously, the committees sought to bring maximum publicity and ostracism upon deliberate violators of the Continental boycott while treating inadvertent violators with mildness.[5]

The committees quickly moved beyond their initial responsibility of enforcing the Continental trade boycott and sought to isolate and immobilize potential opponents. Merchants who refused to open their records to committee inspection faced immediate ostracization. The committees also regulated prices, tried to prohibit gambling, cockfighting, and horse racing as "extravagance," opened people's mail, and after March 1776 began collecting special taxes for military preparation. The Fincastle committee rebuked a man who had publicly denigrated the character of its members, another who had allegedly "damned this committee," and a third man who had declared himself a friend of the King. David Wardrobe, a Scottish teacher in Westmoreland County, wrote a letter to a friend in Scotland describing the hanging in effigy of Lord North that was published without his consent in a Glasgow newspaper and found its way back to Virginia. The committee demanded that Wardrobe be denied use of the vestry house in Cople Parish for a schoolroom and finally extracted a sufficiently penitent and spontaneous statement that significantly stressed the victim's dependence on Virginia for economic sustenance and acknowledged that he was an outsider: "I do most heartily and willingly, on my knees, implore the forgiveness of this country for so ungrateful a return for the advantages I have received from it, and the bread I have earned in it, and hope, from this contrition for my offense, I shall at least be permitted to subsist amongst the people I greatly esteem."[6]

The Nansemond County Committee of Safety also brought the weight of its influence to bear on a particularly stubborn Anglican clergyman, the Reverend John Agnew, who refused to omit prayers for the King from the liturgy or to abandon his outspoken opposition to the Revolutionary movement. On March 2, 1775, he ignored a citation to testify before the committee; in retaliation the committee called on the public to ostracize Agnew. Armed parties of men interrupted his services. On Whitsunday 1775, a crowd of more than 500 waited outside his church and listened to the service through open windows. They heard him pray for the King and royal family and read the scripture lesson on rendering unto Caesar the things that are Caesar's. Then, as he started his sermon, a vestryman, William Cowper, mounted the steps of the pulpit to stop the service. "I am here doing my master's business," the clergyman told Cowper. "*Which* master? Your master in heaven or your master over the water?" Cowper demanded. "I will never be the cause of breeding riot in my master's house," Agnew declared, leaving the church and striding through the crowd outside.[7]

By late June in 1775, Dunmore concluded accurately that "the enemies of government are so numerous and so vigilant" that nearly all loyal subjects "have been so intimidated that they have entirely shrunk away." In the autumn of 1775 Dunmore took refuge in the town of Gosport, near Norfolk, where he had been reinforced with a British regiment from East Florida and a handful of Virginia loyalists. On November 7, 1775, Dunmore issued a proclamation promising slaves belonging to rebels their freedom if they would desert their masters, "bear arms," and join in "reducing this colony to a proper sense of their duty to his Majesty's crown and dignity." By the end of November, 300 slaves responded to Dunmore's call and enlisted in "Dunmore's Ethiopian Regiment," and some 800 blacks served under Dunmore in Virginia. The black loyalist military unit was not nearly large enough to add appreciably to Dunmore's strength, but the news that the Governor had tampered with the institution of slavery and issued arms to black men galvanized Virginians' determination to expel all British authority and demonstrated vividly what seemed to them Dunmore's unspeakable treachery and depravity.[8]

Meanwhile, Norfolk was a town torn apart by the tensions of impending war. In September, with Dunmore encamped only a few miles away in Gosport and British warships on the James River, the Norfolk Committee of Safety interrogated and condemned merchants providing supplies to the British, and John Holt, the town printer, continued to denounce the British in his *Virginia Gazette or Norfolk Intelligencer*. Then, on September 30, 1775, a boatload of British sailors rowed ashore and dismantled and removed Holt's printing press. By the time Dunmore marched into Norfolk on November 16, 1775, many residents had fled. The Scottish merchants who had stayed behind hoped to remain neutral until the storm passed, but Dunmore's refuge in Norfolk among the merchant community accentuated his status as a foreign enemy. "The town is a nest of Tories who are aiding Dunmore to subdue the colony, either by provisioning his ships or actually taking up arms against their fellow countrymen." On the morning of December 9, 1775, Dunmore's regulars, followed by Virginia loyalists and the Ethiopian Regiment, rashly attacked the Virginia militia outside the city and met total defeat. The survivors retreated back into the town and boarded British warships. Of the several hundred blacks taken aboard the British ships, only one hundred survived the smallpox epidemic then raging among the crew. Most of these subsequently served throughout the war in the British Army. Dunmore demanded that the Virginia militia allow women and children who had also fled to the vessels to return to shore and leave the city peaceably. The Virginia commanders did not agree, and shots were exchanged. Many residents who had remained in Norfolk desperately loaded their possessions on wagons and fled the city. On January 1, 1776, the four British ships in Norfolk harbor opened fire, and the Virginians set the torch to the buildings. Plundering broke out, and those who had not already departed huddled at the edge of the town and watched their homes burn. Nearly as pitiful were the loyalists stranded on the British warships, many of them sick and all famished for adequate food and water. The ship carrying Dunmore, H.M.S. *Folley*, commanded by Captain Andrew Hammond, remained in the Chesapeake until August 1776, providing encouragement to loyalists on the eastern shore of Maryland. In February General Henry Clinton, en route to support the North Carolina loyalists at Cape Fear, rendezvoused with Dunmore at Hampton Roads. Clinton concluded that Dunmore's position was untenable and saw no way he could return to the mainland. But Dunmore stayed in the Chesapeake, waiting in vain for General William Howe to recognize his plight and launch an invasion of Virginia.[9]

Dunmore's expulsion and the departure of so many of his identifiable allies in 1776 substantially lightened the planter aristocracy's apprehension created by the mere existence of a loyalist opposition in Virginia. The abandonment of British allegiance and the severing of old loyalties had been difficult for many native Virginians, even though they became staunch revolutionists. There was a handful of loyalist planters, of whom councillors William Byrd III, Richard Corbin, and Ralph Wormeley were the most prominent; but of these only Byrd left the province, and none was molested. The elderly English nobleman Thomas, Sixth Lord Fairfax, who owned a vast Virginia estate, was an entirely passive loyalist. Robert Munford's play *The Patriots* (ca. 1780), though never produced in its own time, reflected what was probably a widespread concern with the difficulty of promoting virtue as well as external political conformity in the midst of a revolution. Munford's earlier play, *The Candidates* (ca. 1770), was an authentic re-creation of election practices in colonial Virginia, and some of the characters in *The Patriots* had actual historical counterparts in Mecklenberg County, Virginia, while others represented generalized social types. Although presented as a comic farce containing three intertwined romantic plots, *The Patriots* was a perceptive, if caricatured, commentary on political behavior. The names in the cast set the tone: Meanwell and Trueman, two moderate Whig planters falsely accused of Toryism; a committee of safety composed of Thunderbolt, Squib, Colonel Strut, Mr. Summons, Brazen, and Skip; Scottish merchants named M'Flint, M'Squeeze, and M'Gripe, pathetic victims of anti-Scottish prejudice; Mr. Tackabout, an actual Tory posing as a Whig; and Captain Flash and Sargeant Trim, dishonest recruiting officials. "What a pity it is that all heads are not capable of receiving the benign influence of the principles of liberty," Munford's Meanwell explained. "Some are too weak to bear it and become thoroughly intoxicated. . . . I hope my zeal against tyranny will not be shown by bawling against it, but by serving my country against her enemies; and never may I signalize my attachment to liberty by persecuting innocent men only because they differ in opinion with me." Hailed before a committee, Trueman punctured the pretensions of his interrogators. "Explain what you mean by the word Tory, gentlemen," he demanded.

Colonel Simple: Tory! Why surely everybody knows what a Tory is—a Tory is—pray, gentlemen, explain to him what a Tory is.
Strut: A Tory, sir, is any one who disapproves of men and measures.
Brazen: All suspected persons are called Tories.
Trueman: If suspicion makes a Tory, I may be one; if a disapprobation of men and measures constitutes a Tory, I am one; but if a real attachment to the true interests of my country stamps me her friend, then I detest the opprobrious epithet of Tory as much as I do the inflammatory distinction of Whig.[10]

Munford did not exaggerate the frustration Virginians felt at knowing there were men in their midst who disapproved of the Revolution but did not openly expose themselves. James Madison wrote to his father in March 1777 about an Orange County man, Benjamin Haley, whose "conversation on public affairs" with two travelers, one a Frenchman, "gave abundant proof of his being an adherent to the king"; because the witnesses, who promptly reported Haley to officials, were travelers who could not be present at the next sitting of court, the committee of safety decided not to prosecute. That evening in the tavern the Frenchman goaded Haley into public debate. "At first he evaded the charges of his antagonist, but after some time said he scorned to be a *counterfeit* and, in answer to some questions that were put to him, signified that we were in a state of rebellion and had revolted from our lawful sovereign. . . . This passed in the presence of 20 or 30 persons and rendered the testimony of the travelers needless." Though convicted of making a seditious statement, Haley was fined only twelve shillings by the court and jailed for one hour. The exposure of hidden loyalist opinion, even when voiced by "a contentious, hot headed fellow who meant, or could do, no harm," remained a serious public responsibility.[11]

43

The Ambiguous Threat
of the Maryland Loyalists

THE Revolution in Maryland swept from power the proprietary establishment and made the province an independent state. Though a victim of the Revolution, the proprietary government was not a direct agent of British authority, and proprietary leaders tried as gracefully as possible to avoid a direct clash with the Maryland Whigs. Individual residents of the state who did overtly support Britain in the War for Independence, therefore, acted without leadership or direct support from Crown officials. The bulk of these Maryland loyalists, however, lived on the eastern shore in such numbers and concentration that local civil officials were unable to intimidate them or suppress their activities. Yet at no time did the eastern shore loyalists constitute more than a serious irritant and embarrassment to the new government, and its retaliation against them was moderate. Proprietary official William Eddis noted this absence of passion. In June 1776 he asked to be exempted from militia duty on the ground that he was a member of the governor's household. The request was denied, and Eddis paid a nominal fine for his refusal to bear arms. "I have been treated with kind attention," he concluded; "it is my endeavor to regulate my conduct with propriety."[1] Eddis, to be sure, was a most proper and discreet young man, and not every proprietary official or other opponent of the Whigs received such civility from Revolutionary committees. Yet there was a widespread willingness in Maryland, as in Virginia, to allow passive opponents of the Revolution, even Daniel Dulany and Robert Eden, to live unmolested during the conflict.[2]

Men of ability and energy, Whig leaders in Maryland capitalized on the proprietary lethargy and loyalist weakness. On November 21, 1774, a provincial Congress met to endorse the Continental Association. A provincial committee of correspondence organized committees of safety in every western shore county by January 1, 1775, but formed none on the eastern shore. On December 1, 1774, when the nonimportation boycott went into effect, enforcement in Baltimore was rigid. Violations were few. When the *Totness* tried to unload a cargo in Talbot County, the committee of safety publicized the fact, and aroused citizens burned the ship to the waterline when it ran aground. Governor Eden appeased the extralegal movement of boycott enforcement by turning provincial arms over to the new Whig militia.[3] Into this vacuum moved a group of Baltimore loyalists led by George Chalmers and Robert and James Christie, who formed their own organization for self-protection. The group persuaded Governor Eden to replace Whig justices of the peace with loyalists, but he refused to arm them. During the summer of 1775, a committee intercepted a letter from James Christie critical of the formation of a Whig militia; the provincial Convention called on all citizens to refuse to do business with Christie, and this pressure effectively ended his political activities. By late 1775 nearly all western shore loyalists had been driven out or silenced. Of the one hundred Maryland loyalists who claimed compensation from the British after the war, forty left the state in 1775, and many of these were wealthy merchants from Baltimore and Ann Arundel counties who had been ruined by the Continental boycott. Also among the early exiles were the more obnoxious opponents of colonial resistance, including Anthony Stewart, whose ship the *Peggy Stewart* had been burned for carrying taxed tea to Annapolis in October 1774; the Reverend Bennett Allen, an utterly dissolute crony of the Calvert family, as well as Henry Addison and Jonathan Boucher.[4]

The senior-level officeholders under the proprietary government were divided in their response to the Revolutionary crisis. Those who owed their posts directly to the proprietor tended to become loyalists, while those who secured positions through the intervention of a powerful Maryland family that had some claim on the proprietor usually transferred their allegiance to the new government. Of 166 high-ranking proprietary officials holding remunerative positions between 1755 and 1775 and living at the creation of an independent government, the Revolutionary allegiances of 136 can be determined with some degree of certainty; 91 were patriots and 45 loyalists. Those with direct ties to Governor Sharpe or Eden or who were members or close allies of one of the three major families allied to the proprietor—the Dulanys, Claggetts, and Calverts—became loyalists by a three-to-one margin. Conversely, those owing their appointments to the influence of some other family, not closely identified with the proprietor, became patriots by a margin of nearly ten to one.[5]

Loyalist activity on the eastern shore was persistent and stubborn but poorly organized and ineffective. Isaac Atkinson, in Somerset County, who organized a loyalist militia drill, was arrested in December 1775 and then released to care for his large family. In Worcester County, in September 1775, Benjamin Shockley and William Townshend organized a loyalist association that was soon suppressed. After Dunmore departed from the Chesapeake in August 1776, Whig committees of safety in eastern-shore counties became more aggressive. A group of seven men who had served on board Dunmore's ship while it harassed the Maryland coast were interrogated, and their statements revealed a consistent pattern of traditional allegiance to the King, dislike of local patriots, and greed for plunder. In spite of persistent efforts by Whig militia to suppress disaffection in Somerset County, loyalists continued throughout the war to organize and to harass the Revolutionary government on the eastern shore. Early in 1777 approximately 500 men in Somerset and Worcester counties banded together to oppose the Revolution, and 200 Maryland regulars were needed to disperse the Tories. Most escaped, and the General Assembly offered to pardon those who surrendered within thirty days, gave up their arms, and took an oath of allegiance. However, the legislature also exempted fourteen known leaders of the uprising from this offer, and all but one of the group were ultimately captured and imprisoned. The evidence against several names on the list was flimsy, and several notorious promoters of the uprising, including Benjamin Shockley, were not included. In March a "Tory Act" imposed a new oath on inactive loyalists and neutrals but set a deadline of

August 1, 1777, for people who had left the state or who had not yet affirmed their allegiance to the new government. Not content with these measures, a self-appointed Whig Club in Baltimore began clamoring for more severe repression, and it organized vigilante harassment of people the club suspected of disloyalty. By slandering several innocent people and by its extralegal activities, the Whig Club soon antagonized the legislature.[6]

William Howe's invasion of Pennsylvania via Chesapeake Bay in late August 1777 precipitated a resurgence of eastern shore loyalist activity, but the militia dispersed a large group of loyalists who intended to join Howe's army. When Howe disembarked at Head of Elk, the northernmost point of Chesapeake Bay in Maryland, he dined in the home of Robert Alexander, a former member of the Maryland Council of Safety and delegate to the Continental Congress until 1776, when he had retired from public life rather than support independence. The path of Howe's invasion forced Alexander to abandon his neutrality. After allowing Howe's army to gorge itself on a vast quantity of his livestock and grain and permitting Howe to use his house as a temporary headquarters, Alexander fled from his home to the British fleet for protection. Even at this critical period, the Maryland legislature remained divided on whether to deprive passive loyalists of the rights to vote, own property, and practice a profession. A compromise law simply imposed a new oath, and some 18,000 people, representing 66 per cent of the population, subscribed to it. Early in 1778 more than 300 loyalists organized a Tory regiment in Somerset County. Some managed to make their way to Philadelphia; others joined a body of Delaware loyalists led by Cheney Clows, who built a fort on the Chester River and defied Delaware officials for several months; while others roamed the eastern shore disrupting civil government and intimidating Whig residents. In February 1778 the Maryland Council of State appointed Luther Martin attorney general. Martin investigated conditions in Somerset County and reported to Governor Thomas Johnson that "the disaffected inhabitants of this county . . . have arrived to so daring a height of insolence and villainy that there appears but very little security for the lives or property of any person who from political or other reasons are obnoxious to them." Civil officials in Somerset County were too weak to enforce laws against aiding the enemy or abusing Whig neighbors, and calling out the militia did little good, for the loyalists simply lapsed into neutrality until the militia departed. Martin prosecuted several prominent eastern shore loyalists in September 1778. One of them, John Tims, was convicted and sentenced to be hanged and drawn and quartered, although the very barbarity of the sentence, or else the decline of the loyalist threat in Maryland after the British evacuation of Philadelphia, prompted the Governor and Council to pardon Tims six months later. In February 1781 the Board of Associated Loyalists in New York City planned a bizarre loyalist uprising in western Maryland. The conspirators rendezvoused in Frederick, Maryland, where the plot was uncovered, and the following July the town became the site of a sensational treason trial in which seven men were sentenced by a local judge to be hanged and drawn and quartered. Luther Martin and Governor Thomas Johnson intervened in the case, commuting four of the death penalties and strictly forbidding drawing and quartering of the three who were to be hanged.[7]

In Maryland, loyalists were numerous and widespread, and the Revolutionary government was hesitant to impose its authority on the disaffected. Because the fighting largely by-passed the state and the loyalists lacked the leadership and the opportunity to pose a real military threat, the potential for bitter division and violence in Maryland was never realized.

44

Georgia, 1778-1781:

Portents of Defeat for

the Southern Loyalists

THROUGHOUT the War for Independence, Georgia remained an immense potential British asset. Georgia's back country loyalists were aggressive and active. Vulnerable to attack by sea from British forces based in East Florida and by land from Indians on the frontier, Georgia was militarily indefensible for the Americans. In James Wright the British possessed an official of unmatched ability in the trying work of restoring British authority to a once-rebellious province. Britain moved vigorously to capitalize on these advantages and enjoyed considerable short-term success. The difficulties that ultimately crippled the British pacification effort in Georgia were rooted in faulty conceptions and errors of command intrinsic to the British conduct of the war.

The lure of easy reconquest of Georgia generated overly optimistic, ambitious, and poorly co-ordinated activity similar to that which marked the early attempts to obtain inexpensive military triumph with the use of loyalist partisans in the Carolinas. South Carolinian and Georgian troops had tried to capitalize on their repulsion of Clinton's attack near Charles Town in June 1776 with an expedition against British East Florida; sickness and lack of provisions forced cancellation of the offensive, leaving Georgia all the more vulnerable to British attack. Thomas Brown, the back country loyalist partisan who had played such an active part in the civil war in South Carolina in 1775, emerged in East Florida as the foremost advocate of the reconquest of Georgia. He soon gained the confidence of East Florida's Governor, Patrick Tonyn. The two men spent the first part of 1776 trying to undercut John Stuart's policy of keeping the Creek Indians at peace. Both were anxious to recapture the Georgia and South Carolina back country and believed that with Creek support it could easily be done. Next, Brown organized a loyalist regiment, the East Florida Rangers. In January 1777, 500 British regulars, 100 of Brown's rangers, and a few Creek braves invaded Georgia but retreated to East Florida when a substantial force gathered to block their advance. For the next year, British forces in East Florida did not feel strong enough to undertake a further attack on Georgia. Brown's rangers formed a defensive force, patrolling the Georgia-Florida border. Meanwhile, bitter internal conflicts raged within the British command. General Augustine Prevost, commander of British regulars in East Florida, objected to Brown's rank and autonomy as commander of the rangers and demanded a unified command over all British and loyalist troops in East Florida. Tonyn and Brown abused John Stuart for his refusal to send the Creeks on the warpath. Stuart contended that without large quantities of supplies and careful co-ordination with British regulars, the Indians would not constitute a credible military force. Both controversies sputtered out. Under pressure from Tonyn, Brown surrendered command of the East Florida Rangers to Prevost; by the time Stuart tried to launch a Creek attack on rebel outposts in Georgia, hunger, apprehension, and dislike of the British had taken serious toll of the Creeks' fighting capacity. Meanwhile, Brown had led a small party into Georgia and returned to East Florida with optimistic reports of a large reservoir of back country loyalists ready to support a British offensive into the region. A second attempted Whig invasion of East Florida in June and July 1778 routed Brown's defensive force before heat and disease forced the small body of South Carolinian and Georgian Continentals to abandon the enterprise. The British and loyalists in East Florida and the Whigs in South Carolina and Georgia presented mutually tempting targets for an invasion. Both sides, however, were too weak to capitalize on the illusory opportunities, and, for both, the first two years of the war were a needlessly debilitating struggle.[1]

The invasion of Georgia by a formidable British force commanded by Colonel Archibald Campbell, in late December 1778 and early January 1779, drastically altered the balance of power and gave the loyalists a fresh opportunity to make Georgia a showcase of pacification and reconciliation to British rule. Campbell's force, composed of 3,500 British regulars, Hessians, and loyalists, outmaneuvered the American defenders of Savannah and captured the city almost without firing a shot. General Prevost, in East Florida, anticipated Campbell's victory and marched overland to Savannah from St. Augustine with a force of 2,000 troops, including Brown's rangers. As a result, the British secured complete control of the Georgia low country by January 17, 1779, and ten days later Campbell led a combined British and loyalist force, which included the East Florida Rangers, in a successful assault on Augusta, one hundred miles inland. The Carlisle Commission had told Campbell before he left New York on the expedition that he should prepare Georgia for the restoration of civil government. Knowing Clinton's distrust of civil government, Campbell pressed his commander as discreetly as possible to have a governor dispatched to Georgia at once. After creating the rudiments of civil rule—a board of police and claims commissioners, to assist needy loyalists—he sailed for England, leaving the acting Governor, Lieutenant Colonel Prevost in charge.[2]

Even before news of Campbell's initial triumph reached London, Colonial Secretary Germain issued orders for Campbell to assume the duties of acting governor. Alexander Innes, Clinton's and Germain's agent in South Carolina in 1776, who served on Campbell's staff, sailed from Georgia on January 23, 1779, and after a swift passage brought the government news of the victory at Savannah on February 23. Although the news bolstered the morale of the ministry at a crucial point in the war, and though Germain busied himself in plans to capitalize on this good fortune, no one bothered to consult former Governor James Wright, an exile in London. For two weeks Wright was completely ignored, and then, without warning, on March 8, 1779, he received orders to return to Georgia and re-establish civil government. Germain's cavalier treatment of Wright was symptomatic of his energetic but wholly unreflective response to news from

America. Wright had spent nearly three years in exile carefully thinking through his convictions about the nature of the Empire and the requirements for restoring British authority in the colonies—a concern to which Germain was profoundly insensitive. Germain's attitude boded ill for Wright's success. Wright's instructions were broad and flexible; they allowed him to reestablish the Assembly and to indemnify loyalists for their losses and promised Georgia special favor from the Crown if the colony would set a precedent by voluntarily contributing to the financial costs of the Empire. Germain failed to inform Clinton that, except for strictly military matters, he no longer had any authority in the province. After belatedly telling the General of this arrangement, Germain wholly ignored the complex and troublesome problems of civil-military relations, which persisted throughout the war because Clinton and Wright shared responsibility for events in the province. When Wright reached the province, in July 1779, civil-military relations had already become inflamed. Prevost had done nothing to prevent or punish looting by British troops. To compensate victims, Wright reorganized the claims commission and gave the commissioners the task of allocating housing in Savannah. The British Army had taken over all the houses it needed when it first occupied the city, and the soldiers now simply defied the orders of the civilian claims commissioners to vacate certain houses needed for civilian personnel. The commissioners told Wright that nothing could be done about the army until an Assembly met and gave legislative sanction to the actions of civil officials.[3]

Even more alarming to Wright was the discovery that Georgia was far from militarily secure and that, apart from conquest of the low country and temporary occupation of Augusta, British troops had done little to restore British control elsewhere in the province. No sooner had Campbell occupied Augusta and established a ring of outposts around the city than he sent emissaries out to urge back-country loyalists to come and assist in pacification. Thomas Brown, who had been injured in the occupation of Augusta, had assured British officers that hundreds of loyalists inhabited the region; but none responded to Campbell's appeal, and the Creek Indians had not accompanied the British in the numbers expected. Therefore, Campbell had withdrawn from

Augusta and returned to Savannah only two weeks after occupying the town. In Augusta he left only a token force that was powerless to prevent the Whigs from controlling the surrounding territory. Back country loyalists who wanted substantial evidence of British determination to hold the region were thoroughly disheartened. Although Campbell's expedition to Augusta had chased patriot militia out of northern Georgia, Colonel Andrew Pickens took command of Whig forces along the South Carolina-Georgia border. Pickens was a back country South Carolinian farmer, a veteran of Indian wars, and a Presbyterian elder so taciturn that, according to one contemporary, he put his words "between his fingers and examined them." Commanding some 400 men, Pickens learned that a force of 700 to 800 North and South Carolina loyalists led by Colonel Thomas Boyd was trying to march south to rendezvous with the British. On February 12, 1779, Boyd repulsed a small Whig band that had attacked his force as it crossed the Savannah River into Georgia, but he was unaware of the presence of Pickens's force a few miles away. Pickens stealthily pursued Boyd and, on the morning of February 14, found the loyalists camped along the banks of Kettle Creek. Pickens's advance party opened fire on the loyalists prematurely, and he lost control of his men as they charged on horseback through a canebrake along the creek. However, his subordinate, Elijah Clarke, reached a hilltop overlooking Boyd's defensive position from which he led an attack that gave Pickens time to regroup his men and overrun the loyalists' lines. A slaughter of the loyalists ensued, and many of the Tories who were captured were summarily hanged in a nearby grove; in all, seventy were killed, including Boyd, and seventy-five others made prisoners.[4]

At the Battle of Brier's Creek, on March 3, 1779, near the Georgia-South Carolina line, Prevost defeated 2,300 Continental troops and North Carolina militia, offsetting the effect of Pickens's victory at Kettle Creek. In March and August 1779 Pickens defeated bands of Creek Indians led by John Stuart's deputy, David Taitt. Taken together, Pickens's victories prevented the British from establishing control over northern Georgia in 1779 and contributed heavily to the sense of military insecurity Wright felt when he again assumed the governorship.

Impatient to finish his work in Georgia and to undertake the next stage of the war, an attack on South Carolina, Prevost was unwilling to leave large numbers of British troops in the Georgia back country. "The more I am able to see into the true state of affairs here," Wright wrote to Germain on August 9, 1779, "the more I am convinced of the wretched situation the province is in and how nearly it was to being totally lost while the army was carrying on their operations in South Carolina." In September and October 1779, during a siege of the city by American and French forces under Admiral d'Estaing, Prevost's troops conducted a brilliant defense of Savannah, but the ordeal so exhausted the British that they were unable to mount fresh operations for several months. When they did move again, it was into South Carolina, to support Clinton's assault on Charles Town early in 1780. Preparations for the South Carolina campaign, in Wright's view, left Georgia "naked and defenseless."[5]

Wright did succeed in his great task, the election of an Assembly, in April 1780. Its members represented only those coastal areas under British control, and it met in Savannah from May 9 until July 10, except for a two-week recess in June. It had to establish procedures for determining land ownership, because the Whigs had taken land records with them when they fled the state. In addition, the Assembly stripped 151 prominent Whigs of their political rights and declared null and void all actions of the Whig government. It also levied a two-and-one-half-per-cent duty on all exports from the province and earmarked this revenue for a contribution to the British Treasury. This genuflection to the principle of the Stamp Act, Wright had been assured, would entitle Georgia to special royal favor; Germain praised Wright for leading "the way in measures which have the fairest tendency to heal the unhappy breach between Great Britain and America." Otherwise Germain ignored Wright's dispatches, including his pleas that sufficient British troops be left in the province to subdue the Whig partisans who controlled most of the back country and destroyed the property of loyalists with impunity. The fall of Charles Town and the British occupation of South Carolina, Germain assured Wright in February 1780, would ease the military pressures on Georgia. "I am sorry to say," Wright retorted pointedly, "the consequences have fallen short of the just expectations of your lordship." Prosecution of the war in South Carolina would increasingly drain British regulars from Georgia and prevent their replacement. Aggravating this problem was the weakness of Thomas Brown's loyalist regiment at Augusta. Brown's experience and stubborn determination made him an able military commander. He was far more successful than any previous British official at motivating groups of Creeks and Cherokees to fight. Increasingly his men became involved in brutal guerrilla conflict. One band of Brown's men tortured the wife of a Whig militia officer named McKay by using the lock on a musket as a thumbscrew; later McKay's savage retaliation against the British shocked his own compatriots. After a long siege, General Andrew Pickens forced Brown to surrender Augusta on June 5, 1781, and, in violation of the terms of capitulation, many of the East Florida Rangers were murdered or beaten by Whig militia before they could reach safety in Savannah. This erosion of British military security in Georgia—after such high hopes of success in 1779—was a microcosm of the entire Southern campaign.[6]

45

Decision in London, 1779

FROM the beginning of 1778 until the autumn of 1779, several deep fissures appeared in the British government's capacity to conduct war. In spite of an obvious need for a painful reappraisal of policy and strategy following news of Saratoga and the French alliance, Germain and the King refused to consider the possibility that the war was lost, and an element of fantasy henceforth permeated official planning. The need to sustain the cohesion of the ministry tended to freeze men in their positions at the worst possible moment. North had known since early 1777 that "the best we can make of" the war in America "is to get out of the dispute as soon as possible"; with news of the French entry into the conflict, North knew that victory was impossible and he tried to resign. The King would not even consider North's departure, and the Cabinet also knew it would be a disaster. As a result of the French alliance with the colonies, the widely rumored plan to dismiss Germain—a step George III had previously endorsed—was quietly dropped. The lack of new leadership and new policies, therefore, made the North ministry increasingly vulnerable to criticism, notwithstanding its still comfortable majority in the House of Commons. "What is still more material" than questions of strategy and resources, the King bluntly told North on January 13, 1778, "is the plan on which [the] administration is to repel the different attacks of opposition when Parliament meets, as to calling for papers, the proposing [of] enquiries, etc." Restraining Parliamentary critics had become a growing preoccupation. For a brief time in early 1778, imperatives of commitment to the American war, maintenance of ministerial stability, and the pronouncement of credible replies to the opposition could be accomplished by an apparently rational and defensible plan of action. First, the British would abandon hope of clear-cut military victory in the northern provinces, withdraw their troops from Philadelphia, and conserve as large a reservoir of manpower as possible in New York City. Drawing on these forces if necessary, Britain would subdue the Southern colonies, starting with Georgia. Finally, the government would send a new conciliation commission to America empowered to accede to virtually all colonial demands short of independence. Some of these plans—invasion of the South, for example—had been under active consideration throughout 1777; Saratoga and the French entry into the war now made them not only desirable but imperative.[1]

Germain moved with customary vigor to adapt Britain's military posture. In the face of intense Cabinet opposition, he successfully proposed a major naval build-up in American waters. The British fleet, Germain argued, must be ready to counter any effort by Admiral d'Estaing to cut British supply lines to North America, and it must also be prepared to pursue the French fleet into the Caribbean should the French shift naval operations to that strategic region. Admiral Samuel Barrington lost the island of Dominica to the French in September 1778, but as soon as d'Estaing sailed for the Caribbean, Clinton dispatched from New York an expedition led by General James Grant to attack the strategically located French island of St. Lucia. Beating d'Estaing to the Caribbean, Grant successfully assaulted the island. Despite numerical superiority in ships and men, the French lost, in 1778, the opportunity to cripple British control of the seas in American waters. To strengthen Clinton's striking force in New York, Germain ordered Clinton to evacuate Philadelphia in May 1778. At this point, Prevost and Campbell seized Georgia.[2]

Britain could not capitalize on these initiatives. In the first place, there had been no co-ordination between these movements and the preparation of the new conciliation commission, headed by Lord Carlisle. North had been so fearful of his Cabinet colleagues that he had arranged the commission secretly, with the assistance of a group of subministers who shared his gloomy outlook on the war. The commission, which was empowered to grant almost any colonial demand short of independence, arrived in America just as Clinton was evacuating Philadelphia, where 3,000 loyalists had to choose between exile and making their own peace with the patriots. The commissioners found the loyalists bitter and Congress intransigent.

Simultaneously, events in England conspired to trigger a corrosive controversy between Admiral Augustus Keppel and Admiral Hugh Palliser that erupted into dangerous political recriminations in London. Palliser had served under Keppel in July 1778, in a crucial but inconclusive naval battle against the French in the English Channel. While the French heavily damaged Keppel's ships, they did not gain enough control of the Channel to threaten invasion. However, British naval vulnerability during the first months of French involvement in the war was a highly emotional issue. When Palliser was anonymously slandered for his conduct in the battle, he brought counter-charges of misconduct against Keppel. After a bitter, partisan court-martial trial, Keppel was found innocent; Palliser demanded a trial of his own, which turned out to be much more dispassionate and which vindicated him. Similarly, Burgoyne, on his return from Saratoga, tried to saddle Germain with the blame for his defeat. In responding to Burgoyne, Germain made disparaging remarks about General William Howe that set the stage for a Parliamentary inquiry into the war under the Howes. The Howe inquiry occurred before the House of Commons in May and June 1779. Witnesses for the two brothers argued that in 1776 and 1777 it had been impossible to defeat the Americans. The Revolution, the pro-Howe argument ran, enjoyed widespread popular support, and loyalists represented an unreliable minority of the populace. Under these conditions, the Howes believed they had done all that could have been reasonably expected of them.[3] Headed by Joseph Galloway, Germain's supporters challenged every one of the Howes' contentions. Four out of five Americans, Galloway contended, were loyal to Britain. Howe had failed utterly to mobilize them effectively, and he had squandered numerous opportunities to defeat the Continental Army. Galloway spoke for an aggressive and newly influential constituency: the loyalist exiles in England, who, after news of Burgoyne's defeat at Saratoga, realized for the first time that Britain could conceivably lose the war. Intensely homesick and humiliated by the lack of interest that the British government showed in their problems and views, the exiles joined eagerly in the campaign to discredit the Howes. In no other way could they dramatize their deep belief that the Revolution enjoyed little popular support, that the colonists yearned for British triumph. Not only did the loyalist spokesmen in the controversy possess firsthand knowledge of the colonies; they also brought compelling emotional force to the debate. When General Charles Grey, one of Howe's witnesses, declared that the American forces could not be defeated, one loyalist objected that his testimony tended to "fix a stigma upon all the Americans" that the exiles were determined "to wipe . . . off." Germain's Parliamentary adroitness, coupled with the loyalists' opinionated intransigence, discredited the Howes' defense of their conduct in America. "We should scarcely know what to do without you," one of Germain's assistants told Galloway, without exaggeration, at the outset of the hearings.[4] Having used the loyalist exile community for political ends, the ministry was now deeply committed to the energetic use of loyalists in the Southern campaign. A cluster of circumstances—the failure of the Howe mission, the spreading pattern of bitterness spawned by the Keppel affair and Germain's public quarrels with Burgoyne and the Howes, the political need to vindicate the loyalist exiles' interpretation of conditions in America—had the effect of dulling the ministry's sensitivity to military realities. For one thing, the war had already ruined the careers of Gage, Burgoyne, William Howe, Keppel, and others. "The ministry had lost the services of too many commanders," Piers Mackesy explains; "its political weaknesses made it clumsy in handling the recalcitrants and frightened of alienating those who remained. Germain could not afford to lose another general. . . . Henceforth the American Secretary was obliged to handle the Commander-in-Chief in America with velvet gloves." Skittish about the opposition, fearful of offending Clinton, uncertain about the extent of British military power, and deeply resentful of attacks on his past military judgment, Germain prepared to launch the invasion of the Carolinas.[5]

The ministry therefore needed arguments and new sources of supporting evidence to check the rising tide of criticism of the war. The potential of loyalist support in the Southern back country was the only evidence that could begin to prove that the war was still worth prosecuting. The country independents in the House of Commons were most sensitive to the ministry's claims. They had expected defeat of the American rebellion to reduce their tax burden. But the terms of North's conciliation plan in 1778 relinquished claim to colonial revenue, and the country independents took alarm. Appealing to their sense of honor, the ministry told the country independents that Britain owed the loyalists a debt of honor that required continued efforts to defeat the American rebels. Germain thus became trapped in an alliance with the loyalist exiles and inescapably wed to their military ideas. James Simpson, a former South Carolina placeman, went to Charles Town in the spring and early summer of 1779 to investigate loyalist strength for General Clinton. "I am of opinion," he wrote Clinton, "whenever the King's troops move to Carolina they will be assisted by very considerable numbers of the inhabitants." Clinton sent Simpson's report on to Germain. Simpson was not an especially objective observer; his only hope of regaining a lucrative Crown post was the restoration of royal government in South Carolina. A faintly obsequious, hedging tone in his report suggested that he was telling Clinton what he thought British officials wanted to hear: "I am not without sanguine expectations that with the proper conduct such a concurrence of many of the respectable inhabitants . . . may be procured, that a due submission to His Majesty's government will be established throughout the country." By the time Parliament reconvened in November 1779, Spain had entered the war, jeopardizing British possessions in the Caribbean and Gulf of Mexico, causing a still wider dispersal of British manpower, and forcing Germain to stake his career and the future of the Empire on the slender hope of effective loyalist exertion in the South.[6]

46

Clinton's War

PLANNING the Southern campaign was not solely Germain's responsibility. Germain gave Clinton the task of timing and directing the seizure of Charles Town and the invasion of the Carolinas. But Clinton was in no psychological condition to benefit from this generous mandate. Certain that the war had not been won in 1776 because his advice to William Howe had been spurned, Clinton now expended much of his energy writing documents that would prove, if things went badly, that he had not been at fault. Yet in spite of his suspicion and defensiveness, Clinton possessed many of the attributes of a first-rate military mind. He had understood in 1776 the folly of trying to rendez-vous British troops with loyalist insurgents in the Carolinas. He had grasped more clearly than any other British general that only a large and mobile British force firmly in control of a province could effect strong mobilization of the loyalists in the area. Now, on the eve of the embarkation to Charles Town, Clinton once again appraised the problem of subduing the American rebellion with loyalist support. Clinton argued that victory could still be won if Britain retained naval superiority in American waters *and* if it could either field a sufficient force in the Northern colonies to engage and defeat Washington or invade and occupy the Southern colonies from the Chesapeake to Georgia. For nearly two years following French entry into the war Clinton had been extremely careful not to move forces by sea while Admiral d'Estaing's fleet was in American waters. Though he did not acknowledge it, a Southern campaign was his only option. South Carolina was a less expensive proposition than land operations in the Chesapeake region, and British resources were increasingly limited. Yet Clinton's reasoning left crucial issues clouded. The movement to the South violated the fundamental strategic doctrine of concentration of force, and it did so at precisely the moment when the French fleet threatened to jeopardize British supply lines. The French had almost isolated New York City and recaptured Savannah in 1778. Dispersal of British forces between New York and the Carolinas in 1780 greatly increased British vulnerability.[1]

As soon as he learned that the siege of Savannah by Admiral d'Estaing had failed, Clinton prepared to sail for Charles Town. Clinton and Vice-Admiral Marriot Arbuthnot left New York on December 26, 1779, with 8,000 men. Landing on the north bank of the Edisto River on February 11, 1780, Clinton skillfully cut off the route of retreat from Charles Town and then overwhelmed the city's defenders. General Benjamin Lincoln, American commander in Charles Town, surrendered his 5,500-man garrison of Continental troops and militia on May 11, 1780. Clinton stayed in Charles Town long enough to consolidate the victory. His work began auspiciously. Two hundred Charles Town residents, including thirty-two artisans eager to do business with the British Army, signed an address welcoming Clinton and Arbuthnot. Within three weeks, rebel militia at Beaufort, Ninety-Six, and Camden capitulated, and many of these men sought and received British parole on the condition that they live peaceably. Clinton and Arbuthnot jointly held the titles of commissioners for restoring civil government. Clinton feared the instability that might plague a civilian administration in militarily occupied territory and hated giving Arbuthnot any credit for political successes. Clinton organized loyalist volunteers in South Carolina into militia companies, and he instructed Cornwallis to establish a civilian board of police to govern occupied Charles Town. On May 22, 1780, Clinton issued a proclamation promising protection to all "faithful and peaceable subjects" and threatening punishment and confiscation for any who tried to dissuade subjects from returning to obedience. A second proclamation, on June 1, granted full pardon to those who returned to British allegiance. There was widespread relief in South Carolina at these generous terms of peace.[2]

Before leaving Charles Town, Clinton made two mistakes that seriously handicapped subsequent British operations in South

Carolina. First, he appointed Major Patrick Ferguson inspector general of loyalist militia, over the protests of several junior officers, who claimed Ferguson had an ungovernable temper and weak judgment—accusations Clinton dismissed as jealous backbiting of the kind he himself had long suffered. Then, on June 3, Clinton issued a third proclamation, which contradicted the generous spirit of his prior announcements; it required all civilians on parole to sign an oath of allegiance to the Crown within seventeen days and declared that all nonsigners would be considered rebels. Many patriots paroled to their homes regarded this proclamation a treacherous denial of prior permission to live peaceably as neutrals. Some fled to the back country to take up resistance again; others took the oath but felt no moral compulsion to obey it; and many notorious rebels took the oath and gained protection of the King's troops, to the chagrin of authentic loyalists. The mood in South Carolina abruptly changed from one of resignation to one of suspicion. Clinton himself somewhat archly observed that the problems created by his final proclamation developed only after he left the province and relinquished direct supervision over British policies there. "By obliging every man to declare and evince his principles," Clinton later wrote, "I gave the loyalists an opportunity of detecting and chasing from among them such dangerous neighbors." Within a month an experienced British officer, Lord Rawdon, reported from the back country that "the unfortunate proclamation of the third of June has had very unfavorable consequences. The majority of the inhabitants in the frontier districts, though ill-disposed to us, . . . were not actually in arms against us; they were therefore freed from the paroles imposed" after the fall of Charles Town, "and nine out of ten of them are now" enlisted with "the rebels."[3]

47

South Carolina under British Rule

BRITISH success in the Southern campaign depended not only on loyalist military success but also on the capacity of loyalist administrators and British officers to re-establish normal patterns of civic life. Just as loyalist militia would play a vigorous role in the reconquest of South Carolina, loyalist appointees in Charles Town and Savannah endeavored with some effect to bring to their provinces the blessings of a benevolent, rational royal rule. But they were hobbled in this task by internal divisions, the lack of clear policy guidelines from New York and London, an ambiguous relationship between military and civil authority, and, most pervasively, the absence of usable constitutional theory concerning the sources of their authority and the requirements of the public good.

The foundation of this effort toward the restoration of civil authority was the Board of Police in Charles Town. The city had three military commandants during British occupation: General James Patterson, during the first weeks after the fall of the city to Clinton; Lieutenant Colonel Isaac Allen, of the New Jersey Volunteers, just before British departure in 1782; and, during most of the occupation, Lieutenant Colonel Nisbet Balfour. They, in turn, were directly answerable to successive British commanders in the South: Clinton, Cornwallis, and, after York-town, General Alexander Leslie. These men delegated wide powers to the Board of Police in Charles Town. The board con-sisted of a coterie of pre-Revolutionary placemen who had re-turned to Charles Town in 1780—James Simpson, Egerton Leigh, and former members of the royal Council and plural officeholders Edward Savage and Thomas Irving. In 1781 former Chief Jus-tice Thomas Gordon also joined the board. In a curious partial throwback to the pre-Revolutionary South Carolina practice of including planting, mercantile, and artisan interests in political organizations, the board included a representative of the planting interest, Alexander Wright, son of Governor Wright of Georgia, and Robert William Powell, a spokesman for the "trading part of the community"—both moderate loyalists who had been exiled from the state in 1778 for refusing to abjure allegiance to the King. Finally, the board included a representative of the British Army, Colonel Alexander Innes. The first head of the Board of Police was James Simpson, former Attorney General; when he left the province in February 1781 his place was taken by former Lieutenant Governor William Bull. Bull possessed far more stature than that of a former placeman; one of the most widely respected men in the pre-Revolutionary period, he had frequently served as acting governor and longed for appointment as governor in his own right. Now more than seventy years of age, he returned to occupied Charles Town as head of the Board of Police, somewhat pathetically yearning for restoration of civil government and appointment as governor. The board was an able and experienced group. Leigh, Simpson, Gordon, and Bull knew intimately the working of the old royal administration and the role of government in promoting the provincial economy. Powell and Wright brought extensive knowledge of commerce and agriculture. Innes, whose reports to Dartmouth in 1775 had charted so graphically the deterioration of royal authority, represented the military, the agency ultimately responsible for British success.[1]

The board acted as a civil court, enforcing the payment of private debts and performance of contract. It also set maximum prices and standard weights for loaves of bread, mediated disputes over compensation due for property appropriated by the British Army, managed sequestered estates belonging to departed Whigs, and disciplined urban slaves. The board also dealt with disputes between merchants and the British Army. The British commissary had confiscated 120 barrels of rice shortly after the occupation of Charles Town. The firm of David Hall and Company protested that the rice was its private property and not subject to confiscation. The army, however, contended that the rice had already passed into the hands of the rebel government and was hence public property and victor's spoils under the terms of capitulation. The board found documentary evidence that the rice had been acquired by the government and rejected Hall's claim, but it did find a load of mahogany seized by the army engineers to be private property. The most sensitive task facing the board was the regulation of slavery. Many slaves had fled their masters and sought the protection of the British Army when it captured Charles Town. In a characteristic eighteenth-century blend of property protection and pursuit of justice, Clinton and later Cornwallis ordered slaves belonging to loyalists returned to their masters, but only on the condition that the masters promise not to inflict punishment on the runaways, who, after all, had trusted in British protection. Until these arrangements could be made, a three-man commission put about one hundred of these slaves to work repairing Charles Town's fortifications. The board further recommended the use of British troops to quell any slave uprisings that occurred in occupied South Carolina, and it published a list of apprehended runaway slaves.[2]

For all its expertise in these administrative matters, however, the Board of Police could not understand the apparent ease with which South Carolinians changed their allegiance from patriot to British after the occupation of Charles Town in 1780, and their willingness to revert to their former loyalties as soon as the fortune of war changed again. Several wealthy figures protected themselves by living in England during the war. South Carolina patriots tolerated this dubious neutrality on the ground that men of substance had a right to be opportunistic in order to protect their fortunes under the extreme conditions of war. Following the same reasoning, many of the signers of the address welcoming Clinton and Arbuthnot to Charles Town did not regard this gesture as a binding expression of their allegiance, nor did the British take much stock in the list of names. Clinton's impolitic proclamation of June 3, 1780, requiring paroled prisoners to support the Crown and the mass deportation and imprisonment at St. Augustine of twenty-nine prominent South Carolina Whigs, to take place in August 1780, seemed to free South Carolinians from any obligation to deal honorably with the British conqueror. Several prominent South Carolina families became divided in allegiance during the occupation without causing serious recriminations. The Pinckneys remained close friends with royal officials like James Simpson and also with a relative by marriage, Daniel Horry, who was a British supporter. Henry Middleton, a former president of the Continental Congress, took an oath of allegiance to the Crown during the occupation, while his son Arthur refused to do so and was exiled to St. Augustine. Even Charles Drayton, William Henry's brother, who tried to remain on good terms with both sides during the occupation, earned only a mild rebuke from a Whig, Charles Cotesworth, who commented that "Charles D. is playing what I suppose he deems to be a sure game, but I look upon it to be a hazardous one; . . . this constant trimming on both sides cannot be deemed an honorable part, and it is in the interests of all parties that it should not be the only safe one." A willingness to curry favor with British officials might not be an honorable course of action, but in a society that could not afford the luxury of recrimination and intense factionalism, supple allegiances were a permissible human vice.[3]

48

Cornwallis's War

BEFORE Clinton departed for New York City on June 8, 1780, he drafted instructions that apparently gave Cornwallis an independent command in the Southern colonies and prescribed only the general military objectives he should pursue. Cornwallis was to complete the pacification of South Carolina, which already seemed well under way, and then conduct an expedition to North Carolina, rally loyalists there, and render the province reasonably secure. He was also put in command of British troops in Georgia and East and West Florida and made responsible for maintaining order in those colonies; and as soon as the entire region from the Carolinas southward was under British rule, Cornwallis was to march his force north to Virginia to support a major offensive in the Chesapeake region. From the outset of his new command, however, there were severe limitations on Cornwallis's capacity to execute these instructions. Clinton took 4,500 men back to New York with him, leaving Cornwallis with at most 3,000 men available for offensive operations. Except for Lieutenant Colonel Banastre Tarleton's British Legion, an elite loyalist corps, Clinton left Cornwallis almost no cavalry, and mounted troops were essential in a campaign to overawe a scattered civilian populace. Two of Cornwallis's principal officers, Tarleton and Ferguson, were ungovernable subordinates. Ferguson refused to be saddled with administrative duties in organizing and training loyalist regiments in South Carolina, and after energetically enlisting and organizing some 1,500 loyalist militia in the strongly pro-British Ninety-Six district, he neglected the work of creating loyalist regiments in the more evenly divided districts of Camden, Cheraw, and Georgetown. Tarleton, a brilliant, mobile, fearless cavalry officer, was a more serious liability. Ranging widely through the interior of South Carolina after the fall of Charles Town, Tarleton caught and defeated the only remaining Continental troops—350 Virginians commanded by Abraham Buford—in the region called the Waxhaws. As the American soldiers tried to surrender, Tarleton's loyalist soldiers cut them down with their swords, thus giving their leader a reputation as a butcher. During their pursuit of Buford's men, the legion galloped across the plantation of a back country landowner and former Revolutionary officer, Thomas Sumter, and, in what Russell F. Weigley calls "a misguided perception of the uses of severity," burned the buildings down. Tarleton's men soon became infamous for their plundering and burning of the homes of noncombatant civilians. Far from cowing the back country, Tarleton's legion provoked the start of what became savage back country warfare, in both South Carolina and Georgia, between irregular patriot militia and loyalist militia, local loyalist partisans, and British troops.[1]

What Tarleton did not realize and could not have known was that the very kind of irregular warfare he was practicing had already brutalized the South Carolina back country. The Cherokee war in 1760 and 1761 had been marked by unusually sadistic killing on both sides. Settlers had fled to the safety of inadequate forts, where disease, hunger, and incompetent administration by the militia increased the suffering. The struggle had left civil government in ruins, and for several years bands of outlaws roamed unchecked, until ruthlessly suppressed by the South Carolina Regulator movement. The back country civil war of 1775 and 1776 renewed the use of ambushes and torture by both loyalists and Whigs. When loyalist partisans from East and West Florida began to filter back into the back country in 1778, on the eve of the reconquest of Georgia, a Charles Town newspaper was probably not exaggerating when it accused them of "the most execrable outrages. . . . They plunder houses, steal horses, abuse women, tie and whip men, and cut their ears off." The British invasion of the state in 1780 and Tarleton's and Ferguson's effectiveness greatly increased the stakes and the passions in this contest—and consequently the killing. In sixty-two small- and medium-sized battles in the South Carolina back country in 1780 and 1781, there were nearly 4,000 casualties. Contributing

significantly to the ferocity of the conflict was the killing of helpless prisoners of war and combatants trying to surrender. On the
morning of May 15, 1781, Whig militia captain John McCord
ordered the summary execution of fourteen loyalist prisoners.
One of the victims, Joseph Cooper, survived the shooting; when
he moved, one of the Whigs ran a sword through his neck and
said he had "never seen a son of a bitch bleed so much in his
life." Miraculously, Cooper survived that wound and managed to
drag a dead companion to whom he was handcuffed to a shady
spot; there two women found Cooper when they were attracted
by the "stench" of his companion's corpse. The following
November, the South Carolina loyalist major "Bloody Bill"
Cunningham, commanding 300 militiamen on a dawn patrol,
found thirty drunken Whigs. Two escaped, but Cunningham's
men surrounded the other twenty-eight and cut them to pieces
with their swords.[2]

In the summer of 1780 Cornwallis could not foresee this
descent into barbarism, and it might have been forestalled if his
army had not been drawn into futile and costly battles in North
Carolina in early 1781. For his part, Cornwallis condemned and
forbade cruelty and plundering by British or loyalist forces, and
he won a stunning conventional victory over General Horatio
Gates at Camden in August 1780; but the victory only increased
the enemy's reliance on guerrilla tactics. Cornwallis recognized
the danger but could not bring himself to abandon the rules of
civilized warfare. "I am clearly of opinion," he admitted to a
loyalist officer from New York, Lieutenant John Cruger, "that in
a civil war there is no admitting of neutral characters, and that
those who are not clearly with us must so far be considered
against us as to be disarmed." He favored hanging for captured
Whig partisans who had previously sworn to the British that they
would live in peace, but he gave orders that civilians who were
only suspected of rebel sympathies were to be disarmed by the
"gentlest methods of which that business will admit." Orders to
embittered loyalist militia to use "gentle" methods in dealing with
suspected rebels were obviously ineffective. Although Cornwallis
had been ordered to secure the Southern colonies with conventional military tactics, the conduct of his subordinates, the limitations of his own manpower, and the violence-prone history of

back country society worked to undermine his effectiveness and ignite a smoldering guerrilla conflict.[3]

So long as Ferguson and Tarleton seemed invincible as they swept through the South Carolina countryside rallying groups of loyalists and taking vengeance on Whig neighbors, the deterioration of Cornwallis's position was not apparent. Cornwallis knew that Ferguson's undisciplined character posed a serious danger. "Between us," he confided to Lieutenant Colonel Nisbet Balfour on July 3, 1780, "I am afraid of his getting to the frontier of North Carolina and playing some cussed trick." Ferguson commanded a nucleus of one hundred experienced loyalist provincial troops from New York and New Jersey and a thousand North and South Carolina loyalist militia. Ranging far to the west and neglecting his communications with Cornwallis, Ferguson became vulnerable to a large force of frontiersmen who had heard of his savage deeds and had gathered on September 25 to pursue him. Only when reports of this movement reached Ferguson on September 27 did he realize the extent of his peril. He stopped at Tate's plantation, near Buffalo Creek, and hoped that his presence would attract fresh loyalist volunteers from the region. Few supporters appeared, and the loyalists headed toward Charlotte. They might have eluded their pursuers completely except that a patriot spy pretending to be a loyalist had loitered around Tate's plantation long enough to learn of Ferguson's route and relay it to some South Carolina Whig militia in the area. Instead of continuing the flight, Ferguson decided that the rocky pinnacle known as King's Mountain provided a magnificent defensive location from which his small force could fight off a numerically superior enemy. He actually believed that the advantages of terrain from the top of King's Mountain would enable him to win a miraculous victory. Discovering Ferguson's position from two captured loyalists on October 5, the mountainmen and South Carolina militia who had been drawn into the pursuit formed battle formation, early the following day, in a long horseshoe arrangement around the base of the mountain. By this time the Whig force had swelled to between 1,400 and 1,800 men. At three o'clock on the afternoon of October 7 the battle began. For all its apparent invincibility, King's Mountain became an extremely difficult position to defend. The trees on the lower slopes provided good cover, and the patriots' buckskin blended with the fall foliage; the steep rocky slopes actually provided further protection, because the loyalists could not position their guns to fire downward at a sufficiently steep angle and their shots went over the heads of the crouching troops below—terrifying at first, but then ineffective. What Ferguson had not known was that the mountainmen were very accurate marksmen and that his men at the top of the mountain made clear targets. Ferguson meanwhile darted conspicuously around the summit waving his sword and encouraging his men. When he realized that he could not hold the mountain with muskets and rifles, he ordered a bayonet charge. Again the apparent advantage of elevation was illusory. As his men charged downward, their momentum and difficult footing turned their hand-to-hand assault into a chaotic scene of tumbling bodies, dead and wounded men spurting blood on the rocks. Momentarily dominating all else was Major Ferguson, mounted on a great white horse, cutting down his own men's surrender flags with his sword, shouting, "Huzza brave boys, the day is our own," and charging into the midst of the combat slashing in all directions with his sword until seven Whig musket balls hit him almost simultaneously. The loyalist Captain Abraham de Peyster, of King William's Regiment, surrendered some 700 survivors. In less than an hour of fighting, more than 157 loyalists died and 163 were seriously wounded. Some of the carnage occurred after Ferguson had fallen, when his men had tried to surrender. Benumbed loyalists were cut down by patriot riflemen amid shouts of "Buford, Buford, Tarleton's quarter." Many of the atrocities were committed by South Carolinians avenging the killing and maiming of their relatives by Ferguson's or Tarleton's men. Not until the Virginian Colonel William Campbell shouted, "For God's sake quit. It's murder to shoot any more," did the killing halt. "The dead lay in heaps on all sides," one witness recalled, "while the groans of the wounded were heard in every direction." Seriously wounded prisoners were simply abandoned and those who could walk forced to march to Bickerstaff's plantation, near Rutherfordton. There nine loyalists accused of plundering, including one man who was clearly innocent, were hanged from a giant oak tree. The others were marched to the Moravian settlements of Salem and Bethabara, where they received medical care. Only 130 of the 700 survivors reached their destination of Hillsborough. The remainder died or escaped. The escapees probably had a significant impact on the future course of the war, for they spread stories of unbelievable suffering and horror among potential loyalists who gave them assistance.[4]

Loyalist strength continued to deteriorate. At dawn on January 17, 1781, Brigadier General Daniel Morgan caught Tarleton's British Legion in an ingenious and superbly executed tactical trap at a popular grazing area known as Cowpens, South Carolina. The British Legion comprised three volunteer troops of loyalist dragoons from Philadelphia and Bucks and Chester counties, in Pennsylvania, who were organized between January and April 1778, during the occupation of Philadelphia. They were tough, hardened men who saw partisan warfare as an opportunity for violence, adventure, and plunder. Though used in South Carolina to keep communications open among British posts, the legion had been the cutting edge of Cornwallis's attack, and Morgan decided to stand and fight only because he knew he could not indefinitely evade the highly mobile force. Selecting his terrain with uncommon foresight, Morgan arranged two lines of green militia across the path of Tarleton's attack, instructing each to fire one volley and then withdraw in order. His Maryland and Delaware Continentals waited in a third line atop a small hill 150 yards behind the first militia line. Tarleton sent his mounted troops, tired from a long predawn pursuit of Morgan, charging into the weak militia lines with what one of his officers called "un-officer-like impetuosity." The militia aimed their volleys at officers, and by the time the legion reached the foot of the hill it had lost both momentum and initiative. Meanwhile, Morgan had two experienced militia companies in reserve, one behind his third line and the other to its right. Tarleton ordered a cavalry charge into the American left, but it was repulsed. Redcoated Scottish infantry accompanying Tarleton's cavalry then marched, with bagpipes screeching, toward the right flank. The militia there pretended to retreat and then suddenly swung around and counterattacked with bayonets. At this critical point, the cavalry in the rear circled a quarter of the way around the battlefield and attacked Tarleton's main force on the American

left, completely routing the British. At the cost of only 12 killed
and 60 wounded, Morgan had captured 400 loyalist troops,
injured 200, and killed 100. This time Morgan's officers prevented vengeful killing of captives. Tarleton escaped capture
and withdrew with the remnants of his force.[5] The next day
Cornwallis learned of the result of the Battle of Cowpens. Three
days later he wrote that Tarleton's defeat "has almost broke my
heart."[6]

From that point, the conquest of North Carolina became a
march through an inhospitable land that cost Cornwallis much
more in time and resources than it did the Americans. He occupied Hillsborough on February 22, 1781, and though many local
loyalists came to town to watch the splendid and welcome sight
of British troops in the streets of the former wartime capital of
the state, few volunteered to fight for the King. Dr. John Pyle,
who was perhaps the most able back country loyalist leader in
North Carolina, assembled between 300 and 400 loyalist recruits
between the Haw and Deep rivers. Cornwallis sent word that
Tarleton and what was left of his British Legion would meet
Pyle en route to Hillsborough and accompany the new recruits to
the town. General "Light Horse Harry" Lee's Virginia dragoons,
clad in green uniforms resembling those of the British Legion,
intercepted Pyle ahead of Tarleton, and the loyalists, mistaking
Lee's men for their friends, allowed themselves to be completely
surrounded. Too late, Pyle realized his mistake and ordered his
men to resist; one hundred were killed and the rest dispersed.
Without significant loyalist help, then, Cornwallis fought an
inconclusive battle near Guilford Courthouse, on March 15,
where General Nathanael Greene tried to use the same formation
that Morgan had utilized at Cowpens. Cornwallis was a commander far superior to Tarleton, and he drove Greene from the
field that day. But in so doing he lost a quarter of his own
army—93 killed and 413 wounded. Thereupon he concluded
that the only course open to him was to march to Wilmington,
where his army could be supplied from sea. Then, in accordance
with his instructions to carry the war into the Chesapeake region,
Cornwallis set out for Virginia and ultimately Yorktown, where
a combined American and French naval and land operation
forced him to surrender in October 1781.[7]

With Cornwallis's departure from the state, the government of North Carolina proved too exhausted to suppress further loyalist guerrilla activity. Colonel David Fanning, an adventurous and irrepressible North Carolina counterpart to Thomas Brown, in Georgia, organized a well-disciplined force of loyalist militia in the summer of 1781. Fanning strictly forbade plundering. He operated throughout the eastern part of the state, gaining strength as he went and defeating every attack by ragged Whig militia. In a brilliantly executed operation on September 12, 1781, Fanning seized Hillsborough and captured Governor Thomas Burke. Fanning took Burke to Wilmington, where the British first threw the Governor into jail and then paroled him to James Island, which he found infested with hostile North Carolina loyalist refugees. In fear for his life, he broke parole and fled back to the mainland. Ironically, the North Carolina loyalists became an effective insurgent force only during the British occupation of Wilmington from January to November 1781. By that time it was too late to affect the course of the war.[8]

Similarly, in South Carolina, loyalists proved to be tenacious fighters in a lost cause. South Carolina, New Jersey, and New York loyalist troops commanded by Lieutenant Colonel John Cruger held the critical British fort at Ninety-Six in May 1781, when Greene laid siege to the post. The battle lasted for almost a month, until Lord Rawdon marched a relief expedition of newly arrived British troops from Charles Town to Ninety-Six. Unable to break the will and courage of Cruger's men before Rawdon arrived, Greene lifted the siege and withdrew. Rawdon decided that the fort at Ninety-Six was not worth the cost of continued fighting, and he marched the loyalist garrison back toward Charles Town, en route turning over command of the loyalists and recently arrived British regulars to Lieutenant Colonel Alexander Stewart. At Eutaw Springs, on August 22, 1781, Greene nearly defeated Stewart and destroyed his army as a fighting force, but the British occupation of Charles Town nonetheless continued for more than a year. In the spring of 1782 Carleton replaced Clinton, in New York City, as commander of the British Army in America. He suspended hostilities and ordered the evacuation of Savannah and Charles Town. Between September and December 1782, the British Navy evacuated 6,300 troops, 3,800 loyalists, and 5,000 slaves from Charles Town. By November 1783, over 20,000 British troops and nearly 30,000 loyalists left New York City on British ships; 10,000 other loyalists had departed earlier.[9]

The Southern campaign had indeed tapped the resource of back country loyalists. Thousands of Georgians and Carolinians had rallied to the Crown between 1779 and 1782 and had endured some of the hardest fighting of the war. But no vital center of loyalist activity had ever developed—no core around which others, motivated by fear, hope, self-interest, or simple inertia, could rally. For all the havoc the Southern campaign spread in the administration of rebel government, organized resistance never ceased. Even in the flush early days of the campaign in the South, the loyalists could never transform their grim sense of desperation into a positive contagion of hope and exultation. Despite their fighting ability and numbers, the loyalists in the South possessed only fragments of social purpose and political capacity.

Epilogue: A Special Kind
of Civil War

AS the fighting sputtered out during the winter of 1781–82 and
peace negotiations ensued, the loyalists entered a new—and in
many ways the most important—phase of their experience, one
that lies beyond the scope of this book. Ahead of them remained
their adjustment to defeat and to Britain's recognition of American independence.

The treatment of the loyalists was the most difficult issue for
British and American negotiators to resolve in 1782. The Crown
insisted on the restoration of all confiscated property and am-
nesty from prosecution for all crimes allegedly committed by the
loyalists in the course of the war. American negotiators were
instructed to refuse any concessions in favor of the loyalists.
Britain broke the impasse by abandoning its rigid defense of the
loyalists' interests, and the Americans responded by agreeing that
Congress would "earnestly recommend" to the states that loyalists who had not borne arms for the British could reclaim their
property and that those who had fought for the Crown or gone
into exile would have one year to purchase back their confiscated
estates from the new owners. The American Secretary for Foreign
Affairs rightly called the loyalist clause of the peace treaty "a
very slender provision . . . inserted [by Britain more] to appease the clamors of these poor wretches than to satisfy their
wants."[1]

Predictably, the peace treaty provided the loyalists scant security. The states ignored Congress's recommendation that they
restore confiscated property, and few prominent refugees dared
try to reclaim their former estates and possessions. Loyalists who

returned unsuspectingly to their homes in Connecticut in 1783 were mobbed and beaten, and in many localities a campaign of hysteria against returning loyalists raged. The frenzy, however, quickly spent itself and subsided.[2] Men like Alexander Hamilton, of New York, and Aedenus Burke, of South Carolina, argued powerfully that the young republic could not endure the corrosive effects of public vengeance. Despite this influential move to calm the public temper, most well-known loyalist exiles discovered that they could not return to their old homes for many years.

Bitterly disappointed by the ambiguous loyalist provisions in the peace treaty, the exiles in London redoubled their efforts to secure redress from the British government. Parliament responded by creating a commission dealing with the losses and services of the American loyalists. Its investigation began in 1783 and lasted for six years. Hearings were held in London and also in Canada, at Halifax, St. Johns, and Montreal. The commission, which heard 3,225 claims for property and income lost on account of claimants' loyalty to the Crown during the Revolution, and granted compensation to 2,291 claimants, did its work well. It eliminated fraudulent and inflated claims and required each claimant to produce witnesses from among other loyalist exiles and Crown officials who could testify to his character, devotion to the Crown during the Revolution, and the pre-Revolutionary value of his estate or Crown office. The claimants did not recoup all of their losses, but the compensation of more than three million pounds amounted to 37 per cent of the successful claimants' estimates of their losses.[3]

Although 55 per cent of the claimants asked for £1,000 or less and were people of "modest means,"[4] the compensation machinery, in the main, served the interests of wealthy loyalists who could afford the time and trouble to file well-documented and convincing claims. Many humble loyalists who migrated to other parts of the Empire secured compensation in the form of land there. Of the 60,000 to 80,000 loyalist exiles, apart from 7,000 who went to England, 30,000 to 40,000 moved to Nova Scotia and Quebec; more than 1,000 black refugees, many of whom had escaped from slavery during the Revolution, finally settled in Sierra Leone, in west Africa; and the remainder went to Bermuda, Jamaica, the Bahamas, and elsewhere in the West Indies.[5] Of all this migration, the loyalist resettlement in Canada had the greatest consequences. These people settled an immense area in Cape Breton, in Nova Scotia, and in the future provinces of New Brunswick and Ontario, as well as the French-speaking province of Quebec. "This thin line of loyalist colonization, extending from the Atlantic to Lake Huron," W. Stewart Mac-Nutt concludes, "held firm for forty years against American assertions of manifest destiny, against all the centrifugal and disruptive forces that a hostile geography and adverse commercial pressures could muster. Somehow or other, these authoritarian and determined Tories created the conscience of a common citizenship that two generations later was to be the most fundamental factor in the making of Canadian confederation."[6]

Much can be said about the American Revolution without taking the loyalists into account. To the extent that the patriots were not primarily interested in punishing the loyalists or the British chiefly concerned with vindicating and protecting their American allies, the loyalists *were* secondary figures in the Revolution. But they were also integral participants. Hauled before committees of safety, villified in Whig ideology, dispossessed, uprooted, and threatened with injury or death if they refused to acquiesce, and enrolled in large numbers in loyalist military regiments, the loyalists witnessed the Revolution at first hand and were the most immediate victims of the upheaval. Multifaceted and constantly shifting, the loyalists' experiences can be readily described. But *explaining* the loyalists' historical significance entails comment on the nature of the Revolution itself.

The Revolution was in some respects a civil war—protracted hostilities between irreconcilably antagonistic segments of society within the same country to exclude one another from political power and social advantage and extirpate one another's beliefs and principles. During the course of the War for Independence, some 19,000 colonists served in forty-two loyalist provincial corps.[7] These troops served as occupation forces in support of the regular British Army in New Jersey, in 1776; the environs of Philadelphia, in 1777 and 1778; the outpost at Augusta, Georgia, between 1779 and 1781; and back country South Carolina, between 1780 and 1782. Loyalist forces bore the burden of battle in the St. Leger and Baum offensives in upstate New York, in 1777, and in Ferguson's disastrous drive into North Carolina, at the end of 1780. When Sumter and Marion resorted to irregular warfare in South Carolina in 1780 and 1781, William Cunningham and other loyalist guerrilla fighters retaliated in kind, just as Butler's Rangers had in the Wyoming and Mohawk valleys during the year following Sullivan's destructive campaign of 1779. David Fanning, in the summer of 1781, perfected a mobile and disciplined loyalist force that temporarily disrupted the Revolutionary government in eastern North Carolina, but only after Cornwallis had failed to pacify the state and had marched north to Yorktown.

In spite of the impressive scope and intensity of this fighting between loyalists and patriots, the loyalists differed significantly from participants in a civil war. Loyalists in arms never enjoyed or really earned the support of a sizable civilian constituency capable of supplying, financing, and supporting military activities with impunity. The loyalists were not fighting to retain control of colonial government or to preserve particular British policies. They were not fervent monarchists or partisans for an eighteenth-century version of British imperialism. They thrust up no charismatic leaders, carried into battle no fully developed and widely shared vision of what America might become under continued British rule, nourished no common hatred of particular Whig leaders. In the beginning, what strength of purpose they shared derived, as John Randolph realized, while a loyalist exile in London, from the intense parochialism insulating some regions and communities and many individuals from the growing national identity that the pre-Revolutionary controversy had strengthened and accelerated among other Americans.[8] Only late in the war, in the loyalist communities of occupied New York City and London, did their common paranoia at the apparent injustices visited on them by American cruelty and British incompetence create a strong group consciousness. This realization of the bitter irony of their situation was the beginning of an ideology that would sustain many loyalist exiles in years to come. It was, at the same time, a useless impediment to those who returned to or remained in the United States.[9]

A more satisfactory way to set the loyalists in historical perspective is to consider the Revolution as a special kind of civil war—a struggle for national liberation.[10] It consisted of a number of stages that have reoccurred in mid-twentieth-century wars against colonialism: a colonial elite embracing an ideology of liberation; then, a struggle for self-determination; and, finally, a debate within the revolutionary party over the organization of the new state. What distinguishes the American Revolution from its mid-twentieth-century African and Asian counterparts is the relative ease and bloodlessness with which it passed through these stages. Yet, like recent colonial societies, pre-Revolutionary America was in a state of profound disequilibrium; their links to an imperial metropolis had endowed colonial leaders with an intellectual and cultural sophistication, an economic prowess, and an awareness of international power politics that were heady stimulants to their aspirations. Patriot leaders in 1775 and 1776 innocently disregarded the practical difficulties of waging war against the greatest military power on earth—an apparent lapse in judgment that the loyalists found inexplicable and that beguiled British officials into believing that they possessed sufficient military power and economic resources to crush the rebellion.

At every point, the loyalists became enmeshed in the tragedy of an ill-conceived exertion of national power. Britain proceeded to fight a limited war in a wilderness setting, across an ocean, where it lacked the manpower and logistical capability to occupy every disaffected locality or to destroy the enemy's main force. It was a struggle in which the pro-British partisans were, at best, politically, numerically, and militarily inferior to those of the rebel government. Such limitations on British power dispirited and disillusioned even those loyalists willing to sacrifice for the Crown, thus costing Britain the very resource on which the ministry had counted to keep the expense of the war within politically acceptable limits. It became a war so futile and contrary to the best traditions of imperial power that only gross misrepresentation of Britain's actual standing in the conflict could induce a suspicious Parliament to continue to finance the venture. Finally, the war so drained Britain of manpower and resources that it sorely tempted her international rivals to intervene, and when Britain finally faced the realities of the situation and negotiated a withdrawal, some loyalists believed they had been cruelly betrayed.[11] Considering the Revolution as a war of national liberation explains why Britain lost the struggle and why many loyalists suddenly found themselves out of phase—applying the assumptions of the 1750's to the conditions of the 1770's. A study of the weaknesses of the imperial connection, this approach, however, fails to touch the deepest roots of American behavior.

In the final analysis, the Revolution was an effort to discover the legitimate sources of authority within American society. British policies restricting colonial autonomy and impinging on traditional liberties forced the colonists to examine in detail and with furious intensity the nature of the compact between themselves and the Crown, and the proper role of Parliamentary power in their political life. They concluded that the ultimate power to review the legitimacy of governmental policy rested in the whole body of the people and could be exercised only by representatives of the people. British actions that transferred more and more decision making from the colonies to London jeopardized this vital theoretical arrangement; subsequent measures coercing recalcitrant colonists raised the specter that British power was brutish and ravenous. Deeply concerned with the need to preserve social coherence and harmony, Whig leaders sought to enlist the entire community in resistance against British authority and in the creation of stable insurrectionary institutions.

This cluster of belief and action—this ideology of constitutionalism and resistance—created fierce antagonisms within colonial society. It turned the rage of the community against royal officials and allies of the Crown, who appeared to have become lackeys of British tyranny, and it created incredibly self-righteous and humorless standards of public virtue. In retaliation, victims of public outrage and dissenters from Whig orthodoxy challenged specific Whig arguments, questioned the prudence and realism of Whig tactics, ridiculed Whig assumptions, and castigated individual agitators for their misdeeds. Loyalist beliefs and preferences, however, never coalesced into a common, vital persuasion with its own logic and momentum. The very nature of the controversy inhibited such a development; except under peculiar circumstances in South Carolina in 1780 and 1781 and among religious pacifists in Pennsylvania in 1777 and 1778, there was little explicit discussion of personal allegiance—the conscious act of making oneself the subject of a ruler. The focus was, rather, on the feelings, expectations, intellectual and cultural heritage, and standards of public morality that subtly shaped the varieties of political behavior and predisposed men to be receptive to certain appeals and to engage in certain kinds of conduct. The opponents of revolution spoke knowledgeably about each of these components of allegiance, and they began the arduous task of justifying continued colonial acquiescence. But events moved too rapidly for them, constantly cutting the ground of their arguments out from under them and frustrating their belated and often clumsy attempts to rally their adherents to action. "Loyalty was the normal condition," Claude H. Van Tyne wrote in the loyalists' defense in 1902; "it was the Whigs . . . who [had to] do the converting, the changing of men's opinions to suit a new order of things which the Revolutionists believed necessary for their own and their country's welfare."[12] All of the historical insight available to Van Tyne had indicated that allegiance to the Crown and acceptance of colonial subordination were the norm for most people on the eve of the Revolution. It is now clear that the entire process of revolution was a consuming, transforming experience that deeply touched the lives of people in every part of the society. Republicanism and revolution became the norm, the common touchstone of American life, by 1775 and 1776. This is not to say that the loyalists were deviants; it is only to say that the search for legitimate political authority in America thrust loyalists and patriots onto diverging courses. "I discern the goddess, but on the other side of the river," William Smith, Jr., wrote of independence in November 1776. "Most men are for plunging into it to embrace her. I am for going over to her in a boat, distrusting my power to swim across the stream."[13] Others feared to cross the river by any means or regarded the water as a forbidden domain.

Abbreviations Used in Notes
and Bibliographical Essay

~~~

Notes

~~~

Bibliographical Essay

~~~

Index

Abbreviations Used in Notes

and Bibliographical Essay

Am Arch	Peter Force, comp., *American Archives*, 9 vols. (Washington: M. St. Clair Clarke and Peter Force, 1837–1853)
Bailyn, *Pamphlets*	Bernard Bailyn, ed., *Pamphlets of the American Revolution, 1750–1776*, vol. 1 (Cambridge: Harvard University Press, Belknap Press, 1965)
CARW	Connecticut Archives, Revolutionary War Series, Connecticut State Library, Hartford
CHR	*Canadian Historical Review*
CO 5	Colonial Office Papers, 5th ser., Public Record Office, London
CRNC	William L. Saunders, ed., *Colonial Records of North Carolina* (Raleigh and Goldsborough, 1886–1898)
CSM Publ	*Publications of the Colonial Society of Massachusetts*
DH	*Delaware History*
Doc Rel CHNY	E. B. O'Callahan *et al.*, eds., *Documents Relative to the Colonial History of the State of New York* (Albany, 1856–1887)
GCR	Allan D. Candler, ed., *Colonial Records of Georgia* (Athens, 1904–1916)
GHQ	*Georgia Historical Quarterly*
HLQ	*Huntington Library Quarterly*
HMPEC	*Historical Magazine of the Protestant Episcopal Church*
HT	Hammond Transcripts on New Hampshire Loyalists, New Hampshire Historical Society, Concord
JAH	*Journal of American History*
JSH	*Journal of Southern History*

LT   American Loyalists: Transcripts of the Commission of Enquiry into the Losses and Services of the American Loyalists, New York Public Library

MA   Massachusetts Archives, State House, Boston

MHM   *Maryland Historical Magazine*

MHS Colls   *Collections of the Massachusetts Historical Society*

MHS Proc   *Proceedings of the Massachusetts Historical Society*

NCHR   *North Carolina Historical Review*

NEQ   *New England Quarterly*

NJH   *New Jersey History*

NYH   *New York History*

NYHS Colls   *Collections of the New-York Historical Society*

NYHSQ   *New-York Historical Society Quarterly*

PH   *Pennsylvania History*

PMHB   *Pennsylvania Magazine of History and Biography*

RIH   *Rhode Island History*

SAQ   *South Atlantic Quarterly*

SCHM   *South Carolina Historical Magazine*

Shipton, *Sibley*   Clifford K. Shipton, *Sibley's Harvard Graduates: Biographical Sketches of Those Who Attended Harvard College,* 12 vols. (Boston, 1933–)

SRNC   Walter Clark, ed., *State Records of North Carolina* (Goldsborough and Winston, 1895–1914)

VH   *Vermont History*

VMHB   *Virginia Magazine of History and Biography*

WMQ   *William and Mary Quarterly,* 3rd ser.

Notes

CHAPTER ONE

1. W. W. Abbot, *The Royal Governors of Georgia, 1754–1775* (Chapel Hill: University of North Carolina Press, 1959), pp. 105–106.
2. Edmund S. Morgan and Helen M. Morgan, *The Stamp Act Crisis: Prologue to Revolution* (Chapel Hill: University of North Carolina Press, 1953), chaps. 8–10.
3. Abbot, *Royal Governors of Georgia,* pp. 84–88.
4. *Ibid.,* chaps. 1 and 4. See also Trevor R. Reese, *Colonial Georgia: A Study in British Imperial Policy in the Eighteenth Century* (Athens: University of Georgia Press, 1963), pp. 121–122.
5. The entire treatment of the Stamp Act crisis in Georgia and Wright's character is based on Abbot, *Royal Governors of Georgia,* chaps. 5 and 6. C. Ashley Ellefson, "The Stamp Act in Georgia," *GHQ,* 46 (March 1962), 1–19, was also useful.
6. Quoted in Abbot, *Royal Governors of Georgia,* p. 112.
7. The phrase is Professor Abbot's, *ibid.,* p. 109.
8. Wright to the Assembly, March 6, 1766, *GCR,* 14:361–362.
9. On this issue, see the careful examination of the *Georgia Gazette* in Ellefson, "Stamp Act in Georgia," pp. 11–14; S. F. Roach, "The *Georgia Gazette* and the Stamp Act: A Reconsideration," *GHQ,* 55 (Winter 1971), 471–491, reveals that the paper's editor, James Johnston, had close economic ties to the Crown and was a tireless publicist for the Governor's side—evidence that does not detract from the shrewdness and intelligence of his position.
10. Abbot, *Royal Governors of Georgia,* pp. 109–111, and Ellefson, "James Habersham and Georgia Loyalism, 1764–1775," *GHQ,* 44 (December 1960), 366–367.
11. Quoted in Abbot, *Royal Governors of Georgia,* p. 119.
12. *Ibid.,* pp. 121–125.
13. Quoted in *ibid.,* p. 123.
14. *Ibid.,* chaps. 6 and 7.
15. *Ibid.,* pp. 162–179.

16. Wright to Hillsborough, August 15, 1769, CO 5, 660:95–98, italics added.
17. Wright to Hillsborough, April 30, 1770, *ibid.,* 661:81–83, italics added.
18. Wright to Hillsborough, May 30, 1768, *ibid.,* 659:79–81. See also Robert G. Mitchell, ed., "Sir James Wright Looks at the American Revolution," *GHQ,* 53 (December 1969), 509–518.
19. Wright to Hillsborough, May 10, 1770, CO 5, 660:191–192.
20. Wright to the Assembly, January 18, 1775, *ibid.,* 664:47–48.

CHAPTER TWO

1. Lawrence Henry Gipson, *The British Empire Before the American Revolution,* 15 vols. (New York: Alfred A. Knopf, 1936–1970), vol. 1, pp. 3–5.
2. Jack P. Greene, ed., *Great Britain and the American Colonies, 1606–1763* (New York: Harper & Row, 1970), pp. xi–xiii introduces these definitions.
3. Richard Pares, *Yankees and Creoles: The Trade Between North America and the West Indies before the American Revolution* (Cambridge: Harvard University Press, 1956), pp. 139–163. See also Lawrence A. Harper, *The English Navigation Acts: A Seventeenth-Century Experiment in Social Engineering* (New York: Columbia University Press, 1939), chaps. 4 and 5; Oliver M. Dickerson, *The Navigation Acts and the American Revolution* (Philadelphia: University of Pennsylvania Press, 1951), chaps. 1–3; and three very useful brief accounts: Stuart Bruchey, ed., *The Colonial Merchant: Sources and Readings* (New York: Harcourt, Brace & World, 1966), pp. 41–45; Carl Ubbelohde, *The American Colonies and the British Empire, 1607–1763* (New York: Thomas Y. Crowell, 1968), pp. 44–74, and Darrett B. Rutman, *The Morning of America, 1603–1789* (Boston: Houghton Mifflin Co., 1971), chap. 4.
4. For the middle range in the spectrum of views in this debate see Charles M. Andrews, "The Government of the Empire 1660–1763," *Cambridge History of the British Empire,* 8 vols. (New York: Macmillan Co., 1929), vol. 1, pp. 405–436, and *The Colonial Period of American History: England's Commercial and Colonial Policy* (New Haven: Yale University Press, 1938), chaps. 9–11; Michael Kammen, *Empire and Interest: The American Colonies and the Politics of Mercantilism* (Philadelphia: J. B. Lippincott Co., 1970), chaps. 3–5; and Thomas C. Barrow, *Trade and Empire: The British Customs*

Service in Colonial America, 1660–1775 (Cambridge: Harvard University Press, 1967), pp. 1–3. For additional bibliography, see Joseph E. Illick, "Recent Scholarship Concerning Anglo-American Relations, 1675–1775," in Alison G. Olson and Richard M. Brown, eds., *Anglo-American Political Relations, 1675–1775* (New Brunswick: Rutgers University Press, 1970), pp. 195–200, 204–210.

5. The authoritative work on the office of royal governor remains Leonard Woods Labaree, *Royal Government in America: A Study of the British Colonial System before 1783* (New Haven: Yale University Press, 1930), chaps. 1–4, 10.

6. David Alan Williams, "Anglo-Virginia Politics, 1690–1735," in Olson and Brown, *Anglo-American Political Relations*, chap. 5.

7. John A. Schutz, *William Shirley: King's Governor of Massachusetts* (Chapel Hill: University of North Carolina Press, 1961), pp. 80–204.

8. Jere R. Daniell, *Experiment in Republicanism: New Hampshire Politics and the American Revolution, 1741–1794* (Cambridge: Harvard University Press, 1970), chap. 1.

9. Jack P. Greene, *The Quest for Power: The Lower Houses of Assembly in the Southern Royal Colonies, 1689–1776* (Chapel Hill: University of North Carolina Press, 1963), especially chaps. 1–5, 19.

10. For an analysis of recent scholarship on these features of colonial politics, see Jack P. Greene, "Changing Interpretations of Early American Politics," in Ray A. Billington, ed., *The Reinterpretation of Early American History* (San Marino, Cal.: Huntington Library, 1966), pp. 151–184.

11. Quoted in Greene, *Quest for Power*, p. 15.

12. See Bernard Bailyn, *The Origins of American Politics* (New York: Alfred A. Knopf, 1968), chap. 2.

13. Quoted in Jack P. Greene, ed., *Settlements to Society, 1584–1763* (New York: McGraw-Hill Book Co., 1966), p. 360.

14. Olson and Brown, *Anglo-American Political Relations, passim.*

15. E. R. Turner, *The Privy Council of England in the Seventeenth and Eighteenth Centuries, 1603–1784*, 2 vols. (Baltimore: Johns Hopkins University Press, 1928), vol. 1, p. 79; vol. 2, pp. 21–22, 50–52, 176–177, 366; Jack P. Greene, ed., "The Case of the Pistole Fee: The Report of a Hearing on the Pistole Fee Dispute before the Privy Council, June 18, 1754," *VMHB*, 66 (October 1958), 399–422; Joseph Henry Smith, *Appeals to the Privy Council from the American Plantations* (New York: Columbia University Press, 1950), pp. 523–664.

16. The most useful analyses of the Board of Trade are Andrews,

Colonial Period of American History: England's Commercial and Colonial Policy, pp. 272–315, 377–423, and Greene, "Introduction," *Great Britain and the American Colonies*, pp. xvii–xlv.

17. Dora Mae Clark, *The Rise of the British Treasury: Colonial Administration in the Eighteenth Century* (New Haven: Yale University Press, 1960), pp. 198–202.

18. Barrow, *Trade and Empire*, pp. 178–184.

19. Carl Ubbelohde, *The Vice-Admiralty Courts and the American Revolution* (Chapel Hill: University of North Carolina Press, 1960), chaps. 1 and 2.

20. John Shy, *Toward Lexington: The Role of the British Army in the Coming of the American Revolution* (Princeton: Princeton University Press, 1965), pp. 45–68, 140–190, 321–374.

21. Carl Bridenbaugh, *Mitre and Sceptre: Transatlantic Faiths, Ideas, Personalities, and Politics, 1689–1775* (New York: Oxford University Press, 1962), chaps. 7 and 8.

22. Of the vast literature on British politics at the accession of George III, the most trenchant comment on the social basis of politics is Richard Pares, *King George III and the Politicians* (Oxford: Oxford University Press, 1953), chap. 1.

23. Sir Lewis Namier, *The Structure of Politics at the Accession of George III*, 2d ed. (London: Macmillan & Co. Ltd., 1957), pp. 1–61; *England in the Age of the American Revolution*, 2d ed. (London: Macmillan & Co. Ltd., 1961), pp. 3–41, 62–83, 171–228.

24. Ian R. Christie, *Myth and Reality in Late-Eighteenth-Century British Politics* (Berkeley: University of California Press, 1970), pp. 31–64.

25. Franklin B. Wickwire, *British Subministers and Colonial America, 1763–1783* (Princeton: Princeton University Press, 1966), chaps. 1–3; Thomas C. Barrow, "Background to the Grenville Program, 1757–1763," and "A Project for Imperial Reform: Hints Respecting the Settlement for our American Provinces, 1763," *WMQ*, 22 (January 1965), 93–104, and 24 (January 1967), 108–126.

26. This survey of British politics is based on some of the scholarship analyzed in Jack P. Greene, "The Plunge of Lemmings: A Consideration of Recent Writings on British Politics and the American Revolution," *SAQ*, 57 (Winter 1968), 141–175, especially by John Norris, *Shelburne and Reform* (London: Macmillan & Co. Ltd., 1963), and by B. D. Bargar, *Lord Dartmouth and the American Revolution* (Columbia: University of South Carolina Press, 1965). See also Bernard Donoughue, *British Politics and the American Revolution, 1773–1775* (London: Macmillan & Co. Ltd., 1964), pp.

36–104. Ian R. Christie, *Crisis of Empire: Great Britain and the American Colonies, 1754–1783* (New York: W. W. Norton & Co., 1966), is very useful, and Michael G. Kammen, *A Rope of Sand: The Colonial Agents, British Politics and the American Revolution* (Ithaca, N.Y.: Cornell University Press, 1968), chaps. 11–14, is unusually analytical and suggestive.

27. Bailyn, *The Ideological Origins of the American Revolution* (Cambridge: Harvard University Press, 1957), pp. 202–203.

28. Jack P. Greene, ed., *The Nature of Colony Constitutions: Two Pamphlets on the Wilkes Fund Controversy in South Carolina by Sir Egerton Leigh and Arthur Lee* (Columbia: University of South Carolina Press, 1970), pp. 42–55.

29. Richard Koebner, *Empire* (Cambridge: Cambridge University Press, 1961), pp. 130–149; Morgan and Morgan, *Stamp Act Crisis*, pp. 7–20; Francis Bernard, *Select Letters on the Trade and Government of America, and the Principles of Law and Polity, Applied to the American Colonies* (London, 1774).

30. Shy, *Toward Lexington*, p. 149.

31. G. H. Guttridge, "Thomas Pownall's *The Administration of the Colonies:* The Six Editions," *WMQ,* 26 (January 1969), 31–46.

CHAPTER THREE

1. On Colden and his role in New York society and politics, I have followed extensively Carole Shammas, "Cadwallader Colden and the Role of the King's Prerogative," *NYHSQ,* 53 (April 1969), 103–126; in addition, Stanley Nider Katz, *Newcastle's New York: Anglo-American Politics, 1732–1753* (Cambridge: Harvard University Press, 1968), and "Between Scylla and Charybdis: James De Lancey and Anglo-American Politics in Early Eighteenth-Century New York," in Olson and Brown, *Anglo-American Political Relations,* pp. 92–108, influenced considerably the foregoing paragraph.

2. Brooke Hindle, *The Pursuit of Science in Revolutionary America, 1735–1789* (Chapel Hill: University of North Carolina Press, 1956), pp. 38–48; Raymond P. Stearns, *Science in the British Colonies of America* (Urbana: University of Illinois Press, 1970), pp. 493–497.

3. Shammas, "Cadwallader Colden," pp. 106–113.

4. *Ibid.,* pp. 115–117.

5. *Ibid.,* pp. 118–122; Milton M. Klein, "Prelude to the Revolution in New York: Jury Trials and Judicial Tenure," *WMQ,* 17 (October 1960), 439–462.

6. Colden to Henry S. Conway, October 26, 1765, *Doc Rel CHNY,* 7: 768–769.

7. Morgan and Morgan, *Stamp Act Crisis,* pp. 197–199, and Shy, *Toward Lexington,* pp. 209–213.

8. Shammas, "Cadwallader Colden," pp. 103–105, 113–115, 122–126; Colden's statement about money is quoted in Milton M. Klein, ed., *The Independent Reflector* (Cambridge: Harvard University Press, 1963), p. 33.

CHAPTER FOUR

1. Quoted in Bailyn, *Origins of American Politics,* p. 4.

2. Douglass Adair and John A. Schutz, eds., *Peter Oliver's Origin and Progress of the American Rebellion: A Tory View* (San Marino, Cal.: Huntington Library, 1961), p. 29.

3. Malcolm Freiberg, "Thomas Hutchinson: the First Fifty Years (1711–1761)," *WMQ,* 15 (January 1958), 36.

4. *Ibid.,* pp. 36–44.

5. Morgan and Morgan, *Stamp Act Crisis,* p. 214; quotations from Hutchinson's letter on the Stamp Act come from Edmund S. Morgan's edition of the document in his article, "Thomas Hutchinson and the Stamp Act," *NEQ,* 21 (December 1948), 480–492.

6. Morgan, "Thomas Hutchinson and the Stamp Act," p. 481.

7. Quoted in Morgan and Morgan, *Stamp Act Crisis,* p. 216.

8. Hutchinson, "Essay on Taxation," MA, 25:121–135, and "Dialogue between an American and European [Englishman]," 28:101–109, State House, Boston. The latter document was called to my attention by Malcolm Freiberg, and he discusses both of them in his "Prelude to Purgatory: Thomas Hutchinson in Massachusetts Politics, 1760–1770" (Ph.D. diss., Brown University, 1950), pp. 216–217.

9. Hutchinson, "Dialogue"; "Essay on Taxation"; Hutchinson to Bernard, October 20, 1770, to John Hely Hutchinson, February 14, 1772, MA, 28:104–106; 25:132–135; 27:26–27, 296–300, italics added. See also Charles F. Mullett, ed., "Roman Precedents and British Colonial Policy in 1770," *HLQ,* 7 (November 1943), 97–104.

10. See Donald C. Lord and Robert M. Calhoon, "The Removal of the Massachusetts General Court from Boston, 1769–1772," *JAH,* 55 (March 1969), 738, n. 9, for documentation. The letters published in 1775 should not be confused with earlier pilfered Hutchinson letters published in pamphlet form in Boston in 1773.

11. Hutchinson to John Hely Hutchinson, February 14, 1772, MA, 27: 296–300. Hutchinson to Abijah Willard, September 7, 1775, quoted

in Mary Beth Norton, *The British-Americans: The Loyalist Exiles in England, 1774–1789* (Boston: Little, Brown & Co., 1972), p. 48.

12. *Dictionary of American Biography* s.v. "Hutchinson, Thomas."

13. This judicious phrase appears in L. Kinvin Wroth and Hiller B. Zobel, eds., *The Legal Papers of John Adams*, 3 vols. (Cambridge: Harvard University Press, 1964), vol. 3, p. 1.

14. For Hutchinson's and Preston's words and an intricate mosaic of the events of the night of March 5, 1770, see Hiller B. Zobel, *The Boston Massacre* (New York: W. W. Norton & Co., 1970), p. 203 and chap. 16, *passim*.

15. Shy, *Toward Lexington*, chap. 7.

16. Wroth and Zobel, *Legal Papers of John Adams*, vol. 3, pp. 14–31.

17. For a detailed account of this controversy, see Lord and Calhoon, "The Removal of the Massachusetts General Court from Boston," pp. 739–748.

18. The account is based on Bailyn's *Ideological Origins of the American Revolution*, pp. 219–222.

19. Thomas Hutchinson, *The Speeches of his Excellency Governor Hutchinson to the General Assembly . . . 1773* (Boston, 1773), pp. 13–14.

CHAPTER FIVE

1. Quoted in Hiller B. Zobel, "Jonathan Sewall: A Lawyer in Conflict," *Publications of the Cambridge Historical Society*, 40 (1964–1966), 127; in addition to Zobel's article I am much indebted for this interpretation of Sewall to Shipton, *Sibley*, 12:306–325.

2. Shipton, *Sibley*, 12:306–307.

3. Zobel, "Jonathan Sewall," pp. 124–127.

4. The preceding three paragraphs are based on Richard B. Morris, "Legalism versus Revolutionary Doctrine in New England," in David H. Flaherty, ed., *Essays in the History of Early American Law* (Chapel Hill: University of North Carolina Press, 1969), pp. 418–432; John D. Cushing, "The Judiciary and Public Opinion in Revolutionary Massachusetts," and Hiller B. Zobel, "Law under Pressure: Boston, 1769–1771," in George A. Billias, ed., *Law and Authority in Colonial America: Selected Essays* (Barre, Mass.: Barre Publishers, 1965), pp. 168–208; John M. Murrin, "The Legal Transformation: The Bench and Bar of Eighteenth-Century Massachusetts," in Stanley N. Katz, ed., *Colonial America: Essays in Politics and Social Development* (Boston: Little, Brown & Co., 1971), pp.

415–449; and Wroth and Zobel, "Introduction," *Legal Papers of John Adams,* vol. 1, pp. xxxviii–xciv.

5. Zobel, "Jonathan Sewall," pp. 131–136.
6. Quoted in Shipton, *Sibley,* 12:307.
7. Quoted in Zobel, "Jonathan Sewall," p. 129.
8. Sewall to Hutchinson (excerpt in Hutchinson's hand), December 11, 1774, Dartmouth Papers, 2:1018, William Salt Library, Stafford, England.
9. Sewall to General Frederick Haldimand, May 30, 1775, in Jack P. Greene, ed., *Colonies to Nation, 1763–1789* (New York: McGraw-Hill Book Co., 1967), pp. 266–268.
10. *Ibid.*
11. [Jonathan Sewall], *A Cure for the Spleen or Amusement for a Winter's Evening: Being the Substance of a Conversation on the Times, over A Friendly Tankard and Pipe* . . . ([Boston], 1775), p. 10.
12. Sewall to Haldimand, May 30. 1775, Greene, *Colonies to Nation,* p. 267.
13. [Jonathan Sewall], "Phileirene," *Massachusetts Gazette and Boston Weekly News Letter,* January 12, 1775; see also January 26; February 9; March 2, 9, and 30; April 6 and 13, 1775.

CHAPTER SIX

1. This treatment of Leigh is adapted from Robert M. Calhoon and Robert M. Weir, " 'The Scandalous History of Sir Egerton Leigh,' " *WMQ,* 26 (January 1969), 47–74.
2. Greene, *The Nature of Colony Constitutions,* pp. 74, 106, 82, 84, 89, 112.

CHAPTER SEVEN

1. For an expanded version of this treatment of Galloway and an evaluation of recent scholarship on John Dickinson and Pennsylvania politics, see Robert M. Calhoon, " 'I have Deduced Your Rights': Joseph Galloway's Concept of his Role," *PH,* 35 (October 1968), 356–378. Since this section was written, John E. Ferling, "Joseph Galloway: A Reassessment of the Motivations of a Pennsylvania Loyalist," *PH,* 39 (April 1972), 163–186, calls into question almost all previous work on Galloway. Ferling reconstructs Galloway's ideas about the nature of the British Empire in the 1750's and shows that his 1774–1775 writings borrowed heavily on his

earlier celebration of imperial power and growth; Ferling therefore concludes that Galloway's pre-Revolutionary views were more consistent and objective than historians have realized. To the extent that previous scholars have made Galloway an opportunist, Ferling's study is a valuable corrective. The purpose of my article was not to denigrate Galloway but to emphasize his emotional vitality and the extent to which he was the victim of his own grandiose vision and aspirations.

2. John Randolph, *Considerations on the Present State of Virginia,* (1774), in Earl G. Swem, ed., *Virginia and the Revolution: Two Pamphlets* (New York: Heartman, 1919), pp. 17–19. In exile during the War for Independence, Randolph realized that "as long as Parliament avow the right of controlling . . . the Americans . . . without limitation," this balanced, classical allegiance to the English constitution would remain precarious; from Mary Beth Norton, ed., "John Randolph's 'Plan of Accommodations,' " *WMQ,* 28 (January 1971), 103–120.

3. [Daniel Leonard and John Adams], *Novanglus and Massachusettensis* . . . (Boston, 1819), p. 152.

CHAPTER EIGHT

1. Lyman H. Butterfield *et al.,* eds., *The Diary and Autobiography of John Adams,* 4 vols. (Cambridge: Harvard University Press, 1961), vol. 2, p. 110; Samuel Johnson, *Dictionary of the English Language* (London, 1755).

2. L. F. S. Upton, *The Loyal Whig: William Smith of New York and Quebec* (Toronto: University of Toronto Press, 1969), chaps. 2–4; Klein, *Independent Reflector,* pp. 1–20. For a brilliant examination of Smith's character as a man "torn between contrapuntal tendencies" of detachment and involvement, see Michael Kammen's introduction to Smith's *The History of the Province of New York* . . ., 2 vols. (Cambridge: Harvard University Press, 1972), vol. 1, pp. xvii–xxxvii.

3. The discussion of the background, content, and significance of the plan is based on Robert M. Calhoon, ed., "William Smith, Jr.'s Alternative to the American Revolution," *WMQ,* 22 (January 1965), 105–118.

4. Quoted in Upton, *Loyal Whig,* p. 60.

5. For an excellent account of Smith's involvement in this business, see *ibid.,* chap. 7.

6. Jack P. Greene's review of Upton, "The Loyal Whig" in *CHR*, 51 (March 1970), 78–80.

7. William W. H. Sabine, ed., *Historical Memoirs of William Smith from . . . 1763 to . . . 1776* (New York: Colburn and Tegg, 1956), pp. 112–113.

8. *Ibid.*, pp. 117–119.

9. *Ibid.*, pp. 156–165.

10. *Ibid.*, pp. 224–228c.

11. *Ibid.*, pp. 228a, 236–237. At least four individuals possessed copies of Smith's plan and transmitted the document to Dartmouth: Dr. James Smith (his brother living in London), Brook Watson (a London merchant and friend of Smith's), General Haldimand, and Thomas Boone (former Governor of South Carolina), as listed in Upton, *Loyal Whig*, p. 92. Contrary to my suggestion that Dartmouth did not appreciate the importance of Smith's proposals ("William Smith, Jr.'s Alternative," p. 111), Dr. James Smith's copy of the plan reached Dartmouth in 1769 and prompted a spirited correspondence between Dartmouth and Rockingham; see Bargar, *Dartmouth*, pp. 48–49. The anonymous author of *America Vindicated from the High Charge of Ingratitude and Rebellion . . .* (Devizes, England, 1774) also incorporated large portions of Smith's plan into his pamphlet.

12. Sabine, *Memoirs of William Smith*, pp. 265–267; Smith to Tryon, November 25, 1774, December 6, 1774, Dartmouth Papers, 2:1002, 1008.

13. Sabine, *Memoirs of William Smith*, pp. 271–277.

CHAPTER NINE

1. Bailyn, *Origins of American Politics*, p. 57. For a definition of the concept of political culture see Lucian W. Pye and Sidney Verba, eds., *Political Culture and Political Development* (Princeton: Princeton University Press, 1965), pp. 7, 513. Jack P. Greene usefully observes that, while political culture encompasses both tangible actions and the intangible implications of those actions, the most important phenomenon to be understood is "that elusive and shadowy cluster of assumptions, traditions, conventions, values, modes of expression, and habits of thought and belief that underlay those visible elements." See Billington, *Reinterpretation of Early American History*, p. 172.

2. For a bibliography of the writings on which this paragraph is based see Greene, "Changing Interpretations of Early American Politics,"

in Billington, *Reinterpretation of Early American History*. The best general reconstruction of pre-Revolutionary politics at the provincial level is Merrill Jensen, *The Founding of a Nation: A History of the American Revolution, 1763–1776* (New York: Oxford University Press, 1968) .

3. Greene, "Changing Interpretations of Early American Politics," p. 173; Richard Buel, "Democracy and the American Revolution: A Frame of Reference," *WMQ*, 21 (April 1964) , 188.

4. William S. Sachs and Ari Hoogenboom, *The Enterprising Colonials: Society on the Eve of the Revolution* (Chicago: Argonaut, 1965) ; Bernard Bailyn, "The Beekmans of New York: Trade, Politics, and Families" and "The Blount Papers: Notes on the Merchant 'Class' in the Revolutionary Period," *WMQ*, 14 (October 1957) , 598–608, and 11 (January 1954) , 98–104; and Carl Bridenbaugh, *Cities in Revolt: Urban Life in America, 1743–1776* (New York: Alfred A. Knopf, 1955) , chap. 7. The systematic and original study of this problem in Marc Egnal and Joseph A. Ernst, "An Economic Interpretation of the American Revolution," *WMQ*, 29 (January 1972) , 3–32, appeared too late for me to use in this connection.

5. Richard L. Merritt, *Symbols of American Community, 1735–1775* (New Haven: Yale University Press, 1966) , p. 180 *et passim;* Lawrence A. Cremin, *American Education: The Colonial Experience, 1607–1783* (New York: Harper & Row, 1970) , pp. 371–378, 387–400.

6. Two of the best introductions to the Great Awakening are the editorial introductions in recent documentary collections, Alan Heimert and Perry Miller, eds., *The Great Awakening; Documents Illustrating the Crisis and Its Consequences* (Indianapolis, Ind.: Bobbs-Merrill Co., 1967) , and Richard L. Bushman, *The Great Awakening; Documents on the Revival of Religion 1740–1745* (New York: Atheneum Publishers, 1970) . I have relied heavily on Perry Miller, "Jonathan Edwards and the Great Awakening" and "The Rhetoric of Sensation" in *Errand into the Wilderness* (Cambridge: Harvard University Press, 1956) , pp. 153–183.

7. Alan Heimert, *Religion and the American Mind from the Great Awakening to the Revolution* (Cambridge: Harvard University Press, 1966) , chaps. 1–4, 8.

8. Heimert's rigid dichotomy between Calvinists and rationalists has generated considerable adverse criticism; see the following reviews of his book: Edmund S. Morgan, in the *WMQ*, 24 (July 1968) , 454–459; Sidney Mead, in the *Journal of Religion*, 48 (July 1968) , 274–288; and Charles W. Akers, in the *NYHSQ*, 51 (July 1967) ,

283–291. Even allowing for several important exceptions to Heimert's generalization—rationalist clergy who genuinely internalized the radicalism of the pre-Revolutionary movement or Calvinists who were politically timid—the preponderance of his evidence demonstrates that evangelical Calvinism provided a ready explanation for the bewildering onslaught of the pre-Revolutionary controversy while rationalism just as readily inculcated an ambivalent response to those events. For a valuable document on this tendency, see A. G. Medlicott, "The Journal of the Reverend Stephen Williams, 1775–1777" (Ph.D. diss., University of Washington, 1962) .

9. Richard Maxwell Brown, *The South Carolina Regulators* (Cambridge: Harvard University Press, 1963) , p. 135.

10. Pauline Maier, "Popular Uprisings and Civil Authority in Eighteenth-Century America," *WMQ,* 27 (January 1970) , 3–35; and Jesse Lemisch, "Jack Tar in the Streets: Merchant Seamen in the Politics of Revolutionary America," *WMQ,* 25 (July 1968) , 371–407.

11. Donald L. Robinson, *Slavery in the Structure of American Politics, 1765–1820* (New York: Harcourt Brace Jovanovich, 1971) , p. 58.

12. Robert M. Weir, " 'The Harmony We Were Famous For': An Interpretation of Pre-Revolutionary South Carolina Politics," *WMQ,* 26 (October 1969) , 282–284.

13. Quoted in Winthrop D. Jordan, *White Over Black: American Attitudes Toward the Negro, 1550–1812* (Chapel Hill: University of North Carolina Press, 1967) , p. 114.

14. David Brion Davis, *The Problem of Slavery in Western Culture* (Ithaca, N.Y.: Cornell University Press, 1966) , pp. 483–493.

15. Robinson, *Slavery in the Structure of American Politics,* chap. 2; and Bailyn, *Ideological Origins of the American Revolution,* pp. 233–237.

16. Jack P. Greene, "Search for Identity: An Interpretation of the Meaning of Selected Patterns of Response in Eighteenth-Century America," *Journal of Social History,* 3 (Spring 1970) , 189–220.

17. Ο Carroll and Dickinson, see Bailyn, *Ideological Origins of the American Revolution,* pp. 89–92. On Adams, see John R. Howe, Jr., *The Changing Political Thought of John Adams* (Princeton: Princeton University Press, 1966) , pp. 35–36. On Rush, see his letter to Ebenezer Hazard, October 22, 1768, Lyman H. Butterfield, ed., *Letters of Benjamin Rush,* 2 vols. (Princeton: Princeton University Press, 1951) , vol. 1, p. 68. In general, see Harry C. Allen, "Anglophobia and Anglophilia," in Marshall F. Fishwick, ed., *American Studies in Transition* (Philadelphia: University of Pennsylvania Press, 1964) , pp. 199–231; and William Lewis Sachse,

The Colonial American in Britain (Madison: University of Wisconsin Press, 1956), pp. 203–206.

18. Quoted in Caroline Robbins, *The Eighteenth-Century Commonwealthman* (Cambridge: Harvard University Press, 1959), p. 364.

19. *Ibid.,* chap. 4; H. Trevor Colbourn, *The Lamp of Experience: Whig History and the Intellectual Origins of the American Revolution* (Chapel Hill: University of North Carolina Press, 1965), chaps. 1–3; David L. Jacobson, ed., *The English Libertarian Heritage: From the Writings of John Trenchard and Thomas Gordon* (Indianapolis, Ind.: Bobbs-Merrill Co., 1965); and Pauline Maier, *From Resistance to Revolution: Colonial Radicals and the Development of American Opposition to Britain, 1765–1776* (New York: Alfred A. Knopf, 1972), pp. 31–32.

20. The classic exposition and analysis of the Country Ideology is J. G. A. Pocock, "Machiavelli, Harrington, and English Political Ideologies in the Eighteenth Century," *WMQ,* 22 (October 1965), 549–583.

21. Jacobson, *English Libertarian Heritage,* pp. 106, 126–127; Robbins, *Eighteenth-Century Commonwealthman,* p. 124.

22. Bailyn, *Origins of American Politics,* pp. 107–117; Weir, " 'The Harmony We Were Famous For,' " *passim.*

23. Quoted in Richard L. Bushman, *From Puritan to Yankee: Character and the Social Order in Connecticut, 1690–1765* (Cambridge: Harvard University Press, 1967), p. 195.

24. Edmund S. Morgan, "The Puritan Ethic and the American Revolution," *WMQ,* 24 (January 1967), 3–18.

25. Printed in Eli W. Caruthers, *A Sketch of the Life and Character of the Reverend David Caldwell . . .* (Greensboro, 1842), pp. 273–284.

26. Quoted in Kammen, *A Rope of Sand,* p. 167.

CHAPTER TEN

1. Catherine Fennelly, "William Franklin of New Jersey," *WMQ,* 6 (July 1949), 361–382, provides essential background and narrative, while Larry R. Gerlach, "Revolution or Independence? New Jersey, 1760–1776" (Ph.D. diss., Rutgers, 1968), is a masterful and exhaustive study of William Franklin's public career and the context of New Jersey politics. My conjecture concerning Franklin's struggle to establish his identity, first written in 1964, coincides with Gerlach's assessment of the same issue, "Revolution or Independence?" pp. 205–206.

2. William Franklin to Benjamin Franklin, November 13, 1765, Leonard W. Labaree *et al.,* eds., *The Papers of Benjamin Franklin,* 16 vols. (New Haven: Yale University Press, 1968), vol. 12, p. 367.

3. Gerlach, "Revolution or Independence?" pp. 16–30, 200–206. On Franklin's political education, see particularly William Franklin to the Lords of Trade, December 5, 1763, January 20, 1764, and February 8, 1764, *New Jersey Archives* (Newark, 1880–1940), 9:398–404.

4. William Franklin to Conway, September 23, November 30, and December 18, 1765; to Coxe, September 4, 1765; to the Lords of Trade, November 13, 1765, *New Jersey Archives,* 9:492–495, 507–508, 497–498, 505–507.

5. Quoted in Gerlach, "Revolution or Independence?" p. 260.

6. William Franklin to the Lords of Trade, December 18, 1765, *New Jersey Archives,* 9:525.

7. Gerlach, "Revolution or Independence?" p. 267.

8. William Franklin to Benjamin Franklin, November 13, 1765, Labaree *et al., Papers of Benjamin Franklin,* vol. 12, p. 369. *Pennsylvania Gazette* and *Pennsylvania Journal,* October 3, 1765.

9. William Franklin to Benjamin Franklin, April 30, 1766, Labaree *et al., Papers of Benjamin Franklin,* vol. 13, p. 256.

10. William Franklin to Shelburne, October 22, 1767, to Hillsborough, June 14, 1768, *New Jersey Archives,* 9:642–643; 10:32–33.

11. William Franklin to Hillsborough, November 23, 1768, *New Jersey Archives,* 10:64–95.

12. Gerlach, "Revolution or Independence?" pp. 405–407.

13. William Franklin to the Council and Assembly, January 13, 1775, *New Jersey Archives,* 10:538–541.

14. William Franklin to Benjamin Franklin, July 22 and August 6, 1784, Benjamin Franklin Papers, B:F85.X22, American Philosophical Society, Philadelphia.

15. Robert W. Barnwell, "Loyalism in South Carolina, 1765–1785" (Ph.D. diss., Duke University, 1941), p. 25; Bull to the Commissioners of Loyalist Claims, Audit Office Papers 13, 125:689–690, Public Record Office. Bull hedged against confiscation of his estate by deeding it, for the duration of the conflict, to his Whig nephew Stephen Bull, who after the war declined to restore it to his uncle.

16. Bull to Hillsborough, March 2, 1770, CO 5, 393:43–46.

17. Bull to Hillsborough, August 23, 1770, *ibid.,* 393:165–169.

18. Bull to Hillsborough, December 12, 1769, *ibid.,* 393:21–24.

19. Bull to Hillsborough, March 3, 1766, Transcripts of Records Pertaining to South Carolina, 31:32–34, British Public Record Office.

20. Daniell, *Experiment in Republicanism,* p. 45.
21. *Ibid.,* pp. 35–65.
22. Wentworth to Hillsborough, April 12, 1770, CO 5, 937:21–25.
23. Quoted in Daniell, *Experiment in Republicanism,* p. 55.
24. John Wentworth to Paul Wentworth, November 15, 1768, Wentworth Letterbooks, 1:152–155, New Hampshire Department of Records and Archives, Concord, New Hampshire.
25. John Wentworth to Paul Wentworth, September 17, 1769, *ibid.,* pp. 269–276.
26. Wentworth to Rockingham, September 17, 1769, *ibid.,* p. 281.
27. Wentworth to Rockingham, February 16, 1769, *ibid.,* pp. 203–205. Wentworth to John Temple, Temple-Bowdoin Papers, 2:14, Massachusetts Historical Society.
28. Wentworth to John Henniker, January 12, 1769, Wentworth Letterbooks, 1:179.
29. Wentworth to Rockingham, February 16, 1769, *ibid.,* pp. 203–205; Wentworth to the Assembly, June 13, 1775, CO 5, 939:339–341.
30. Quoted in Shipton, *Sibley,* 13:672–673.
31. Quoted in L. S. Mayo, *John Wentworth* (Cambridge: Harvard University Press, 1921), p. 19.
32. For this important distinction see Daniell, *Experiment in Republicanism,* pp. 54–55.
33. Quoted in Mayo, *Wentworth,* pp. 123–124.
34. Wentworth to Hillsborough, November 15, 1771, CO 5, 937:209–222.
35. Wentworth to Dr. Anthony Belham, August 9, 1768, Wentworth Letterbooks, 1:129–137; long portions of this uniquely candid and valuable letter are quoted in Mayo, *Wentworth,* pp. 122–124, and Richard F. Upton, *Revolutionary New Hampshire* (Hanover, N.H.: Dartmouth College, 1936), p. 1.

CHAPTER ELEVEN

1. Aubrey C. Land, *The Dulanys of Maryland* (Baltimore: Maryland Historical Society, 1955), chaps. 1–2.
2. *Ibid.,* p. 153.
3. Quoted in Bailyn, *Pamphlets,* pp. 603–604.
4. Land, *The Dulanys of Maryland,* chaps. 12–16.
5. Quoted in Bailyn, *Pamphlets,* p. 604.
6. Land, *The Dulanys of Maryland,* p. 244.
7. Bailyn, *Pamphlets,* pp. 600–603.
8. *Ibid.,* pp. 610–652.
9. The entire foregoing discussion is based on Charles A. Barker, *The*

Background of the Revolution in Maryland (New Haven: Yale University Press, 1940) ; Land, *The Dulanys of Maryland;* James Haw, "Maryland Politics on the Eve of the Revolution: The Provincial Controversy, 1770–1773," *MHM*, 65 (Summer 1970), 103–129; and David Curtis Skaggs, "Maryland's Impulse Toward Social Revolution, 1750–1776," *JAH*, 54 (March 1968), 771–786.

10. Land, *The Dunlanys of Maryland,* chap. 19.
11. Elihu S. Riley, ed., *Correspondence of "First Citizen"* . . . *and "Antilon"* . . . (Baltimore, 1902), pp. 34, 71.
12. Quoted in Bailyn, *Pamphlets,* p. 606.
13. Quoted in Haw, "Maryland Politics," p. 119.
14. Riley, *Correspondence of "First Citizen" and "Antilon,"* pp. 38–39.
15. Land, *The Dulanys of Maryland,* chap. 20.
16. Quoted in *ibid.,* p. 315, italics added.

CHAPTER TWELVE

1. William Smith *et al.* to the Bishop of London, June 30, 1775, and Smith to the Bishop of London, July 8, 1775, William S. Perry, ed., *Historical Collections of the Protestant Episcopal Church,* 5 vols. (Hartford, Conn., 1870–1878), vol. 2, pp. 470–475.
2. William Smith, *A Sermon on the Present Situation of American Affairs* . . . (Philadelphia, 1775), p. 19.
3. Perry, *Historical Collections,* vol. 2, p. 472.
4. See the biographical sketch in Labaree *et al., Papers of Benjamin Franklin,* vol. 4, pp. 467–468.
5. Benjamin Rush, *Autobiography,* ed. George W. Corner (Princeton: Princeton University Press, 1948), pp. 262–265.
6. [William Smith], *A Brief View of the Province of Pennsylvania* . . . (London, 1758), p. 9.
7. Smith to Josiah Tucker, December 18, 1765, transcript in Notes and Papers on the Commencement of the American Revolution, Rev. William Smith Papers, Historical Society of Pennsylvania, Philadelphia.
8. William Smith *et al., Four Dissertations on the Reciprocal Advantages of a Perpetual Union Between Great Britain and her Colonies* . . . (Philadelphia, 1766), pp. 1–12.
9. William Smith, memorandum in Notes and Papers on the Commencement of the American Revolution, Rev. William Smith Papers.
10. *Am Arch,* 4th ser., 1:427.
11. Smith, *Sermon on the Present Situation of American Affairs,* pp. 7–20.

12. William Smith, *The Works of William Smith, D.D. . . .* , 2 vols. (Philadelphia, 1803), vol. 2, p. 123; *Am Arch,* 4th ser. 5:544; the latter quotation was called to my attention by Professor Don R. Byrnes, author of a careful study, "The Pre-Revolutionary Career of Provost William Smith, 1751–1778" (Ph.D. diss., Tulane University, 1969).

13. John W. Thornton, ed., *The Pulpit in the American Revolution . . .* (Boston, 1860), p. 247; there are recent editions of this sermon in Edmund S. Morgan, ed., *Puritan Political Ideas, 1558–1794* (Indianapolis, Ind.: Bobbs-Merrill Co., 1965), pp. 352–372, and in A. W. Plumstead, ed., *The Wall and the Garden: Selected Massachusetts Election Sermons, 1670–1775* (Minneapolis: University of Minnesota Press, 1968), pp. 349–372; but the Thornton volume remains the best collection of Revolutionary sermons.

14. Plumstead, *The Wall and the Garden,* pp. 3–37.

15. Andrew Eliot, *A Sermon Preached before his Excellency Francis Bernard . . .* (Boston, 1765), pp. 10, 15, 18, 34–36, 38, 41–42; the pagination of the copy of this sermon that I consulted at the Houghton Library, Harvard University, differs from the edition cited by Bernard Bailyn in his "Religion and Revolution: Three Biographical Studies," *Perspectives in American History,* 4 (1970), 85–169.

16. Bailyn, "Religion and Revolution," p. 88; I have relied heavily on Bailyn's masterful reconstruction of Eliot's personality and intellect, based on a large, complicated body of sermons and printed and manuscript letters; but in his effort to refute Alan Heimert's jaundiced view of Eliot, Bailyn dismisses theology as a central motive for Eliot's political ambivalence. Eliot's view of human nature and his temporizing ministry seem to me inseparably intertwined with his explicitly political ideas.

17. *Ibid.,* pp. 87–93.

18. Quoted in Caroline Robbins, "The Strenuous Whig: Thomas Hollis of Lincoln's Inn," *WMQ,* 7 (July 1950), 430.

19. Bailyn, "Religion and Revolution," pp. 98–102; Eliot to Hollis, December 10, 1767; September 27, 1768; and January 29, 1769, *MHS Colls,* 4th ser., 4:402–461, *passim.*

20. Eliot to Hollis, January 26, 1771, *ibid.,* 454–455; Eliot to Blackburne, December 15, 1767, Andrew Eliot Papers, Houghton Library, Harvard University.

21. Quoted in Shipton, *Sibley,* 10:151, and Bailyn, "Religion and Revolution," p. 106.

CHAPTER THIRTEEN

1. Samuel Quincy to Josiah Quincy, August 26, 1768, Samuel Quincy Papers, Massachusetts Historical Society.
2. Bailyn, *Ideological Origins of the American Revolution,* pp. 121–122; the careers of the Quincy brothers corresponded exactly with John Murrin's generalization about the political motivation of Boston attorneys in the pre-Revolutionary period. See above, chap. 5, n. 4.
3. Samuel Quincy to Josiah Quincy, August 26, 1768, Samuel Quincy Papers.
4. Samuel Quincy to Josiah Quincy, June 1, 1774 and May 13, 1775, *ibid.*
5. This section on Beverley is based upon my "A Sorrowful Spectator of These Tumultuous Times: Robert Beverley Describes the Coming of the Revolution," *VMHB,* 73 (January 1965), 41–55, and reprints portions of my "'Unhinging Former Intimacies': Robert Beverley's Perception of the Pre-Revolutionary Controversy, 1761–1775," *SAQ,* 68 (Spring 1969), 246–261.

CHAPTER FOURTEEN

1. There is an unusually rich historical literature on this topic: Frederick B. Tolles, *Meeting House and Counting House: The Quaker Merchants of Colonial Philadelphia, 1682–1763* (Chapel Hill: University of North Carolina Press, 1948); Sydney V. James, *A People Among Peoples: Quaker Benevolence in Eighteenth-Century America* (Cambridge: Harvard University Press, 1963); Theodore Thayer, *Israel Pemberton: King of the Quakers* (Philadelphia: University of Pennsylvania Press, 1943); Peter Brock, *Pacifism in the United States: From the Colonial Era to the First World War* (Princeton: Princeton University Press, 1968), pt. 1; and Richard Bauman, *For a Reputation of Truth: Politics, Religion, and Conflict among the Pennsylvania Quakers, 1750–1800* (Baltimore: Johns Hopkins University Press, 1971).
2. Robert F. Oaks, "Philadelphians in Exile: The Problem of Loyalty during the American Revolution," *PMHB,* 96 (July 1972), 304, n. 24.
3. Arthur J. Mekeel, "The Society of Friends (Quakers) and the American Revolution" (Ph.D. diss. Harvard University, 1940), pp. 110–111.

4. Bauman, *For a Reputation of Truth,* p. 148.
5. Tolles, *Meeting House and Counting House,* p. 3.
6. *Ibid.,* chap. 1.
7. Quoted in Bauman, *For a Reputation of Truth,* pp. 15–16.
8. *Ibid.,* pp. 128–134.
9. *Ibid.,* p. 143.
10. Mack Thompson, *Moses Brown: Reluctant Reformer* (Chapel Hill: University of North Carolina Press, 1962), chap. 4.
11. *Ibid.,* pp. 108–114; John Brown to the Rhode Island General Assembly, May 5, 1775, photostat, Miscellaneous Manuscripts, Rhode Island Historical Society, Providence.
12. Moses Brown to John Brown, June 16, 1775, Moses Brown Papers, Rhode Island Historical Society.

CHAPTER FIFTEEN

1. For an introduction to the study of moderate loyalist thought, see Calhoon, " 'Unhinging Former Intimacies,' " pp. 246–248; and my review of Aubrey C. Land, ed., William Eddis, *Letters from America* (Cambridge: Harvard University Press, 1969), in *Studies in Burke and His Time,* 13 (Winter 1971–1972), 2168–2171. Two studies of British attempts at reconciliation throw considerable light on the frustration of colonial attempts: Weldon A. Brown, *Empire or Independence* ([Baton Rouge]: Louisiana State University Press, 1941), and a particularly valuable recent article, Herbert A. Meistrich, "Lord Drummond and Reconciliation," *Proceedings of the New Jersey Historical Society,* 80 (1963), 256–277. For corrections and amplification, see Milton M. Klein, "Failure of a Mission: The Drummond Mission of 1775," *HLQ,* 35 (August 1972), 343–380. Michael G. Kammen, "Intellectuals, Political Leadership, and Revolution," *NEQ* 41 (December 1968), 583–593, raises important questions about the social roots of ambivalence and moderation on the eve of the Revolution.
2. Edward Burd to E. Shippen, July 14, 1774, Lewis Burd Walker, ed., *The Burd Papers . . . 1763–1828* (n.p., 1899), p. 67; *Pennsylvania Gazette,* May 18, 1774; [Richard Wells], *A Few Political Reflections . . .* (Philadelphia, 1774), pp. 3–4; Andrew Eliot to Thomas Hollis, September 27, 1768, December 25, 1769, *MHS Colls,* 4th ser., 4:423, 445–446; *Pennsylvania Packet,* September 19, 1774; "Letters of Thomas Wharton, 1773–1783," *PMHB,* 33 (October 1904), 437–440, 446–447.
3. Eliot to Blackburne, December 15, 1767, Andrew Eliot Papers;

Pennsylvania Ledger, January 28, 1775; [Wells], *A Few Political Reflections,* p. 18; Tryon to Dartmouth, August 7, 1775, Additional Manuscripts, 38650, pp. 1–2, British Museum, London; Thomas Combe to Rockingham, February 5 and November 5, 1774, Rockingham Papers, R 1, nos. 1480 and 1529, Sheffield City Library, Sheffield, England.

4. Jeremy Belknap, *A Sermon on Military Duty* . . . (Salem, New Hampshire, 1773), p. 6; [Wells], *A Few Political Reflections,* p. 36; John Tucker, *A Sermon Preached* . . . *before his Excellency Thomas Hutchinson* . . . *May 29, 1771* (Boston, 1771), p. 21; Gad Hitchcock, *A Sermon Preached before his Excellency Thomas Gage* . . . *May 25, 1774* . . . (Boston, 1774), p. 24; Daniel Shute, *A Sermon Preached before his Excellency Francis Bernard* . . . *May 25, 1768* . . . (Boston, 1768), p. 60.

5. *Massachusetts Gazette and Boston Weekly News-Letter,* February 2, 1775; Shipton, *Sibley,* 10:151; Jeremy Belknap, Extracts and Remarks on the Correspondence of J[ohn] W[entworth] and T[homas] W. W[aldron], Jeremy Belknap Papers, Massachusetts Historical Society; Wingate to Timothy Pickering, April 28, 1775; Charles E. L. Wingate, *The Life and Letters of Paine Wingate* (Medford, Mass.: Mercury Publishing Co., 1930), 1:159–162; fourteen members of the New York Assembly to Gage, May 5, 1775, CO 5, 92:168–169.

6. *Pennsylvania Gazette,* September 7, 1774; "Jeremy Belknap's Reasons Against Subscribing the Covenant, June 28, 1774," *MHS Proc,* 2:484–486; Nathaniel Peaslee Sargeant to Thomas Cushing, May 22, 1775, Robert Treat Paine Papers, Massachusetts Historical Society.

7. J. J. Zubly, *The Law of Liberty* . . . (Philadelphia, 1774), pp. vi–vii; Simeon Howard, *A Sermon Preached before the Ancient and Honorable Artillery Company* . . . *June 7, 1773* . . . (Boston, 1773), p. 38; Diary of Reverend David Hall, April 5, 1770, Massachusetts Historical Society; Andrew Eliot to John Eliot, May 4 and August 1, 1775, Andrew Eliot Papers; see also the letters of Isaac Smith, Jr., in *MHS Proc,* 59 (1925), 117–138; John Eliot to Jeremy Belknap, February 18, 1775, *MHS Colls,* 6th ser., 4:83–84; and Jeremy Belknap, A Prayer, June 26, 1774, Jeremy Belknap Papers.

8. Zubly, *Law of Liberty,* pp. 11, 18–19, 25–26. The Reverend John Joachim Zubly, a Swiss immigrant, was a Presbyterian clergyman in Georgia; see Marjorie Daniel, "John J. Zubly . . .," *GHQ,* 19 (March 1935), 1–16.

9. Zubly, *Law of Liberty,* pp. 24–25; Howard, *Sermon before Artillery Company,* pp. 30–36.

10. Jones to James Duane, December 7 and July 13, 1775, James Duane Papers, New-York Historical Society, New York; Gill to Rev. Mr. Hawley, August 18, 1770, S. P. Savage Papers, Massachusetts Historical Society.

11. Quoted in Upton, *Loyal Whig,* title page and p. 110.

12. Morgan and Morgan, *Stamp Act Crisis,* p. 149; William A. Benton, *Whig Loyalism: An Aspect of Political Ideology in the American Revolutionary Era* (Teaneck, N.J.: Fairleigh Dickinson University Press, 1969), pp. 93, 160; Kammen, *Rope of Sand,* p. 163. Johnson to Thomas Pownall, November 3, 1772; to Richard Jackson, August 3, 1774; and to Sally Johnson, November 21, 1774, William Samuel Johnson Papers, Connecticut Historical Society.

13. Carl Becker, "John Jay and Peter Van Schaack," *Everyman His Own Historian* (New York: F. S. Crofts, 1935), p. 288; Benton, *Whig Loyalism,* p. 134; Van Schaack to ? , January 3, 1775; and to [William Laight], September 2, 1774, Peter Van Schaack Papers, Columbia University Library, New York; and Van Schaack to John Maunsell, May 7, 1775, Henry C. Van Schaack, *The Life of Peter Van Schaack . . .* (New York, 1842), pp. 37–39.

14. *Ibid.,* pp. 54–58. "Inalienable" in the second paragraph is spelled "unalienable" in the published version of this document.

CHAPTER SIXTEEN

1. The succeeding quotations on Samuel Peters are from "A Narrative," Samuel Peters Papers, vol. 1, item 3, microfilm; New-York Historical Society; Oscar Zeichner, *Connecticut's Years of Controversy, 1750–1776* (Chapel Hill: University of North Carolina Press, 1949), pp. 325–326, discusses this manuscript, cautions against accepting Peters's more extravagant claims, and cites other useful accounts of the episode. I have used Peters's statements that seem internally consistent and plausible but in any event am concerned more with Peters's peculiar view of events than with his objective veracity.

2. Ezra Stiles's secondhand but probably reliable characterization of the event, F. B. Dexter, ed., *The Literary Diary of Ezra Stiles,* 3 vols. (New York: Charles Scribner's Sons, 1909), vol. 1, pp. 466–467.

3. For a more elaborate, embroidered, but still useful version of

Peters's experience in Connecticut, see the Appendix to his *General History of Connecticut* . . . (London, 1788), pp. 246–276.

4. Glenn Weaver, "Anglican-Congregational Tension in Pre-Revolutionary Connecticut," *HMPEC,* 26 (September 1957), 269–285.

5. Bushman, *Puritan to Yankee, passim;* and Albert E. Van Dusen, *Connecticut* (New York: Random House, 1961), chap. 7.

6. Bushman, *Puritan to Yankee,* pp. 267–281; Joseph J. Ellis, "Anglicans in Connecticut, 1725–1750: The Conversion of the Missionaries," *NEQ,* 44 (March 1971), 66–81.

CHAPTER SEVENTEEN

1. Peter Gay, *The Enlightenment: An Interpretation, The Rise of Modern Paganism* (New York: Alfred A. Knopf, 1967), p. 3.

2. *Ibid.,* pp. 16–19.

3. Leonard Krieger, *Kings and Philosophers, 1689–1789* (New York: W. W. Norton & Co., 1970), p. 138.

4. Charles A. Barker, *American Convictions: Cycles of Public Thought, 1660–1815* (Philadelphia: J. B. Lippincott Co., 1970), chap. 8; and Peter Gay, *The Enlightenment: An Interpretation, The Science of Freedom* (New York: Alfred A. Knopf, 1969), pp. 555–568.

5. John Dunn, "The Politics of Locke in England and America in the Eighteenth Century," in John W. Yolton, ed., *John Locke: Problems and Perspectives* (Cambridge: Cambridge University Press, 1967), pp. 45–80, quotation from p. 52; and Dunn, *The Political Thought of John Locke* (Cambridge: Cambridge University Press, 1969), chap. 5.

6. W. H. Greenleaf, *Order, Empiricism, and Politics: Two Traditions of English Political Thought, 1500–1700* (London: Oxford University Press, 1964), chap. 2; and Dunn, *The Political Thought of John Locke,* chap. 6.

7. Perry Miller, *The New England Mind: From Colony to Province* (Cambridge: Harvard University Press, 1953), pp. 419–420; Herbert Schneider and Carol Schneider, eds., *Samuel Johnson, President of King's College: His Career and Writings,* 4 vols. (New York: Columbia University Press, 1929), vol. 2, p. 281; Robert Middlekauff, *The Mathers: Three Generations of Puritan Intellectuals, 1596–1728* (New York: Oxford University Press, 1971), p. 297.

8. Quoted in Dunn, "The Politics of Locke in England and America," p. 64.

9. An explicit example is John Adams, "Original Draft Reply to the . . . Friendly Address to all Reasonable Americans," John Adams

Papers, microfilm reel 344, Massachusetts Historical Society, cited in Thomas R. Adams, *American Independence, The Growth of an Idea: A Bibliographical Study of the American Political Pamphlets Printed between 1764 and 1776 Dealing with the Dispute between Great Britain and Her Colonies* (Providence, R.I.: Brown University Press, 1964), p. 83.

10. Gladys Bryson, *Man and Society: The Scottish Inquiry of the Eighteenth Century* (Princeton: Princeton University Press, 1956), pp. 11, 121–130; John M. Werner, "David Hume and America," *Journal of the History of Ideas,* 33 (July–September 1972), 439–456.

11. John Clive and Bernard Bailyn, "England's Cultural Provinces: Scotland and America," *WMQ,* 11 (April 1954), 200–213.

12. Bryson, *Man and Society,* pp. 114–147.

13. Norman S. Fiering, "President Samuel Johnson and the Circle of Knowledge," *WMQ,* 28 (April 1971), 231–236.

14. Wilbur S. Howell, "The Declaration of Independence and Eighteenth-Century Logic," *WMQ,* 18 (October 1961), 463–484.

15. Philip C. Foner, ed., *The Complete Writings of Thomas Paine,* 2 vols. (New York: Citadel Press, 1945), vol. 1, pp. 4–5.

16. Bailyn, *Ideological Origins of the American Revolution,* pp. 288–289.

17. *Ibid.,* pp. 287–288; [Chalmers], *Plain Truth* . . . (Philadelphia, 1776), pp. 1–6, 10–12; [Inglis], *The True Interest of America* . . . (Philadelphia, 1776), pp. 11, 15, 18, 22–23, 34.

CHAPTER EIGHTEEN

1. Bridenbaugh, *Mitre and Sceptre,* chaps. 6–8; Barker, *American Convictions,* pp. 115–124.

2. Quoted in Richard J. Hooker, "The Anglican Church and the American Revolution" (Ph.D. diss., University of Chicago, 1943), p. 75.

3. Quoted in Bridenbaugh, *Mitre and Sceptre,* p. 167.

4. Frederick V. Mills, "Anglican Expansion in Colonial America, 1761–1775," *HMPEC,* 39 (September 1970), 315–324. The pioneering work in this field is W. W. Sweet, "The Role of the Anglicans in the American Revolution," *HLQ,* 11 (November 1947), 51–70.

5. Bruce E. Steiner, "New England Anglicanism: A Genteel Faith?" *WMQ,* 27 (January 1970), 136–144.

6. Schneider and Schneider, *Samuel Johnson,* vol. 2, p. 28, and vol. 3, pp. 520–521.

7. Jack M. Sosin, "The Proposal in the Pre-Revolutionary Decade for

Establishing Anglican Bishops in the Colonies," *Journal of Ecclesiastical History,* 13 (April 1962) , 80, 81, 84.

8. Denzil T. Clifton, "Anglicanism and the Negro in Colonial America," *HMPEC,* 39 (March 1970) , 29–70.

9. John Calam, *Parsons and Pedagogues: The S.P.G. Adventure in American Education* (New York: Columbia University Press, 1971) , p. 63.

10. *Ibid.,* chaps. 3 and 4.

11. Richard J. Hooker, ed., *The Carolina Backcountry on the Eve of the Revolution: The Journal and Other Writings of Charles Woodmason, Anglican Itinerant* (Chapel Hill: University of North Carolina Press, 1953) , pp. 88–117.

12. Quoted in Gerald J. Goodwin, "The Anglican Reaction to the Great Awakening," *HMPEC,* 35 (December 1966) , 355.

13. Joseph J. Ellis, "The Puritan Mind in Transition: The Philosophy of Samuel Johnson," *WMQ,* 28 (January 1971) , 26–45; quotation from p. 30.

14. Schneider and Schneider, *Samuel Johnson,* vol. 2, p. 434, italics added.

15. See Edward Bass, manuscript, Sermon on Genesis 7:17, E. C. Chorley Collection, Yale University Library, Box 9.

16. Edward Bass, manuscript, Sermon on Proverbs 57:14, Episcopal Diocesan House Library, Boston.

17. Henry Caner, *The Great Blessing of Stable Times . . .* (Boston, 1763) , pp. 7–8; Caner, *Joyfulness and Consideration, or the Duties of Prosperity and Adversity . . .* (Boston, 1761) , pp. 8–9, 13–14, 24, 28.

18. Edward Bass, manuscript, Sermon on Romans 6:25, Episcopal Diocesan House Library, Boston.

19. Edward Bass, manuscript, Sermon on Ephesians 5:7, Episcopal Diocesan House Library, Boston; [Thomas Bradbury Chandler], *A Friendly Address to All Reasonable Americans . . .* (New York, 1774) , p. 5, italics added.

CHAPTER NINETEEN

1. Jonathan Bouchier, ed., *Reminiscences of an American Loyalist, 1738–1789; Being the Autobiography of the Reverend Jonathan Boucher . . .* (Boston: Houghton Mifflin Co., 1925) , pp. 118–124.

2. The reconstruction of Boucher's experience in this and succeeding paragraphs is largely based upon Arthur D. Middleton, "The Colonial Virginia Parson," *WMQ,* 26 (July 1969) , 425–440; Ralph

Emmett Fall, "The Reverend Jonathan Boucher: Turbulent Tory (1738–1804)," *HMPEC,* 36 (December 1967), 323–356; Philip Evanson, "Jonathan Boucher: The Mind of an American Loyalist," *MHM,* 58 (June 1963), 123–136; James Haw, "Maryland Politics," pp. 109–113; Michael D. Clark, "Jonathan Boucher's *Causes and Consequences,*" in Lawrence Leder, ed., *The Colonial Legacy: The Loyalist Historians* (New York: Harper & Row, 1971), pp. 89–117; and "Jonathan Boucher: The Mirror of Reaction," *HLQ,* 33 (November 1969), 19–32.

3. Boucher, *Reminiscences,* pp. 41, 57–59.

4. Quoted in Jordan, *White Over Black,* p. 280.

5. Boucher, *Reminiscences,* pp. 42–47.

6. Robert G. Walker, "Jonathan Boucher: Champion of the Minority," *WMQ,* 2 (January 1945), 3–14.

7. Boucher to John James, June 22, 1767, "Letters of Jonathan Boucher," *MHM,* 7 (December 1912), 348.

8. Boucher to James, November 28, 1767, *ibid.,* p. 352.

9. Boucher, *Reminiscences,* p. 92.

10. Haw, "Maryland Politics," pp. 104–112.

11. Boucher to James, August 7 and 19, 1759, "Letters of Jonathan Boucher," *MHM,* 7 (March 1912), 6–9, 23; Boucher, *Reminiscences,* p. 27.

12. Boucher, *Reminiscences,* pp. 28–29.

13. *Ibid.,* pp. 34–38.

14. Boucher to James, August 5, 1762, "Letters of Jonathan Boucher," *MHM,* 7 (June 1912), 151–153.

15. Evanson, "Jonathan Boucher," pp. 123–124. Boucher to James, March 9, 1767, and July 25, 1769, "Letters of Jonathan Boucher," *MHM,* 7 (December 1912), 338–339; and *MHM,* 8 (March 1913), 39–40.

16. Boucher to Washington, August 2, 1768; December 18, 1770; July 4, and November 19, 1771; January 19, 1773, S. M. Hamilton, ed., *Letters to Washington . . . ,* 5 vols. (Boston and New York, 1898–1902), vol. 3, pp. 324–328; vol. 4, pp. 41–46, 69–73, 83–86, 175–180. For a valuable commentary on this correspondence, see Douglas Southall Freeman, *George Washington: A Biography,* 7 vols. (New York: Charles Scribner's Sons, 1948–1957), vol. 3, *Planter and Patriot,* pp. 203, 263, 285–286, 311.

17. Boucher, *Reminiscences,* pp. 66–74.

18. Bailyn, *Ideological Origins of the American Revolution,* p. 314; the following discussion of Boucher's "Sermon on Civil Liberty,

Passive Obedience, and Nonresistance" follows Bailyn's acute dissection on pp. 314–318.

19. Jonathan Boucher, *A View of the Causes and Consequences of the American Revolution* (London, 1897), pp. 511–518.

20. *Ibid.*, pp. 523–534.

21. *Ibid.*, pp. 504–509, 512–513, 519–520, 549.

22. Clark, "Jonathan Boucher: The Mirror of Reaction," pp. 19–20. An article that appeared after my section on Boucher was in final form, Anne Young Zimmer and Alfred H. Kelly, "Jonathan Boucher: Constitutional Conservative," *JAH*, 58 (March 1972), 897–922, establishes with greater precision and detail than any previous scholarship what Boucher actually believed about the American Revolution and colonial society. Professors Zimmer and Kelly successfully discredit the view that Boucher was "a high Tory and reactionary political theorist who derived his ideas almost entirely from . . . Robert Filmer"; they demonstrate that his published sermons, in *A View of the Causes and Consequences of the American Revolution,* were not exact copies of the sermons he wrote between 1763 and 1775; they reveal Boucher's extensive use of philosophical and religious ideas that were not authoritarian; they stress his advanced views on the equality of blacks and Indians with white men; in sum, they find Boucher "an eighteenth-century constitutional conservative" who incidentally espoused some advanced and some archaic political and social ideas. They do not, I believe, directly refute Clark's or Bailyn's carefully qualified depictions of Boucher's organic conservatism or contradict my exploratory examination of his self-image and emotional development, but their article does raise serious questions about the premises of all prior scholarship on Boucher.

23. Boucher, *Reminiscences,* pp. 114–115.

24. Quoted in Clark, "Jonathan Boucher's *Causes and Consequences,*" pp. 96–97, 104; from *MHM,* 7:295 and 8:44.

25. Boucher, *Causes and Consequences,* pp. 372–373.

26. Boucher to William Eden, January 7, 1776, "Letters of Jonathan Boucher," *MHM,* 8 (December 1913), 338–343.

27. The phrase is from Bailyn, *Ideological Origins of the American Revolution,* p. 312.

CHAPTER TWENTY

1. Shipton, *Sibley,* 8:737–743.

2. *Ibid.*, p. 744; Robert Zemsky, *Merchants, Farmers, and River Gods* (Boston: Gambit, 1971), chap. 9; quotation from p. 228.

3. This treatment of the controversy is based on Shipton's masterful reconstruction, *Sibley,* 8:747–754; I disagree with only one point in this account. "The House itself suggested rioting as the next step," Shipton states, after Hutchinson refused to recommend Oliver's dismissal. What the House told Hutchinson was that "we can assure you that the continuance of the Chief Justice in his place will increase the uneasiness of the people out of doors and endanger the public tranquillity." One man's incitement to riot, I suppose, is another's considered assessment of the public temper. See p. 750 and *Journal of the Massachusetts House of Representatives . . .* (Boston, 1773–1774), p. 167.

4. Adair and Schutz, *Peter Oliver's Origin and Progress of the American Rebellion,* pp. ix, 35–37, 40–42.

5. *Ibid.,* p. 65, italics added.

6. *Ibid.,* pp. 44, 74, 55, 4, italics added.

7. [Peter Oliver], "An Address to the Soldiers of Massachusetts Bay," *Boston Weekly News-Letter,* January 11, 1776, reprinted in Adair and Schutz, *Peter Oliver's Origin and Progress of the American Rebellion,* pp. 158–168, quote from p. 161.

8. Quoted in Shipton, *Sibley,* 7:757–758.

9. Peter Oliver, Journal . . . 1776–1780, entries for October 22, 1776, and June 21, 1777, Egerton Manuscripts, 2672, pp. 125–127, 177, British Museum, London.

CHAPTER TWENTY-ONE

1. Bruce E. Steiner, *Samuel Seabury, 1729–1796: A Study in the High Church Tradition* (Athens: Ohio University Press, 1971), p. 89, and chaps. 2–4, *passim.*

2. *Ibid.,* pp. 90, 123, 124; Chandler to Johnson, January 1, 1768, Schneider and Schneider, *Samuel Johnson,* vol. 1, pp. 432–434.

3. Samuel Seabury, *Letters of a Westchester Farmer,* ed. Clarence H. Vance (White Plains, N.Y.: Westchester County Historical Society, 1930), *passim* and pp. 62, 140, 31.

4. Samuel Seabury, *A Discourse on II Timothy 3:16 . . .* (New York, 1777); because of its bearing on his pre-Revolutionary thought, I have used the 1773 manuscript copy, Fulham Palace Papers, 50:207–226, Lambeth Palace, London.

5. Seabury to the Secretary of the S.P.G., December 17, 1769, S.P.G. Papers, B 2, 176, S.P.G. Archives, London.

6. Vance, *Letters of a Westchester Farmer,* p. 72.

7. *Ibid.,* p. 151.

8. *Ibid.*, pp. 156, 162.
9. *Ibid.*, pp. 104, 106–107, 108.
10. *Ibid.*, pp. 109–110.
11. *Ibid.*, pp. 111–121, 129, 132–145; quotation from p. 116, italics added.
12. Seabury's memorial to the Connecticut General Assembly recounting the experience is printed in E. E. Beardsley, *Life and Correspondence of . . . Reverend Samuel Seabury* (Boston, 1881), pp. 36–42; Seabury to the Secretary of the S.P.G., December 29, 1776, quoted by Beardsley, pp. 45–47.

CHAPTER TWENTY-TWO

1. The foregoing is based on a luminous study in intellectual, religious, and educational history, David Churchill Humphrey, "King's College in the City of New York, 1754–1776" (Ph.D. diss., Northwestern University, 1968), pp. 257–303.
2. Cooper to Boucher, March 22, 1770, in Herbert B. Howe, ed., "Colonel George Washington and King's College," *Columbia University Quarterly*, 24 (June 1932), 140–141, cited in Humphrey, "King's College," p. 282.
3. See King's College to George III *et al.*, October 12, 1771, quoted extensively in Humphrey, "King's College," pp. 259–262.
4. [Myles Cooper, Charles Inglis *et al.*], "A Whip for the American Whig, #2," *New York Gazette* (Gaine's), April 11, 1768. Humphrey, "King's College," makes extensive use of the "Whip for the American Whig" series and demonstrates the value of this source.
5. "A Whip for the American Whig, #32," *New York Gazette,* November 14, 1768; see also nos. 3 (April 18, 1768), 4 (April 25, 1768), 5 (May 2, 1768), 6 (May 9, 1768), 7 (May 16, 1768), 29 (October 24, 1768), 41 (January 23, 1769), and 49 (March 17, 1769).

CHAPTER TWENTY-THREE

1. Wiswall to the Secretary of the S.P.G., January 5, 1771, September 16, 1774, and May 30, 1775; and Wiswall to Admiral Thomas Graves, May 22, 1775, John Wiswall Letterbook, microfilm, Massachusetts Historical Society.
2. Wiswall to Henry Bellew, January 15, 1776, *ibid.*
3. Clark to the Secretary of the S.P.G., October 15, 1774, William Clark Papers, Episcopal Diocesan Library, Boston.

4. [Thomas Bradbury Chandler], *The American Querist; or Some Questions Proposed Relative to the Present Disputes between Great Britain and her American Colonies* . . . (New York, 1774), pp. 7, 6, 4, 5, 32.

5. Henry Caner to John Wentworth, June 16, 1774, Henry Caner Letterbook, Bristol University Library, Bristol, England.

6. *Debates at the Robin-Hood Society in the City of New York on Monday Night 19th of July, 1774* (New York, 1774), pp. 5–6.

7. *The Triumph of the Whigs* . . . (New York, 1775), p. 8.

8. Samuel Andrews, *A Discourse Showing the Necessity of Joining Internal Repentance with the External Profession of It* . . . (New Haven, 1775), pp. 5–18.

9. [Myles Cooper], *The Patriots of North America: A Sketch* (New York, 1775), p. 3.

10. Chandler to Inglis, October 3, 1775, Dartmouth Papers, 2:1546.

11. An untitled broadside proposing a "Grand Congress of Controul," Broadside Collection, Library of Congress.

12. *A Dialogue between a Southern Delegate and his Spouse* . . . ([New York], 1774) as excerpted in "Who's Afraid of Catherine Macaulay?" *WMQ,* 21 (October 1964), 593–595.

CHAPTER TWENTY-FOUR

1. Richard D. Brown, *Revolutionary Politics in Massachusetts: The Boston Committee of Correspondence and the Towns, 1772–1774* (Cambridge: Harvard University Press, 1970), pp. 202, 216, and 203 and chaps. 8–9, *passim*. Oscar Handlin and Mary Handlin, eds., *The Popular Source of Political Authority: Documents on the Massachusetts Constitution of 1780* (Cambridge: Harvard University Press, 1966), pp. 6 and 4–12, *passim*.

2. Albert Matthews, ed., "Documents Relating to the Last Meetings of the Massachusetts Royal Council, 1774–1776," *CSM Publ,* 32 (1937), 473, italics added.

3. See Maier, *From Resistance to Revolution,* pp. 284–287.

4. Shipton, *Sibley,* 13:338–340; *CSM Publ,* 32:485–489. The more extensive resignation from the Council bearing Thomas Oliver's signature, dated September 2, 1774, in the Boston Public Library, ms. 938, is not an authentic document. See Oliver Elton, "Lieutenant Governor Thomas Oliver, 1734–1815," *CSM Publ,* 28:57.

5. Williams *et al.* to [Gage], September 20, 1774, House of Lords Record Office, London.

6. *CSM Publ,* 32:472, 476; Shipton, *Sibley,* 9:213–216.

7. *CSM Publ,* 32:476–478; Samuel Paine to William Paine, June 22, 1775, William Paine Manuscripts, American Antiquarian Society, Worcester, Massachusetts.

8. *CSM Publ,* 32:478–479, italics added.

9. Robert J. Taylor, *Western Massachusetts in the Revolution* (Providence, R.I.: Brown University Press, 1954), pp. 63–66; Shipton, *Sibley,* 8:325–326, italics added.

10. *Ibid.,* 323; George Shelton, *A History of Deerfield, Massachusetts,* 2 vols. (Deerfield, 1896), vol. 2, pp. 685, 697; Margaret Miller, "A Whig Parson and Tory Colonel at Hatfield," *History and Proceedings of the Pocumtuck Valley Memorial Association,* 5 (1912), 418–431.

11. Gardiner to [Oliver Whipple], May 9, 1776, Gardiner-Whipple-Allen Manuscripts, 2:7, Massachusetts Historical Society.

12. Oliver to [Elisha Hutchinson], December 7, 1775, in P. O. Hutchinson, ed., *The Diary and Letters of Thomas Hutchinson,* 2 vols. (London: Low, Marston, Searle and Rivington, 1883–1886), vol. 1, p. 582; Richard D. Brown, "The Confiscation and Disposition of Loyalists' Estates in Suffolk County, Massachusetts," *WMQ,* 21 (October 1964), 549–550.

CHAPTER TWENTY-FIVE

1. Zeichner, *Connecticut's Years of Controversy,* pp. 193–197.

2. Deposition of Ephraim Hinman, December 20, 1775; and Richard Mansfield to the Derby Committee of Inspection, March 11, 1776, Chauncy Family Collection, Yale University Library.

3. Wallace Brown, *The King's Friends: The Composition and Motives of the American Loyalist Claimants* (Providence, R.I.: Brown University Press, 1966), pp. 65–66.

4. Adair and Schutz, *Peter Oliver's Origin and Progress of the American Rebellion,* p. 157.

5. Zeichner, *Connecticut's Years of Controversy,* chap. 12.

6. David S. Lovejoy, *Rhode Island Politics and the American Revolution, 1760–1776* (Providence, R.I.: Brown University Press, 1958), chap. 9.

7. Joel A. Cohen, "Rhode Island Loyalism and the American Revolution," *RIH,* 27 (October 1968), 97–100.

8. *Ibid.,* pp. 100–102.

9. *Ibid.,* pp. 102–103.

10. *Ibid.,* pp. 103–105; see also Ralph Adams Brown, *"The Newport Gazette:* Tory Newssheet," *RIH,* 13 (October 1954 and January 1955), 11–21, 97–108.

11. "Proceedings of the third Hillsborough County Congress . . . ," May 24, 1775, Benjamin Whiting File, HT.

12. Daniell, *Experiment in Republicanism,* pp. 100–101.

13. Jere R. Daniell, "Lady Wentworth's Last Days in New Hampshire," *Historical New Hampshire,* 23 (Spring 1968), 14–25.

14. Atkinson to the Committee of the Provincial Congress, July 6, 1775, and Atkinson to Wentworth, July 7, 1775, Photostat Collection, Massachusetts Historical Society.

15. Richard F. Upton, *Revolutionary New Hampshire,* p. 53.

16. Avery J. Butters, "New Hampshire History and the Public Career of Meshech Weare, 1713–1786" (Ph.D. diss., Fordham University, 1961).

17. Otis G. Hammond, "The Tories of New Hampshire in the War of the Revolution," *Proceedings of the New Hampshire Historical Society,* 5 (1917), 286–291.

18. Adam Stuart File, HT; Butters, "Meshech Weare," p. 210.

19. *New Hampshire State Papers* (Concord and Manchester, 1872–1943), 8:156; Hammond, "The Tories of New Hampshire," pp. 306–307.

20. *New Hampshire State Papers,* 13 (1884), 458–461.

21. All of the documentation on Asa Porter may be found in the Asa Porter File, HT. Several of these documents are published in *New Hampshire State Papers,* 8:413–414, 416, 418, 436, 568, 577–578, 585, 609, 612, 717, and in *Am Arch,* 5th ser., 3:686.

22. See Gordon S. Wood, *The Creation of the American Republic, 1776–1787* (Chapel Hill: University of North Carolina Press, 1969), pp. 156–157.

CHAPTER TWENTY-SIX

1. Lee Nathaniel Newcomer, *The Embattled Farmers: A Massachusetts Countryside in the American Revolution* (New York: Columbia University Press, 1953), pp. 32–34, 39, 90–91; *Am Arch,* 5th ser., 1:245–246.

2. Framingham Committee of Correspondence to the General Court, September 4, 1776, and Nathaniel Brinley to the General Court [*ca.* September 1776], MA, 181:190–192.

3. Artemas Ward to   ?   , June 13, 1775, and to the [Rutland,

Massachusetts] Committee of Correspondence, June 18, 1775, Chamberlain Collection, Boston Public Library.

4. "A Copy of the Proceedings of the Committee against the Reverend Jacob Bailey of Pownallboro," Samuel Peters Papers, 1:item 25, italics added.

5. Documents relating to the case of Edward Perry are in MA, 137: 25–35.

6. Cambridge Committee of Safety to the Selectmen of Lynn, May 11, 1775, MA, 154:3, 5; and Miscellaneous Revolutionary Records, Essex Institute, Salem, Massachusetts.

7. Groton Committee of Safety to the Massachusetts Committee of Safety, July 3, 1775, MA, 154:25.

8. Northboro Committee of Correspondence to   ?   , May 17, 1775, MA, 154:11.

9. Resolution of the Massachusetts Committee of Safety, May 19, 1775, and letter to the Sudbury Committee of Correspondence, May 30, 1775, MA, 154:12, 14.

10. Farmington Committee of Safety to the Connecticut General Assembly, June 19, 1776, CARW, vol. 5, pt. 2, p. 410.

11. Records of the Medway, Massachusetts, Committee of Correspondence, June 5–8, 1775, Chamberlain Collection.

12. John Bartlett Brebner, *The Neutral Yankees of Nova Scotia* (New York: Columbia University Press, 1937), pp. 115–118, 132–135; Sunbury, Nova Scotia Committee of Safety to the Massachusetts General Assembly, June 20 and September 24, 1776, MA, 181:247–249.

13. *The Recantations of Robert Hooper [et al.], [ca.* early May 1775] Broadside Collection, Library of Congress.

14. Enoch Bartlett to [the Haverhill, Massachusetts, Committee of Correspondence], September 9, 1774, Miscellaneous Manuscripts, Massachusetts Historical Society, and to Nathaniel Peabody, September 23, 1774, Peabody Papers, New Hampshire Historical Society.

CHAPTER TWENTY-SEVEN

1. Bradley Chapin, *The American Law of Treason: Revolutionary and Early National Origins* (Seattle: University of Washington Press, 1964), pp. 38–45.

2. Connecticut Superior Court Records, Fairfield County, April–May 1777, Connecticut State Library, Hartford.

3. *Ibid.,* May 1778.

4. Miscellaneous Papers, 1:27–28, Suffolk County Courthouse, Boston.

Testimony of Elnathan Mitchell and Elisha Smith, May 6, 1777; Justices of the Peace of Derby, Connecticut, to the General Assembly, June 8, 1778; and John Davis to the General Assembly, May ?, 1778, CARW, 8:174; 13:275–276. Suffolk County Justices of the Peace to the Sheriff of Suffolk County, June 2, 1777; Edward Winslow to [the Massachusetts General Court], July 2, 1777; John Stetson to the [Massachusetts General Court], September 7, 1777; Great Barrington, Massachusetts Justices of the Peace to ？ ， December 13, 1777, MA, 154:124; 183:78–80; 154:221–222, 176–177. Petitions addressed to the Massachusetts Council or Board of War and those addressed to the House of Representatives are identified here as petitions to the General Court.

5. Prince Barker to the Massachusetts General Court, August 15, 1777; Jov[?]tt Bullough to [the Massachusetts General Court], September 3, 1777, MA, 154:148, 177.

6. Suffolk Court Files, 608:24 (case 102523) ; CARW, vol. 5. pt. 2, p. 393. Massachusetts Superior Court of Judicature, Hampshire and Berkshire Counties, 1778–1780, Suffolk County Courthouse. Minute Books of the Superior Court of Judicature, vol. 19 (no pagination) , Connecticut Superior Court Records, Windham County, March 1777.

7. Resolution of the Connecticut General Assembly, January 1779, CARW, 14:342. Charles Whitworth to [the Massachusetts General Court], November 3, 1777; Charles Perrin to [the Massachusetts General Court], October 10, 1777, MA, 154:198, 191. Suffolk County Files, 1082:126 (case 152873) , Suffolk County Courthouse. Richard H. Phelps, *A History of Newgate of Connecticut . . .* (Albany, N.Y., 1860) , pp. 42–46.

CHAPTER TWENTY-EIGHT

1. Paul H. Smith, "The American Loyalists: Notes on their Organization and Numerical Strength," *WMQ,* 25 (April 1968) , 259, 270. Ephraim Hawley to the Connecticut General Assembly, [*ca.* May 1777], CARW, 8: 172. Connecticut Superior Court Records, Fairfield County, April 1777. [Richard Mansfield], "The Catechism," Chauncy Family Collection. On Mansfield see Rena Vassar, "The Aftermath of the Revolution: Letters of Anglican Clergy in Connecticut, 1781–1785," *HMPEC,* 41 (December 1972) , 429–461. His "Catechism" contains twenty-six questions and answers.

2. Stephen Parker to [the Massachusetts General Court], May 11, 1776, MA, 181:3–4. Titus Butler to the Connecticut General Assembly, April 7, 1779; John Baker to the Connecticut General Assembly,

January 26, 1779; Stephan Gorham to the Connecticut General Assembly, February 22, 1780; Thomas Osbourn to the Connecticut General Assembly, [*ca.* April 1777]; William Mitchell to the Connecticut General Assembly, May 10, 1777, CARW, 14:363, 353; 20: 92; 7:170; 8:164.

3. Judah and Benjamin Leaming to the Connecticut General Assembly, May 8 and 16, 1777; Abel Skidmore, William Allen, and Matthew Sherman to the Connecticut General Assembly, February 9, 1778; Prosper Brown to the Connecticut General Assembly, May 10, 1782, CARW, 8:157–159; 13:233; 23:354–355.

4. David Washburn to the Connecticut General Assembly, October 2, 1779; Samuel Roberts to the Connecticut General Assembly, February 6, 1782; Nathan Turrill to the Connecticut General Assembly, October 2, 1778, CARW, 20:95; 23:300; 13:290. John Jennings to the Massachusetts General Court, January 4, 1779, MA, 184:292.

5. Documents relating to the case of John McKee, October 7 and 8, 1776, May 8, 1777, CARW, 5:421–423; 8:155–156. Nathan Daton to the Connecticut General Assembly, January 10, 1778; Ashbel Humphrey to the Connecticut General Assembly, June 4, 1782; Solomon Ferris to the Connecticut General Assembly, October 9, 1779, CARW, 13:195; 23:302; 20:105.

6. Edward Winslow to [the Massachusetts General Court], July 2, 1777; Hopestill Capen to "the Court of Enquiry," August 29, 1776, and to Joseph Otis, December 11, 1776; Jonathan Hicks and Josiah Jones to the Provincial Congress, June 15, 1775, MA, 183:78; 154: 70–71; 180:51–52.

7. Andrew Leet to the Connecticut General Assembly, February 26, 1778, Miscellaneous Manuscripts, Massachusetts Historical Society, vol. 15; Patience Capen to [the Massachusetts General Court], March 13, 1778; and William Apthorp to [the Massachusetts General Court], June 8, 1779, MA, 184:30; 185:200.

8. Isaac Royall to James Bowdoin, November 19, 1778, and August 25, 1779, Temple-Bowdoin Papers, 3:99–100. Isaac Royall to   ?   , March 26, 1779; Samuel Mather to Rev. Dr. Mather, September 23, 1783, Chamberlain Collection. William Peck to the Connecticut General Assembly; Darling Whelply to the Connecticut General Assembly, October 9, 1779, CARW 20:102, 103; 20:102; Robert Cutts Shannon File, HT.

9. Documents relating to the case of Henry Stone and Ebenezer Tisdale, March 1777; Selectmen of Waltham to the General Court, May 1775, MA, 182:182–190; 180:4–5.

10. Daniel Ringe File, HT. William E. Nelson, "Emerging Notions of Modern Criminal Law in the Revolutionary Era," *New York University Law Review*, 62 (May 1967), 471.

11. Depositions relating to Ralph Isaac and others, October 15, 1776, CARW, 5:429–430. Oliver Parker File, HT.

12. Suffolk Court Files, 1083:144 (case 152967); 611:80 (case 102638). Massachusetts Supreme Judicial Court Records, Berkshire County, 1781–1782, pp. 99–100. Jonathan Smith, "Toryism in Worcester County," *MHS Proc*, 48 (1914), 25, italics added.

13. Benjamin Whitcher, Adam Stuart, and Seth Fogg Files, HT; deposition concerning Abiel Wood, MA, 138:182. Suffolk Court Files, 610: 102–107 (case 102601).

14. Connecticut Superior Court Records, Windham County, March 3, 1778. Eleazer Fitch to the Connecticut General Assembly, October 26, 1778, CARW, 13:295.

CHAPTER TWENTY-NINE

1. Van Dusen, *Connecticut*, p. 165.

2. *Ibid.*, p. 166. Frederick G. Mather, *The Refugees of 1776 from Long Island to Connecticut* (Albany, N.Y.: Lyon, 1913), pp. 200–224 *passim*. Albert E. Van Dusen, "The Trade of Revolutionary Connecticut" (Ph.D. diss., University of Pennsylvania, 1948), pp. 360–362. Connecticut Superior Court Records, Fairfield County, February 1777, April 1777, February 1778. Stamford Committee of Inspection to the Connecticut General Assembly, October 1776; James and Samuel Richards to the Connecticut General Assembly, June 4, 1778, CARW, 5:434; 10:356.

3. John R. Cuneo, "The Early Days of the Queen's Rangers, August 1776–February 1777," *Military Affairs*, 22 (Summer 1958), 65–74.

4. Papers relating to the trial of Moses Dunbar, photostats, Connecticut State Library, are cited in Van Dusen, *Connecticut*, pp. 144–145.

5. Mather, *Refugees of 1776*, pp. 204–205.

6. Charles S. Hall, *The Life and Letters of Samuel Holden Parsons* (New York: Otseningo Publishing Company, 1905), pp. 242–243, 257.

7. John Mackay to Jonathan Trumbull, October 23, 1779, CARW, 15: 26.

8. Ashbel Humphrey to the Connecticut General Assembly, June 4, 1782, CARW, 23:302. See also the memorials to the Connecticut General Assembly, of Joseph Seelye, May 10, 1777; of Robert

Thompson, May 9, 1777; of Samuel Rogers, January 12, 1778; of Samuel Hawley, January 2, 1778; of John Moorhouse, February 7 and October 8, 1778; of Benjamin Mead *et al.*, January 2, 1782; of Henry Stephens, May 24, 1782; of John Bates *et al.*, April 29, 1782, CARW, 8:149, 165, 193, 201; 13:249, 300; 23:319, 362, 370. See also Jonathan Ketchum to Henry Clinton, October 18, 1780, British Headquarters Papers, photostat no. 3078, New York Public Library.

9. This treatment of politics in the New Hampshire Grants follows closely Chilton Williamson, *Vermont in Quandary, 1763–1825* (Montpelier: Vermont Historical Society, 1941).

10. *Ibid.*, pp. 44–50, and chaps. 7 and 8, *passim*. Charles A. Jellison, *Ethan Allen: Frontier Hero* (Syracuse, N.Y.: Syracuse University Press, 1969), pp. 201–203; *Vermont State Papers* (Montpelier, 1924–), 6:21–23; *Connecticut Courant*, March 2 and 30, 1779.

11. Gwilym R. Roberts, "An Unknown Vermonter: Sylvanus Ewarts, Governor Chittenden's Tory Brother-in-law," *VH*, 29 (April 1961), 92–102; Piers G. Mackesy, *The War for America, 1775–1783* (London: Longmans and Green, 1964), p. 134; Richard J. Hargrove, "The Burgoyne Expedition of 1777: Ticonderoga and Bennington" (M.A. thesis, Duke University, 1967), chap. 5.

12. Roberts, "An Unknown Vermonter," pp. 96–97.

13. Hamilton V. Bail, "Zadock Wright: That 'Devilish' Tory of Hartland," *VH*, 36 (Autumn 1968), 186–203; Zadock Wright deposition, n.d., Miscellaneous Manuscripts, New Hampshire Historical Society.

14. James, *A People Among Peoples*, chap. 13, and "The Impact of the American Revolution on Quakers' Ideas about their Sect," *WMQ*, 19 (July 1963), 360–382; Brock, *Pacifism in the United States*, chap. 5; Mack Thompson, ed., "Moses Brown's 'Account of Journey to Distribute Donations 12th Month 1775,' " *RIH*, 15 (October 1956), 97–121; Henry J. Cadbury, "Quaker Relief during the Siege of Boston," *CSM Publ*, 34:39–179.

15. Thompson, *Moses Brown*, pp. 135–145; [Timothy Davis] to "Dear Friends," July 16, 1775, Moses Brown Papers.

16. Brock, *Pacifism in the United States*, pp. 229–230, 250; Christopher Starbuck to Moses Brown, January 17, 1777, and Moses Brown to John Fothergill, November 15, 1776, Moses Brown Papers; *Memorandum Written by William Rotch in the Eightieth Year of His Age* (Boston, 1916), pp. 2–7, 27–31.

17. Brock, *Pacifism in the United States*, pp. 241–245. Arthur J. Mekeel, "New England Quakers and Military Service in the Ameri-

can Revolution," in Howard H. Brinton, ed., *Children of Light* (New York: Macmillan Co., 1938), 241–275, *passim* and 263, 271. Jabez C. Bowen to Moses Brown, June 13, 1778; and Moses Brown to Jabez Bowen, July 1, 1778, Moses Brown Papers. New England Meeting for Sufferings to the Massachusetts General Court, October 9, 1779; and Moses Peck *et al.* to the General Court, June 28, 1779, MA, 185:383–386, 241. See also James, "The Impact of the American Revolution on Quakers' Ideas about their Sect," p. 382; Thompson, *Moses Brown,* p. 137; Job Scott, *Journal of . . . Life, Travels, and Gospel Labours . . .* (New York, 1797), pp. 53–71; and George Dill[wyn] to   ? , September 1, 1778, John Carter Brown Library, Providence, Rhode Island.

18. William G. McLoughlin, *New England Dissent, 1630–1833: Baptists and the Separation of Church and State,* 2 vols. (Cambridge: Harvard University Press, 1971), vol. 1, pp. 553–579, and "Mob Violence against Dissent in Revolutionary Massachusetts," *Foundations,* 14 (October–December 1971), 294–317.

19. Comfort Benedict to the General Assembly, March 25, 1780; Samuel Dible *et al.* to Jonathan Trumbull, March 24, 1778, CARW, 20: 96; 13:285; Connecticut Superior Court Records, Fairfield County, April 4, 1779.

CHAPTER THIRTY

1. The entire discussion of the Otis family and Barnstable follows John J. Waters, *The Otis Family in Provincial and Revolutionary Massachusetts* (Chapel Hill: University of North Carolina Press, 1968), *passim.*

2. *Ibid.,* p. 194.

3. The entire discussion of Edward Bacon is based on documents published in Francis T. Bowles, "The Loyalty of Barnstable in the Revolution," *CSM Publ,* 25 (1922–1924), 265–345, and on Waters, *The Otis Family,* p. 194.

4. Bowles, "Loyalty of Barnstable," pp. 289–292.

5. *Ibid.,* pp. 330–331.

6. *Ibid.,* pp. 310–312. See Archibald S. Foord, *His Majesty's Opposition, 1714–1830* (Oxford: Oxford University Press, 1964), pp. 334–337.

7. John M. Bumstead, "Orthodoxy in Massachusetts: The Ecclesiastical History of Freetown, 1683–1776," *NEQ,* 43 (June 1970), 274–284.

8. Bruce G. Merrit, "Loyalism and Social Conflict in Revolutionary Deerfield, Massachusetts," *JAH,* 57 (September 1970), 277–289.

CHAPTER THIRTY-ONE

1. Ambrose Serle, quoted in Ira D. Gruber, *The Howe Brothers and the American Revolution* (New York: Atheneum Publishers, 1972), p. 109.
2. Don Higginbotham, *The War of American Independence: Military Attitudes, Policies, and Practice, 1763–1789* (New York: Macmillan Co., 1971), pp. 160–164.
3. Gruber, *The Howe Brothers and the American Revolution,* p. 9.
4. *Ibid.,* pp. 10–15.
5. *Ibid.,* pp. 43–53, 56–61.
6. *Ibid.,* pp. 118–119.
7. *Ibid.,* p. 126.

CHAPTER THIRTY-TWO

1. Leonard Lundin, *Cockpit of the Revolution: The War for Independence in New Jersey* (Princeton: Princeton University Press, 1940), 158–161 and chap. 5 *passim.*
2. *NYHS Colls,* 16 (1883), 96–102; Vincent Flanagan and Gerald Kurland, "Stephen Kemble: New Jersey Loyalist," *NJH,* 90 (Spring 1972), 5–26.
3. Paul H. Smith, "New Jersey Loyalists and the British 'Provincial' Corps in the War for Independence," *NJH,* 87 (Summer 1969), 69–78.
4. Lundin, *Cockpit of the Revolution,* p. 74.
5. *Ibid.,* pp. 163–164.
6. Adrian C. Leiby, *The Revolutionary War in the Hackensack Valley: The Jersey Dutch and the Neutral Ground* (New Brunswick, N.J.: Rutgers University Press, 1962), pp. 19–25.
7. *Ibid.,* p. 26.
8. *Ibid.,* p. 30.
9. *Ibid.,* pp. 34–35.
10. *Ibid.,* pp. 37–41.
11. *Ibid.,* pp. 106–107.
12. *Ibid.,* pp. 143–149.

CHAPTER THIRTY-THREE

1. The entire discussion of New York City politics and society to this point is based on Bernard Mason, *The Road to Independence: The Revolutionary Movement in New York, 1773–1777* (Lexington:

University of Kentucky Press, 1966), pp. 45–57; and Thomas Jefferson Wertenbaker, *Father Knickerbocker Rebels: New York City During the Revolution* (New York: Charles Scribner's Sons, 1948), chaps. 2–4. For a valuable firsthand account, see the claim of Margaret Hill, LT, 45:101–103; and for a useful study, see L. S. Launitz-Schürer, Jr., "Whig-Loyalists: The De Lanceys of New York," *NYHSQ,* 56 (July 1972), 179–198.

2. Oscar T. Barck, *New York City during the War for Independence with Special Reference to the Period of British Occupation* (New York: Columbia University Press, 1931), chap. 4.

3. *Ibid.,* chaps. 5 and 6; on conditions on the periphery of British-occupied territory in Westchester County, see depositions of Marcus Christian, Eden Hunt, James Oakley, Anne Ryer, and John Pine in Westchester County, Court of Oyer and Terminer Records, August 19–23, 1783, New York Public Library.

4. Upton, *Loyal Whig,* pp. 120–121.

5. *Ibid.,* p. 121.

6. *Ibid.,* pp. 117–121.

7. William Bradford Willcox, *Portrait of a General: Sir Henry Clinton in the War of Independence* (New York: Alfred A. Knopf, 1962), p. 332.

8. Upton, *Loyal Whig,* pp. 130–135, 218–223. Symptomatic of the regressive and self-deluding tendencies of the New York loyalist community, Judge Thomas Jones's bitter recriminations blind Smith and Clinton in his *History of New York City during the Revolutionary War* (New York: New-York Historical Society, 1879).

CHAPTER THIRTY-FOUR

1. David Hawke, *In the Midst of a Revolution* (Philadelphia: University of Pennsylvania Press, 1961), chaps. 9 and 10 *passim.* Jensen, *The Founding of a Nation,* p. 685.

2. Wood, *Creation of the American Republic,* pp. 85–89; Jack R. Pole, *Political Representation in England and the Origins of the American Republic* (London: Macmillan & Co. Ltd., 1966), p. 273.

3. Henry J. Young, "Treason and its Punishment in Revolutionary Pennsylvania," *PMHB,* 90 (July 1966), 278–291, and "The Treatment of the Loyalists in Pennsylvania" (Ph.D. diss., Johns Hopkins University, 1955), pp. 13–14, 74–79, 82–93.

4. Brock, *Pacifism in the United States,* pp. 259–265.

5. *Ibid.,* pp. 267–271; Young, "The Treatment of the Loyalists in Pennsylvania," pp. 141–146. See also John Ettwein, "A Short Ac-

count of the Disturbances in America and of the Brethren's Conduct and Suffering in this Connection," in Kenneth G. Hamilton, *John Ettwein and the Moravian Church during the Revolutionary Period* (Bethlehem, Penn.: Times Publishing Co., 1940), pp. 131–140.

6. Mekeel, "The Society of Friends and the American Revolution," pp. 173–175; Oaks, "Philadelphians in Exile," pp. 298–302; Rufus M. Jones, *The Quakers in the American Colonies* (New York: Macmillan Co., 1923), p. 565.

7. Oaks, "Philadelphians in Exile," pp. 322–325.

8. *Ibid.*, p. 324; James, "The Impact of the American Revolution on Quakers' Ideas about their Sect," p. 382 *et passim.*

9. John M. Coleman, "Joseph Galloway and the British Occupation of Philadelphia," *PH,* 30 (July 1963), 280.

10. *Ibid.*, pp. 272–286, *passim.*

11. *Ibid.*, pp. 287–289.

12. *Ibid.*, pp. 289–294.

13. Jacob E. Cooke, "Tench Coxe: Tory Merchant," *PMHB,* 96 (January 1972), 48–81; Willard O. Mishoff, "Business in Philadelphia during the British Occupation, 1777–1778," *PMHB,* 61 (April 1937), 165–181.

14. Coleman, "Joseph Galloway and the Occupation of Philadelphia," pp. 295–299. For the tenacity with which Galloway's supporters clung to these expectations, see Isaac Ogden to Joseph Galloway, November 22, 1778, Balch Papers, New York Public Library.

CHAPTER THIRTY-FIVE

1. Quoted in James Westfall Thompson, "Anti-Loyalist Legislation during the American Revolution," *Illinois Law Review,* 3 (June–October 1908), 157.

2. Young, "Treason and its Punishment in Revolutionary Pennsylvania," pp. 289–291.

3. *Ibid.*, p. 293.

4. *Ibid.*, p. 287.

5. *Ibid.*, pp. 293–295.

6. *Ibid.*, pp. 295–298; Cooke, "Tench Coxe," p. 85.

7. Young, "Treason and its Punishment in Revolutionary Pennsylvania," p. 299. See in general Thomas R. Meehan, "Courts, Cases, and Counselors in Revolutionary and Post-Revolutionary Pennsylvania," *PMHB,* 91 (January 1967), 3–34.

8. Henry C. Mercer, "The Doans and their Times," *Collections of the Bucks County Historical Society,* 1 (1908), 270–282.

9. Richard C. Haskett, "Prosecuting the Revolution," *AHR,* 59 (April 1954) , 578–581.
10. *Ibid.,* pp. 581–587.
11. Deposition of William Tatem, Stewart Collection, no. 0341, Savitz Library, Glassboro State College, N.J.
12. Harold Bell Hancock, *The Delaware Loyalists* (Wilmington: Historical Society of Delaware, 1940) , pp. 11–22.
13. Harold Bell Hancock, "Thomas Robinson: Delaware's Most Prominent Loyalist," *DH,* 4 (January 1950) , 1–36.
14. Harold Bell Hancock, "The New Castle County Loyalists," *DH,* 4 (September 1951) , 315–353; *The Delaware Loyalists,* p. 55.

CHAPTER THIRTY-SIX

1. Brown, *The King's Friends,* p. 252. *Minutes of the Committee and . . . First Commission for Detecting and Defeating Conspiracies in New York . . . , NYHS Colls,* 57 (1924) , 29.
2. Alexander C. Flick, *Loyalism in New York during the American Revolution* (New York: Columbia University Press, 1901) , chap. 6; Bernard Mason, *The Road to Independence,* appendix, pp. 254–257, demonstrates the unreliability of Flick's attempts at quantification, but I believe that Flick's chapter on the machinery of suppression stands up fairly well.
3. Flick, *Loyalism in New York,* p. 124.
4. *Ibid.,* pp. 125–130. *NYHS Colls,* 57:47–48, 93–94, 163–165.
5. *NYHS Colls,* 57:34–41.
6. *NYHS Colls,* 58 (1925) , 379–385.

CHAPTER THIRTY-SEVEN

1. Sung Bok Kim, "A New Look at the Great Landlords of Eighteenth-Century New York," *WMQ,* 28 (October 1970) , 581–614.
2. Patricia U. Bonomi, *A Factious People: Politics and Society in Colonial New York* (New York: Columbia University Press, 1971) , pp. 179–211.
3. Beatrice G. Reubens, "Pre-emptive Rights in the Disposition of a Confiscated Estate—Philipsburgh Manor, New York," *WMQ,* 22 (July 1965) , 435–456.
4. Ms. Reubens finds no conclusive evidence that Philipse exacted quarter-sales (*ibid.,* p. 439) , but Ms. Bonomi, citing Reubens's article, says that he did, "with at least the same regularity as other New York landlords" (Bonomi, *Factious People,* p. 226) . Perhaps

his one-third/one-sixth formula amounted to quarter-sales. Philipse's testimony to the Claims Commissioners is in LT, 41:601–616.

5. Reubens, "Pre-emptive Rights," p. 444.
6. Staughton Lynd, *Class Conflict, Slavery, and the United States Constitution: Ten Essays* (Indianapolis, Ind., and New York: Bobbs-Merrill Co., 1967), pp. 63–67.
7. *Ibid.,* pp. 68–70.
8. *Ibid.,* pp. 71–77.
9. *Ibid.,* pp. 25–61.

CHAPTER THIRTY-EIGHT

1. See Jack M. Sosin, "The Use of Indians in the War of the American Revolution: A Reassessment of Responsibility," *CHR,* 46 (June 1965), 101–121.
2. This section is based on Barbara Graymont, *The Iroquois in the American Revolution* (Syracuse, N.Y.: Syracuse University Press, 1972); see also Hazel C. Mathews, *The Mark of Honour* (Toronto: University of Toronto Press, 1965), chap. 5.
3. Mabel G. Walker, "Sir John Johnson," *Mississippi Valley Historical Review,* 3 (December 1916), 318–346.
4. Graymont, *The Iroquois in the American Revolution,* p. 190.
5. *Ibid.,* p. 256.

CHAPTER THIRTY-NINE

1. William H. Nelson, *The American Tory* (Oxford: Oxford University Press, 1961), p. 91.
2. Alice P. Kenney, "The Albany Dutch: Loyalists and Patriots," *NYH,* 42 (October 1961), 331–350.
3. Alice P. Kenney, *The Gansevoorts of Albany: Dutch Patricians in the Upper Hudson Valley* (Syracuse, N.Y.: Syracuse University Press, 1969), p. 273.
4. Kenney, "The Albany Dutch," pp. 345–347.

CHAPTER FORTY

1. Paul H. Smith, *Loyalists and Redcoats: A Study in British Revolutionary Policy* (Chapel Hill: University of North Carolina Press, 1964), pp. 14–19. See also, *CRNC,* 10:1145–1146; 9:1160–1164; Robert L. Ganyard, "North Carolina during the American Revolution: The First Phase, 1774–1777" (Ph.D. diss., Duke University, 1962), pp. 120–148; and Hugh F. Rankin, *The North Carolina*

Continentals (Chapel Hill: University of North Carolina Press, 1971), pp. 28–31.

2. Smith, *Loyalists and Redcoats,* pp. 14–18.

3. *Ibid.,* pp. 19–22. See also Ganyard, "North Carolina during the American Revolution," pp. 240–241, for an illuminating assessment of Martin's character.

4. Charles G. Sellers, "Making a Revolution: The North Carolina Whigs, 1765–1775," in J. Carlyle Sitterson, ed., *Studies in Southern History* (Chapel Hill: University of North Carolina Press, 1957), pp. 32–40; Ganyard, "North Carolina during the American Revolution," pp. 144–145, 170.

5. H. Roy Merrens, *Colonial North Carolina in the Eighteenth Century* (Chapel Hill: University of North Carolina Press, 1964), chap. 4.

6. Ganyard, "North Carolina during the American Revolution," pp. 121–135; Robert O. DeMond, *Loyalists in North Carolina during the Revolution* (Durham, N.C.: Duke University Press, 1940), chap. 2. See also Charles G. Sellers, "Private Profits and British Colonial Policy: The Speculations of Henry McCulloh," *WMQ,* 8 (October 1951), 535–551.

7. Laura Page Frech, "The Wilmington Committee of Public Safety and the Loyalist Rising of February, 1776," *NCHR,* 41 (January 1964), 21–33.

8. Rankin, *North Carolina Continentals,* pp. 34–40; *CRNC,* 22:950.

9. Rankin, *North Carolina Continentals,* pp. 40–45.

10. *Ibid.,* pp. 45–50.

11. Smith, *Loyalists and Redcoats,* pp. 25–31.

CHAPTER FORTY-ONE

1. B. D. Bargar, ed., "Charleston Loyalism in 1775: The Secret Reports of Alexander Innes," *SCHM,* 63 (July 1963), 132.

2. "Dr. Milligen's Report on the State of South Carolina," Transcripts of Records Pertaining to South Carolina, 35:230–234, British Public Record Office.

3. Edmund Berkeley and Dorothy S. Berkeley, *Dr. Alexander Garden of Charlestown* (Chapel Hill: University of North Carolina Press, 1969), pp. 265–266.

4. David D. Wallace, *The Life of Henry Laurens* (New York: Putnam, 1915), pp. 207–212.

5. David H. Villers, "The Smythe Horse Affair and the Association," *SCHM,* 70 (July 1969), 137–148.

6. David D. Wallace, *South Carolina: A Short History* (Chapel Hill: University of North Carolina Press, 1951), p. 258.
7. Bargar, "Charlestown Loyalism in 1775," p. 131.
8. Printed in the *Southern Literary Review*, 4 (July–October 1843), 141–145; George C. Rogers, "The Conscience of a Huguenot," *Transactions of the Huguenot Society of South Carolina*, 67 (1962), 1–11.
9. Thomas Brown, quoted in James H. O'Donnell, ed., "A Loyalist View of the Drayton-Tennent-Hart Mission to the Upcountry," *SCHM*, 67 (January 1966), 17.
10. The entire treatment of the back country struggle is based upon Gary D. Olson, "Loyalists and the American Revolution: Thomas Brown and the South Carolina Backcountry, 1775–1776," *SCHM*, 68 (October 1967), 201–219, and 69 (January 1968), 45–56. Several key documents are printed in R. W. Gibbes, ed., *Documentary History of the American Revolution, 1764–1776* (New York, 1855), pp. 184–186, 196–197, 200–203, 254–255, 289–291. Olson's two long articles on Brown in South Carolina and Georgia (see chap. 44, n. 1) comprise a splendid history of Southern back country loyalism and an ideal complement to Smith's *Loyalists and Redcoats*.
11. Olson, "Thomas Brown and the South Carolina Backcountry," p. 210.
12. *Ibid.*, pp. 210–211.
13. *Ibid.*, pp. 210–213.
14. *Ibid.*, pp. 214–215.
15. *Ibid.*, pp. 217–219.

CHAPTER FORTY-TWO

1. Edmund Randolph, *History of Virginia*, ed. Arthur H. Shaffer (Charlottesville: University of Virginia Press, 1970), pp. 193–194. On the nature of Virginia politics on the eve of the Revolution, see Greene, *Quest for Power*, pp. 22–31; Carl Bridenbaugh, *Seat of Empire* (Williamsburg, Va.: Colonial Williamsburg, 1958); and Charles S. Sydnor, *Gentlemen Freeholders: Political Practices in Washington's Virginia* (Chapel Hill: University of North Carolina Press, 1952).
2. Thad W. Tate, "The Coming of the Revolution in Virginia: Britain's Challenge to Virginia's Ruling Class, 1763–1776," *WMQ*, 19 (July 1962), 323–343.
3. J. H. Soltow, "Scottish Traders in Virginia, 1750–1775," *Economic History Review*, 2d ser., 12 (August 1959), 83–98.

4. Patrick Henderson, "Smallpox and Patriotism: The Norfolk Riots, 1768–1769," *VMHB*, 73 (October 1965), 413–424. On the continuation of these stresses, see Joseph S. Ewing, ed., "The Correspondence of Archibald McCall and George McCall, 1777–1783," *VMHB*, 73 (July and October 1965), 312–353, 425–454.

5. Thomas Jefferson Wertenbaker, *Norfolk: Historic Southern Port* (Durham, N.C.: Duke University Press, 1931), chap. 3.

6. Larry Bowman, "The Virginia County Committees of Safety, 1774–1776," *VMHB*, 79 (July 1971), 322–333; Peter M. Mitchell, "Loyalist Property and the Revolution in Virginia" (Ph.D. diss., University of Colorado, 1965), chap. 2.

7. *Virginia Historical Register*, 5 (1852), 38–39; LT, 59:610–656; Bowman, "The Virginia County Committees of Safety," p. 329.

8. Smith, *Loyalists and Redcoats*, p. 19, n. 28; Benjamin Quarrels, "Lord Dunmore as Liberator," *WMQ*, 15 (October 1958), 494–507.

9. Wertenbaker, *Norfolk*, pp. 58–80; W. H. Moomaw, "The British Leave Virginia," *VMHB*, 66 (April 1958), 147–160.

10. Rodney M. Baine, *Robert Munford: America's First Comic Dramatist* (Athens: University of Georgia Press, 1967), chap. 6; Cortlandt Canby, ed., "Robert Munford's *The Patriots*," *WMQ*, 6 (July 1949), 450, 458–465, 472, 481, 484, 486.

11. Madison to his father, March 29, 1777, in William T. Hutchinson and William M. E. Rachal, eds., *The Papers of James Madison*, 2 vols. (Chicago: University of Chicago Press, 1962), vol. 1, pp. 190–191 and 192 n.

CHAPTER FORTY-THREE

1. Aubrey C. Land, *Letters from America*, ed. William Eddis (Cambridge: Harvard University Press, 1969), pp. 149–150.

2. Richard A. Overfield, "The Loyalists of Maryland during the American Revolution" (Ph.D. diss., University of Maryland, 1968), p. 117.

3. *Ibid.*, pp. 77–78.

4. *Ibid.*, pp. 100–116. On the range and intensity of antiloyalist surveillance, see "Committee of Observation Records for Frederick County and Elizabethtown" in *MHM*, 10–13 (1915–1917), *passim.*

5. Anne Alden Allen, "Patriots and Loyalists: The Choice of Political Allegiances by the Members of Maryland's Proprietary Elite," *JSH*, 38 (May 1972), 783–792.

6. Overfield, *Loyalists of Maryland*, pp. 134–144, 185–191, 195.

7. *Ibid.*, pp. 204–243; Janet B. Johnson, *Robert Alexander: Maryland*

Loyalist (New York: G. P. Putnam's Sons, 1942) , pp. 96–106; Paul S. Clarkson and R. Samuel Jett, *Luther Martin of Maryland* (Baltimore: Johns Hopkins University Press, 1970) , pp. 41–47.

CHAPTER FORTY-FOUR

1. Gary D. Olson, "Thomas Brown, Loyalist Partisan, and the Revolutionary War in Georgia, 1777–1782," *GHR,* 54 (Spring and Summer 1970) , 1–19, 183–207.
2. *Ibid.,* pp. 10–12; Patrick J. Furlong, "Civilian-Military Conflict and the Restoration of the Royal Province of Georgia, 1778–1782," *JSH,* 38 (August 1972) , 415–419.
3. *Ibid.,* pp. 419–426. On the durability of Wright's civilian following, see C. Ashley Ellefson, "Loyalists and Patriots in Georgia during the American Revolution," *The Historian,* 24 (May 1962) , 347–356.
4. Clyde R. Ferguson, "General Andrew Pickens" (Ph.D. diss., Duke University, 1960) , chap. 2.
5. Furlong, "Civilian-Military Conflict," p. 426.
6. *Ibid.,* pp. 429–434; Hugh McCall, *The History of Georgia,* 2 vols. (Savannah, Ga.: Seymour and Williams, 1811–1816) , vol. 2, pp. 307–308.

CHAPTER FORTY-FIVE

1. There is much literature on this year in British politics, but most of the points made in this paragraph come from Smith, *Loyalists and Redcoats,* chap. 6, especially pp. 79–82.
2. Gerald S. Brown, *The American Secretary: The Colonial Policy of Lord George Germain, 1775–1778* (Ann Arbor: University of Michigan Press, 1963) , chap. 9; Mackesy, *War for America,* pp. 155–157.
3. *Ibid.,* pp. 237–243.
4. Norton, *The British-Americans,* p. 161.
5. Mackesy, *War for America,* p. 244.
6. Alan S. Brown, ed., "James Simpson's Reports on the Carolina Loyalists, 1779–1780," *JSH,* 21 (November 1955) , 513–519.

CHAPTER FORTY-SIX

1. Willcox, *Portrait of a General,* pp. 296–299.
2. Smith, *Loyalists and Redcoats,* pp. 126–130.
3. *Ibid.,* pp. 131–133.

CHAPTER FORTY-SEVEN

1. George Smith McCowen, *The British Occupation of Charleston, 1780–1782* (Columbia: University of South Carolina Press, 1972), pp. 13–23.
2. *Ibid.,* pp. 24–42.
3. *Ibid.,* pp. 70–73 and chap. 3, *passim.*

CHAPTER FORTY-EIGHT

1. Franklin and Mary Wickwire, *Cornwallis: The American Adventure* (Boston: Houghton Mifflin Co., 1970), pp. 131–146; Russell F. Weigley, *The Partisan War: The South Carolina Campaign of 1780–1782* (Columbia: University of South Carolina Press, 1970), pp. 7, 14.
2. Richard Maxwell Brown, "Backcountry Violence (1760–1785) and its Significance for South Carolina History," a paper read to the Conference on Early American History, Georgetown University, April 9, 1965.
3. Wickwire and Wickwire, *Cornwallis,* pp. 174–175.
4. *Ibid.,* pp. 205, 213–215, 217; and Christopher Ward, *The War of the Revolution,* 2 vols. (New York: Macmillan Co., 1952), vol. 2, p. 744.
5. Don Higginbotham, *Daniel Morgan: Revolutionary Rifleman* (Chapel Hill: University of North Carolina Press, 1961), pp. 136–141; Robert D. Bass, *The Green Dragoon, The Lives of Banastre Tarleton and Mary Robinson* (New York: Holt, Rinehart & Winston, 1957), pp. 46–48.
6. Wickwire and Wickwire, *Cornwallis,* p. 269.
7. Rankin, *North Carolina Continentals,* pp. 289–292; Wickwire and Wickwire, *Cornwallis,* chaps. 13 and 14, *passim.*
8. Rankin, *North Carolina Continentals,* pp. 363–365; DeMond, *Loyalists in North Carolina,* pp. 144–152.
9. Higginbotham, *War of American Independence,* pp. 371–375, is an excellent assessment of Greene and the last stages of the war in South Carolina. David Syrett, *Shipping and the American War, 1775–1783* (London: Athlone Press, 1970), p. 238.

EPILOGUE

1. Norton, *The British-Americans,* p. 180.
2. L. F. S. Upton, "The Return of the Un-Americans: The Reaction to the Loyalists in 1783," a paper read to the meeting of the Organization of American Historians, Washington, April 8, 1972.

3. Norton, *The British-Americans,* pp. 185–216.
4. Brown, *The King's Friends,* p. 267.
5. Wallace Brown, *The Good Americans: The Loyalists in the American Revolution* (New York: William Morrow & Co., 1969) , chap. 7.
6. W. Stewart MacNutt, "New England's Tory Neighbors," *CSM Publ,* 43:360.
7. Smith, "The American Loyalists: Notes on their Organization and Numerical Strength," pp. 259–267.
8. Norton, ed. "John Randolph's 'Plan of Accommodations,' " p. 105.
9. For a highly original study of this matter by a political scientist, see David V. J. Bell, "Nation and Non-Nation: A New Analysis of the Loyalists and the American Revolution" (Ph.D. diss., Harvard University, 1969) .
10. I am indebted for this concept to Thomas C. Barrow, "The American Revolution as a Colonial War for Independence," *WMQ,* 25 (July 1968) , 452–464.
11. On these patterns of war, see Smith, *Loyalists and Redcoats,* chap. 10; and David V. J. Bell and Allan E. Goodman, "Vietnam and Revolution," *Yale Review,* 61 (Autumn 1971) , 26–34.
12. Claude H. Van Tyne, *The Loyalists in the American Revolution* (New York: Macmillan Co., 1902) , pp. 2–3. For a different view of this issue, see Norton, *The British-Americans,* pp. 7–8.
13. Upton, *The Loyal Whig,* p. 119.

Bibliographical Essay

THIS essay will discuss the major books and articles that deal exclusively with the loyalists—writings that have not appeared very often in the notes but that have contributed much to the content and interpretation of this book. The starting place for the study of the loyalists is Lorenzo Sabine, *Biographical Sketches of Loyalists of the American Revolution with an Historical Essay* (Boston: Little, Brown & Co., 1864). Sabine collected biographical information on approximately 6,000 loyalists; his long historical essay attempted an unprecedented interpretation of the character of colonial politics, and his assessment of loyalist motives anticipated the findings of recent scholarship. Subsequent refinements on Sabine's method of biographical sketches are to be found in James H. Stark, *The Loyalists of Massachusetts and the Other Side of the American Revolution* (Boston: J. H. Stark, 1910), Edward A. Jones, *The Loyalists of Massachusetts: Their Memorials, Petitions, and Claims* (London: St. Catherine Press, 1930), Jones, *The Loyalists of New Jersey* (Newark: New Jersey Historical Society, 1927), and Wilbur H. Siebert, *Loyalists in East Florida, 1774-1785* (DeLand: Florida State Historical Society, 1929). Similarly massive in scope and important in its findings is Moses Coit Tyler, *The Literary History of the American Revolution* (New York: G. P. Putnam's Sons, 1897); Tyler's chapter 13, "The Party of the Loyalists and their Literature," is a classic essay that also appeared in *The American Historical Review*, 1 (1895), 24–49, and depicted loyalist publicists as intelligent, constructive, and responsible men; in chapters 14 through 17 and 27 through 29, Tyler summarizes competently a large body of their writings.

Claude H. Van Tyne, in *The Loyalists in the American Revolution* (New York: Macmillan Co., 1902) treats the loyalists as a problem in institutional history, discussing the laws passed to punish and control them and the difficulties they created for British officials. Van Tyne's book and A. C. Flick, *Loyalism in New York* (New York: Columbia University Press, 1901), became the models for a spate of state studies: Wilbur H. Siebert, *The Loyalists of Pennsylvania* (Columbus: Ohio

State University, 1920) ; Isaac S. Harrell, *Loyalism in Virginia* (Durham, N.C.: Duke University Press, 1926), and "North Carolina Loyalists," *NCHR*, 3 (October 1926), 575–590; Harold Bell Hancock, *The Delaware Loyalists* (Wilmington: Historical Society of Delaware, 1940) ; Robert O. DeMond, *The Loyalists in North Carolina during the American Revolution* (Durham, N.C.: Duke University Press, 1941) ; and Robert W. Barnwell, "Loyalism in South Carolina 1765–1785" (Ph.D. diss., Duke University, 1941). In addition to these thorough, monographic works, two long essays complete the list of early state-level studies: Epaphroditus Peck, *The Loyalists of Connecticut* (New Haven: Yale University Press, 1934), a pedestrian account; and Otis G. Hammond, *The Tories of New Hampshire* (Concord: New Hampshire Historical Society, 1917), a highly illuminating evaluation.

Several recent state studies that pay close attention to the nature of legal proceedings against the loyalists are Richard A. Overfield, "The Loyalists of Maryland during the American Revolution" (Ph.D. diss., University of Maryland, 1968) ; Henry J. Young, "The Treatment of the Loyalists in Pennsylvania" (Ph.D. diss., Johns Hopkins University, 1955) ; Peter M. Mitchell, "Loyalist Property and the Revolution in Virginia" (Ph.D. diss., University of Colorado, 1965) ; Richard C. Haskett, "Prosecuting the Revolution," *The American Historical Review*, 59 (April 1954), 578–587; and Joel A. Cohen, "Rhode Island Loyalism and the American Revolution," *RIH*, 27 (October 1966), 97–112. James Westfall Thompson, "Anti-Loyalist Legislation during the American Revolution," *Illinois Law Review*, 3 (June and October 1908), 81–90, 147–165; and Bradley Chapin, *The American Law of Treason: Revolutionary and Early National Origins* (Seattle: University of Washington Press, 1964), are important supplements to this work in the legal history of the loyalists. Richard D. Brown, "The Confiscation and Disposition of Loyalists' Estates in Suffolk County, Massachusetts," *WMQ*, 21 (October 1964), 534–550; and Richard B. Morris, *The American Revolution Reconsidered* (New York: Harper & Row, 1967), pp. 77–79, appraise the scholarship on the confiscation of loyalist property. North Callahan has written two volumes on the loyalists, *Royal Raiders* and *Flight from the Republic* (Indianapolis, Ind.: Bobbs-Merrill Co., 1963 and 1967). The first volume covers much the same ground as this book. While I have had reservations about the craftsmanship and interpretive value of Callahan's *Royal Raiders* (see my review, *VMHB*, 72 [July 1964], 364–365), the two chapters on violence and legal disorder now seem to me the best general treatments of these topics available.

Two monumental works, Lawrence H. Gipson, *The British Empire be-*

fore the American Revolution, 14 volumes (New York: Alfred A. Knopf, 1936–1971) ; and Clifford K. Shipton, *Sibley's Harvard Graduates,* 12 volumes to date (Boston: Massachusetts Historical Society, 1933–), though not explicitly concerned with the loyalists, surpass even Sabine's *Sketches* in the sheer volume of their research on the opponents of the American Revolution; both authors argue forcefully that the loyalists and many British officials were men of intelligence, responsibility, and courage. Gipson chronicles in impressive detail the history of the British Empire from 1748 to 1776. He depicts "The Great War for Empire," as he labeled the Seven Years' War, as a crucible from which the Empire emerged too successful and vibrant to be readily governed or administered. Gipson's doctoral dissertation, recently republished as *American Loyalist: Jared Ingersoll* (New Haven: Yale University Press, 1971), contains a sprightly essay on the past half century of loyalist scholarship; volume 13, pp. 173–454, of his *British Empire* is an up-to-date and discerning appraisal of Revolutionary and British imperial historiography that reconciles his sympathetic attitude toward the British Empire with his generous appreciation of recent scholarship on patriot motivation and belief. Shipton's *Harvard Graduates* is a continuation of a project begun by John L. Sibley in the nineteenth century to preserve biographical information about every Harvard graduate from the colonial period. Sibley wrote three volumes, covering the classes of 1642 to 1689; and since 1933, Shipton has extended the series from the class of 1690 to 1763. From volume 7 onward, many of Shipton's Harvard men lived during the Revolution, and 15 to 20 per cent of the men in these volumes who lived during the Revolutionary era were either loyalists, neutralists, or very reluctant Whigs who suffered for their political conservatism.

Shipton includes not only major biographical interpretations of Thomas Hutchinson (class of 1727), Andrew and Peter Oliver (1724 and 1730), and other prominent figures but also equally valuable portraits of relatively minor opponents of the Revolution like Josiah Edson (1730), Eli Forbes (1751), and Mather Byles (1751). There is no better access to the intricacies of Massachusetts society in the eighteenth century than Shipton's sketches, and for the student of the loyalists these volumes are all the more useful because Shipton is a stubborn, if discriminating, admirer of the loyalists. For a candid statement of the author's purpose and method see the introductions to volumes 7 and 9 and his letter to the editor, *WMQ,* 10 (April 1953) 348–350.

The modern re-evaluation of the loyalists began with Julian P. Boyd in *Anglo-American Union: Joseph Galloway's Plans to Preserve the*

Bibliographical Essay

British Empire (Philadelphia: University of Pennsylvania Press, 1941) ; and Leonard Woods Labaree in "The Nature of American Loyalism," *Proceedings of the American Antiquarian Society,* 54 (April 1944), 15–58, an essay that he recast in more rigorous, incisive terms as "The Tory Mind," in *Conservatism in Early American History* (New York: New York University Press, 1948) . Labaree synthesizes in these writings two great schools of scholarship: first, the work of institutional historians who depicted the Empire as a benevolent, rational enterprise; and second, the findings of progressive historians who detected sharp class conflict in colonial America and cast the loyalists as conservative oligarchs who failed to accommodate themselves to the rising democratic forces during the Revolution. Labaree sensed the limitations of the imperial and progressive perspectives on the problem of the loyalists, and he called on scholars to turn their attention to "factors of personality, of individual conditioning, of sub-conscious motivation, and of sheer human inertia" that helped shape the loyalist experience. Edmund S. and Helen M. Morgan, *The Stamp Act Crisis: Prologue to Revolution* (Chapel Hill: University of North Carolina Press, 1953) ; and W. W. Abbot, *The Royal Governors of Georgia, 1754–1775* (Chapel Hill: University of North Carolina Press, 1959), adopted such an approach in their sensitive portrayals of prominent defenders of British authority. William H. Nelson, *The American Tory* (Oxford: Oxford University Press, 1961) is a brilliant extended essay on the roles of personality, temperament, ambition, political and social style, and impulses of self-preservation in loyalist experiences. Gracefully written and modest in its claims, Nelson's book anticipated many of the findings of more exhaustively documented studies published later in the decade. The work of Adrian C. Leiby, Alice P. Kenney, Staughton Lynd, Barbara Graymont, and Peter Brock—cited in the notes for Part Five—confirm Nelson's suggestion that the loyalists in the middle colonies represented "cultural minorities." Nelson's sketches of prominent loyalists and his summary of their political thought are lively and perceptive. His conclusion that some of the loyalists were custodians of an "organic conservatism" that was ill suited to survive in the American political culture pointed toward Bernard Bailyn's use of high-Anglican ideologues as astute commentators on the radical implications of Whig ideology. Nelson, however, neglects loyalist spokesmen in the South, and he bases his treatment of Hutchinson on the numerous quotations in a somber nineteenth-century biography by James K. Hosmer, *Life of Thomas Hutchinson, Royal Governor of the Province of Massachusetts Bay,* a sample of sources that altogether ignore Hutchinson's emotionality and quickness of mind and therefore have subtly warped Nelson's interpretation of Hutchinson.

Indeed, Nelson's brevity and lucidity, the essential qualities of his style, make many of the figures in his book appear remarkably self-possessed, reasonable, and deliberate. A number of recent studies by William A. Benton, Wallace Brown, Paul H. Smith, and Mary Beth Norton have therefore sought to penetrate deeper and grapple more directly with the problem of loyalist attitudes, beliefs, and aspirations. William A. Benton, in *Whig-Loyalism: An Aspect of Political Ideology in the American Revolutionary Era* (Teaneck, N.J.: Fairleigh Dickinson University Press, 1969), isolates nine men who played an active part in behalf of colonial resistance during some stage of the pre-Revolutionary controversy but became loyalists in 1776, among them William Smith, Jr., Daniel Dulany, William Samuel Johnson, Daniel Leonard, Peter Van Schaack, and William Byrd III. The book narrates clearly the complex and interesting lives of these men during the Revolutionary period, but it never comes to grips with the reasons for their support of resistance and opposition to independence. Nonetheless, *Whig-Loyalism* is an important book for the questions it asks. When Ralph Ketcham, in a severely critical review, declared that Benton "doesn't take ideas in history seriously" he touched the heart of the problem. Benton seems to argue that something other than formal political ideas governed the conduct of his nine subjects—a desire for personal autonomy, an insistence on reflection, an aversion to harsh and judgmental rhetoric, and perhaps a principled opportunism. But he is never able to explore these imperatives in any depth because the evidence he has found in the writings of his Whig-loyalists takes the form of conventional discourse on political events and ideas. Therefore Benton's abundant quotations from their writings on politics do not support his thesis very rigorously. Part Two of this book is based on much of the same evidence as that which Benton used, and while I disagree with some of his classifications and assumptions, his ambitious study made my work much easier.

A very different sort of pioneering attempt to get beneath the surface of loyalist historical materials is Wallace Brown, *The King's Friends: The Composition and Motives of the American Loyalist Claimants* (Providence, R.I.: Brown University Press, 1966). Brown subjects the claims for compensation filed by loyalist exiles in London and Canada to quantitative analysis and produces a useful profile of their property losses, occupations, geographical distribution, military service, and other variables. Unfortunately, he is not entirely convincing in his ingenious argument that the 2,908 claimants were in some respects a representative numerical and geographic sample of the larger body of 250,000 to 500,000 loyalists. Nevertheless, Brown's thorough knowledge of the claims has enabled him to write valuable chapters on the nature of the loyalist opposition to the Revolution in each colony. In *The Good Americans: The Loyalists in the American Revolution* (New York: William Morrow & Co., 1969), Brown utilizes biographical data and personal testimony from the claims and other sources to write a full-scale history of the loyalist experience. His chapters on loyalist motivation, the plight of loyalist exiles in England during the war, and the resettlement of departed loyalists in Canada, the West Indies, and elsewhere in the Empire sensitively portray the spare and fleeting moods of resignation and determination that many loyalist sources convey. Brown's articles "The American Farmer during the Revolution: Rebel or Loyalist?" *Agricultural History*, 42 (October 1968), 327–338, and "Viewpoints of a Pennsylvania Loyalist," *PMHB*, 91 (October 1967), 419–433, are a useful supplement to his two books.

Exploiting the rich archival resources of the William L. Clements Library and the growing body of scholarship on British military policy in the Revolution, Paul H. Smith, in *Loyalists and Redcoats: A Study in British Revolutionary Policy* (Chapel Hill: University of North Carolina Press, 1964), exposes the inability of British ministers and generals to appraise accurately loyalist military potential and the requirements for mobilizing and sustaining provincial forces. On the state of methodology in recent loyalist studies, see Eugene R. Fingerhut's "Uses and Abuses of the American Loyalists' Claims: A Critique of Quantitative Analyses," and Paul H. Smith, "The American Loyalists: Notes on Their Organization and Numerical Strength," both in *WMQ*, 25 (April 1968), 245–258 and 259–277. Finally, Mary Beth Norton, *The British-Americans: The Loyalist Exiles in England 1774–1789* (Boston: Little, Brown & Co., 1972),* and her "The Loyalists' Image of England: Ideal and Reality," *Albion*, 3 (Summer 1971), 62–71, reconstruct in impressive detail and intricacy the life of the loyalist expatriate community in England. For a valuable historiographical essay on Canadian and United States scholarship on the loyalists, see Wallace Brown, "The View at Two Hundred Years: The Loyalists of the American Revolution," *Proceedings of the American Antiquarian Society*, 80 (1970), 25–47.

The notes for this volume cite a wide sample of the published and

---

* *The British-Americans* was published after the manuscript for this book had been completed. In a few cases where Professor Norton had kindly called my attention to documents I have quoted, I have cited her book as a source for these, and my treatment of the exiles in England in the Epilogue is also based on her book.

manuscript sources on the loyalists. The Loyalist Papers Project, a cooperative enterprise of British, Canadian, and United States scholars, will soon publish a definitive listing of loyalist manuscripts. In a few years the Project will publish every scrap of surviving documentation on the loyalists in letterpress and microcard editions. By making this mass of data available to scholars everywhere, the Loyalist Papers Project will make possible an entirely new kind of scholarship on the loyalists—vastly more sophisticated, thorough, and interrelated than most previous scholarship.* In the meantime, the most convenient published loyalist sources and the commentary on that material include Morton and Penn Borden, eds., *The American Tory* (Englewood Cliffs, N.J.: Prentice-Hall, 1972) ; M. L. Bradbury, "Loyalism and Allegiance," in Lawrence H. Leder, ed., *Dimensions of Change: Problems and Issues of American Colonial History* (Minneapolis, Minn.: Burgess Publishing Co., 1972) ; Lawrence H. Leder, ed., *The Colonial Legacy: Loyalist Historians* (New York: Harper & Row, 1971) ; Leslie F. S. Upton, ed., *Revolutionary versus Loyalist: The First American Civil War, 1774–1784* (Waltham, Mass.: Blaisdell Publishing Co., 1968) ; G. N. D. Evans, ed., *Allegiance in America: The Case of the Loyalists* (Reading, Mass.: Addison-Wesley Publishing Co., 1969) ; and Bernard Mason, ed., *The American Colonial Crisis: The Daniel Leonard–John Adams Letters to the Press, 1774–1775* (New York: Harper & Row, 1972) .

* See Robert M. Calhoon, "Loyalist Studies at the Advent of the *Loyalist Papers Project*," *NEQ*, 46 (June 1973) .

Index